T0227339

No Code Required

No Code Required
Giving Users Tools to Transform the Web

Edited by

Allen Cypher

Mira Dontcheva

Tessa Lau

Jeffrey Nichols

AMSTERDAM • BOSTON • HEIDELBERG • LONDON
NEW YORK • OXFORD • PARIS • SAN DIEGO
SAN FRANCISCO • SINGAPORE • SYDNEY • TOKYO

Morgan Kaufmann Publishers is an imprint of Elsevier

Morgan Kaufmann Publishers is an imprint of Elsevier.
30 Corporate Drive, Suite 400, Burlington, MA 01803, USA
This book is printed on acid-free paper.

Material in the work originally appeared in:

For Chapter 3, *Proceedings of the 18th Annual ACM Symposium on User Interface Software and Technology* (© ACM 2005),

For Chapter 4, *Proceedings of the SIGCHI Conference on Human Factors in Computing Systems* (© ACM 2006), and *"CoScripter: automating & sharing how-to knowledge in the enterprise,"* in *Proceedings of the Twenty-Sixth Annual SIGCHI Conference on Human Factors in Computing Systems* (© ACM 2008),

For Chapter 5, *Proceedings of the 17th Annual ACM Symposium on User Interface Software and Technology* (© ACM 2004),

For Chapter 8, *"Clip, connect, clone: combining application elements to build custom interfaces for information access,"* by: Jun Fujima, Aran Lunzer, Kasper Hornbaek, Yuzuru Tanaka. (© ACM 2004) and *Proceedings of the 17th Annual ACM Symposium on User Interface Software and Technology* (©UIST 2004),

For Chapter 10, *"Programming by a sample: leveraging Web sites to program their underlying services,"* by: Björn Hartmann, Leslie Wu, Kevin Collins, Scott R. Klemmer. (© ACM 2007) and *Proceedings of the 20th Annual ACM Symposium on User interface Software and Technology* (©UIST 2007),

For Chapter 12, *"Summarizing personal Web browsing sessions,"* in *Proceedings of the 19th Annual ACM Symposium on User Interface Software and Technology,* by: Mira Dontcheva, Steven M. Drucker, G. Wade, David Salesin, and Michael F. Cohen* (©UIST 2006) and *"Relations, cards, and search templates: user-guided Web data integration and layout,"* in *Proceedings of the 20th Annual ACM Symposium on User interface Software and Technology* by Mira Dontcheva, Steven M. Drucker, David Salesin, and Michael F. Cohen* (©ACM 2007),

For Chapter 13, *"Zoetrope: interacting with the ephemeral Web,"* in *Proceedings of the 21st Annual ACM Symposium on User Interface Software and Technology* (© ACM 2008),

For Chapter 15, *"Translating keyword commands into executable code,"* in *Proceedings of the 19th annual ACM Symposium on User Interface Software and Technology* (© ACM 2006), *"Koala: capture, share, automate, personalize business processes on the Web,"* in *Proceedings of the SIGCHI Conference on Human Factors in Computing Systems* (© ACM 2007), and *"Inky: a sloppy command line for the Web with rich visual feedback,"* in *Proceedings of the 21st Annual ACM Symposium on User interface Software and Technology* (© ACM 2008),

For Chapter 23, *"Two studies of opportunistic programming: interleaving Web foraging, learning, and writing code,"* in *Proceedings of the 27th International Conference on Human Factors in Computing Systems* (© ACM 2009).

Library of Congress Cataloging-in-Publication Data
Application submitted

British Library Cataloguing-in-Publication Data
A catalogue record for this book is available from the British Library.

ISBN: 978-0-12-381541-5

For information on all Morgan Kaufmann publications,
visit our Web site at www.mkp.com or www.elsevierdirect.com.

Printed in the United States of America
10   11   12   13   5   4   3   2   1

Contents

For video demonstrations, please visit this book's companion Web site at www.mkp.com /nocoderequired.

Foreword

There is no question that the Web has become an integral part of modern life for people around the world, connecting us to each other and to seemingly infinite portals of information in real time.

In the era of Web 2.0, barriers to participation have been lowered further and further, and we've seen the birth of myriad new people to connect, learn, share, and collaborate. From blogs to social networks, people are enjoying an increasingly rich online life.

And while the Web has dramatically enriched our lives, we have only just scratched the surface of its potential. Through the rapid expansion and enhancement of the information to which we have access, we've also lost a great deal of freedom and flexibility over it; although most people may not have noticed this yet, as "newer" is often perceived as "better."

Many of the basic abilities we have when consuming and sharing information in the physical world have yet to make the jump to the digital realm. Most Web sites do not yet provide us the ability to integrate our own personal context into the presentation of information and the tools uniquely available to each of us. For instance, before the Web, planning a holiday trip often involved clipping articles and pictures from magazines, collecting brochures, taking tips and hints from friends, writing down details from travel agents, highlighting ratings and reviews of restaurants and hotels from travel books that we've bought or borrowed, noting suggestions on the best seats on an airplane from coworkers, and assembling all this information in one place, often the kitchen table, to finalize travel plans and itinerary.

It was a social experience with a great deal of interaction and discussion, integrated your own personal context (e.g., magazine subscriptions you had, books you owned, previous travel experiences, etc.), and was not overly constrained by the media or medium, from any one source (e.g., there were no technical or legal barriers to "mashing up" pictures of hotels with ratings from your guide books), as one could easily pull from all sources at once.

This experience – the ease of cutting and arranging articles and integrating context and tools from disparate sources – is not yet readily possible for people on the Web today. Users can only access the bits and pieces of information per Web page that have been explicitly included by the owner of that page; and while users can open multiple windows at once and switch between them, it becomes confusing, vexing, and often contradictory. Users have become frustrated by these limitations.

There's increasing demand for flexibility and better tools that put the user in control of their online experience – providing the ability to create, combine, compare, customize, manage, share, and track information to fit their own unique individual needs and interests.

Just in time, exciting tools are coming out of academic and corporate research and development labs that have the potential to give users unprecedented control over information and experiences on the Web. The hope is that users can become much more than simply passive consumers of the content provided to them. They can be tinkerers, hackers (in the good sense), and remixers who build, use, and share tools to suit their needs, including making that kitchen table into an interactive suite of information.

These tools are aiding in the evolution of the Web from isolated silos of information and functionality to a platform that provides intuitive and accessible tools and capabilities that allow for the kind of individual control and access to personal context that we've come to appreciate in the physical world.

No Code Required presents these next set of tools that are allowing users, as information omnivores, to participate in the building and remixing of *their* Web. You'll find the latest thinking, research, and efforts underway empower the masses to take the Web into their own hands and to provide people everywhere the tools and capabilities to and make it not only *say* but also *do* what they want. Leaders in their respective fields, the experts in this book provide us with the tools and the know-how to change the end user from consumer to developer, organizer, editor, or even travel agent.

As researchers and developers, we can all play a role in shaping our collective future. The sky is the limit. This book will help take us there.

Chris Beard
Chief Innovation Officer, Mozilla

Preface

The last few years have seen a dramatic upsurge in research in end user programming. Much of this renewed interest is due to the popularity of the Web. The Web browser is rapidly replacing the personal computer's desktop as the platform for many computer activities, and users can now find information, make purchases, and communicate with each other through a Web browser.

As Chapter 1 explains, the Web browser has turned out to be an ideal platform for end user programming. Researchers and students at a variety of institutions have been exploring how Web browsers can be changed or augmented to better support everyday users' tasks. Some of these systems have even been released for public use. Unfortunately, there was no common community linking researchers in this area together. As a result, there was relatively little collaboration between different groups and papers describing work in this area were published in a variety of different academic venues. Not only was this hurting the productivity of the field, but it was preventing the potential beneficiaries, such as Web users and developers, from accessing these technologies. As researchers working this area ourselves, the four of us felt that it was time to foster a community for researchers in end user programming on the Web.

"End-User Programming on the Web" workshop at ACM SIGCHI

We began by organizing a workshop at the SIGCHI conference (ACM Conference on Human Factors in Computing Systems) in April 2009. The goals of this workshop were three-fold: (1) to bring together researchers from a variety of institutions and establish a sense of community, (2) to discuss common problems and share lessons from our work, and (3) to plan the publication of an edited book on this topic. The goal of the book was to make it easy for researchers to read about the latest approaches and innovations in the field and to make this interesting topic more readily available to a larger audience.

The one-day workshop was attended by 32 participants representing 20 different institutions across three continents (Asia, Europe, and North America). Participants were selected based on short position papers that were submitted in advance of the workshop. We personally invited a number of people to submit position papers on the basis of their previously published work, and we also conducted an open call for position papers from the research community at large. The authors of all submissions related to end user programming on the Web were invited to attend the workshop, with the condition that attendees were also required to prepare a book chapter by our prespecified deadlines.

We began the workshop with each participant giving a one-minute talk about their work in the space of end user programming on the Web. We then asked five attendees to give longer presentations covering some of the key projects and areas of interest to our research community. The remainder of the workshop was spent alternating between break-out groups and full-group discussion in areas of interest to our research community and specific topics regarding the book. Several of these breakout sessions were instrumental in helping us establish a coherent organization for the book.

Overview of the book

This book brings together the state of the art in interface and language design, system architectures, research methodologies, and evaluation strategies for end user programming on the Web. The book compiles seventeen systems (Chapters 3–19) and offers a concise system summary at the end of each system chapter that lists such characteristics as intended users, domain, and scripting ability, and enables direct comparison between all of the systems. Video demonstrations of the systems are available on the Morgan Kaufmann Web site at www.mkp.com/nocoderequired.

No Code Required may be seen as a companion publication to three previous edited volumes:

1. Cypher, A. (Ed.). (1993). *Watch what I do: Programming by demonstration.* Cambridge, MA: MIT Press.
2. Lieberman, H. (Ed.). (2001). *Your wish is my command.* San Francisco, CA: Morgan Kaufmann.
3. Lieberman, H., Paterno, F., & Wulf, V. (Eds.). (2005). *End user development,* Springer.

Introduction (Chapters 1–2)
Chapters 1 and 2 look back at the field of end user programming since its beginnings in the 1980s and discuss the resurgence of this research area in the Web domain. They point to the extensibility of the Web browser and the open nature of HTML as differentiating factors that have enabled end user customization and automation across many different tasks and applications on the Web.

Customizing and automating (Chapters 3–7)
The second section of the book focuses on approaches for enabling automation and customization of the Web. We survey five systems – Chickenfoot (Chapter 3), Creo (Chapter 4), CoScripter (Chapter 5), Highlight (Chapter 6), and Atomate (Chapter 7) – that leverage a variety of techniques, including inventing a new human readable scripting language, allowing programming by example, and leveraging a large knowledge base of semantic information.

Mashups (Chapters 8–11)
This section includes four systems – C3W (Chapter 8), Mash Maker (Chapter 9), d.mix (Chapter 10), and ITL (Chapter 11) – that mix information from multiple Web sites and applications to create mashups. Their approaches vary from proposing a specialized platform to building on top of the Web browser and mapping the interface to existing Web services.

Visualization and exploration (Chapters 12–14)
In contrast to the systems described earlier in the book, the three systems in this section – Web Summaries (Chapter 12), Zoetrope (Chapter 13), and RecipeSheet (Chapter 14) – focus on providing end user customization tools for visualizing and exploring the large amounts of data that live on the Web.

Natural language (Chapters 15–17)
Any type of Web customization is possible through code, but writing code – at least as it exists today – is not the right interface for most Web customization tasks. The three systems in this section – Inky (Chapter 15), PLOW (Chapter 16), and MOOIDE (Chapter 17) – propose new approaches to programming that are inspired by or incorporate natural language.

Accessibility (Chapters 18–19)
A large portion of Web content does not conform to accessibility standards, making it difficult for visually impaired users to use the Web. The systems in this section – Social Accessibility

(Chapter 18) and TrailBlazer (Chapter 19) – leverage third-party tagging and demonstrations to improve Web accessibility.

User studies (Chapters 20–23)

We conclude the book with four ethnographic user studies that provide a deep understanding for the target end users and their needs for Web use, code reuse, and debugging.

About the Editors

Allen Cypher, PhD, Research Staff Member, User Experience Research, IBM Almaden Research Center. Allen Cypher has been creating tools to bring the power of programming to nonprogrammers for 20 years. His Eager system from 1988 observed users' actions and automatically wrote programs to automate repetitive activities. Eager was one of the first intelligent agents. In 1993, he edited *Watch What I Do: Programming by Demonstration.* In the 1990s, he co-developed a visual programming language called Stagecast Creator that enabled children to create their own games and simulations and publish them on the Web. His current work with CoScripter is aimed at bringing end user programming to the Web. Dr. Cypher received an A.B. in Mathematics from Princeton University in 1975, a PhD in Computer Science from Yale University in 1980, and spent 4 years as a post-doctoral student in the Psychology department at the University of California, San Diego. He was in the Advanced Technology Group at Apple Computer for 9 years, and has been at the IBM Almaden Research Center for the past 7 years.

Mira Dontcheva, PhD, Research Scientist, Adobe Systems. Mira Dontcheva is a research scientist at Adobe Systems. Her research focuses on new interfaces and tools that help people make use of the vast amount of information found on the Web in the context of their daily activities. Before joining Adobe in 2008, Mira completed her PhD in Computer Science at the University of Washington with David Salesin, Michael Cohen, and Steven Drucker. Her thesis focused on novel interaction techniques for managing and repurposing Web content. Mira was an undergraduate at the University of Michigan in Ann Arbor and completed her B.S.E. in Computer Engineering in 2000.

Tessa Lau, PhD, Research Staff Member, IBM Almaden Research Center. Tessa has been doing research on end user programming since 1997, resulting in more than a dozen technical papers on the various aspects of EUP. Tessa's research goal is to develop innovative interfaces for enhancing human productivity and creativity through the use of techniques drawn from artificial intelligence. Her research interests include intelligent user interfaces, machine learning, artificial intelligence, human-computer interaction, programming by demonstration, and email classification. She also contributed a chapter about her SMARTedit system to the second EUP book, *Your Wish Is My Command.* PhD, University of Washington's Department of CS&E.

Jeffrey Nichols, PhD, Research Staff Member, IBM Almaden Research Center. Jeffrey currently leads the Highlight project, which is building technology that allows users to easily create their own mobile versions of existing Web sites. His research interests are in the field of human-computer interaction, with a specific focus on automated design, mobile computing, end user programming, and ubiquitous computing. He received his PhD in December 2006 from the Human-Computer Interaction Institute in Carnegie Mellon University's School of Computer Science. His thesis described the first system to automatically generate interfaces that are consistent with a user's previous experience and provided the first evidence from user studies that automatically generated interfaces can be more usable than human-designed interfaces in certain situations. He received a B.S. degree in computer engineering from the University of Washington in 2000.

Contributors

Eytan Adar
University of Michigan, School of Information & Computer Science and Engineering, Ann Arbor, Michigan

Moin Ahmad
Massachusetts Institute of Technology Media Laboratory, Cambridge, Massachusetts

James Allen
Institute for Human and Machine Cognition, Pensacola, Florida

Paul André
University of Southampton, School of Electronics and Computer Science, Southampton, United Kingdom

Chieko Asakawa
IBM Research – Tokyo, Yamato, Kanagawa, Japan

John Barton
IBM Almaden Research Center, San Jose, California

Michael Bernstein
Massachusetts Institute of Technology Computer Science and Artificial Intelligence Laboratory, 32 Vassar Street, Cambridge, Massachusetts

Jeffrey P. Bigham
Department of Computer Science, University of Rochester, Rochester, New York

Nate Blaylock
Institute for Human and Machine Cognition, Pensacola, Florida

Jim Blythe
Information Sciences Institute, University of Southern California, Marina del Rey, California

Michael Bolin
Massachusetts Institute of Technology Computer Science and Artificial Intelligence Laboratory, Cambridge, Massachusetts

Yevgen Borodin
Computer Science Department, Stony Brook University, Stony Brook, New York

Joel Brandt
Computer Science Department, Stanford University, Stanford, California

Lydia B. Chilton
Massachusetts Institute of Technology Computer Science and Artificial Intelligence Laboratory, Cambridge, Massachusetts

Victoria H. Chou
Massachusetts Institute of Technology Computer Science and Artificial Intelligence Laboratory, Cambridge, Massachusetts

Elizabeth F. Churchill
Yahoo! Research, Sunnyvale, California

Michael F. Cohen
Microsoft Research, Redmond, Washington

Kevin Collins
Stanford University, San Francisco, California

Allen Cypher
IBM Almaden Research Center, San Jose, California

William de Beaumont
Institute for Human and Machine Cognition, Pensacola, Florida

Mira Dontcheva
Adobe Systems, San Francisco, California

Steven M. Drucker
Microsoft Research, Redmond, Washington

Clemons Drews
IBM Almaden Research Center, San Jose, California

Rob Ennals
Intel Labs, Berkeley, California

James A. Fogarty
Computer Science & Engineering, University of Washington, Seattle, WA

Björn Hartmann
University of California, Berkeley, California

Alexander Faaborg
Massachusetts Institute of Technology Media Laboratory, Cambridge, Massachusetts

George Ferguson
Department of Computer Science, University of Rochester, Rochester, New York

Jun Fujima
Fraunhofer IDMT, Childrens Media Department, Erfurt, Germany

Lucien Galescu
Institute for Human and Machine Cognition, Pensacola, Florida

Melinda Gervasio
SRI International, Menlo Park, California

Philip J. Guo
Stanford University, Stanford, California

Eben Haber
IBM Almaden Research Center, San Jose, California

Will Haines
SRI International, Menlo Park, California

Kasper Hornbæk
Department of Computer Science, University of Copenhagen, Copenhagen S, Denmark

Zhigang Hua
IBM Almaden Research Center, San Jose, California

M. Cameron Jones
Yahoo! Research, Sunnyvale, California

Hyuckchul Jung
Institute for Human and Machine Cognition, Pensacola, Florida

Eser Kandogan
IBM Almaden Research Center, San Jose, California

David Karger
Massachusetts Institute of Technology Computer Science and Artificial Intelligence Laboratory, Cambridge, Massachusetts

Shinya Kawanaka
IBM Research – Tokyo, Yamato, Kanagawa, Japan

Masatomo Kobayashi
IBM Research – Tokyo, Yamato, Kanagawa, Japan

Scott R. Klemmer
Department of Computer Science, Stanford University, Stanford, California

Tessa Lau
IBM Almaden Research Center, San Jose, California

Kristina Lerman
University of Southern California, Information Sciences Institute, Marina del Rey, California

Gilly Leshed
Information Science, Cornell University, Ithaca, New York

Joel Lewenstein
Stanford University, Stanford, California

Henry Lieberman
Massachusetts Institute of Technology Media Laboratory, Cambridge, Massachusetts

James Lin
Google Inc., Mountain View, California

Greg Little
Massachusetts Institute of Technology Computer Science and Artificial Intelligence Laboratory, Cambridge, Massachusetts

Aran Lunzer
Meme Media Laboratory, Hokkaido University, Sapporo, Japan

Tara Matthews
IBM Almaden Research Center, San Jose, CA

Robert C. Miller
Massachusetts Institute of Technology Computer Science and Artificial Intelligence Laboratory, Cambridge, Massachusetts

Brennan Moore
Massachusetts Institute of Technology Computer Science and Artificial Intelligence Laboratory, Cambridge, Massachusetts

Les Nelson
Palo Alto Research Center, Palo Alto, California

Jeffrey Nichols
IBM Almaden Research Center, San Jose, California

Mary Beth Rosson
College of Information Sciences and Technology, The Pennsylvania State University, University Park, Pennsylvania

David Salesin
Adobe Systems, San Francisco, California

Daisuke Sato
IBM Research – Tokyo, Yamato, Kanagawa, Japan

Christopher Scaffidi
School of Electrical Engineering and Computer Science, Oregon State University, Corvallis, Oregon

m.c. schraefel
School of Electronics and Computer Science, University of Southampton, Southampton, United Kingdom

Mary Shaw
Carnegie Mellon University, Institute for Software Research, School of Computer Science, Pittsburgh, Pennsylvania

Aaron Spaulding
SRI International, Menlo Park, California

Mary Swift
Department of Computer Science, University of Rochester, Rochester, New York

Hironobu Takagi
IBM Research – Tokyo, Yamato, Kanagawa, Japan

Yuzura Tanaka
Meme Media Laboratory, Hokkaido University, Sapporo, Japan

Max Van Kleek
Massachusetts Institute of Technology Computer Science and Artificial Intelligence Laboratory, Cambridge, Massachusetts

Matthew Webber
Massachusetts Institute of Technology Computer Science and Artificial Intelligence Laboratory, Cambridge, Massachusetts

Daniel S. Weld
Department of Computer Science and Engineering, University of Washington, Seattle, Washington

Eric Wilcox
IBM Almaden Research Center, San Jose, CA

Leslie Wu
Department of Computer Science, Stanford University, Stanford, California

Chen-Hsiang Yu
Massachusetts Institute of Technology Computer Science and Artificial Intelligence Laboratory, Cambridge, Massachusetts

Nan Zang
College of Information Sciences and Technology, The Pennsylvania State University, University Park, Pennsylvania

Introduction

We begin this book with two chapters that set the context for the field of end user programming since its inception in the 1980s, and look to the Web as the new focus of this growing research area. Both chapters point to the Firefox browser and its extensibility model as one of the differentiating factors in end user programming on the Web as compared to the desktop. Firefox's extensible platform combined with the simplicity and openness of HTML provide a consistent interface across many different tasks and applications, thereby enabling end user customization and automation in real settings. Cypher describes specific Web scenarios and the pain points that can be improved through end user programming, whereas Chilton et al. categorize existing browser extensions and the types of customizations that are available today.

End user programming on the Web

1

Allen Cypher
IBM Research – Almaden

ABSTRACT

This introduction explains who end users are and why they want to program. In the past 25 years, there have been two main approaches to enable end users to create their own programs: scripting languages and programming by demonstration. After outlining the challenges that confront these approaches, we shall see how the Web has removed some of the most significant barriers, opening the way for the recent progress that is detailed in this book.

THE ORIGINS OF END USER PROGRAMMING

For as long as there have been computers to program, there have been attempts to make programming easier, less technical, and available to a broader audience. The term "end user programming" proposes that although most computer users do not know how to program, they would appreciate having some of the power of programming, if only it could be obtained with little effort.

Back in the 1960s, *using* a computer meant *programming* a computer. There was no need for the concept of "end user programming" because all end users were programmers. By the 1980s, this was beginning to change. I had a friend who – in 1980 – wrote her comparative literature thesis on punch cards. She was not a programmer, but the ability to add a sentence and not have to retype a chapter was revolutionary and compelling, and she was willing to spend some effort to get some of the capabilities that had previously been available only to programmers. Then the Macintosh came out in 1984 and changed everything. Soon, computers meant "desktop computers," command languages were replaced by direct manipulation, and "end users" came into existence. These end users of computers had no desire to become programmers; they wanted to use computers to edit documents, create graphics, and, eventually, to communicate via email. Instead of programming, their goal was *computer literacy*, which meant knowing how to point-and-click in a word processor or spreadsheet.

Nonetheless – as we shall see – it is inevitable that end users will encounter tasks that are painfully repetitive, or that require an inordinate number of actions to accomplish a simple goal. In these situations, end users could simplify their interaction with the computer, if only they could program. So, in the modern world of computer literacy, there is a need for end user programming.

This chapter defines end user programming, summarizes the current state of the field, and shows how the Web has removed many of the obstacles to widespread adoption of end user programming.

WHAT IS END USER PROGRAMMING?
Who are end users?

I consider the term *end user* to refer to the vast majority of personal computer users whose use of a computer consists of taking advantage of currently available software. The range of what they can do with a computer is determined by that software. The word *end* distinguishes this group from computer programmers, because programmers use computers to create tools and applications for others to use.

End users have jobs in real estate, retail sales, car repair, and the performing arts. In their spare time, they are gardeners, cyclists, sports fans, and knitters. They use computers to communicate with their friends, to manage their photos, to find information, and to buy things.

Why do end users want to program?

Let's begin with a variety of scenarios where end users could benefit from end user programming. These are situations in everyday computer use where it would be helpful if the computer could automate part of an activity. I will use real examples from my own experience, and I will briefly describe in more general terms the motivations for end user programming that these scenarios exemplify. Chapter 2, "Why we customize the Web," offers a different perspective on why end users want to program.

1) Forward phone to home

I frequently work from home, so I like to forward my work phone to my home number. Fortunately, we have VOIP phones at work, so it is possible to use a Web site to forward the phone. The Web site offers many capabilities and many options. But I only use *one* of those capabilities, and I use it often. This activity requires nine actions, with a great deal of waiting because the Web site is slow. I would like to be able to click once and let my computer take care of forwarding the phone. See Figure 1.1.

Motivation: Many capabilities and options. In general, Web site developers need to meet the needs of all of their users, so they need to include long lists of capabilities – such as "Configure your Cisco Personal Address Book" – that are useful for someone, but are just complicating clutter to others. And even a single activity, such as paying for a purchase, may require a variety of options to handle arbitrary user preferences, such as paying with Visa, MasterCard, or PayPal. Chapter 5, "Collaborative scripting for the Web," describes a tool for automating activities with many actions.

Motivation: Unique personal information. Even if there were a special Web page for forwarding one's phone, Cisco is not going to know my home phone number. It takes a custom end user program to create "Forward Allen Cypher's work phone to his home number."

2) Pay my monthly credit card bill

Every month, I look over my credit card bill on the Web, and then schedule an automated payment for 3 days before the due date. This activity requires 15 actions. What I would really like is to click once to see the bill, and then when I'm ready, click one more time to complete the activity. See Figure 1.2.

Motivation: Poorly designed applications and Web sites. Fifteen actions is an awful lot for paying a bill, and it's likely that your credit card company has a better Web site. One reason end users create programs is to streamline and improve poorly designed applications and Web sites. It may happen that a software developer will eventually fix the problem, but it's a problem for you *now*.

3) Send text alerts

I often forget to check my personal information manager for email, so I sometimes don't see an important message until it's too late. My iPhone makes an audible beep when a text alert arrives, so I would like to get a text alert whenever I receive an urgent email from a friend.

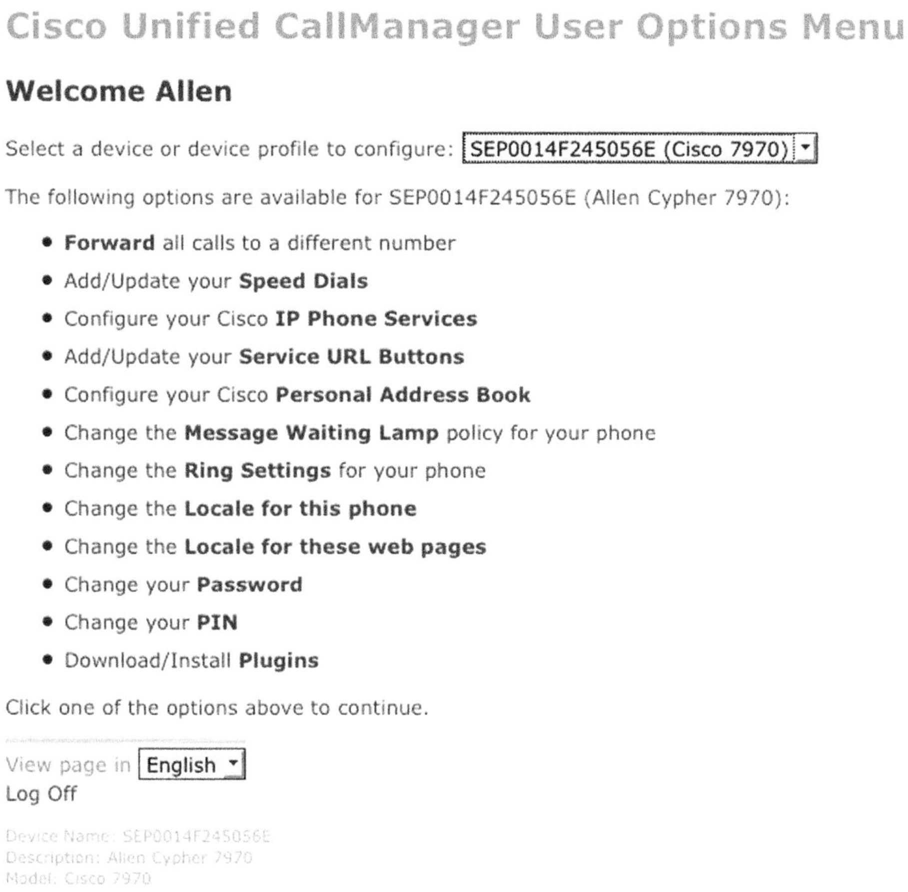

Cisco Unified CallManager User Options Menu

Welcome Allen

Select a device or device profile to configure: SEP0014F245056E (Cisco 7970) ▾

The following options are available for SEP0014F245056E (Allen Cypher 7970):

- **Forward** all calls to a different number
- Add/Update your **Speed Dials**
- Configure your Cisco **IP Phone Services**
- Add/Update your **Service URL Buttons**
- Configure your Cisco **Personal Address Book**
- Change the **Message Waiting Lamp** policy for your phone
- Change the **Ring Settings** for your phone
- Change the **Locale for this phone**
- Change the **Locale for these web pages**
- Change your **Password**
- Change your **PIN**
- Download/Install **Plugins**

Click one of the options above to continue.

View page in English ▾
Log Off

Device Name: SEP0014F245056E
Description: Allen Cypher 7970
Model: Cisco 7970

(a)

FIGURE 1.1

Forward phone to home.

(Continued)

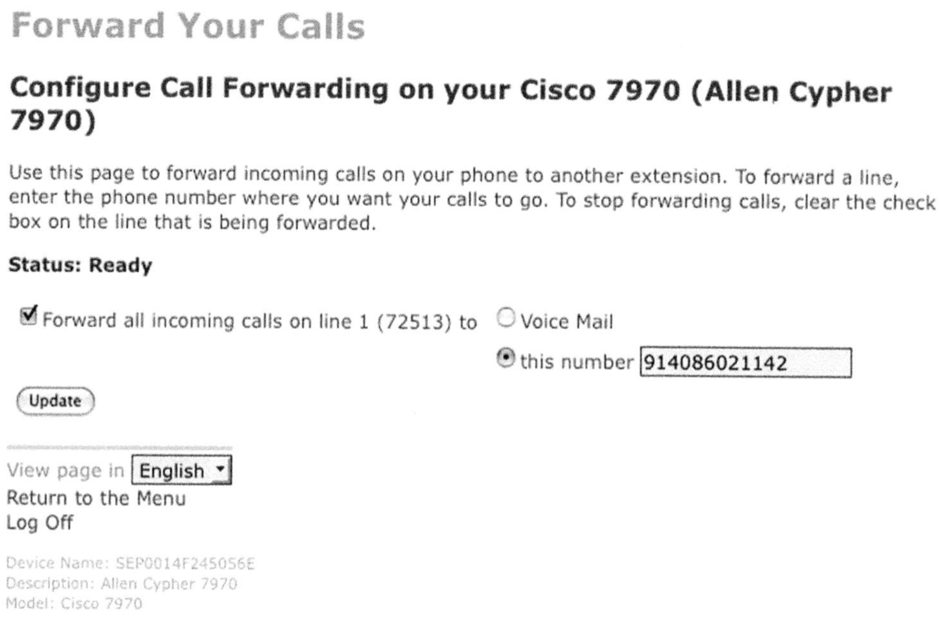

Forward Your Calls

Configure Call Forwarding on your Cisco 7970 (Allen Cypher 7970)

Use this page to forward incoming calls on your phone to another extension. To forward a line, enter the phone number where you want your calls to go. To stop forwarding calls, clear the check box on the line that is being forwarded.

Status: Ready

☑ Forward all incoming calls on line 1 (72513) to   ○ Voice Mail

◉ this number 914086021142

(Update)

View page in [English ▾]
Return to the Menu
Log Off

Device Name: SEP0014F245056E
Description: Allen Cypher 7970
Model: Cisco 7970

(b)

FIGURE 1.1—Cont'd

Motivation: Triggering automated responses. Chapter 7, "Mixing the reactive with the personal," describes an end user programming system called Atomate that lets users automate a wide variety of tasks of the form "Do A when situation B occurs." See Figure 1.6.

4) Gather hotel information

When I planned a trip to Florence and needed to find a hotel, I wanted to consult a variety of Web sites, read some reviews, select various hotels that seemed promising, and gather information about their location and price, a photo, and a sentence or two from a helpful review. A single button wouldn't work in this case, but I would have appreciated assistance in the repetitive parts of this task, and I wish there had been a way to organize all of this information. See Figure 1.3.

Motivation: Information gathering. Information gathering is such a prevalent and important use of the Web that it constitutes a new genre of activities that can be supported well by end user programming. Chapter 12, on Web summaries, addresses this genre directly.

5) Add nutritional information

Whenever I see a recipe on the Web, I wish the ingredients were accompanied by nutritional information. That information is available on other Web sites, but it requires of great deal of repetitive

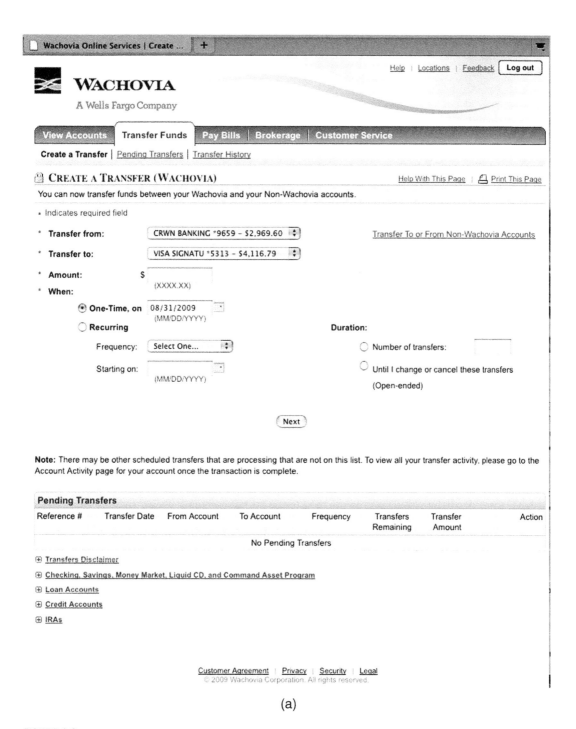

(a)

FIGURE 1.2

Pay my monthly credit card bill and the fifteen required actions.

(Continued)

1. Go to "www.wachovia.com/myaccounts"
2. Enter your "finance password" into the "Password" textbox.
3. Click the "Login" button.
4. Click the "VISA SIGNATU" link.
5. Select the "current month" from the "Current Period" listbox.
6. Click the "Go" button.
7. Copy the "Ending Balance."
8. YOU look over the statement to see if all of the charges are correct.
9. Click the "Transfer Funds" link.
10. Select the item that starts with "CRWN BANKING" from the "Transfer from:" listbox.
11. Select the item that starts with "VISA SIGNATU" from the "Transfer to:" listbox.
12. Paste into the "Amount:" textbox.
13. Select the fourth from last "when" date.
14. Click the "Next" button.
15. Click the "Submit" button.

(b)

FIGURE 1.2—Cont'd

effort to compile the information. See Figure 1.4. Another end user might want to add price information from a local grocery store.

Motivation: Mashups. End users may have personal needs that are not addressed by a single application or Web site, so they may want to "mash up" multiple sites. Chapter 4, "A goal-oriented Web browser," addresses this scenario directly, and mashups are considered in several other chapters as well.

What is end user programming?

As the examples above have illustrated, applications and Web sites are created to address specific needs and provide specific capabilities. But invariably, users find that in order to meet their own specific needs, they have to perform mundane, repetitive actions. Although it might be possible to meet these needs by writing a program, end users are not computer geeks, and one can't rely on the fascination of programming to lure them into learning a traditional programming language.

In short, end user programming is programming by people who are not professional programmers. The program is often something that only this one person wants. And because end users are engaged in performing real-world tasks, the solution often needs to be accomplished right away, while the user is performing the task.

The challenge to researchers in this field is to find ways to make limited forms of programming sufficiently understandable and pleasant that end users will be willing and able to program. The goal is to bring programming to "the rest of us," and advances in end user programming come when systems achieve an elegant balance between power and ease of use.

The gray areas

I would like to exclude solutions that are too limited in scope and power to be called programming. For instance, check boxes in a preference dialog can customize an application to better suit individual preferences, but they don't qualify as end user programming.

Montebello Splendid Hotel, Florence

Hotel Class: ★★★★★

Via Garibaldi 14
Florence 50123 Italy
Phone: 055-27471

Official site: www.montebellosplendid.com

The Montebello Splendid occupies a restored 19th
century villa in the heart of Florence. The hotel is
about two blocks from the central train station
and... more ▾

Amenities
Wheelchair Accessible, Meeting Facilities,
Babysitting, Broadband Access, Restaurant in
Hotel, Hot Tub, Air Conditioning, Television... see
all

$202
CHECK RATES

★★★★☆ Average
Rating (19)

Read 10 Reviews

Write a Review

In 13 Trip Plans　|　✚ Add to Trip

Travelers think it's best for:
Singles (1 person thinks so)
Family (1)

Tell us what YOU think

PHOTO ALBUM | IMAGE SEARCH

Add your photos of this Hotel

Montebello Splendid Hotel Deals from $202

Check Price and Availability

Check-in
| mm/dd/yy 🔲 |

Check-out
| mm/dd/yy 🔲 |

Check on Orbitz

Check on Priceline-europe

Check on Hotels.com

Check on Priceline

Check on Expedia

Check on Travelocity

Florence Hotel Deals

SPONSOR LINKS

350 **Hotel** a **Firenze** - Italia
Booking.com/hotel-a-firenze-italia　　Prenota online,
risparmi fino al 50% Nessun addebito, paga in albergo.

Florence **Hotels**
www.HotelinFirenze.com　　Budget to 5 star **Hotels** in
Florence. Discount online rates, book now.

Hotels in Florence, Italy
Venere.com/florencehotels　　View photos, maps, reviews,
rates and book: pay when you check out.

Florence, Italy hotel deals

Reviews of Montebello Splendid Hotel

10 Reviews | Write a Review

 ★★★★★
The Best!!!!
by A Yahoo! Contributor
We loved everything about the
place no complaints! The service
was amazing! Rocco, Francesca
and the rest of the staff was
class and more... more ▾

 ★★★★★
Great stay!
by A Yahoo! Contributor
Rooms are very nicely decorated
and have a very comfortable bed.
We enjoyed also the food at the
restaurant, both breakfast and
dinner... more ▾

 ★★★★★
Simply amazing
by Ozhen
One of the best hotels I've stayed
in. This hotel is simply amazing.
Elegant lobby, beautiful rooms
and the staff members were top
notch... more ▾

FIGURE 1.3

Gather hotel information.

Easy Tiramisu

SUBMITTED BY: KALLISTA   PHOTO BY:  Asli Ocak

"Yummiest dessert ever! And very easy to make. This is my family's favorite. One serving is not enough! Believe me! Don't substitute the mascarpone with double cream. There is no tiramisu without mascarpone. And use the best quality coffee."

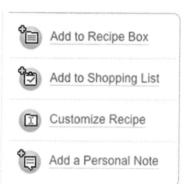

RECIPE RATING:

★ ★ ★ ★ ★

Read Reviews (49)

Review/Rate This Recipe

Add to Recipe Box

Add to Shopping List

Customize Recipe

Add a Personal Note

PREP TIME   15 Min
READY IN   1 Hr 15 Min
Original recipe yield 1 - 8x8 inch dish

Upload A Photo

SERVINGS (Help)

 Servings   Calculate

◉ US   ○ METRIC

INGREDIENTS (Nutrition)

- 3 egg yolks
- 1/4 cup white sugar
- 2 teaspoons vanilla extract
- 1 1/8 cups mascarpone cheese
- 24 ladyfingers
- 1 1/2 cups brewed coffee
- 1 tablespoon unsweetened cocoa powder

DIRECTIONS

1. In a medium bowl, beat yolks with sugar and vanilla until smooth and light yellow. Fold mascarpone into yolk mixture. Set aside.

2. Dip ladyfingers briefly in coffee and arrange 12 of them in the bottom of an 8x8 inch dish. Spread half the mascarpone mixture over the ladyfingers. Repeat with remaining cookies and mascarpone. Cover and chill 1 hour. Sprinkle with cocoa just before serving.

(a)

FIGURE 1.4

Add nutritional information.

(Continued)

(b)

FIGURE 1.4—Cont'd

```
=$A$34*G2
=FLOOR(B2/12,1)
=IF(D2=0,C2,C2+1)
=SUM(Q15,S15,$P$21)
```

FIGURE 1.5

Some typical spreadsheet formulas.

I would also like to exclude approaches that are too hard and technical to be considered an advance in making programming accessible to nonprogrammers. This includes cases where the users who adopt the approach do not represent typical end users; for instance, they may be scientists or accountants. There is good work in this area: LabView (see http://www.ni.com/labview) is a successful tool that enables end users to wire together laboratory instrumentation.

Another gray area is applications for end users that include programming as part of the application, to enable additional capabilities for advanced users. Adobe Photoshop includes a history mechanism that records each user action, and it is possible to group recorded actions into a macro for automation. Microsoft Word can be extended with the Visual Basic scripting language. But in neither of these cases is scripting essential to use of the application, nor is it a typical activity for the typical user. Perhaps one could call this amateur programming.

The special case of spreadsheet programming

Spreadsheet programmers are an important and unique subgroup of end user programmers; they are important because of their size – estimated at over 50 million people (Scaffidi, Shaw, & Myers, 2005) – and are unique because they are not averse to technical, mathematical solutions. Because spreadsheets are used to manipulate numeric data, spreadsheet programmers are comfortable with mathematical formulas and are not intimidated by abstraction. Figure 1.5 shows some typical spreadsheet formulas.

Indeed, spreadsheet applications like Microsoft Excel can be considered to be *programming environments*, and the custom spreadsheets that users of Excel create are *programs*. So it is not that spreadsheet creators need occasional access to programming capabilities to enhance their interaction with the spreadsheet application; programming is the fundamental activity in spreadsheet creation.

It is interesting to note that a whole continuum of spreadsheet users has evolved. Bonnie Nardi did a seminal study on the ecology of spreadsheet programming in her book, *A Small Matter of Programming* (Nardi, 1993), which was published in 1993. She describes the rich network of users that arises around spreadsheets, from expert programmers to individuals who only use spreadsheets created by others and do not do any formula writing themselves.

Despite the phenomenal success of end user programming with spreadsheets, it is crucial not to assume that the solutions appropriate for this audience will also be appropriate for typical end users. I am continually dismayed by researchers who want to use spreadsheets as a paradigm for all classes of end user programmers.

That said, there is significant research in the spreadsheet domain that is likely to be applicable to all types of end user programming. In particular, Margaret Burnett's work on the Surprise-Explain-Reward strategy – as a technique for motivating end user programmers to test their spreadsheet programs – is likely to be effective for Web-based end user programming as well (Wilson et al., 2003).

TWO APPROACHES TO END USER PROGRAMMING

What is it about conventional programming languages that makes them daunting and unpalatable to ordinary end users? The answer is that the text you have to write to get something done is very remote from what is being done. To click a button, you have to write something like this:

```
    theEvent.initMouseEvent("mousedown", true, true, contentWindow, 1,
  (contentWindow.screenX + clickLocH), (contentWindow.screenY + clickLocV),
  clickLocH, clickLocV, ctrlP, false, false, false, 0, null)
```

The syntax is obscure and unforgiving, and many of the details are abstract and only indirectly related to the simple action being performed. In short, traditional programming languages are *obscure, abstract,* and *indirect.* Don Norman (1986) has explained the analogous problem in user interfaces as a gulf of evaluation, and programming language researchers have referred to this issue as the "closeness of mapping" (Green & Petre, 1996).

There have been two main approaches in end user programming to deal with the difficulties of programming languages: scripting and programming by demonstration. Of the 17 systems presented in this book, 9 use scripting and 11 use programming by demonstration. Each of these approaches offers novel means of overcoming the difficulties of traditional programming while retaining some of its power. There is a third approach – visual languages – but it has had limited success. One example is LabView, but it requires sophisticated users, and much of the actual programming for LabView is done by professional programmers outside of the visual tool. Another example is Stagecast Creator (Cypher & Smith, 1995), but it is intended specifically for children.

Scripting languages

Scripting languages approach end user programming by still using a programming language, but by making that language simpler and easier to use. To accomplish this, they may restrict their solutions to a limited domain – such as spreadsheets or Web pages – and offer only limited power within that domain.

The syntax of scripting languages

Although a programming language needs to be able to express arbitrary commands like the `initMouseEvent` command shown previously, a scripting language may only need to express a few actions, such as click and type; and a few objects, such as button and textbox. So instead of the myriad possibilities of commands using the obscure format of the initMouseEvent command, a scripting language can use simplified formats like click the button. The CoScripter system in Chapter 5 uses this simplified format, whereas the Chickenfoot system in Chapter 3 uses a hybrid of the simplified and complex formats.

Scripting languages walk a fine line between power and ease of use. The formulas used in spreadsheets have opted for considerable power, at the expense of requiring significant effort to learn. For instance, a "$" preceding a symbol in a formula means that the symbol will not be modified when the formula is moved to a different cell. Although it is true that it is easier to learn to write =SUM[A1:A12] than to create commands like the initMouseEvent shown previously, this is still a far cry from the simplicity required to turn most computer users into end user programmers. The Clip Connect Clone system in Chapter 8 uses spreadsheet formulas to connect and transform data from one Web page so that it can be used in another page, but this may limit its applicability, since many users of Web browsers are not spreadsheet programmers.

Structure editors

One approach that has helped make scripting languages easier is the structure editor, where the end user creates commands by selecting words from menus, and the editor guarantees that only legal combinations of words can be selected. Figure 1.6 shows the structure editor used in Atomate, which is described in Chapter 7.

Programming by demonstration

Instead of writing programs, the end user of a Programming by Demonstration (PbD) system demonstrates an activity, and the system writes a program to perform that activity. This simplifies program creation in three ways. First, it eliminates *indirectness*, because the user interacts directly with an application by clicking its buttons, typing into its boxes, and dragging its objects. There is no need to know that the button that was clicked is the dijit_form_ComboBox_0.downArrowNode. Second, it deals with *abstractness* by working with concrete instances of a program's execution, rather than working directly with the abstractions. Third, it minimizes the problems of an *obscure syntax* by having the system write the commands for the user.

The classic challenges that must be addressed in creating programs from user demonstrations are (1) inferring the user's intent, and (2) presenting the created program to the user.

Inferring intent

Suppose I have a list of addresses that I want to add to my online address book (see Figure 1.7). After adding a few by hand, I wish I had a program that would finish this activity for me. In 1988, Witten and Mo's (1993) TELS system used PbD to automate this kind of activity.

Ideally, one would teach a PbD system just as one would teach another person: as you select the word "John," you say "copy the first name and paste it into the *First Name* box in the Address Book." Actually, with a human assistant, you would probably just say "copy this information into

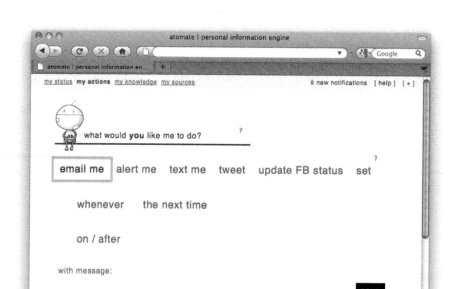

FIGURE 1.6

Atomate's structure editor.

John Bix, 2416 22 St., N.W., Calgary, T2M 3Y7. 284-4983
Tom Bryce, Suite 1, 2741 Banff Blvd., N.W., Calgary, T2L IJ4. 229-4567
Brent Little, 2429 Cheroka Dr., N.W., Calgary, T2L 2J6. 289-5678
Mike Hermann, 3604 Caritre Street, N.W., Calgary, T2M 3X7. 2340001
Helen Binnie, 2416 22 St., Vancouver, E2D R4T. (405)220-6578
Mark Willianms, 456 45 Ave., S.E., London, F6E Y3R, (678)234-9876
Gorden Scott, Apt. 201, 3023 Blakiston Dr., N.W., Calgary, T2L IL7. 289-8880
Phil Gee, 1124 Brentwood Dr., N.W., Calgary, T2L IL4. 286-7680

FIGURE 1.7

A list of unformatted addresses.

the address book." Both approaches rely on the fact that a human understands semantic concepts – people's names, addresses, and phone numbers – and has enough experience with them to be able to identify those items in the text.

Semantic knowledge

The main reason this task is difficult for a PbD system is that the system doesn't understand real-world semantic knowledge. This problem is actually not unique to PbD or even to end user programming; it is a challenge for all programmers. A professional programmer who wants to make a program that will take postal address information from a page of text and use it to fill in an address form on a Web page has to deal with exactly the same problem: how do you write a computer program that will figure out which part of the text is the first name, the last name, the street number, the street address, and so on?

Witten and Mo's system did what a programmer might do: it looked for patterns in the *syntax,* such as a series of digits, followed by a space, followed by a series of letters, and then a space followed by the letters "Dr.," or "Rd.," or "Ave." that corresponded to the semantics.

An end user might try to do the same thing with a scripting language; the huge improvement in ease of use that comes with a PbD system is that the *system* infers the syntactic pattern. Instead of writing a program, the end user just gives examples of what the system should do, and the PbD system writes the program.

Semantic challenges come in a variety of forms. Consider a mashup that annotates a corporation's list of approved hotels with the rating assigned by a travel Web site, such as TripAdvisor. (see Figure 1.8). A human can determine that "Holiday Inn Philadelphia Historic Dst." is the same as "Holiday Inn Philadelphia - Historic District," but this is problematic for a computer program. Once again, even professional programmers will find it challenging to handle this issue.

Multiple interpretations

When a user selects *Bix* in the example above, there are many syntactic inferences that the system could make about why that word was selected: because it is the second word, the first three-letter word, the first word that is followed by a comma and a space, or perhaps the second capitalized word. Examples such as *Henry van der Zanden* illustrate the complexity of the challenge.

While generating syntactic rules for semantic concepts may account for many of the inferences that PbD systems need to make, there are plenty more that are not a matter of semantics. For example, consider the possible reasons why I might click on a link on a Web page. In order to do the right thing the next time I run my PbD-generated program on that Web site, it's important to make the correct inference. When I visit my banking Web site, I always look at the charges for the second date in the list, since that is the most recently completed bill (see Figure 1.9a). Inferring from my demonstration that I always want to match the text "February 3, 2009" would be wrong; I want to always select the *second* item. However, when I check the current traffic on http://cbs5.com, I always pick the information for South Bay. Sometimes this is the fourth item in the list, sometimes it's the sixth, and sometimes it doesn't appear at all (see Figure 1.9b). There is no way to know which inference is correct from observing a single demonstration.

Presenting programs to the user

As the examples in Figure 1.9 show, a PbD system can't always make the correct inference from a single example. Sometimes, the best that PbD systems can do is to generate the "reasonable" alternatives and let the user pick the right one. A PbD system is nonetheless a great help to an end user, because *recognizing* the command for the correct inference is much easier than *writing* that

(a)

Hotel	Wired Internet Access Included?	Wireless Internet Access Included?
Holiday Inn Philadelphia Historic Dst. 400 Arch St., Philadelphia, PA 19106 800-843-2355 Rate this hotel	Yes	Yes
Radisson Plaza Warwick Philadelphia 1701 Locust St., Philadelphia, PA 19103 800-333-3333 Rate this hotel	Yes	Yes
Hilton Philadelphia City Avenue 4200 City Ave., Philadelphia, PA 19131 /1\ 215 879 4000	No 9.95 USD per day	No 9.95 USD per day

(b)

8 Holiday Inn Philadelphia - Historic District ★★★☆☆

Hotel photos | Map this hotel | Amenities | Details

#**30** of 87 hotels in Philadelphia

196 reviews

" Great hotel close to attractions " Nov 12, 2009

" Fantastic stay in a great location! " Nov 11, 2009

CHECK RATES!
Rooms available from under
$200

9 Comfort Inn Downtown/Historic Area ★★★☆☆

Hotel photos | Map this hotel | Amenities | Details

#**29** of 87 hotels in Philadelphia

143 reviews

" Filthy " Nov 12, 2009

" Great Location and Great Staff " Nov 11, 2009

CHECK RATES!
Rooms available from under

FIGURE 1.8

Determining that "Holiday Inn Philadelphia Historic Dst." is the same as "Holiday Inn Philadelphia - Historic District."

command yourself. In order for users to choose an interpretation, PbD systems need to be able to present their inferences to the user. A representation of a program is important to users for other reasons as well. It may allow the user to edit the program, verify the program's correctness, understand it, and trust that the program will do the right thing. *Presenting programs to the user* is therefore an important part of a PbD system. The problem of presenting abstractions to the user is still a major challenge for PbD systems and user interfaces in general, and it has not been simplified by the Web.

HOW THE WEB HAS REMOVED BARRIERS TO END USER PROGRAMMING

The most dramatic effect that the Web has had on end user programming is that it has removed several long-standing barriers that have kept end user programming from being useful in practice in the real world.

Open access to applications

The early work on end user programming was done at a time when desktop applications were distributed as proprietary source code that could not be modified, and user actions in the applications could not be recorded or even scripted. When Witten and Mo built their TELS system in 1988, they had to write their own text editor. This meant that no one was using TELS in their daily work. All testing had to be done in short, contrived experimental sessions, and regardless of the success and usefulness of their system, it would never be available for daily use.

We are in a very different world today. Thanks to the open source movement, the Firefox browser – as a prime example – is freely and readily available to anyone with an Internet connection. What is most important for end user programming is that this browser has a complete system for extending its capabilities. This means that any researcher can now get full access to the internal workings of the browser and the Web pages it displays. There are millions of people around the world who use this browser for their activities on the Web, and more and more of their daily activities take place on the Web. Testing can now be ecologically valid – conducted on real tasks as their users are performing them – and if a system is successful, it can now be easily given to real users for real use. The potential for widespread adoption of end user programming technology is now a reality. As an indication of the

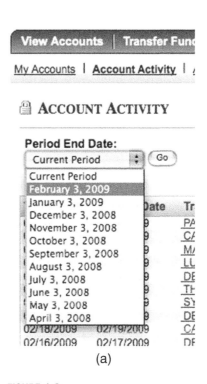

(a)

FIGURE 1.9

Match the ordinal or match the text? The correct inference for the selection in (a) is *the second item*, whereas the correct inference for the selection in

(Continued)

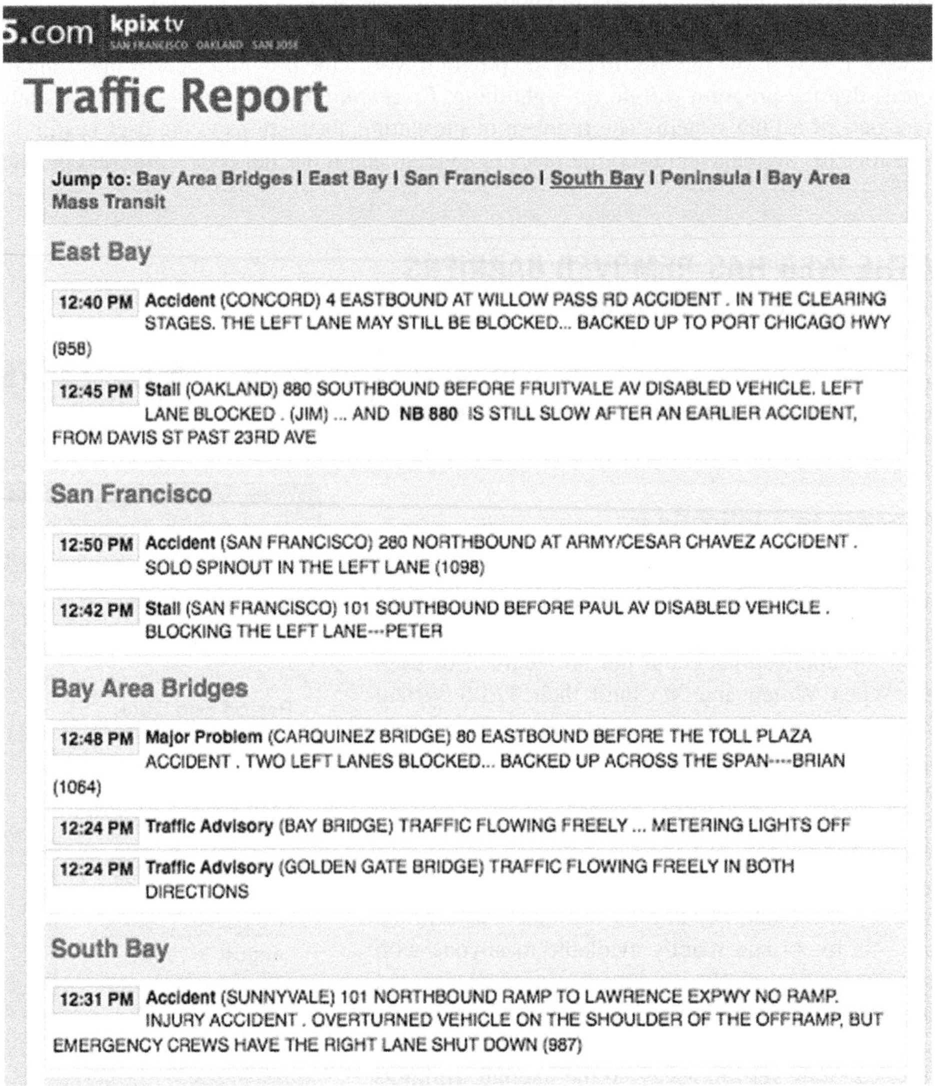

5.com **kpix** tv
SAN FRANCISCO OAKLAND SAN JOSE

Traffic Report

Jump to: Bay Area Bridges I East Bay I San Francisco I South Bay I Peninsula I Bay Area Mass Transit

East Bay

12:40 PM **Accident** (CONCORD) 4 EASTBOUND AT WILLOW PASS RD ACCIDENT . IN THE CLEARING STAGES. THE LEFT LANE MAY STILL BE BLOCKED... BACKED UP TO PORT CHICAGO HWY (958)

12:45 PM **Stall** (OAKLAND) 880 SOUTHBOUND BEFORE FRUITVALE AV DISABLED VEHICLE. LEFT LANE BLOCKED . (JIM) ... AND **NB 880** IS STILL SLOW AFTER AN EARLIER ACCIDENT, FROM DAVIS ST PAST 23RD AVE

San Francisco

12:50 PM **Accident** (SAN FRANCISCO) 280 NORTHBOUND AT ARMY/CESAR CHAVEZ ACCIDENT . SOLO SPINOUT IN THE LEFT LANE (1098)

12:42 PM **Stall** (SAN FRANCISCO) 101 SOUTHBOUND BEFORE PAUL AV DISABLED VEHICLE . BLOCKING THE LEFT LANE---PETER

Bay Area Bridges

12:48 PM **Major Problem** (CARQUINEZ BRIDGE) 80 EASTBOUND BEFORE THE TOLL PLAZA ACCIDENT . TWO LEFT LANES BLOCKED... BACKED UP ACROSS THE SPAN----BRIAN (1064)

12:24 PM **Traffic Advisory** (BAY BRIDGE) TRAFFIC FLOWING FREELY ... METERING LIGHTS OFF

12:24 PM **Traffic Advisory** (GOLDEN GATE BRIDGE) TRAFFIC FLOWING FREELY IN BOTH DIRECTIONS

South Bay

12:31 PM **Accident** (SUNNYVALE) 101 NORTHBOUND RAMP TO LAWRENCE EXPWY NO RAMP. INJURY ACCIDENT . OVERTURNED VEHICLE ON THE SHOULDER OF THE OFFRAMP, BUT EMERGENCY CREWS HAVE THE RIGHT LANE SHUT DOWN (987)

(b)

FIGURE 1.9—Cont'd

(b) is the "South Bay" item.

importance of Firefox to the end user programming community, 10 of the 17 systems described in this book are implemented as Firefox extensions.

Cross-application scripting

Until recently, all applications that were available to end users ran on top of a common desktop platform, such as the Microsoft Windows operating system or the Apple Macintosh operating system. These platforms are also proprietary, and they only provide limited access to their workings and to user actions. Researchers (Piernot & Yvon, 1993) have been concerned for a long time with finding ways to enable cross-application end user programming, because in practice, many of the tasks that users want to automate involve more than just a single application.

The popularity of the Web means that many different kinds of applications, such as word processors, email, and chat programs, as well as online banking and retail shopping, are now implemented on a single platform: the Web browser. As a result, end user programming developers have direct access to all of the data in every Web page in the browser, so the barriers to cross-application scripting have vanished.

The modern end user

The Web is only partially responsible for another enabling change for end user programming: the advent of the modern end user. The end user of today differs dramatically from the end user of the 1980s. My nephew, who is 13 years old, cannot remember a time when he did not know how to use a computer. He learned how to use a mouse before he learned how to talk. Unlike many adults who are afraid that they will do something wrong, if he doesn't know what a button does, he presses it. Users who are unafraid of technology and who are willing to try something new constitute a much more receptive audience for end user programming.

Social networks

Another trait of modern end users is that they create and share Web content, through sites like YouTube and Wikipedia. And they readily join communities with common interests, from friends on Facebook to a forum for paragliding enthusiasts. The consequence of this is that end users are ready and willing to create and share scripts, if only the tools become available that make it sufficiently easy to do so. The Chickenfoot and CoScripter systems in Chapters 3 and 5 both have Web sites where users can contribute scripts. Furthermore, users may be further motivated to put in the effort to create scripts when they know that others in their community may benefit from the scripts. The rich variety of roles that Nardi observed in the spreadsheet world may arise in Web-based social networks as well.

Semantic information

As was noted previously, the inability to apply semantic information when inferring intent has been a major obstacle to progress in PbD systems. In the age of the Internet,

1. large-scale semantic information is being collected in knowledge bases like ConceptNet (see http://conceptnet.media.mit.edu);
2. programmers are writing *data detector*s (Nardi, Miller, & Wright, 1998) to recognize semistructured information like addresses, and *data mining* techniques annotate Web pages with the detected semantic information;
3. Web sites are formatting semantic information on their pages with *microformats* (see http://microformats.org); and, most importantly,
4. this information and these programs are readily available, free of charge, and are being continually updated.

As a result, it is now becoming possible for PbD systems to circumvent the entire problem of trying to approximate semantics with syntactic patterns. The Citrine system (Stylos, Myers, & Faulring, 2004), for instance, can take a line of text like that in Figure 1.7 and, in a single action, paste the appropriate parts into the various fields of a Web form (see Figure 1.10). There will still be plenty of idiosyncratic tasks for PbD systems to automate, but now those systems won't be annoyingly "stupid" because they don't have access to basic semantic concepts. This semantic information could potentially help scripting languages as well, if they have access to data detectors.

Semantic information and HTML

No discussion of the transformative power of the Web would be complete without a consideration of its underlying language: HTML. The simplicity of HTML is largely responsible for the widespread adoption of the Web. However, along with being simple, HTML is also impoverished. In the move from the desktop to the Web, developers lost the ability to drag and drop, to precisely arrange page layout, to draw anywhere on the page, and to update a small part of a page. Nuanced interactions were replaced with jumping from page to page.

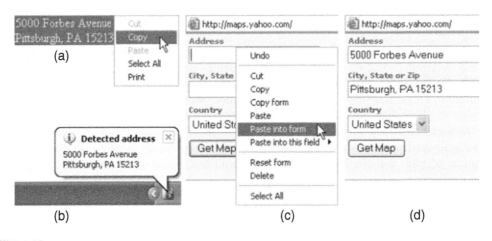

FIGURE 1.10

Citrine's address detector.

This simplicity offers – at least temporarily – a great opportunity for end user programming. Any Web page written in HTML uses the same small set of interface elements, and because HTML is a *declarative* language, most of these elements have a semantically meaningful tag, which identifies them as buttons, textboxes, and pull-down menus (e.g., <a> for a link; <input type=submit> for a button). This immediately solves the problem for PbD systems of inferring the semantics of interface elements.

However, HTML is now being augmented with techniques that bring back the richness of interaction of desktop applications, and these new techniques pose a challenge for the future success of end user programming. Adobe Flash, for instance, allows for rich user interactions, but no HTML appears on the part of a Web page that uses Flash. When users click and type in Flash, programming by demonstration systems get no indication at all that anything has happened. Similarly, the use of JavaScript, the AJAX programming style, and Web toolkits like YUI and Dojo are replacing the *declarative* format of HTML with *procedures*, or programs. For example, the buttons and textboxes in Dojo all use the semantically meaningless <div> tag, and the only way to determine the semantics of a JavaScript procedure is to read and understand the program.

As an example, consider the calendar widget in Figure 1.11. A click on the "26" in the calendar may get recorded as

```
click at (119, 252) in the "Date Selection" window
```

In terms of the semantics of the calendar widget, this click actually means

```
set the "Payment Date" to "August 26, 2009".
```

In fact, because the date highlighted in blue ("31") in this widget is the "Payment Due Date," a highly specific interpretation of the user's click would be

```
set the "Payment Date" to 3 business days before the "Payment Due Date"
```

Fortunately, the problem posed by toolkits may also afford its own solution. Toolkits enable Web site developers to use semantically rich user interface objects without having to build them by hand. This means that if just one person goes to the trouble of documenting the meaning of the items in a toolkit, then that information is available for every Web site that uses the toolkit. It is also fortunate that the need for Web site accessibility – for blind users in particular – is a strong motivation for adding just this sort of semantic annotation to a toolkit. The ARIA specification (see http://www.w3.org/WAI/intro/aria) is a standard for adding semantic annotations to toolkits, AJAX, and JavaScript. Chapter 18 describes a project that can make these semantic annotations available everywhere on the Web.

HTML is still the dominant language on Web pages, and hopefully end user programming will gain success and widespread adoption soon. If a large

August	2009
Su	**Mo**	**Tu**	**We**	**Th**	**Fr**	**Sa**
26	27	28	29	30	31	1
2	3	4	5	6	7	8
9	10	11	12	13	14	15
16	17	18	19	20	21	22
23	24	25	26	27	28	29
30	**31**	1	2	3	4	5

◀ **Today: Mon, Aug 31 2009** ▶

FIGURE 1.11

Calendar widget.

number of end users recognize its importance, there will be a reason for developers to maintain the scriptability, recordability, and accessibility of their sites.

SUMMARY

We have seen that the Web has removed many of the barriers to making end user programming successful in practice, by providing a common platform that enables the modern end user to create and share programs, and by making semantic information widely available.

WHAT'S NEXT? MOBILE END USER PROGRAMMING

As Internet-enabled smartphones and other mobile devices become more prevalent, the way end users interact with the Web is changing. There are several reasons why the customization offered by end user programming will be particularly valuable for end users of mobile devices: (1) the devices have small screens, so it's important that only relevant information be displayed; (2) without a full keyboard, user input is difficult and constrained, so it is important that users can express their specific needs with just a click or two; and (3) because mobile devices are used while people are on the move and their attention may be limited, there is an even greater need for simple displays and simple interaction. The Highlight system in Chapter 6 and the Atomate system in Chapter 7 illustrate the power of applying end user programming to mobile devices.

This book presents the latest research in end user programming, which is just the beginning in a new era of empowerment for all users of the computing technology that is transforming our interaction with the world and with each other.

Acknowledgments

I would like to thank Jeff Nichols and Chris Scaffidi for their thoughtful and provocative reviews of an earlier draft of this chapter. I would also like to thank Tessa Lau – my colleague for the past 5 years – for her work and ideas that have advanced my understanding of end user programming, particularly regarding social aspects of the Web.

Why we customize the Web

2

Lydia B. Chilton, Robert C. Miller, Greg Little, Chen-Hsiang Yu
MIT CSAIL

ABSTRACT

The Web is increasingly an application platform comparable to the desktop, but its openness enables more customizations than were possible on the desktop. This chapter examines the kinds of customization seen on the Web, focusing on the highly extensible Mozilla Firefox Web browser, and compares and contrasts the motivations for Web customization with desktop customization.

INTRODUCTION

The modern Web has grown into a platform to rival the desktop, offering not only a wealth of information and media, but also applications. The combination of private data, public data, and desktop-quality applications has created a powerful computing environment. As people use the Web to shop, plan events, consume media, manage their personal information, and much more, they also want to customize the sites they use to shape them around their preferred workflow.

Fortunately, the openness, flexibility, and common standards of the Web platform enable customizations that would not have been possible on the desktop. Web pages primarily use HTML markup to display their user interfaces, and the Document Object Model (DOM) representation for HTML inside a Web browser makes it possible to inspect and modify the page. Similarly, many Web applications are divided into individual pages with unique identifiers (URLs). State changes in the user interface are triggered by clicking hyperlinks or submitting forms, so customizations can observe state changes and cause them automatically, even without the application's help. On the desktop, by contrast, customizations must be explicitly supported by the application developer, by providing a programming interface or customization interface. The openness of the Web platform has been a fertile ground for third-party customization systems, many of which are described in this book.

This chapter looks at the landscape of Web customization, particularly for the Mozilla Firefox Web browser. We use the term *customization* in a broad sense to refer to any modification to a Web site by an end user or third party (not the original Web developer). In this chapter, however, we focus on customizations hosted by the Web browser. Customizations of this sort may automate interaction with the site – clicking links, filling in forms, and extracting data automatically. They may change the site's appearance by adding, removing, or rearranging page components. Or they may combine a site with other Web sites, commonly called a *mashup*.

Our focus on browser-hosted customizations glosses over customization features provided by Web sites themselves, such as customizable portals like iGoogle and My Yahoo. Also outside the scope of this chapter is the rich world of mashups hosted by third-party Web sites, such as the classic HousingMaps mashup of craigslist and Google Maps (http://www.housingmaps.com), as well as Web-hosted programming systems like Yahoo Pipes (http://www.pipes.yahoo.com).

One reason we focus on browser-hosted customizations is that many of the systems described in this book fall into this category. Another reason is that the Web browser is the component of the Web platform that is closest to the user and most under the user's control, as opposed to Web sites, which might be controlled by corporate entities or be more subject to legal or intellectual property restrictions. As a result, browser-hosted customizations may be the best reflection of user preferences and needs, and the best expression of user freedom, so this is where we focus our attention.

We will show that users customize the Web for many of the same reasons users customize desktop applications: to better suit their needs by making tasks less repetitive or aspects of browsing less annoying. On the Web, some of these problems arise because tasks span multiple sites, and others because Web sites may be underdeveloped and have usability problems or missing functionality. A final reason to customize the Web, not previously seen on the desktop, is to "bend the rules," circumventing legal restrictions or the intentions of the site.

The rest of this chapter is organized as follows. We start by looking back at previous research, particularly about customization on the desktop, which uncovered motivations and practices that continue to be true on the Web. We then survey some examples of customizations for Firefox, drawing from public repositories of Firefox extensions, Greasemonkey, Chickenfoot, and CoScripter scripts. We follow with a discussion of motivations for customization revealed by these examples, some of them unique to the Web platform.

CUSTOMIZATION ON THE DESKTOP

Early research on customization was exclusively on desktop customization. In many ways, Web customization achieves the same basic goal as traditional customization: making the interface match the user's needs. Yet the Web's unique platform and culture bring about several differences from traditional customization. Some of the barriers to desktop customization aren't as prevalent on the Web; the types of changes that users make on the Web are different, and customization on the Web is driven by a wider set of motivations.

In a study of the WordPerfect word processor for Windows, Page et al. describe five types of customization found on the desktop (Page, Johnsgard, & Albert, 1996). Most common was (1) setting general preferences; followed by (2) using or writing macros to enhance functionality of the application; (3) granting easier access to functionality, typically by customizing the toolbar with a shortcut; (4) "changing which interface tools were displayed," for example, showing or hiding the Ruler Bar; and (5) changing the visual appearance of the application. These categories are certainly relevant to Web customization, particularly enhancing functionality and granting easier assess to existing functionality.

Wendy Mackay studied a community of customization around a shared software environment, MIT's Project Athena, and identified four classes of reasons why users customized (Mackay, 1991). The top technological reason cited was that "something broke," so that the customization was actually a patch. The top personal reasons cited were first that the user noticed they were doing something repetitively, and second that something was "getting annoying." All of these reasons can be found in Web customization as well.

In the same study, Mackay describes barriers to customization reported by users. The most reported barrier overall was lack of time, but the chief technical reasons were that it was simply too difficult and that the application programming interfaces (APIs) were poor. End user programming systems for the Web have tried to ease the technical burden. Additionally, customizable Web sites all use the same technology, and have the same structure – the Document Object Model of HTML, modifiable with JavaScript – which reduces the need to rely on APIs.

In a study of users sharing customizations stored in text files (Mackay, 1990), Mackay highlights how important it is that authors of customizations share their work with nonprogrammers who want customizations but don't know how to write them. The same culture of sharing is just as important and widely prevalent on the Web. Mackay describes a group of "translators" who introduce the nonprogrammers to existing customizations. The Web has its own channels for distributing customizations that rely not just on repositories of customizations (like blogs and wikis) but also on personal interactions (email, forums, comments, and so on).

Mackay recommends that users "want to customize patterns of behavior rather than lists of features." Desktop applications today still concentrate on customizing lists of features, such as the commands available on a toolbar. End-user programming on the Web, however, leans heavily toward what Mackay recommends – adding new features, combining features in new ways, and streamlining the process of completing tasks, as is seen in the examples later in this chapter.

The classic end user programming system Buttons (MacLean et al., 1990) is a customization tool built around macros that can be recorded and replayed by pressing a single button. MacLean et al. point out that there is a "gentle slope" of customizability where technical inclination governs ability and willingness to customize. Web customization exhibits a similar slope. At the very basic level, users have to know about and trust browser extensions in order to even run browser-hosted customizations. To start writing customizations, a user must become familiar with an end user programming tool. At the programming level, it may be necessary for customizers to know about the HTML DOM, JavaScript, and browser APIs, such as Firefox's XPCOM components.

CUSTOMIZATION ON THE WEB

More recently, researchers have studied practices of customization on the Web, particularly mashup creation and scripting. The authors of Chapter 20 found through surveys of mashup developers that mapping sites (specifically Google Maps and Yahoo Maps) were among the most popular to mash up with other sites, and that many programming obstacles to mashup creation still exist. Wong and Hong surveyed mashup artifacts rather than the people who created them, examining two public directories of Web-hosted mashups (ProgrammableWeb and Mashup Awards) in order to discover interesting characteristics and dimensions for classifying existing mashups (Wong & Hong, 2000). Although aggregation of data from multiple sites was a very common feature, Wong and Hong also found mashups designed to personalize a site, filter its contents, or present its data using an alternative interface. This chapter takes a similar approach to Wong and Hong, surveying customizations in four public repositories, but focusing on browser-hosted customizations.

The CoScripter system in particular has been the subject of two studies of Web customization practice. Leshed et al. (2008) studied how CoScripter was used by internal IBM users, whereas Bogart et al. (2008) looked at much wider use on the Web after CoScripter was released to the public. Some of the findings from these two studies are cited in the next section.

EXAMPLES OF WEB CUSTOMIZATION

We now turn to a brief informal survey of examples of Web customization found on today's Web. These examples are mostly drawn from the public repositories of four customization systems, all designed for the Mozilla Firefox Web browser:

- *Firefox extensions* (https://developer.mozilla.org/en/Extensions) add new user interface elements and functionality to the browser, generally using JavaScript and HTML or XUL (Firefox's user interface language).
- *Greasemonkey* (http://www.greasespot.net) allows user-provided JavaScript code to be injected into a Web page and customizes the way it looks or acts.
- *Chickenfoot* (see Chapter 3) is a JavaScript programming environment embedded as a sidebar in the browser, with a command library that makes it easier to customize and automate a Web page without understanding the internal structure of the Web page.
- *CoScripter* (see Chapter 5) allows an end user to record a browsing script (a sequence of button or link clicks and form fill-in actions) and replay it to automate interaction with the browser, using a natural language-like representation for the recorded script so that knowledge of a programming language like JavaScript is not required.

Each of these systems has a public repository of examples, mostly written by users, not the system's developers. Firefox extensions are hosted by a Mozilla Web site (https://addons.mozilla.org/en-US/firefox/), whereas Greasemonkey has a public scripts wiki (http://userscripts.org), as do Chickenfoot (http://groups.csail.mit.edu/uid/chickenfoot/scripts/index.php/Main_Page) and CoScripter (http://coscripter.researchlabs.ibm.com). CoScripter is worth special mention here, because *all* CoScripter scripts are stored on the wiki automatically. The user can choose to make a script public or private, but no special effort is required to publish a script to the site, and the developers of CoScripter have been able to study both public and private scripts.

Other browser-hosted customization techniques exist. *Bookmarklets* are small chunks of JavaScript encoded into a JavaScript URL, which can be invoked when a Web page is visible, to change how that page looks and acts. Bookmarklets have the advantage of being supported by all major browsers (assuming the JavaScript code in the bookmarklet is written portably). Other browser-specific systems include User JavaScript for the Opera browser (http://www.opera.com/browser/tutorials/userjs), which is similar to Greasemonkey, and Browser Helper Objects for Internet Explorer (http://msdn.microsoft.com/en-us/library/bb250436.aspx), which are similar to Firefox extensions.

Since this survey focuses mainly on customizations for Firefox that users have chosen to publish in a common repository, it may not reflect all the ways that Web customization is being used in the wild, but these examples show at least some of the variety, breadth, and, in particular, varying motivations that drive users to customize the Web.

The rest of this section describes the following six interesting dimensions of Web customizations:

- The kind of site customized
- The nature of the customization (shortcut, simplification, mashup, etc.)
- Generic customizations (for any Web site) vs. site-specific ones
- Customizations for one-shot tasks vs. repeated use
- The creator of the customization, who is not always an end user of the site
- The relationship between the customization and the targeted site – sometimes collaborative, sometimes breaking the rules

Kind of Web site. Many scripts target Web sites for personal information management (PIM), such as email, calendars, and to-do lists, probably because users of these sites spend much time using them. Gmail alone has spawned a rich community of customizers. One popular Firefox extension, Better Gmail, bundles up several Greasemonkey scripts that change how Gmail works, among them keyboard macros, saved searches, and forced use of a secure connection. Folders4Gmail (Figure 2.1) is a Greasemonkey script that allows Gmail's flat labels to be organized into a hierarchy of folders. Google Account Multi-Login speeds up switching between different Gmail accounts with different usernames and passwords.

Other customizations target media sites, particularly for video and photo sharing. Since YouTube is widely used for posting and watching music videos, YouTube Lyrics (Figure 2.2) adds a box to video pages that searches for and displays the lyrics to the song. Other scripts and extensions support downloading videos from YouTube, and combining The Internet Movie Database (IMDb) with Bit-Torrent (a popular technology for downloading movies online). Better Flickr bundles up several scripts that enhance the usability of the Flickr photo-sharing site, including a photo magnifier, short-cuts for replying to other users' comments, and a rich text editor for comments. GMiF embeds a Google Map in a Flickr photo page to display the location of a geotagged photo.

A third major category of customized sites are search engines. The GooglePreview extension (Figure 2.3) inserts Web page thumbnails into Google and Yahoo search results, and SurfCanyon reranks search results (Google, Yahoo, craigslist, LexisNexis) and filters out undesirable sites.

PIM, media, and search may be important areas of customization for two reasons: first, because users' interaction with these sites may be highly idiosyncratic and personalized; and second, because the developers of these sites sometimes have their hands tied for legal or practical reasons, preventing them from implementing features that end users may demand. Customization is thus forced to pick up the slack.

A fourth kind of site commonly customized is online games. Travian Beyond is a Greasemonkey script for the Travian Web-based multiplayer game, which adds shortcuts and provides more sensible defaults

(a)   (b)

FIGURE 2.1

Folders4Gmail converts Gmail's flat list of labels (a) into a tree (b).

Green Day Wake Me Up When September Ends

FIGURE 2.2

YouTube Lyrics adds a lyrics box to YouTube music videos.

FIGURE 2.3

GooglePreview shows Web page thumbnails in search result listings.

to improve the usability of the game's original interface. Scripts for other gaming sites are more interested in bending (or breaking) the rules of the game – automatically farming gold, for example, or disabling ads to make the free version of a game feel more like playing the premium version.

Customization is certainly not limited to Web sites in the four areas mentioned, however, and it seems likely that the tail of the distribution is long.

Kind of customization. Many scripts are *shortcuts*, making a frequent or repeated task in the site more efficient. A classic example of a shortcut is Gmail Delete Button, a Greasemonkey script that added a delete button to Gmail's interface. When this script was created, deleting a message was possible but inconvenient. The Greasemonkey script simply makes the function accessible with one click. Another shortcut is a script that changes links to Gmail and Google Calendar so that they simply switch to an existing Gmail or Google Calendar tab rather than opening a new one (initially prototyped in Chickenfoot, and subsequently a popular Firefox extension). Other notable Chickenfoot examples include a script that adds a recently-viewed-pages box to MediaWiki, and one that forces all YouTube videos viewed into high-quality mode whenever available. Many CoScripter scripts surveyed by their developers also fall into this category. Because CoScripter was widely deployed and used within IBM before being made public, Bogart et al. found that many popular shortcuts automate internal IBM systems, such as voicemail, telephony, and business processes (Bogart et al., 2008).

A particular kind of shortcut is *automatic form fill-in*, which fills in a form with defaults. Major Web browsers, including Firefox, already provide this ability for login forms, but generally don't have good support for users who must manage multiple accounts per site. The Google Account Multi-Login mentioned previously is one script for this problem. Another is a Chickenfoot script for the Mailman mailing list system, which automatically selects the right password to use for administering a mailing list. For general form fill-in, several Firefox extensions exist, the most widely installed probably being Google Toolbar. Many CoScripter and Chickenfoot scripts also do form fill-in for specific sites and purposes, under more control by the user than a generic extension.

Simplification customizations reduce clutter and distraction, or eliminate unnecessary features. One Chickenfoot script simplifies iGoogle (Google's home page portal) by removing the logo and search box, which otherwise occupy half the screen. Another script used by one of the authors on Gmail hides the fact that there are unread messages in the Drafts folder (turning off the boldface and removing the unread message count). For general Web browsing, two very popular Firefox extensions are Adblock Plus and Flashblock, which remove advertisements and Flash objects from Web pages.

Finally, *mashups* combine two or more Web sites or services. The YouTube Lyrics script mentioned previously is a mashup between YouTube and a number of lyrics search engines. The GMiF extension (Figure 2.4) embeds a Google Map into a Flickr page to show where the photo was taken (assuming geographical metadata is found in the photo). The Delegate to Remember The Milk extension allows a Gmail message to be forwarded to the Remember The Milk to-do list site with a single click. Chickenfoot mashups include a script that posts the currently viewed item on Amazon to a Gnolia wishlist and a price comparison script for the online used textbook exchange, MIT412 (http://mit412.com), and Barnes & Noble. Finally, Chickenwire, a Chickenfoot-based mashup created by two of the authors, supports connecting YouTube and Wikipedia, so that Wikipedia pages about songs or movies can be linked to YouTube music videos or movie clips.

FIGURE 2.4

GMiF mashes up Flickr with Google Maps.

Generic vs. site-specific customization. The examples so far have targeted specific Web sites, such as Gmail, YouTube, Flickr, and Wikipedia, or specific Web interfaces, such as MediaWiki and Mailman. But other customizations are designed to change the overall experience of browsing the Web. Generic simplifiers like Adblock Plus, and generic form fill-in tools like Google Toolbar, certainly fall into this category. A generic shortcut is the Interclue extension, which pops up a preview of a hyperlink's destination when the mouse hovers over the link.

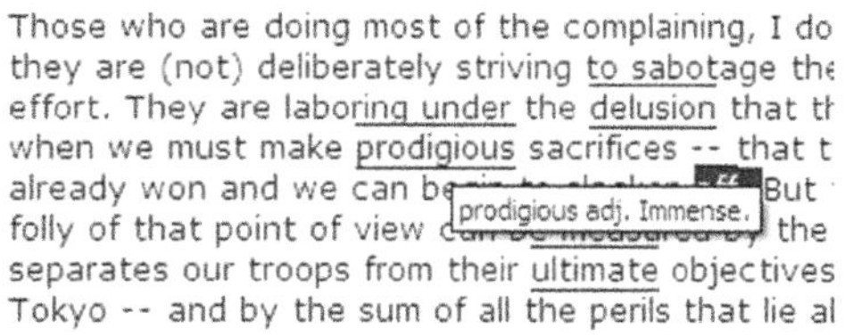

Other generic scripts focus on reading on the Web. A vocabulary-builder script for Chickenfoot (Figure 2.5) highlights words from a vocabulary list wherever they happen to be found in Web pages, and pops up definitions on mouseover, so that students can learn words in context. The LookItUp Greasemonkey script can pop up the dictionary definition of any selected word. For foreign languages, the Globefish extension helps a reader by translating selected text, and helps a writer with idioms and awkward phrasing by measuring the popularity of a phrase with Web searches. Finally, the Froggy extension developed by one of the authors reduces distraction and splits paragraphs into sentences, to help nonnative English readers increase comprehension of the text.

Those who are doing most of the complaining, I do they are (not) deliberately striving to sabotage the effort. They are laboring under the delusion that th when we must make prodigious sacrifices -- that t already won and we can be ... But folly of that point of view ... the separates our troops from their ultimate objectives Tokyo -- and by the sum of all the perils that lie al

prodigious adj. Immense.

FIGURE 2.5

Vocabulary word highlighting using a Chickenfoot script.

Other scripts help with text entry. The Virtual Keyboard Interface Greasemonkey script displays an onscreen keyboard under a textbox, for entering special characters, avoiding keyloggers, and accessibility. Chickenfoot scripts allow any textbox to be resized and add commands for joining paragraphs (removing hard line breaks) and for splitting them (inserting hard line breaks).

Another common generic script concatenates a series of Web pages, such as a multipage article or a list of search results, using a table of contents or Next link to discover the subsequent pages. An early Chickenfoot example did this, as do the Greasemonkey scripts GoogleAutoPager and AutoPagerize.

Because generic customizations essentially add functionality to the overall browser experience, they raise questions about whether the browser itself should evolve to include these features, and if not, why not. Similar questions arise about site-specific customizations; why doesn't the site itself implement these features, particularly when a customization has proved popular? Sometimes the site eventually does, but sometimes it can't, for legal or practical reasons.

One-shot vs. repeated use. Most of these examples have been designed for repeated use over time by the same user, and have little value if used only once. Another kind of script is intended for a *one-shot task* that may never be needed by the user again. One-shot scripts generally use automation or scraping to do a large task. These scripts are worth creating when the size of the task is large enough that the effort put into writing the script pays off in reduced manual effort (Potter, 1993).

An example of a one-shot task is a Chickenfoot script that clears the bounce flag on all subscribers to a Mailman mailing list. Mailman's interface makes this task tedious to do manually, first because subscribers are divided up into pages by initial letter (A, B, C, . . .), forcing the user to visit 26 or more pages for a large mailing list; and second, because each bounce flag is a checkbox next to the subscriber's email address, with no command for selecting or deselecting all checkboxes at once. The Chickenfoot script automates stepping through the pages, clearing all the checkboxes.

Other examples of one-shot automation include clean-up tasks for a wiki, transferring course grades from a college information system to a grad school application, scraping school tuition data into a spreadsheet, and calculating scores for a school contest. These examples are Chickenfoot scripts written by one or more of the authors. One-shot automation is hard to find in public repositories, since it rarely seems worth publishing. Also, the programming system used must have a low threshold to make it practical to create the one-shot script in the first place. One-shot Firefox extensions seem highly unlikely, because building a Firefox extension is a serious investment. Chickenfoot and CoScripter are easier to use for that purpose.

Creator of the customization. Most customizations are created by *users* of the Web sites they target, albeit those with more programming skills than the average user. But the customizer is not always an end user. For example, several popular Firefox extensions have been published by Web sites themselves, including Google Toolbar, Yahoo Toolbar, eBay Sidebar, and Remember The Milk for Gmail. These extensions may not strictly fit the definition of *customization* we use in this chapter, since they are provided by the original Web developer rather than a third party. They extend the Web site deeper into the browser, to run code with stronger permissions and more functionality (e.g., storing data locally or mashing up data with other sites), or to provide a more persistent, browser-level interface that follows the user around while they browse elsewhere on the Web.

Another situation arises when the customizer is not just an end user but also the *owner* of the site. Open source systems like Mailman and MediaWiki may be locally installed in an organization, and the source code for the system may be technically available to be changed, and yet Web customization may still be a more viable route. The authors have written many Chickenfoot scripts for systems that their organization owns and controls, including the Mailman bounce-flag script, a script for MediaWiki editing that provides a save-and-continue-editing command, and several scripts for the Flyspray bug database that provide simplification and shortcuts (see the section, "Making a bug tracker more dynamic," in Chapter 3). Many CoScripter scripts created for internal IBM use may also fall in this category, because IBM owns and controls many of the systems that IBM's own employees find it necessary to customize.

Finally, the customizer may be neither an end user nor a developer, but a researcher exploring new ideas in Web user interfaces. The four customization systems surveyed here have proven to be fertile ground for research prototypes, many of which are described in this book. Firefox extensions created for research purposes include Web summaries (Chapter 12), Transcendence (Bigham et al., 2008), and Intel MashMaker (Chapter 9). IE Browser Helper Objects were used by Creo (Chapter 4). Notable research uses of Greasemonkey include Accessmonkey (Bigham & Ladner, 2007), PrintMonkey (Baldwin, Rowson, & Coady, 2008), SparTag.us (Hong et al., 2008), Kalpana (Ankolekar & Vrandecic, 2008), and table browsing for small screens (Tajima & Ohnishi, 2008). In our own group, Chickenfoot has been used in Kangaroo (see the section, "Adding faces to Webmail," in Chapter 3), Smart Bookmarks (Hupp & Miller, 2007), and Inky (see Chapter 15). CoScripter has contributed to Highlight (Chapter 6) and Vegemite (Lin et al., 2009).

Is it an arms race? A final consideration is the relationship between the customization and the targeted Web site. Some customizations bend the rules of a site. In a survey of public CoScripter scripts, Bogart et al. (2008) found that 18% of scripts sampled were designed to circumvent an assumption made by the site that a human user was clicking on a button or hyperlink. One example is Automated Click for Charity, a script that visits charity Web sites and clicks on links to trigger donations without viewing the ads that pay for those donations. Other examples include ballot stuffing for online polls and automatic players for online lotteries or multiplayer games.

Many Web sites have Terms of Service agreements for their users, and these agreements may forbid certain kinds of automation. Sites may defend against customizations by technical means (such as CAPTCHA tests that distinguish humans from scripts) or legal means. One case concerned a Firefox extension that injects a button into Amazon music and video pages, linking to downloadable content on the illicit file-sharing site The Pirate Bay. The site hosting the extension was reportedly taken down by a cease and desist order from Amazon (Kravets, 2008).

Conversely, sites can welcome and support customizations. Gmail is noteworthy in this regard, providing the Gmail API for Greasemonkey to make Greasemonkey scripts easier to write and more robust to future changes.

Sites can also pay attention to what customizers are saying with their customizations, and respond with improvements. Gmail is notable here too. The Gmail Delete Button mentioned as our first example has become obsolete, because Gmail now includes a delete button.

WHY WE CUSTOMIZE

The basic reason users make customizations is that users want applications that were written for "just anybody" to be optimized for their work habits and preferences. On the Web, this means that users want (1) individual sites to have the features they need, (2) sites to be able to work together for certain tasks, and (3) improvements to Web browsing in general, that is, customizations that affect all sites that they visit. In addition, many Web sites are less developed than most desktop software. Some sites get launched before they are fully functional, and some sites don't get regularly updated and have interfaces that could be improved from the user standpoint.

From surveying existing Web customizations, we can say that some of the prevalent reasons Mackay found for users making desktop software customizations in her 1991 paper are still true on the Web today.

Mackay identified one of the top reasons to customize being that the user became aware of doing something repetitive. Many customizations on the Web have been written to eliminate redundant actions. For users who are constantly clicking away ads, there are ad blocking customizations. For users who spend time looking up uncommon words, there are customizations that add definitions for certain words in a tool tip. For users who commonly search for icons, a customization adds a single button to Google that searches for small (icon-sized) images. For users who repetitively look at the large product images while shopping online, there are customizations to load all the full-size images automatically.

Additionally, Mackay reported that feeling annoyed was a reason for customization. The Web has seen customizations to work around the annoyance of not being able to bookmark pages such as airline fare results. There are customizations to reduce the saliency of ads on a page to make reading the content less annoying. For users who find it annoying that Ctrl-S doesn't "save and continue" in MediaWiki edit pages, there is a customization to bind the shortcut to that action on all MediaWiki edit pages.

Many repetitive tasks span multiple pages: shopping comparisons, looking up words in an online dictionary, and looking up airfares, for example. Web customizations can navigate through a sequence of pages or mash up multiple Web sites, whereas it is uncommon for desktop customizations to use more than one application. GooglePreview inserts Web page thumbnails in Google and Yahoo search results.

Some of the customizations we have seen are changes to individual sites that fix usability problems that the sites could fix eventually. Users who make these changes don't want to wait; they want to stay ahead of the curve. This includes simple changes like moving the login interface to the top of the page where it is more useful, and adding a delete button to Gmail, which is a change Gmail eventually made.

One way in which Web customization is unique is that for some sites, customization is the only way to get certain features, because the site will never provide them. Legal restrictions prevent some sites from adding features, and some commercial sites have an disincentive to provide certain features. Bogart et al. refer to customizations that circumvent the intentions of a site as "changing the rules" (Bogart et al., 2008). Because legal restrictions prevent Wikipedia from hosting copyrighted content, one customization keeps its own list of links to YouTube videos relevant to each Wikipedia page and includes those videos every time the user visits a Wikipedia page. YouTube doesn't allow users to download its video content largely for legal reasons, but there are several customizations that make it trivial to download the videos as they stream. There are also customizations to recommend torrent sites for particular movies on IMDb. Among the CoScripter customizations designed to change the rules, the most devious may be a script to automate voting on a poll whose winner receives money. Other changing-the-rules customizations include injecting one shopping site with price comparisons to other sites, and scrubbing ads out of applications such as Gmail or sponsored search results in search engines.

In summary, users customize the Web for some of the same reasons users usually customize: to better suit their needs by making tasks less repetitive or aspects of browsing less annoying. On the Web, some of these problems arise because tasks span multiple sites, and some of them arise because Web sites can be underdeveloped and have usability problems or missing functionality. Lastly, an important reason to customize the Web is to "bend the rules," circumventing legal restrictions or the intentions of the site.

SUMMARY AND FUTURE DIRECTIONS

This chapter has shown a variety of motivations for customization in the Web browser. Customizations were fundamentally enabled by both the inherent openness of Web technology and the particular decision by Mozilla developers to make Firefox highly extensible. The threshold of customization was lowered still further by Greasemonkey, Chickenfoot, and CoScripter, all of which were built on top of Firefox's extension mechanism.

Although one can expect the world of Web customization to continue to grow in size and richness, challenges remain. One continuing problem is robustness. Web sites change over time, in appearance and organization and internal structure. Customizations that target a changing Web site will decay unless maintained and updated. If the Web site commits to supporting customizations, as Gmail does through its Greasemonkey API, then this problem can be mitigated, but it seems unlikely that more than a tiny fraction of Web sites will ever do this. Customization systems that target the rendered user interface of the site (as Chickenfoot and CoScripter do) may prove more robust to change than those that operate on internal HTML/JavaScript interfaces (like Greasemonkey), but this remains to be proven.

Another perennial challenge comes from programming platforms that run inside the browser but do not provide the same degree of reflection and modification as HTML and JavaScript. Java applets are probably the oldest example, but Adobe Flash/Flex and Microsoft Silverlight are becoming widely used as well. Currently these platforms are used more for embedding components (like video players or ads) in a mostly HTML site, rather than implementing the entire site, but as the trend toward richer interactive experience continues, site developers may find the new platforms very enticing. A site whose entire functionality is provided by Flash or Silverlight can't be customized using the systems described in this chapter. New approaches may be required, lest we slip back toward the closed and less customizable world of the desktop.

We have focused on browser-hosted customizations in this chapter, but a serious limitation of this approach is that the user's customizations don't easily move with them as they use different browsers on different computers. CoScripter has an advantage here, because it stores all scripts on a wiki so that any Firefox browser with CoScripter installed can access them. Mozilla Weave (https://mozillalabs.com/weave/) is an effort to solve this problem in general, by synchronizing Firefox extensions and other preferences across multiple installations of the browser.

Finally, although we made a distinction in this chapter between "desktop" and "Web," in fact the Web platform we considered might better be called the "Web desktop" – the Web as seen by a conventional Web browser like Mozilla Firefox running on a conventional desktop or laptop computer with a big screen, keyboard, and pointing device. The future of the Web platform is much more diverse. Web browsers will turn up in a variety of different devices and contexts, including cell phones, netbooks, TV set-top boxes, home media servers, and wall displays. Mobile Web customization is already an active area of research, as demonstrated by Creo (Chapter 2) and Highlight (Chapter 6), but much work remains to be done to give users the power to customize the Web of the future.

Customizing and Automating

2

In this section we look at five systems that customize and automate the Web experience in different ways. Chickenfoot proposes a scripting interface for controlling and augmenting Web page interfaces, making it possible to modify any bookstore page with local library book availability information. Creo and Miro leverage a vast knowledge base to generate personalized semantic hypertext, like dynamically linking the names of foods to their nutritional information. CoScripter helps knowledge workers collaboratively automate repetitive tasks, such as ordering office supplies. Highlight lets users create a mobile version of any Web site, whereas Atomate makes it possible to quickly set up contextualized reminders for a task.

There are many similarities and differences between these systems. Chickenfoot, CoScripter, and Atomate all aim to simplify the underlying Web scripting language (i.e., JavaScript) by introducing keyword-based scripting languages that can be both read by a machine and understood by a human. CoScripter, Highlight, and Creo use a programming by example approach that lets users demonstrate the type of automation they would like to script. Highlight enables users to clip parts of Web pages as part of a demonstration, whereas Creo leverages a large knowledge base of semantic information to generate a script from a single demonstration. CoScripter also explores the social component of end user programming through sharing and reuse with a wiki. The Atomate system proposes that programming by example is not only valuable in automating information gathering and procedural tasks but also in personal information management tasks, such as setting up reminders, organizing notes, and coordinating social events between people.

Rewriting the Web with Chickenfoot

Robert C. Miller, Michael Bolin, Lydia B. Chilton, Greg Little, Matthew Webber, Chen-Hsiang Yu
MIT CSAIL

ABSTRACT

On the desktop, an application can expect to control its user interface down to the last pixel, but on the World Wide Web, a content provider has no control over how the client will view the page, once delivered to the browser. This creates an opportunity for end users who want to automate and customize their Web experiences, but the growing complexity of Web pages and standards prevents most users from realizing this opportunity. This chapter describes Chickenfoot, a programming system embedded in the Firefox Web browser, which enables end users to automate, customize, and integrate Web applications without examining their source code. One way Chickenfoot addresses this goal is a technique for identifying page components by keyword pattern matching. We motivate this technique by studying how users name Web page components, and present a heuristic keyword matching algorithm that identifies the desired component from the user's name. We describe a range of applications that have been created using Chickenfoot and reflect on its advantages and limitations.

INTRODUCTION

The World Wide Web has become a preferred platform for many kinds of application development. Over the past decade, applications that formerly would have been designed for the desktop – calendars, travel reservation systems, purchasing systems, library card catalogs, map viewers, crossword puzzles, and even Tetris – have made the transition to the Web, largely successfully.

The migration of applications to the Web opens up new opportunities for user interface customization. Applications that would have been uncustomizable on the desktop sprout numerous hooks for customization when implemented in a Web browser, without any effort on the application developer's part. Displays are represented primarily by machine-readable HTML or XML, navigation and commands are invoked by generic HTTP requests, and page designs can be reinterpreted by the browser and tailored by style sheets. Unlike desktop applications, Web applications are much more exposed and open to modification. Here are some of the customization possibilities that arise when an application is moved to the Web.

Transforming a Web site's appearance. Examples of this kind of customization include changing defaults for form fields, filtering or rearranging Web page content, and changing fonts, colors, or element sizes. Web sites that use Cascading Style Sheets (CSS) have the potential to give the end user substantial control over how the site is displayed, since the user can override the presentation with personal style sheet rules.

Automating repetitive operations. Web automation may include navigating pages, filling in forms, and clicking on links. For example, many conferences now use a Web site to receive papers, distribute them to reviewers, and collect the reviews. A reviewer assigned 10 papers must download each paper, print it, and (later) upload a review for it. Tedious repetition is a good argument for automation. Other examples include submitting multiple queries and comparing the results, and collecting multiple pages of search results into a single page for easy printing or additional sorting and filtering.

Integrating multiple Web sites. The simplest kind of integration is just adding links from one site to another, but much richer integration is possible. For example, many retailers' Web sites incorporate maps and directions provided by a mapping service directly into their Web pages, to display their store locations and provide driving directions. But end users have no control over this kind of integration. For example, before buying a book from an online bookstore, a user may want to know whether it is available in the local library, a question that can be answered by submitting a query to the library's online catalog interface. Yet the online bookstore is unlikely to provide this kind of integration, not only because it may lose sales, but because the choice of library is inherently local and personalized to the user. This is an example of a *mashup*, a combination of data or user interface from more than one site.

These examples involve not only *automating* Web user interfaces (clicking links, filling in forms, and extracting data) but also *customizing* them (changing appearance, rearranging components, and inserting or removing user interface widgets or data). The openness and flexibility of the Web platform enables customizations that would not have been possible on the desktop.

Previous approaches to Web automation used a scripting language that dwells outside the Web browser, such as Perl, Python, or WebL (Kistler & Marais, 1998). For an end user, the distinction is significant. Cookies, authentication, session identifiers, plugins, user agents, client-side scripting, and proxies can all conspire to make the Web look significantly different to an agent running outside the Web browser. Highly interactive Web applications like Google Mail and Google Maps – sometimes called AJAX applications (Garrett, 2005) because they use asynchronous Java-Script and XML – have made this situation worse.

But perhaps the most telling difference, and the most intimidating one to a user, is the simple fact that outside a Web browser, a Web page is just raw HTML. Even the most familiar Web portal can look frighteningly complicated when viewed as HTML source.

Chickenfoot is a programming system we have developed that provides a platform for automating and customizing Web applications through a familiar interface – as Web pages rendered in a Web browser. The challenge for Chickenfoot is simply stated: a user should not have to view the HTML source of a Web page to customize or automate it.

Chickenfoot addresses this challenge in three ways. First, it runs inside the Web browser, so that the rendered view of a Web page is always visible alongside the Chickenfoot development environment. Second, its language primitives are concerned with the Web page's user interface, rather than its internal details. For example, Chickenfoot uses commands like `click`, `enter`, and `pick` to interact with forms. Third, it uses novel pattern matching techniques to allow users to describe components of a Web page (targets for interaction, extraction, insertion, or customization) in terms that make sense for the rendered view. For example, `click` identifies the button to be clicked using keywords from its text

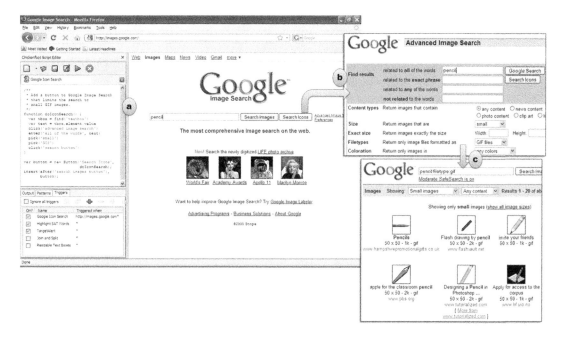

FIGURE 3.1

Chickenfoot in action. (a) Chickenfoot sidebar showing a complete script that customizes Google Image Search with a new "Search Icons" button, which (b) automatically fills out the Advanced Search form to (c) display only small GIF images matching the query.

label, rather than the name it was given by the Web page designer. Figure 3.1 shows Chickenfoot in action, with a script for Google Image Search that uses some of these commands.

Chickenfoot is implemented as an extension for the Mozilla Firefox Web browser, written in Java, JavaScript, and XUL. It consists of a development environment, which appears as a sidebar of Firefox, and a library built on top of JavaScript. Chickenfoot customizations are essentially JavaScript programs, so Chickenfoot currently does not support nonprogramming users. We assume that a Chickenfoot user has *some* knowledge of JavaScript and HTML – not an unreasonable assumption, because many power users showed the ability and willingness to learn these during the explosive growth of the Web. The problem Chickenfoot is addressing is not learning JavaScript and HTML syntax, but rather reading and understanding the complex HTML used by today's Web applications.

Naturally, many users would benefit from a Web automation system that avoids the need to learn programming language syntax. While Chickenfoot is only one step towards this goal, we regard it as a crucial one, since it provides a level of expressiveness and completeness unavailable in special purpose Web automation systems.

One system similar to Chickenfoot in implementation is Greasemonkey (http://www.greasespot. net), a Firefox extension that can run user-written JavaScript on Web pages just after they are loaded in the browser. Though Greasemonkey enables mutation and automation of Web pages in the browser, it still requires users to understand the HTML underlying the page. Platypus (http://platypus.mozdev.org) is another Firefox extension, designed to work with Greasemonkey, that allows some customization of rendered Web pages, but not automation or integration of multiple Web sites.

The rest of this chapter is organized as follows. First we give an overview of the Chickenfoot language and development environment, and describe a range of applications we have built using Chickenfoot. Then we delve deeper into a novel aspect of Chickenfoot: the pattern matching used to identify Web page elements for automation or customization. We describe a survey of Web users that motivated the design of the pattern matching, and present the algorithm we developed as a result. Finally we discuss some experience and lessons learned from the Chickenfoot project, review related work, and conclude.

CHICKENFOOT

Chickenfoot is an extension to the Mozilla Firefox Web browser, consisting of a library that extends the browser's built-in JavaScript language with new commands for Web automation, and a development environment that allows Chickenfoot programs to be entered and tested inside the Web browser. This section describes the essential Chickenfoot commands, including pattern matching, form manipulation, page navigation, and page modification. The section concludes by describing the development environment (Figure 3.1a).

Language

Chickenfoot programs are written in JavaScript, using the JavaScript interpreter built into Mozilla Firefox. As a result, Chickenfoot users have access to the full expressiveness of a high-level scripting language, with a prototype-instance object system, lexically scoped procedures, dynamic typing, and a rich class library.

Because Chickenfoot uses JavaScript, Web developers can transfer their knowledge of JavaScript from Web page development over to Chickenfoot. Chickenfoot predefines the same variables available to JavaScript in Web pages – for example, `window`, `document`, `location`, `frames`, `history` – so that JavaScript code written for inclusion in a Web page can generally be used in a Chickenfoot script that operates on that Web page. JavaScript has its own ways of visiting new pages (`location`), manipulating form controls (`document.forms`), and modifying page content (using the Document Object Model, or DOM). These mechanisms can be used by Chickenfoot scripts in addition to the Chickenfoot commands described in the next few sections. We have found that the native JavaScript mechanisms generally require reading and understanding a Web page's HTML source. But by providing access to them, Chickenfoot provides a smooth escape mechanism for script developers that need to do something more low-level.

Pattern matching

Pattern matching is a fundamental operation in Chickenfoot. To operate on a Web page component, most commands take a pattern describing that page component.

Chickenfoot supports three kinds of patterns: keywords, XPath, and regular expressions. A keyword pattern consists of a string of keywords that are searched in the page to locate a page component, followed by the type of the component to be found. For example, "Search form" matches a form containing the keyword "Search," and "Go button" matches a button with the word "Go" in its label. The component type is one of a small set of primitive names, including link, button, textbox, checkbox, radiobutton, listbox, image, table, row, cell, and text (for text nodes). When a keyword pattern is used by a form manipulation command, the type of page component is often implicit and can be omitted. For example, click("Go") searches for a hyperlink or button with the keyword "Go" in its label. Case is not significant, so click("go") has the same effect. Keyword patterns are one example of *sloppy programming* (see Chapter 15).

An XPath pattern uses the XPath pattern matching syntax to identify nodes in the HTML document. For example, the XPath pattern "//b" finds all elements in the page that are tagged with <b> (bold); "//b//a" finds hyperlinks inside bold elements; and "//div[@class='box']" finds <div> elements that have the class attribute "box". The XPath syntax is far more powerful and precise than keyword patterns, but harder to learn and use correctly, and often requires close examination of the page's HTML to create, understand, and debug a pattern. XPath patterns are generally used to identify parts of a page for modification or extraction; form manipulation is often easier to do with keyword commands instead.

The third kind of pattern, regular expressions, search the visible text content of the page, using JavaScript's regular expression syntax and semantics. For example, /[A-Z]\w+/ finds capitalized words in the page. For the purpose of matching, the page content is divided into *paragraph blocks* by hard line breaks (
 elements) and HTML block-level element boundaries. The pattern is applied separately to each paragraph. Thus /^\w+/ matches words at the start of a block, and /ISBN: .*/ will match only part of a block, not the entire page after "ISBN" first appears.

Chickenfoot's find command takes one of these patterns and searches for it in the current page. A keyword pattern is represented simply as a string, whereas XPaths and regular expressions are represented by XPath and RegExp objects:

```
find("Search form") // finds a form with "Search" somewhere in it
find(new XPath("//b//a")) // finds hyperlinks in bold
find(/\w+/) // finds words in the page
```

Find returns a Match object, which represents the first match to the pattern and provides access to the rest of the matches as a JavaScript iterator. Here are some common idioms using find:

```
// test whether a pattern matches
if (find(pattern).hasMatch) { ... }
// count number of matches
find(pattern).count
// iterate through all matches
for each (m in find(pattern)) { ... }
```

A Match object represents a contiguous region of a Web page, so it also provides properties for extracting that region. If m is a Match object, then m.text returns the plain text it represents, that is, the text that would be obtained by copying that region of the rendered Web page and pasting it to a text editor that ignored formatting. Similarly, `m.html` returns the source HTML of the region, which is useful for extracting the region with formatting intact. Finally, `m.element` returns the DOM `Element` object represented by the region, if the region contains a single outermost element. This `element` can be used to get and set element attributes, for example: `find("link").element.href`.

The `find` command is not only a global procedure, but also a method of `Match` (returned by a previous `find`) and `Tab` (which identifies a Firefox tab or window). Invoking `find` on one of these objects constrains it to return only matches within the page or part of a page represented by the object. Here are some common idioms:

```
// nested finds
for each (t in find("table")) {
    for each (r in t.find("row")) {

        ...

    }
}
// find in a different tab
otherTab.find(pattern)
```

Clicking

The `click` command takes a pattern describing a hyperlink or button on the current page and causes the same effect as if the user had clicked on it. For example, these commands click on various parts of the Google home page:

```
click("Advanced Search") // a hyperlink
click("I'm Feeling Lucky") // a button
```

Keyword patterns do not need to exactly match the label of the button or hyperlink, but they do need to be unambiguous. Thus, `click("Lucky")` would suffice to match the "I'm Feeling Lucky" button, but in this case, `click("Search")` would be ambiguous between the "Google Search" button and the "Advanced Search" link, and hence would throw an exception. Exact matches take precedence over partial matches, however, so if there was a single button labeled Search, then the `click` command would succeed.

Another way to eliminate ambiguity is by prefixing the pattern with an index, like "first", "second", "third", and so on, so `click("second Search")` will click on the second search button.

When a button or link has no text label, but an image instead, then the search can use keywords mentioned in the image's alt and title attributes, if any. The keyword matching algorithm is described in more detail later in this chapter.

The `click` command can take a `Match` object instead of a pattern, if the button or hyperlink to be clicked has already been found. For example, to identify the "I'm Feeling Lucky" button using an XPath pattern, the user might write something like this:

```
click(new XPath("//input[@name='btnI']"))
```

This example illustrates why XPath is generally less readable than keywords.

Form manipulation

The `enter` command enters a value into a textbox. Like `click`, it takes a pattern to identify the textbox, but in this case, the keywords are taken from the textbox's caption or other visible labels near the textbox. For example, to interact with the Amazon login page, a script might say:

```
enter("e-mail address", "rcm@mit.edu")
enter("password", password)
```

When the page contains only one textbox, which is often true for search forms, the keyword pattern can be omitted. For example, this sequence does a search on Google:

```
enter("EUP book")
click("Google Search")
```

Checkboxes and radio buttons are controlled by the `check` and `uncheck` commands, which take a keyword pattern that describes the checkbox:

```
check("Yes, I have a password")
uncheck("Remember Me")
```

The `pick` command makes a selection from a listbox or drop-down box (which are both instantiations of the HTML `<select>` element). The simplest form of `pick` merely identifies the choice by a keyword pattern:

```
pick("California")
```

If only one choice in any listbox or drop-down on the page matches the keywords (the common case), then that choice is made. If the choice is not unique, `pick` can take two keyword patterns, the first identifying a listbox or drop-down by keywords from its caption, and the second identifying the choice within the listbox:

```
pick("State", "California")
```

Like `find`, all the clicking and form manipulation commands are also methods of `Match` and `Document`, so that the keyword search can be constrained to a particular part of a page:

```
f = find("Directions form")

f.enter("address", "32 Vassar St")
f.enter("zip", "02139")
f.click("Get Directions")
```

The form manipulation commands described so far permit setting the value of a form widget, which is the most common case for Web automation. To read the current value of a widget, a script can use `find` to locate it, and then access the value of its Element object in conventional JavaScript fashion, for example:

```
find("address textbox").element.value
```

Chickenfoot also provides a `reset` command, which resets a form to its default values, though `reset` is rarely needed.

Other input

Chickenfoot can also simulate more low-level mouse and keyboard input. The `click` command can simulate a mouse click on any page component. By default it searches only through buttons and hyperlinks, but this default can be overridden by specifying a component type. For example, instead of using `check` or `uncheck` to set a checkbox, one can toggle it with `click`:

```
click("Remember Me checkbox")
```

Similarly, the `keypress` command sends low-level keystrokes to a particular page component. Unlike `enter`, which takes a string of text to fill a textbox, `keypress` takes a sequence of keywords describing individual keypresses. Valid keywords include characters (a, A, %, etc.), key names (enter, f1, home, tab, backspace, etc.), and modifier keys (shift, ctrl, control, etc.). The key sequence is interpreted from left to right, and modifier keys affect the first character or key name that follows them; for example, `"ctrl x c"` produces Control-X followed by "c". Examples include:

```
keypress("password", "enter") // presses Enter on the password textbox
keypress("ctrl s") // sends Ctrl-S to the only textbox on the page
keypress("E U P space b o o k") // types "EUP book" in the only textbox
```

The last `keypress` command above is almost equivalent to `enter("EUP book")`, except that `enter` discards the old contents of the textbox, if any, whereas `keypress` inserts the keystrokes wherever the textbox's selection happens to be.

Navigation and page loading

In addition to loading pages by clicking on links and submitting forms, Chickenfoot scripts can jump directly to a URL using the `go` command:

```
go("http://www.google.com")
```

If the string is not a valid URL, `go` automatically adds the prefix "http://".

Conventional browser navigation operations are also available as Chickenfoot commands: `back`, `forward`, and `reload`.

The `openTab` command opens a page in a new tab, returning a `Tab` object representing the tab:

```
google = openTab("www.google.com")
```

To retrieve a page without displaying it, the `fetch` command can be used. It returns a `Tab` object representing the invisible page:

```
google = fetch("www.google.com")
```

The JavaScript `with` statement is convenient for performing a sequence of operations on a different tab, by implicitly setting the context for Chickenfoot pattern matching and form manipulation:

```
with (fetch("www.google.com")) {
    enter("syzygy")
    click("Google Search")
}
```

A tab created with `openTab` and `fetch` can be brought to the front by calling its `show` method and closed with its `close` method. The `Tab` object representing the current tab is stored in a read-only variable, `tab`.

Pages retrieved by `go`, `openTab`, `fetch`, and `click` are loaded asynchronously by the browser, while the Chickenfoot script continues to run. Thus, a script can fire off several `fetch` requests in parallel, without forcing each request to complete before the next one starts. When a subsequent Chickenfoot command needs to access the content of a page, such as `find`, the command automatically blocks until the page is fully loaded. The `wait` and `ready` commands make this blocking available to programmatic control. Both commands take a `Tab` object or an array of `Tabs` as an argument. With no arguments, the default is the current tab. `Wait` blocks until at least one of the specified tabs is fully loaded, and returns that tab. `Ready` returns a loaded tab only if it has already completed, otherwise it immediately returns `null`.

Page modification

Chickenfoot offers three primitive commands for changing the content of Web pages: `insert`, `remove`, and `replace`.

The `insert` command takes two arguments: a location on a page and a fragment of Web page content that should be inserted at that location. In its simplest form, the location is a keyword pattern, and the Web page content is simply a string of HTML. Since insertion must use a single point in the page, not a range of content, the `before` or `after` commands must be used to reduce the pattern match to a point:

```
insert(before("textbox"), "<b>Search: </b>")
```

The location can also be a `Match` object:

```
t = find("textbox")
insert(after(t), "<b>Search: </b>")
```

The page content to be inserted can also be a `Match` or `Node`, allowing content to be extracted from another page and inserted in this one:

```
map = mapquest.find("image") // where mapquest is a tab showing a map
insert(after("Directions"), map)
```

The `remove` command removes page content identified by its argument, which can be a pattern or `Match` object. For example:

```
remove("Google image")
```

The `replace` command replaces one chunk of page content with another. It is often used to wrap page content around an existing element. For example, the following code puts every number in the page in boldface:

```
for each (num in find(/\d+/)) {
    replace(num, "<b>"+num.text+"</b>")
    }
```

Widgets

When a Chickenfoot script needs to present a user interface, it can create links and buttons and insert them directly into a Web page. Hyperlinks are created by the `Link` constructor, which takes a chunk of HTML to display inside the hyperlink and an event handler to run when the link is clicked:

```
new Link("<b>Show All</b>", showAll)
```

The event handler should be a JavaScript function object. Buttons are created similarly by the `Button` constructor.

Other widgets can be created by inserting HTML, e.g.:

```
insert(..., "<input type=checkbox>")
```

If an `onclick` attribute is included in this HTML element, however, the code it contains will execute like conventional, untrusted JavaScript code downloaded with the page. Commands defined by Chickenfoot would be unavailable to it. Instead, the right way to add a Chickenfoot handler to a button is to use the `onClick` command:

```
onClick(button, showAll)
```

Keyboard handlers can also be attached using the `onKeypress` command, which takes an optional page component, a key sequence (specified using words as in the `keypress` command) and a handler function:

```
onKeypress("ctrl s", saveWikiPage)
onKeypress("username textbox", "tab", fillInPassword)
```

Development environment

Figure 3.2 shows a screenshot of the development environment provided by Chickenfoot, which appears as a sidebar in Firefox. At the top of the sidebar is a text editor used to compose Chickenfoot code. The editor supports multiple tabs editing different script files. This simple interface goes a long way toward making the Web browser's JavaScript interpreter more accessible to the user. Previously, there were only two ways to run JavaScript in a Web browser: by embedding it in a Web page (generally impossible if the page is fetched from a remote Web site, since the user cannot edit it), or by encoding it as a *bookmarklet*, in which the entire program is packed into a one-line URL. The Chickenfoot sidebar makes it much easier for an end user to write and run scripts. Recent Web debugging tools, such as Firebug (http://getfirebug.com), now include multiline script editors for a similar reason.

The bottom of the sidebar has three tabbed panels. The Output panel is an output window that displays output printed by the Chickenfoot `output` command, error messages and stack traces, and the result of evaluating a Chickenfoot script (i.e., the value of the last expression). If the "Record Actions" checkbox is enabled, then the Output panel also displays Chickenfoot commands corresponding to the manual actions that the user does in the browser, like `click("Search button")` or `enter("Username", "rcm")`. This feature enables some degree of self-disclosure (DiGiano & Eisenberg, 1995). A manual browsing sequence can be used as the basis for a script by recording it into the Output panel and copying it into a script.

The Patterns panel displays an interface for developing patterns, which allows the user to enter a pattern and highlight what it matches in the current page. This panel also displays the types of page components that can be used for keyword commands (`link`, `button`, `textbox`, etc.).

The Triggers panel allows a Chickenfoot script to be installed into the browser for regular use. For automatic invocation, a script can be associated with a *trigger*, which is a URL pattern, such as `http://www.amazon.com/*`. Whenever a page is loaded, if its URL matches a trigger, then the associated script executes automatically. If a page matches multiple triggers, the associated scripts execute in the fixed order given by the Triggers panel. Trigger scripts can also be invoked manually by right-clicking on a page and selecting "Run Trigger on This Page". The Triggers panel provides an interface for adding and removing trigger scripts and enabling and disabling triggers.

Finally, the Triggers panel provides a "Package Script as Firefox Extension" command, which binds one or more trigger scripts and supporting files, together with an embedded version of the Chickenfoot library, and exports the result as a Firefox extension (XPI) file. Any Firefox user can install this extension in their browser to use the triggers without having to install Chickenfoot first. Thus, customizations developed in Chickenfoot can be easily exported as full-fledged Firefox extensions.

FIGURE 3.2

Chickenfoot sidebar.

Security

All current Web browsers, including Firefox, implement a security model for JavaScript to protect Web users from malicious downloaded scripts. A major part of this security model is the *same-origin policy*, which prevents JavaScript code downloaded from one Web server from manipulating a Web page downloaded from a different server. This restriction is clearly too severe for Chickenfoot, because its primary purpose is integrating and customizing multiple Web sites. As a result, Chickenfoot scripts run at a privileged level, where they have access to the entire Web browser, all pages it visits, and the user's filesystem and network. Users must trust Chickenfoot code as much as they trust any other desktop application. As a result, Chickenfoot scripts cannot be embedded in downloadable Web pages like other JavaScript. But Chickenfoot code *can* inject new behavior into downloaded pages, for example, by inserting new widgets and attaching event handlers to them.

KEYWORD MATCHING ALGORITHM

One of the novel aspects of Chickenfoot is the use of keyword patterns to identify page elements, such as `"Search button"` and `"address textbox"`. A heuristic algorithm resolves a keyword pattern to a Web page component. Given a name and a Web page, the output of the algorithm is one of the following: (1) a component on the page that best matches that name, (2) *ambiguous match* if two or more components are considered equally good matches, or (3) *no match* if no suitable match can be found.

Some components, like buttons and hyperlinks, have a label directly associated with the component, which makes the keyword search straightforward. Other components, like textboxes, checkboxes, and radio buttons, typically have a label appearing nearby but not explicitly associated with the component, so Chickenfoot must search for it. (HTML supports a <label> element that explicitly associates labels with components like these, largely to help screen reader software, but this element is unfortunately rarely used by Web sites.) This section outlines the algorithm for locating a textbox given a keyword pattern. Other components are handled similarly, but with different heuristics for finding and ranking labels.

The first step is to identify the text labels in the page that approximately match the provided name, where a *label* is a visible string of content delimited by block-level tags (e.g., <p>, <br>, <td>). Button labels and `alt` attributes on images are also treated as visible labels. Before comparison, both the name and the visible labels are normalized by eliminating capitalization, punctuation, and extra white space. Then each label is searched for keywords occurring in the name. Matching labels are ranked by edit distance, so that closer matches are ranked higher.

For each matching label, we search the Web page for textboxes that it might identify. Any textbox that is roughly aligned with the label (so that extending the textbox area horizontally or vertically would intersect the label's bounding box) is paired with the label to produce a candidate *(label, textbox)* pair.

These pairs are further scored by several heuristics that measure the degree of association between the label and the textbox. The first heuristic is pixel distance: if the label is too far from the textbox, the pair is eliminated from consideration. Currently, we use a vertical threshold of 1.5 times the height of the textbox, but no horizontal threshold, because tabular form layouts often create large horizontal gaps between captions and their textboxes. The second heuristic is relative position: if the label appears below or to the right of the textbox, the rank of the pair is decreased, because these are unusual places for a caption. (We do not completely rule them out, however, because users sometimes use the label of a nearby button, such as "Search", to describe a textbox, and the button may be below or to the right of the textbox.) The final heuristic is distance in the document tree: each *(label, textbox)* pair is scored by the length of the shortest path through the DOM tree from the *label* node to the *textbox* node. Thus labels and textboxes that are siblings in the tree have the highest degree of association.

The result is a ranked list of (*label, textbox*) pairs. The algorithm returns the textbox of the highest-ranked pair, unless the top two pairs have the same score, in which case it returns *ambiguous match*. If the list of pairs is empty, it returns *no match*.

USER STUDY OF KEYWORD MATCHING

To explore the usability of the keyword pattern matching technique, we conducted a small study to learn what kinds of keyword patterns users would generate for one kind of page component (textboxes), and whether users could comprehend a keyword pattern by locating the textbox it was meant to identify.

Method

The study was administered over the Web. It consisted of three parts, always in the same sequence. Part 1 explored free-form generation of names: given no constraints, what names would users generate? Each task in Part 1 showed a screenshot of a Web page with one textbox highlighted in red, and asked the user to supply a name that "uniquely identified" the highlighted textbox. Users were explicitly told that spaces in names were acceptable. Part 2 tested comprehension of names that we generated from visible labels. Each task in Part 2 presented a name and a screenshot of a Web page, and asked the user to click on the textbox identified by the given name. Part 3 repeated Part 1 (using fresh Web pages), but also required the name to be composed only of "words you see in the picture" or "numbers" (so that ambiguous names could be made unique by counting, e.g., "2nd Month").

The whole study used 20 Web pages: 6 pages in Part 1, 8 in Part 2, and 6 in Part 3. The Web pages were taken from popular sites, such as the *Wall Street Journal*, The Weather Channel, Google, AOL, MapQuest, and Amazon. Pages were selected to reflect the diversity of textbox labeling seen across the Web, including simple captions (Figure 3.3a), wordy captions (Figure 3.3b), captions displayed as default values for the textbox (Figure 3.3c), and missing captions (Figure 3.3d). Several of the pages also posed ambiguity problems, such as multiple textboxes with similar or identical captions.

Subjects were unpaid volunteers recruited from the university campus by mailing lists. Forty subjects participated (20 females, 20 males), including both programmers and nonprogrammers (24 reported their programming experience as "some" or "lots," while 15 reported it as "little" or "none," meaning at most one programming class). All but one subject were experienced Web users, reporting that they used the Web at least several times a week.

Results

We analyzed Part 1 by classifying each name generated by a user into one of four categories: (1) *visible,* if the name used only words that were visible somewhere on the Web page (e.g., "User Name" for Figure 3.3a); (2) *semantic,* if at least one word in the name was not found on the page, but was semantically relevant to the domain (e.g., "login name"); (3) *layout,* if the name referred to the textbox's position on the page rather than its semantics (e.g., "top box right hand side"); and (4) *example,* if the user used an example of a possible value for the textbox (e.g., "johnsmith056"). About a

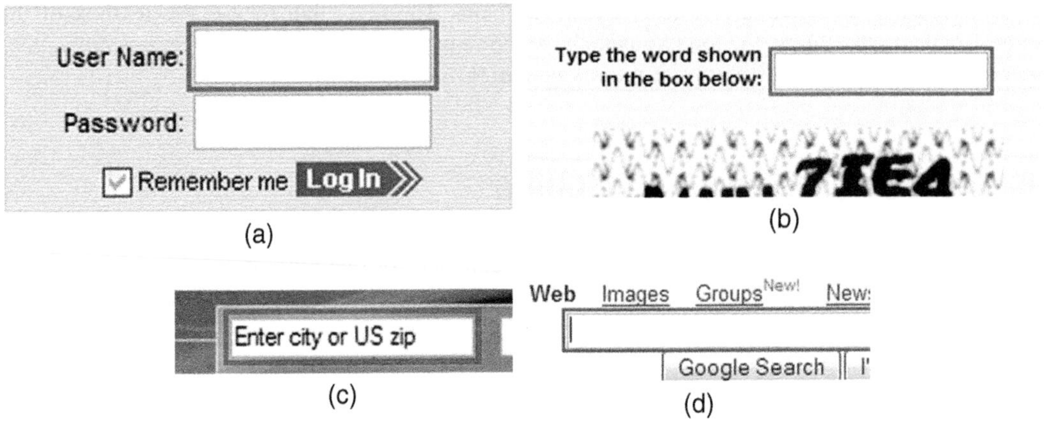

FIGURE 3.3

Some of the textboxes used in the Web survey.

third of the names included words describing the type of the page object, such as "field", "box", "entry", and "selection"; we ignored these when classifying a name.

Two users consistently used *example* names throughout Part 1; no other users did. (It is possible these users misunderstood the directions, but because the study was conducted anonymously over the Web, it was hard to ask them.) Similarly, one user used *layout* names consistently in Part 1, and no others did. The remaining 37 users generated either *visible* or *semantic* names. When the textbox had an explicit, concise caption, *visible* names dominated strongly (e.g., 31 out of 40 names for Figure 3.3a were visible). When the textbox had a wordy caption, users tended to seek a more concise name (so only 6 out of 40 names for Figure 3.3b were visible). Even when a caption was missing, however, the words on the page exerted some effect on users' naming (so 12 out of 40 names for Figure 3.3d were visible).

Part 2 found that users could flawlessly find the textbox associated with a visible name, as long as the name was unambiguous. When a name was potentially ambiguous, users tended to resolve the ambiguity by choosing the first likely match found in a visual scan of the page. When the ambiguity was caused by both visible matching and semantic matching, however, users tended to prefer the visible match: given "City" as the target name for Go.com, 36 out of 40 users chose one of the two textboxes explicitly labeled "City"; the remaining 4 users chose the "Zip code" textbox, a semantic match that appears higher on the page. The user's visual scan also did not always proceed from top to bottom; given "First Search" as the target name for eBay.com, most users picked the search box in the middle of the page, rather than the search box tucked away in the upper right corner.

Part 3's names were almost all visible (235 names out of 240), since the directions requested only words from the page. Even in visible naming, however, users rarely reproduced a caption exactly; they would change capitalization, transpose words (writing "Web search" when the caption read "Search the Web"), and mistype words. Some Part 3 answers also included the type of the page object ("box", "entry", "field"). When asked to name a textbox that had an ambiguous caption (e.g., "Search" on a page with more than one search form), most users noticed the ambiguity and tried to resolve it with one of two approaches: either counting occurrences ("search 2") or referring to other nearby captions, such as section headings ("search products").

Observations from the user study motivated several features of Chickenfoot's pattern matching. Chickenfoot does not insist on exact matches between patterns and captions, tolerating missing words, rearrangements, and capitalization changes. Chickenfoot also supports counting for disambiguation, such as using "search 2" or "second search box".

APPLICATIONS

This section describes a few of the example scripts we have created using Chickenfoot. These examples cover the three types of Web page customization discussed in the introduction (*transforming, automating,* and *integrating*), and some examples have aspects of two or more types.

Highlighting vocabulary words

We start with a simple example that *transforms* the presentation of Web pages. Students studying for college placement exams, such as the SAT, often work hard to expand their vocabulary. One way to make this learning deeper is to highlight vocabulary words while the student is reading, so that the context of use reinforces the word's meaning. One of our Chickenfoot scripts takes a list of vocabulary words and definitions (posted on the Web) and automatically highlights matching words in any page that the user browses (see Figure 3.4). The script uses a `title` attribute to pop up the word's definition as a tooltip if the mouse hovers over it:

```
for each (w=find(/\w+/)) {
    if (w.text in vocab) {
        html = "<span style='background-color: yellow' title='"
               + vocab[w.text] + "'>"
               + w + "</span>"
        replace(w, html)
    }
}
```

Sorting tables

A feature that some Web sites have, but many lack, is the ability to sort a table of data by clicking one of its column headers. A Chickenfoot script can add this functionality automatically to most tables, by replacing every table header cell it finds with a link that sorts the table. This is another example of a *transforming* customization.

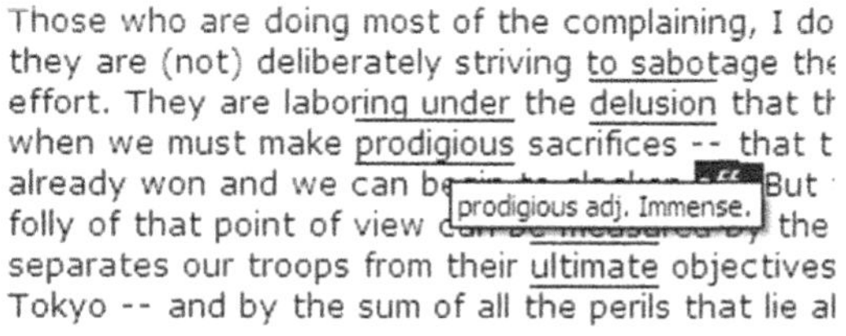

Those who are doing most of the complaining, I do they are (not) deliberately striving to sabotage the effort. They are laboring under the delusion that th when we must make prodigious sacrifices -- that t already won and we can be *prodigious adj. Immense.* But folly of that point of view the separates our troops from their ultimate objectives Tokyo -- and by the sum of all the perils that lie al

FIGURE 3.4

Vocabulary word highlighting.

Most of the script is concerned with managing the sort, but here is the part that replaces headers with links:

```
column=0
for each (h in table.find(new XPath("//th//@text"))) {
    f = makeRowSorter(table,column++)
    replace(h, new Link(h, f))
}
```

The `makeRowSorter` function returns a function that sorts the specified table by the specified column number.

Concatenating a sequence of pages

Search results and long articles are often split into multiple Web pages, mainly for faster downloading. This can inhibit fluid browsing, however, because the entire content isn't accessible to scrolling or to the browser's internal Find command. Some articles offer a link to the complete content, intended for printing, but this page may lack other useful navigation.

We have written a Chickenfoot script that detects a multipage sequence by searching for its table of contents (generally a set of numbered page links, with "Next" and "Previous"). When a table of contents is found, the script automatically adds a "Show All" link to it (Figure 3.5). Clicking this link causes the script to start retrieving additional pages from the sequence, appending them to the current page. In order to avoid repeating common elements from subsequent pages (such as banners, sidebars, and other decoration), the script uses a conservative heuristic to localize the content, by searching for the smallest HTML element that contains the list of page links (since the content is nearly always adjacent to this list) and spans at least half the height of the rendered page (since the content nearly always occupies the majority of the page). The content element from each subsequent page is inserted after the content element of the current page.

In terms of types of Web customization, this example not only *transforms* the page (by inserting additional content into it), but also *automates* it (by clicking on "Next" links on behalf of the user).

Integrating a bookstore and a library

An example of *integrating* two Web sites is a short script that augments book pages found in Amazon with a link that points to the book's location in the MIT library:

```
isbn = find(/ISBN.*: *(\d+)/).range[1]
with (fetch("libraries.mit.edu")) {
```

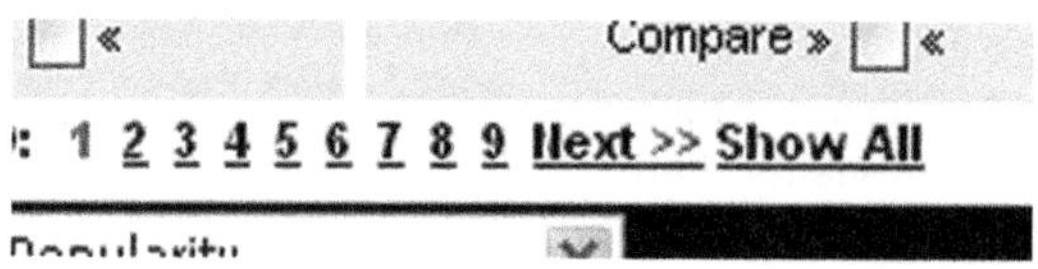

FIGURE 3.5

"Show All" link injected for page concatenation.

```
      // run on MIT library site
      pick("Keyword")
      enter(isbn)
      click("Search")
      link = find("Stacks link")
}
// now back to Amazon
if (link.hasMatch) {
      insert(before("Available for in-store pickup"), link.html)
}
```

Figure 3.6 shows the result of running this script.

Making a bug tracker more dynamic

For issue tracking in the Chickenfoot project, we use the Flyspray bug tracker (http://flyspray.org), which has the advantage of being free and simple. One downside of Flyspray is that some of its interfaces are inefficient, requiring several clicks and form submissions to use. For example, when we meet to discuss open bugs, we often use Flyspray's list view (Figure 3.7a), which displays bugs in a compact tabular form. But changing a bug's properties from this view – particularly, its priority, severity, or assigned developer – requires five clicks and waiting for three different pages to load. What we want instead is direct manipulation of the list view, so that bug properties can be edited immediately without leaving the view.

FIGURE 3.6

A link to a local library injected into a bookstore Web page.

ID	Category	Severity	Priority	Summary
495	Bug	High	Immediate	can't click on javascript: links
178	Usability	Low	High	Open File should default to Chickenfoot profile directory.
219	Documentation	Medium	High	Examples on the web site are broken
478	Documentation	Low	High	SAT word example is broken
493	New feature	Low	High	dynamically-scoped withTab
500	Bug	Critical	immediate	FF2 native libraries break 64-bit Ubuntu
476	Platform bug/Plugin conflict	High	Urgent	Load ChickenSleep manually
411	Usability	Medium	Normal	Recorder should be on all the time
412	Bug	Medium	Normal	Recorder records lots of spurious commands

(a)

FIGURE 3.7a

Flyspray bug summary display.

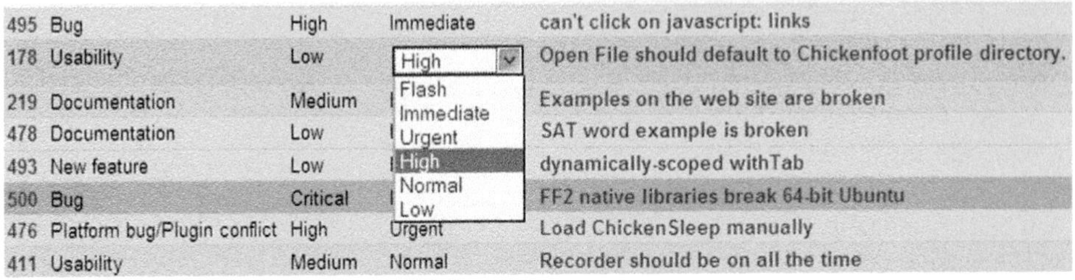

495	Bug	High	Immediate	can't click on javascript: links
178	Usability	Low	High ▼	Open File should default to Chickenfoot profile directory.
219	Documentation	Medium	Flash	Examples on the web site are broken
478	Documentation	Low	Immediate Urgent	SAT word example is broken
493	New feature	Low	High	dynamically-scoped withTab
500	Bug	Critical	Normal Low	FF2 native libraries break 64-bit Ubuntu
476	Platform bug/Plugin conflict	High	Urgent	Load ChickenSleep manually
411	Usability	Medium	Normal	Recorder should be on all the time

(b)

FIGURE 3.7b

Flyspray augmented by a Chickenfoot script so that bug properties can be edited in place.

We added this behavior to Flyspray using a Chickenfoot script, which replaces values in the table with a drop-down menu (Figure 3.7b). The script automatically discovers the available choices for each drop-down menu by opening the edit page for some bug (invisibly, using fetch) and extracting the HTML for each of its drop-down menus:

```
firstBug = find(new XPath("//td[@class='project_summary']/a"))

with (fetch(firstBug.element.href)) {
    click("Edit this task")
    priorityMenu = find("Priority listbox").html
    severityMenu = find("Severity listbox").html
    assignedToMenu = find("Assigned To listbox").html
    ... // for other fields
    close() // closes the fetched edit page
}
```

The script then attaches an onClick handler to each cell of the table, so that when a cell is clicked, the value is replaced with the appropriate drop-down menu for that column (Figure 3.7b). If the user changes the value of the property using the drop-down menu, then the script drills into the edit page for that bug (again, invisibly) and changes it:

```
with(fetch(href)) {
    click("Edit this task")
    pick("Priority", newValue)
    click("Save Details")
    wait() // make sure changes are saved before closing tab
    close()
}
```

The overall effect of this script is to make Flyspray, a traditional Web application driven entirely by form submission, feel more like a modern AJAX-driven Web application, which responds immediately and updates the server in the background. This example not only *transforms* Flyspray's interface, by adding drop-down menus, but also *automates* it when a drop-down menu is changed.

It's also worth considering why we used Chickenfoot in this case. Unlike the previous examples, which modified third-party Web sites, we control our own installation of Flyspray, which is an open source system written in PHP. Technically, we could modify Flyspray ourselves to add this feature. The main reason we chose not to was the complexity barrier of understanding and using Flyspray's internal interfaces, which we had never seen since we did not originally develop it. With Chickenfoot, however, the interface we needed to understand and use was the Flyspray *user* interface, which was simple and already very familiar to us as users of Flyspray. Writing the Chickenfoot script took less than an hour; delving into Flyspray and making it AJAX-capable would have been considerably longer.

Adding faces to Webmail

Usable security is an active area of research that aims to make computer security easier to use, and use correctly, for end users (Cranor & Garfinkel, 2005). One interesting and underexplored problem in this area is *misdirected email*, such as pressing "Reply All" when you meant to press "Reply", or mistyping an email address. Sending email to the wrong recipients is an access control error, since it inadvertently grants access to the email's contents to a different group of people than intended. One example of this error made headlines when a lawyer for the drug company Eli Lilly, intending to send a confidential email about settlement discussions to another lawyer, accidentally sent the message to a *New York Times* reporter who happened to have the same last name as the intended recipient (NPR, 2008), resulting in a front-page story (Berenson, 2008). Note that even secure email suffers from this error, because a digitally signed and encrypted message can be sent, securely, to the wrong people.

Using Chickenfoot, we have devised a novel solution to this problem that displays the faces of the recipients directly in the mail composition window of a Webmail system. The faces appear automatically as the user is composing the message, acting as a peripheral interface that informs the user without demanding direct attention. Figure 3.8 shows our interface, called Kangaroo, extending the IMP Webmail system. Our studies have found that the face display makes a substantial difference in users' ability to detect whether an email is misdirected (Lieberman & Miller, 2007).

Kangaroo is implemented as a collection of Chickenfoot scripts. One script triggers whenever a mail composition page appears, to automatically add the Face section to the page. This script triggers on URLs used by Gmail and IMP (the Webmail system MIT uses), but it could be readily extended to other Webmail systems. The script also attaches event handlers to the To, Cc, and Bcc boxes on the page, so that Kangaroo is notified when the user edits the recipient list. The same simple keyword patterns (e.g., `"To textbox"`) are sufficient to identify these controls across the three Webmail systems Kangaroo currently supports, so the porting costs to new Webmail systems are likely to be minimal.

A second set of scripts in Kangaroo are concerned with finding faces to display. The database that maps between email addresses and faces is cached locally in the user's Web browser, rather than at a server. This database is populated automatically by Chickenfoot scripts that automate searches of various Web services, including Google Images and Facebook. Another set of scripts expands mailing list addresses into their subscribers wherever possible, using Web interfaces for Mailman and Athena Blanche (a mailing list system used internally at MIT). New scripts can be

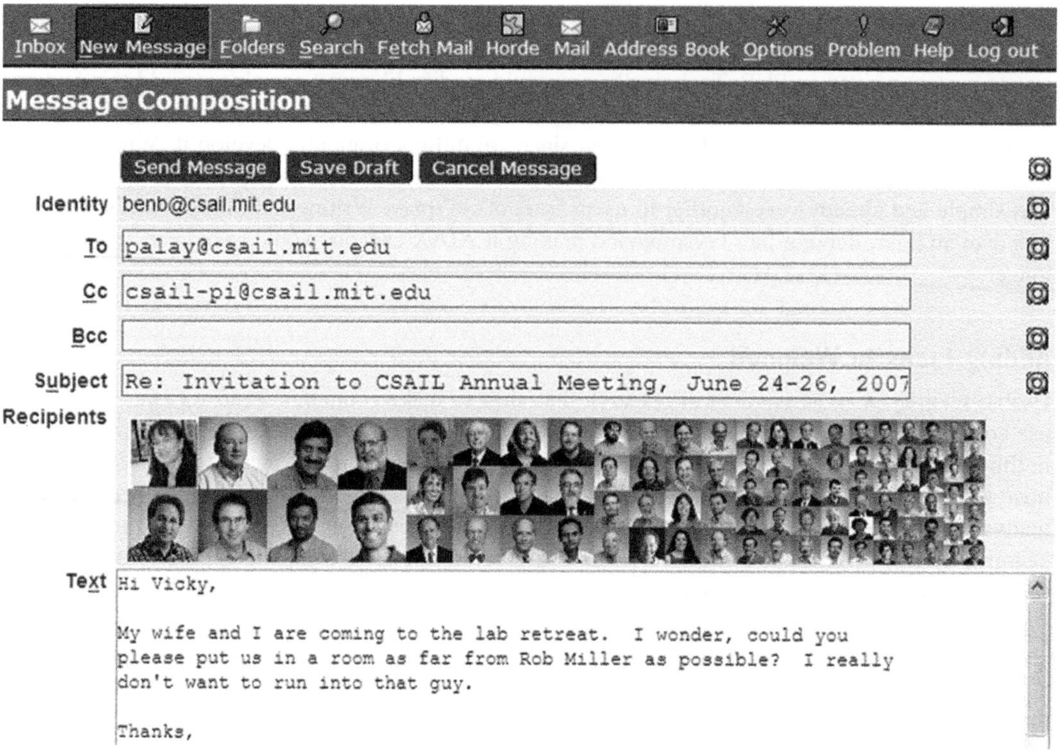

FIGURE 3.8

Kangaroo recipient-visualization interface, augmenting the IMP Webmail system. In this example, the user pressed "Reply All" by mistake, so the crowd of faces is a highly salient reminder about who will read the message.

added to support new sources of faces and new kinds of mailing lists. For example, to use Kangaroo in a corporate email environment, the corporate ID database and mailing list server could readily be connected.

Kangaroo is an example of a substantial and interesting application built on top of Chickenfoot that embodies several of Chickenfoot's key ideas: *transforming* an existing Web application (in this case, Gmail), *automating* and *integrating* multiple Web applications (like Mailman and Facebook), and programming at the level of *rendered user interfaces* ("To textbox") rather than application programming interfaces (APIs). We also use Chickenfoot's trigger-packaging functionality to make Kangaroo downloadable as a standalone Firefox extension (http://groups.csail.mit.edu/uid/kangaroo/).

In addition to Kangaroo, our research group has used Chickenfoot as a prototyping tool for several other research systems, including minimal-syntax programming (see Chapter 15), bookmarks for modern AJAX sites (Hupp & Miller, 2007), a command line for Web applications (Miller et al., 2008), and a tool that improves page readability for nonnative English readers. Chickenfoot has proven to be a flexible and useful tool for exploring new ideas in Web user interface.

DISCUSSION

This section reflects on some of the lessons learned and surprises encountered over several years of developing and using Chickenfoot, and mentions some of the open areas of future work.

A guiding design principle, mentioned in the introduction of this chapter, was that Chickenfoot users should not have to look at the HTML source of a Web page to automate and customize it. This is a hard goal to achieve, and Chickenfoot only gets some of the way there. Some success can be seen in the Kangaroo system mentioned earlier, which uses keyword patterns effectively to customize Webmail systems in a portable way. But in other cases, getting a good, unambiguous keyword pattern for some Web page controls can be very hard, so users fall back on less robust counting patterns ("third textbox") or XPath. It's not uncommon for users to use a Web page inspector, like Firebug, to help analyze and understand the Web page, and then take what they learned to write a Chickenfoot script.

An aspect of Chickenfoot that turned out to be much more important, however, was the *synchronous*, *page-independent* nature of Chickenfoot scripts, relative to ordinary JavaScript or Greasemonkey. A Chickenfoot script can be written as a simple, straight-line sequence of commands, even if those commands end up affecting different pages. The Chickenfoot interpreter automatically handles waiting for pages to load, which substantially reduces the complexity burden on the programmer. In ordinary JavaScript, this simple script might need to be torn apart into many little pieces in event handlers.

Although originally designed for end user customization of Web applications, Chickenfoot has been put to a few uses that we never anticipated, but that turn out to be very fruitful. One use already mentioned is as a testbed for our own research prototypes. Some of these prototypes customize the *browser itself* with new toolbar buttons or menu items, not just changing the Web sites it displays. This is made possible by two incidental facts: first, Firefox's user interface is mostly written in XUL (an XML-based user interface language) and JavaScript, which is very similar to the HTML/JavaScript model used in Web sites; and second, Chickenfoot scripts run with the same privileges as browser-level JavaScript, so they have permission to modify XUL and attach event listeners to it. Thus Chickenfoot can be used to prototype full-fledged Firefox extensions. One area of ongoing work is to generalize Chickenfoot's library of commands and patterns so that it works as well on XUL as it does on HTML.

Another unexpected but popular use of Chickenfoot on the Web is for functional Web testing, that is, scripts that exercise various functions of a Web application to check that they work correctly. Unlike the scenario Chickenfoot was envisioned for, in which end users customize Web sites they did not themselves create, functional Web testing is done by the Web site's own developers, who have deep knowledge of the site and its internal interfaces. Chickenfoot turns out to be a useful tool for these users nevertheless, for several reasons. First, it is based on JavaScript, so it was familiar to them, and it could directly access and call JavaScript interfaces inside the Web page. Second, a testing script written at the level of the rendered interface (e.g., click "search button") is decoupled from the internal implementation of that interface, allowing the internal interfaces to change without having to change the testing code. And finally, Chickenfoot's synchronous programming model, which automatically blocks the script while pages load, makes it easy to write test scripts.

Future work

Chickenfoot's current commands and pattern language seem well designed for *automation*, but are still weak for *data extraction*, also called Web scraping. The keyword pattern approach should be applicable here, for identifying captioned data (like "List Price: $27.95") and tabular data with labeled rows and columns. Currently, most data extraction in Chickenfoot is done with XPaths or regular expressions.

Complex or large Web pages are hard to automate efficiently and effectively with Chickenfoot. For example, nested `<iframe>` elements (which embed other HTML documents into a Web page) cause problems for XPath pattern matching, because Chickenfoot uses the XPath matcher built into Firefox, which expects only one tree with one root, and which cannot dig into an `<iframe>`. For keyword patterns and regular expressions, Chickenfoot searches all embedded documents, but then the problem becomes efficiency. Chickenfoot is written in JavaScript, and traversing large DOM trees is very slow using Firefox's current JavaScript engine. But browser developers are devoting significant resources to improving the performance of JavaScript and DOM manipulation (Paul, 2008), since they are so critical to modern Web applications, so we can anticipate that this situation will improve in the future.

A final question concerns security. Can a malicious Web site do harm to a user who is using Chickenfoot scripts? Can a malicious Chickenfoot script be installed, possibly as a Trojan horse that pretends to do something useful? The answer to both questions is probably yes, although no cases of either have been observed in the wild so far. Chickenfoot's design includes some decisions aimed at mitigating security risks. For example, Chickenfoot code cannot be embedded in Web pages like ordinary JavaScript, and Chickenfoot puts none of its own objects or interfaces into the namespace seen by ordinary Web page JavaScript. For comparison, Greasemonkey's architecture had to be rewritten to fix security holes related to the fact that Greasemonkey scripts were injected into the same namespace as the remote, untrusted JavaScript (Pilgrim, 2005).

Chickenfoot also benefits from features of Firefox designed to make general Firefox extension development safer. For example, when a Chickenfoot script obtains a reference to an object from the Web page (like the Document object, or Window, or a Node), the reference is hidden by a security wrapper called XPCNativeWrapper, which protects against certain kinds of attacks. But Chickenfoot code runs with full privileges, like other Firefox extensions or indeed like any executable run on the desktop, so it should be subjected to a high level of scrutiny. A thorough and detailed security audit of Chickenfoot remains to be done.

RELATED WORK

Several systems have addressed specific tasks in Web automation and customization, including building custom portals (Sugiura & Koseki, 1998), crawling Web sites (Miller & Bharat, 1998), and making multiple alternative queries (Fujima et al., 2004a; Bigham et al., 2008). Chickenfoot is a more general toolkit for Web automation and customization, which can address these tasks and others as well.

One form of general Web automation can be found in scripting language libraries, such as Perl's WWW::Mechanize or Python's ClientForm. These kinds of scripts run outside the Web browser, where they cannot easily access pages that require session identifiers, secure logins, cookie state, or client-side JavaScript to run.

In an attempt to access these "hard-to-reach pages" (Anupam et al., 2000), some systems give the user the ability to record macros in the Web browser, where the user records the actions taken to require access to a particular page, such as filling out forms and clicking on links. Later, the user can play the macro back to automate access to the same page. LiveAgent (Krulwich, 1997) takes this approach, recording macros with a proxy that sits between the user's browser and the Web. The proxy augments pages with hidden frames and event handlers to capture the user's input, and uses this information to play back the recording later. Unfortunately, the proxy approach is also limited – for example, pages viewed over a secure connection cannot be seen, or automated, by the proxy. WebVCR (Anupam et al., 2000) is another macro recorder for Web navigation, which skirts the proxy problem by using a signed Java applet to detect page loads and instrumenting the page with event-capturing JavaScript after the page loads. Because part of WebVCR runs as an applet inside the browser, it can record all types of navigation. But neither LiveAgent nor WebVCR enable the user to modify the pages being viewed.

CoScripter (see Chapter 5) also uses the macro recording model, but unlike these earlier systems, CoScripter runs directly in the browser as a Firefox extension. In addition, recorded CoScripter scripts are displayed to the user as a list of actions that can be read and edited by humans, such as "click on the Google Search button." CoScripter executes these instructions in a manner similar to Chickenfoot keyword pattern matching.

Toolkits such as WBI (Barrett, Maglio, & Kellem, 1997) and Greasemonkey focus on giving the user the ability to modify pages before, or just after, they are loaded in the user's Web browser. WBI uses a proxy to intercept page requests, letting user-authored Java code mutate either the request or the resulting page. Giving users the ability to automate pages with Java and all its libraries is a powerful tool; however, WBI is still hampered by the limitations of a proxy.

Though both WBI and Greasemonkey enable the user to mutate pages, neither of them eliminates the need to inspect the HTML of the page to mutate it. For example, the sample scripts on the Greasemonkey site are full of XPath patterns that identify locations in Web pages. These scripts are difficult to create because they require the author to plumb through potentially messy HTML to find the XPath, and they are difficult to maintain because they are not resilient to changes in the Web site. Chickenfoot avoids this problem by giving users a high-level pattern matching language based on keyword matching that enables the user to identify pages without knowledge of the page's HTML structure, facilitating development and increasing readability and robustness. In Chickenfoot, users can fall back on XPath expressions to select elements and JavaScript to manipulate a page's DOM, but they are not restricted to these low-level tools.

WebL (Kistler & Marais, 1998), a programming language for the Web, also focused on giving users a higher-level language to describe Web page elements. In WebL, the user provides names of HTML elements to create *piece-sets*, where a piece-set is a set of *piece* objects, and a piece is a contiguous text region in a document. WebL provides various methods to combine piece-sets called *operators*, including set operators such as `union` and `intersection`, positional operators such as `before` and `after`, and hierarchical operators such as `in` and `contain`. Although these operators help produce more readable scripts, the language does not eliminate the need to inspect a Web page for the names of its HTML elements, as the user must provide those to construct the basic pieces on which the operators work.

Another drawback of WebL, and of most of the aforementioned tools (with the exception of the macro recorders), is that they do not allow scripts to be developed inside the Web browser. We consider the ability to experiment with a Web site from the script development environment one of the greatest advantages of Chickenfoot – the user does not have to wait to see how it will affect the appearance of the Web page, because Chickenfoot gives immediate feedback on the rendered page. LAPIS (Miller & Myers, 2000), a predecessor of Chickenfoot, took a similar approach, giving the user an interactive environment in which to experiment with pattern matching and Web automation. Unfortunately, the LAPIS Web browser does not support Web standards like JavaScript, cookies, and secure connections, so it fails to provide the user with a complete Web experience.

In the time since Chickenfoot was originally released, many new systems have appeared for creating mashups between Web services. Examples include Marmite (Wong & Hong, 2006), Web Summaries (see Chapter 12), Intel MashMaker (see Chapter 9), Yahoo Pipes (http://pipes.yahoo.com/pipes/), and Vegemite (Lin et al., 2009). Most of these systems are themselves Web services, rather than browser extensions, so they have less access to the user's own data and less ability to transform the user's experience in small or personalized ways, like adding a bit of data, a keyboard shortcut, or a new link into an existing Web page. These mashup systems tend to have much richer support than Chickenfoot for data extraction and manipulation, however.

SUMMARY

Chickenfoot is a programming system for Web automation, integrated into the Firefox Web browser. Chickenfoot enables the user to customize and automate Web pages without inspecting their source, using keyword pattern matching to name page components. We showed that keyword patterns correspond closely to the names users actually generate for page components, and we presented a heuristic algorithm that implements keyword matching.

As of 2009, Chickenfoot is still being actively developed and used. The latest version is available at http://groups.csail.mit.edu/uid/chickenfoot/.

Acknowledgments

We thank all the students who have worked on Chickenfoot over the years, including Michael Bernstein, Prannay Budhraja, Vikki Chou, Mike Fitzgerald, Roger Hanna, Darris Hupp, Eric Lieberman, Mel Medlock, Brandon Pung, Philip Rha, Jon Stritar, Kevin Su, and Tom Wilson, as well as other members of the UID group who provided valuable feedback on the ideas in this chapter, including ChongMeng Chow, Maya Dobuzhskaya, David Huynh, Marcos Ojeda, and Vineet Sinha. This work was supported in part by the National Science Foundation under award number IIS-0447800, and by Quanta Computer as part of the T-Party project. Any opinions, findings, conclusions, or recommendations expressed in this publication are those of the authors and do not necessarily reflect the views of the sponsors.

This chapter is based on a paper that originally appeared as "Automation and Customization of Rendered Web Pages," in Proceedings of the 18th Annual ACM Symposium on User Interface Software and Technology (UIST 2005), © ACM, 2005. See http://doi.acm.org/10.1145/1095034.1095062.

CHICKENFOOT

Intended users:	Script programmers
Domain:	All Web sites
Description:	Chickenfoot is a system for automating and customizing Web sites by writing scripts that run inside the Web browser. The command language and pattern language are designed to work at the level of the Web site's rendered user interface, rather than requiring knowledge of the low-level HTML.
Example:	Before buying a book from an online bookstore, a user may want to know whether it is available in the local library. A Chickenfoot script can automatically answer this question by submitting a query to the library's online catalog interface, retrieving the location of the book, and injecting it directly into the Web page for the online bookstore, in the user's browser.
Automation:	Yes.
Mashups:	Yes, Chickenfoot can combine multiple Web sites within the browser.
Scripting:	Yes. Users can write scripts in JavaScript using Chickenfoot's command library, in an ordinary text editor.
Natural language:	No.
Recordability:	Yes. Recorded actions are displayed in an output panel, where they can be copied into a script.
Inferencing:	Yes. Heuristics are used to match a script command against the page. For example, click("search") triggers a heuristic search for a clickable element on the page that is labeled with the keyword "search".
Sharing:	Chickenfoot has a wiki where users post scripts and helpful library functions.
Comparison to other systems:	Similar to CoScripter in its ability to automate Web sites, although CoScripter has better support for recording scripts and a wiki integrated into its user interface.
Platform:	Implemented as an extension to Mozilla Firefox Web browser.
Availability:	Freely available at http://groups.csail.mit.edu/uid/chickenfoot/. Source code is available under the MIT license.

A goal-oriented Web browser

Alexander Faaborg, Henry Lieberman
MIT Media Laboratory

ABSTRACT

Many users are familiar with the interesting but limited functionality of data detector interfaces like Microsoft's Smart Tags and Google's AutoLink. In this chapter we significantly expand the breadth and functionality of this type of user interface through the use of large-scale knowledge bases of semantic information. The result is a Web browser that is able to generate personalized semantic hypertext, providing a goal-oriented browsing experience.

We present (1) Creo, a programming-by-example system for the Web that allows users to create a general purpose procedure with a single example; and (2) Miro, a data detector that matches the content of a page to high-level user goals.

An evaluation with 34 subjects found that they were more efficient using our system, and that the subjects would use features like these if they were integrated into their Web browser.

INTRODUCTION

In this chapter we describe a programming-by-example system for the Web named Creo, and a data detector named Miro. Working together, Creo and Miro provide the user with a goal-oriented Web browsing experience. We describe an evaluation of our software based on data from 34 users, and evaluations of our software's user interface during an iterative design process.

Finally, we conclude with a discussion of how large-scale knowledge bases of semantic information can be leveraged to improve human–computer interaction.

CONTRIBUTIONS

This chapter presents five contributions. First, the chapter demonstrates how a programming-by-example system can be used to automate repetitive tasks on the Internet, saving users time.

The central problem of programming-by-example systems is generalization. The second contribution is to show how two large knowledge bases of semantic information, MIT's ConceptNet and Stanford's TAP (The Alpiri Project), can be leveraged to improve generalization.

The chapter's third contribution is to show how a programming-by-example system can work together with a data detector, solving both recording and invocation in an integrated way.

Commercially available data detectors like Microsoft Smart Tags and Google AutoLink limit users in both the types of data that can be detected and the services that can be performed on those types of data. This chapter's fourth contribution is to show how combining a programming-by-example system with a data detector enables users to control the services associated with their data.

Finally, this chapter demonstrates how a Web browser can proactively detect a user's potential goals while they browse the Web. Although current Web browsers sit between the user and the Web, the very thin amount of interface they do provide (*Back*, *Next*, *Stop*, *Refresh*, *Home*) has little to do with the user's higher-level goals. The overall contribution of this chapter is to demonstrate how the integration of large knowledge bases of semantic information, a programming-by-example system, and a data detector can result in a goal-oriented Web browser.

TEACHING COMPUTERS THE STUFF WE ALL KNOW

Computers lack common sense. Current software applications know literally nothing about human existence. Because of this, the extent to which an application understands its user is restricted to simplistic preferences and settings that must be directly manipulated. Once software applications are given access to commonsense knowledge, hundreds of thousands of facts about the world we live in, they can begin to employ this knowledge to understand their users' intentions and goals.

Open Mind

Since the fall of 2000, the MIT Media Lab has been collecting commonsense facts from the general public through a Web site called Open Mind (Singh, 2002; Singh et al., 2002; Singh, Barry, & Liu, 2004). Currently, the Open Mind Common Sense Project has collected over 806,000 facts from over 19,000 participants. These facts are submitted by users as natural language statements of the form "tennis is a sport" and "playing tennis requires a tennis racket." Although Open Mind does not contain a complete set of all the commonsense knowledge found in the world, its knowledge base is sufficient to be useful in real-world applications.

ConceptNet

Using natural language processing, the Open Mind knowledge base was mined to create ConceptNet (Liu & Singh, 2004), a large-scale semantic network currently containing over 250,000 commonsense facts. ConceptNet consists of machine-readable logical predicates of the form:

```
(IsA "tennis" "sport")
(EventForGoalEvent "play tennis" "have racket")
```

ConceptNet is similar to WordNet (Fellbaum, 1998) in that it is a large semantic network of concepts, however ConceptNet contains everyday knowledge about the world, whereas WordNet follows a more formal and taxonomic structure. For instance, WordNet would identify a "dog" as a type of "canine," which is a type of "carnivore," which is a kind of "placental mammal." ConceptNet identifies a "dog" as a type of "pet" (Fellbaum, 1998).

Stanford TAP

The Stanford TAP knowledge base was created to help bootstrap the Semantic Web (Guha & McCool, 2002; Guha & McCool, 2003a, 2003b; Guha, McCool, & Miller, 2003; McCool, Guha, & Fikes, 2003). Unlike the Open Mind knowledge base, which was generated through the contributions of knowledge from volunteers on the Web, TAP was generated by creating 207 HTML scrapers for 38 Web sites rich with instance data. TAP has extracted knowledge from over 150,000 Web pages, discovering over 1.6 million entities and asserting over 6 million triples about these entities (McCool et al., 2003). This knowledge covers a wide variety of topics, including music, movies, actors, television shows, authors, classic books, athletes, sports, sports teams, auto models, companies, home appliances, toys, baby products, countries, states, cities, tourist attractions, consumer electronics, video games, diseases, and common drugs. The instance data found in TAP is a good complement to commonsense knowledge bases like ConceptNet or CYC (Lenat, 1995). For instance, "CYC knows a lot about what it means to be a musician. If it is told that Yo-Yo Ma is a cellist, it can infer that he probably owns one or more cellos, plays the cello often, etc. But it might not know that there is a famous cellist called Yo-Yo Ma" (Guha & McCool, 2002). For this project, the TAP knowledge base has been modified to match the formatting of ConceptNet.

A GOAL-ORIENTED WEB BROWSER

Using the knowledge in ConceptNet and TAP, we have created a toolbar for Microsoft Internet Explorer that matches the semantic context of a Web page to potential user goals. For instance, imagine a user is viewing a Web page that contains a recipe for blueberry pudding cake. The user's browser will notice a pattern of foods on the page, and present the user with two suggestions: order the foods, or view their nutritional information. When the user selects one of these buttons, all of the foods on the page turn into hyperlinks for the selected action. For instance, by pressing the "Order Food" button, each food in the recipe will be converted into a hyperlink for that food at the user's favorite online grocery store. Alternatively, the user can view the nutritional information for each of the foods at their favorite Web site for nutritional information (Figure 4.1).

After being presented with this example, a critical reader likely has two significant questions: (1) How does the browser know how to interact with the user's favorite grocery store? and (2) How does the browser know which of the terms in the recipe are foods? The answer to the first question is by enabling users to train a Web browser to interact with their favorite sites using a programming-by-example system named Creo (Latin, "to create, make"). The answer to the second question is by leveraging the knowledge bases of ConceptNet and TAP to create a next generation data detector named Miro (Latin, "to wonder"). The following two sections discuss both of these topics in detail.

It is important to note that while this "recipe to grocery store" example is used throughout the chapter for the purposes of clarity, Creo can automate interactions with other kinds of sites on the Web (not just grocery stores), and Miro can detect any type of data described in ConceptNet and TAP (not just foods).

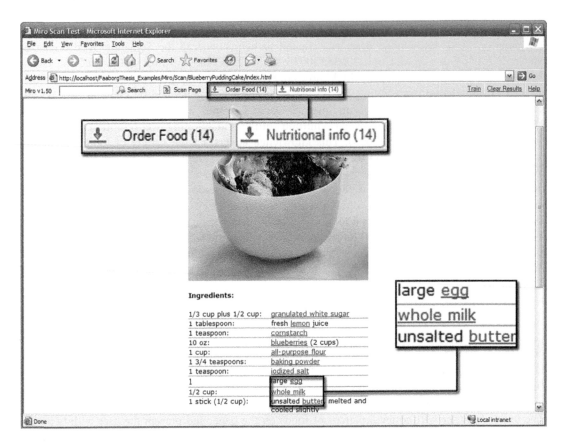

FIGURE 4.1

Automatically associating a user's high-level goals with the content of a Web page.

PROGRAMMING BY EXAMPLE

Traditional interfaces leave the user with the cognitive burden of having to figure out what sequence of actions available to them will accomplish their goals. Even when they succeed in doing this for one example, the next time the same or a similar goal arises, they are obliged to manually repeat the sequence of interface operations. Because goals tend to re-occur over time, the user is faced with having to tediously repeat procedures. A potential solution to this dilemma is programming by example (Lieberman, 2001). A learning system records a sequence of operations in the user interface, which can be associated with a user's high-level goal. It can then be replayed in a new situation when the goal arises again. However, no two situations are exactly alike. Unlike simple macro recordings, programming-by-example systems generalize the procedure. They replace constants in the recording with variables that usually accept a particular kind of data.

Previous research

The TrIAs (Trainable Information Assistants) by Mathias Bauer (Bauer, Dengler, & Paul, 2000; Lieberman, 2001) is a programming-by-example system that automates information gathering tasks on the Web. For instance, TrIAs can aggregate information from airline, hotel, weather, and map sites to help a user with the task of scheduling a trip.

Turquoise, by Rob Miller and Brad Myers (1997), is a programming-by-example system that allows nontechnical users to create dynamic Web pages by demonstration. For instance, Turquoise can be used to create a custom newspaper by copying and pasting information, or to automate the process of aggregating multiple lunch orders into the same order.

Similar to Turquoise, the Internet Scrapbook, by Atsushi Sugiura and Yoshiyuki Koseki (1998; Lieberman, 2001) is a programming-by-example system that allows users with few programming skills to automate their daily browsing tasks. With the Internet Scrapbook, users can copy information from multiple pages onto a single personal page. Once this page is created, the system will automatically update it as the source pages change.

Web Macros, created by Alex Safonov, Joseph Konstan, and John Carlis (1999), allows users to interactively record and play scripts that produce pages that cannot be directly bookmarked.

A new approach to generalization

Knowing how to correctly generalize is crucial to the success of programming by example. Past systems have either depended on the user to correctly supply the generalization, or they have attempted to guess the proper generalization using a handcrafted ontology, representing knowledge of a particular, usually narrow, domain. Our contribution is to solve both problems of generalizing procedures and proactively seeking invocation opportunities by using large knowledge bases of semantic information.

Creo

Creo allows users to train their Web browser to interact with a page by demonstrating how to complete the task. If a user decides that they are spending too much time copying and pasting the ingredients of recipes, they can easily train Creo to automate this action. To do so, the user hits the *Start Recording* button.

Creo turns red to indicate that it is in recording mode, and it captures the user's action of navigating to FreshDirect (http://www.freshdirect.com).

Next, the user searches FreshDirect for an example food, "Diet Coke." Creo detects that this was an example, and automatically generalizes the concept to "food brand."

Since these are the only two steps needed for locating a particular food at the grocery store, the user can now finish the recording and give it a name: "Order Food." By providing a single example, "Diet Coke," the user has created a general purpose recording.

In the opening example, terms like "egg," "whole milk," and "blueberries" were being linked to the grocery store, even though these are not "food brands." The reason for this is that Creo actually associates a range of generalizations with the user's input, but only displays the most general of the

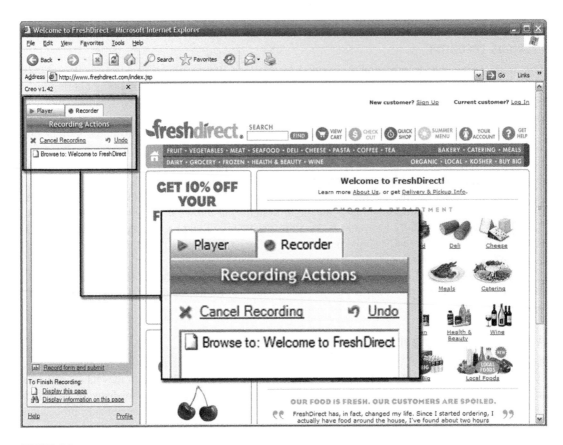

FIGURE 4.2

Creo learns how to interact with a Web site by watching the user's demonstration.

FIGURE 4.3

Creo automatically generalizes the user's input.

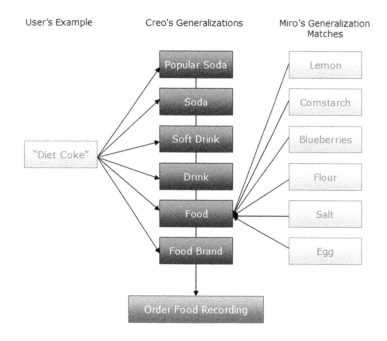

FIGURE 4.4

Foods in the recipe are matched to the user's recording.

generalizations for clarity. In this particular case, "food" was the second most general generalization of "Diet Coke," as shown in Figure 4.4.

Although this step is not required to create functional recordings, users can directly control the selected generalizations for a piece of input by clicking on the *Ask->Food brand* link shown in Figure 4.5 and clicking on the *Scan* tab.

The contextual help for this tab reads, "The Miro Toolbar will look for words that can be used in this recording when you click the Scan button." By checking and unchecking items, users can directly control Creo's generalizations. For the user's example of "Diet Coke," Creo automatically selected the generalizations of food brand, food, drink, soft drink, soda, and popular soda.

Because Creo has access to ConceptNet and TAP, users can create general purpose recordings with a single example, allowing their Web browser to automate interactions with their favorite sites.

The topic of generalization also comes into play in invoking recordings: if the user creates a recording that works on certain kinds of data, seeing that data in a new situation presents an opportunity for the Web browser to invoke the recording.

DATA DETECTORS

The purpose of data detectors is to recognize meaningful words and phrases in text, and to enable useful operations on them (Pandit & Kalbag, 1997). Data detectors effectively turn plain text into a form of hypertext.

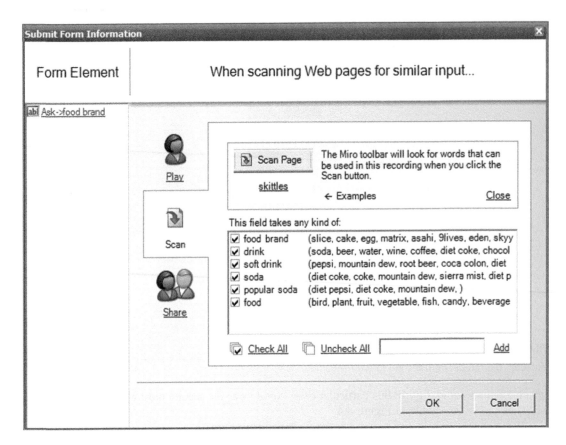

FIGURE 4.5

The user can control which generalizations are active with checkboxes.

Previous research

The majority of data detector research occurred in the late 1990s.

In 1997, Milind Pandit and Sameer Kalbag (1997) released the Intel Selection Recognition Agent. The Intel Selection Recognition Agent was able to detect six types of data: geographic names, dates, email addresses, phone numbers, Usenet news groups, and URLs. These pieces of data were then linked to actions created by a programmer, like opening a Web browser to a URL or sending an email message to an email address.

In 1998, Bonnie Nardi, James Miller, and David Wright (1998) released Apple Data Detectors, which increased the types of data detected from 6 to 13. Apple Data Detectors were able to recognize phone numbers, fax numbers, street addresses, email addresses, email signatures, abstracts, tables of contents, lists of references, tables, figures, captions, meeting announcements, and URLs. Additionally, users could supply their own lists of terms they wanted Apple Data Detectors to recognize. Similar to the Intel Selection Recognition Agent, creating an action associated with data required programming.

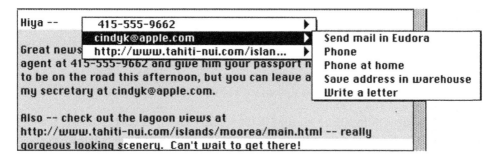

FIGURE 4.6

Apple Data Detectors (1998).

Also in 1998, Anind Dey, Gregory Abowd, and Andrew Wood (1998) released CyberDesk. CyberDesk detected eight kinds of data: dates, phone numbers, addresses, names, URLs, email addresses, GPS positions, and times. Although this was less than the types supported by Apple Data Detectors, CyberDesk provided a more advanced framework for actions, including the ability to chain actions together, and to combine different pieces of data into the same action. CyberDesk also allowed for data detection on mobile devices. For instance, CyberDesk provided the ability to associate a GPS position with the action of loading a URL.

Like the Intel Selection Recognition Agent and Apple Data Detectors, the only way to create new actions with CyberDesk was to program them.

The functionality of these data detectors has been integrated into several consumer products. Released in 1999 by aQtive, onCue monitored information copied to the clipboard and suggested relevant Web services and desktop applications. Like earlier data detectors, onCue did not perform any level of semantic analysis, and it simply associated words with various search engines, an encyclopedia, and a thesaurus. However, onCue differed from previous data detectors in that it was also able to detect different structures of information, such as lists and tables, and then suggest relevant ways to visualize that information, including dancing histograms, pieTrees, and the charts available in Microsoft Excel. Both the service and recognizer components in the onCue framework (called Qbits) required a developer to program (Dix, Beale, & Wood, 2000). Microsoft Office XP (released in 2001) provided data detection with a feature called Smart Tags, and the Google Toolbar 3.0 (released in 2005) added data detection to Web browsing, with a feature called AutoLink. Microsoft's Smart Tags currently recognizes eight types of data, although a developer can program additional data types and actions. Google's AutoLink currently recognizes three types of data: addresses, ISBNs, and Vehicle Identification Numbers. The actions associated with these types of data are controlled by Google.

Back to the future

One similarity of all of the research on data detectors in the late 1990s is each paper's future work section.

Programming by example and end user programming

First, all of the research mentioned the importance of programming by example and end user programming. The creators of the Intel Selection Recognition Agent wrote, "We would like to enhance the Selection Recognition Agent along the lines of Eager [a Programming by Example system], allowing it to detect the repetition of action sequences in any application and automate these sequences" (Pandit & Kalbag, 1997). The creators of Apple Data Detectors wrote that a "goal is to complete a prototype of an end-user programming facility to enable end users to program detectors and actions, opening up the full Apple Data Detectors capability to all users" (Nardi et al., 1998). Finally, the creators of CyberDesk wrote that they were "investigating learning-by-example techniques to allow the CyberDesk system to dynamically create chained suggestions based on a user's repeated actions" (Dey et al., 1998).

Grammex (Grammars by Example), released in 1999 and created by Henry Lieberman, Bonnie Nardi, and David Wright (1998), allowed users to create data detectors through programming by example. Like Creo, Grammex allowed users to define the actions to associate with data by providing demonstrations. However, Grammex was limited to the few Macintosh applications that were "recordable" (sending user action events to the agent) (Lieberman et al., 1998). Similar to the data detectors preceding it, Grammex based its data detection on patterns of information. For instance, Grammex could learn how to detect email addresses if the user showed it several examples with the format *person@host*. Unfortunately, very few types of data outside of URLs, email addresses, and phone numbers actually have a detectable structure, limiting the usefulness of such a system. This leads to the second "future work" topic mentioned by data detector researchers of the late 1990s: semantics.

Semantics

The creators of Apple Data Detectors noted that relying on pattern detection has many limitations: "It is easy to imagine a company might choose a syntax for its product order numbers – a three-digit department code followed by a dash followed by a four-digit product code – that would overlap with U.S. telephone number syntax, thus leading Apple Data Detectors to offer both telephone number and part-ordering actions…We can do little about these overlapping syntaxes without performing a much deeper, semantic interpretation of the text in which the pattern appears" (Nardi et al., 1998). The creators of CyberDesk also discussed the topic of semantic interpretation, writing that they were interested in "incorporating rich forms of context into CyberDesk, other than time, position, and meta-types" (Dey et al., 1998).

Miro

Miro expands the types of data that can be detected from the previous range of three types (Google's AutoLink) and thirteen types (Apple Data Detectors), to the full breadth of knowledge found in ConceptNet and TAP.

It is important to note that the pages Miro reads are just normal pages on the Web. The pages do not contain any form of semantic markup. All of the semantic information is coming from the ConceptNet and TAP knowledge bases.

LEVERAGING COMMONSENSE KNOWLEDGE TO UNDERSTAND THE CONTEXT OF TEXT

Miro builds on three years of research on applying large-scale knowledge bases to understanding the context of text, and using this commonsense knowledge to improve the usability of interactive applications (Lieberman et al., 2004).

Related work

ARIA (Annotation and Retrieval Integration Agent) is a software agent that leverages ConceptNet to suggest relevant photos based on the semantic context of an email message (Lieberman & Liu, 2002).

ConceptNet has also been shown to be useful for determining the affective quality of text, allowing users to navigate a document based on its emotional content (Liu, Selker, & Lieberman, 2003). Also in the domain of text analysis, by using ConceptNet to understand the semantic context of a message the user is typing, predictive text entry can be improved on mobile devices (Stocky, Faaborg, & Lieberman, 2004).

In the domain of speech recognition, this same approach can also be used to streamline the error correction user interfaces of speech recognition systems (Lieberman et al., 2005). Additionally, ConceptNet can be used to detect the gist of conversations, even when spontaneous speech recognition rates fall below 35% (Eagle & Singh, 2004).

Both ConceptNet and TAP have also been found to be incredibly useful in the domain of search, demonstrated by the prototypes GOOSE (Goal-Oriented Search Engine) (Liu, Lieberman, & Selker, 2002) and ABS (Activity Based Search) (Guha et al., 2003).

Dealing with the ambiguity of natural language

The most significant challenge that Miro faces in its task of data detection is dealing with the ambiguity of natural language. For instance, because of the way Open Mind was created, the following two statements are in ConceptNet:

```
(IsA "apple" "computer")
(IsA "apple" "fruit")
```

It is important to deal with ambiguity well, because incorrectly matching a user's goals leads to a very poor user experience:

> *Mr. Thurrott typed the word "nice." Up popped a Smart Tag offering to book a flight to Nice, France using Microsoft's Expedia website. When he typed the word "long," up popped a Smart Tag from ESPN offering more information on Oakland Athletics centerfielder Terrence Long. As Thurrott put it, "Folks, this is lame."*

(Kaminski, 2001)

Google's AutoLink team avoided this problem entirely by opting to only detect three kinds of data that are already designed to be unique (addresses, ISBNs, and VINs).

Miro begins to address this problem by leveraging the semantic context of surrounding terms. For instance, the term "apple" by itself is ambiguous, but if it is surrounded by terms like "Dell" and "Toshiba," the meaning becomes clearer. However, algorithms to re-rank a term's semantic value based on the surrounding context are far from perfect. In general, our current algorithm performs much better on semistructured data (like a list of items) compared to parsing paragraphs of text. For instance, if someone wrote a blog entry about how they "spilled apple juice all

FIGURE 4.7

The ambiguity of "apple."

over a brand new apple MacBook Pro," Miro will have difficulty understanding the apples. Although Miro does occasionally make mistakes, we believe the benefit it provides users is valuable nonetheless. Using large knowledge bases of semantic information to determine the specific semantic value of a particular term remains an interesting challenge for future research.

PUTTING END USERS IN CONTROL OF THEIR DATA AND SERVICES

Both Microsoft and Google have received a strong outcry of criticism for their data detectors, Smart Tags, and AutoLink (Kaminski, 2001; Mossberg, 2001). The equality of the criticism is surprising given the considerable difference between Microsoft's and Google's current public images. Microsoft actually pulled the feature Smart Tags from Internet Explorer 6 shortly before the release of Windows XP because of public outcry. In an article in the *Wall Street Journal*, columnist Walter Mossberg wrote, "Using the browser to plant unwanted and unplanned content on these pages – especially links to Microsoft's own sites – is the equivalent of a printing company adding its own editorial and advertising messages to the margins of a book it has been hired to print. It is like a television-set maker adding its own images and ads to any show the set is receiving" (Mossberg, 2001).

Together, Miro and Creo solve this problem by enabling end users to define the services associated with particular types of data.

IMPLEMENTATION

This section briefly covers the implementation of Creo and Miro. Further information can be found in Alexander Faaborg's masters thesis, *A Goal-Oriented User Interface for Personalized Semantic Search* (Faaborg, 2005).

AN EXTENSION FOR INTERNET EXPLORER 6?

Although the author of this chapter is currently a principal designer on Firefox at Mozilla, he notes that development work on Creo and Miro began long before the release of Firefox 1.0. While the system detailed in this chapter was built to be part of IE6, Firefox's excellent support for extension development would have made implementing Creo and Miro considerably easier today. Examples of end user programming systems for the Web implemented as Firefox extensions (and in general implemented after Firefox's initial release in late 2004) can be found throughout this book, in Chapter 1, Chapter 2, Chapter 3, Chapter 5, Chapter 6, Chapter 9, and Chapter 15.

Implementation of Creo

Recording actions on the Web

Unlike many of the previous programming-by-example systems for the Web, which are implemented using a proxy server, Creo is integrated directly into a Web browser. Creo's integration with Internet Explorer provides two core functions: (1) *monitoring*, the ability to directly capture the user's actions, and what the user is currently looking at; and (2) *impersonation*, the ability to recreate actions inside the Web browser and make it appear as if an actual user was completing them.

The basic set of actions that Creo must be able to monitor and impersonate consists of capturing navigation events (monitoring), navigating (impersonation), scraping a form (monitoring), filling out a form (impersonation), being instructed to scrape text from a Web site (monitoring), and scraping text from a Web site (impersonation).

From a Web site's perspective, there is no difference between the user completing actions by controlling their Web browser, and Creo completing actions by controlling the Web browser. Aside from the fact that Creo is faster (which actually caused problems with some Web sites, so it was subsequently slowed down), Creo does a perfect job of impersonating the user's actions. This, of course, does not include CAPTCHA tests or completing any other type of higher-level perceptual or cognitive challenges.

Generalizing information

What differentiates programming-by-example systems like Creo from basic macro recorders is their ability to generalize information. First, Creo determines if the input should be generalized or remain static based on three heuristics: (1) if the input consists of personal information, (2) if the name of the text field matches a predetermined list of fields that should remain static, and (3) the number of generalizations of the input. If Creo determines that the input should be generalized, it looks up the relevant IsA relationships for the input in ConceptNet and TAP. For instance, the input "Diet Coke" is found in ConceptNet and TAP in statements like:

```
(IsA "diet coke" "food brand")
```

As shown in the earlier example, the full list of generalizations of Diet Coke consists of food brand, food, drink, soft drink, soda, and popular soda. These generalizations are written to the recording's XML file, and leveraged by Miro when determining if the recording should be activated based on the semantic context of a Web page.

Implementation of Miro

Miro determines the user's potential goals based on the Web page they are looking at by matching the generalizations of terms and phrases on the page to the set of generalizations associated with recordings created using Creo. For instance, the recipe page shown earlier activated the "Order Food" and "Nutritional Information" recordings because many of the terms on the Web page generalized to "food," and this generalization described a variable in both the "Order Food" and "Nutritional Information" recordings.

When Miro converts a plain text term or phrase into a hyperlink for a particular recording, the hyperlink does not reference a resource found on the Internet. Instead, the hyperlink references a URI that instructs the Web browser to invoke the recording, with the term or phrase used as a variable.

Limitations of Creo and Miro

Creo's current implementation results in a number of limitations to its use. First, Creo cannot record interactions with Flash, Java Applets, or other non-HTML elements of Web pages. This limitation is similar to the challenges facing the development of third-party Software Agents for client-side applications. To be able to automate a procedure, the agent must be able to capture the user's actions.

Secondly, Creo is currently not able to generalize navigation events. However, many of the programming-by-example systems for the Web discussed earlier have implemented this ability.

The third limitation of Creo is its ability to automate procedures that change based on the variables provided. Creo is able to automate multistep, multivariable procedures, like purchasing stock, ordering a pizza, or sending PayPal. However, Creo cannot currently automate procedures that change based on dependencies of the variables provided, like making the travel arrangements for a trip.

Because of the breadth of ConceptNet and TAP, Miro is able to avoid many terminological issues like the different spelling of words, synonyms, and in some cases, concepts described in phrases. However, the knowledge in ConceptNet and TAP is by its very nature common and generic. Subsequently, Miro is unable to detect specialized domain information, such as particular part numbers, job codes, or customer numbers, unless this information is provided in an additional knowledge base.

Whereas Creo is able to automate recordings that take multiple variables, the current implementation of Miro is not yet able to combine multiple pieces of information from a Web page into a single invocation.

EVALUATION

In this section we describe two sets of evaluations: (1) a series of evaluations done during the iterative design process of Creo conducted with a total of 10 subjects, and (2) a final evaluation conducted with 34 subjects to assess how Creo and Miro can improve a user's efficiency when completing a task.

Evaluating the user interface design

While designing Creo and Miro, we realized that the critical factor to their success would not be technical limitations, since systems built on top of ConceptNet and TAP have worked fine in the past. Instead, the critical factor to their success would be usability. We followed an iterative design process during Creo's creation, formally evaluating each iteration, before designing the next. The first version of Creo's user interface was evaluated with three users during a paper prototyping session. The second version of Creo's user interface was evaluated with four user interface designers, using a computer prototype. The third version of Creo's user interface was evaluated in a usability test with three novice users, using a fully functional prototype running as part of Internet Explorer.

Determining the software's ability to improve the user's efficiency

The purpose of the fourth user evaluation was to (1) conclude if the overall system made users more efficient when completing a task, (2) conclude if users understood the utility of the software, and (3) determine whether they would use software applications like Creo and Miro if they were included in their Web browser.

The evaluation was run with 34 subjects, 17 male and 17 female. In Part 1 of the evaluation, 17 people were in the experimental group and 17 people were in the control group. The average age of the subjects was 29.3 years, with a range of 19 to 58 years; 26% of subjects had no programming experience, and all subjects were familiar with using the Web. Subjects were compensated $10.

Part 1: Evaluating Miro

In the first part of the experiment, subjects were asked to order 11 ingredients in a recipe for blueberry pudding cake. The experimental group of subjects had access to the Miro toolbar, which could recognize common foods and automatically link them to the subject's grocery store. The control group of subjects completed the same task, but used Internet Explorer with Miro turned off. Subjects in the control group were allowed to complete the task however they naturally would. All of the subjects were instructed to complete the task at a natural pace, and not to treat the experiment like a race. We hypothesized that the experimental group would be able to complete the task significantly faster than the control group.

Part 2: Evaluating Creo

In the second part of the experiment, all of the subjects were asked to create a recording with Creo that could order any type of food at a grocery store. Subjects completed this task after being shown an example of how Creo works. We showed the subjects a single demonstration of how to train Creo to look up a movie at The Internet Movie Database (IMDb). We chose to do this because unlike the three preceding usability studies, for this evaluation we were interested in capturing the average time it took a slightly experienced subject to create a simple recording. We hypothesized that subjects would be able to successfully complete this task in a trivial amount of time.

Results

The experimental group completed the task in Part 1 in an average time of 68 seconds, with a standard deviation of 20 seconds. The control group completed the task in an average time of 139 seconds with a standard deviation of 58 seconds. These results are statistically significant ($p < .001$). These results are also consistent with the study conducted by the Intel Selection Recognition Agent authors, finding that interface "saved both time and effort, in some cases over 50%" (Pandit & Kalbag, 1997).

The range of results from the control group in Part 1 is due to the fact that subjects were asked to complete the task however they naturally would. There was a large amount of variability in the way subjects transferred information between the recipe and the grocery store site. Some subjects relied heavily on keyboard shortcuts, using alt-tab to switch windows and tab to switch which control on

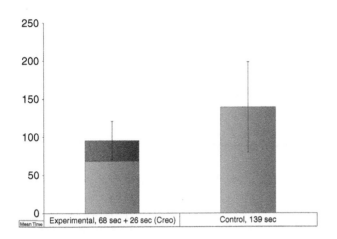

FIGURE 4.8

The time it took the control and experimental groups to complete the task.

the grocery store page had the focus. Some subjects double-clicked to select a word, and triple-clicked to select a full line. Other subjects retyped every ingredient instead of copying and pasting. Since they would often hold three to four ingredients in their own memory at a time, this usually turned out to be faster.

In Part 2, subjects completed the task in 26 seconds, with a standard deviation of 5 seconds. This means that even for interacting with a list of 11 items, it would be faster to train Creo first, and then use Miro to turn the information into hyperlinks. In Figure 4.8, the time for Part 2 is represented as an overhead cost for the experimental group's time for Part 1.

The debriefing questionnaire contained several Likert scale questions asking the subject's impressions of the software's usability (Figure 4.9 and Figure 4.10), and if they would actually use the software.

Asked if they would use the software, 85% of subjects responded that they would use Creo, and 100% of subjects responded that they would use Miro. We have implemented a way for users to easily share the functionality of recordings they create with Creo without sharing any of their personal information (which Creo automatically detects and stores separately). So it is technically possible for a subset of users to use Creo, and for everyone to use Miro.

Limitations of the evaluation

Although subjects responded favorably to debriefing questions asking if they would use Creo and Miro if they were integrated into their Web browsers, it remains an open question if users in real-world environments would devote the necessary time to apply these tools.

The 34 users in our study were demographically diverse in age and gender. However, the fact that 74% of the subjects reported some level of programming experience may limit this study's external validity. Unexpectedly, we found that subjects with programming experience had more difficulty using Creo than subjects without any programming experience. Although at first this seems counterintuitive, we believe it has to do with the subject's expectations. Specifically, subjects with technical experience had more difficulty believing that Creo could generalize their single example. This is because they were familiar with how computers normally function.

To analyze how Creo and Miro make users more efficient compared to using a conventional Web browser, this evaluation focused on a single example of using Creo and Miro. We did not study the breadth of tasks that Creo and Miro can perform for two reasons: (1) the ConceptNet and TAP knowledge bases are rapidly growing, and (2) the respective teams at MIT and Stanford responsible for the creation of these knowledge bases have already performed evaluations of their breadth

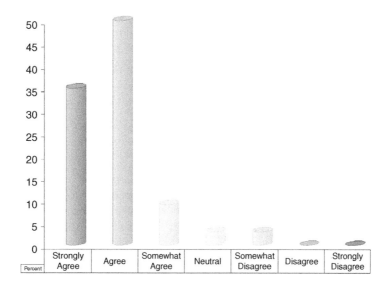

FIGURE 4.9

Did the subjects find Miro easy to use?

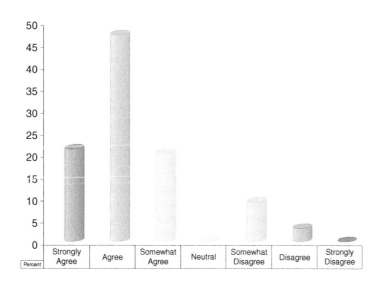

FIGURE 4.10

Did the subjects find Creo easy to use?

(Singh, 2002; Singh et al., 2002; Singh et al., 2004; Liu & Singh, 2004; Guha & McCool, 2002; Guha & McCool, 2003b; Guha et al., 2003; McCool et al., 2003). We believe the task users were asked to perform, while only in a single domain, represents a common use of Creo and Miro. However, further studies should be conducted to assess the overall effectiveness of Creo and Miro in real-world situations.

FUTURE WORK
When things go wrong

Although the ConceptNet and TAP knowledge bases are very large, they are certainly not complete. To assist the user with situations where Miro fails to detect a specific piece of information, we have developed a Training Wizard. This wizard consists of a three-step process: (1) ask the user what information should have been detected, (2) ask the user what the information is (by having them fill out a sentence), and (3) ask the user which recording from Creo should have been activated. In most cases, Miro can provide intelligent defaults for at least two of these three steps, creating a collaborative learning interface between Miro and the user. In the first step, Miro performs predictive text entry on what the user types, based on the terms on the current Web page. In the second step, Miro attempts to describe the concept itself. In some cases Miro will know what the concept is, but not how it relates to the current set of recordings created by Creo. In the third step, Miro attempts to check which recordings should have been activated based on the information in the previous step. This is useful when providing new pieces of information. For instance, once the user tells Miro that "Eastern Standard Tribe" is a book, Miro knows what to do with books.

For the situations where a recording breaks because of a change with a Web site, we have developed a debugging mode.

Learning from the Web

We are exploring using natural language processing to enable Miro to learn new pieces of information by reading Web pages. Miro takes the text of the page the user is on and (1) performs sentence boundary detection, (2) isolates the nouns and words used for pattern matching, (3) lemmatizes the text, and (4) matches the text against 11 different patterns. For instance, the sentence "The Killers is a really great band" can be easily parsed to (IsA "the killers" "band"). When Miro finds a new piece of information that matches the current set of recordings, it displays the activated recording (as if the knowledge came out of ConceptNet or TAP), and then watches to see if the user clicks on it. We believe an approach like this could be used to quickly grow broad knowledge bases, if a system like Miro were to be used by a large number of users.

SUMMARY

In their 1998 article, the creators of Apple Data Detectors described the goal-oriented nature of their system: "When users invoke it on a region of text in a document, they are saying, in effect, 'Find the important stuff in here and help me do reasonable things to it'... Direct manipulation is a wasteful, frustrating way for users to interact with machines capable of showing more intelligence" (Nardi et al., 1998). Creo and Miro further enhance this type of goal-oriented user interface, by (1) enabling users to define their own services by example, and (2) increasing the types of data that can be detected to any information stored in the semantic knowledge bases ConceptNet and TAP.

Creo and Miro, like many other interactive applications (Lieberman & Liu, 2002; Lieberman et al., 2004; Lieberman et al., 2005; Liu et al., 2002; Liu et al., 2003; Stocky et al., 2004; Eagle & Singh, 2004) would not be able to generalize information and anticipate their users' goals without access to the knowledge stored in ConceptNet and TAP. This chapter has demonstrated the effect these knowledge bases can have on the research areas of programming-by-example and data detection. However, we believe many other types of interactive applications can benefit from access to this knowledge as well. Usability is improved by making it easier for humans to understand computers. However the reverse is true as well. ConceptNet and TAP improve usability by making it easier for computers to understand humans.

Acknowledgments

Thanks to James Hendler, Pattie Maes, and Rob Miller for their advice. Thanks to Push Singh and Hugo Liu for ConceptNet, and Rob McCool and R.V. Guha for TAP. The authors would also like to thank Alan Dix.

© ACM, 2006. This is a minor revision of the work published in *Proceedings of the SIGCHI Conference on Human Factors in Computing Systems* (Montréal, Québec, Canada, April 22–27, 2006), 751-760. See http://doi.acm.org/10.1145/1124772.1124883.

CREO/MIRO

Intended users:	All users
Domain:	All Web sites
Description:	Creo is a programming-by-example system for a Web browser that uses commonsense knowledge to generalize interactions. Miro is a companion "data detectors" system that analyzes a Web page and automatically detects opportunities for invoking Creo procedures.
Example:	Use Creo to record a procedure to order a food item from an online grocery store. Then, if you browse a recipe, Miro can automatically order the recipe ingredient items from the store.
Automation:	Yes. Mainly used to automate repetitive activities.
Mashups:	Yes.
Scripting:	Yes.
Natural language:	Yes. Natural language on Web pages is analyzed by tools integrated with the commonsense inference.
Recordability:	Yes.
Inferencing:	Yes. A novel ability is the use of a commonsense knowledge base and an instance knowledge base to generate candidate generalizations. For example "Diet Coke" can be generalized to "a cola," "a soft drink," "a drink," etc.
Sharing:	Yes.
Comparison to other systems:	Comparable to CoScripter and other programming-by-example systems in the browser environment.
Platform:	Microsoft Internet Explorer. PC and compatibles.
Availability:	Available only for sponsor organizations of the MIT Media Lab and selected academic collaborators.

Collaborative scripting for the Web

5

Allen Cypher,[1] Clemens Drews,[1] Eben Haber,[1] Eser Kandogan,[3] James Lin,[4] Tessa Lau,[1]
Gilly Leshed,[2] Tara Matthews,[1] Eric Wilcox[1]

[1]*IBM Research – Almaden*
[2]*Cornell University*
[3]*MIT CISAIL*
[4]*Google, Inc.*

ABSTRACT

Today's knowledge workers interact with a variety of Web-based tasks in the course of their jobs. We have found that two of the challenges faced by these workers are automation of repetitive tasks, and support for complex or hard-to-remember tasks. This chapter presents CoScripter, a system that enables users to capture, share, and automate tasks on the Web. CoScripter's most notable features include ClearScript, a scripting language that is both human-readable and machine-understandable, and built-in support for sharing via a Web-based script repository. CoScripter has been used by tens of thousands of people on the Web. Our user studies show that CoScripter has helped people both automate repetitive Web tasks, and share how-to knowledge inside the enterprise.

INTRODUCTION

Employees in modern enterprises engage in a wide variety of complex, multistep processes as part of their daily work. Some of these processes are routine and tedious, such as reserving conference rooms or monitoring call queues. Other processes are performed less frequently but involve intricate domain knowledge, such as making travel arrangements, ordering new equipment, or selecting insurance beneficiaries. Knowledge about how to complete these processes is distributed throughout the enterprise; for the more complex or obscure tasks, employees may spend more time discovering how to do a process than to actually complete it.

However, what is complex or obscure for one employee may be routine and tedious for another. Someone who books conference rooms regularly should be able to share this knowledge with someone for whom reserving rooms is a rare event. The goal of our CoScripter project is to provide tools that facilitate the capture of how-to knowledge around enterprise processes, share this knowledge as human-readable scripts in a centralized repository, and make it easy for people to run these scripts to learn about and automate these processes.

Our "social scripting" approach has been inspired by the growing class of social bookmarking tools such as del.icio.us (Lee, 2006) and dogear (Millen, Feinberg, & Kerr, 2006). Social bookmarking systems began as personal information management tools to help users manage their bookmarks. However they quickly demonstrated a social side-effect, where the shared repository of bookmarks became a useful resource for others to consult about interesting pages on the Web. In a similar vein, we anticipate CoScripter being used initially as a personal task automation tool, for early adopters to automate tasks they find repetitive and tedious. When shared in a central repository, these automation scripts become a shared resource that others can consult to learn how to accomplish common tasks in the enterprise.

RELATED WORK

CoScripter was inspired by Chickenfoot (Bolin et al., 2005), which enabled end users to customize Web pages by writing simplified JavaScript commands that used keyword pattern matching to identify Web page components. CoScripter uses similar heuristics to label targets on Web pages, but CoScripter's natural language representation for scripts requires less programming ability than Chickenfoot's JavaScript-based language.

Sloppy programming (Little & Miller, 2006) allowed users to enter unstructured text which the system would interpret as a command to take on the current Web page (by compiling it down to a Chickenfoot statement). Although a previous version of CoScripter used a similar approach to interpret script steps, feedback from users indicated that the unstructured approach produced too many false interpretations, leading to the current implementation that requires steps to obey a specific grammar.

Tools for doing automated capture and replay of Web tasks include iMacros[1] and Selenium.[2] Both tools function as full-featured macro recorder and playback systems. However CoScripter is different in that scripts are recorded as natural language scripts that can be modified by the user without having to understand a programming language.

CoScripter's playback functionality was inspired by interactive tutorial systems such as Eager (Cypher, 1991) and Stencils (Kelleher & Pausch, 2005a). Both systems used visual cues to direct user attention to the right place on the screen to complete their task. CoScripter expands upon both of those systems by providing a built-in sharing mechanism for people to create and reuse each others' scripts.

THE COSCRIPTER SYSTEM
CoScripter interface

CoScripter consists of two main parts: a centralized, online repository of scripts (Figure 5.1), and a Firefox extension that facilitates creating and running scripts (Figure 5.2). The two work together to provide a seamless experience. Users start by browsing the repository to find interesting scripts; the site supports full-text search as well as user-contributed tags and various sort mechanisms to help users identify scripts of interest.

---

[1] http://www.iopus.com/imacros/firefox/
[2] http://seleniumhq.org/

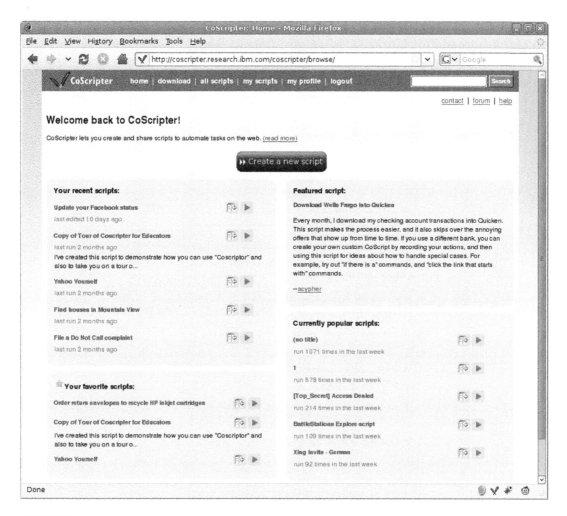

FIGURE 5.1

CoScripter script repository.

Once a script has been found, the user can click a button to load the script into the CoScripter sidebar. The sidebar provides an interface to step through the script, line by line. At each step, CoScripter highlights the step to be performed by drawing a green box around the target on the Web page. By clicking CoScripter's "step" button, the user indicates that CoScripter should perform this step automatically and the script advances to the following step.

Scripts can also be run automatically to completion. The system iterates through the lines in the script, automatically performing each action until either a step is found that cannot be completed, or the script reaches the end. Steps that cannot be completed include steps that instruct the user to click a button that does not exist, or to fill in a field without providing sufficient information to do so.

FIGURE 5.2

CoScripter sidebar (Firefox extension).

CoScripter also provides the ability to record scripts by demonstration. Using the same sidebar interface, users can create a new blank script. The user may then start demonstrating a task by performing it directly in the Web browser. As the user performs actions on the Web such as clicking on links, filling out forms, and pushing buttons, CoScripter records a script describing the actions being taken. The resulting script can be saved directly to the repository. Scripts can be either public (visible to all) or private (visible only to the creator).

Scripting language

CoScripter's script representation consists of a structured form of English which we call ClearScript. ClearScript is both human-readable and machine-interpretable. Because scripts are human-readable, they can double as written instructions for performing a task on the Web. Because they are machine-interpretable, we can provide tools that can automatically record and understand scripts in order to execute them on a user's behalf.

For example, here is a script to conduct a Web search:

- go to "http://google.com"
- enter "sustainability" into the "Search" textbox
- click the "Google Search" button

Recording works by adding event listeners to clicks and other events on the HTML DOM. When a user action is detected, we generate a step in the script that describes the user's action. Each step is generated by filling out a template corresponding to the type of action being performed. For example, `click` actions always take the form "click the *TargetLabel TargetType*". The TargetType is derived from the type of DOM node on which the event listener was triggered (e.g., an anchor tag has type "link", whereas an `<INPUT type="text">` has type "textbox"). The TargetLabel is extracted from the source of the HTML page using heuristics, as described later in the "Human-readable labels" section.

Keyword-based interpreter

The first generation CoScripter (described in (Little et al., 2007), previously known as Koala) used a keyword-based algorithm to parse and interpret script steps within the context of the current Web page. The algorithm begins by enumerating all elements on the page with which users can interact (e.g., links, buttons, text fields). Each element is annotated with a set of keywords that describe its function (e.g., `click` and `link` for a hypertext link; `enter` and `field` for a textbox). It is also annotated with a set of words that describe the element, including its label, caption, accessibility text, or words nearby. A score is then assigned to each element by comparing the bag of words in the input step with the bag of words associated with the element; words that appear in both contribute to a higher score. The highest scoring element is output as the predicted target; if multiple elements have the same score, one is chosen at random.

Once an element has been found, its type dictates the action to be performed. For example, if the element is a link, the action will be to `click` on it; if the element is a textbox, the action will be to enter something into it. Certain actions, such as enter, also require a value. This value is extracted by removing words from the instruction that match the words associated with the element, along with common stopwords such as "the" and "in"; the remaining words are predicted to be the value.

The design of the keyword-based algorithm caused it to always predict some action, regardless of the input given. Whereas this approach worked surprisingly well at guessing which command to execute on each page, the user study results below demonstrate that this approach often produced unpredictable results.

Grammar-based interpreter

The second generation CoScripter used a grammar-based approach to parse script steps. Script steps are parsed using a LR(1) parser, which parses the textual representation of the step into an object representing a Web command, including the parameters necessary to interpret that command on a given Web page (such as the label and type of the interaction target).

The verb at the beginning of each step indicates the action to perform. Optionally a value can be specified, followed by a description of the target label and an optional target type. Figure 5.3 shows an excerpt of the BNF grammar recognized by this parser, for click actions.

Human-readable labels

CoScripter's natural language script representation requires specialized algorithms to be able to record user actions and play them back. These algorithms are based on a set of heuristics for accurately generating a human-readable label for interactive widgets on Web pages, and for finding such a widget on a page given the human-readable label.

CoScripter's labeling heuristics take advantage of accessibility metadata, if available, to identify labels for textboxes and other fields on Web pages. However, many of today's Web pages are not fully accessible. In those situations, CoScripter incorporates a large library of heuristics that traverse the DOM structure to guess labels for a variety of elements. For example, to find a label for a textbox, we might look for text to the left of the box (represented as children of the textbox's parents that come before it in the DOM hierarchy), or we might use the textbox's name or tooltip.

Our algorithm for interpreting a label relative to a given Web page consists of iterating through all candidate widgets of the desired type (e.g., textboxes) and generating the label for the widget. If the label matches the target label, then we have found the target, otherwise we keep searching until we have exhausted all the candidates on the current page.

```
Click ::= click {on} the TargetSpec
TargetSpec ::= TargetLabel {TargetType}
TargetLabel ::= "String"
TargetType ::= link | button | item | area
```

FIGURE 5.3

Excerpt from CoScripter's grammar.

Some labels may not be unique in the context of a given page, for example, if a page has multiple buttons all labeled "Search". Once a label has been generated, we check to see whether the same label can also refer to other elements on the page. If this is the case, then the system generates a disambiguation term to differentiate the desired element from the rest. The simplest form of disambiguator, which is implemented in the current version of CoScripter, is an ordinal (e.g., the *second* "Search" button). We imagine other forms of disambiguators could be implemented that leverage higher-level semantic features of the Web page, such as section headings (e.g., the "Search" button in the "Books" section); however, these more complex disambiguators are an item for future work.

Variables and the personal database

CoScripter provides a simple mechanism to generalize scripts, using a feature we call the "personal database." Most scripts include some steps that enter data into forms. This data is often user-specific, such as a name or a phone number. A script that always entered "Joe Smith" when prompted for a name would not be useful to many people besides Joe. To make scripts reusable across users, we wanted to provide an easy mechanism for script authors to generalize their scripts and abstract out variables that should be user-dependent, such as names and phone numbers.

Variables are represented using a small extension to the ClearScript language. Anywhere a literal text string can appear, we also support the use of the keyword "your" followed by a variable name reference. For example:

- Enter your "full name" into the "Search" textbox

Steps that include variables are recorded at script creation time if the corresponding variable appears in the script author's personal database. The personal database is a text file containing a list of name-value pairs (lower left corner of Figure 5.2). Each name–value pair is interpreted as the name of a variable and its value, so that, for example, the text "full name = Mary Jones" would be interpreted as a variable named "full name" with value "Mary Jones". During recording, if the user enters into a form field a value that matches the value of one of the personal database variables, the system automatically records a step containing a variable as shown above, rather than recording the user's literal action. Users can also add variables to steps post hoc by editing the text of the script and changing the literal string to a variable reference.

Variables are automatically dereferenced at runtime in order to insert each user's personal information into the script during execution. When a variable reference is encountered, the personal database is queried for a variable with the specified name. If found, the variable's value will be substituted as the desired value for that script step. If not found, script execution will pause and ask the user to manually enter in the desired information (either directly into the Web form, or into the personal database where it will be picked up during the next execution).

Debugging and mixed-initiative interaction

CoScripter supports a variety of interaction styles for using scripts. The basic interaction is to step through a script, line by line. Before each step, CoScripter highlights what it is about to do; when the "Step" button is clicked, it takes that action and advances to the next step. Scripts can also run to completion; steps are automatically advanced until the end of the script is reached, or until a step is reached that either requires user input, or triggers an error.

In addition to these basic modes, CoScripter also supports a mixed-initiative mode of interaction. The mixed-initiative mode helps people learn to use scripts. Instead of allowing CoScripter to perform script steps on the user's behalf, the user may perform actions herself. She may either deviate from the script entirely, or may choose to follow the instructions described by the script. If she follows the instructions and manually performs an action recommended by CoScripter as the next step (e.g., clicking on the button directly in the Web page, rather than on CoScripter's "Step" button), then CoScripter will detect that she has performed the recommended script step and advance to the following step.

CoScripter can be used in this way as a teaching tool, to instruct users on how to operate a user interface. CoScripter's green page highlighting helps users identify which targets should be clicked on, which can be extremely useful if a page is complex and targets are difficult to find in a visual scan. After the user interacts with the target, CoScripter advances to the next step and highlights the next target. In this way, a user can learn how to perform a task using CoScripter as an active guide.

Mixed-initiative interaction is also useful for debugging or on-the-fly customization of scripts. During script execution, a user may choose to deviate from the script by performing actions directly on the Web page itself. Users can use this feature to customize the script's execution by overriding what the script says to do, and taking their own action instead. For example, if the script assumes the user is already logged in, but the user realizes that she needs to log in before proceeding with the script, she can deviate from the script by logging herself in, then resume the script where it left off.

EVALUATING COSCRIPTER'S EFFECTIVENESS

We report on two studies that measure CoScripter's effectiveness at facilitating knowledge sharing for Web-based tasks across the enterprise. For our first study, we interviewed 18 employees of a large corporation to understand what business processes were important in their jobs, and to identify existing practices and needs for learning and sharing these processes.

In a second study, we deployed CoScripter in a large organization for a period of several months. Based on usage log analysis and interviews with prominent users, we were able to determine how well CoScripter supported the needs discovered in the first study, and learn how users were adapting the tool to fit their usage patterns. We also identified opportunities for future development.

STUDY 1: UNDERSTANDING USER NEEDS
Participants

We recruited 18 employees of the large corporation in which CoScripter was deployed. Since our goal was to understand business process use and sharing, we contacted employees who were familiar with the organization's business processes and for whom procedures were a substantial part of their everyday work. Our participants had worked at the corporation for an average of 19.4 years (ranging from a few weeks to 31 years, with a median of 24 years). Twelve participants were female. Seven participants served as assistants to managers, either administrative or technical; six held technical positions such as engineers and system administrators; three were managers; and two held human resource positions. The technology inclination ranged from engineers and system administrators on the high end to administrative assistants on the low end. All but two worked at the same site within the organization.

Method

We met our participants in their offices. Our interviews were semistructured; we asked participants about their daily jobs, directing them to discuss processes they do both frequently and infrequently. We prompted participants to demonstrate how they carry out these procedures, and probed to determine how they obtained the knowledge to perform them and their practices for sharing them. Sessions lasted approximately one hour and were video-recorded with participants' permission (only one participant declined to be recorded).

Results

We analyzed data collected in the study by carefully examining the materials: video-recordings, their transcripts, and field notes. We coded the materials, marking points and themes that referred to our exploratory research goals: (1) common, important business processes; and (2) practices and needs for learning and sharing processes.

Note that with our study method, we did not examine the full spectrum of the interviewees' practices, but only those that they chose to talk about and demonstrate. Nonetheless, for some of the findings we present quantified results based on the coded data. In the rest of this chapter, wherever a reference is made to a specific participant, they are identified by a code comprised of two letters and a number.

What processes do participants do?

We asked our participants to describe business processes they perform both frequently and infrequently. The tasks they described included Web-based processes, other online processes (e.g., processes involving company-specific tools, email, and calendars), and non-computer-based processes. Given that CoScripter is limited to a Firefox Web browser, we focused on the details of Web-based tasks, but it is clear that many business processes take place outside a browser.

We found that there was a significant amount of overlap in the processes participants followed. Seventeen participants discussed processes that were mentioned by at least one other participant. Further, we found that a core set of processes was performed by many participants. For example, 14 participants described their interactions with the online expense reimbursement system. Some other frequently mentioned processes include making travel arrangements in an online travel reservation system, searching for and reserving conference rooms, and purchasing items in the procurement system. *These findings show that there exists a common base of processes that many employees are responsible for performing.*

Despite a common base of processes, we observed considerable personal variation, both within a single process and across the processes participants performed. A common cause for variation within a single process was that the exact input values to online tools were often different for each person or situation. For example, DS1 typically travels to a specific destination, whereas LH2 flies to many different destinations. We observed variations like these for all participants. Secondly, there were a number of processes that were used by only a small number of people. Eleven participants used Web-based processes not mentioned by others. For instance, TD1, a human resource professional, was the only participant to mention using an online system for calculating salary base payments. *These findings suggest that any process automation solution would need to enable personalization for each employee's particular needs.*

Our participants referred to their processes using various qualities, including familiarity, complexity, frequency, involvement, etc. Some of these qualities, such as complexity, were dependent on the task. For example, purchasing items on the company's procurement system was a challenging task for most participants. Other qualities, such as familiarity and frequency, varied with the user. For example, when demonstrating the use of the online travel system, we saw CP1, a frequent user, going smoothly through steps which DM1 struggled with and could not remember well. We observed that tasks that were *frequent* or *hard-to-remember* for a user may be particularly amenable to automation.

Frequent processes. Participants talked about 26 different processes they performed frequently, considering them tedious and time-consuming. For example, JC1 said: "[I] pay my stupid networking bill through procurement, and it's the same values every month, nothing ever changes." Automation of frequent processes could benefit users by speeding up the execution of the task.

Hard-to-remember processes. At least eight participants mentioned processes they found hard to remember. We observed two factors that affected procedure recall: its complexity and its frequency (though this alignment was not absolute). In general, tasks completed infrequently, or which required the entry of arcane values, were often considered hard to remember. For example, this company's procurement system required the entry of "major codes" and "minor codes" to complete a procurement request. One user of that system said, "It's not so straightforward, so I always have to contact my assistant, who contacts someone in finance to tell me these are the right codes that you should be using." Alternatively, although AB1 frequently needed to order business cards for new employees, it involved filling out multiple data fields she found hard to remember. *Automation could benefit users of hard-to-remember tasks by relieving the need to memorize their steps.*

How do participants share knowledge?

An important goal of our interviews was to develop an understanding of the sharing practices that exist for procedural knowledge. Thus, we asked participants how they learned to perform important processes, how they captured their procedural knowledge, and how and with whom they shared their own procedural knowledge.

Learning. Participants listed a variety of ways by which they learned procedures, most of them listing more than one approach. Figure 5.4 shows the different ways people learned procedures. Note that the categories are not mutually exclusive. Rather, the boundaries between contacting an expert, a colleague, and a mentor were often blurred. For example, KR1 needed help with a particular system and mentioned contacting her colleague from next door, who was also an expert with the system. Participants often said they would start with one learning approach and move to another if they were unsuccessful. Interestingly, although each participant had developed a network of contacts from which to learn, they still use trial and error as a primary way of getting through procedures: 13 out of 18 participants mentioned this approach for obtaining how-to knowledge. *This finding indicates that learning new procedures can be difficult, and people largely rely on trial and error.*

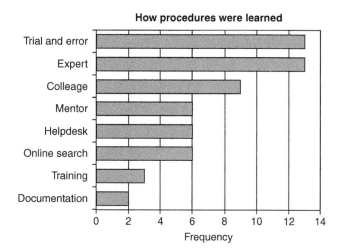

FIGURE 5.4

Frequency of ways participants learned new processes.

For maintaining the acquired knowledge, 15 out of 18 participants kept or consulted private and/ or public repositories for maintaining their knowledge. For the private repositories, participants kept bookmarks in their browsers as pointers for procedures, text files with "copy-paste" chunks of instructions on their computer desktops, emails with lists of instructions, as well as physical binders, folders, and cork-boards with printouts of how-to instructions. Figure 5.5 shows sample personal repositories. *Users create their own repositories to remember how to perform tasks.*

One participant noted an important problem with respect to capturing procedural knowledge: "Writing instructions can be pretty tedious. So, if you could automatically record a screen movie or something, that would make it easier to [capture] some of the instructions. It would be easy to get screenshots instead of having to type the stories." *This feedback indicates that an automatic procedure recording mechanism would ease the burden of capturing how-to knowledge (for personal or public use).*

Sharing. Eleven participants reported that they maintain public repositories of processes and "best practices" they considered useful for their community of practice or department. However, though these repositories were often made available to others, others did not frequently consult them. DS2 said, "I developed this, and I sent a link to everyone. People still come to me, and so I tell them: well you know it is posted, but let me tell you." Having knowledge spread out across multiple repositories also makes it harder to find. In fact, seven participants reported that they had resorted to more proactive sharing methods, such as sending colleagues useful procedures via email.

Our results show that experts clearly seek to share their how-to knowledge within the company. Nonetheless, we observe that sharing is time-consuming for experts and shared repositories are seldom used by learners, suggesting that sharing could be bolstered by new mechanisms for distributing procedural knowledge.

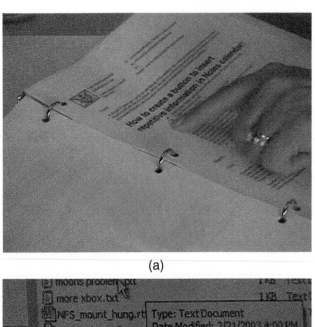

(a)

(b)

FIGURE 5.5

Ways participants maintain their procedural knowledge: a physical binder with printouts of emails (a); a folder named "Cookbook" with useful procedures and scripts (b).

Summary

Our initial study has shown that there is a need for tools that support the automation and sharing of how-to knowledge in the enterprise. We observed a core set of processes used by many partici-pants, as well as less-common processes. Processes that participants used frequently were considered routine and tedious, whereas others were considered hard to remember. Automating such procedures could accelerate frequent procedures and overcome the problem of recalling hard-to-remember tasks. Our data also suggest that existing solutions do not adequately support the needs of people learning new processes. Despite rich repositories and social ties with experts, mentors, and colleagues, people habitually apply trial and error in learning how to perform their tasks. New mechanisms are needed for collecting procedural knowledge to help people find and learn from it.

We also found that people who were sources of how-to knowledge needed better ways for capturing and sharing their knowledge. These people were overloaded by writing lengthy instructions, maintaining repositories with "best practices," and responding to requests from others. Also, distribution of their knowledge was restricted due to limited use of repositories and bounds on the time they could spend helping others. As such, automating the creation and sharing of instructions could assist experts in providing their knowledge to their community and colleagues.

STUDY 2: REAL-WORLD USAGE

In the second study, we analyzed usage logs and interviewed users to determine how well CoScripter supported the needs and practices identified in the first study. The purpose of this study was three-fold: (1) determine how well CoScripter supported the user needs discovered in Study 1, (2) learn how users had adapted CoScripter to their needs, and (3) uncover outstanding problems to guide future CoScripter development.

Log analysis: recorded user activity

CoScripter was available for use within the IBM corporation starting from November 2006 through the time of this research (September 2007). Usage logs provided a broad overview of how CoScripter had been used inside the company, while the interviews in the following section provided more in-depth examples of use. In this section we present an initial analysis of quantitative usage, with a content analysis left to future work. The data reported here excludes the activities of CoScripter developers.

Script usage patterns

Users were able to view scripts on the CoScripter repository anonymously. Registration was only required to create, modify, or run scripts. Of the 1200 users who registered, 601 went on to try out the system. A smaller subset of those became regular users.

We defined active users as people who have run scripts at least five times with CoScripter, used it for a week or more, and used it within the past two months. We identified 54 users (9% of 601 users) as active users. These users, on average, created 2.1 scripts, ran 5.4 distinct scripts, ran scripts 28.6 times total, and ran a script once every 4.5 days. Although 9% may seem to be a relatively low fraction, we were impressed by the fact that 54 people voluntarily adopted CoScripter and derived enough value from it to make it a part of their work practices.

We defined past users as those who were active users in the past, but had not used CoScripter in the past two months. This category included 43 users (7%). Finally, we defined experimenters as those who tried CoScripter without becoming active users, which included 504 users (84%). The logs suggested that automating frequent tasks was a common use, with 23 scripts run 10 or more times by single users at a moderate interval (ranging from every day to twice per month).

Collaborating over scripts

One of the goals of CoScripter is to support sharing of how-to knowledge. The logs implied that sharing was relatively common: 24% of 307 user-created scripts were run by two or more different users, and 5% were run by six or more users. People often ran scripts created by others: 465 (78%) of the user population ran scripts they did not create, running 2.3 scripts created by others on average. There is also evidence that users shared knowledge of infrequent processes: we found 16 scripts that automated known business processes within our company (e.g., updating emergency contact info), that were run once or twice each by more than ten different users.

In addition to the ability to run and edit others' scripts, CoScripter supports four other collaborative features: editing others' scripts, end-user rating of scripts, tagging of scripts, and adding free-form comments to scripts. We found little use of these collaborative features: fewer than 10% of the scripts were edited by others, rated, tagged, or commented on. Further research is needed to determine whether and how these features can be made more valuable in a business context.

Email survey of lapsed users

To learn why employees stopped using CoScripter, we sent a short email survey to all the experimenters and past users, noting their lack of recent use and asking for reasons that CoScripter might not have met their needs. Thirty people replied, and 23 gave one or more reasons related to CoScripter. Of the topics mentioned, ten people described reliability problems where CoScripter did not work consistently, or did not handle particular Web page features (e.g., popup windows and image buttons); five people said their tasks required advanced features not supported in CoScripter (most commonly requested were parameters, iteration, and branching); three people reported problems coordinating mixed initiative scripts, where the user and CoScripter alternate actions; and two had privacy concerns (i.e., they did not like scripts being public by default). Finally, seven people reported that their jobs did not involve enough tasks suitable for automation using CoScripter.

INTERVIEWS WITH COSCRIPTER USERS

As part of Study 2, we explored the actual usage of CoScripter by conducting a set of interviews with users who had made CoScripter part of their work practices.

Participants

Based on usage log analysis, we chose people who had used one or more scripts at least 30 times. We also selected a few people who exhibited interesting behavior (e.g., editing other peoples' scripts or sharing a script with others). We contacted 14 people who met these usage criteria; 8 agreed to an interview.

Seven interviewees were active CoScripter users, one had used the tool for 5 months and stopped 3.5 months before the interview. Participants had used CoScripter for an average of roughly 4 months (minimum of 1, maximum of 9). They had discovered the tool either via email from a co-worker or on an internal Web site promoting experimental tools for early adopters. Seven participants were male, and they worked in 8 sites across 4 countries, with an average of 10 years tenure at the company. We interviewed four managers, one communications manager, one IT specialist, one administrative services representative, and one technical assistant to a manager/software engineer. Overall, our participants were technology savvy, and five of them had created a macro or scripts before CoScripter. However, only two of them claimed software development expertise.

Method

We conducted all but one of our interviews over the phone, because participants were geographically dispersed, using NetMeeting to view the participant's Firefox browser. Interviews lasted between 30 and 60 minutes and were audio-recorded with participants' permission in all cases but one.

We conducted a semistructured interview based on questions that were designed to gather data about how participants used CoScripter, why they used it, and what problems they had using the tool. In addition to the predetermined questions, we probed additional topics that arose during the interview, such as script privacy and usability. We also asked participants to run and edit their scripts so we could see how they interacted with CoScripter.

Results

Automating frequent or hard-to-remember tasks

Four participants described CoScripter as very useful for automating one or more frequent, routine tasks. Each person had different tasks to automate, highlighting various benefits of CoScripter as an automation tool. Table 5.1 lists the most frequent routine tasks that were automated.

Those four subjects described instances where CoScripter saved them time and reduced their effort. For example, CR 1 said, "Two benefits: one, save me time – click on a button and it happens – two, I wouldn't have to worry about remembering what the address is of the messaging system here." PV1 also appreciated reduced effort to check voicemail inboxes: "I set up [CoScripter] to with one click get onto the message center." AM1 used his service pack registration script for a similar reason, saying it was "really attractive not to have to [enter the details] for every single

Table 5.1 Description of Routine Tasks Automated by CoScripter

User	Scripted Task	Sharing	Frequency Run
JL1	Send a page via an online paging tool	Private	M–F: 6 runs/day, Sa–Su: 3 runs/day
PV1	Log in to two technical support voicemail inboxes and check for new messages (2 scripts)	Public	Many runs/day
AM1	Fill in a form to register service packs for clients (form data is same for each client)	Private	20–30 runs/day
CR1	Change call forwarding and phone status messages (9 scripts)	Public	Several runs/day

service pack I had to register." JL1 runs his script many times during non-business hours. He would not be able to do this without some script (unless, as he said, "I didn't want to sleep").

These participants, none of whom have significant software development experience, also demonstrate an important benefit of CoScripter: it lowered the barrier for automation, requiring minimal programming language skills to use.

Though most participants interacted with CoScripter via the sidebar or the wiki, JL1 and PV1 invoked CoScripter in unexpected ways. JL1 used the Windows Task Scheduler to automatically run his script periodically in the background. Thus, after creating his script, JL1 had no contact with the CoScripter user interface. PV1 created a bookmark to automatically run each of his two scripts, and added them to his Firefox Bookmarks Toolbar. To run the scripts, he simply clicked on the bookmarks – within a few seconds he could check both voicemail inboxes.

In addition to automating frequent tasks, CoScripter acted as a memory aid for hard-to-remember tasks. For example, DG1 created scripts for two new processes he had to do for his job. Both scripts used an online tool to create and send reports related to customer care. Creating the report involved a number of complicated steps, and CoScripter made them easier to remember:

> *[CoScripter] meant I didn't have to remember each step. There were probably six or seven distinct steps when you have to choose drop-downs or checkboxes. It meant I didn't have to remember what to do on each step. Another benefit is I had to choose eight different checkboxes from a list of about forty. To always scan the list and find those eight that I need was a big pain, whereas [CoScripter] finds them in a second. It was very useful for that.*

After using CoScripter to execute these scripts repeatedly using the step-by-step play mode (at least 28 times for one script, 9 times for the other) for five months, DG1 stopped using them. He explained, "It got to the point that I memorized the script, so I stopped using it." This highlights an interesting use case for CoScripter: helping a user memorize a process that they want to eventually perform on their own.

Participant LH1 found CoScripter useful in supporting hard-to-remember tasks, by searching the wiki and finding scripts others had already recorded: "I found the voicemail one, it's really useful because I received a long email instruction on how to check my voicemail. It was too long so I didn't read it and after a while I had several voicemails and then I found the [CoScripter] script. It's really useful."

Automation limitations and issues. Despite generally positive feedback, participants cited two main issues that limited their use of CoScripter as an automation tool, both of which were named by lapsed users who were surveyed by email: reliability problems and a need for more advanced features.

Four out of eight participants noted experiencing problems with the reliability and robustness of CoScripter's automation capability. All of these participants reported problems related to CoScripter misinterpreting instructions. Misinterpretation was a direct result of the original keyword-based interpreter (Little et al., 2007), which did not enforce any particular syntax, but instead did a best-effort interpretation of arbitrary text. For example, one user reported running a script that incorrectly clicked the wrong links and navigated to unpredictable pages (e.g., an instruction to "click the Health link," when interpreted on a page that does not have a link labeled "Health", would instead click a random link on the page). Another user reported that his script could not find a textbox named in one of the instructions and paused execution. Misinterpretation problems were exacerbated by the dynamic and unpredictable nature of the Web, where links and interface elements can be renamed or moved around in the site.

Five users reported wanting more advanced programming language features, to properly automate their tasks. In particular, participants expressed a desire for automatic script restart after mixed-initiative user input, iteration, script debugging help, and conditionals.

Sharing how-to knowledge

Our interviews revealed some of the different ways CoScripter has been used to share how-to knowledge. These included teaching tasks to others, promoting information sources and teaching people how to access them, and learning how to use CoScripter itself by examining or repurposing other peoples' scripts.

Participants used CoScripter to teach other people how to complete tasks, but in very different ways. The first person, LH1, recorded scripts to teach her manager how to do several tasks (e.g., creating a blog). LH1 then emailed her manager a link to the CoScripter script, and the manager used CoScripter to complete the task. The second person, DG1, managed support representatives and frequently sent them how-to information about various topics, from generating reports online to using an online vacation planner. DG1 used CoScripter to record how to do the tasks, and then copied and pasted CoScripter's textual step-by-step instructions into emails to his colleagues.

DG1's use of CoScripter highlights a benefit of its human-readable approach to scripting. The scripts recorded by CoScripter are clearly readable, since DG1's colleagues were able to use them as textual instructions.

Another participant, MW1, a communications manager, used CoScripter to promote information that is relevant to employees in a large department and to teach them how to access that information. He created one script for adding a news feed to employees' custom intranet profiles and a second script to make that feed accessible from their intranet homepage. He promoted these scripts to 7000 employees by posting a notice on a departmental homepage and by sending links to the scripts in an email. Before using CoScripter, MW1 said he did not have a good method for sharing this how-to information with a wide audience. With such a large audience, however, correctly generalizing the script was a challenge; MW1 said he spent 2 to 3 hours getting the scripts to work for others. Still, MW1 was so pleased that he evangelized the tool to one of his colleagues, who has since used CoScripter to share similar how-to knowledge with a department of 5000 employees.

Participants used CoScripter for a third sharing purpose: three people talked about using other peoples' scripts to learn how to create their own scripts. For example, PV1 told us that his first bug-free script was created by duplicating and then editing someone else's script.

Sharing limitations and issues. Though some participants found CoScripter a valuable tool for sharing, these participants noted limitations of critical mass and others raised issues about the sharing model, generalizability, and privacy, which were barriers to sharing.

Sharing has been limited by the narrow user base (so far) within the enterprise. As CR1 said, critical mass affected his sharing ("I haven't shared [this script] with anyone else. But there are other people I would share it with if they were CoScripter users."), and his learning ("I think I would get a lot more value out of it if other people were using it. More sharing, more ideas. Yet most of the people I work with are not early adopters. These people wouldn't recognize the difference between Firefox and Internet Explorer."). DG1, who sent CoScripter-generated instructions to his co-workers via email, could have more easily shared the scripts if his coworkers had been CoScripter users.

We also saw problems when users misunderstood the wiki-style sharing model. For example, PV1 edited and modified another person's script to use a different online tool. He did not realize that his edits would affect the other person's script until later: "I started out by editing someone else's script and messing them up. So I had to modify them so they were back to what they were before they were messed up, and then I made copies." A second participant, PC1, had deleted all the contents of a script and did not realize this until the script was discussed in the interview: "That was an accident. I didn't know that [I deleted it]. When I look at those scripts, I don't realize that they are public and that I can blow them away. They come up [on the sidebar] and they look like examples."

Easy and effective ways to generalize scripts so that many people can use them is essential to sharing. Though users are able to generalize CoScripter scripts, participants told us it is not yet an easy process. For example, MW1 created a script for 7000 people, but spent a few hours getting it to work correctly for others. Also, although CoScripter's personal database feature allows users to write scripts that substitute user-specified values at runtime, not all processes can be generalized using this mechanism. For example, PV1 copied another person's script for logging into voicemail in one country and modified it to log in to voicemail in his country, because each country uses a different Web application.

Finally, sharing was further limited when participants were concerned about revealing private information. Three participants created private scripts to protect private information they had embedded in the scripts. AC1 said: "There is some private information here – my team liaison's telephone number, things like that. I don't know, I just felt like making it private. It's not really private, but I just didn't feel like making it public." Others used the personal database variables to store private information and made their scripts public. This privacy mechanism was important to them: "Without the personal variables, I would not be able to use the product [CoScripter]. I have all this confidential information like PIN numbers. It wouldn't be very wise to put them in the scripts." However, one participant was wary of the personal variables: "The issue I have with that is that I don't know where that is stored. . .If I knew the data was encrypted, yeah."

Summary

These findings show that, while not perfect, CoScripter is beginning to overcome some of the barriers to sharing procedural knowledge uncovered in Study 1. First, CoScripter provides a single public repository of procedural knowledge that our interviewees used (e.g., several participants used scripts created by other people). Second, CoScripter eliminates the tedious task of writing instructions (e.g., DG1 used it to create textual instructions for non-CoScripter users). Third, CoScripter provides mechanisms to generalize instructions to a broad audience so that experts can record their knowledge once for use by many learners (e.g., MW1 generalized his scripts to work for 7000 employees).

GENERAL ISSUES AND FUTURE WORK

By helping users automate and share how-to knowledge in a company, CoScripter is a good starting point for supporting the issues uncovered in Study 1. User feedback, however, highlights several opportunities for improvement. While some of the feedback pointed out usability flaws in our particular implementation, a significant number of comments addressed more general issues related to knowledge sharing systems based on end user programming. Participants raised two issues that highlight general automation challenges – reliability challenges and the need for advanced features – and four collaboration issues that will need to be addressed by any knowledge sharing system – the sharing model, script generalization, privacy, and critical mass.

One of the most common complaints concerned the need for improved reliability and robustness of the system's automation capability. These errors affected both users relying on the system to automate repetitive tasks, and those relying on the system to teach them how to complete infrequent tasks. Without correct and consistent execution, users fail to gain trust in the system and adoption is limited.

Users also reported wanting more advanced programming language features, such as iteration, conditionals, and script debugging help, to properly automate their tasks. These requests illustrate a tradeoff between simplicity – allowing novice users to learn the system easily – and a more complex set of features to support the needs of advanced users. For example, running a script that has iterations or conditionals might be akin to using a debugger, which requires significant programming expertise. A challenge for CoScripter or any similar system will be to support the needs of advanced users while enabling simple script creation for the broader user base.

Our studies also raise several collaboration issues that must be addressed by any PBD-based knowledge sharing tool: the sharing model, privacy, script generalization, and critical mass. The wiki-style sharing model was confusing to some users. Users should be able to easily tell who can see a script and who will be affected by their edits, especially given the common base of processes being performed by many employees. A more understandable sharing model could also help address privacy concerns, as would a more fine-grained access control mechanism that enables users to share scripts with an explicit list of authorized persons. Finer-grained privacy controls might encourage more users to share scripts with those who have a business need to view them. For generalization, we learned that personal database variables were a good start, but we are uncertain as to what degree this solution appropriately supports users with no familiarity of variables and other programming concepts. One way to better support generalization and personalization could be to enable users to record different versions of a script for use in different contexts, and automatically redirect potential users to the version targeted for their particular situation. Finally, a small user base limited further use of the system. We hope that solving all the issues above will lower the barriers to adoption and improve our chances of reaching critical mass.

Finally, one important area for future work is to study the use of CoScripter outside the enterprise. While we conducted the studies in a very large organization with diverse employees and we believe their tasks are representative of knowledge workers as a whole, the results we have obtained may not be generalized to users of CoScripter outside the enterprise. CoScripter was made available to the public in August 2007 (see http://coscripter.researchlabs.ibm.com/coscripter), and more research on its use is needed to examine automation and sharing practices in this larger setting.

SUMMARY

In summary, we have presented the CoScripter system, a platform for capturing, sharing, and automating how-to knowledge for Web-based tasks. We have described CoScripter's user interface and some of its key technical features. The empirical studies we have presented show that CoScripter has made it easier for people to share how-to knowledge inside the enterprise.

Acknowledgments

We thank Greg Little for the initial inspiration for the CoScripter project and Jeffrey Nichols for invaluable discussions and architectural design.

COSCRIPTER

Intended users:	All users
Domain:	All Web sites
Description:	CoScripter is a system for recording, automating, and sharing browser-based activities. Actions are recorded as easy-to-read text and stored on a public wiki so that anyone can use them.
Example:	Look for houses for sale in your area. The user records visiting a real estate Web site and filling in number of bedrooms and maximum price. Then, every few days, the user can run the recorded script with a single click and see what houses are currently available.
Automation:	Yes. Mainly used to automate repetitive activities.
Mashups:	Possibly. Not its main use. Some support for copying and pasting information between Web sites.
Scripting:	Users can record CoScript commands or write them manually in the CoScripter editor.
Natural language:	No, although the scripting language is designed to be English-like, with commands such as click the "Submit" button.
Recordability:	Yes. Most scripts are created by recording actions in the Web browser.
Inferencing:	Heuristics are used to label Web page elements based on nearby text. This technique was invented in the Chickenfoot system.
Sharing:	Yes. Scripts are shared on a public wiki, but they can be marked "private." A personal database allows a shared script to use values particular to the individual running the script.
Comparison to other systems:	The scripting language is based on Chickenfoot's language. CoScripter excels at recording arbitrary actions in the browser in a way that is easily understood by people and is also executable by CoScripter.
Platform:	Implemented as an extension to the Mozilla Firefox Web browser and a custom wiki built with Ruby on Rails.
Availability:	Freely available at http://coscripter.researchlabs.ibm.com/coscripter. Code also available as open source under the Mozilla Public License.

Highlight
End user re-authoring of existing Web sites

6

Jeffrey Nichols, Zhigang Hua, Tessa Lau, John Barton
IBM Research – Almaden

ABSTRACT

Today's Web pages provide many useful features, but unfortunately nearly all are designed first and foremost for the desktop form factor. At the same time, the number of mobile devices with different form factors and unique input and output facilities is growing substantially. The Highlight "re-authoring" environment addresses these problems by allowing users to start with sites they already use and create mobile versions that are customized to their tasks and mobile devices. This re-authoring is accomplished through a combination of demonstrating desired interactions with an existing Web site and directly specifying content to be included on mobile pages. The re-authored Web sites can be deployed to mobile devices through a new server-side architecture that makes use of a remote control metaphor in which the mobile device controls a fully functional browser that is embedded within a proxy server. The system has been tested successfully with a variety of existing sites. A small study suggests that novice users may be able to use the system to create useful mobile applications.

INTRODUCTION

Use of the Web from mobile devices is becoming increasingly popular, especially with the release of powerful new devices such as the Apple iPhone, Palm Pre, and T-Mobile G1 that offer easy browsing of desktop-sized pages on a small device. Many popular Web sites also now offer mobile versions. However, there are two challenges that current mobile devices and Web sites do not address:

- Existing mobile sites do not always offer streamlined access to the functionality each user wants; and
- Web site designs for desktop browsing are not always appropriate for scenarios when the user is on the go.

A possible solution to both of these problems is to create technologies that allow users to create their own mobile Web sites by re-authoring existing Web sites. Using this approach, users choose the features that they want included in their mobile sites, avoiding the problem of missing functionality that exists in many of today's mobile sites. Re-authoring can also allow users to remove irrelevant content, skip over pages that are not needed, and break up complex pages into multiple simpler pages. These types of changes allow users to streamline the desktop browsing experience into something more appropriate for mobile situations. Figure 6.1 and other figures throughout this chapter show some examples of mobile applications that might be re-authored from existing sites.

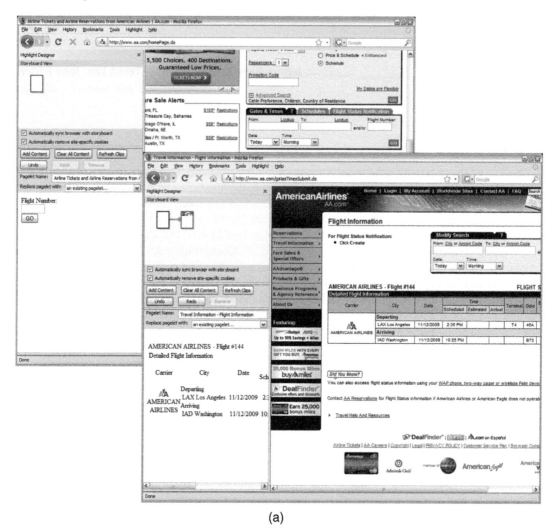

(a)

FIGURE 6.1

An example of Highlight being used to create a two-page mobile flight tracking application from the American Airlines Web site. (a) Shows the Highlight user interface and the original Web pages that the mobile application is constructed from.

(Continued)

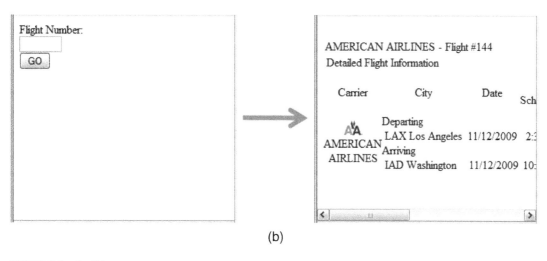

(b)

FIGURE 6.1—Cont'd

(b) Shows the two mobile pages in the flight tracking application.

Our Highlight system enables end users to *re-author* mobile Web applications from existing Web sites simply by demonstrating how to complete their task in a desktop browser. Highlight uses the *trace* of a user's interaction with an application as the basis for creating a task-specific mobile version of that application. By interacting with only the controls needed to accomplish a task, a user defines the set of controls that should be surfaced in the mobile Web application. Unfortunately, traces are not always sufficient to capture the richness of interaction needed. Our Highlight Designer tool lets users interactively "clip" portions of the original Web site for display in the mobile version, and generalize flow by specifying additional paths through the application. A before/after example of using Highlight to create a flight tracking application for the American Airlines Web site can be seen in Figure 6.1.

A key aspect of Highlight is that it leverages a user's existing knowledge of Web sites. We believe that many of the tasks users perform on the Web are repetitive, particularly those performed in enterprise Web applications. A user that is an expert at using a particular Web site is uniquely qualified to know how the site is used and what features of that site could be useful in a mobile version. By making the authoring interfaces as simple as demonstrating how to perform a task using a desktop browser, we are lowering the barrier to creating mobile Web applications. This enables end users to create their own customized mobile Web experience, optimized for the tasks they need to perform and the mobile device they use to access the content.

In summary, this chapter describes the following contributions:

- Algorithms for converting the trace of an interaction into a mobile Web application;
- Highlight Designer, an implemented interactive tool for creating and modifying mobile Web applications; and

- An empirical evaluation, showing that end users were able to create useful applications with Highlight, and that our approach saves significant bandwith over existing Web applications.

We begin by describing Highlight's user interface through a walkthrough of a user constructing a mobile version of the amazon.com interface. We then describe how we implemented some of the key features of the authoring environment, followed by a discussion of Highlight's architecture. In the next section we evaluate Highlight through an informal study of novice users creating applications using the system, in terms of the breadth of existing sites that it can support, and the benefits to users through use of a Highlight mobile application as compared to existing Web pages. Then we put Highlight in context with the related work in this area. We conclude with a discussion of the current system and directions for future work.

BACKGROUND

Early work on creating mobile interfaces focused primarily on two approaches:

- Automatically modifying existing interfaces based on heuristic rules or machine learning algorithms; and
- Creating tools that allow Web site builders to model their site and use those models to create new versions of their site for multiple mobile devices.

Many of the first systems to create mobile interfaces attempted to use the automatic approach. Digestor (Bickmore & Schilit, 1997a) used sets of heuristic rules to modify pages, such as "replace each text block with its first sentence." While Highlight does not use the same automatic approach, it may be useful to support some of the operations suggested by Digestor. Other automatic approaches have analyzed users' browsing history to improve mobile interfaces (e.g., (Anderson, Domingos, & Weld, 2001)), such as by increasing the prominence of links that users often follow. In most cases, these systems made use of a proxy server between the mobile browser and Web server to modify content for mobile consumption, such as the Top Gun Wingman (Fox et al., 1998) and Power Browser (Buyukkokten et al., 2000).

Highlight relies on users' recollections of their browsing history to pick the most useful elements of the Web site, and thus the authoring environment might be augmented by including some indication of previous history in its interface. These automatic schemes were also limited to making small changes to the interface, whereas Highlight can make radical changes because the user is directly involved in the process.

Other systems have used a model-based approach to creating mobile Web interfaces. Vaquita (Bouillon, Vanderdonckt, & Souchon, 2002) provides a tool and some heuristic rules for reverse engineering a Web page into a XIML presentation model that could later be transformed for use on other devices. In contrast, the MDAT system (Banavar et al., 2004) starts with the designer creating a generic interface model for their Web page and then provides tools to transform the generic interface for use on a variety of different devices. Unlike Highlight, these systems require significant knowledge of abstract modeling and programming to use.

A few projects have investigated the idea of allowing end users to create their own user interfaces from those found on Web sites. Clip, Connect, Clone for the Web (C3W) (Fujima et al., 2004a) is a system that allows users to clip elements from existing Web pages onto a separate panel and then link the elements together to create useful combined applications. Unlike Highlight, however, interfaces created in C3W exist entirely on one page and were not designed to work on a mobile device.

With d.mix (described in Chapter 10), users can create mashups by combining elements found in existing Web applications. It supports creation of mobile interfaces, but this mobilization feature appears to require users to create and edit scripts written in the Ruby programming language.

Another relevant system is Adeo (see Chapter 4), which allows mobile phone users to run previously recorded macros in a Web browser on a remote machine and receive back the results on their phone. Inputs can be provided to the macros at the start, but otherwise macros run completely independent of the phone and only return when they have completed. Adeo's architecture has an element of the remote control metaphor used by Highlight, although in Adeo the browser is treated more like a function that returns a result instead of as an interactive entity. We believe that Adeo could be built using Highlight, however the reverse would not be possible.

PageTailor (Bila et al., 2007) is a tool that allows users to remove, resize or move Web page elements while browsing on a mobile device. The tool runs directly on the mobile device, and studies have shown that its modification algorithms are robust to Web site changes over long periods of time. While PageTailor can modify the content of pages, it does not allow users to specify the transitions between pages as Highlight does. PageTailor also requires the mobile device to download most of the content of every Web page, because the modification algorithms are run directly on the mobile device. Highlight only requires the mobile device to download the content required for the user-designed application because its modification algorithms are run on a proxy server.

Common to all of these approaches, and the approach of Highlight, is the idea that content will need to be modified for use on the mobile device. Researchers have also been designing new interaction techniques in an attempt to replicate the experience of browsing a Web page on a typical PC browser within the constraints of the mobile browsing environment. WebThumb (Wobbrock et al., 2002), Collapse-to-Zoom (Baudisch et al., 2004), OPA Browser (Arase et al., 2007), and the Apple iPhone's multitouch interface are all examples of this work. While these techniques have had some success, we believe there is still a place for content modification approaches such as that of Highlight. Modified interfaces should always be smaller and easier to navigate than regular Web pages. If the modified pages contain the correct content and features, then they are likely to be easier to use. We hope that by involving the user in the design process, the modified pages will contain the correct content in an easy-to-use format.

THE HIGHLIGHT SYSTEM

Re-authoring is performed through the Highlight Designer extension to the Firefox Web browser running on a typical PC. A user begins by visiting an existing site and demonstrating an interaction with the site to include in the mobile application. As the user interacts, the Designer automatically adds content to the current "pagelet," a mobile version of the current page, and creates new pagelets as needed. While demonstrating an interaction, the user may choose to explicity add additional content from the existing Web page and rearrange or remove elements already in the current pagelet. A storyboard-style interface gives the user a visual overview of the application and allows the user to return to previous locations in the mobile application. This enables the user to demonstrate alternate actions that might be taken while interacting with the mobile application or to help the Designer generalize its knowledge of interactions that were previously observed. Once the user has finished, a description of the application can be saved to a proxy server that will allow access to the application from mobile devices.

A novel feature of Highlight is that it allows users to author both the content of mobile pages and the sequences of interactions that characterize the transitions between pages. This feature allows users to create mobile applications with a page structure that differs from that of the existing Web site. For example, a mobile application can skip over unnecessary Web pages, allowing users to perform a minimum of interactions in order to complete their task.

Interface walkthrough

We illustrate the use of our system by walking through an example scenario in which Amy creates a mobile application using the Highlight Designer to buy a single item from amazon.com.

The Designer opens in a Firefox sidebar to the left of the main browser window (see Figure 6.2). This sidebar contains three main parts: a storyboard that contains a node-and-arrow overview of the application being created, a toolbar, and a preview browser showing the current pagelet. Amy starts by typing "amazon.com" into the browser's location bar and loading the retail site. Highlight records this event as one of the initial events required to set up the application. She then selects "Books" from the category drop-down list, types her search term into the search box and presses the "Go" button to initiate the search. As she performs these actions, the Designer automatically clips the widgets with which she is interacting, as well as a label or other descriptive text that explains their use. Thus, the Designer adds the drop-down list, the search box, labels for both, and the search button to the current pagelet, and those items are displayed in the sidebar's preview browser. All of these clips are made automatically, just by virtue of Amy's trace of interactions with the Web site.

The search resulted in a list of hits being displayed in the main browser. Amy wants to clip all of these results for display in the mobile application. She clicks the "Add Content" button in Highlight. Now, as she moves the mouse over the browser, portions of the Web page are highlighted in red, indicating the region of the page that would be clipped. Amy moves the mouse such that all of the results are contained within the red box, and clicks to clip that region. These search results appear in the preview browser. In addition, a new pagelet is automatically constructed ("Search results"), and added to the storyboard. The storyboard now contains two pagelets, one containing the search interface, and a second containing the list of search results.

Next, Amy clicks on one of the items for sale. The item page is displayed in the main browser. On this page, she is interested in the item information such as the name and the purchase price. She uses the "Add Content" button again to clip the region containing these details to her application, adding a third pagelet ("Item Details") to the storyboard (see Figure 6.3).

Amy wants to be able to purchase the item with her application, so she clicks the "Add to Shopping Cart" button on the item description page. The next page is an overview of the current shopping cart. Amy's goal is to create an application for buying a single item, so she decides not to include any content from this page and clicks on the "Proceed to Checkout" button. Highlight chooses not to create a pagelet that includes this button because the page would have only included one button.

Highlight Sidebar   Main Browser Window

Storyboard View

Toolbar

Preview Browser

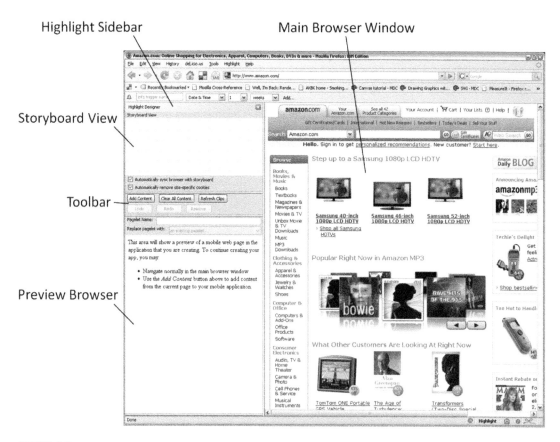

FIGURE 6.2

The Highlight Designer interface embedded as a sidebar in a Mozilla Firefox Web browser before the user has started creating an application.

Highlight does not create such pages by default because they typically add an additional navigation step without any interactive value. The click on the "Proceed to Checkout" button is recorded as part of the transition to the next pagelet, however, which ensures that it will automatically happen when the mobile application is executed.

The next page requires a login/password to continue. By typing in her amazon.com username and password, these widgets are automatically clipped and used to populate the fourth pagelet in the application ("Sign in"). On the next page, which is a confirmation of the order, she uses the "Add Content" button to create a new pagelet with information such as the final price of the order and the shipping address. At this point, Amy could click the "Place Your Order" button to place the order, which would also automatically add that button to her pagelet. Because she is just specifying an example, however, she does not actually want to buy the item. Instead she uses the "Add Content"

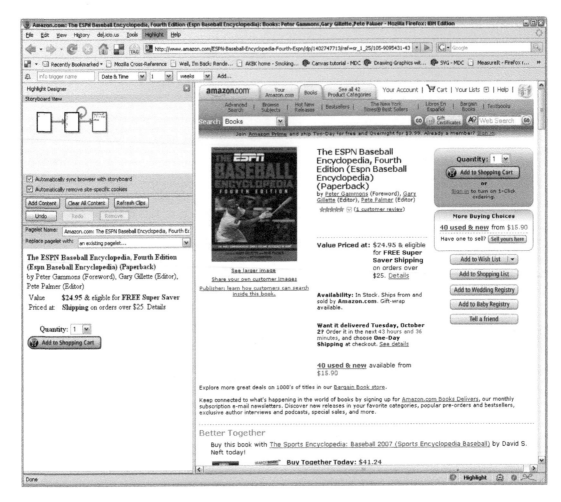

FIGURE 6.3

The Highlight Designer window after the creation of the "Item Details" pagelet.

button in the sidebar to highlight the "Place Your Order" button and add it to the current pagelet, which completes the basic structure of her application.

At any point, Amy can test her application by double-clicking on the pagelets in the storyboard to return to previous pages. Currently, this is the only interaction supported with the storyboard interface. Returning to the "Search results" pagelet, the main browser navigates back to the search result page, and the clipped search results are refreshed in the preview browser. Amy clicks on a different item this time. When she does this, Highlight detects that she has performed an action that looks very similar to an action she performed previously, and asks if she wishes to generalize them. By saying "yes", Amy is indicating that a click on the title link of *any* of the items in the search result pagelet should lead to the "Item Detail" pagelet. The next time she returns to the search result page and clicks on a different item, she will automatically be redirected to the appropriate "Item Detail" pagelet.

As a final step, Amy can add the functionality of navigating across multiple pages of search results, which is available on the amazon.com site by clicking links at the bottom of the page. Amy can start adding this functionality by returning to the search result pagelet in the storyboard, and then clicking on the "Next" link at the bottom of the search results page. Clicking on the link takes the main browser to the next page of search results. Amy now has two options to create the interface that she desires. She could use the "Add Content" button to add the search results content to her pagelet, as she did previously. The Designer will recognize that this new pagelet is similar to the previous search results pagelet, and it will ask Amy if she would like to use her previous pagelet. Answering "yes" to this question creates a looping edge from the "Search results" pagelet back to itself. Alternately, Amy could have explicitly specified that the "Search results" pagelet should be used by selecting it from the drop-down list in the preview browser. To make the rest of the search page navigation links work, Amy can click one of the other links. The Designer will detect that this link click is similar to the "Next" click, and ask if she wants to generalize. By answering "yes," Amy will tell Highlight to generalize all of the search navigation links.

Through a mixture of demonstrating how she interacts with the application, and using clipping regions to select desired content on each page, Amy has constructed an application that allows her to search for and purchase items via a lightweight Web interface suitable for use on mobile devices. When this interface is loaded into her mobile device (see Figure 6.4b), she will be able to search for items by name, navigate through the list of search results, see item details for a particular item, and purchase that item. The interface is optimized for the task that Amy wishes to do with this Web site, and contains only the subset of the amazon.com application that is relevant to her task.

Implementation

Highlight Designer works by recording the actions a user takes in the browser, and converting these actions into a mobile application description. Mobile applications are represented as a directed graph of "pagelets." Each pagelet represents one page that might be seen on the mobile device. Pagelets are described in two parts:

- *Content operations* that describe how the pagelet's content will be constructed from the content of the page on the existing site.
- *Transition events* that describe the navigation element in the pagelet that causes a transition to the next pagelet. These events also store the sequence of interactions that were demonstrated on the existing Web site to reach the page from which the next pagelet's content will be clipped. Each transition is represented by an arrow on the storyboard view.

Content operations

The most common content operation is extracting some content from the existing Web page and adding it to a pagelet. When a user interacts with a form field, such as a textbox or a radio button, this field is clipped and added to the Highlight application. In addition, a descriptive label is generated for some elements whose function is not obvious from their appearance alone; these include textboxes, drop-down listboxes, checkboxes, and radio buttons. The label is determined by first looking for labels or captions specified in the HTML; if these are not present, heuristic rules (borrowed from CoScripter, see Chapter 5) are used to extract textual content close to the target element that might plausibly constitute that element's label.

Content can also be clipped using the "Add Content" tool, rather than by directly interacting with the page. This form of clipping is used to add read-only content to the mobile application, such as a flight status or a weather report, or to add multiple related interactive elements simultaneously, such as the search results in the Amazon application. Another use is to add content for future use that

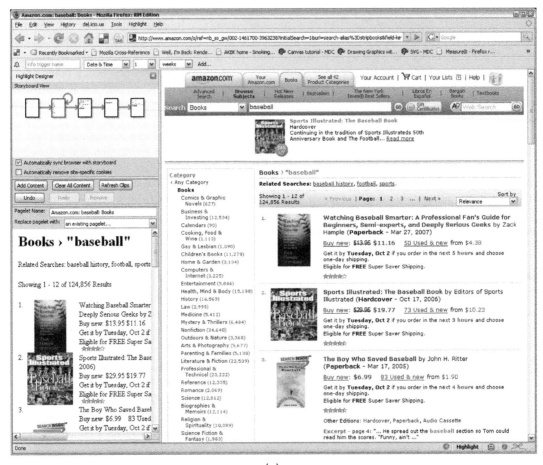

(a)

FIGURE 6.4

(a) The Highlight Designer running inside of the Mozilla Firefox Web browser. This screenshot was taken from the "Search results" pagelet after construction of the Amazon item purchasing example.

(Continued)

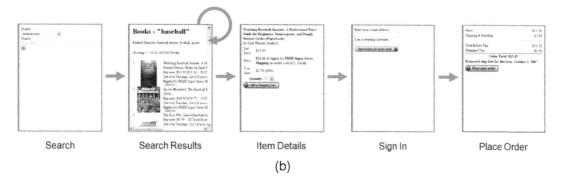

Search	Search Results	Item Details	Sign In	Place Order

(b)

FIGURE 6.4—Cont'd

(b) An overview of the final Amazon mobile application.

should not be activated at this time, such as the "Place your order" button in our Amazon scenario. When the "Add Content" button is selected, moving the cursor around on the Web page causes a red box to be drawn around the HTML element currently in focus. By moving the mouse, the user can select the target element to be clipped. Multiple elements can be clipped by invoking "Add Content" for each item.

The Designer also supports the "move" and "remove" content operations, which allow users to modify content already added to the pagelet. These operations are supported by interactions in the preview browser. Clicking on an item will select it, and then that item can either be dragged to move it to a new location or removed by clicking the "Remove" button.

Transition events

The Designer also records the series of interactive steps that the user demonstrated in order to transition from one pagelet to the next and stores this in a transition event. For example, in the amazon.com walkthrough the transition event from the "Item Details" pagelet to the "Sign in" pagelet would contain the steps "click on the Add to Shopping Cart button" and "click on the Proceed to Checkout button." The following steps would have been recorded from the "Sign in" pagelet to the final "Confirm Order" pagelet: "enter <username> into the Login: textbox," "enter <password> into the password textbox," and "click the Login button." Note that all of the user's operations are stored in the transition event, even those that may have caused some content to be clipped into the pagelet. All of these steps are included in the transition event so that the Designer can keep the browser and application in sync when the user double-clicks in the storyboard interface. Each transition event contains steps that were recorded from when the user created or navigated to the current pagelet and end when the user creates or navigates to a new pagelet.

Identifying elements on a Web page

Both content operations and transition events must be able to identify Web page elements in a repeatable manner. This allows the same content to be clipped for a pagelet every time it is shown and allows the steps specified by an event to be replicated properly on the Web page.

The Highlight Designer uses a combination of two approaches to identify Web page elements: XPath expresssions (Clark & DeRose, 1999) and a heuristic representation ("slop") pioneered by the CoScripter system described in Chapter 5. XPath has the capability of precisely describing any element on a Web page, but its expressions are often prone to failure if the page structure changes even slightly. CoScripter's slop uses textual descriptions and heuristics to identify elements on the page (e.g., "the Advanced link" refers to an <a> element containing the text "Advanced"). CoScripter slop is much more robust to page changes, however it was designed to identify small functional elements, such as textboxes and buttons, so it is not capable of describing non-interactive content regions on the page. Because slop interpretation is heuristic, it is possible that in some cases the interpreter will produce an incorrect match, creating an application that does not work even though it might appear that it should.

Slop is a good match for transition events because it was designed to represent traces of interactions with Web pages. Currently we record both the slop representation and an XPath expression for each event. If the XPath expression fails to find the correct element, then we can recover by trying to interpret the slop instead.

However, slop is less useful for representing content operations such as clipping a region of the page. Because CoScripter's focus has been on capturing user interactions with a Web page, it does not contain instructions for selecting arbitrary content on the page. Although we have enhanced the slop interpreter in Highlight to be able to understand human-written instructions, such as "clip the table containing Flight Status", we have yet to devise intelligent algorithms for recording slop based on user demonstrations. Thus, Highlight relies on XPath expressions to specify elements that are the targets of content operations. It is an area of future work to incorporate more robust methods for describing regions to be clipped.

Generalizing transition events and pagelets

We observed early on in the development of the Designer that many Web applications have repetitive site and page structures, such as the search pages we saw in the amazon.com application example. There are two types of repetition that we wanted to support with the Highlight Designer:

- *Repetitive site structure* – Some sites have multiple paths to get to the same type of page. For example, the "Item details" page on amazon.com can be reached both from searching and browsing through the site's product hierarchy.
- *Repetitive page structure* – Some pages, such as pages of search results, contain repetitive blocks of content. Often there will be similar interaction elements in each of these blocks, such as a link on a heading, that lead to a similar page.

To support creating a mobile application for Web sites with these characteristics, we wanted to add a set of lightweight interactions that would allow users to specify that an existing pagelet should be re-used and that a set of links all lead to the same pagelet.

We created two techniques for allowing users to specify that a pagelet should be re-used. These methods are both needed once the user has navigated to a new page and is about to clip content to create a new pagelet. The first method is explicit. If the user immediately recognizes that they wish to re-use a pagelet, then they can select that pagelet from a drop-down list in the sidebar and the existing pagelet will immediately be applied. The second method is implicit. If the user does not recognize that an existing pagelet might be reused, then they will begin clipping content from the new page into the pagelet. The Designer will analyze the XPath locations of the content as it is clipped, and if it appears to match a previous pagelet then the system will offer to replace the new pagelet with the old one. To reduce annoyance, the system will only ask this question once for each new pagelet.

In order to specify that a set of links all should lead to the same pagelet, the user must first specify a trace using one of the links in the set. In the amazon.com example above, remember that Amy clicked on the first result and created a pagelet for the result item before returning to the search results pagelet. When the user returns to the results pagelet and clicks on another link in the set, Highlight will analyze the new event and compare it to previous events. Specifically, it will look for similarities in the event interactions that caused the mobile pagelet to advance to a next page.

Our current algorithm for detecting similarities in events is as follows. First, we test to see if the events were of the same type. Clicking a link cannot be the same as pressing a submit button, for example. Second, we examine the XPath expressions of the elements involved in the two events. For example, in the amazon.com example the XPaths for the two search result links were:

```
First link:  /HTML[1]/.../TBODY[1]/TR[1]/TD[1]/A[1]
Second link: /HTML[1]/.../TBODY[1]/TR[2]/TD[1]/A[1]
```

The Designer considers events to be generalizable if the XPath expressions differ only in the indices, such as for the TR element in the amazon.com example. This means that the elements are located in much the same place in the Web page but are offset by some repetition of structure. Often this will occur when items are located in the same relative location within different cells of a table. The particular indices at which the elements differ are saved.

If the events are generalizable, then the system will identify the pagelet to which the previous event leads and ask the user if that pagelet should be the target for all similar links. If the user says "yes," then the two events are combined into a single event. The new event remembers the XPath indices that differed between the two events that created it and any future interaction with an element that has an XPath that differs only in those indices will cause the mobile application to follow that event. In our experience, this mechanism has worked well for a variety of search result pages, and has also been shown to be useful in other contexts, such as category browsing pages with many links. This heuristic does have limitations, however, particularly in situations where repeating chunks of content are not completely identical. For example, some forms of eBay searches will return a list of results, but the format of each particular item in the list will vary depending on the auction type for that item.

Our XPath-based algorithms for identifying similarities between links and pages are similar to the XPath-based algorithms used by Dontcheva's Relations, Card, and Search Templates system (see Chapter 12), Karma (Tuchinda, Szekely, & Knoblock, 2008), and many other Web systems. These algorithms are all susceptible to failure because of changes in the page, which is a limitation that we will discuss later in this chapter.

Architecture

To make mobile applications available outside of the Designer, we have implemented a proxy server component that serves mobile applications based on existing sites. When the user wishes to access a mobile application, they navigate their mobile browser to the proxy server's main page,

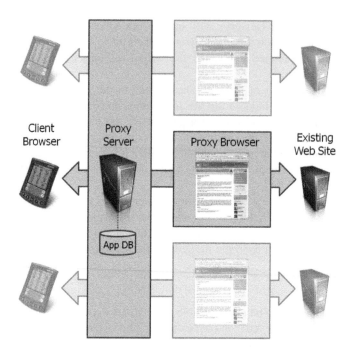

FIGURE 6.5

The Highlight system architecture. Mobile devices are shown on the left and existing Web servers are on the right. The proxy server system is located in the middle. A new proxy browser instance is launched for each client in order to maintain security and privacy between different clients' sessions.

select their application from a list of available applications, and then proceed to use the application.

The proxy server is implemented as a typical Web server that contains a fully functional Firefox Web browser as a component (Nichols et al., 2008) (see Figure 6.5). Selecting an application establishes a session with the server and causes the proxy server's Firefox browser to automatically navigate to the page of the existing Web site that corresponds with the first pagelet in the mobile application, execute the content operations of that pagelet, and return the HTML of this content to the mobile device. Subsequent requests from the mobile device are matched to a transition event for the current pagelet, any form data from the mobile device is filled in appropriately, and then the proxy browser advances to the next page based on the interactions specified by the event. Thus, the interface between the proxy server and the mobile device is similar to a remote control in that each request by the mobile browser specifies a series of user interface operations for the proxy browser to perform in order to get the contents of the next mobile page. For example, the proxy server might fill in some form fields, press the submit button, and navigate through several subsequent pages before constructing the next mobile page.

The use of a proxy server provides several advantages. First, only the clipped content is sent to the mobile device, resulting in fast load times despite slow network connections. Second, because the browser running on the proxy is a full-fledged desktop browser, any "client-side" JavaScript from the existing Web site can be executed in place, rather than relying on the mobile device's (often poor) JavaScript support. This feature enables the proxy server to serve mobile versions of Ajax applications, although the Highlight Designer does not yet support authoring mobile applications that make use of Ajax.

INTEGRATION WITH COSCRIPTER

Since Highlight makes use of traces of user interaction with Web applications to construct interfaces, we extended it to make use of a large repository of such traces as collected in the CoScripter project (see Chapter 5).

CoScripter is a programming by demonstration system for Firefox that records user actions performed in the browser and saves them as pseudo-natural-language scripts. CoScripter's representation for scripts is a plaintext language with steps consisting of commands such as "go to http://google.com", "type coscripter into the search box", and "click the Search button". These steps are both human- and machine-understandable, resulting in scripts that are easy for people to understand yet interpretable by a machine.

Scripts are automatically saved to a central wiki for sharing with other users. The CoScripter community has created thousands of scripts for Web-based tasks such as checking stock prices, creating trouble tickets, and managing queues in a call center (see Chapter 5).

This repository of scripts provides a wealth of information about the tasks people do with Web applications. It also provides an excellent starting point for the creation of Highlight applications, particularly if we could enable CoScripter users to import their scripts into Highlight and, with little or no effort, be able to complete their tasks from a mobile device.

Thus, we added the capability to Highlight to create a new application from a CoScript. When a script is loaded, Highlight uses CoScripter's interpretation component to programmatically run through the script, clicking on buttons and entering text as if the user had done these actions directly. Meanwhile, Highlight records the actions and uses them to construct an initial application.

One piece missing from the CoScripter language was the ability to specify portions of the content of the Web page to be clipped, akin to using Highlight's "Add Content" tool. Thus, we extended CoScripter's language with an additional type of instruction to describe regions to be clipped. These instructions take the form "clip the table containing Flight Status", and are parsed by Highlight and turned into an XPath expression that selects the smallest table element in the document that contains both the words "Flight" and "Status".

With this addition to the CoScripter language, users are able to import scripts directly from the CoScripter wiki into Highlight and have a fully functional mobile application with no additional authoring work. Once the script has been imported into Highlight, any of Highlight Designer's interactive features can be used to modify the application in order to customize it further for one's mobile device.

This integration reduces the cost of authoring mobile applications even further, because Highlight users are able to take advantage of already-created scripts for completing common tasks on the Web. The clipping feature has also been useful for other applications, such as authoring scripts that assist blind users while navigating through Web pages (for example, the TrailBlazer system described in Chapter 19).

INFORMAL USER STUDY

We conducted an informal user study to help us understand whether users would understand interacting with the system and be able to create applications of their own.

Three subjects in different age groups from our research lab participated in the study. The subjects were not regular users of the mobile Web, either because they did not own devices that were capable of it or they did not believe its benefits were worth paying for the service. They all were able to recall instances in which they would have liked to access the Web in a mobile setting, however, for example to look up nearby restaurants, get directions, get movie times for a local theater, view current traffic, or access Web-based email.

We gave the subjects a very brief verbal introduction to the system and then asked them to create two mobile applications that would allow them to explore the system's capabilities. For the first application, we asked subjects to create a two-pagelet mobile application from mapquest.com. The first pagelet was to contain the fields for entering an address and the second pagelet was to contain some information about that location. Note that we would have asked our subjects to clip the resulting map, but the maps on mapquest.com are generated from client-side JavaScript and are not easily replicated by simply copying their HTML. At the time, we did not have Designer support for clipping portions of a Web page as an image.

The second application was a three-pagelet simplified version of Google Image Search. The first pagelet was to contain the search textbox and button, the second pagelet was to contain the grid of search results, and the final pagelet was to contain the full-size version of an image selected from the results (see Figure 6.6 for a finished example of this application). Subjects were required to create a mobile application that skipped over a page of the existing site (an extra page exists in Google Image Search to show the image in the context of the page in which it was found) and to use the generalization features of the Designer in order to complete their application.

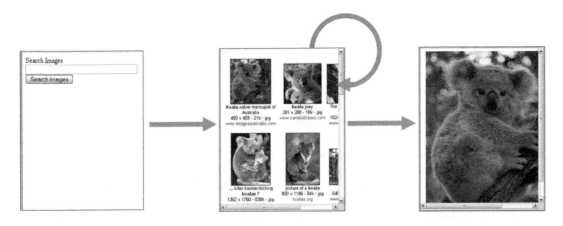

FIGURE 6.6

An overview of the pagelets and structure of the Google Image Search mobile application.

All of our subjects were able to build the first two applications, though there was a noticeable learning curve to using the tool. In particular, users were initially unclear on when to expect the system to add content for them as compared to when they should add content explicitly. After creating the applications, users seemed to form a clearer model of what the system was capable of doing automatically. We also found that the Designer's capabilities for allowing users to make and then fix mistakes were lacking. Users would often explore a site to understand the possible interactions before choosing one for their application. Although the Designer has some capabilities for changing and rearranging the content within a pagelet, it needs more facilities for changing the storyboard structure after the initial recording.

After creating the two applications, we asked users to think of an interesting mobile application that they would like and then try to create it using the Designer. With just this instruction, our subjects were able to successfully create applications for the *San Francisco Chronicle*'s Bargain Bites Web site and the weather.com 10-day forecast. The subject who created the Bargain Bites Web site was particularly happy, because the subject had been manually creating a mobile version of this site and syncing it with a PDA.

Our third subject attempted to create a traffic application from the www.beatthetraffic.com Web site, but unfortunately this site used a great deal of client-side JavaScript code that the Designer was not able to correctly interact with in order to play back the application. A different subject also attempted to create a mobile application from Gmail, but Gmail's Ajax features prevented the Designer from working correctly.

Although the subjects occasionally ran into difficulties while learning to use the system, they encountered few problems with the Designer's UI while creating their third application. At the conclusion of the study, all of the subjects reported that they were excited about the technology and wanted to use it in their everyday lives.

BREADTH AND BENEFITS

Using the Highlight Designer, we have created working mobile applications for a wide range of both popular and niche Web sites. These sites include aa.com, amazon.com, ebay.com, google. com, mapquest.com, sfgate.com, weather.com, and many others (see Table 6.1 for a more extensive list). We believe that the set of sites we have explored is large and varied enough to be representative of a significant portion of Web sites. In our experience, the Designer works best with pages that use a minimal amount of client-side JavaScript. The Designer seems to work with pages that use scripting for small UI features, such as highlighting an item when the mouse moves over it, but will likely break if the page's DOM is manipulated or new content is loaded via an XmlHttpRequest. We are exploring how to extend the Designer to work with pages that contain these features.

In order to understand the benefits of using a Highlight mobile application, we compared performing a task using a Highlight mobile application to performing the same task using the original interface on a mobile Web browser with desktop browser features, such as Minimo or Opera Mobile. Some of the problems with mobile Web browsing include small screens that are only able to display a few UI elements at a time and slow networks and processors that result in delayed page rendering.

Table 6.1 A Comparison of Interactive Elements and the Amount of Data Downloaded for Applications Created Using the Highlight Designer and the Desktop Web Sites Used for the Same Task

Description	Interactive Elements			Size (kB)		
	Original	Highlight	Percent	Original	Highlight	Percent
Check status of AA flight	736	3	0.4%	711	3.6	0.5%
Update Facebook status	217	5	2.3%	296	0.5	0.2%
Find nearby Wi-fi hotspot	74	18	24.3%	1072	2.8	0.3%
Get weather in my area	486	6	1.2%	1079	7	0.6%
Sprint cellphone usage	175	6	3.4%	739	4.6	0.6%
Log today's exercise	128	4	3.1%	393	0.9	0.2%
Update Fitday food diary	169	38	22.5%	145	12.7	8.8%
Get calories for food	88	16	18.2%	63	11.5	18.3%
Real estate in my area	274	35	12.8%	1036	194.1	18.7%
Show trip itineraries	77	17	22.1%	726	42.7	5.9%
Find Amazon book price	823	4	0.5%	844	4.1	0.5%

The small screens found on today's mobile devices make it difficult to navigate interfaces that have many clickable elements. For example, the front page of American Airlines' Web site has 298 distinct elements that can be clicked on or interacted with. One benefit to using Highlight is that task-driven mobile interfaces can reduce screen clutter to only those controls that are necessary for the task at hand. To measure the value of this claim, we calculated the total number of interactive elements (form fields, links, and buttons) that are displayed in the original application versus the Highlight application, throughout the course of performing each task (see Table 6.1). While not a perfect measure, this number approximates the complexity of the interface in terms of the number of options the user must sift through in order to complete her task.

The results show that the number of interactive elements in the Highlight application is drastically reduced compared to the original application. The reduction is greatest for large, multi-purpose Web sites where Highlight's task focus makes it possible for the user to concentrate on the elements that are required for the task at hand, and ignore all the elements used to access irrelevant portions of the application.

Another problem with mobile Web browsing is slow networks and costly page rendering. To show how Highlight addresses this problem, we have measured the amount of bandwidth required to download the set of pages (and associated content, such as images and scripts) required to complete a task using Highlight vs. the original Web site (see Table 6.1). All Highlight applications were significantly smaller than their unmodified counterparts. The applications that exhibited the least reduction in size were all ones that forwarded lists of results to the mobile device (e.g., choices of food items or listings of real estate) – all of which represented data that would have had to be transmitted to the client device in any case.

DISCUSSION

In this chapter, we have described a method of designing mobile Web interfaces based on user demonstrations of an interaction trace through an existing Web site. While the Designer allows users to then expand upon and improve their mobile application, we have observed that quite often a single trace is sufficient for creating a useful mobile application. This is especially apparent through the integration of Highlight with CoScripter. CoScripts are linear traces by nature, and we were able to find a number of existing scripts that could be turned into useful applications (many of which are listed in Table 6.1).

Of course, without the Designer it would be impossible to create applications with non-linear structures or with the ability to perform a search and navigate through the results. An important capability of the Designer is allowing the user to demonstrate two different interactions and have them generalized across a larger set of possible interactions. Our current generalization scheme is a heuristic based on the format of XPath expressions, which has been successful but could be improved. In particular, we would like to design an algorithm that detects repetitive chunks of content in the pagelet and then generalizes based on the detected repetition.

A current limitation of the Designer is its inability to support automating sites that use a lot of client-side JavaScript, particularly Ajax sites. We believe that it may be possible to extend the Designer to support these sites by extending it to also record the changes that occur in the Web site as the user interacts. Currently, the Designer only records the user's input and makes assumptions about the changes that can result in the interface based on the operation. An example assumption is that a new pagelet is only needed after a user clicks on a link or presses a submit button; these events typically trigger a new page to be loaded. For an Ajax site, a new page may never be loaded and the transition to a new pagelet may occur following any type of interaction. Recording changes to the Web page may allow us to track when pagelet changes should occur and allow the creation of applications from Ajax sites.

We have also taken into account the problem of re-authoring Ajax Web pages with the design of Highlight's mobile application deployment system (Nichols et al., 2008). This system takes as input a mobile application description for each application, and these descriptions are written in JavaScript and make use of standard Web APIs such as the HTML DOM API. Using a programming language as the basis for the application descriptions gives programmers the freedom to create applications for sites that are more complicated than the authoring environment can currently support. The authoring environment also generates application descriptions in the same format, which programmers can modify and extend.

The Designer has a few other limitations as well. Currently the clipping algorithms are not able to completely copy CSS style information from the source page into the mobile page. We plan to add this feature to Highlight at some point in the future, but we have encountered several challenges while experimenting with the feature. In particular, certain style attributes should not be copied in certain situations, such as relative vs. absolute position. We need to develop a complete set of heuristics to describe which attributes should be copied in which situations.

Another issue for Highlight mobile applications is robustness to changes in the underlying Web site. Highlight primarily relies on XPath mappings to find elements to clip and manipulate, and changes to the Web site can easily invalidate these mappings. One possible solution to this problem is to rely more on slop-based solutions for identifying elements, though this would only help if the desired element is still on the page and may create even more problems if the sloppy recognition algorithms clip the wrong element. Other solutions may also be possible, including asking the mobile user for help when run-time errors occur. One of our goals in the design of Highlight was to significantly lower the cost of creating these mobile applications, and so it is our hope that users will also find it easy to fix mobile applications when they break due to changes in the underlying site.

With many data entry tasks, some fields will always contain the same value (e.g., your address), whereas some fields (e.g., the item you are searching for) will change each time the task is run. Currently, Highlight prompts the user to enter data into every field in the mobile application, placing an unnecessary burden on the user. However, in future work we plan to improve this process by learning from the user's previous behavior on this task and identifying fields that always contain the same value on every run through the task. One option would be to prefill form fields with the most common value, enabling the user to change it if necessary but accept the default with no effort; another more drastic change would be to remove constant-valued fields from the pagelet displayed to the user, while still filling in the target value on the proxy server.

We found in our user studies that the user interface of the Designer is not very forgiving when users make mistakes or want to explore the existing Web site. One of our initial assumptions was that users would be experts with the sites they are mobilizing, but this may not always be the case and certainly it should be possible to recover from mistakes. We may be able to address some of these issues by providing more interaction through the storyboard interface, such as by allowing extra pagelets to be removed. It may also be valuable to provide a separate interface that shows a verbal description of the interaction steps that have been recorded, similar to CoScripter, and allows the user to edit their application at a different level.

One future goal of the Highlight project is to create a platform for uploading, sharing, and editing Highlight applications among a large group of users. In our current deployment framework, users can upload applications to our server and all uploaded applications are available to every user. So far there are no facilities for reopening the mobile application in our authoring environment or otherwise making edits to the uploaded application however. Providing these editing features and creating a better platform for viewing and exploring the uploaded applications will be important for creating a community of Highlight users.

The prospect of sharing Highlight applications introduces a question about the possibility of unintentionally sharing personal information through an uploaded application. For example, an application could contain a username, password, credit card number, or other sensitive information that the author would not want to share with the entire world. Our current Designer does not save information entered during recording by default, however it is still the responsibility of the user to check their application to make sure it does not contain any sensitive personal information. In the future, we may add features to help users check what information an application is storing and making available to others.

The Highlight Designer is explicitly not a model-based tool. When users create applications however, they do identify both the interactive elements of a useful application and the contextual information that is needed to use the application. This information could be useful for creating a model of the Web site. If multiple applications were created for the same site, then we might be able to combine information from those applications to create a more detailed model. Such a model could allow previous work in model-based research to be more easily applied to existing sites.

SUMMARY

We have presented Highlight, a system enabling end users to create task-based mobile Web applications simply by demonstrating how to perform a task on an existing application. Highlight uses the trace of a user's interaction to automatically clip the relevant controls for presentation in the mobile application, and enables users to visually point and select noninteractive content for inclusion in the application as well. Moreover, we have integrated Highlight with an existing repository of traces from the CoScripter system, which can be used to create Highlight applications with little or no additional effort. An informal user study suggests that novice users may be able to use Highlight to create useful mobile applications of their own choosing. An empirical evaluation shows that for a range of tasks, Highlight is capable of creating an application that is smaller and easier to use on mobile devices. In short, we believe Highlight enables ordinary users to mobilize their tasks and take them on the road wherever they go.

Acknowledgments

We thank our user study participants for helping us evaluate Highlight, and the CoScripter team for their valuable comments.

This work is based on an earlier work: "Highlight: A System for Creating and Deploying Mobile Web Applications," in *Proceedings of the Symposium on User Interface Software and Technology 2008* (Nichols, Hua, & Barton, 2008) and "Mobilization by Demonstration: Using Traces to Re-author Existing Web Sites," in *Proceedings of Intelligent User Interfaces 2008* (Nichols & Lau, 2008).

HIGHLIGHT

Intended users:	All users, though some tasks require programming skill
Domain:	All Web sites
Description:	Highlight allows anyone to create a personalized mobile version of an existing Web site through a programming-by-demonstration style interaction. Mobile Web sites created in Highlight can be accessed from any mobile device that can view basic Web pages. Programmers can also extend the mobile sites by writing JavaScript in a structured format.
Example:	Imagine that an airline you will be flying on soon has a flight tracking tool on their desktop Web site, but there is no mobile version. To create a mobile version to use during your upcoming trip, you sit down in front of your normal desktop Web browser, navigate to the airline's Web site, and track a flight. Based on your interactions with the Web site, a mobile site is built that supports the task of flight tracking for this airline.
Automation:	Yes, though typically only portions of a task would be automated while the rest is done manually.
Mashups:	No, although adding mashup support is possible.
Scripting:	No.
Natural language:	No.
Recordability:	Yes, using Highlight's end user authoring environment.
Inferencing:	Heuristics are used throughout Highlight's end user authoring environment to guess which content should be included and to determine the structure of the mobile Web sites.
Sharing:	Mobile Web sites created by users are shared on the Highlight Web site, but more in-depth sharing and collaboration features have yet to be explored.
Comparison to other systems:	Highlight uses CoScripter's recording and playback libraries.
Platform:	Highlight's end user authoring environment runs in Mozilla Firefox only. Mobile Web sites created in Highlight can be accessed by any HTML 1.0 compatible Web browser.
Availability:	Not currently available.

Mixing the reactive with the personal

7

Opportunities for end user programming in personal information management (PIM)

Max Van Kleek,[1] **Paul André,**[2] **Brennan Moore,**[1] **David Karger,**[1] **m.c. schraefel**[2]

[1]MIT CSAIL
[2]ECS, University of Southampton

ABSTRACT

The transition of personal information management (PIM) tools off the desktop to the Web presents an opportunity to augment these tools with capabilities provided by the wealth of real-time information readily available. In this chapter, we describe a personal information assistance engine that lets end users delegate to it various simple context- and activity-reactive tasks and reminders. Our system, Atomate, treats RSS/ATOM feeds from social networking and life-tracking sites as sensor streams, integrating information from such feeds into a simple unified RDF world model representing people, places, and things and their time-varying states and activities. Combined with other information sources on the Web, including the user's online calendar, Web-based email client, news feeds and messaging services, Atomate can be made to automatically carry out a variety of simple tasks for the user, ranging from context-aware filtering and messaging, to sharing and social coordination actions. Atomate's open architecture and world model easily accommodate new information sources and actions via the addition of feeds and Web services. To make routine use of the system easy for nonprogrammers, Atomate provides a constrained-input, controlled natural language interface (CNLI) for behavior specification, and a direct-manipulation interface for inspecting and updating its world model.

INTRODUCTION

The end user programming systems presented in this book feature the common goal of empowering users who are nonprogrammers to construct custom computational processes that help them with various types of tasks. In this chapter, we examine the application of end user programming techniques to the management of personal information – a task which, for most of us, ordinarily consumes significant time and effort. Since different individuals' needs and strategies surrounding their personal information vary greatly, empowering users to construct their own custom automation is of great promise to this problem.

The focus of our approach has been to consider actions performed automatically when certain conditions arise, which we refer to as *reactive automation*. Our motivation for examining reactive automation in personal information management (PIM) derives from the fact that the majority of PIM tools we rely upon daily are still designed to facilitate user-initiated, manual access to and manipulation of information. By contrast, human personal assistants, such as secretaries and administrative assistants, work autonomously on behalf of their supervisors, taking calls, handling visitors, managing contacts, coordinating meetings, and so on. For personal information management tools to approach the helpfulness of human personal assistants, these tools will need to demand less explicit attention from users and gain a greater ability to initiate and carry out tasks without supervision.

In this chapter, we introduce Atomate, a Web-based reactive personal information assistance engine that uses information streams about people, places, and events to drive end user constructed custom automation. Unlike the personal agents portrayed in Semantic Web scenarios, Atomate requires no complex inference, learning, or reasoning – data available from the feeds can be used directly to drive useful behaviors.

The transition of personal information management (PIM) tools to the Web presents an unprecedented opportunity to give tools greater capabilities. The Web is a data-rich environment with an increasing amount of machine-readable (semistructured) information that systems can leverage directly to take action. In particular, the rise of social networking and life-tracking Web sites have brought to the Web a wealth of near-real-time information about what people are doing, where they are, and the relationships between individuals, places, and things. Today, these social networking sites and services are geared toward human consumers, that is, letting people view each other's activities. Atomate, however, treats feeds from these sites as sensor streams, and by doing so, demonstrates that these Web data feeds can also be used to drive adaptive, context-reactive behaviors that perform various simple actions without user supervision.

Atomate relies on two key components: the first is a uniform internal RDF (Berners-Lee, Hendler, & Lassila, 2001) data model that simplifies the integration of heterogeneous information. The second is an interface that makes it easy for end users to create behaviors and annotate the data model. To make this possible, we introduce a constrained-input, controlled natural language interface (CNLI)[1] designed to let nonprogrammers accurately and easily specify actions to be performed. Although the use of CNLIs has previously been explored for ontology authoring and semantic annotation, Atomate is the first system to use CNLIs for scripting personal reactive automation.

In the rest of this chapter, we first present examples of Atomate behaviors and how they are expressed. These examples are followed by a brief discussion of related work, and a detailed description of Atomate's architecture. We then describe a user study to evaluate the creation of rules with Atomate, and discuss results and ongoing work.

ATOMATE WALKTHROUGH

We present three scenarios illustrating how a user interacts with Atomate to script useful simple reactive automation.

---

[1]Controlled natural languages are subsets of natural language whose grammars and dictionaries have been restricted in order to reduce or eliminate both ambiguity and complexity. See: http://sites.google.com/site/controllednaturallanguage/.

Scenario: Simple contextual reminding

There are certain household chores Xaria needs to do on particular days of the week, but like many busy individuals, she has trouble remembering what day of the week it is. Because she sometimes works late, setting a regular calendar alarm would cause her to be reminded either on her way home or while she's still at the office. With Atomate, she can set up a reminder action to trigger precisely at the right time (right after she gets home), and to be delivered to her via a variety of mechanisms – an SMS text message to her mobile phone, email, or a desktop notification.

To set up a reminder to take out the trash when she gets home on Tuesday evenings, Xaria clicks on the Atomate tab in her Firefox browser, and clicks "My tasks". This pulls up the interface visible in Figure 7.1. She first specifies what she wants done: she selects "alert me" (Figure 7.2), which defaults to a combination of desktop notification and an SMS text message. The next two options are "whenever" or "next time", which let her specify recurring or one-shot actions. Because she has to take the trash out every week, she chooses "whenever" (Figure 7.2).

Clicking on "whenever" makes visible the situation specifier, visible as the "who does what" line (Figure 7.2.3). This interface is used to specify situational constraints that characterize the conditions under which the action should be taken. Such constraints could pertain to the user's state (such as his or her location) as well as the state of any other entity Atomate has in its world model. Such entities

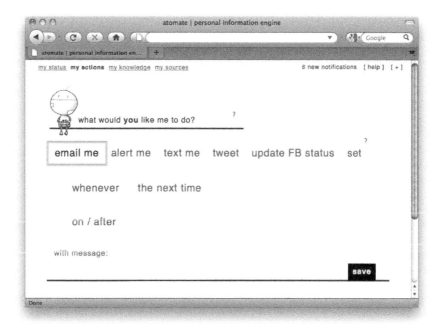

FIGURE 7.1

Atomate's interface for creating new behaviors. A new behavior is created by specifying the action first (top row), situations under which the behavior should act (second row), temporal constraints, and optional action parameters, such as the message to be delivered.

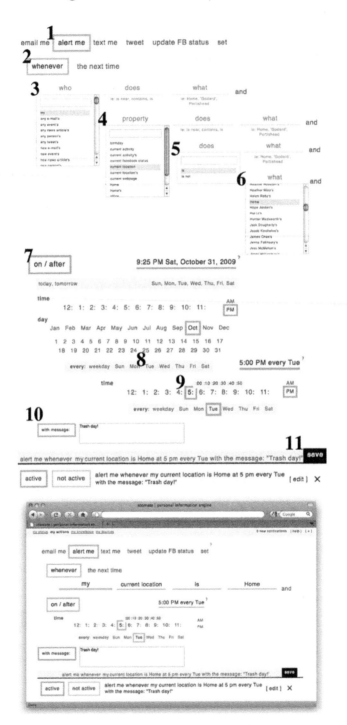

FIGURE 7.2

Xaria filing out the situational conditions for the statement "alert me whenever my current location is Home on/after 5 PM every Tue with the message: 'Trash day!'" The top portion of this figure shows a pieced together view of each click in the rule creation process. The bottom portion shows an in-browser view of the final statement.

typically include the user's friends, acquaintances, calendar events, all of the locations the user commonly visits, Web sites, music tracks, news articles, and emails. This world model is built from information arriving from all of Atomate's various Web-based information streams, such as via RSS/ATOM feeds and REST APIs, as described later in "Data Feeds". Returning to the scenario, since Xaria wants to be reminded when she gets home, she specifies a constraint pertaining to her location: she clicks the "who" slot, which produces a list of possessive forms of people's names, and clicks the top choice, "my (Xaria's)". This produces a list of properties pertaining to her entity, including "current activity", "birthday", "current location", and so on. She selects "current location" (Figure 7.2.4). This moves the entity selector to the predicate position (labeled "does") and displays a list of all predicates that take a location as the first argument, such as "is", "is near", "is not near". She selects "is" (Figure 7.2.5), and this moves the selector to the object (labeled "what") slot, where she selects "Home" (Figure 7.2.6). (Xaria could have equivalently selected "my", and subsequently "home", which also refers to her home.)

At its current state, the behavior would execute whenever she got home. To constrain the behavior to execute only on Tuesday evenings, she selects the "on/after" button (Figure 7.2.7). This produces a calendar widget, where she selects "every Tuesday" (Figure 7.2.8) and a time (Figure 7.2.9). Finally, she adds a message by clicking "message" (Figure 7.2.10) and typing "Trash day!".

She verifies that the behavior is what she intended by reading the simplified English rendering of the rule visible at the bottom of the screen: "Alert me when my location is Home on/after 5 PM every Tue with the message: Trash day!". She hits Save (Figure 7.2.11) and the behavior appears in her Atomate's list of tasks.

Note that, in this example, it is likely that Xaria intends on having the system remind her *once* on Tuesday upon reaching her home, *not* constantly while at home on Tuesday evenings. This assumption is common to most kinds of behaviors that users create in the system, and thus Atomate's rule chainer is designed to work on changes of state.

Scenario: Social coordination

In this second scenario, we illustrate how Atomate can be used in a simple social coordination task.

Ben is often overloaded with things to do and misses events on his calendar – sometimes because he's forgotten about them, while other times he was not sure he wanted to attend them to begin with. In either case, he wants to be notified which of his friends (if any) are attending events he's scheduled but not attending, to both serve as a reminder and potentially help him decide whether or not to go.

To set up an appropriate event, Ben opens Atomate and creates a "New task". He begins by clicking "notify me" and "whenever" to specify that he wishes to be alerted whenever the condition is met. Then he constructs the first condition clause specifying that he wishes the behavior to execute when he's missing an event on his calendar, by selecting, in sequence, "[my] [current calendar event's] [location] [is not] [my] [location]". Next, he adds a second clause to restrict notifications to when his friends arrive at that event: "[any friend's] [location] [is] [my] [current calendar event's] [location]". Ben verifies that the rule looks correct by inspecting the English rendering and hits save.

Since Ben did not specify a message, Atomate will tell him about the situation that caused the rule to trigger. Atomate uses the same mechanism for previewing rules in English to render notifications in simplified English as well. For example, if Ben was missing Liz's birthday party that his friend John is attending, the notification would appear "Ben's current location is not Liz's Birthday Party location. John Smith is at Liz's Birthday Party."

Note that for this rule to work, Ben needs to have provided two types of data sources: a location data source for him and his friends, and his online calendar.[2] His location data source is configured to set the "current location" property on entities representing him and his friends in Atomate's knowledge base, while his calendar is configured to update the "current calendar event" property on the entity representing him. The "Extending Atomate" section describes how new data sources can be configured to update properties automatically.

Scenario: Extending the system

The final scenario illustrates how Atomate can be easily extended to new data sources.

Sherry prefers buying groceries from a local organic grocer, but the availability of produce items there changes every few days. Recently, her grocer started posting the arrival of fresh items on a simple static Web page. Since she never remembers to manually check the page before going shopping, she sets up an Atomate script to inform her to not buy available organic items whenever she arrives at the supermarket.

Her grocer does not publish an RSS feed, so Sherry uses Dapper[3] to construct a data mapper to scrape data off of the grocer's site every couple days. Once she constructs it, she copies the address of the resulting RSS feed to her clipboard, and clicks on the "My Feeds" section of "Atomate" (Figure 7.3). She selects "Create a data source" and names it "Harvest Feed". She then pastes the dapper feed URL into the appropriate field.

When she does this, Atomate retrieves the feed and displays retrieved entries in the interface below. Seeing that Atomate has misidentified the type of entry as "News Story", Sherry clicks on the "type:" property to change it. Because Atomate does not yet know about produce, she creates a new type for these items; to do this, she clicks "new type" and names it "Fresh Produce".

Behind the scenes, these actions cause Atomate to create an *rdfs:Class*[4] for the new type, with the label "Fresh Produce", and to attach a property to the data source ("Harvest Feed") so that the arrival of new entries from this source will result in the creation of entities of the proper type in the world model in the future. Thus, in this way, new RDF classes can be spontaneously created from data arriving from new sources; and multiple sources can be configured to create the same data types. Sherry can further customize the names of the other properties of each of the fresh produce items, or filter out unnecessary properties by unselecting the row(s) corresponding to the properties she wishes to filter.

Next, she constructs a rule to use the new information. She goes to "My tasks" and creates a rule to trigger based on her location and available fresh produce items: "Notify me when my location is Super Market Shop and any Fresh produce item's posted date is within the past 24 hours".

---

[2]Examples of services that could be used for location include Plazes (http://plazes.com) and Google Latitude (http://latitude.google.com). As most of these services do not provide indoor localization, we have also created our own Wi-fi-based room-granularity location-sensing service called OIL (Organic Indoor Location). For calendaring, any of the popular online calendaring services like Google Calendar would suffice.

[3]Dapper – the Data Mapper: http://www.dapper.net/open.

[4]In RDF, the entity used to represent classes of other entities is defined in http://www.w3.org/TR/rdf-schema/.

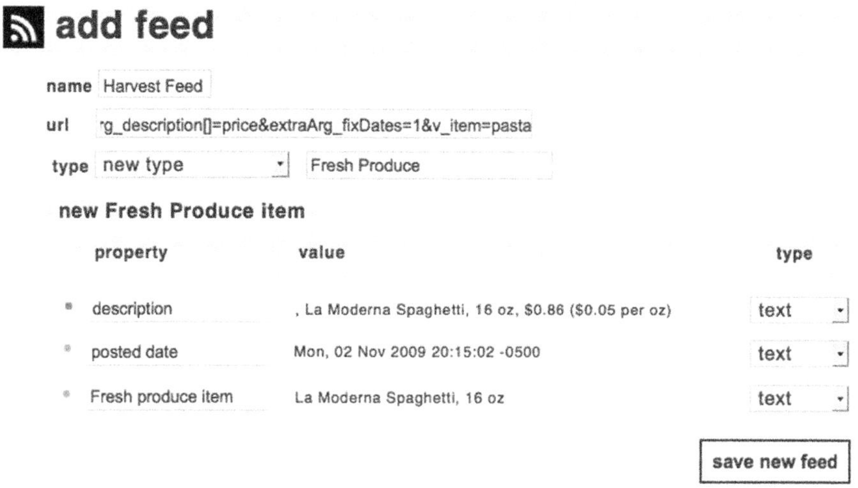

add feed

name | Harvest Feed

url | `g_description[]=price&extraArg_fixDates=1&v_item=pasta`

type | new type ▾ | Fresh Produce

new Fresh Produce item

	property	value	type
●	description	, La Moderna Spaghetti, 16 oz, $0.86 ($0.05 per oz)	text ▾
●	posted date	Mon, 02 Nov 2009 20:15:02 -0500	text ▾
●	Fresh produce item	La Moderna Spaghetti, 16 oz	text ▾

save new feed

FIGURE 7.3

Scenario 3: Sherry adding a new data source to Atomate.

RELATED WORK

Architecturally, Atomate can be viewed as a type of blackboard system, an architecture for sensor-fusion and pattern-directed problem solving using heterogeneous information sources (Winograd, 2001). Atomate's information sources (e.g., Web sites), correspond to a blackboard's "experts," whereas its end user authored behaviors correspond to the pattern-directed programs in these systems.

Toward end-user–specified reactive behaviors, a number of research systems have emerged from the context-aware and ubiquitous computing communities, including the Context Toolkit (Salber, Dey, & Abowd, 1999) and ReBA (Kulkarni, 2002). A number of these projects have looked at different interfaces for making it easy to specify such behaviors; the iCAP, for example, proposed and studied sketching-based interfaces for programming home automation (Sohn & Dey, 2003). CAMP, meanwhile, explored a whimsical, magnetic-poetry metaphor (Truong, Huang, & Abowd, 2004).

Atomate's approach to rule creation, meanwhile, was inspired by research systems examining the use of simplified natural languages for knowledge capture and access on the Semantic Web (Berners-Lee et al., 2001). In particular, the CLOnE (Funk et al., 2001) and ACE (Attempto Controlled English) (Fuchs, Kaljurand, & Kuhn, 2008) work introducing controlled natural languages (CNL), and related GINO (Bernstein & Kaufmann, 2006) and GINSENG interfaces for guided input interfaces for CNLs were the basis of Atomate UI's design.

Other relevant research from the semantic Web community includes work on rule representations (such as SWRL and RuleML), and efficient chainers and reasoners for rule systems. In the future, we aim to transition Atomate's internal rule representation to one of these standard representations and chainers to enable greater interoperability and more efficient rule evaluation.

Atomate also borrows inspiration from the "Web mashup," systems that have explored the potential for combining data from multiple Web sites. A survey of 22 mashups (Wong & Hong, 2008) concluded that most mashups provided new visualizations based on "mashed-up" data from heterogeneous feeds, but found no mashups designed to deliver reactive behaviors (e.g., actions) based on this same data. Atomate demonstrates thus that reactive mashups are both easily created and potentially useful for saving people time and effort. Because Atomate actually allows the user to extend the system and add new data sources, Atomate requires capabilities similar to end user mashup construction environments, such as Intel's Mash Maker (Ennals et al., 2007).

ATOMATE

In the following sections, we describe details of Atomate's design, explaining at a high level how data flows through the system, followed by a description of the data model, the rule chainer, and the user interface.

Data flow

Atomate works in a reactive loop, as illustrated in Figure 7.4, consisting of the steps of data retrieval, world model update, and behavior execution. These behaviors, in turn, can cause changes to the knowledge base that cause more behaviors to run.

Step 1: Retrieving new data. Atomate's feeder component periodically retrieves from Atomate's RDF model a list of all the data sources the user has created, and pulls data from each. For most data sources (corresponding to RSS/ATOM feeds), pulling data corresponds to a simple GET operation of the particular feed in question. For data sources that provide push (asynchronous callbacks), the feeder registers a callback on startup and waits for asynchronous notifications.

Step 2: Updating the world model. For each item retrieved from a source, the feeder updates the corresponding entity in the world model, or creates a new entity if no such corresponding item is found. This updating is fully deterministic as established through per-source mappings created by the user when he or she sets up the data source. For example, a Twitter feed would cause new *Tweet* entities to be created in the RDF knowledge base, whereas entries from Facebook would cause updates to and creation of new *Person* entities.

Step 3: Triggering. Updates to entities in the knowledge base are noticed by the rule chainer. When such updates occur, the rule chainer retrieves all *Rule* entities from the knowledge base. It evaluates each rule antecedent, and fires all rules whose triggered antecedents depend on the entities that changed. Rule antecedents can be either entirely time-based or based on the state of entities in the world model.

The effects of rule firings depend on the type of rule: rules can either cause updates to properties of entities in the knowledge base (if its consequent consists of a "set" clause), trigger a message or notification to be sent to the user, or cause a tweet or other message to be posted via a Web service. For other actions, Atomate can be extended to call arbitrary Web services as described in "Extending Atomate". If the knowledge base is updated as a result of an action firing, the chainer is informed and the rule trigger evaluation starts again.

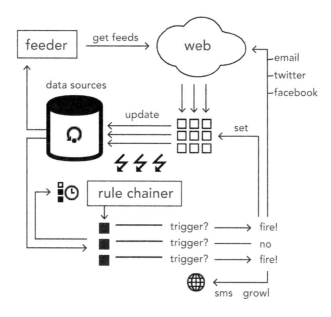

FIGURE 7.4

Atomate data flow. Atomate pulls data from the Web and updates the world model. Model updates are fired and picked up by the rule chainer, which evaluates triggers for user-specified behaviors (rules). Triggered rules that depend on changed entities are fired. The effects of such behaviors can be to update the world model (Set) or to call external services.

Atomate's world model

Atomate internally represents all data it manipulates as RDF entities, including information about things in the physical world (people, places, events), digital items such as messages, articles, tweets, and emails, as well as Atomate-specific rules, predicates, and data sources. The uniform representation reduces overall system complexity and makes it possible for users to examine, access, and update parts of the world model using the entity inspector user interface, which acts as a "global address book" for the system. For example, through this interface users can redefine or add their own predicates and actions by creating new entities of the appropriate types, and define how Atomate should connect to and interpret information from new external data sources.

Rules

Behaviors in Atomate are represented internally as rules, consisting of an antecedent (which characterizes the conditions under which the rule should execute) and the consequent (which specifies the action to be taken).

Specifying conditions for behavior execution

As described earlier, behavior antecedents can consist of two types of constraints: time constraints and situational constraints. Each behavior may have one time constraint, one or more situational constraints, or both a time and one or more situational constraints. The time constraint is simply an expression of when the behavior should execute. Like most calendar alarms, Atomate supports recurring time constraints based on day of week and time of day (e.g., "every Tuesday", "every day at 3 pm").

Situational constraints, on the other hand, specify that particular conditions in the world model must be met for the rule to execute. Since Atomate's world model is designed to mimic (in a greatly simplified form) the dynamics of the real world, constraints on the world model correspond, in Atomate's terms, to situational constraints on the real world. These constraints could pertain to the user, people the user knows, or any other entities (people, places, events, music tracks, resources) being tracked by the system.

Situational constraints are expressed as conjunctions ("ands") of clauses, each with one binary relational predicate applied to two arguments. The simplest such binary relational predicate is "is", which merely checks to see whether the two arguments are the same or equal. Each argument of a binary relational predicate can be either a simple primitive type (number, date, or string) or a *path query* into Atomate's world model. Each path query originates at either a single specific entity, or any entity of a particular type through "any" expressions (e.g., "any Person", "any Event" or "any email"). Atomate also supports the restricted wildcard expression "new", which is evaluated like "any" but only for newly created entities, to make it convenient to write rules that trigger based on the arrival of new information (e.g., "new email", "new instant message", etc.). These wildcard expressions expand the expressiveness of Atomate's antecedents beyond propositional logic and allow for the construction of general rules that work over any (including yet unseen) entities of a particular type. The tail of a path query consists of properties which are traversed from the origin node(s) to values. For example, "[any email's] [author's] [current location]" would be a path query starting from all email entities to the locations of the authors of those entities. Atomate supports path queries of arbitrary lengths. A rule is considered triggered when an interpretation (i.e., a set of mappings) can be found from entities to clause predicate arguments such that resolved values from those entities (through path queries) satisfy each corresponding clause predicate.

The use of "any" versus "new" can yield very different behaviors; for example, a rule with antecedent "[new email's] [author's] [location] [is] [my] [current location]" would trigger at most once: upon arrival of a new email if the email's author was co-located with the user at the time the email arrived. The use of "any" instead of "new", meanwhile, (i.e., "[any email's] [author's] [location] [is] [my] [current location]") would trigger whenever the author of any email (including those previously received) became co-located with the user.

Atomate supports a third type of expression, "that", which is used to refer to entities that were implicitly referenced in preceding clauses. Implicit references arise in two situations: at the end of a path query (e.g., "my current location") or via the wildcard expression "any" (e.g., "any Location") described earlier. The subsequent use of "that Location" in either case would allow the specific entity (either the value of my current location) or the value being bound to "any Location" to be applied to another predicate; "that" binds to only the last such reference.

Expressing actions to be taken

The default set of actions provided in Atomate are "email", "alert", "text", "post a tweet", "update Facebook status", and "Set". The *Set* function updates the property of an entity in the system to a particular specified value, and is typically used to associate information arriving from a particular source to the property value of another entity in the world model.

When an action is called, the antecedent that caused the rule to fire is provided as an argument. This information can be used to make the action adaptive, or to include a helpful message to the user about why the action was taken.

Triggering and scheduling

The goal of the rule chainer is, for every given behavior, to determine whether predicates can be satisfied by some entity (or entities) under the current state of the world model. This corresponds to determining whether nodes named in each clause, when de-referenced by the appropriate path queries, yield values that satisfy the predicates in the antecedent. If the clause contains wildcard expressions (such as "any", or "new", described previously), the chainer must search over all nodes of an appropriate type to determine satisfaction. Computationally, Atomate's approach is naive; it is a forward rule chainer that uses a brute-force approach to evaluate such rule triggers. While it is likely that an efficient solution to this problem exists, our implementation searches the entire space of instances of a particular type in the worst-case scenario to evaluate triggers.

One assumption embodied in the trigger surrounds when rules are considered for execution. As introduced in Scenario 1, most behaviors exhibit the assumption that they will fire once when the rule's antecedents become satisfied. Atomate's rule chainer implements this assumption as follows: when an entity is updated in the knowledge base, the chainer is informed of the change, in particular the entity, property, and value(s) affected. Then, upon evaluating the triggers for all behaviors, the chainer only fires rules if the values that caused them to trigger corresponded to any of the update operations.

Our ongoing work seeks to apply previous work in reasoning engines to make evaluation of triggers more efficient, and to relax the assumption surrounding rule execution to support ongoing behaviors.

User interface

The Atomate interface consists of two integrated interfaces: the delegation interface, where users construct, activate, and monitor the execution of reactive behaviors in the system, and the entity explorer interface, where entities can be viewed, edited, and linked.

"My stuff": The entity explorer

The entity explorer, visible in Figure 7.5, displays all entities in the system, filtered by type. It is designed to act as a general "global address book" for the user, a single unified interface to reference information obtained from Web sources about people, places, events, articles, and so on. Clicking on any of the type names along the top displays a list of all the entities of that type. Clicking further on any item expands the item and displays its properties. Property values can be edited by clicking on them, which opens an auto-completing, incremental-search entity selector box. This box can be used to assign a primitive typed-value (an integer, string, or date), a single, or multiple entities as values.

FIGURE 7.5

The entity inspection UI lets users view and annotate entities in the world model.

Entities can also be set as values of properties by dragging the entity from any list to the property value slot.

The "me" object displays the user's own entity object and state, which, because of its importance, is promoted in the interface to the top (type) selector. Users can use this interface to quickly update properties of their own entity's state, which may cause relevant behaviors they have scripted to trigger.

Rule creation and management interface

Scenarios 1-3 stepped through the rule creation user interface in detail. This interface was designed to be as easy to use as reminder-alarm dialog boxes often visible in PIM calendaring tools, such as Outlook, and yet provide more expressive, context-aware reminder capabilities.

Scenario 1 walked through one example of using the rule creation interface visible in Figure 7.2. This interface has two sections, a section for choosing an action and a section for stating the condition(s) required to make that action occur. The user may choose for an action to occur "whenever" the conditions are satisfied or only "the next time" and then is guided through crafting the "who does what" clause, shown in Figures 7.2.3–7.2.6. Atomate continually modifies the displayed options such that an invalid rule cannot be created. The user may add additional clauses by clicking "and." To specify a time constraint, the calendar widget shown in Figures 7.2.8–7.2.9 can be used, which becomes visible upon clicking the "at/on/after" button. At any time, the user may add a message by clicking "with message" and entering the message in the text field provided. While a user is creating a rule, it is incrementally displayed next to the save button in plain English to reduce the likelihood of error. After reviewing their rule, the user may alter their rule or click "save" to have it recorded and displayed below the rule creation interface in the rule management interface where it may be toggled active or inactive, and edited or deleted.

Implementation

Atomate is implemented as a Firefox browser add-on, and is written entirely in JavaScript. Atomate's RDF data storage layer is kept in-browser using the client-side persistence API mozStorage,[5] which stores all data in an SQLite[6] file in the user's Firefox profile. Atomate's RDF-JS object relation mapper (ORM) allows RDF nodes to be treated like other JavaScript objects in the code, enabling such objects to be serialized and inherit methods through *rdfs:subClass* chains. (Code for entity instance methods are serialized in the triple-store as string properties.) The rule scheduler, database engine and feeder are packaged in a Firefox XPCOM component, and remains a singleton per Firefox process (which is limited by Firefox to one per user). The Atomate UI, meanwhile, resides in a Web page, which calls upon the components and renders/lays out the UI using jQuery.[7]

The advantage to having Atomate in the browser is that the many JavaScript client libraries and APIs available for letting sites access data, such as Facebook Client-Connect[8] and GData JS,[9] can be readily used to obtain data.[10] New data sources with custom client libraries can be added by Web developers without any need for special integration work.

EXTENDING ATOMATE

Since there are an enormous number of Web sites that publish potentially useful information for use in Atomate scripts, it was impossible to anticipate and pre-integrate all possible data sources that users might need. Instead, we opted to make it easy for users to extend Atomate to use arbitrary new sources and actions as they become available.

The architecture of Atomate was designed to support extension in three ways. The first is the introduction of new capabilities (actions) and relation comparison functions (predicates) for user behaviors. The second is the addition of data sources for supplying new information about types of things Atomate already knows about. The third is to extend Atomate to entirely new types of information and representations, as illustrated in Scenario 3. In this section, we describe in greater detail how new sources are added to introduce new information into Atomate's world model.

Adding predicates and actions

New predicates can be added to Atomate to, for example, add more sophisticated support for comparing entities of certain types, while new action functions can be used to extend Atomate's

---

[5]mozStorage APIs for Mozilla Firefox: https://developer.mozilla.org/en/Storage.
[6]SQLite Database Engine: http://sqlite.org.
[7]jQuery Framework for JavaScript: http://jquery.org.
[8]Client Connect for Facebook: http://wiki.developers.facebook.com/index.php/JavaScript_Client_Library.
[9]Google Data APIs: http://code.google.com/apis/gdata/.
[10]To comply with Facebook's Terms of Service, Atomate tags and refreshes or expires data it has gathered from Facebook within a 24-hour period.

capabilities. Currently geared toward end users comfortable with writing JavaScript, adding a predicate or action involves merely creating a new entity of the appropriate type (i.e., *Predicate* or *Action*), specifying required argument types, and attaching an implementation property with a string value consisting of the appropriate JavaScript implementation.[11] Such an implementation may call an external Web service to perform the relevant action or comparison evaluation.[12]

Adding new data sources

The most common form of extension is adding new data sources to provide instances of existing types. For the purposes of this discussion, we assume that Atomate had no prior record of the schema or representation used by this new data source.

Adding a new source requires two steps: adding the source to Atomate's world model, and telling Atomate how to interpret retrieved data. The first step is simple: if the data source exports an RSS/ATOM or other public XML feed, a new Data Source entity is created with the source URL pointing to that feed. If the data source provides its data in a proprietary format, embedded in HTML, or using a custom library, the user can either write a wrapper themselves in JavaScript, or use a third-party service such as Dapper, Babel,[13] or Yahoo Pipes[14] to convert data into an RSS feed first.

The second step is to establish a mapping between the new type and an existing Atomate type. We model our approach to that of Piggybank (Hyunh, 2007), which lets the user construct a visualization from multiple sources with dissimilar schemas using drag and drop gestures. Atomate first retrieves and displays a selection of raw (unaligned) items from the new source. Next, the user selects the Atomate type that best matches the type of the entities retrieved from the new source. For a microblogging service such as Twitter, for example, the user could select the closest entity, such as *Tweet*. Atomate then inserts in the display of each record of the new source items the properties that are found in instances of the chosen destination type. Atomate automatically maps properties in the destination type that match source type properties exactly. For the remaining properties, the user can manually match properties by dragging property names on top of other property names. Behind the scenes, Atomate creates a mapping descriptor to the data source that is used to structurally convert incoming items on its feed prior to being added to the knowledge base.

Atomate does not require all properties in either source or target schemas to be aligned; new properties can be introduced into the type by leaving source properties unpaired. Similarly, properties of the target type can be left unpaired; this will cause entities from the particular source to have undefined values for these properties.

Extending Atomate's schemas

If Atomate does not already have an appropriate class to represent a particular type, a new class can be created directly at the time the new source is added. This process, illustrated in Scenario 3,

---

[11]We omit details on the requirements of such a function for sake of brevity, but a tutorial geared at advanced users of the system is included in Atomate's online documentation.

[12]As predicates are re-evaluated frequently, they should be made efficient and properly cache computed values.

[13]Babel translator service: http://simile.mit.edu/babel.

[14]Yahoo Pipes: http://pipes.yahoo.com.

is done by performing the same steps as described above for adding a new data source. Then, when entities are retrieved from the source and displayed as described above, the user types the name of a new class instead of selecting an existing class as a target destination type. The user can customize the names of property fields and set property field destination types as in the alignment case described above. (Atomate initially guesses the value types by trying to coerce values in the new feed.) The user may optionally specify a superclass by selecting one during this process.

To complete the process of adding a schema, the user needs to specify at least one property to uniquely identify the entity to update when a new piece of information arrives from each source. Defining inverse functional properties serves as Atomate's simple solution to the *entity resolution* problem, and avoids the need to deal with ambiguity in updates to the world model. For example, for schemas representing a person, their email address and phone number could be a useful choice for such a property, because email addresses or phone numbers usually uniquely identify individuals.

Automatically updated properties

The introduction of new sources and types just described result in the creation of new entities and classes to the Atomate knowledge base. In many situations it is useful to assign created values as property values of some other entity in the system. For example, if a user adds new entities of type "GPS observation" from his car's navigation system, hooking up these values to the user's "current location" property would enable rules that condition on the user's current location property to work unmodified with this new data source.

This is where the *Set* action described earlier comes in. To create properties that automatically update in response to the arrival of new information items, a user creates a new rule using the *Set* action. *Set* takes as argument an entity, property, and value. The "that" expression described in the "Rules" section is particularly useful in *Set* rules, as it allows for the succinct expression of general property-update rules. For example, for the previous scenario, the rule "whenever [any GPS Observation's] [user id] is [any Person's] [gps service username], set [that Person's] [current location] to [that GPS Observation's] [location]." would connect the locations associated with any new GPS Observations to appropriate Person entities in the knowledge base.

EVALUATION

Since a user's ability to easily and correctly create rules using Atomate's UI is potentially the greatest obstacle toward successful adoption of the system, our first goal was to investigate whether users could understand and create rules. Secondly, we were interested in users' thoughts about the potential value for such a system – if and how they may use it now, and future desires for functionality. To answer these questions, we performed two studies as follows:

Study 1: Design review. An informal design review was held with 15 user interface researchers (some of whom have experience in designing end user programming interfaces) to discuss the rule creation process and interface. Asked to think about both personal and lay-user preferences, this discussion was used as early feedback and an opportunity to alter the surfacing, presentation, or explanation of the components before the rule creation study.

Study 2: Rule creation. This study was designed to test our hypothesis that a constrained natural language input interface allows end users to easily and quickly create rules of varying complexity, and to enquire about the system's current or future value to users. Using an example data set (consisting of locations, events, contacts, and emails), we asked users to create nine rules (see Figure 7.6 for a full list). These rules ranged from simple to complex, and tested a range of possible behaviors (one-off/repeat reminding, different predicates and actions, multiple clauses, etc.).

We estimated the study would take 10 minutes, at 1 minute for each of the nine rules and another for the survey. We first piloted the study with three colleagues in our lab, observing as they thought aloud through the study, before releasing it to a wider audience online. A 2-minute video was available to explain the system before use.

We used one of four categories to classify each created rule. "Correct" – the rule does exactly what the instructions specified; "half-correct" – the rule would work but may fire too often as the result of it being inadequately specific, or it was obvious what the participant was trying to achieve; "incorrect" – the rule would not achieve the role as set out in instructions; or "missing" – the participant did not complete a rule. Though accuracy was of course desirable,

Rule 1	You have a meeting with a colleague tomorrow at 3pm. Set a reminder.
Rule 2	You have to provide a work status report every Thursday at 2pm. Set a reminder.
Rule 3	Set up an alert that notifies you whenever anyone you know is near your house.
Rule 4	Set an alert that notifies you when your boss, John von Neumann, arrives at his office.
Rule 5	You often forget to bring your shopping list with you to the store. Have Atomate text you your new shopping list (1. eggs. 2. bread. 3. milk) to you when you arrive at your local grocery store (Harvest Market).
Rule 6	You have been buying too many books from Amazon.com. Remind yourself every time you visit amazon.com to check your local public library for the book.
Rule 7	You are working on an urgent project with Vannevar Bush and want to make sure to not miss new emails about it. Have Atomate alert you when you receive a new email from him containing the word "MEMEX" in the subject line.
Rule 8	Have Atomate automatically update your Facebook status when you are at a concert.
Rule 9	Have Atomate send you a text message when you have an activity scheduled in 5 minutes that is not close to where you are.

FIGURE 7.6

The nine rules participants were asked to create in the evaluation.

one of the goals of this study was the process participants went through to create rules, and the (potentially creative or misunderstood) solutions they may come up with, for us to refine the system for extended use. Thus, we were particularly interested in the "half-correct" and "incorrect" rules as these would point to areas or concepts that participants found difficult to comprehend or input, allowing future improvement.

An exit survey measured quantitative response to how easy the system was to use and how useful it was deemed to be, qualitative feedback on the ease of use of the system, and thoughts as to how and when participants would like to use it now or in the future.

RESULTS

Study 1: Design review. Feedback from the design review resulted in a number of changes to the interface to make the rule creation process clearer and more intuitive. These included: labeling the three autocomplete boxes with examples, and simplifying the time and date entry fields.

Study 2: Rule creation. Three colleagues performed the rule creation study in our lab, talking aloud so we could get feedback on what was confusing or unclear about the system. Positively, the feedback mostly concerned minor improvements as opposed to higher-level concerns about the grammar or interface. Based on those concerns, we improved feedback on what an alert or email would display and on whether a rule was one-time or to be repeated; and we clarified our instructions before advertising the study online.

In total, 33 participants began the study, but because of time limitations or technical issues with smaller screens, 26 participants fully completed all rules and the final survey. The group's age ranged from 25 to 45 years, 14 of whom had some previous programming experience. In the sections below, we first examine how participants used the system, including measures of accuracy and ease of use, and discuss how these results suggest design changes, and secondly, look at whether and in what ways participants thought such a system would be useful to them.

Accuracy and ease of use

As in the previous section, we classified each answer into one of four categories: correct, half-correct, incorrect, or missing. Figure 7.7 details these scores as a percentage of all answers. The first six rules were correct over 75% (and mostly over 85%) of the time. The final three were more problematic and raised some interesting issues. Rule 7 (Memex mail): Many participants achieved "half-correct" answers on this rule, leaving out one of the two clauses needed (either "from V Bush" or "subject contains 'Memex'"). Rule 8 (concert): This was an intentionally tricky rule, and open to interpretation on how each person would set up their Atomate system. The "correct" way was to specify a current activity type of concert, but many participants used "current activity's description contains 'concert'". This could feasibly work, but only if, when setting up the concert feed, they make sure to precede each description with the word "concert", otherwise it would most likely just look like "nine inch nails @ middle east, 9pm". The incorrect rules here were varied, and in feedback, participants said when they could not quite grasp the correct way to do it; they just moved on with whatever they had. Rule 9 (event in 5 minutes): The half-correct and incorrect rules for rule 9 mainly missed the second desired clause ("and that event's location is near me"), meaning the rule would fire for all events starting soon, regardless of location.

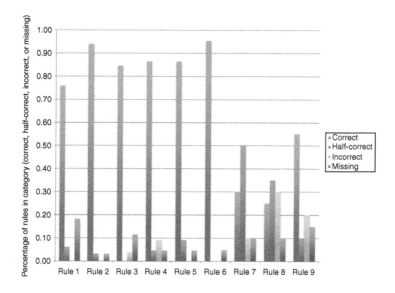

FIGURE 7.7

Percentage of created rules that were correct, half-correct, incorrect, or missing.

Figure 7.8.1 details responses to the question, "After reading and understanding the instructions for each rule, how easy was it to create the rule?" Feedback suggests (as we intended) that the rules were of varying complexity, but overall it was encouraging that with only 2 minutes of training in the form of a video, 65% of participants found it easy to create rules. However, 35% said they found it difficult, and we discuss improvements in "Ongoing Work".

The half-correct and incorrect answers, along with feedback from the survey, suggest a number of both simple design changes to improve the system and interesting directions for future work.

Simple improvements were implemented to address some of the issues we observed. These included an easier and more prominent way to "and" clauses together to form a rule and alterations to the language displayed in the interface, such as changing "at" to "on / after" for adding dates, and changing "if" to an option of "whenever" or "the next time" for adding clauses.

We are working on several improvements to the rule creation process described in the "Evaluation" section including rule sharing and approaches at specifying rules by demonstration. As a specific example, to mitigate the problem of clause omission, which causes rules to act too often (e.g., with insufficient specificity), we are working on a rule simulation environment which will let the user immediately see the effects of a rule on the user's recent past.

Usefulness

The second goal of our study was to explore how helpful or useful participants would find the current implementation, and what other uses they would like Atomate to perform.

After completing the example rule creation, users were asked, "Do you think Atomate would be useful to you?" (Figure 7.8.2). On a scale of 1 (Not Useful) to 7 (Very Useful), the mean response was 5.5. Participants valued a number of uses of Atomate, such as forwarding certain emails to a

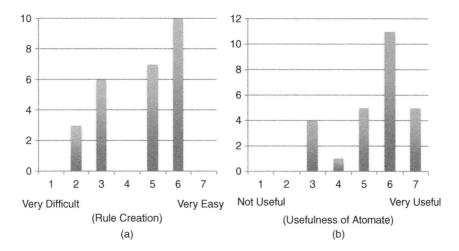

FIGURE 7.8

Results from the rule creation survey. (a) How easy was it to create each rule? (b) Do you think Atomate would be useful to you?

phone, emailing me the weather forecast when I am in a new location, or giving reminders at certain dates (pay credit card when due) or for certain events and locations (bring earplugs to a concert, remind me to thank people for gifts when in their vicinity). A number of participants also reported they thought it may encourage more social uses of the Web, easing the barriers for acts of sharing. One participant said:

> "When done manually, letting your friends know every time you're at a bar could be tedious…but with automation it would be more of a friendly standing invitation and may actually drive me to use social networking sites more."

A number of creative future uses for Atomate were also posited. The ability to add sensors to other objects was widely desired, such as a Roomba vacuum cleaner, a microwave, a fridge, or even toilet paper! Integration with cell phones was also seen as valuable, declining calls if in a certain location, or replying to missed calls when in transit.

In summary, the majority of participants found it easy to create rules, and thought the system would provide value, positing potential supported uses. A number of rule creation mistakes and feedback suggested both short- and long-term design improvements. We discuss some of the longer-term improvements in the following section.

ONGOING WORK

In this section, we describe our current work toward extending Atomate to make it easier to use and more versatile.

Extending the rule language

Ternary and higher-arity predicates are often useful for expressing such value-modified predicates as "within N minutes of" or "within N miles of"; thus, we are adding support for such predicates in the chainer and UI. Second, to realize an initial goal of better supporting message filtering/routing applications, we will support "engage-able" actions through "while" rules. Unlike the "next time"/"whenever" rules described earlier, "while" rules will enable something when a rule triggers, and disable it automatically when the rule ceases triggering. For example, "while my location is home, send notifications through my computer" would allow Atomate's notification policy to change based on the user's location.

Simulation and by-demonstration UI

To reduce the likelihood of errors at rule creation time, we are developing an interface that will immediately simulate, when a rule is specified, the conditions under which it will fire. This simulation will display and replay a recent history of the user's world model, to demonstrate what caused the behavior to fire. Such a simulation we believe would help users identify, for example, when they've left out a clause in a rule antecedent that would cause it to fire more frequently than desired, or if their antecedent is too restrictive. In addition to firing simulation, we wish to provide a "programming by demonstration" approach to start specifying rules. The idea is to use the visualization idea just mentioned to let the user select situations in which they want the new behavior to execute.

Community sharing (the Atom Garage)

While advanced users and enthusiasts may extend the system to new data sources and property-updating rules in the ways described, casual end users are unlikely to bother. To allow the effort of the few "power users" of Atomate to benefit the casual users, we are building an online repository where users can upload entities of their choice, and publish them with descriptors so that they can be easily found.

Publishing your life stream (peRSSona)

To make it easy for users to share updates about their activities, location, and state with their friends, Atomate can be configured to publish state changes to particular entities in its world model as RSS 1.0 feeds. This feature, which we call *your peRSSona*, will be configurable to provide differing degrees of disclosure for their activities. For example, a user might publish a public feed containing information about how they preferred to be contacted but not their precise activity, while posting different perRSSonas containing more detailed activity information for their trusted friends – information such as their whereabouts, music listening, and Web page browsing history.

From pull to push: PubSubHubbub

Atomate's current method of polling of ATOM/RSS feeds is inefficient because feeds are pulled repeatedly, which causes entries previously seen to be repeatedly parsed. The current architecture requires that Atomate subscribe to a potentially large number of feeds, hundreds, for example, if the user is to track the location and activity state changes of all her friends. To reduce load on clients, we are adding support for PubSubHubbub,[15] which feed clients use to register for change notifications at "hubs" for a number of feeds. New information is pushed to clients only when changed, saving clients from polling repeatedly and repeatedly re-obtaining data they already have.

DISCUSSION AND CONCLUSION

We have presented Atomate, a system to allow end users to utilize Web-based data sources to create reactive automation. The system comprises a uniform internal data model, and a constrained-natural-language interface to create rules. Through an evaluation, we have demonstrated that the majority of participants found it easy to create rules, and thought Atomate would provide value in a number of personal-information-related settings.

Some of the reactive behaviors demonstrated in this paper bear resemblance to scenarios proposed by Berners-Lee et al. in the original vision for the Semantic Web (Berners-Lee et al., 2001). However, there are a number of differences between Atomate and these Semantic Web agents. First, unlike the agents in the Semantic Web scenarios, which can "roam from page to page to carry out sophisticated tasks for users," Atomate acts directly based on the state of its model and information on incoming feeds, and lacks a sophisticated description logic inference engine, or capacities to learn, search, or act on the user's behalf beyond the rules set up by the user. However, the comparative simplicity of Atomate's approach makes it easier to understand, and potentially more predictable than approaches that use more sophisticated reasoning mechanisms.

Furthermore, the Web of today is very different from the Web portrayed in Semantic Web scenarios. Very few of today's "Web 2.0" RSS/ATOM feeds employ RDF; instead, they "shoehorn" data into simpler schemas intended for news article syndication, often embedding HTML into fields and overloading field semantics. This has not been a problem until now, as feeds have been consumed exclusively by humans through feed aggregators. But these behaviors cause a wealth of challenges for Atomate, directly complicating the process of adding new data sources to the system. Because of the lack of semantics and this scheme-overloading behavior observed in RSS feeds, users of Atomate have to manually assign, for each new data source, mappings between fields and the schemata used in the rest of the system. In schema overloading situations, feeds have to first be "scraped" to extract data from overloaded fields and to eliminate presentation markup (using a tool such as Yahoo Pipes) before being added to the system. Finally, users have to grapple with obscure concepts such as unique IDs (inverse functional properties) in order to make it possible for the system to identify entities to update provided the arrival of new information along any particular feed.

Given the positive responses from participants of our study surrounding the perceived usefulness of the system, we anticipate that reactive automation driven by data from Web feeds and APIs will soon emerge in various forms. To make use of feeds for such applications easier, content publishers and designers of content delivery and publishing platforms for the Web should consider ways to improve the quality of feeds to make them more suitable for such applications.

---

[15]The PubSubHubbub Project: http://code.google.com/p/pubsubhubbub/.

First, data feeds should avoid the schema overloading, appropriation, and presentation markup embedding practices just described, as this creates the need for an additional "scraping/extraction" step to syntactically clean up and unpack feeds prior to use. Second, metadata could be added to facilitate the process of schema integration. Life-logging services in particular could add metadata describing what it is that the feed represents – the type of activity or state (locations, music listening, Web page viewing, hours slept), and even more importantly, an identifier of the person or agent that is the subject of observation. Of additional benefit for interfaces supporting constrained natural language expression of entities would be natural language labels (common names) to use to describe observed entities or observations in the interface. Finally, the use of URIs, or an indication of the inverse functional properties to use in the schema of a feed, would eliminate the need for users to specify this manually in the interface.

We note that such recommendations would be easy to implement using RSS 1.0/RDF which seemingly has fallen out of favor among content publishing platforms and feed readers. The richer RDF representation would allow data items to be presented in their original schemas, since RDF permits a natural incorporation of definitions and properties from external schemata within a RSS-schema structure documents. With RSS 1.0, information about different subjects could be combined in the same feed, reducing the fragmentation that occurs with the more restrictive feed types.

AVAILABILITY

Atomate, including its source, is available as free, open source software under the MIT License at http://atomate.me/. The authors currently view Atomate as primarily a proof of concept, and hope that other developers will download, examine, use, appropriate, extend, and improve upon the ideas presented therein. A forum, bug tracker, and message board for researchers and developers is available there for discussing ideas and collaboration opportunities.

Acknowledgments

Atomate was developed with support from MIT CSAIL, the National Science Foundation, the Web Science Research Initiative, and a Royal Academy of Engineering Senior Research Fellowship. We would like to thank Jamey Hicks, Ora Lassila, Mark Adler, Wendy Mackay, and Michel Beaudoin-Lafon for their helpful ideas, input, and suggestions.

ATOMATE

Intended users:	All users
Domain:	All Web sites
Description:	Atomate is a reactive personal information assistant that lets individuals easily create activity- and context-sensitive reminders and actions driven by heterogeneous information streams. Atomate users construct behaviors through a constrained natural language UI (CNLI), which resembles a simplified form of English. The CNLI is designed to let nonprogrammers easily specify actions for the system to take, and the situations in which to take them.
Example:	Atomate can be used to remind you of a calendar event. For instance, you may have a meeting with a colleague, but you only want to be reminded if the colleague is actually in their office. Atomate lets users set the rule: "when I have an upcoming meeting in my calendar with [colleague], alert me if that colleague enters the office, and I am not near his office."
Automation:	Yes, although currently the system is restricted to notifying the user or posting new information (e.g., to Twitter).
Mashups:	Partially. Atomate combines information from multiple sites internally to make decisions.
Scripting:	Yes, through the rule editor interface.
Natural language:	Yes, through Atomate's English-like CNLI.
Recordability:	No, users must specify actions to take and when to take them.
Inferencing:	Yes. All rules/behaviors are specified by users, but heuristics are employed when introducing new information sources.
Sharing:	Yes, Atomate users can share their actions as feeds.
Comparison to other systems:	Unlike Chickenfoot and CoScripter, Atomate works with Web information that is "off the page" (e.g., RSS feeds). Like Inky, we support a simplified natural language interface, but use a different constrained-input approach.
Platform:	Implemented as an extension to the Mozilla Firefox browser.
Availability:	Code is available under the MIT license at: http://code.google.com/p/list-it.

Mashups

Many Web tasks involve combining information from multiple sources, for example plotting open rentals on a map or adding legroom descriptions to a list of flights. The chapters in this section propose alternative methods for mixing data from different sources. C3W (clip, connect, and clone for the Web) presents a specialized platform for clipping, connecting, and cloning pieces of Web pages to help users make decisions more easily, such as which bus to take to a movie theater. Mash Maker is a Firefox plugin that allows users to create overlay mashups by interactively extracting and placing data. The d.mix system presents an approach that leverages available Web site services instead of extracting data directly from the HTML Web pages. Finally, the Integrated Task Learning system looks beyond the Web browser and proposes a system that lets users automate tasks and mix data across a variety of desktop applications.

Clip, connect, clone

Combining application elements to build custom interfaces for information access

8

Jun Fujima,[1] **Aran Lunzer,**[1] **Kasper Hornbæk,**[2] **Yuzuru Tanaka**[1]

[1]*Meme Media Laboratory, Hokkaido University*
[2]*Department of Computer Science, University of Copenhagen*

ABSTRACT

Many applications provide a form-like interface for requesting information: the user fills in some fields, submits the form, and the application presents corresponding results.

Such a procedure becomes burdensome if (1) the user must submit many different requests, for example in pursuing a trial-and-error search; (2) results from one application are to be used as inputs for another, requiring the user to transfer them by hand; or (3) the user wants to compare results, but only the results from one request can be seen at a time. We describe how users can reduce this burden by creating custom interfaces using three mechanisms: clipping of input and result elements from existing applications to form cells on a spreadsheet; connecting these cells using formulas, thus enabling result transfer between applications; and cloning cells so that multiple requests can be handled side by side. We demonstrate a prototype of these mechanisms, initially specialized for handling Web applications, and show how it lets users build new interfaces to suit their individual needs.

INTRODUCTION

This paper describes a prototype that supports end users in reducing the burden in certain kinds of information access. The prototype lets users create custom interfaces by clipping, connecting, and cloning elements from existing applications. It is currently specialized to the handling of Web applications, yet the underlying mechanisms are also suitable for applications of other kinds.

The motivation for this work arises from three kinds of challenge that are commonly observed in the use of applications for information access.

First, it can be laborious for users to find the interface elements of interest. For example, the input fields for a Web application may be on a page that also includes many other items; similarly, the page of results delivered by that application may include details that the user does not need. If the application is used repeatedly, even the effort of locating the relevant input fields and the relevant results can become a burden. We would like users to be able to create simplified versions of the applications they are using.

Second, users often want further information related to the results they have found. This may involve using results from one application as inputs to another. For example, in planning an evening out, a user may invoke one Web application to discover what films are currently showing, choose a film, see which cinemas are showing it, look up the address of a cinema to feed into a transport enquiry, and so on. Repeating all these steps for each of several films would be hard work; it would be preferable if the user could create connections that automatically transfer the data between applications.

Third, the results obtained from one request can have increased value when seen in the context of other results. For example, the filmgoer might want to consider a variety of cinemas and screening times, to compare the cost and convenience of getting to each one. However, comparing results is difficult if each request causes the previous result to disappear from view. We would like to help users handle alternative requests side by side, so that it becomes easy to submit many requests and to compare their results.

This paper extends an earlier poster presentation (Fujima et al., 2004b) in describing C3W (clip, connect, and clone for the Web), a prototype that provides integrated support for addressing these three challenges. We show how C3W allows a user to create a custom information-access interface based on one or several Web applications, then use this interface to view and control many alternative requests side by side. Providing support for such side-by-side handling is the central theme of our work on subjunctive interfaces (Lunzer, 1999; Lunzer & Hornbæk, 2003b; Lunzer & Hornbæk, 2004); C3W represents a substantial advance in this work, being the first system to make subjunctive-interface facilities available for a whole class of applications that normally handle just one request at a time.

The section, "Examples and Explanations" demonstrates our prototype and explains its capabilities. The facilities needed to generate this kind of system are discussed in the "Implementation Requirements" section, whereas "Related Work" places our work in the context of prior research. The contributions are summed up in the "Conclusion" section, where we also discuss how to move beyond the limitations of the existing prototype.

EXAMPLES AND EXPLANATIONS

In the following, we explain the main features of C3W through two examples.

A useful union of two applications

Suppose an investor in Japan wants to look up the stock price of U.S.-quoted companies, but to see them in Japanese yen rather than dollars. Perhaps no single Web application offers such a lookup, but the investor knows that the CNN Money site offers a stock price lookup in dollars, and Yahoo! has a currency conversion page that can certainly deal with dollars and yen. Furthermore, suppose the investor wants to see several companies' prices at the same time.

Figure 8.1 shows an interface, built using C3W, that fulfils these needs. We will now describe the three main techniques used in building it.

Clipping

This interface was assembled from two previously created, simpler interfaces: one for the stock-price lookup and one for the currency conversion. Figure 8.2 shows how elements were initially clipped from the Yahoo! site; Figure 8.3 shows these clipped elements arranged by the user on what we call a C3Sheet, along with a second C3Sheet for the CNN lookup. All the cells on these sheets act as portals (in the sense of Olston & Woodruff, 2000) onto the Web pages from which they were clipped. Thus the top three cells on the currency-conversion sheet (on the left in Figure 8.3) retain their roles as input devices, so that specifying a new value in any one will cause a re-evaluation of the Yahoo! conversion and will update the bottom text field to show the new converted amount.

Holding down the Alt key brings up a red rectangle that follows the mouse to highlight the region of the nearest surrounding HTML tag; this indicates which portion of the page will be clipped if a mouse drag is started.

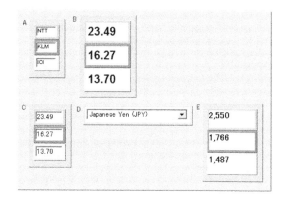

FIGURE 8.1

A user-built interface that takes company stock codes as input (in the cells marked A), and finds their dollar prices (B) and the equivalent yen amounts (E). Cells A and B were created by clipping elements from a stock-price lookup application; C, D, and E were clipped from a currency exchange application. The user connected these applications by giving C a formula that copies the value in B. The user has also cloned cell A to deal with three cases in parallel, which has caused the automatic cloning of all cells that depend on A. Each set of clones uses the same layout and color-coding, to emphasize their correlations – for example, the current dollar price of NTT is $23.49, and the current value of this many dollars is ¥2,550.

Here the user has started dragging the conversion input field, to drop it on a C3Sheet. After also clipping the drop-downs that specify the source and destination currencies, the user enters a sample dollar amount and presses the "Convert" button. The lower part shows the clipping of the converted-amount text from its place on the result page.

Note that the cells need not be clipped in the order in which they are encountered. In particular, if the user had only decided to wrap this application after having obtained some result, he or she could have clipped the result field first, and then gone back to the previous page to clip the parameters that led to it.

Each of the C3Sheets in Figure 8.3 works as a reusable application, which could be saved on a user's local disk or distributed to other users for their immediate use. This illustrates how clipping enables the creation of simplified versions of an application.

Connecting

The next stage in building the example in Figure 8.1 is to create a combination in which the two applications are connected. To do this, the user starts with another empty C3Sheet and repeats the clipping process – this time clipping the cells from the existing C3Sheets. Notice that there is

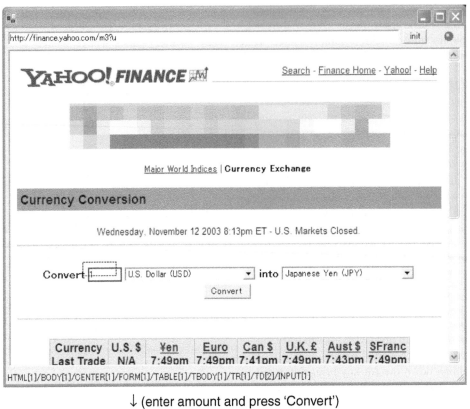

↓ (enter amount and press 'Convert')

Symbol	U.S. Dollar	Exchange Rate		Japanese Yen	Bid	Ask	Historical Charts
USDJPY=X	10	7:49pm	108.5600	1,088	108.5600	108.6100	3m, 1y, 2y, max

FIGURE 8.2

Clipping elements from a currency conversion application. At the top is the default input page for the conversion, on view in C3W's specialized Web browser.

no need to clip the source currency selector if the desired currency is always the same; the user must simply ensure that the selector is set to that currency when the other cells are clipped. The cells may be laid out like this:

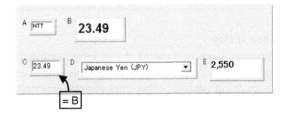

Here the upper two cells (A and B) come from the stock price application, whereas the lower three are from the currency conversion. The user has already taken the final step necessary in connecting the applications together: establishing that the conversion amount cell (C), rather than its previous status as a user input field, is to take its value from cell B. This is done by adding the simple formula "=B" to cell C. Now whenever B's value changes, as the result of a new stock price lookup, C is automatically updated and a currency conversion is triggered. If the user wanted instead to convert the price of 100 shares, this could be done by making C's formula "=B*100".

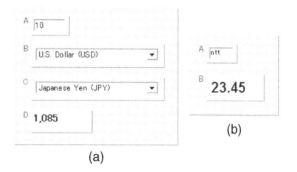

(a)

(b)

FIGURE 8.3

Left: C3Sheet with the elements clipped in Figure 8.2. Right: C3Sheet for a stock-price lookup. The cells' different font sizes reflect the visual nature of the clipping operation; these are the fonts used in the elements that were clipped. However, each cell created from a Web-page element is in essence a fully functioning Web browser, so the user is free to adjust the font size.

This C3Sheet also works as a reusable application, accepting a stock code in cell A and producing a converted price in E. It could be configured to reevaluate automatically every few minutes to reflect the latest stock price and conversion rate. In addition, because it includes the destination currency selector, it will perform conversions into whichever currency the user chooses; for example, a Danish investor might want Danish krone (DKr) conversions.

This illustrates how connecting enables the automated transfer of results from one application to another.

Cloning

The third stage in our example is when the user decides to track several companies' stock prices in parallel. The interface shown previously can be extended to support this, by cloning the relevant cells.

Using a pop-up menu on cell A, the user asks for an additional scenario, and then one more. This causes A to be cloned twice, with the new instances appearing directly beneath the original and initially holding the same stock code. At the same time, cloning automatically takes place for every cell that depends on the stock code – namely the dollar price (B), the input to the currency conversion (C), and the conversion result (E). Each cell that is cloned shows its instances in the same layout, and with the same colored borders. Thus when the user types a new stock code into any instance of cell A, it is easy to tell where the results for that stock will appear.

A cell that has not been cloned remains as a single instance that participates in all scenarios. An example of this is the single instance of the destination currency selector in Figure 8.1. Selecting a new currency will cause all scenarios to be reevaluated – for example, one could switch all the conversions simultaneously to euros. Alternatively, the user can specify that this cell should also have separate instances for each scenario; then each scenario could be given a distinct setting, for example to convert the NTT price into yen, the KLM price into euros, and the ICI price into pounds.

This illustrates how cloning enables side-by-side handling of requests that normally can only be handled separately.

A more ambitious combination

We now present a more complex example. Consider someone who lives in Copenhagen and likes to make use of the city's many cinemas. It would be useful for this person to have an application that helps in planning a film outing. The C3Sheet shown in Figures 8.4 and 8.5 was built by clipping from three Web applications with the following facilities:

1. A personal page that lists favorite places and has links to pages describing them. It includes a drop-down selector listing cinemas by their familiar names; the user can select a cinema and then navigate to a description page containing the cinema's official name and address.
2. The film section of a large Copenhagen events site, which includes a search box where the user can enter the name of a film currently on release and obtain a page with a description of the film and links to further details. One link leads to a page detailing where and at what times the film is being screened.
3. A travel-planning site allows a user to specify start and destination addresses, and the proposed travel time (either for arrival or departure). The site then presents one or more recommended itineraries.

The user wants to be able to select a film, a cinema, and the earliest acceptable screening time; the application should then find the first satisfactory screening of that film at the chosen cinema, and submit an itinerary request from the user's home to the cinema, arriving fifteen minutes before the film starts. A combination that achieves this is shown in Figure 8.4. Figure 8.5 then shows a simple example of cloning: the user has created a further scenario to handle a second film name, and can now work with the two scenarios in parallel.

The two examples described in this section illustrate the potential capabilities of C3W. In the following section we provide some details of C3W's implementation, as guidelines for practitioners wishing to develop similar systems.

IMPLEMENTATION REQUIREMENTS

Many software platforms and toolkits could be used to implement a system supporting the operations shown above. C3W, which primarily addresses Web applications, is built on the PlexWare platform (K-Plex, Inc., San Jose and Tokyo; http://www.kplex.com). Before we illustrate how clipping, connecting, and cloning are supported in C3W, we will explain briefly some implications of choosing this platform.

PlexWare is an implementation of the IntelligentPad meme media architecture (Tanaka & Imataki, 1989; Tanaka, 2003). In IntelligentPad, information and processing components are

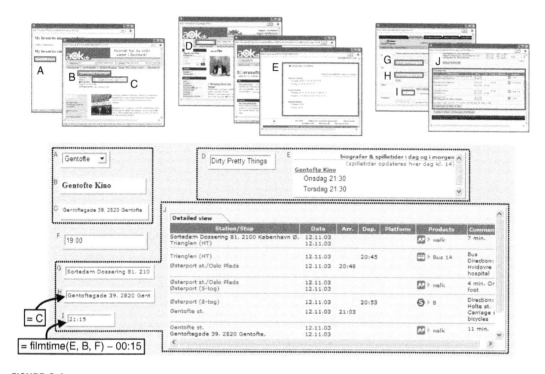

FIGURE 8.4

Using three Web applications in combination to provide travel information for film outings. The cell relationships established by clipping from the pages shown as thumbnails at the top are as follows: selecting a cinema in the list in cell A triggers navigation that places the cinema's name and address in B and C, respectively; entering a film name in D causes E to hold a list of that film's Copenhagen-area screenings for today and tomorrow; cells G, H and I serve as start address, destination, and arrival time for a travel enquiry that gives an itinerary in J. Cell F is an independently created cell in which the user specifies the earliest desired film start time. The applications have been connected by giving cell H (destination) a formula that copies the cinema address from C, and cell I (arrival time) a formula based on a user-written function for finding in cell E the first screening time relevant to cinema name B and time F. Any change to the cinema choice in A, film name in D, earliest start time in F, or starting address in G will trigger reevaluation leading to a new itinerary.

represented as 2D visual objects called pads. Each pad holds its state data in named slots, which also form its interface for functional connection to other pads. By the direct-manipulation pasting of one pad onto another, a user defines a child–parent relationship between them and can also connect one slot in the child to one slot in the parent. This simple form of linkage is enough to enable pad compositions to act as compound multimedia documents, or hierarchically structured applications. The compositions are also easy to decompose – again by direct manipulation – to be reused or reedited.

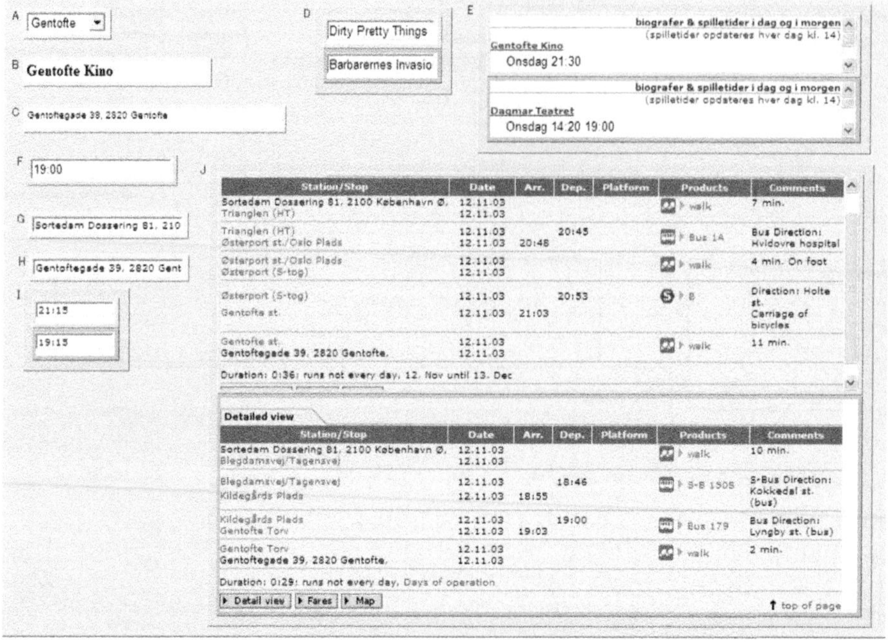

FIGURE 8.5

The composite Web application shown in Figure 8.4, after the user has cloned cell D. Cloning has been propagated automatically to all the cells that depend directly or indirectly on D: the screening times (E), derived arrival time (I), and the itinerary (J). The user may now wish to experiment by entering alternative film names in either instance of cell D, or could change some other input parameter and obtain new timings and itineraries for both films simultaneously.

Within PlexWare, many powerful Microsoft controls – such as Internet Explorer (IE) and Excel – have been encapsulated as pads. Through our collaboration with K-Plex, we had access to the source code involved in such encapsulation and were able to modify this code to extend the capabilities of the encapsulated controls. In addition, though not described in detail in this paper, we were able to implement mechanisms for extracting and reusing elements within general pad compositions, enabling us to explore how non-Web applications may also be included in C3Sheet constructions.

Clipping

The activity that we call clipping is the fundamental mechanism by which a user extracts elements from existing applications for use in a custom interface. Any implementation of clipping requires detailed cooperation between the existing applications and the interface-construction environment. The necessary components are as follows:

1. *An interaction mechanism by which the user identifies an element that is to be clipped, and installs it as a cell in the custom interface:* Our support for clipping from Web pages is implemented by cooperation between an IE pad, with some extensions that we added, and a C3Sheet object. The extended IE supports the extraction of any Web-page region that can be expressed using an HTML-Path (Tanaka, Kurosaki, & Ito, 2002). An HTML-Path is a specialization of an XPath expression; it can specify any self-contained HTML tag (such as an input field, table row, or even a whole document), and also supports regular expressions for defining portions of text nodes. Once the user has steered an interactive highlight to the desired region of the page, that region can be dragged and dropped onto a C3Sheet to define a new cell.

2. *A visual representation for the custom interface and the cells within it, where each cell can exhibit the behavior of its source region in the original application:* Earlier we mentioned that each cell in C3W is in essence a fully functional Web browser – a Web-browsing pad – that works as a portal onto the region of the page from which the element was clipped. Therefore the cell has the interaction behavior that the element would normally have within the full Web page: input fields, menus, buttons, and the like all work as usual, as do display elements.

3. *A way of capturing the dependency relationships between separately clipped cells, so that changes in input values result in reevaluation of results:* The most complex aspect of clipping is the capture of dependency relationships between cells. Cells in C3W are typically extracted from navigations that span multiple Web pages, and carry detailed information enabling the C3Sheet to determine their mutual relationships and to reexecute the navigation when necessary.

We now give further details of the processes that support clipping in C3W.

Capturing the dependency relationships between elements

As the user navigates using our browser, a navigation path of the following form is recorded:

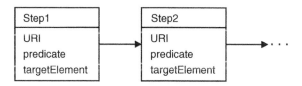

The path is a sequence of steps representing encountered documents. A step consists of the URI of the document, a "predicate" specifying any conditions that the user has specified on that document, and a "targetElement" specifying the interaction that took the browser to the next document (if any). The predicate conditions correspond to values specified in elements such as INPUT or SELECT; the targetElement is typically an A (anchor) or FORM. All these attributes are recorded using HTML-Path expressions, as described above.

When the user clips elements from the documents, the path is augmented with "extract" attributes. The following figure shows how navigation actions within the Yahoo! currency conversion application contribute to the recorded path, and a specific example of the attribute values recorded when the user clips the entry field for the starting-currency amount on the top page, puts the value "10" into that field, presses the "Convert" button (to submit the form), then clips the converted amount on the result page:

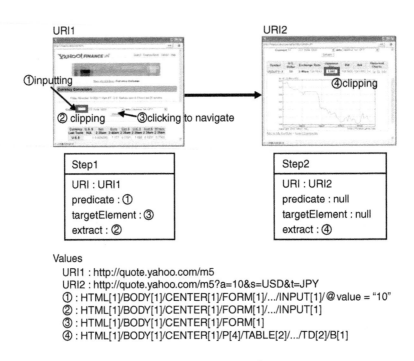

Values

URI1 : http://quote.yahoo.com/m5
URI2 : http://quote.yahoo.com/m5?a=10&s=USD&t=JPY
① : HTML[1]/BODY[1]/CENTER[1]/FORM[1]/.../INPUT[1]/@value = "10"
② : HTML[1]/BODY[1]/CENTER[1]/FORM[1]/.../INPUT[1]
③ : HTML[1]/BODY[1]/CENTER[1]/FORM[1]
④ : HTML[1]/BODY[1]/CENTER[1]/P[4]/TABLE[2]/.../TD[2]/B[1]

Whenever a user drops a new element on a C3Sheet, it brings with it the full multistep navigation path describing how it was extracted. The C3Sheet compares this path against the paths for existing cells, and thus determines their dependency relationships. In our Yahoo! example the conversion result cell becomes a dependant of the currency amount cell, with a single navigation step between them. If a currency selection field were also extracted as a cell, the result would be a dependant of that cell too.

Note that this analysis of navigation paths is not affected by the order in which the cells are created. This is why, as mentioned in the section, "Clipping", a user need not decide in advance which navigations he or she will want to reuse, but can do so in retrospect – that is, after having seen some initial results. In such a case the user could clip the desired result elements, then backtrack to earlier pages and clip the input elements. By the same token, C3W can support clipping from a branched navigation – for example, pursuing two different links from a film information page to clip both actor information and local reviews.

Replaying derivations

Later, when a new value is supplied for some cell that is acting as an input, C3W must replay the appropriate navigation steps to obtain the results for any dependent cells. For this it uses an instance of Web browser that it holds behind the scenes, iteratively executing the following procedure for each navigation step:

1. Set up any conditions specified by predicate attributes.
2. Set up any values connected to input cells; propagate any values connected to output cells.
3. Access the element specified by the targetElement attribute, to jump to the next step. This jump goes to a URI that depends on the user's input values at the time of replay, and may therefore override the URI attribute value originally recorded for each step.

Note that, in contrast to the formulas specified by users to connect applications, the details of the dependencies between input and result cells extracted from a given application are typically hidden. To help users understand these hidden relationships it would be possible to create a dummy formula for each result cell, revealing which other cells it depended on and perhaps some clues about the kind of derivation involved (e.g., whether it is a Web navigation or a pad-based calculation). These dummy formulas could also contribute to a global mechanism for helping the user to trace dependencies through the sheet.

Although the specifics for clipping from other kinds of application are different, the facilities required are equivalent. For example, if the user is creating cells by clipping pads from within large IntelligentPad composites, then instead of a Web navigation path, each cell includes a precise description of its pad's position within the hierarchical structure of the source composite; instead of holding a Web browser behind the scenes to re-evaluate the navigation, the C3Sheet must maintain a working copy of the relevant parts of the composites.

Connecting

Connecting refers to applying formulas to cells, so that derivations normally driven by direct user input can instead be driven by changes in the values of other cells.

Formulas in the C3W prototype are handled by a hidden instance of an Excel spreadsheet. A C3Sheet cell with label x corresponds to the cell at location $x1$ on the Excel sheet – that is, the cell labeled C is mapped to C1, and so on. When the user adds a formula to a C3Sheet cell, the formula is first scanned for references to other cell labels, these references are converted to spreadsheet cell locations, and the derived formula is then attached to the appropriate cell on the spreadsheet.

A cell on a C3Sheet always corresponds to some clipped unit of HTML, including its enclosing tag. However, in transferring values between the C3Sheet and Excel, a distinction is made between two types of cell: those whose essential content can be characterized as a simple character string, and those that have a more complex, typically nested, structure. For the former category, Excel only handles the inner content string. This applies not just to simple textual-result cells and input fields, but also to cells whose main function depends on a single string property – such as the HREF property of an A (anchor) tag, or the SRC property of an IMG (image) tag. Thus for simple elements a user can write simple formulas, such as "=B*100" for passing a stock price result into a currency conversion input, while complex elements can be handled using Excel's full macro-language capabilities – for example to realize the specialized string handling for the "filmtime" function shown in Figure 8.4.

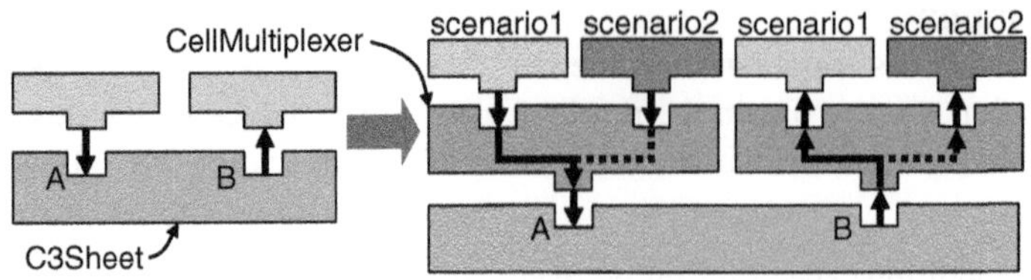

FIGURE 8.6

The use of CellMultiplexers to support cloning in a single-layer composite pad. On the left is the basic composite pad; on the right is a setup for two scenarios. The child pads connected to slots A and B have both been cloned, and the clone pairs are connected to the parent through separate cooperating CellMultiplexers. When the CellMultiplexers are handling scenario 1, the parent is connected (indirectly) to the scenario-1 instances of its children; when handling scenario 2, the other instances are connected.

In the current prototype, the distinction between simple and complex cell types is made on the basis of hard-coded rules. However, realizing that there will be exceptions, in the future we may make it a user-selectable option. Meanwhile we are considering what kind of built-in function library could help users build formulas for complex structure analysis, and are also examining how to incorporate interactive, direct manipulation techniques that will let users identify elements within structured data without having to write code.

Cloning

The cloning facilities are based on our work on Subjunctive Interfaces (Lunzer, 1999; Lunzer & Hornbæk, 2003b; Lunzer & Hornbæk, 2004). Computer users often want to compare alternative scenarios, but few applications provide good support for the side-by-side viewing that would facilitate such comparison; equipping an application with a subjunctive interface allows users to set up multiple scenarios, then view and control those scenarios in parallel.

C3W's support for parallel viewing and control of scenarios is derived from the widget-multiplexer approach (Lunzer & Hornbæk, 2003a). Using widget multiplexers involves reserving a dedicated region of the computer screen for each widget that appears in the normal, single-scenario application interface. As the user creates additional scenarios, each multiplexer displays simultaneously, side by side, how its widget would appear in each scenario. In general, if there are n scenarios then each multiplexer displays n copies of its widget. The exception is when a widget would have identical appearance in all scenarios, in which case only a single display is needed. All multiplexers lay out their scenario-specific displays in the same way; by the principles of "small multiples" visualizations (Tufte, 1990), this helps users to locate all the information that comprises each scenario.

The cloning facilities of C3W work as follows:

- The user can create a new scenario by cloning some chosen input cell. This introduces an independent calculation passing through all the cells on the sheet. However, because formula-based derivation is unidirectional, only the chosen cell and those cells that depend on it need to prepare and show multiple displays. The other cells still have the same value in every scenario.

- Entering a new value in one display of a cloned cell will only affect the scenario corresponding to that display. Entering a new value in an uncloned cell will affect all scenarios simultaneously.
- When multiple scenarios are on view, the user can choose to clone a previously uncloned cell so that it has separate displays for each scenario. Any cells that depend on the newly cloned cell, but were not cloned before, will now be cloned.
- The user can delete a scenario. This removes the clones associated with that scenario from all cloned cells.

The fact that C3W is implemented on the PlexWare platform as a set of cooperating pads allows us to support multiplexing in a particularly straightforward way. Each cell is a pad, that is, a child of the C3Sheet pad, and has a slot connection to a cell-specific slot within the parent. For each cloned cell, we introduce between the cell and the parent C3Sheet a specialized pad called a CellMultiplexer. The CellMultiplexer is responsible for creating and deleting clones of the cell, and for time-multiplexing the connection between a cell's various clones and the C3Sheet. Figure 8.6 illustrates the principle of a CellMultiplexer, showing two child pads that are each cloned to support two scenarios.

The various CellMultiplexers within a single application (i.e., attached to the same C3Sheet) coordinate their displays so that the clones belonging to a given scenario all have the same color of border, and the scenarios are laid out in the same way. The coloring and layout policy is a simplified version of that described in (Lunzer & Hornbæk, 2004). As seen in the examples in the section "Examples and Explanations", cell clones in C3W have the same size as their original cell, which imposes a practical limit on the number of clones – especially for large cells, such as the itinerary in Figures 8.4 and 8.5. We are working to improve this and other aspects of the usability of the cloning facilities.

RELATED WORK
Automating access to Web applications
Clipping elements from Web applications relates to the highly active research area on automated extraction of information from the Web.

Recording and replaying Web interaction
Much usage of the Web is repetitive; users often want to revisit pages that they have accessed before. Many projects start from the observation that bookmarks, the basic mechanism for supporting revisitation, are not enough. Hunter Gatherer (Schraefel et al., 2002) is one such project, supporting users in collecting not just links to pages that they want to revisit, but copied portions of those pages. The copies can include text, images, links, or other active components such as forms; the active components retain the behavior that they have within the original Web pages.

One benefit of being able to copy just selected regions within pages is that the user can construct a simplified interface, free from the clutter of surrounding elements that are irrelevant to that user or to a particular instance of use. This was one goal in the development of WebViews (Freire, Kumar, & Lieuwen, 2001), in allowing users to create customized views suited to small screen devices, and also of WinCuts (Tan, Meyers, & Czerwinski, 2004), which lets users create live copies of arbitrary subregions of general windowed applications.

WebViews is not only a system for replicating components of Web pages; like the WebVCR (Anupam et al., 2000) system that it extends, its key feature is so-called smart bookmarks that point not to a single location within the Web, but encapsulate a series of Web-browsing actions. Smart bookmarks can therefore be used to record hard-to-reach Web pages, that have no fixed URIs and can only be reached by navigation. However, the decision to make a smart bookmark must be taken before the user starts the navigation that is to be recorded; this is in contrast to C3W's support for extracting elements retrospectively, which we have not found in other published work.

When a user records a smart bookmark, he or she can indicate if some field in a form (e.g., a password) is to be requested at playback time, rather than stored with the bookmark. However, in essence the job of a smart bookmark is to arrive at the destination Web page and to deliver to the user's display either the whole page or some chosen parts thereof; intermediate pages are not seen. In this respect C3W offers greater flexibility, since the user can clip arbitrary regions of any page encountered during the course of a navigation, either to reveal intermediate results or to capture inputs. And because each clipped region is treated as a portal (Olston & Woodruff, 2000) onto the original Web page, inputs to be used during replay can be based on arbitrary form widgets – including menus, checkboxes and the like – rather than just textual input fields.

For presenting results, too, the portal approach has some benefits. For example, in the cinema interface shown in Figures 8.4 and 8.5, the carefully designed itineraries provided by the travel-planning application can be viewed in full detail. However, if the user wants to use the contents of such a semistructured display as a source of values for further processing, he or she must typically write a complex extraction function – as exemplified by the "filmtime" function in the same application. In such a case, it may be preferable for the system to include some automated facilities for formalizing the semistructured content.

Formalized extraction of content

Many researchers are working on how to extract structured data, suitable for storage in databases or processing by agents, from Web pages that were designed for human readers; (Kuhlins & Tredwell, 2003) and (Laender et al., 2002) are recent surveys of this area.

Lixto (Baumgartner, Flesca, & Gottlob, 2001a) and InfoBeans (Bauer, Dengler, & Paul, 2000) are two research systems that, like C3W, aim to define what data is to be extracted by generalizing from example selections made by a human user. The goal is a definition that will extract equivalent information from Web pages with different contents, and perhaps with different structures – because information providers on the Web often make changes to their pages (such as adding or removing menu items, or slightly altering how items are grouped) that, while causing no difficulty for human readers, can easily confuse a formal system. The HTML-path expressions used by C3W are not robust against such changes in page structure. The XPath expressions used by WebViews include additional conditions that help to make the extraction more robust, and the system also uses various heuristics to work around common kinds of structural change. The scripts used by InfoBeans can incorporate context, landmark, and characterization conditions to increase their robustness; if a script still fails to locate suitable content, the system includes TrIAs (Trainable Information Agents) that can start a dialogue with the current user to obtain further example-based training.

However, no amount of heuristics or training can guarantee to find the intended elements in the face of arbitrary changes. Here again, the fact that C3W encourages the display of intermediate results rather than hiding them in a processing pipeline can be of some benefit. For example, if some change in a Web resource causes values that are normally numeric to be replaced by strings, our portal-based clipping at least increases the likelihood that the user will see that something has gone wrong, rather than being puzzled by (or, worse, failing to notice) the outcome of strange derived values flowing through an unseen pipe.

Passing information between applications

In C3W, separate Web applications can be connected with the help of formulas on input elements. Other systems for working with Web applications offer alternative approaches: Lixto provides a visual patch-panel mechanism; InfoBeans allow the user to define "channels" for each InfoBox component, which are then used to connect them; earlier work on wrapping Web applications as pads within an IntelligentPad environment (Ito & Tanaka, 2003) allowed the applications to be connected using the pads' slot-based communication mechanism. In Snap (North & Shneiderman, 2000), a system supporting construction of customized visualizations, users connect visualization components by using dialog-box mechanisms to set up parameterized queries between them.

The cell-and-formula approach of C3Sheets is based on the spreadsheet model; other well-known spreadsheet-based systems include Forms/3 (Burnett et al., 2001), Information Visualization Spreadsheets (Chi et al., 1998), and C32 (Myers, 1991). In general, such projects selectively adopt or abandon various features of what could be called the traditional spreadsheet. The use of formulas in C3Sheets, for example, conforms to the tradition that each formula determines the value of just one cell. On the other hand, our implementation is not alone in breaking free of the restriction that cells should contain only text or numbers, or the idea that cells should be positioned and named according to a tabular grid.

Handling multiple scenarios in parallel

As explained in the "Cloning" section, the cloning mechanisms in C3W reflect our interest in supporting the viewing, comparison, and update of alternative scenarios. This applies not only to the kind of information exploration addressed in this paper, but also in design, such as when investigating the influence of image placement on the layout of a document, or in simulation, such as when testing how alternative population growth scenarios would affect a country's economy. But such comparison is seldom well supported; Terry and Mynatt (2002) speak of the "single-state document model" of most of today's applications, and the implicit barrier that this imposes on a user who wants to explore and compare alternatives. In addressing this issue for simple design tasks, Terry et al. (2004) demonstrate an interface that lets a user set up and work with multiple designs in parallel, although their interface is limited in its support for viewing scenarios side by side.

In the domain of Web browsing we have found little work supporting interactive comparison of scenarios. One isolated example is the Comparative Web Browser (CWB) (Nadamoto & Tanaka, 2003), an interface that offers comparison and synchronized browsing between similar Web pages. However, CWB displays the pages in full, which makes it less scalable than the C3W approach in which the user is able to clone just chosen cells, and where those cells may have been taken from several Web pages.

Relative to our own previous work on subjunctive interfaces, a key advance embodied in C3W is that the widget multiplexers themselves are generic; they can handle any client that is a cell, and in C3W a cell can contain any clipped region of a Web page. This makes it the first system to offer subjunctive-interface facilities for an entire class of applications.

CONCLUSION

We have introduced C3W, a prototype that supports users in creating custom interfaces for accessing information through Web applications. C3W exemplifies three mechanisms that together help users to overcome inconveniences and restrictions imposed by the original applications, as follows:

1. Clipping: By drag-and-drop manipulation, a user can select and extract input and result elements from the pages of a Web application. Placing the elements on a substrate (a C3Sheet) turns them into cells that work as portals onto the original Web pages; cells containing clipped input elements support user input, and cells containing result elements display the corresponding results. Thus the user can create a compact, reusable interface that excludes unnecessary features of the Web application.
2. Connecting: A single C3Sheet can hold input and result cells for multiple applications. The user can define formulas for input cells, so that they obtain their values from the contents of other cells. By defining formulas that refer to the result cells of other applications, the user can create connections between applications that were not originally designed to work together.
3. Cloning: The user can set up multiple scenarios – that is, different settings for the inputs, leading to different results – to be shown in parallel. Each cell displays, side by side, its contents in the various scenarios. So even if the original application could only handle one scenario at a time, the user can efficiently explore and compare the different results available through that application. This also works for applications that have been connected using formulas.

As demonstrated in this chapter, even the current prototype lets us build useful interfaces for our own needs, and helps us to explore the wider promise of this approach. That said, there are several areas to be addressed in going beyond this stage of development.

First, the existing C3Sheet implementation has many interface features that should be improved. We are considering how to incorporate strategies found in other spreadsheet-like interfaces, such as for partial automation of cell sizing and layout, for more informative labeling of cells (including the ability for a user to provide clarifying annotations), and for assistance in creating formulas. We are also working to improve the usability of cloning operations, and the scalability of the cloned-cell displays.

Second, our support for Web applications can be improved by incorporating techniques demonstrated in other projects, such as for enhancing the robustness of element identification in the face of changes to the underlying pages, and for capturing a broad range of user actions across applications of different types. Content formalization techniques can be applied to help users extract richer data types from Web-page elements for use in formulas.

Third, the broader benefits of the C3Sheet approach depend on supporting not just Web applications and IntelligentPad composites, but other kinds of application for information access or derivation. Obvious candidates for inclusion are local database applications, spreadsheets, and statistical packages. Their integration, through implementation of the facilities outlined in the section, "Implementation Requirements", is likely to be achievable through the use of existing APIs and object broker services.

All the previously mentioned development directions will naturally need to be backed up with user evaluations. In the first instance we are working with colleagues who rely on combined use of Web applications in the course of their (noncomputing) research; our hope is to confirm that using C3Sheets will benefit their work, and to improve our understanding of the facilities that must be made available.

Thus we regard the work reported in this paper as initial steps towards facilities that, while not technically hard to achieve, could make a profound difference to how people can benefit from the many potentially cooperating applications available to them.

Acknowledgments

We are grateful to the many reviewers who provided helpful comments. In our examples we used a stock-price application provided by CNN (http://money.cnn.com/data/markets/), currency exchange from Yahoo! (http://finance.yahoo.com/currency-converter), film lookup from Alt om København (http://www.aok.dk/Copenhagen/Film/), and itinerary search from Rejseplanen (http://www.rejseplanen.dk/).

© ACM, 2004. This is a minor revision of the work published in *Proceedings of the 17th Annual ACM Symposium on User Interface Software and Technology (UIST 2004)*, Santa Fe, NM, 175–184, http://doi.acm.org/10.1145/1029632.1029664. It is based on work carried out during a visit by the first author from the Meme Media Laboratory to the University of Copenhagen, where the second author was then working. Since then, C3W development has continued at Hokkaido University.

POSTSCRIPT TO 2009 REPRINT

From 2004 to early 2009 the first author led the continued development of C3W at the Meme Media Laboratory, Hokkaido University. One direction of this work was the further integration of the IntelligentPad-based Web clipping and connection mechanisms with Microsoft Office applications, enabling users to create Word documents or Excel spreadsheets with embedded content extracted dynamically from Web applications (Fujima, Yoshihara, & Tanaka, 2007). Another direction was the packaging of C3W's clipping and replay mechanisms as a Dynamic Link Library suitable for use by applications built with the Microsoft .NET framework. One such application is the RecipeSheet (Lunzer & Hornbæk, 2006b), a spreadsheet-like end user programming environment that emphasizes support for specifying and viewing alternative cases in parallel. With its specialized mechanisms for accessing Web resources, the RecipeSheet has allowed us to explore further the benefits of cloning as initially demonstrated in C3W. This work is described in detail by Lunzer and Hornbæk in a separate chapter of this book (Chapter 14).

A number of other chapters also present systems that extend the kinds of capabilities demonstrated early on with C3W. For example, the Web Summaries project, pursued by Dontcheva and others (Chapter 12), provides advanced features for supporting users in extracting information from Web sites: users can assemble data into a structured dataset, create associations between extracted elements, and construct a personalized representation of the assembled contents. The elements to be extracted can be identified not just by "structural rules" based on XPaths, but also simple "content-based" rules that examine the elements' textual contents. The card-like view of the extracted contents is reminiscent of C3W's cells, but is further structured by the use of templates with which users can make personalized layouts of the data.

Mash Maker (Chapter 9) provides end users with an alternative approach to information gathering, based on augmenting existing Web pages with information delivered by previously coded widgets that the user chooses to invoke. It is not assumed that these users can develop new widgets for themselves, though Mash Maker provides the tools that help expert users to develop wrappers for extracting information from pages, and to specify how that information is to be delivered in widgets. These expert users are also expected to define how information should be passed from one application to another.

A number of research groups have developed ways of capturing processing behavior offered by Web sites. Like C3W, CoScripter (Chapter 5) records replayable scripts based on actions carried out by a user to demonstrate the behavior of interest. The scripts recorded by CoScripter have the property of being both human- and machine-readable, helping users to confirm that a script reflects the actions that were intended, or to edit it if not. Instead of an XPath-based approach to identifying interactive elements within Web pages, CoScripter uses various analysis mechanisms and heuristics to generate human-readable locators for those elements. These locators are more robust against minor page-layout changes than an unforgiving XPath, but have their own sources of brittleness; the search for dependable wrapper techniques is not over yet. Scripts generated by CoScripter can also be deployed within Highlight (Chapter 6), a system for creating customized versions of Web sites suitable for mobile devices. However, neither of these projects focuses on the challenges in connecting diverse applications.

The application d.mix (Chapter 10) does provide some support for end users to compose behavior from existing Web applications to create new ones. It depends on expert users doing the work of creating and maintaining so-called site-to-service maps for the existing applications, which requires profound knowledge of the original page APIs and of script programming. Once this is done, it becomes straightforward for users to extract chosen behavioral elements and combine them in simple ways.

Many projects beyond those presented in this book are addressing similar challenges. Marmite (Wong & Hong, 2007), for example, is one project that focuses on improving the robustness and flexibility of techniques for extracting data from Web sites. Vegemite (Lin et al., 2009), like C3W, encourages a view of existing Web sites not just as sources of data but as tools for performing computations, and offers a framework for letting end users combine such computations to create ad hoc mashups. Vegemite is centered on a spreadsheet-like VegeTable, into which data from Web sites can be extracted by scripts created by direct manipulation and programming-by-demonstration techniques.

Advances on the concept we referred to as cloning are also found in some recent work. Transcendence (Bigham et al., 2008), for example, supports a user in identifying input fields for which various alternative input values are to be tried; Transcendence then coordinates the execution of the corresponding queries, and merges their results. Meanwhile Hartmann et al. (2008) take the mechanisms for parameter control in multiple scenarios off the computer screen into the real world, with mechanisms for integrating application logic with simple hardware controllers.

We close with some comments on the directions we see ahead. The fact that the Web has largely moved on from the days of static content delivery, with dramatically increased use of active contents driven by frameworks, such as JavaScript, Flash, and Silverlight, presents significant new challenges for any reuse of Web-delivered data and behavior. We are watching with interest the drive towards the Semantic Web, in the hope that it will lead to new standards for annotating the properties and intended use of such active content. In the meantime we are working to make some of C3W's mechanisms available within this increasingly dynamic Web, by investigating how to deliver them in the form of Web services. Our overall goal remains unchanged: to support users in creating distributable, reeditable, ad hoc compositions of Web application behavior in line with the philosophy of meme media software (Tanaka, 2003).

C3W

Intended users:	All users
Domain:	Form-driven Web sites
Description:	C3W is a system for creating a custom information–access interface based on one or more Web applications, then reusing this interface to view and control many alternative requests.
Example:	Open a stock price Web site. The user clips the input field used for specifying a company code, supplies a sample code to request its price, then clips the price display from within the result page. Similarly, the user opens a currency conversion application, clips the currency amount input field and clips the converted amount from the result of a sample conversion. Then using a formula the user can connect these two applications, feeding the stock price result to the currency conversion input. By cloning an input cell, the user can create new scenarios with distinct input values that are displayed alongside each other.
Automation:	Yes.
Mashups:	Possibly. Although the system doesn't output new Web applications, the result can be used as new local applications.
Scripting:	No.
Natural language:	No.
Recordability:	Yes. Recorded user actions are represented as XML-based descriptions called navigation paths.
Inferencing:	No.
Sharing:	Yes. The newly created custom applications can be shared among IntelligentPad users.
Comparison to other systems:	C3W was an early demonstration of how to enable users to wrap and connect the behavior of Web applications just by visual manipulation. Its clipping mechanisms are used in RecipeSheet.
Platform:	Implemented as an IntelligentPad application.
Availability:	An older version is available at: http://km.meme.hokudai.ac.jp/plaza/ (description currently in Japanese only).

Intel® Mash Maker

9

Rob Ennals
Intel Research

ABSTRACT

Intel® Mash Maker is a mashup creation tool that was initially developed at Intel Research and is now being developed by Intel's Software Solutions Group.

Mash Maker allows a user to customize and improve Web pages by applying mashups that add additional content. Such "overlay mashups" add content that is visually distinguished from the host Web page, but is integrated into the normal page layout.

Mash Maker allows a user to apply a mashup to a Web page without having to trust the mashup or even know what the mashup does. Mash Maker suggests user-created mashups that a user might want to apply to the page that they are currently browsing. A user can try out one of these mashups to see if they like it, while knowing that it cannot do anything harmful, besides read the information on the current page.

Mash Maker uses a three-level structure to create mashups. Information is extracted from Web sites using wrappers that are written collaboratively by users in a wiki-like model. Widgets written in Java-Script query this information and add new information and visualizations to the page. A user can then arrange several widgets on a page to create a mashup which they publish and share with other users.

INTRODUCTION

Intel Mash Maker (Ennals & Gay, 2007; Ennals et al., 2007) is a browser extension for Firefox or Internet Explorer. Mash Maker allows a user to customize existing Web pages by applying mashups that add additional content. Such "overlay mashups" add content that is visually distinguished from the host Web page while being integrated into the normal page layout.

Mash Maker encourages users to take a "try it and see" approach to finding mashups that they like. As a user browses the Web, Mash Maker suggests mashups that it believes the user will find useful. If a mashup looks interesting then the user can turn it on, see if the added content looks useful, and turn it off again if they do not like it.

Mash Maker uses a three-level architecture (Figure 9.1) to create mashups: *wrappers* extract structured information from the HTML of a Web page; *widgets* query information that has been extracted from a page and publish new information and visualizations, and *mashups* specify what widgets should be added to a page, what their settings should be, and how their output visualizations should be integrated into the layout of a page.

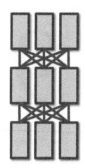

Mashups
Enhance a particular kind of page by inserting one or more widgets

Widgets
Visualize and manipulate data extracted from a page. Import data from other sources

Wrappers
Extract data from Web sites for use by widgets

FIGURE 9.1

Wrappers, widgets, and mashups.

Most users interact with Mash Maker in a passive way, browsing to the sites that they normally use and occasionally turning on a suggested mashup. More skilled users may occasionally create a new mashup or edit a wrapper. Only expert users are expected to write their own widgets.

In this chapter, we discuss several of the key concepts behind Mash Maker:

1. **Overlay mashups:** Mash Maker allows a user to customize existing Web pages by applying mashups that add new content.
2. **Mashup suggestions:** Mash Maker tries to suggest mashups that a user will find useful.
3. **Collaborative creation of Web wrappers:** Mash Maker uses a wiki model in which each page type has a single canonical wrapper that can be edited by anyone.
4. **The shared data tree:** Mash Maker widgets communicate by reading and writing a shared data tree.
5. **Untrusted widgets:** Mash Maker restricts what a widget can do, allowing them to be untrusted.
6. **Copy and paste:** Mash Maker allows a user to combine Web sites using a simple "copy and paste" metaphor.

Intel Mash Maker was originally created at Intel Research and is now being developed and maintained by the Intel Software Solutions Group. You can download Intel Mash Maker from the following URL: http://mashmaker.intel.com.

EXAMPLE: NEWS ON A MAP

We will begin with an example of what it is like to browse the Web using Mash Maker.

Alice has the Mash Maker browser extension installed in her Web browser and opens the front page of CNN news. Mash Maker looks through its database of wrappers and finds that a wrapper called "CNN Home Page" knows how to extract information from this page. Mash Maker also finds that a mashup called "News Map" can be applied to pages that match "CNN Home Page". Because other users who used this mashup said they liked it, Mash Maker suggests the mashup to Alice using a toggle button on its toolbar.

Alice isn't sure what the "News Map" mashup does, or whether she will like it, but since it looks like it might be interesting, she turns on the mashup to see what it does.

When Alice turns on the "News Map" mashup, Mash Maker enhances the CNN home page by inserting a map into the existing page layout (Figure 9.2). This map shows the locations of all the stories on the CNN front page. Alice can browse around the map to see what is going on in different

Mashup Button
Click on any mashup to
toggle it

Map Widget
Inserted into the normal
page layout. Shows the
locations of the news
stories on the page

FIGURE 9.2

Showing CNN news stories on a map.

parts of the world, and can click on one of the pins on the map to see more information about a particular story.

After a while, Alice decides that she doesn't want to enhance the CNN home page in this way, and so she turns the mashup off by clicking on its toggle button again.

This example made use of the three layers of the Mash Maker architecture:

- A *wrapper* called "CNN Home Page" extracted the names and URLs of the stories on the front page and made this information available for use by widgets. The wrapper also specified good places where additional visualizations could be inserted into the page layout.
- A *mashup* called "News Map" was linked to the "CNN Home Page" wrapper. This mashup contains configured instances of the "Linked Data" and "Google Maps" widgets, and specifies a good place to insert the Google Maps map into the page layout.
- Two *widgets* called "Linked Data" and "Google Maps" made enhancements to the page. "Linked Data" followed the links for each of the stories,[1] applied a wrapper to each story, and published the information extracted from each story page for other widgets to see. "Google Maps" looked for published information that had addresses, and showed it all on a map.

---

[1]To improve performance, Linked Data caches all of its fetched data on a shared server. The map will appear immediately provided that the cache already contains the data for the linked story pages.

EXAMPLE: LEGROOM FOR FLIGHT LISTINGS

Bob wants to book a flight and is viewing a list of potential flights on Expedia. Mash Maker sees that this page can be handled by the "Expedia Flights" wrapper, and that the "Legroom" mashup is associated with this wrapper. Because Bob has rated the Legroom mashup highly in the past, Mash Maker suggests it to Bob.

When Bob turns on the "Legroom" mashup, Mash Maker enhances the Expedia search results by adding legroom information to each of the flight entries on the page (Figure 9.3). The legroom information is the range of legroom amounts that the airline offers for economy class seats. Bob decides that he would like legroom information to be present on Expedia searches by default, so he clicks the "pin" icon on the Mash Maker toolbar. The next time Bob does an Expedia search, the "Legroom" mashup will be applied as soon as the page has loaded.

As with the previous example, this example uses all three layers of the Mash Maker architecture.

- A wrapper called "Expedia Flights" extracts the airline for each flight, and specifies a location where additional information should be inserted.

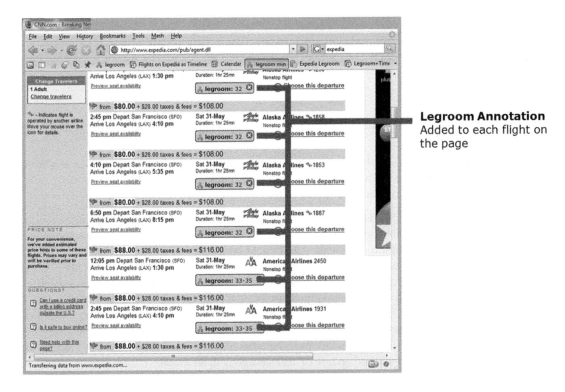

Legroom Annotation
Added to each flight on the page

FIGURE 9.3

Adding legroom to Expedia.

- A mashup called "Legroom" enhances the page by adding configured instances of the Paste, Correct, and Join widgets.
- The Paste widget loads a remote page that contains legroom information from every airline, applies an extractor to it, and publishes the resulting information for use by other widgets. The Correct widget allows users to contribute alternative canonical names for airlines, to cope with the fact that the pasted page doesn't use the same airline names as the Expedia page. For each flight, the Correct widget publishes a corrected airline name. The Join widget joins the corrected airline name with the airline in the pasted legroom table and then publishes a legroom field for each flight.
- The mashup specifies that the legroom field published by the Join widget should be made visible to the user, and specifies where it should be placed in the page layout.

OVERLAY MASHUPS

Mash Maker allows a user to enhance the Web sites that they browse by applying mashups that add additional content. In addition to the two examples given earlier there are many other possibilities. For example one might add price comparison information to a shopping site to see what the prices were like on other sites, add a button to every phone number that calls the number if you click it, or annotate craigslist housing ads to show the ratings of the nearest restaurants.

There has been a lot of prior work on building tools that modify existing Web sites. OreO (Brooks et al., 1995) and WBI (Barrett, Maglio, & Kellem, 1997; Maglio & Barrett, 2000) use a proxy to modify Web pages without requiring support from the Web browser. Other tools such as Greasemonkey and Chickenfoot (Chapter 3) run as extensions to the Web browser that modify Web pages on the client. Mash Maker was initially implemented as a Web proxy (Ennals & Gay, 2007) and was then re-implemented as a browser extension (Ennals et al., 2007).

Unlike previous work, Mash Maker only allows a mashup to add new content to an existing page. A mashup cannot edit or remove content. In addition, any content added to a page is surrounded by a blue border to visually distinguish it from the page's original content. We refer to this restricted class of mashups as *overlay mashups*.

By restricting itself to overlay mashups, Mash Maker excludes some mashups that can be created in tools such as Chickenfoot. For example, a Chickenfoot mashup can change the text on a Web site, make text boxes resizable, add keyboard shortcuts to a Web site, or provide automatic login for Web sites.

There are three reasons why Mash Maker restricts mashups to be overlay mashups:

- **To make it clear what a mashup does:** Unlike previous work, Mash Maker assumes that a user will apply a mashup to a Web site without knowing in advance what it is that the mashup does, or whether they should trust it. Because Mash Maker visually distinguishes the content it added, a user can quickly see what a mashup has done and thus evaluate whether it is useful.
- **To prevent mashups misbehaving:** Since Mash Maker assumes that a user will be applying an untrusted mashup to a Web site without knowing what it does, it is important that Mash Maker restrict the extent to which mashups can do things that are unexpected or harmful. Restricting ourselves to overlay mashups makes this easier.

- **To reduce legal concerns:** If a mashup can modify a page in an arbitrary way, what happens if a mashup modifies a page in a way that the content owner does not approve of? One of the reasons why Mash Maker restricts itself to overlay mashups is to reduce the likelihood that a content owner sees a mashup as an unlawful derived work. Since all additional content is visually distinguished from the page, and the mashup does not modify existing page content, one could argue that Mash Maker is a browser that overlays additional content about a page, rather than a tool that modifies someone else's content.

More generally, if mashups are to become widespread then it is important that they be structured in a way that is beneficial or at least acceptable to content owners. This is the primary reason why Mash Maker cannot, at present, remove content from a Web page. If content could be removed then users could upset content owners by removing advertisements.

MASHUP SUGGESTIONS

As the user browses the Web, Mash Maker suggests mashups that it believes the user might like. Suggested mashups appear as toggle buttons on Mash Maker's toolbar (Figures 9.1 and 9.4). A user can turn a particular mashup on or off by clicking on the button for that mashup. Mash Maker assumes that a user does not know what existing mashups will be useful for them, but that they will recognize useful mashups when they see them applied to a page.

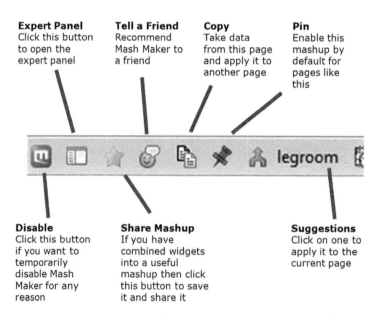

Expert Panel
Click this button to open the expert panel

Tell a Friend
Recommend Mash Maker to a friend

Copy
Take data from this page and apply it to another page

Pin
Enable this mashup by default for pages like this

Disable
Click this button if you want to temporarily disable Mash Maker for any reason

Share Mashup
If you have combined widgets into a useful mashup then click this button to save it and share it

Suggestions
Click on one to apply it to the current page

FIGURE 9.4

The Mash Maker toolbar.

Mash Maker builds on a lot of prior work that recommends content based on user browsing behavior (Teevan, Dumais, & Horvitz, 2005; Seo & Zhang, 2000; Rucker & Polanco, 1997; Kelly & Teevan, 2003; Gasparetti & Micarelli, 2007). The key feature that distinguishes Mash Maker from previous systems is that it recommends mashups rather than Web pages. Mash Maker bases its suggestions on the wrapper that matches the page currently being viewed, the user's recent browsing history, the mashups the user seemed to like previously, and the behavior of other users.

If a user decides that they like a mashup, they can *pin* it by clicking on the pin button on the toolbar (Figure 9.4). Once a mashup is pinned, it will be enabled by default whenever the user visits a Web page that matches the current wrapper.

It is possible for a user to apply multiple mashups to the same page simultaneously. When a user has several mashups turned on, all mashups will add their content to the page. In some cases, one mashup can use information added by another mashup. For example if a user turns on a mashup that annotates apartment listings with nearby restaurants, and then turns on a mashup that displays everything with an address on a map, then the restaurants will also be shown on the map. If the new combination of mashups is itself an interesting mashup, then the user can save the new mashup by clicking on the share button on the toolbar (Figure 9.4).

Mash Maker's suggestion system is largely orthogonal to the rest of the system. One could conceivably use Mash Maker's suggestion toolbar to automatically suggest mashups created with a tool such as Chickenfoot (Chapter 3). The advantage of combining Mash Maker's suggestion system with Mash Maker's restricted *overlay mashups* is that a user can easily see what a mashup has done, it is easy to remove a mashup without reloading the page if the user decides they do not like it, and it is harder for a mashup to do something undesirable.

If the suggestion toolbar does not suggest an interesting mashup, a user can also use Mash Maker's more conventional Web-based gallery to find mashups. The gallery allows one to search for mashups by keyword and can show either mashups associated with a particular wrapper, or mashups for arbitrary pages. Clicking on a mashup in the Web gallery takes the user to an example Web page with that mashup enabled.

There is a trade-off between privacy and suggestion accuracy. If Mash Maker knows more about user behavior then it can potentially be better at suggesting mashups, but this would be at the cost of sacrificing user privacy. In the current implementation, the client tells the server when a user turns a mashup on or off, or pins it – but it does not report browsing history, or any exact URLs. The Mash Maker client will sometimes take browsing history into account when suggesting a mashup, and will prefer mashups that use a service from a site the user recently browsed, but browsing history is not reported to the central server.

COLLABORATIVE CREATION OF WEB WRAPPERS

To apply a mashup to a Web page, Mash Maker needs to extract machine-readable data that it can use as input to the mashup. For example, if a mashup wants to add a map to an apartment listing site showing the location of each apartment, then Mash Maker needs to extract the apartment addresses from the Web site. Although standards such as microformats and RDFa exist to allow a Web site to expose machine-readable data directly in its HTML, at the time of writing most Web sites do not do this. Mash Maker thus extracts machine-readable information from raw HTML using user-created *wrappers*.

A wrapper (Laender et al., 2002) is a set of rules that can be used to extract machine-readable data from a Web site. Though some authors have had some success extracting data from a Web site without any human assistance (Crescenzi & Mecca, 2004; Simon & Lausen, 2005; Chang & Lui, 2001; Arasu & Garcia-Molina, 2003), most systems, including Mash Maker, require some form of user guidance to teach the wrapper-generator what a Web page means (Kushmerick, Weld, & Doorenbos, 1997; Ashish & Knoblock, 1997; Muslea, Minton, & Knoblock, 1999; Zheng et al., 2008; Irmak & Suel, 2006; Baumgartner, Flesca, & Gottlob, 2001b).

Mash Maker's Web wrapper system has two unusual features. Firstly, Mash Maker organizes its wrappers in a *wiki-style* model in which there is a single canonical Web wrapper for any given Web page layout, and any user can edit any wrapper. Secondly, wrappers created by Mash Maker include *drop zones* that indicate where additional content should be inserted into the page layout.

In Mash Maker's wiki-style wrapper model, any page is handled by one canonical wrapper, and any user can edit any wrapper. If a user believes that the canonical wrapper is not extracting the information they need then they must modify that wrapper, rather than creating a new one. CoScripter (Chapter 5) independently developed a similar wiki model for sharing scripts.

Mash Maker's wiki-style model differs from the more conventional model in which multiple users create their own competing wrappers for different Web sites and writers of mashups pick the wrappers that work well for them. One advantage of the wiki model is that it removes the need for a user to look through a list of potentially broken wrappers in order to find the one that works best with their Web page. For example, if a user wants to create a new mashup that visualizes the data on a particular Web page using a calendar, then they can just drag a calendar widget onto the page, without having to choose what wrapper to use. Choosing a wrapper can be a confusing process: "I just want to apply the calendar to this page. Why do I have to choose something from this list?"

Another advantage of the wiki model is that it is easier to recover when a change to the structure of a Web page breaks a wrapper. In a study conducted by Dontcheva et al (2007a), 74% of tested Web sites underwent a significant structural change of the kind that would be likely to break a wrapper within the 5-month test period. If a broken wrapper was owned by a particular person then it would be necessary for every mashup creator to either wait for the wrapper owner to fix their wrapper, or to move their mashups to a new wrapper, adding the old wrapper to the set of dead wrappers that mashup authors need to avoid. With the wiki approach, the first user to notice that the wrapper has broken can open Mash Maker's wrapper editor and fix the problem for all mashups. Although techniques exist to repair a broken wrapper automatically (Raposo et al., 2005; Meng, Hu, & Li, 2003; Chidlovskii, 2001), these techniques are not yet bulletproof.

The big disadvantage of the wiki model is that it opens Mash Maker up to potential vandalism (Denning et al., 2005). If anyone can edit a wrapper, then anyone can break a wrapper. A common problem during the early days of Mash Maker deployment was that a novice user would decide to experiment with the wrapper editing tools and break something high profile, such as Google search, without realizing that their changes were affecting all users. Mash Maker's mechanisms for dealing with this problem are the same as those taken by text wikis such as Wikipedia (Riehle, 2006) – a history is recorded so that bad edits can be rolled back, and sensitive wrappers can be locked. In the future, one could potentially also use wrapper verification (Kushmerick, 2000) to prevent users from saving wrappers that had obviously been broken.

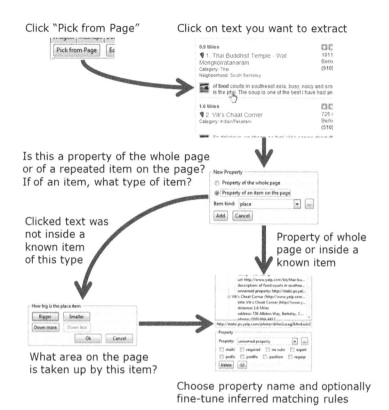

FIGURE 9.5

Teaching Mash Maker what something means.

Mash Maker's wiki model for Web wrappers is largely orthogonal to its other features. Mash Maker could have used the more conventional "roll your own" model, in which case a user would be required to choose a suitable wrapper when creating a mashup. Similarly, Mash Maker's wrapper database can be useful for other tools; indeed Yahoo! SearchMonkey uses Mash Maker as one of its methods for extracting data from Web pages (Goer, 2008). Mash Maker's wiki model is also largely independent of Mash Maker's particular choice of wrapper editor. One could potentially adapt other wrapper editors to support Mash Maker's wiki model by adding support for revision tracking and other collaborative features.

Like Chickenfoot (Chapter 3) and Greasemonkey, Mash Maker uses URL regular expressions to determine what pages a wrapper is applicable to. Users will not usually edit this regular expression themselves. Instead they provide example URLs that the wrapper should apply to, and Mash Maker automatically computes a regular expression that matches the known examples. If several wrappers match a URL, then Mash Maker chooses the one with the highest *priority* – where the priority is a user-editable number. More sophisticated techniques exist for determining what wrapper to apply to

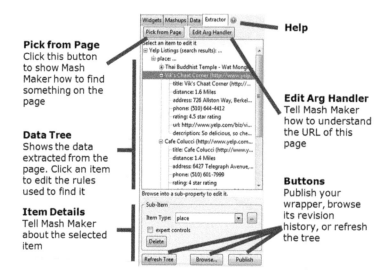

Pick from Page
Click this button to show Mash Maker how to find something on the page

Data Tree
Shows the data extracted from the page. Click an item to edit the rules used to find it

Item Details
Tell Mash Maker about the selected item

Help

Edit Arg Handler
Tell Mash Maker how to understand the URL of this page

Buttons
Publish your wrapper, browse its revision history, or refresh the tree

FIGURE 9.6

The wrapper editor (the UI calls a wrapper an extractor).

a page. Zheng et al. (2007) automatically cluster pages based on the similarity of their page layouts. Dontcheva et al. (2006) choose the wrapper with the highest number of matching rules. Although regular expressions can be difficult for end users, they have the advantage of being cheap and predictable.

EXAMPLE: EDITING A WRAPPER FOR YELP

Carl is looking at business reviews on Yelp and has an idea for a useful mashup he could apply to the page. Carl opens the *expert panel* (Figure 9.6) and sees that the current wrapper for this page does not extract the address of a business.

Carl follows the process in Figure 9.5 to teach Mash Maker how to extract the address of a business. He clicks "pick from page" to tell Mash Maker that there is something on the page that he would like to extract. He then clicks on the address of one of the businesses on the current page. Mash Maker asks Carl whether what he clicked on is a property of the whole page, or a property of a repeated item on the page. Carl says that the name is a property of a repeated item, and that the repeated item is a "business review."

A previous user had already shown Mash Maker how to find business reviews on the page, and the address that Carl clicked on was inside one of the business reviews that the wrapper already knew about. If this was not the case then Mash Maker would have asked Carl to show it what area of the page was occupied by the business review that the address was part of.

From this one example, Mash Maker attempts to infer a rule that will find an address for every business review on the page. If Mash Maker infers this rule incorrectly, then Carl can help Mash

Maker out by either giving more examples or manually editing the underlying rules that Mash Maker has generated (revealed by turning on the "expert controls" option).

THE WRAPPER EDITOR

A Mash Maker wrapper extracts three kinds of information from a page:

- A *top level property* is something that appears once on a page. It has a name and a textual value.
- An *item* has a type and a set of *item properties*. A page may contain several items with the same type, and may contain items with multiple types. All items with the same type are found using the same matching rules. In our example we had items of type "business review."
- An *item property* has a name and textual value and is contained inside an item.

Mash Maker's wrapper editor works in a similar way to other user-guided wrapper editors, such as Pictor (Zheng et al., 2008), Lixto (Baumgartner, Flesca, & Gottlob, 2001b), WIEN (Kushmerick, Weld, & Doorenbos, 1997), STALKER (Muslea, Minton, & Knoblock, 1999), Dapper.net, and Irmak/Suel (Irmak & Suel, 2006). A user gives examples of things on the page that they think are interesting, and Mash Maker attempts to infer extraction rules from these examples. If Mash Maker's inference does the wrong thing, then a user can either provide more examples or manually edit the inferred rules.

It addition to specifying where information can be found on a page, Mash Maker wrappers also specify the *drop zones* on a Web page where extra content should be added. A drop zone is a place on a Web page where it is good to insert additional content without disturbing the layout of the Web page. Since the best drop zones on a Web page are largely independent of the particular content being inserted, it makes sense that drop zones be factored into the wrapper, rather than requiring each mashup to specify its own layout from scratch. A mashup is free to ignore the drop zones in the wrapper and place content in other locations if the author thinks that is appropriate.

Mash Maker uses wrappers to extract data from a Web page even if a Web site provides programmatic APIs that can be used to query its data. This is for several reasons. Firstly, if an API was used, then it would still be necessary to use a wrapper to determine where the data was on the page (as done by d.mix (Hartmann et al., 2007)). Secondly, since the Web page is already loaded, it is more efficient to get the information from the HTML rather than accessing an external API. A mashup may however use APIs to bring in additional information from other sources that should be added to the current page.

Mash Maker wrappers do not follow "next" links to extract information from other pages on the same Web site. The purpose of a Mash Maker wrapper is only to extract information from the current page. If a mashup wants to obtain large amounts of information from a Web site then it can use a widget that loads that information using an API.

It is useful if wrappers agree on a common vocabulary to describe their data. For example, if one wrapper says "price" whereas another says "cost", then it becomes harder to write widgets that can work across multiple Web sites. Mash Maker encourages wrapper authors to choose type and property names that conform to a common ontology. This ontology is editable by all users using a collaborative ontology editor. Mash Maker's collaborative ontology editor is significantly more primitive than systems like Protege (Tudorache et al., 2008) or Freebase.com. It allows users to specify type names, associated property names, and simple subtype relationships, but lacks higher-level features. Unlike the ontology editor of FreeBase Mash Maker allows anyone to edit the properties that can be associated with a type, not just its owner. The motivation is to encourage people to reuse existing types rather than creating new ones.

Mash Maker does not currently use any kind of data detector (e.g., Miro (Chapter 4)) to detect objects on a page. Mash Maker does however take advantage of microformats when they are available.

THE SHARED DATA TREE

As mentioned in the introduction, Mash Maker uses a three-level architecture for creating mashups (Figure 9.1). Wrappers extract data from Web pages, widgets create additional data and visualizations, and mashups connect multiple widgets together and place their content in drop zones in the page layout. These three layers are largely independent: A wrapper may support many mashups, a widget may accept data from many wrappers, a mashup may use many widgets, and a widget may be used by many mashups.

Several other mashup tools allow one to create a mashup by composing multiple components. Good examples include Yahoo! Pipes, Microsoft Popfly, Clip Connect Clone (Chapter 8), and Marmite (Wong & Hong, 2006), all of which use some form of dataflow model. Pipes and Popfly adopt a visual dataflow programming model (Ingaiis, 1988; Koelma, van Balen, & Smeulders, 1992; Raeder, 1985) in which wires are drawn between widgets to allow data to flow between them, Clip Connect Clone allows one to specify dataflow using a spreadsheet metaphor, and Marmite behaves like Apple's Automator by allowing one to create a mashup as a sequence of stages, each of which acts on the output of the previous stage. Mash Maker instead uses a tuple space–inspired (Gelernter, 1989) publish/subscribe model (Eugster et al., 2003) in which widgets communicate by reading and writing a shared data tree. The difference is similar to the difference between the Blackboard and Pipeline models in software engineering.

Mash Maker maintains a *data tree* for every Web page currently open in the browser, showing a structured view of the data on the Web page. Initially the data tree contains the information extracted from the page by the wrapper. Any widgets on the page can query the data on the page, add additional information to the data tree, and modify or remove information. An expert user can view the data tree for the current page using its tab in the expert side panel (Figure 9.7).

The data tree is the only means by which widgets can communicate with each other. The Mash Maker API allows a widget to ask

FIGURE 9.7

A data tree showing additions from widgets.

to be notified when the result of a query changes due to actions by another widget. For example, the map widget asks to be notified when the set of objects with addresses changes. This allows the map widget to dynamically update its map when other widgets add or remove objects with addresses.

The mental model is that adding a widget to a page creates an *improved page*, which can itself be enhanced further by adding more widgets. A widget is not expected to distinguish between information that was originally on the page and information that has been added to the page by other widgets. For example a price comparison widget does not care if the dollar price of an item was calculated by a separate currency conversion widget.

Mash Maker could have used the same visual dataflow approach that is used by Yahoo! Pipes and Microsoft Popfly. Under this model, the wrapper would be treated as being just another box in the network whose extracted data could be fed to other boxes. Work started on Mash Maker before Pipes or Popfly were publicly known, so no deliberate decision was taken to use a different model. There are however advantages of the "shared tree" model for the domain in which Mash Maker works.

One motivation for the "shared tree" model is that it allows a user to create a mashup by adding the features that they think that they want, without having to think about how they should fit into a logical structure. The widgets find each other by looking for information that they want that other widgets are providing. This works well for simple cases (e.g., find home country and visualize on a map), but for more complex mashups one may have to use a widget's settings panel (Figure 9.8) to tell it which other widget it should be talking to.

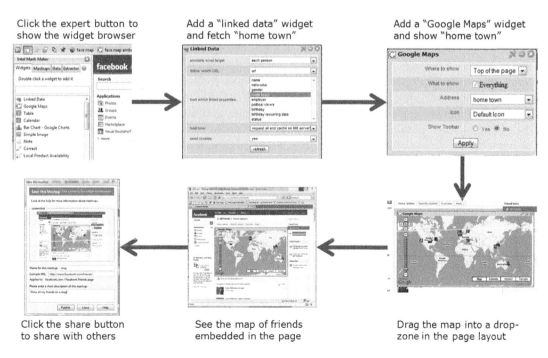

FIGURE 9.8

Steps to creating a mashup that shows Facebook friends.

Another motivation for the "shared tree" model is that it makes it easier for the physical location of a widget on the page to correspond to where its primary visualization will be inserted. If a visual dataflow model is used, then some layouts of boxes will make the wires hard to read. Since Mash Maker's boxes are not connected by wires, this problem does not arise.

In addition to manipulating the data tree, a widget can also publish content that can be inserted into the layout of the page. Content can currently be either text, a clickable action icon, or an iframe that can contain arbitrary Web content. Figure 9.2 shows a map visualization running in an iframe that has been published by the Map widget. Figure 9.3 shows text annotations that have been associated with objects on a page.

A widget has no control of how its content will be integrated into the layout of the page, because the only view it has of the page is the data tree. It is entirely up to the user creating the mashup to insert content into the page layout appropriately. They can do this by either dropping content into drop zones described by the wrapper, or placing content at a physical location relative to the node that it is associated with. This separation allows widgets to focus on the high-level data processing task they are concerned with, without having to worry about how they might integrate into any particular layout.

Each widget can have a settings panel that can be used to configure their behavior. For some settings the default choice will usually be correct (e.g., a map widget should map everything on the page with an address), but for other settings a user is likely to want to set things manually in order to get good results (e.g., which property of an object should be used to decide its icon on the map). The options provided by a widget's settings panel are entirely up to the widget – indeed the settings panel can contain arbitrary HTML.

Once a user has created a mashup that they think is useful, they can publish it by clicking on the "share" button. A user will then be prompted to enter a short description of their mashup and will be shown the preview screenshot that Mash Maker will save with the mashup (Figure 9.8). Once a mashup has been published, Mash Maker can suggest it to other users.

Figure 9.8 shows the process of creating a mashup that adds a map to the Facebook friends list. The map shows the location of each of the user's friends, based on the "home town" information they provided in their profile. In this example the user opens the expert sidebar, double-clicks on two widgets to add them to the page, adjusts their settings appropriately, and then drops the map into an appropriate drop zone on the page. Once the user has created a mashup that they like, they can click the "share" button to make it available to other users looking at pages that are interpreted by the same wrapper.

UNTRUSTED WIDGETS

Mash Maker has to be particularly careful about security, because mashups have access to private data and users are encouraged to run untrusted mashups without investigating them beforehand.

Since Mash Maker runs inside the browser, it has access to all the information that the browser shows to the user. This includes Web pages that require logins, Web pages on intranets, and content that is generated dynamically inside the browser. The advantage of this approach is that it allows Mash Maker to mash up useful content that would not be easily accessible to a mashup that ran on a separate server (e.g., Pipes or Popfly). The disadvantage is that some of this information may be private information that should not be leaked to third parties.

Without proper precautions, one could easily open doors for hackers to steal confidential data. For example a mashup could scan email messages for passwords and use an external API to send them to a site run by an attacker. In the absence of security controls, any data that is visible on a Web site could be scraped by a wrapper and sent to a malicious Web site by a widget.

Other browser extension mashup tools like Greasemonkey and Chickenfoot (Chapter 3) suffer from this problem to a lesser extent. Unlike Mash Maker, Greasemonkey and Chickenfoot do not suggest mashups to users automatically. Instead, their model is more similar to installing desktop software; a user browses a list of recommended mashups hosted on a trusted Web site, picks one that seems useful and trustworthy, and installs it. By contrast, Mash Maker encourages users to turn on unvetted mashups written by unknown third parties, with little information available about them other than their name.

Mash Maker addresses this problem by distinguishing between *trusted* and *untrusted* widgets. A trusted widget is one that has been checked by the Mash Maker administrators to make sure it cannot leak data to an untrusted server. The choice of which widgets are trusted is subjective. The Google Maps widget is considered to be trusted, even though it sends addresses to Google. If the addresses were highly confidential and Google was considered to be untrusted then one might not want this widget to be applied to a page.

If a widget is not trusted, then it is not permitted to see any data that is fetched with cookies or HTTP authentication enabled. This restriction also prevents an untrusted widget being applied to information that another widget fetched with cookies. For example, if a calendar widget inserted information from your personal calendar then this could not be viewed by an untrusted widget. The intention is to restrict an untrusted widget to only be able to see content that it could see if it was running on another machine and prevent it from seeing content that was personalized for the current user. No mashups can be applied to a URL served as HTTPS.

One loophole in the "no cookies" security model is that an untrusted widget will still be able to see content that is private to a local intranet. The correct solution would be to consider any page fetched from a corporate intranet to be a "secure" page that cannot be seen by untrusted widgets, however it is difficult to determine what pages are on the intranet rather than being on the outside Web. In particular, simply checking whether a page can be fetched from a remote server is not sufficient, because some intranets provide private information on pages that have the same URL as a nonprivate page that is externally accessible. Mash Maker does not currently have a solution for this problem, and so Mash Maker is not recommended for use on corporate intranet Web pages.

A Mash Maker widget is implemented rather like a Google gadget. A widget is a piece of JavaScript code that runs inside its own iframe, embedded on the page. The browser's same-origin policy prevents a widget from being able to directly manipulate the page that is being mashed up. This is in contrast to Greasemonkey, which injects mashup scripts directly onto the page.

Mash Maker provides extensions to the standard browser JavaScript API to allow widget code to query the shared data tree and publish information and visualizations. The implementation is similar to MashupOS (Howell et al., 2007) and SMash (Keukelaere et al., 2008) – although it was created independently.

COPY AND PASTE

As a special case, Mash Maker allows a user to create a mashup by using a copy-and-paste metaphor to combine Web sites. To create a mashup that inserts content from site A into site B, the user browses to site A, clicks the "copy" button on the toolbar (Figure 9.4), and then browses to site B and clicks "paste". For example, to add legroom information to a flight listing, one can browse to a Web site that gives legroom information for different airlines, click "copy", and then browse to a list of flights and click "paste".

Mash Maker will try to guess how to combine the two sites together and create an appropriate mashup. In the current version of Mash Maker, the support for copy and paste is fairly simple. Mash Maker will look at the information extracted from the two Web sites and try to find a matching property that can be used for a simple join. The resulting mashup is implemented by adding an instance of the "paste" widget to the page. If the copy and paste result was not as desired then the user can tweak it using the settings panels on the Join widget. Subsequent to the release of Mash Maker, this concept has been improved on by Karma (Tuchinda, Szekely, & Knoblock, 2008a), which uses more intelligent techniques to guess how Web sites should be combined.

The core idea of using copy and paste to create Web sites was inspired by previous work on Web clipping tools (Lingam & Elbaum, 2008; schraefel & Zhu, 2002). While Mash Maker uses Web wrappers to extract data from a copied Web site, d.mix (Hartmann et al., 2007) takes a more elegant approach by determining an API that could be used to obtain information from the source site. In contrast, Mash Maker's copy and paste system combines a pair of pages.

Dontcheva et al. (2007) take a more general approach in which the pages that should be joined together are found using a Web search.

SUMMARY

Mash Maker combines several novel ideas into a complete system: an overlay mashup extends a Web page by adding new content that is visually distinguished but integrated into the page layout; suggestions allow users to find useful mashups as they browse. The collaborative wiki model for wrapper creation allows a mashup to keep working even when the wrapper it depends on breaks. The shared data tree allows a user to create a mashup by adding a set of widgets to each other and letting them work out how to help each other. The untrusted widget model allows a user to apply a mashup to their page without having to trust it. And the copy and paste model allows a user to combine Web sites together by simply choosing which Web sites have information that they like.

Mash Maker was originally developed as a technology demonstration at Intel Research and is now being developed and maintained by a group in the Intel Software Solutions Group. At the time of writing, the preview version of Mash Maker has around 18,000 registered users, of whom 822 have created or edited a wrapper, and 387 have created a mashup. The Mash Maker database has 1190 mashups.

INTEL MASH MAKER

Intended users:	All users
Domain:	Web pages with structured content
Description:	Intel® Mash Maker is a browser extension that allows a user to customize Web pages by applying mashups that add additional content. Such "overlay mashups" add content that is visually distinguished from the host page while being integrated into the normal page layout.
Example:	When booking a flight, a user may wish to know how much legroom each flight is likely to provide. When the user browses a flight listing Mash Maker will suggest a mashup that adds legroom information to each flight on the page. If the user decides that they like this mashup then they can "pin" it so that it is always enabled for pages that list flights.
Automation:	Mash Maker automates the task of collecting and compositing information from different sources.
Mashups:	Yes, Mash Maker can combine information from multiple Web sites within the browser.
Scripting:	No, though expert users can write new "widgets" in JavaScript.
Natural language:	No.
Recordability:	No.
Inferencing:	Simple heuristics are used to infer what mashups a user might like, and to infer how widgets should be connected together to create a mashup.
Sharing:	Yes, mashups can be published to a Web site. Published mashups can be suggested to other users and users may vote for mashups that they like.
Comparison to other systems:	Like other systems, Mash Maker is a browser plugin that modifies existing Web pages. Mash Maker mashups are more restricted, since they can only add content to a page. This restriction prevents most malicious mashups and encourages users to try untrusted mashups that Mash Maker suggests.
Platform:	Implemented as an extension to the Mozilla Firefox browser.
Availability:	Publicly available at http://mashmaker.intel.com.

Programming by a sample

Leveraging Web sites to program their underlying services

10

Björn Hartmann,[1] **Leslie Wu,**[2] **Kevin Collins,**[2] **Scott R. Klemmer**[2]

[1]*University of California, Berkeley*
[2]*Stanford University*

ABSTRACT

Many popular Web sites offer a public API that allows Web developers to access site data and functionality programmatically. The site and its API offer two complementary views of the same underlying functionality. This chapter introduces *d.mix*, a Web development tool that leverages this *site-to-service* correspondence to rapidly create Web-service based applications. With d.mix, users browse annotated Web sites and select elements on the page they would like to access programmatically. It then generates code for the *underlying Web service calls* that yield those elements. This code can be edited, executed, and shared in a wiki-based hosting environment. The application d.mix leverages prexisting Web sites as example sets and supports rapid composition and modification of examples.

INTRODUCTION

Web hosting and search have lowered the time and monetary costs of disseminating, finding, and using application programming interfaces (APIs). The number and diversity of application building blocks that are openly available as Web services is growing rapidly (Papazoglou et al., 2007). Programmableweb.com lists 4452 mashups leveraging 1521 distinct APIs as of November 2009 (the most popular being Google Maps, Flickr, YouTube, and Amazon). These APIs provide a rich selection of interface elements and data sources. Many serve as the programmatic interface to successful Web sites, where the site and its API offer complementary views of the same underlying functionality. In such cases, the Web site itself is often a complete example of the functionality that can be realized with its associated API. This chapter describes how modeling the correspondence between site and service can enable a Web site to serve as an automatic code example corpus for its service API.

Many small Web applications are created opportunistically, leveraging elements from third-party Web services (Chapter 23). These applications, commonly known as mashups, are created by amateurs who are learning the ropes, by designers creating a rapid prototype, by hobbyists, and by professionals creating in-house applications. A broad shift of this paradigm is that the designer's effort and creativity are reallocated: less time is spent building an application up brick by brick, while more time and ingenuity is spent finding and selecting components, and then creating and shaping the "glue" between them (Hartmann et al., 2008). Automatically generating relevant examples has the potential to significantly speed up component selection and integration and lower the expertise threshold required to build software.

Integrating site and service

To enable rapid authoring of API-based Web applications, this chapter introduces *d.mix* (see Figure 10.1), a Web-based design tool with two notable attributes. The first is a technique for users to compose Web applications by browsing existing sites, visually specifying elements to borrow from them, and combining and modifying them. We call this technique *sampling*. Sampling is enabled by a programmable proxy system providing a *site-to-service map* that establishes the correspondence between elements shown on a site and the Web service calls needed to replicate these elements programmatically. Second, a server-side *active wiki* hosts scripts generated by the proxy. This active wiki provides a configuration-free environment for authoring and sharing of applications. By virtue of displaying the actual underlying code to users, d.mix also allows developers with sufficient technical expertise to drill down into source code as needed.

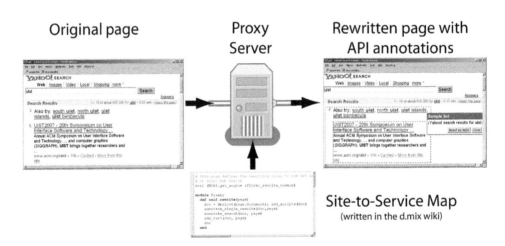

FIGURE 10.1

With d.mix, users browse Web sites through a proxy that marks API-accessible content. Users select marked elements they wish to copy. Through a site-to-service map, d.mix composes Web service calls that yield results corresponding to the user's selection. This code is copied to the d.mix wiki for editing and hosting.

Foraging for examples

As the number and size of programming libraries increase, locating and understanding documentation and examples is playing an increasingly prominent role in developers' activities (Stylos & Myers, 2006). To aid users in foraging for example code, d.mix co-locates two different kinds of information on one page: examples of what information a Web site offers; and information about how one would obtain this information programmatically.

Because problems often cut across package and function boundaries, example-based documentation provides value by aiding knowledge crystallization (gathering of relevant data and distinguishing it from irrelevant data) and improving information scent (the cues that describe the likely utility of the provided information) (Pirolli & Card, 1999). For this reason, examples and code snippets are a popular resource (see Chapter 23). This approach of documentation through examples complements more traditional, index-based documentation. d.mix enables developers to dynamically generate code snippets for a Web service API as they browse the canonical example of its functionality: the Web site itself.

The approach used by d.mix draws on prior work in *programming by example*, also known as *programming by demonstration* (Cypher, 1993; Lieberman, 2001; Nardi, 1993). In these systems, the user demonstrates a set of actions on a concrete example – such as a sequence of image manipulation operations – and the system infers application logic through generalization from that example. The logic can then be reapplied to other similar cases.

Although d.mix shares much of its approach with programming-by-example systems, it differs in the procedure for generating examples. Instead of specifying logic by demonstrating *novel* examples, with d.mix, designers choose and parameterize *found* examples. In this way, the task is more one of programming by *example modification*, which Nardi highlights as a successful strategy for end user development (Nardi, 1993). Modification of a working example also speeds development because it provides stronger scaffolding than starting from a blank slate (Chapter 23).

The rest of this chapter is structured as follows. We first introduce the main interaction techniques of d.mix through a scenario. Subsequently, we explain the d.mix implementation. We then describe applications we created with d.mix, feedback from Web professionals, and an initial laboratory study. We conclude with a discussion of related research and commercial systems, limitations of the current implementation, and an outlook to future work.

HOW TO PROGRAM BY A SAMPLE

A scenario will help introduce the main interaction techniques. Jane is an amateur rock climber who frequently travels to new climbing spots with friends. Jane would like to create a page that serves as a lightweight Web presence for the group. The page should show photos and videos from their latest outings. She wants content to update dynamically so she doesn't have to maintain the page. She is familiar with HTML and has some JavaScript experience, but does not consider herself an expert programmer.

Jane starts by browsing the photo and video sharing sites her friends use. David uses the photo site Flickr and marks his pictures with the tag "climbing". Another friend also uses Flickr, but uses image sets instead of tags. A third friend shares her climbing videos on the video site YouTube.

To start gathering content, Jane opens David's Flickr profile in her browser and navigates to the page listing all his tags. She then presses the *sample this* button in her browser bookmark bar (Figure 10.2a). This reloads the Flickr page, adding dashed borders around the elements that she can sample.

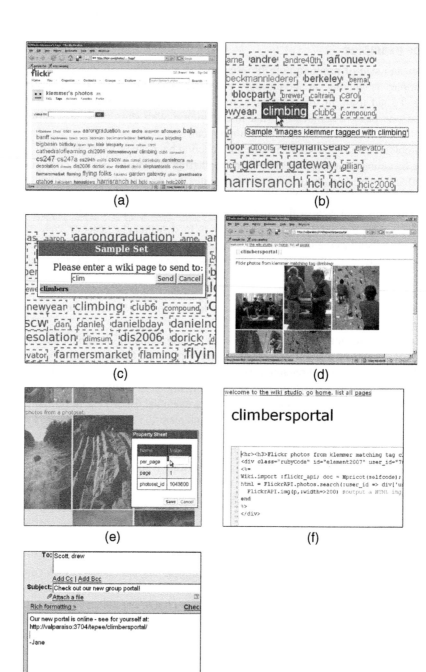

FIGURE 10.2

She right-clicks on the tag "climbing", to invoke a context menu of possible actions for the selected screen element. In this case, there is only one possible action: to copy the set of images that David has tagged with "climbing" (Figure 10.2b).

A floating dialog asks her to specify which page on the d.mix wiki she would like to send the sampled content to (Figure 10.2c). This dialog permits her to either create new pages or add content to existing pages. She enters a new name, "ClimbersPortal", to create a new page.

Her browser then loads the newly created page in the d.mix programmable wiki (Figure 10.2d). The rendered view now shows the specified images she sampled; the source view of the page contains the corresponding API call to the Flickr Web service.

Continuing her information gathering, Jane samples Sam's climbing photo set on Flickr. Her wiki page now displays both David's photos and several images from Sam. Jane would like the page to display only the latest three images from each person. She right-clicks on Sam's images to invoke a *property sheet,* a graphical field editor for object attributes, showing that the content came from a Flickr photo set (Figure 10.2e). This sheet gives parameters for the user ID associated with the set and for the number of images to show. Changing the parameters reloads the page and applies the changes.

Jane then opens Karen's YouTube video page. For Karen's latest video, d.mix offers two choices: copy this *particular* file, or copy the *most recent* video in Karen's stream. Because Jane wants the video on her page to update whenever Karen posts a new file, she chooses the latter option.

Next, Jane would like to lay out the images and add some text. In the d.mix wiki, she clicks on "edit source," which displays an HTML document, in which each of the three samples she inserted corresponds to a few lines of Ruby script, enclosed by a structuring *<div>* tag (Figure 10.2f). She adds text and a table around the images. Remembering that David also sometimes tags his images with "rocks", she modifies the query string in the corresponding script accordingly to broaden the search criteria.

When she is satisfied with the *rendered view* of her active wiki page, Jane emails the URL of the wiki page to her group members to let them see the page (Figure 10.2g).

IMPLEMENTATION

In this section, we describe d.mix's implementation for sampling, parametric copying, editing, and sharing.

"Sample this" button rewrites pages

Two buttons are present in d.mix, *sample this* and *stop sampling*, that can be added to a browser's bookmark bar to enable or disable sampling mode (Figure 10.3). *Sample this* is implemented as a bookmarklet – a bookmark containing JavaScript instead of a URL – that sends the current browser location to the d.mix server. The browser is then redirected to load a page through the d.mix proxy which combines

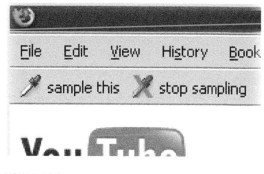

FIGURE 10.3

the target site's original Web markup with annotations found using the *site-to-service map* (see Figure 10.1). The map contains information about the correspondence between HTML elements on the current page and API calls that can retrieve that same content programmatically.

While it would be straightforward for site operators to provide the site-to-service map through extra markup in their page source, the original Web site *need not* provide any support for d.mix. The active wiki maintains a collection of site-to-service maps, contributed by knowledgeable developers. These maps describe the programmatically accessible components associated with a particular set of URLs (see Figure 10.4). Each map defines a partition of a Web site into page types through regular expression matches on URLs. For each page type, the map then defines the correspondence between the markup found on a page and the API method invocations needed to retrieve the equivalent content programmatically. It does so by searching for known markup patterns — using Xpath[1] and CSS[2] selectors — and recording the metadata that will be passed to Web services as parameters, such as a user or photo ID, a search term, or a page number.

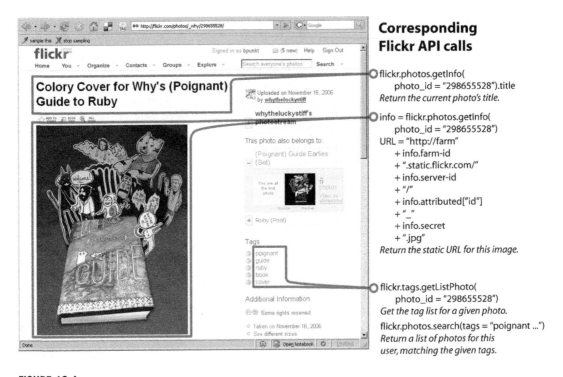

FIGURE 10.4

The site-to-service map defines a correspondence between HTML elements and Web service API calls. The shown example highlights this mapping for three items on a Flickr photo page.

---

[1]XML Path Language: http://www.w3.org/TR/xpath.
[2]Cascading Style Sheets: http://www.w3.org/Style/CSS/.

For example, on Flickr.com, pages with the URL pattern http://flickr.com/photos/ <*username*>/tags contain a list of image tags for a particular user, displayed as a tag cloud. Programs can access a user's tags by calling the API method *flickr.tags.getListUser* and passing in a *user ID*. Similarly, photos corresponding to tags for a given user can be retrieved by a call to *flickr.photos.Search*.

When the user is in sampling mode, d.mix's programmable HTTP proxy rewrites the viewed Web page, adding JavaScript annotations. These annotations serve two functions. First, d.mix uses the site-to-service map to derive the set of components that can be sampled on the current page. Second, d.mix's annotation visually augments those elements with a dashed border as an indication to the user.

In the other direction, the *stop sampling* button takes a URL of a proxy page, extracts the non-proxy URL of the target site from it, and redirects the browser to this page, ending access through the proxy.

d.mix is implemented in the Ruby programming language. We chose Ruby to leverage its metaprogramming libraries for code generation and dynamic evaluation, and for MouseHole,[3] a Ruby-based HTTP proxy. Largely for expediency, the d.mix research prototype also uses Ruby as the user-facing scripting language inside the d.mix active wiki. One could also use a different scripting language for the active wiki, such as PHP.

Annotating Web pages

HTML elements (e.g., an image on a photo site) are annotated with d.mix with a set of potential actions. It presents these options to the user in a context menu. Each menu entry corresponds to a Ruby script method. The site-to-service mapping uses elements' *class* and *ID* to determine which options are available.

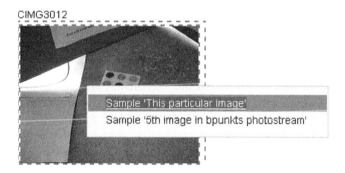

FIGURE 10.5

---

[3]MouseHole scriptable proxy: http://rubyforge.org/projects/mousehole/.

As an example, consider a *tag cloud* page found on Flickr. All tags are found inside the following structure:

```
<p id="TagCloud">
<a href="...">Tag1</a>
<a href="...">Tag2</a>...
</p>
```

The site-to-service mapping script to find each element and annotate it is:

```
@user_id=doc.at("input[@name='w']")["value"]
doc.search("//p[@id='TagCloud']/a").each do |link|
tag = link.inner_html
src = generate_source(:tags=>tag, :user_id=>@user_id)
annotations += context_menu(link, "tag description", src)
end
```

In this example, the Ruby code makes use of an HTML parser library, Hpricot,[4] to extract the user's ID from a hidden form element. It then iterates over the set of links within the tag cloud, extracts the tag name, generates source code by parameterizing a source code stub for *flickr.photos.search,* and generates the context menu for the element.

The d.mix mapping code scrapes Web pages as the developer visits them in order to extract the needed information for code generation. Scraping can be brittle because matching expressions can break when site operators change class or ID attributes of their pages. Still, scraping is common practice in Web development (Hartmann, Doorley, & Klemmer, 2008) as it is often the only technique for extracting data without the site operator's cooperation. An important design decision in d.mix is to scrape at *authoring-time*, when the designer is creating pages such as the Flickr-and-YouTube mashup in the scenario. By scraping parameters first, d.mix's user-created pages can then make API calls at *runtime*, which tend to be more stable than the HTML format of the initial example pages.

Authoring and maintaining the site-to-service map

The keystone of the sampling approach is the site-to-service map. For d.mix to be aware of the functionality of a Web service, a corresponding map must be created and maintained. For the d.mix research prototype, the authors implemented the necessary rewrite and code generation rules for three popular sites (see Figure 10.6). Though these rules are relatively concise, authoring them requires expertise with DOM[5] querying. The appeal of the sampling approach is that the one-time – or at least infrequent – effort of creating the map is hopefully very small relative to the recurring benefits reaped every time a user creates a new site with d.mix.

Additionally, we see four approaches a production tool could employ to ease the creation of site-to-service maps. First, a declarative, domain-specific language could be devised to express mappings. Second, visual DOM selection tools like Solvent[6] could enable markup selection by

---

[4]Hpricot HTML parser library: http://github.com/hpricot/hpricot/.
[5]Document Object Model: http://www.w3.org/DOM.
[6]Solvent Firefox extension for screen scraping: http://simile.mit.edu/wiki/Solvent.

API	Supported Actions	Site-to-Service map code size
flickr	• Get images from a user's photo stream, with or without metadata • Get images from an image set • Get images from individual photo pages • Get images matching tags, global or per user, from tag clouds and photo pages • Get images by global image ID • Get images from full-text search	355 lines
YAHOO!	• Single Web search result • Web search result set	54 lines
You Tube	• Retrieve a user's videos • Retrieve most recent videos • Single search result • Search result set	115 lines

FIGURE 10.6

The site-to-service map implemented by the authors supports three services.

demonstration. Third, given such direct manipulation tools, one could build and maintain the map through *crowdsourcing*, splitting the modeling task into many small subtasks (e.g., identifying a single API call correspondence) that can be completed through volunteer efforts. The success of community-created sites like Wikipedia demonstrates that large-scale volunteer effort can create significant works (Krieger, Stark, & Klemmer, 2009). Finally, the map may not have to be authored by users at all – Web companies may have incentive to publish them themselves. Companies expose their Web APIs because they want them to be used. Since these companies designed both their site and their API, it would be relatively straightforward for them to embed site-to-service map annotations directly into the generated HTML pages, without requiring an intermediate proxy.

Server-side active wiki hosts and executes script

In d.mix's active wiki, developers can freely mix text, HTML, and CSS to determine document structure, as well as Ruby script to express program logic. The wiki format offers two primary benefits. First, the preconfigured, server-side environment enables rapid experimentation with code and sharing of created pages. Second, the wiki offers the opportunity to view, copy, and include any existing wiki page to leverage the practice of programming by example modification (Nardi, 1993). Like other wiki environments, the active wiki also offers page versioning.

When a d.mix user creates a new page that remixes content from multiple data sources, another end user can just as easily remix the remix. Currently, this involves copying and pasting the generated code from one wiki page to another. To further lower the threshold for reuse, each wiki page itself could contain an automatically generated site-to-service map that allows sampling elements from wiki pages in the same manner users sample from other supported sites. Users of d.mix can also contribute new site-to-service maps for their own Web sites, or submit fixes to mappings as Web sites evolve.

When a developer sends code to the wiki through sampling, she has to provide a page name that will receive the generated code. For a new name, a page containing the generated code is created. For an existing name, the generated code is appended to the existing page. The browser then displays a rendered version of the wiki page, which includes executing the specified Web API calls (see Figure 10.2d). In this rendered version, HTML, CSS, and JavaScript take effect, the embedded Ruby code is evaluated, and its output is inserted into the page.

To switch from the rendered view to the source view containing Web markup and Ruby code, a user can click on the *edit* button, as in a standard wiki. The markup and snippets of script are then shown in a browser-based text editor, which provides syntax highlighting and line numbering. As browser-based development environments such as Mozilla Bespin[7] mature, we expect that the functionality and usability gap between such Web-based editors and integrated development environments on the desktop will narrow. In d.mix wiki code, snippets of Ruby are encapsulated in a reserved tag <%= #code %> to distinguish them from plain text. Clicking on the *save* button saves the document source as a new revision, and redirects the user back to the rendered version of the wiki page.

Pasted material can be parameterized and edited

In comparison to a standard copy-and-paste of Web content, the notable advantage of d.mix's *parametric copy* is that it copies a richer representation of the selected data. This allows the arguments of each API call to be changed after pasting. The d.mix wiki offers graphical editing of parameters through property sheets to enable a level of customization without having to modify the generated source code directly. The structure of these property sheets, implemented as layers floating above the rendered page in JavaScript, is determined during the code generation step. In our current implementation, property editors are generated for each argument of each Web service API call. It may be valuable to provide additional parameters such as formatting commands in the future.

As a test of the complexity of code that can be written in a wiki environment, we implemented all site-to-service mapping scripts as wiki pages. This means that the scripts used to drive the programmable proxy and thus create new wiki pages are, themselves, wiki pages. To allow for modularization of code, a wiki page can import code or libraries from other wiki pages, analogous to "#include" in the C language.

The generated code makes calls into d.mix modules that broker communication between the active wiki script and the Web services. For example, users' Ruby scripts often need to reference working API keys to make Web service calls. Modules in d.mix provide a default set of API keys so that users can retrieve publicly accessible data from Web services without having to obtain personal keys. Although using a small static number of Web API keys would be a problem for large-scale deployment (many sites limit the number of requests one can issue), we believe our solution works well for prototyping and for deploying applications with a limited number of users.

---

[7]Mozilla Bespin Web code editor: https://bespin.mozilla.com/.

ADDITIONAL APPLICATIONS

In this section, we review additional applications of d.mix beyond the use case demonstrated in the scenario.

Existing Web pages can be virtually edited

The same wiki-scripted programmable HTTP proxy that d.mix employs to annotate API-enabled Web sites can also be used to remix, rewrite, or edit existing Web pages to improve usability, aesthetics, or accessibility, enabling a sort of *recombinant* Web. As an example, we have created a rewriting script on our wiki that provides a connection between the event-listing site Upcoming[8] and the calendaring site 30 Boxes.[9] By parsing an event's microformat on the site and injecting a graphical button, users can copy events directly to their personal calendar. Because this remix is hosted on our active wiki, it is immediately available to any Web browser.

Another example is reformatting of Web content to fit the smaller screen resolution and lower bandwidth of mobile devices. Using d.mix, we wrote a script that extracts only essential information – movie names and show times – from a cluttered Web page. This leaner page can be accessed through its wiki URL from any mobile phone browser (see Figure 10.7). Note that the reformatting work is executed on the server and only the small text page is transmitted to the phone. The server-side infrastructure of d.mix made it possible for one author and a colleague to develop, test, and deploy this service in 30 minutes. In contrast, client-side architectures, such as Greasemonkey,[10] do not work outside the desktop environment. The Highlight system in Chapter 6 presents an alternative architecture for reformatting Web sites for mobile consumption.

Web applications to monitor and control physical spaces

The scenario presented in this chapter focused on data-centric APIs from successful Web sites with large user bases. Though such applications present the dominant use case of mashups today, we also see opportunity for d.mix to enable development of situated ubiquitous computing applications. A wide variety of ubicomp sensors and actuators are equipped with embedded Web servers and publish their own Web services. This enables d.mix's fast iteration cycle and "remix" functionality to extend into physical space. To explore d.mix design opportunities in Web-enabled ubicomp applications, we augmented two smart devices in our laboratory to support API sampling: a camera that publishes a video feed of lab activity and a network-controlled power outlet. Combining elements from both servers, we created a wiki page that allows remote monitoring of lab occupancy to turn off room lights if they were left on at night (see Figure 10.8).

---

[8]Upcoming event listings: http://upcoming.yahoo.com.
[9]30 Boxes calendar: http://30boxes.com.
[10]Greasemonkey Firefox extension: http://addons.mozilla.org/en-US/firefox/addon/748.

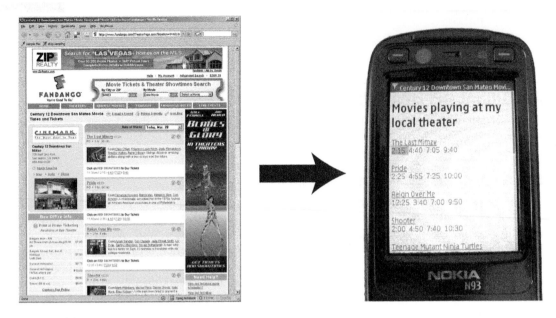

FIGURE 10.7

The rewriting technology in d.mix can be used to tailor content to mobile devices. Here, essential information is extracted from a movie listings page.

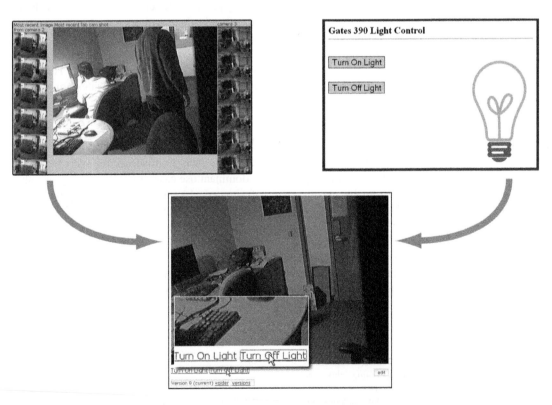

FIGURE 10.8

An example of a d.mix ubiquitous computing mashup: Web services provide video monitoring and lighting control for an office.

More important than the utility of this particular example is the architectural insight gained: because the Web services of the camera and power outlet were open to us, we were able to embed API annotations directly into the served Web pages. This proof of concept demonstrated that Web service providers can integrate support for API sampling into their pages, obviating the need for a separate site-to-service map on the d.mix server.

FEEDBACK FROM WEB PROFESSIONALS

As d.mix matured, we met weekly with Web designers to obtain feedback for a period of 8 weeks. Some of these meetings were with individuals, others were with groups; the largest group had 12 members. Informants included attendees of Ruby user group meetings, Web developers at startup companies in Silicon Valley, and researchers at industrial research labs interested in Web technologies.

Informants repeatedly raised scaling concerns for mashups. One informant noted that many Web services impose limits on how many API calls a user can make in a given amount of time. This feedback suggests that *social norms* of acceptable use may place a stronger limit on the number of d.mix applications and users a d.mix server can support than available processing power.

As the reach of mashups expands, informants were interested in how users and developers might find relevant services. Several informants noted that while services are rapidly proliferating, there is a dearth of support for search and sensemaking in this space. Prior work on software customization (Mackay, 1990; MacLean et al., 1990) has explored the social side of end-user–created software, and recent work on CoScripter (see Chapter 5) has made strides in enabling sharing of end user browser automations. Additional efforts in this direction are a promising avenue for future work.

Informants saw the merits of extending the d.mix approach beyond PC-based browsers. A researcher at an industrial research lab expressed interest in creating an "elastic office," where Web-based office software is adapted for mobile devices. This focus on mobile interaction kindled our interest in using a mashup approach to tailoring Web applications for mobile devices.

Informants also raised the broader implications of a mashup approach to design. A user experience designer and a platform engineer at the offices of a browser vendor raised end user security as an important issue to consider. At another Web startup, a Web developer brought our attention to the legal issues involved in annotating sites in a public and social way.

Our recruiting method yielded informants with more expertise than d.mix's target audience; consequently, they asked questions about the *complexity ceiling* (Myers, Hudson, & Pausch, 2000) of the tool. In a group meeting with 12 Web designers and developers, informants expressed interest in creating annotations for a new API, and asked how time-consuming this process was. We explained that annotation in d.mix requires about 10 lines of (complex) code per HTML element; this was met with a positive response. For future work informants suggested that d.mix could fall back to HTML scraping when sites lack APIs.

EVALUATION

Our evaluation of d.mix was guided by the following questions:

1. Is the sampling approach embodied in d.mix *accessible* to Web developers? Is the mental model of sampling and modifying what was sampled clear?

2. Is the sampling approach *useful*? Can pages of sufficient complexity and value be created with d.mix?
3. What is the *usability* of the current interaction techniques?

To answer these questions, we conducted a first-use evaluation study with eight participants: seven were male, one female; their ages ranged from 25 to 46 years. We recruited participants with at least some Web development experience. All participants had some college education; four had completed graduate school. Four had a computer science education; one was an electrical engineer; three came from the life sciences. Recruiting developers with Ruby experience proved difficult – only four participants had more than a passing knowledge of this scripting language. Everyone was familiar with HTML; six participants were familiar with JavaScript; and six were familiar with at least one other scripting language. Four participants had some familiarity with Web APIs, but only two had previously attempted to build a mashup. Our participants thus match our target audience along the dimensions of familiarity and expertise with Web development practices although they were more expert in general engineering and computer science.

Study protocol

Study sessions took approximately 75 minutes. We wrote a site-to-service mapping for three Web sites – Yahoo Web search, Flickr photo sharing, and YouTube video sharing. For each site, d.mix supported annotations for a subset of the site's API (see Figure 10.6). For example, with Flickr, participants could perform full-text or tag searches and copy images with their metadata, but they could not extract user profile information. Participants were seated at a single-screen workstation with a standard Web browser. We first demonstrated d.mix's interface for sampling from Web pages, sending content to the wiki, and editing those pages. Next, we gave participants three tasks to perform.

The first task tested the overall usability of our approach – participants were asked to sample pictures and videos, send that content to the wiki, and change simple parameters of pasted elements, such as how many images to show from a photo stream. The second design task was similar to our scenario – it asked participants to create an information dashboard for a magazine's photography editor. This required combining data from multiple users on the Flickr site and formatting the results. The third task asked participants to create a meta-search engine – using a text input search form, participants should query at least two different Web services and combine search results from both on a single page. This task required generalizing a particular example taken from a Web site to a parametric form by editing the source code d.mix generated. Figure 10.9 shows two pages produced by one participant, who was Web design–savvy but a Ruby novice. After completing the tasks, participants filled out a qualitative questionnaire on their experience and were debriefed verbally.

Successes

On a high level, all participants understood and successfully used the workflow of browsing Web sites for desired content or functionality, sampling from the sites, sending sampled items to the wiki, and editing items. Given that less than one hour of time was allocated to three tasks, it is notable that all participants successfully created pages for the first two tasks. In task 3, five participants created

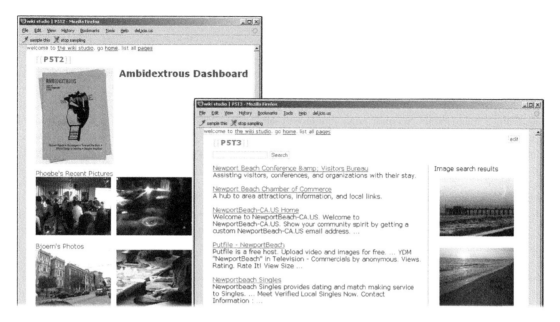

FIGURE 10.9

Two pages a participant created during our user study. Left image: Information dashboard for a magazine editor, showing recent relevant images of magazine photographers. Right image: Meta-search engine showing both relevant Web pages and image results for a search term.

working meta-search engines (see Figure 10.9). However, for three of the participants without Ruby experience, its syntax proved a hurdle; they only partially completed the task.

Our participants were comfortable with editing the generated source code directly, without using the graphical property editor. Making the source accessible to participants allowed them to leverage their Web design experience. For example, multiple participants leveraged their knowledge of CSS to change formatting and alignment of our generated code to better suit their aesthetic sensibility. Copy and paste within the wiki also allowed participants to reuse their work from a previous task in a later one.

In their post-test responses, participants highlighted three main advantages that d.mix offered compared to their existing toolset: elimination of setup and configuration barriers, enabling of rapid creation of functional Web application prototypes, and lowering of required programming expertise.

First, participants commented on the advantage of having a browser-based editing environment. There was "minimum setup hassle," since "you don't need to set up your own server." One participant's comments sum up this point succinctly: "I don't know how to set up a Ruby/API environment on my Web space. This lets me cut to the chase." Second, participants also highlighted the gain in development speed. Participants perceived code creation by selecting examples and then modifying them to be faster than writing new code or integrating third-party code snippets. Third, participants felt that d.mix lowered the expertise threshold required to work with Web APIs because they were not required to search or understand an API first. A Web development consultant saw value in d.mix because he felt it would enable his clients to update their sites themselves.

Shortcomings

We also discovered a range of challenges our participants faced when working with d.mix. Universally, participants wished for a larger set of supported sites. This request is not trivial because creating new annotations requires manual programming effort. However, we believe the amount of effort is reasonable when amortized over a large number of users. Other shortcomings fall into four categories. First, inconsistent ways in which d.mix annotated pages caused confusion about how to sample from a given page. Second, participants had difficulty switching between multiple languages interspersed in a single wiki page. Third, documentation and error handling in the wiki was insufficient compared to other tools. Fourth, wiki-hosted applications may not scale well beyond prototypes for a few users.

Inconsistent models for sampling

Participants were confused by limitations in what source elements were "sampling-aware." For example, to specify a query for a set of Flickr images in d.mix, the user currently must sample from the *link* to the image set, not the *results*. This suggests that the d.mix architecture should always enable sampling from both the *source* and from the *target* page. Also, where there is a genuine difference in effect, distinct highlighting treatments could be used to convey this.

Participants complained about a lack of visibility as to whether a given page would support sampling or not. Since rewriting pages through the d.mix proxy introduces a page-load delay, participants browsed the Web sites normally, and only turned on the sampling proxy when they had found elements they wished to sample. Only after this action were they able to find out whether the page was enhanced by d.mix. One means of addressing this shortcoming is to provide feedback within the browser as to whether the page may be sampled; another would be to minimize the latency overhead introduced through the proxy so that users can always leave their browser in sampling mode.

Multi-language scripting

Dynamic Web pages routinely use at least three different notation systems: HTML for page structuring, JavaScript for client-side interaction logic, and a scripting language, such as PHP, Python, or Ruby, for server-side logic. This mix of multiple languages in a single document is a general source of both flexibility and confusion for Web developers. The d.mix implementation exacerbated this complexity. An interaction between Ruby scripts and generated HTML tags wrapping these scripts prevented users from adding Ruby variables inside the attributes of the wrapping tag, a non-obvious restriction that confused users.

Lack of documentation and error handling

Many participants requested more complete documentation. One participant asked for more comments in the generated code explaining the format of API parameters. A related request was to provide structured editors inside property sheets that offered alternative values and data validation.

Participants also commented that debugging their wiki pages was hard, since syntax and execution errors generated "incomprehensible error messages." The current version of d.mix catches and displays Ruby exceptions along with the source code that generated the exception, but it does not interpret or explain the exceptions. Debugging is further hampered by the absence of the common *read-eval-print* command line for inspecting state and experimenting with changes in dynamic languages.

How to deploy applications outside the wiki environment?

Participants valued the active wiki for its support of rapid prototyping. However, because of a perceived lack of security, robustness, and performance, participants did not regard the wiki as a viable platform for larger deployment. One participant remarked, "I'd be hesitant to use it for anything other than prototyping" and two others expressed similar reservations.

RELATED WORK

Existing work in three areas supports d.mix: tools for end user modification of the Web, tools that lower the threshold of synthesizing new Web applications, and research on locating, copying, and modifying program documentation and examples. We discuss each area in turn.

Tools for end user modification of Web experiences

Greasemonkey, Chickenfoot (Chapter 3), and CoScripter (Chapter 5) are client-side Firefox browser extensions that enable users to rewrite Web pages and automate browsing activities.

Greasemonkey enables the use of scripts that alter Web pages as they are loaded; users create these scripts manually, generally using JavaScript to modify the page's Document Object Model. Chickenfoot builds on Greasemonkey, contributing an informal syntax based on keyword pattern matching; the primary goal of this more flexible syntax was to enable users with less scripting knowledge to create scripts. CoScripter further lowers the threshold, bringing to the Web the approach of creating scripts by generalizing the demonstrated actions of users (an approach pioneered by EAGER (Cypher, 1991; Myers, 1993)).

Of this prior work, CoScripter and d.mix are the most similar; d.mix shares with CoScripter the use of programming-by-demonstration techniques and the social-software mechanism of sharing scripts server-side on a wiki page. There are several important ways that d.mix distinguishes itself. First, d.mix stores and executes all code on a server. In this way, d.mix takes an infrastructure service approach to support end user remixing of Web pages. This approach obviates the need for users to install any software on their client machine – the increasing use of the Web as a software platform provides evidence as to the merit of this approach. Second, d.mix generates and stores API calls as its underlying representation. Chickenfoot and CoScripter focus on automating Web browsing and rewriting Web pages using the DOM in the page source – they do not interact with Web service APIs directly. Third, CoScripter shields users from the underlying code representation. The approach used by d.mix is more akin to Web development tools, such as Adobe's Dreamweaver HTML editor,[11] which use visual representations when they are expedient yet also offer source code editing. Often, experts can perform more complex tasks by directly editing the source code; it also avoids some of the "round-trip" errors that can arise when users iteratively edit an intermediate representation.

---

[11]Adobe Dreamweaver HTML editor: http://www.adobe.com/products/dreamweaver.

Tools for end user synthesis of Web experiences

In the second category, there are several tools that lower the expertise threshold required to create Web applications that *synthesize* data from multiple pre-existing sources. Most notably, Yahoo! Pipes,[12] Kapow,[13] and Marmite (Wong & Hong, 2007) employ a data flow approach for working with Web services.

Yahoo! Pipes draws on the data flow approach manifest in Unix pipes, introducing a visual node-and-link editor for manipulating Web data sources. It focuses on visually rewriting RSS feeds. Kapow offers a desktop-based visual editing environment for creating new Web services by combining data from existing sites through API calls and screen scraping. Services are deployed on a remote "mashup server." The main difference between these systems and d.mix is that Kapow and Pipes are used to create Web services meant for programmatic consumption, not applications or pages intended directly for users.

The Marmite browser extension offers a graphical language for sequentially composing Web service data sources and transformation operations; the interaction style is somewhat modeled after Apple's Automator[14] system for scripting desktop behaviors. Marmite combines a visual dataflow language for expressing data transformations with a spreadsheet view, which shows the current data set at a given step. The user experience benefit of this linked view is an improved understanding of application behavior. Unlike d.mix, Marmite applications run client side, and cannot be shared as easily. An additional distinction is that the Marmite programming model is one of starting from a blank slate, whereas d.mix's is based on example modification. Clearly, both approaches have merit, and neither is globally optimal. A challenge of composition, as the Marmite authors note, is that users have difficulty "knowing what operation to select" – we suggest that the direct manipulation embodied in d.mix's programming-by-demonstration approach ameliorates this gulf-of-execution (Hutchins, Hollan, & Norman, 1985) challenge.

IBM's QEDWiki (now part of IBM Mashup Center)[15] uses a widget-based approach to construct Web applications in a hosted wiki environment. This approach suggests two distinct communities – those that create the widget library elements, and those that use the library elements – echoing prior work on a "tailoring culture" within Xerox Lisp Buttons (MacLean et al., 1990). QEDWiki and d.mix have a shared interest in supporting different "tiers" of development, with two important distinctions. First, d.mix does not interpose the additional abstraction of creating graphical widgets; with d.mix, users directly browse the source site as the mechanism for specifying interactive elements. Second, d.mix better preserves the underlying modifiability of remixed applications by exposing script code on demand.

Finding and appropriating documentation and code

The literature shows that programmers often create new functionality by finding an example online or in a source repository (Fairbanks, Garlan, & Scherlis, 2006; Hartmann, Doorley, & Klemmer, 2008; Kim et al., 2004) – less code is created *tabula rasa* than might be imagined. Recent research

---

[12]Yahoo! Pipes feed composition tool: http://pipes.yahoo.com.
[13]StrikeIron Kapow Web Data Services: http://strikeiron.com/kapow.
[14]Apple Automator: http://developer.apple.com/macosx/automator.html.
[15]IBM Mashup Center: http://www-01.ibm.com/software/info/mashup-center/.

has begun to more fully embrace this style of development. The Mica (Stylos & Myers, 2006) and Assieme (Hoffmann, Fogarty, & Weld, 2007) systems augment existing Web search with tools specifically designed for finding API documentation and examples. Although Mica, Assieme, and d.mix all address the information foraging issues (Pirolli & Card, 1999) involved in locating example code, their approaches are largely complementary.

Several tools have offered structured mechanisms for deeply copying content. Most related to d.mix, Citrine (Stylos, Myers, & Faulring, 2004) introduced techniques for structured copy and paste between desktop applications, including Web browsers. Citrine parses copied text, creating a structured representation that can be pasted in rich format, for example, as a contact record into Microsoft Outlook. The idea of structured copy is extended by d.mix into the domain of source code.

In other domains, Hunter Gatherer (schraefel et al., 2002) aided in copying Web content; clip, connect, clone enabled copying Web forms (Chapter 8); and WinCuts (Tan, Meyers, & Czerwinski, 2004) and Façades (Stuerzlinger, Chapuis, Phillips, & Roussel, 2006) replicate regions of desktop applications at the window management level. Broadly speaking, d.mix differs from this prior work by generating code that retrieves content from Web services rather than copying the content itself.

LIMITATIONS AND FUTURE WORK

The primary concern of this chapter is an exploration of authoring by sampling. There are security and authentication issues that a widely released tool would need to address. Most notably, the current d.mix HTTP proxy does not handle cookies of remote sites as a client browser would. This precludes sampling from the "logged-in Web" – pages that require authentication beyond basic API keys. Extending d.mix to the logged-in Web comprises two concerns: sampling from pages that require authentication to view, and then subsequently performing authenticated API calls to retrieve the content for remixed pages. To sample from logged-in pages, both client-side solutions (e.g, a browser extension that forwards a full DOM to d.mix to be rewritten) and server-side solutions (e.g., by utilizing a "headless" browser like Crowbar[16]) are possible. To perform API calls authenticated with private tokens, the private variable mechanism of CoScripter (Chapter 5) could be adapted. Implementation of private data would also require the addition of access permissions through user accounts to the d.mix wiki.

A second limitation is that using d.mix is currently limited to sites and types of content that are amenable to Web scraping. Scraping is only reliable if the site generates static HTML, as opposed to HTML with AJAX, which modifies page content dynamically based on state, or Flash, which does not offer any ability to inspect its content. In addition, the type of content that users can sample also has to be a static element of the page DOM. We have not yet researched whether a sampling approach could be used to reuse dynamic page aspects like animations or interaction patterns.

Third, d.mix makes a fundamental assumption that API and Web site mirror each other, and that the site provides good coverage of possible API calls. This is not always the case. For example, Web developers have used the Google Maps API to create more sophisticated visualizations than the Google Maps site offers. Conversely, not all content on a site may be accessible programmatically. The

---

[16]Crowbar headless browser: http://simile.mit.edu/wiki/Crowbar.

Google site offers browsing of the entire result set for a given query, whereas the current API only returns a maximum of 60 matches. A comprehensive tool should offer support both for working with content that *is* accessible through APIs and content that *is not* (Hartmann, Doorley, & Klemmer, 2008); d.mix could be combined with existing techniques for scraping by demonstration.

Lastly, while d.mix is built on wikis, a social editing technology, we have not yet evaluated how use by multiple developers would change the d.mix design experience. Prior work on desktop software customization has shown that people share their customization scripts (Mackay, 1990). It would be valuable to study code-sharing practices on the Web.

SUMMARY

We have introduced the technique of programming by a sample. The application d.mix addresses the challenge of becoming familiar with a Web service API and provides a rapid prototyping solution structured around the acts of sampling content from an API-providing Web site and then working with the sampled content in a wiki. Our system is enabled on a conceptual level by a mapping from HTML pages to the API calls that would produce similar output. It is implemented using a programmable proxy server and wiki. Together with our past work (Hartmann et al., 2006; Hartmann, Doorley, & Klemmer, 2008), we regard d.mix as a building block toward new authoring environments that facilitate prototyping of rich data and interaction models.

Acknowledgments

We thank Leith Abdulla and Michael Krieger for programming and production help, whytheluckystiff for Ruby support, and Wendy Ju for comments. This research was supported through NSF grant IIS-0534662, a Microsoft New Faculty Fellowship for Scott Klemmer, an SAP Stanford Graduate Fellowship for Björn Hartmann, and a PC donation from Intel.

D.MIX

Intended users:	All users
Domain:	Web service-backed Web sites
Description:	With d.mix, users browse annotated Web sites and select elements to sample. The sampling mechanism used by d.mix generates the underlying service calls that yield those elements. This code can be edited, executed, and shared in d.mix's wiki-based hosting environment. This sampling approach leverages pre-existing Web sites as example sets and supports fluid composition and modification of examples.
Example:	Jane would like to create a Web site for her rock climbing club, showing off pictures and videos of their trips. The content lives in service-backed Web sites. With d.mix, Jane can browse to the relevant sites, and "sample" it – sampling copies the underlying service calls that would generate this content. She can then paste this code into d.mix's wiki-based hosting environment, and use it to create a custom site.
Automation:	No, d.mix relies on Web service calls rather than automation.
Mashups:	Yes! Users of d.mix will often want to compose and integrate content from multiple sites.
Scripting:	Yes, in d.mix's active wiki, people can freely mix text, HTML, CSS, JavaScript and Ruby to create new custom sites.
Natural language:	No, sampling is accomplished through direct manipulation.
Recordability:	No, though direct manipulation is used to specify samples.
Inferencing:	No, a manually specified site-to-service map is used to infer underlying service calls.
Sharing:	Yes, the wiki-based hosting environment lets users share code; the site-to-service maps are also globally shared.
Comparison to other systems:	Like Chickenfoot and CoScripter, lowers the programming threshold by piggybacking on the existing Web. Differs in its focus on content creation rather than automation.
Platform:	Implemented in Ruby, using the MouseHole proxy.
Availability:	Contact the authors.

A world wider than the Web

End user programming across multiple domains

11

Will Haines,[1] **Melinda Gervasio,**[1] **Jim Blythe,**[2] **Kristina Lerman,**[2] **Aaron Spaulding**[1]

[1]*SRI International*
[2]*USC Information Sciences Institute*

ABSTRACT

As Web services become more diverse and powerful, end user programming (EUP) systems for the Web become increasingly compelling. However, many user workflows do not exist exclusively online. To support these workflows completely, EUP systems must allow the user to program across multiple applications in different domains. To this end, we created Integrated Task Learning (ITL), a system that integrates several learning components to learn end user workflows as user-editable executable procedures. In this chapter, we illustrate a motivating cross-domain task and describe the various learning techniques that support learning such a task with ITL. These techniques include dataflow reasoning to learn procedures from demonstration, symbolic analysis and compositional search to support procedure editing, and machine learning to infer new semantic types. Then, we describe the central engineering concept that ITL uses to facilitate cross-domain learning: pluggable domain models, which are independently generated type and action models over different application domains that can be combined to support cross-domain procedure learning. Finally, we briefly discuss some open questions that cross-domain EUP systems will need to address in the future.

A WORLD WIDER THAN THE WEB

Today's rapid proliferation of Web services has prompted an increasingly varied use of the Web to support users' everyday tasks (Cockburn & McKenzie, 2001). In the office, Web services now support many business processes: travel authorization and reimbursement, calendaring, and room reservation are just some of the processes that often rely on dedicated Web-based applications. At home, we visit a variety of Web sites to purchase books, make travel arrangements, and manage our finances. However, many user workflows, particularly in business environments, still involve non-Web applications (Dragunov et al., 2005). Even as some applications begin to transition to the Web – for example, email and calendar tools – the workflows will continue to involve multiple, disparate domains. Thus, any EUP tool, particularly those designed for the business environment, must accommodate procedures learned over a variety of applications, in Web domains and beyond.[1]

Consider Alice, who is responsible for maintaining a Web site listing all the publications by the members of a university laboratory.[2] Anyone in the lab who produces a report notifies Alice by email. The email message contains the citation for the report as well as an attached electronic version of the work. The attachment may be in a single-file format, like Word or PDF, or in a multifile format such as LaTeX. Alice saves the files, and if the paper is not already a PDF, she must convert it before renaming the file to conform to a standard naming scheme. She then uploads the PDF file using the site administrator's Web interface. This includes filling out a form with the citation information for the paper, uploading the paper, and verifying that the uploaded paper is downloadable. Finally, Alice replies to the email message, copying a direct URL link to the paper into the message for the author's benefit.

This is a task Alice repeats several dozen times a year, and she would clearly benefit by automating it. Unfortunately, since it touches several different applications, including an email client, the file system, word-processing software, PDF converters, and a Web browser, any EUP tool designed for a single application would be able to automate only part of Alice's workflow. For example, Alice could use a Web EUP system to automate the segment involving uploading the paper and citation information to the Web site. However, she must still manually process the email, perform the file operations, fill in the Web form, and reply to the email. Additional single-application EUP systems could potentially automate more segments, but they would require Alice not only to learn several different interfaces but also to manually link the data from one system to another. In contrast, an EUP tool that works across different applications could potentially automate the entire workflow, benefiting Alice much more significantly.

While cross-domain EUP would clearly be valuable here, it also presents many design and implementation challenges. There are many reasons why most EUP systems tackle a single application domain: it is much easier to engineer instrumentation and automation for a single platform, the relations between different domain actions are straightforward, and the procedures that can be learned are bounded by the single domain. Nevertheless, we argue that the benefits provided by cross-domain EUP make it well worth attempting to meet the unique challenges that such a system presents.

In this chapter, we present Integrated Task Learning (ITL), our approach for learning procedures across domains using EUP (Spaulding et al., 2009). ITL provides a suite of complementary learning and reasoning capabilities for acquiring procedures, some of which are shown in Figure 11.1. This includes inducing generalized procedures from observed demonstrations in instrumented applications, providing template-based procedure visualizations that are easily understandable to end users, and supporting procedure editing. To incorporate other domains, including Web domains, ITL also includes facilities for semantically mapping actions across domains. We begin by describing each of these capabilities in turn. Then we discuss the implications of such an approach on domain modeling, instrumentation, and automation. Finally, we present avenues for future work and conclusions.

---

[1]In this chapter, we use the terms *application* and *domain* interchangeably, with the recognition that the Web, while typically involving a single client application, encompasses a rich variety of domains.

[2]This use case was adapted from a real user workflow discovered in a contextual inquiry user study (Beyer & Holtzblatt, 1998) we conducted in 2008 to observe office workers performing potentially automatable tasks on their computers.

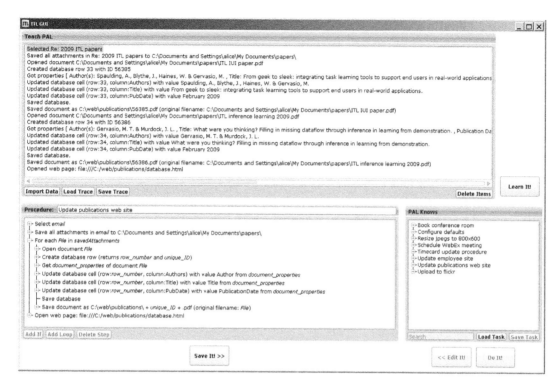

FIGURE 11.1

The ITL user interface. This interface provides a user with the ability to demonstrate (top), edit (bottom left), and execute (bottom right) procedures. Here, the demonstration trace and editor reflect a simplified version of Alice's *publications upload* procedure. The "PAL Knows" pane also displays some other tasks for which ITL already learned procedures.

LEARNING PROCEDURES FROM DEMONSTRATION

To automate her *publications upload* task with ITL, Alice uses programming by demonstration (PBD) (Cypher & Halbert, 1993; Lieberman, 2001). Alice shows the system how she performs the task, and ITL generalizes the observed actions into an automated procedure that Alice can use to perform the task in the future. Figure 11.1 shows Alice's demonstration in the "Teach PAL" panel and the procedure learned from it in the "Procedure: Update publications web site" panel. Alice's demonstration is generalized in two ways: *parameter generalization*, whereby the action arguments are variablized (e.g., *row_number* replaces *33*), and *structure generalization*, whereby control flow constructs are induced (e.g., we introduce the loop: *For each File...*). This generalization lets Alice apply the same procedure to any email message with an arbitrary number of attachments. In ITL, this PBD capability is provided by the LAPDOG component (Gervasio, Lee, & Eker, 2008; Gervasio & Murdock, 2009). We now elaborate on the learning process by which LAPDOG generalizes an observed demonstration into a procedure.

Parameter generalization

LAPDOG was designed specifically to learn *dataflow procedures*. In the dataflow paradigm, actions are characterized in terms of their inputs and outputs, and within a procedure, the outputs of actions generally serve as inputs to succeeding actions. Thus, to be executable, the inputs of every action in a dataflow procedure must be supported by previous outputs.

In the simplest case, an input is directly supported by a previous action's output or an input to the entire procedure. For example, in Alice's scenario, the email message upon which the *saveAttachments* action operates is the email message that the user passes into the procedure upon invocation. A more complex case involves inputs that are supported by elements or combinations of previous outputs. For example, in Alice's procedure, the values used for the *Authors*, *Title*, and *PubDate* fields of the database record need to be extracted from the *DocumentProperties* tuple that is the output of the *getProperties* action. Figure 11.2 graphically depicts a variety of support relationships induced by LAPDOG over Alice's demonstration.

In the direct support case (e.g., the row *378* output by *newDBEntry* serving as an input to *updateCell*) LAPDOG captures the support relationship by replacing the matching action arguments with the same variable, in this case *$row*. In the indirect support case, LAPDOG captures the support relationship by using expressions. For example, the support provided by the *Title* field of the properties tuple output by *getProperties* to the *title* input to *updateCell* is captured by using the variable *$propsTuple* for the output of *getProperties* and using the tuple access operation (*get "Title" $propsTuple*) as the input to *updateCell*.

```
saveAttachments +E123 +C:\\ -[ C:\\A.doc C:\\B.doc]
getProperties +C:\\A.doc -‹Author="John Smith" Title="EUP for
    Intranets" PubDate="July 2009"›
newDBEntry -378 -ID48392
updateCell +378 +"Paper Title" +"EUP for Intranets"
```

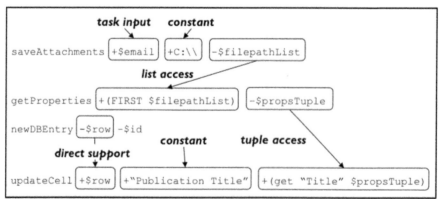

FIGURE 11.2

Examples of dataflow supports found by LAPDOG.

In general, there may be multiple possible supports for any input. LAPDOG generates them all, efficiently maintaining the alternative hypotheses in a structure that parallels the original demonstration except that every action argument is represented by its set of alternative supports. With multiple examples (i.e., demonstrations of the same procedure), LAPDOG can eliminate incorrect hypotheses. However, ITL is often used to acquire long, complex procedures for which users are unlikely to provide multiple demonstrations. To address this situation, LAPDOG employs a number of heuristics to select the best generalization given only one demonstration. This includes preferring support from action outputs to support from procedure inputs, preferring more recent supports, and preferring direct support to support through expressions. These heuristics not only make sense intuitively, but they have also proven to be appropriate in practice.

Structural generalization

The learned procedure in Figure 11.1 includes a loop over the attachments of the email message. Within the dataflow paradigm, such loops over the elements of a collection (i.e., a set or a list) are common. When the loop is over a collection that is explicitly observed in the demonstration (i.e., the collection is the output of some action), LAPDOG can use the known collection to detect loops. For example, when Alice opens the first email attachment, LAPDOG detects the start of a potential loop, by virtue of the attachment being part of a collection. When Alice opens the second email attachment, LAPDOG collects all the actions until that second attachment is opened; the collected actions form the hypothesized body of the loop. Since Alice repeats this sequence of actions for the second attachment, LAPDOG induces a loop to be performed over all the attachments of the input email message. Figure 11.3 shows the complete SPARK-L (Morley & Myers, 2004) procedure learned from the demonstration in Figure 11.1, including the induced loop.

As with parameter generalization, there may be multiple possible structural generalizations of a demonstration trace. LAPDOG creates a separate generalized program for each hypothesis and applies the heuristic of preferring the shortest program (i.e., induce loops whenever possible) to select the final generalization. In practice, this heuristic has worked well because a demonstration including actions repeated over all the objects in a collection is typically meant to process the entire collection rather than just the specific number of elements observed. LAPDOG is currently limited to inducing loops over collections of objects; it does not yet learn conditional or counting loops. However, LAPDOG is able to leverage this specific looping context to learn loops over a rich variety of collections, including loops over either ordered or unordered collections (lists or sets), loops over one or more lists in parallel, and loops that themselves accumulate the outputs of the individual iterations into lists (Eker, Lee, & Gervasio, 2009).

Learning cross-domain dataflow procedures

The dataflow paradigm adopted by ITL is a natural fit to many information-oriented domains, with most Web services and desktop applications being easily characterized in terms of their actions' inputs and outputs. This facilitates the use of ITL to learn procedures across these domains, since users can just demonstrate their procedures as they would naturally execute them and ITL can rely on the dataflow between actions and across domains to guide reasoning and learning. Since the learned procedures themselves may be characterized in terms of their inputs and outputs, demonstration and learning over learned procedures becomes a straightforward extension.

```
{defprocedure do_TASK1238608548125
 cue: [do: (TASK1238608548125 +$email_1
  -$savedAttachments_5 )]
 precondition: (True)
 body:
 [seq:
 [do: (|selectEmail| $email_1)]
 [do: (|saveAttachments| $email_1
  "C:\\Docs\\itl\\Desktop\\"
 $savedAttachments_5)]
 [forin: $X7 $savedAttachments_5
  [seq:
  [do: (|openFile| $X7)]
  [do: (|getProperties| $X7
  $document_properties_6)]
  [do: (|newDbEntry| $row_number_7
  $unique_ID_8)]
  [do: (|updateCell| $row_number_7 "Authors"
  (get "Author" $document_properties_6))]
  [do: (|updateCell| $row_number_7 "Title"
  (get "Title" $document_properties_6))]
  [do: (|updateCell| $row_number_7 "PubDate"
  (get "PublicationDate"
   $document_properties_6))]
  [do: (|saveDatabase|)]
  [do: (|saveFileAs| $X7
  "C:\\Docs\\itl\\Desktop\\"
  $unique_ID_8)]
  ] $unique_ID_8 $Generated_9
 $document_properties_6 $Generated_10
 $row_number_7 $Generated_11 ]
 [do: (|openUrl|
  "www.ai.sri.com/itl/database.html")]]
  ...
 }
```

FIGURE 11.3

The SPARK-L source for Alice's entire procedure, as learned from the demonstration in Figure 11.1.

Even engineered procedures or procedures acquired through other means potentially become available to ITL, provided they can be characterized in terms of the dataflow they support. However, this cross-domain integration through dataflow can be achieved only if there exists an appropriate mapping between the input and output types of the actions in each domain. In later sections, we discuss how we address this concern with a machine learning approach to semantic mapping as well as with the ITL framework's extensible type system.

VISUALIZING AND EDITING PROCEDURES

Once a demonstration is successfully generalized, an end user like Alice can simply execute the newly learned procedure to perform her task. However, the life cycle of a procedure rarely ends at demonstration. As conditions change, procedures may need to change as well. Thus, a complete framework for end user programming should support the viewing and editing of procedures in addition to learning from demonstration. To this end, ITL provides an editor that visualizes procedures and allows users to make a number of postdemonstration modifications.

Before Alice starts modifying her procedure, let us first consider how the hard-to-read procedural code in Figure 11.3 becomes the human-readable display that she sees in Figure 11.1. Then, we will discuss how she makes edits that will improve the procedure's generality.

Visualization using templates

Programming by demonstration aims to build general procedures out of concrete examples, and as such, it inevitably involves abstraction. For nonprogrammers, dealing with abstract procedures is difficult because end users tend to think of programs as the set of concrete actions that they experience at runtime, rather than as more general abstract control structures (Pane, Ratanamahatana, & Myers, 2001). Rode and Rosson demonstrated this difficulty in the Web domain (Rode & Rosson, 2003), and based on our deployment of ITL, we also conclude that in complex, cross-domain environments the user's need to understand abstract procedures is both vital and difficult to support.

To leverage the end user's tendency to conceive of procedures in terms of runtime actions, we can combine appropriately abstracted actions with human-readable annotations to make procedure visualizations more concrete. First, in ITL, we aim to define the domain model in terms of atomic user interactions. This level of abstraction affords a straightforward mapping from a domain action to a human-readable *displayed step* that reflects an atomic graphical user interface (GUI) interaction with the end user. ITL implements this mapping using a template approach that annotates domain actions to specify a human-readable display format as well as to create pointers to "live" application properties that must be queried at runtime to fill in missing display data. Figure 11.4 illustrates how this approach displays the *selectEmail* action when Alice replies to a publication request.

The action template indicates that when the *selectEmail* action is being rendered for the demonstration trace, it should display as "Selected" concatenated to the display value of the *email* parameter. Next, we include a template for the *Email* data type, which queries the application to find an application-specific representation – in this case, the email's subject. If the *Email* happened to be a variable, we would instead display just the variable's human-readable name.

Also important to note is the fact that this template does not present all parts of an action to the user – in particular, the output argument of the *selectEmail* action is never shown. Our research indicates that some parameters simply complicate a user's understanding of the overall procedure flow (Spaulding et al., 2009). For example, although the procedure executor might need to know a window's onscreen pixel position to execute a procedure, such information is irrelevant to most end users. As such, adding the ability to suppress parameters and even entire actions to a "details" view is another simple way to improve user comprehension of complex procedures.

For any given domain, determining exactly which actions and parameters to display and how exactly to display them is best discovered through iterative testing with end users. In our experience, every attempt to determine this information a priori has been unsuccessful, so any approach must be flexible and respond well to iterative refinement. To date, the ITL framework's action metadata approach has provided us with the necessary flexibility to craft readable procedures.

```
Raw Source:
selectEmail +email:
 [recipients:["alice@ai.sri.com"],
 sender:faculty@ai.sri.com,
 subject: "Re: 2009 ITL Papers",
 body:"...",
 attachments:[attach1]]
-emailID:12345
```

Action Template:
```
selectEmail := if for trace
 then Selected "$email"
 else Select "$email"
```

Apply Action Template:
```
Selected
 "[recipients:["alice@ai.sri.com"],
 sender:faculty@ai.sri.com,
 subject: "Re: 2009 ITL Papers",
 body:"...",
 attachments:[attach1]]"
```

Data Type Template:
```
Email := $Email.subject
```

Apply Data Type Template:
```
Selected "Re: 2009 ITL Papers"
```

FIGURE 11.4

Action template application – before and after.

Typed dataflow and editing

Given an understandable representation of their procedures, users want to make changes that span a range of complexity – from simple edits, like changing constant parameters in steps, to complex modifications, like adding conditionals and iterative loops. Simple edits may be required when the task to be performed by an existing procedure changes slightly or to correct an initial hypothesis from another learning component. Further, support for multiple domains increases the chance that users will also need to add new steps to procedures, modify step ordering, or change the structure of the procedure. This occurs because some domains are less reliant on a graphical interface where demonstration-based techniques are natural. In these nongraphical domains, users may want to supplement demonstration by instead choosing available actions from a menu, or describing them and composing within an editor.

In the dataflow-oriented model, full user support for editing poses many of the same challenges faced by demonstration-based learning. For example, users may insert an action but omit auxiliary steps or queries that provide inputs for that action. In a dataflow model, those missing steps must themselves make use of inputs that are established earlier in the procedure. The use of typing in the domain specification allows one to frame the problem of inferring missing steps as compositional search over a graph of data types in which queries or steps are composed to form a path from existing inputs to those that are needed.

An editing tool for a typed dataflow model should provide several complementary kinds of support. First, it should allow users to perform edits, not only to add or delete steps, but also to add conditions or loops by suggesting candidates based on queries and lists that are available. Another desirable characteristic is to allow users to copy steps between procedures, facilitating best practices, while using the dataflow model to ensure that the resulting procedure is executable. Finally, it should warn the user if the newly edited procedure is missing critical inputs or otherwise has potential flaws, and it should use dataflow information to suggest potential fixes.

In ITL, the Tailor component supports the procedure editing capabilities (Blythe, 2005; Spaulding et al., 2009) of the user interface. Tailor allows users to add or delete steps, add conditions and iterative loops, and copy steps between procedures. It searches over possible queries and actions arranged in the same space to find plausible missing steps, composing steps and queries if needed.

Tailor uses compositional search over a graph of data types to infer missing steps or queries when users add steps. For example, rather than demonstrate a new step, Alice can ask the editor to add a step that she describes as "copy project leader." Using the templates described above, Tailor can match this description to the *addCC* action, which requires a recipient. By searching from known inputs, Tailor can identify "leader of project that funds the work" as the most plausible match. Building procedures by demonstration and description can both be ambiguous individually, but they complement each other well because they do not cause the same ambiguities.

Support for copying steps between procedures

Description is a powerful technique for editing; however, our research indicates that users find the process of describing a brand new step difficult and do not perform it often, preferring instead to copy or move steps from a library of available actions (Spaulding et al., 2009). Suppose Alice demonstrated her procedure on PDF documents and now wishes to handle Word documents as well, by first converting them to PDF. Instead of demonstrating a new procedure, Alice can utilize another previously learned procedure that converts a Word file into PDF by copying over the relevant steps. Tailor supports this by changing the arguments of the copied command to refer to each email attachment, after searching for plausible matches.

By copying all or part of a procedure, as illustrated in Figure 11.5, users can reuse long demonstrations or complex constructs, such as conditions and loops. The procedures learned in ITL use no global variables, so the variables in the steps that are copied must be replaced by terms in the target procedure, either by (1) changing them to an existing variable, (2) changing them to a constant, or (3) adding auxiliary steps to establish a new variable. The same search technique used to recognize new steps supports a wide range of other activities, including copying steps, generating potential fixes for flaws, and adding conditions or loops. Tailor finds potential replacements of all three kinds using its compositional search method (Blythe & Russ, 2008). The search naturally prefers to use an existing variable or constant for each copied variable, because it leads to a shorter solution. In ITL, we extended this capability to enable copying sequences of steps, by composing the variable mappings of the component steps. We also added domain-specific heuristics that replace variables with constants when the intended value is known.

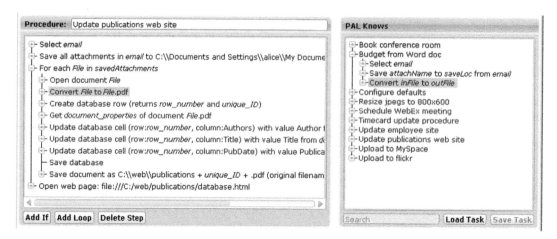

FIGURE 11.5

Alice copies the step to convert a file to PDF by dragging it from another procedure for which it was demonstrated (right side) to the active procedure (left side). The editor suggests the objects in the new procedure to which the step applies.

Support for adding conditions and loops

Alice's newly modified procedure is syntactically correct, but it will attempt to convert every attachment into PDF, whether or not it is a Word document. To have the `convertFileType` step be applied only to Word documents, Alice needs to make this step conditional on the file's extension. As with creating steps, we have found that users prefer to select an appropriate condition from a list of alternatives rather than to supply a description of the condition. The ITL editing interface allows the user to select a set of steps to put into a loop or condition, without providing any initial information about the loop or condition itself. This simplifies the interface and reduces the cognitive burden on the user, who may find it difficult to describe a conditional or loop without assistance.

Tailor again uses compositional search and heuristics to generate a set of reasonable candidate specifications. Once it generates a set of candidates for a new action, condition, loop, or change to a parameter value, the interface can present them as options. Here it is critical that the user can understand both the current procedure and the available alternatives in order to make a reasoned choice. The alternatives are displayed within the procedure visualization described above and use templates to provide a uniform view. By presenting the user with appropriate bounds, the editor makes it easier to create complex control structures and limits the user's capacity to make errors.

In our example, Alice selects the step that converts Word to PDF and clicks "Add If" to add a condition around it. As shown in Figure 11.6, Tailor searches for plausible conditions, preferring those that use objects referenced in or just before the step to be made conditional. Depending on the known properties and actions, it may suggest conditions involving the document's type, author, age, or size as well as conditions on the conference or journal. Alice chooses `"file extension = .doc"` to make the action conditional. Tailor also adds the step to retrieve the file's extension.

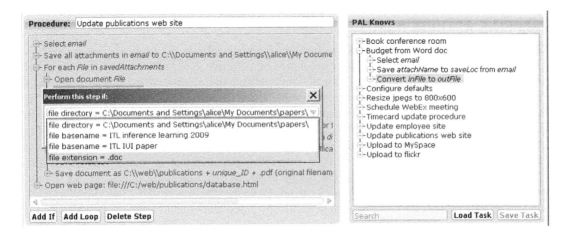

FIGURE 11.6

Alice chooses from a set of conditions to place on *convertFileType*, to make it be applied only to Word documents.

Support for editing errors or flaws

Users often make errors when editing procedures, despite help from structured editors. After the user makes a modification, Tailor checks the procedure for simple errors, such as a step that has been deleted even though it produced a value that was needed later in the procedure (Blythe, 2005). To make this check, Tailor performs a symbolic analysis of the procedure, aiming to find important errors before the procedure is executed. This means that it does not know, for example, which of several conditional branches may be taken during execution or how and when a loop will terminate. ITL's execution engine is also capable of interleaving many concurrent actions, and this means that one cannot prove that global variables will be unavailable when a step is to be run (Morley & Myers, 2004). Because of this, Tailor provides a warning for an unbound global variable only at the time that a modification removes or reorders a step or query that provides a value.

For each warning, Tailor uses templates to provide a set of potential fixes that may include reordering steps, removing them, or undoing the user's last edit. In some cases, modifications requiring several coordinated edits can be made by picking one edit and choosing the appropriate recovery steps. Further, Tailor can use compositional search to suggest steps that may be added to provide missing inputs.

For example, if the `convertFileType` action that Alice made conditional creates a PDF file as output and that output is used outside the scope of the conditional, she will see a warning that the PDF file does not exist unless the input document has the extension ".doc". Tailor can help Alice fix this potential error by making the later actions also be conditional on the PDF file's existence. We are currently investigating how best to help users add steps along alternative branches of a condition, for example, to warn the user if the procedure is unable to produce a PDF file.

MAPPING ACTIONS ACROSS DOMAINS

Online data sources, such as Web services, could be incorporated into ITL by direct instrumentation. However, in many cases, it may be easier and more cost-effective to instead generate special purpose information extractors over these data sources.[3] For our example, suppose Alice also wishes to automate her task of compiling all the papers published by the members of a particular project. In ITL, Alice can teach ITL one procedure for extracting the names of the members of the project from the project Web page, another for extracting all the papers from the publications Web page, and then create a conditional to output only the publications authored by project members. Key to this is the ability to extract structured information from Web pages – that is, names and publication information – and to be able to map the names extracted from the project page to the authors extracted from the publications page in order to complete the dataflow. In ITL, this ability to translate online data sources into actions with semantically typed inputs and outputs is provided by the PrimTL component, which automatically creates semantic definitions for data contained in online data sources, which can then be interpreted and executed by ITL.

Semantic mapping with PrimTL

The Semantic Mapper in PrimTL uses machine learning techniques to leverage existing knowledge in order to semantically type data from new sources. The learner relies on background knowledge captured in the domain model, in particular the set of known semantic types, such as *PersonName* and *Year*, that can be used to describe the inputs and outputs of actions. We assume that the learner can populate the domain model with examples of each type by querying known data sources.

The data returned by online sources usually has some structure or format. PrimTL learns this structure and uses it to recognize new instances of the same semantic type. What makes this problem difficult is the wide variety of formats that represent the same semantic type and inconsistent use of a format within a given source. Similar to other data validating approaches, such as Topes (Scaffidi, Myers, & Shaw, 2008), PrimTL uses a domain-independent data representation language to model the structure of data as a sequence of tokens or token types (Lerman, Minton, & Knoblock, 2003). Tokens are strings generated from an alphabet containing different syntactic types (e.g., alphabetic, numeric), which the tokens inherit. The symbolic representation of data as a sequence of tokens and syntactic token types is concise and flexible, and we can easily extend it by adding new semantic or syntactic types as needed.

PrimTL can efficiently learn data structure from examples of the data type. Consider the list in Figure 11.7, which gives examples of semantic types *PersonName* and *PhoneNumber*. PrimTL will learn that the set of examples for *PersonName* is described well by patterns "Caps Caps" (two capitalized words) and "Caps 1Upper. Caps" (capitalized word, followed by an initial, period, and another capitalized word). Similarly, PrimTL will learn a description of the semantic type *PhoneNumber* that consists of patterns "(650) 859 - Number", "(310) 448 - Number", as well as the more general "(Number) Number - Number".

---

[3]See also Chapter 8 (Intel Mash Maker) for another take on this approach.

The learned patterns can be used to recognize new instances of the same type by evaluating how well the patterns describe them (Blythe, Kapoor, Knoblock, Lerman, & Minton, 2008). PrimTL allows the user to specify the data she wants to extract from a Web source, and then it uses its learned patterns to map the extracted data to known semantic data types. In Alice's *publications upload* task, the member names extracted from the project Web page and the authors extracted from the publications page are mapped into compatible semantic types, allowing the former to be compared against the latter when filtering the publications.

By semantically typing the inputs and outputs of Web sources, PrimTL creates well-defined actions for ITL, allowing a wider variety of online data sources to be used in procedures acquired by demonstration or editing. While mashup tools such as Yahoo! Pipes allow users to combine sources, our approach is more general: using PrimTL, users can demonstrate and edit procedures that incorporate live data and use it in conditions and loops.

(a) **PersonName**	(b) **PhoneNumber**
Melinda T. Gervasio	(650) 859-4411
Will D. Haines	(650) 859-6153
Aaron Spaulding	(650) 859-3911
Jim Blythe	(310) 448-8788
Kristina Lerman	(310) 448-8714

FIGURE 11.7

Some examples for learning the semantic types *PersonName* and *PhoneNumber*.

CREATING PLUGGABLE DOMAIN MODELS

The previous sections describe a number of complementary techniques that ITL uses to learn procedures across multiple domains. To accomplish this learning, ITL must encode the domain knowledge that supports reasoning across different applications. By engineering this knowledge appropriately, one can make it much easier for a suite of learning components to interact and support the full life cycle of procedure creation, editing, and execution.

Our earliest domain modeling approach, realized in the CALO cognitive desktop assistant, was to commit to a master shared ontology of all the objects and relations in the desktop world and also all the actions or tasks involving them (Chaudhri et al., 2006). Such an approach is very powerful, supporting deep reasoning over tasks spanning different applications (Gervasio & Murdock, 2009). However, this power comes at a very high engineering and maintenance cost. Knowledge engineers must develop an all-encompassing ontology, and as such any changes to the ontology must be carefully vetted to avoid unintended consequences and significant re-engineering. In a large, distributed EUP system comprising applications that are only loosely, if at all, connected, these concerns present an unacceptable cost. For ITL, we instead decided to use an extensible architecture that models each domain as a separate, pluggable module. Here, we discuss the issues that arise when specifying such domain models, and we suggest some guidelines for their development.

Action-oriented domain model

EUP is concerned primarily with automating user workflows, so the domain actions must be a primary focus of modeling. Recall that ITL uses a dataflow model of actions, wherein each action is a named operation with a set of typed input and output parameters such that, in a procedure, outputs of actions serve as inputs to succeeding actions. Notationally, we represent an action as *name [parameters]* where parameters are of the form +/−*paramName:paramType*, with "+" indicating an input and "−" indicating an output.

Let us consider some of the actions necessary to learn Alice's task with ITL. To model her workflow, we need to select an email and save its attachments in an email client. We need to open files, look at their properties, and possibly convert types in a document viewer like Word or Acrobat. In a database application, we need to add rows and update cells. Finally, we need to open a Web page in the browser to verify that everything worked correctly. Figure 11.8 shows these dataflow actions in pseudo code.

In ITL, we allow each application to specify its set of actions in its own module. Thus, for the Alice scenario, we end up working with an action model composed of four modules, one for each application domain. Application developers can create and modify each module individually without breaking the others. Note, however, that several of the modules have data types in common; we discuss this issue in more detail in the section entitled Extensible Type System.

Modeling human-level actions

Key to successful procedure representation and learning is to capture actions at the right level of granularity, as this has a big impact on learning. Based on our experience, we believe that actions should be modeled at the level at which humans would typically describe their own actions and should expose the objects that humans would find relevant to the actions as arguments (Spaulding et al., 2009). For example, in an email application, it is preferable to model the actions *selectEmail* and *saveEmailAttachment* rather than low-level actions like *moveMouse* and *rightClick*, or high-level actions like *replyToFaculty*.

Capturing actions at a low level generally results in more compact action models, which simplify instrumentation. However, low-level actions result in incomprehensible learned procedures, for example, a procedure composed entirely of mouse drags and clicks (Spaulding et al., 2009). Such procedures are difficult to learn and nearly impossible for end users to read or edit. On the other hand, capturing actions at too high a level often imposes an impractical reasoning burden on the instrumentation to divine the user's intent from what can actually be observed. Further, it is difficult for users to manipulate such high-level actions when editing because they cannot break them down into smaller units should they want to realign them.

When one models actions that match how users think of themselves interacting with applications, one is more likely to strike the right balance between the cost of instrumentation and

```
Email:
selectEmail +email:Email -emailID:Int
saveAttachments +email:Email
       +saveDirectory:Path
       -attachments:list<File>

Document Viewer:
openFile +file:File
getProperties +file:File
       -props:map<string,string>
convertFileType +file:File +type:string
       -converted:File

Database:
newDBEntry -rowID:int -uniqueID:int
updateCell +rowID:int +cellID:string
       newCellValue:string

Browser:
openURL +url:URL
```

FIGURE 11.8

Examples of dataflow actions.

user comprehension of procedures. Such comprehension is an essential prerequisite to creating systems that allow users to later modify and debug their procedures (Spaulding et al., 2009).

Beyond actions: Modeling objects and relations

While an action-oriented domain model presents a number of advantages for a cross-domain EUP system, actions often do not capture the full scope of information in the world. As such, supplemental modeling of the objects in a domain and the relations between them can often simplify action modeling while also improving our ability to learn and reason over procedures. For example, suppose that Alice sends the email confirming an uploaded publication not only to the paper's authors but also to their supervisors. Without knowledge of the relation "X supervises Y," a learner cannot capture this requirement in a procedure. Relations and properties are also needed for the tests that decide control flow in conditional branches.

Referring explicitly to properties and relations of objects does require additional mechanisms to be defined to support querying for object properties or relations when a procedure is executed. Compared with an alternative approach that represents each object as a static tuple of its properties, this approach provides two distinct advantages. First, the properties themselves may be most natural for users to view and edit in the domain application's interface, which necessitates that the system can query that application to pick up changes. Second, the object properties may be *live*, that is, they may change concurrently within the domain application. Live data could invalidate a tuple representation, which is simply a snapshot of the value at a given time. In short, explicit references can be useful anywhere one wants a pointer rather than a copy.

Extensible type system

Recall that we define an action in ITL as taking a set of *typed* inputs and outputs. These types are used to allow the learners to make reasonable comparisons and substitutions between actions operating on compatible types of data. Figure 11.9 shows a variety of types, ranging from simple primitives such as *string* to more complex types such as *Email*.

As with actions, it is preferable to allow application domain models to specify arbitrary types. However, since the type system is critical to capturing dataflow across applications, it is important that types be compatible across applications. For example, in Alice's procedure, the email client provides the `File` used by the document viewer, so they must have compatible representations.

We can achieve this agreement either by having the two domains use the same name for these object types, or by providing a central module that asserts the equivalence of the types. Providing shared type names or conversions does not in itself solve the problem of bridging information across multiple domains by matching types. This problem is similar to the ontology alignment or database integration problems (Euzenat & Valtchev, 2004; Parent & Spaccapietra, 1998). Although there are a number of sophisticated approaches, our general strategy in ITL is to maintain a lightweight central type system that is relatively easy for

```
Named EmailAddress string

Object Email:
  List<EmailAddress> recipients
  EmailAddress sender
  string subject
  string body
  List<File> attachments
```

FIGURE 11.9

Building the `EmailAddress` and `Email` types.

domain model developers to align to, and to rely on PrimTL to automatically align types into our system (Lerman, Plangprasopchock, & Knoblock, 2007).

A lightweight type system allows for easier type alignment; however, it is also useful to allow domain developers to create arbitrarily complex types to support their domain models. To accommodate increased expressiveness while maintaining ease of alignment, ITL implements a hierarchical type system that lets application domain models build up *complex data types* from *primitive data types* (Spaulding et al., 2009). For example, consider the complex *Email* type used in Alice's procedure as depicted in Figure 11.9.

Complex types are built by aggregating string, integer, float, Boolean, and named primitives into lists or tuples. Lists are ordered groups of identically typed parameters, such as the list of email attachments. Tuples are records of typed fields used to represent complex domain objects, such as *Email* above. Named types are structurally represented by another type but are not considered equivalent to that type. For example, *EmailAddress* is represented by a string but should not be considered equivalent to an arbitrary string. This representational scheme allows one to build arbitrarily complex data types while still supporting reasoning over the simpler primitive components (Chaudhri et al., 2006).

OPEN QUESTIONS IN CROSS-DOMAIN END USER PROGRAMMING

Cross-domain EUP is a powerful approach that enables users to extend automation beyond the Web and into the rich desktop applications that pervade so much of our everyday lives. In this chapter, we presented Integrated Task Learning, our approach to cross-domain EUP. Clearly, there are both significant benefits and considerable costs associated with an extensible cross-domain EUP system such as ITL, and in this chapter we explored in detail some of these issues. However, there remain a number of other challenges and avenues for future work.

Interleaved demonstration and editing

EUP in ITL currently primarily involves learning from demonstration, with procedure editing occurring as a postprocessing stage, and data source integration happening orthogonally. However, EUP workflows may not always unfold this way. Consider the case where the user already has a library of smaller procedures that can be composed into what she wants. It may be more natural for the user to use direct manipulation to first construct the procedure, and then to use demonstration to fill in any remaining gaps, including gaps requiring the integration of new data sources. More generally, users will likely want to be able to switch seamlessly back and forth between demonstration and editing as circumstances dictate. Supporting such programming workflows would greatly enhance the usability of an EUP system.

Mixed-initiative learning

Learning in ITL is currently heavily user driven, with the user indicating when to learn from a demonstration and how to correct a learned procedure. Though ITL supports the user by suggesting the most likely generalizations and modifications and by ensuring that no errors are introduced during editing, the user is still ultimately in control of the learning process. There are often situations, however, where ITL could learn more efficiently if it could sometimes ask the user for additional guidance. There may also be cases where offline reasoning suggests procedure merges, subtask extraction, and other refactoring to improve procedure understandability and performance. Unsupervised learning techniques may even be applicable for automatically acquiring procedures based on repeated patterns in a user's activities. By allowing ITL some of the initiative in the learning process, we could potentially learn a larger, more effective set of procedures.

Procedure sharing

In addition to supporting the reuse of one's own procedures, an EUP system should support procedure reuse across users. Given that making procedures understandable to the author is already difficult, making them understandable to others is even more challenging. This problem is compounded when there is a wide range in the computational literacy of the user population. Advanced users may be comfortable with complex structures, such as conditionals and iteration, but these may confuse novice users. A simple approach that we have explored is to allow users to explicitly define arbitrary sections within a procedure and to enter descriptions summarizing the procedure and individual steps. Similar to comments in code, this metadata can help users understand and evaluate shared procedures; however, they will be useful only if users feel motivated to add them to their procedures. Automated reasoning and learning approaches, in combination with recent work on leveraging social annotations, may lead to more powerful approaches to procedure sharing.

Another issue that arises with shared procedures is that a given procedure may contain certain types of personal data, such as names, email and mailing addresses, passwords, and credit card information. These types of information will need to be identified and hidden to protect the original author and to be personalized for new users. A possible approach is to use the notion of a personal data store for these data types, as CoScripter does (Leshed et al., 2008), and use semantic mapping capabilities, such as those provided by PrimTL, to find appropriate instantiations for new users.

Consistency in a heterogeneous environment

A widely recognized interface design principle, consistency (Nielsen & Molich, 1990), is difficult enough to achieve in an unregulated environment like the Web. When attempting to integrate Web applications with desktop applications, achieving consistency becomes even more challenging. One option is to return to the native application to edit procedure parameters. Although this leverages users' familiarity with that application and makes sense for certain dialogs (such as *Save As* options), it is problematic for other operations like defining loops. A second option, managing editing operations entirely within the EUP tool, raises new questions. Should the EUP system follow platform conventions, Web standards, or some other standard entirely? An extensible visualization system like the one in ITL should allow us to test various approaches with end users, but there are currently no clear answers.

SUMMARY

Our Integrated Task Learning system for cross-domain EUP supports programming by demonstration, editing by direct manipulation, and online data source integration. It leverages a variety of artificial intelligence techniques, including structure induction, compositional search, knowledge base inference, and pattern recognition to facilitate these EUP approaches. To support this variety of algorithms, ITL learns dataflow models using a centralized action-oriented domain model and a lightweight, extensible type system. This design streamlines instrumentation and automation while allowing diverse methods for learning, reasoning over, and visualizing cross-domain procedures. In short, ITL demonstrates that by modeling the world around us in a modular, extensible fashion, one can facilitate learning and expand the scope of end user workflow automation to the Web and beyond.

Acknowledgments

We thank Tom Lee, Steven Eker, and Janet Murdock for helping conceptualize and realize LAPDOG; Vijay Jaswal for working out the type system engineering details that hold the ITL system together; and the various other members of the ITL team for helping to bring Integrated Task Learning to life.

This material is based upon work supported by the Defense Advanced Research Projects Agency (DARPA) under Contract No. FA8750-07-D-0185/0004. Any opinions, findings, and conclusions or recommendations expressed in this material are those of the author(s) and do not necessarily reflect the views of DARPA or the Air Force Research Laboratory (AFRL).

ITL

Intended users:	All users
Domain:	All domains, including non-Web applications.
Description:	ITL learns procedures across multiple instrumented applications. It relies on programming by demonstration, editing by instruction, direct manipulation, and semantic type learning to bridge actions across different applications. Learned procedures are presented to the user in a human-readable format.
Example:	Imagine a user who maintains a publications Web site. After receiving email from a group member containing one or more publications, she can teach ITL to save the attachment(s), convert them to PDF if necessary, add entries into a publications database, copy citation information from the documents, and upload them to a Web site.
Automation:	Yes, ITL can automate both simple and complex tasks.
Mashups:	Yes, ITL is designed to combine information and coordinate tasks across many applications, not just Web browsers.
Scripting:	Yes, ITL includes a procedure visualization and editing component that provides intelligent assistance.
Natural language:	No, though this will be explored in future work.
Recordability:	Yes.
Inferencing:	Yes, heuristics are used to infer connections between steps, and to suggest edits and fixes to procedures.
Sharing:	No. Users in some domains have shared libraries of procedures, but a general facility for sharing is not yet completed.
Comparison to other systems:	ITL's primary contribution is its ability to learn procedures incorporating other applications along with Web-based domains. While the core ideas are similar to Intel Mash Maker and other mashup systems, its type inference to support this capability is unique, as are its editing and correction assistance.
Platform:	ITL is a standalone application that runs on Windows, Mac, and Linux. Target domains/applications must be instrumented.
Availability:	Not publicly available. Contact the authors for research use.

Visualization and Exploration

4

The systems in this section focus on enabling rich visualization and exploration of the data that lives on Web pages. The Web Summaries system lets users semiautomatically collect and organize data from multiple Web pages using personalized cards and task-oriented search templates. The Zoetrope system provides an interface for exploring Web data over time through interactive lenses that can be placed directly on Web pages and combined to answer specific questions, such as how weather affects traffic. The RecipeSheet system extends the C3W system described in the previous section to provide parallel exploration of alternative scenarios. This ability is especially important when the user is looking for a collection of items and wants to change a parameter that affects all scenarios.

From Web Summaries to search templates

Automation for personal tasks on the Web

12

Mira Dontcheva,[1] **Steven M. Drucker,**[2] **David Salesin,**[1,3] **Michael F. Cohen**[2]

[1]*Adobe Systems*
[2]*Microsoft Research*
[3]*University of Washington*

ABSTRACT

This chapter describes the Web Summaries system, which is designed to aid people in accomplishing exploratory Web research. Web Summaries enables users to produce automation artifacts, such as extraction patterns, relations, and personalized task-specific search templates, in the context of existing tasks. By leveraging the growing amount of structured Web pages and pervasive search capabilities Web Summaries provides a set of semiautomatic interaction techniques for collecting and organizing personal Web content.

INTRODUCTION

As the amount of content delivered over the World Wide Web grows, so does the consumption of information. And although advancements in search technologies have made it much easier to find information on the Web, users often browse the Web with a particular task in mind, such as arranging travel plans, making purchases, or learning about a new topic. When users have a task in mind, they are often concerned not only with finding but also with collecting, organizing, and sharing information. This type of browsing, which we call *exploratory Web research*, typically lasts a long time, may span several sessions, involves gathering large amounts of heterogeneous content, and can be difficult to organize ahead of time, as the categories emerge through the tasks themselves (Sellen, Murphy, & Shaw, 2002). Current practices for collecting and organizing Web content such as using bookmarks or tabs, collecting content in documents, storing pages locally, or printing them out (Jones, Bruce, & Dumais, 2002) require a great deal of overhead, as pages must be saved manually and organized into folders, which distracts from the real task of analyzing the content and making decisions.

In our work we break out of the Web page paradigm and consider the individual pieces of content inside of the Web page to be the basic unit that must be collected, as it is the information inside the

Web page that is of most importance. If the goal is to let people more easily accomplish their information tasks, then tools must support the manipulation of information, not Web pages.

There are a few examples of systems that give users access over the content inside of a Web page, such as Hunter Gatherer (schraefel et al., 2002), Internet Scrapbook (Sugiura & Koseki, 1998), and C3W (Chapter 8), but it is the Semantic Web that promises to truly transform the way people manipulate information. Unfortunately, the Semantic Web remains unrealized largely because it requires a large collaborative effort in defining an appropriate data representation and adopting that representation. Content providers are not yet willing to invest in embedding semantic information into the existing Web and coordinating their efforts with others.

We take advantage of three trends in the World Wide Web – the growing number of structured Web pages, the vast rise in online collaboration, and pervasive search technologies – and present a new approach for collecting and organizing Web content in a set of semiautomatic interaction techniques and algorithms that allow people to not only collect and organize Web content more quickly and easily but also enable them to build a form of the Semantic Web as they accomplish their own tasks.

OVERVIEW

Our goal in the design of the Web Summaries system was to make the process of collecting information as easy as possible and thereby allow the user to focus on the task at hand rather than worry about organizing and keeping track of content. Because we wanted to aid users through automation while still supporting existing habits, we implemented Web Summaries as an extension to the Firefox Web browser and presented it to the user through a toolbar (see Figure 12.1), which provides Web page clipping functionality, and a summary window (see Figure 12.2), which presents Web clippings through predefined or user-generated layout templates. When users find a Web page they want to save to their summary, they can clip content by interactively selecting parts of the Web page. For each set of user clippings, the system creates *extraction patterns*. These extraction patterns encode the information the user clipped in the context of the Web page structure. Since many Web sites today present content using templates, we can use structural patterns to automatically extract corresponding information from Web pages that use the same template. For example, clipping information about one hotel allows the user to automatically clip information about other

FIGURE 12.1

Web Summaries offers semiautomatic gathering of Web content through a browser toolbar.

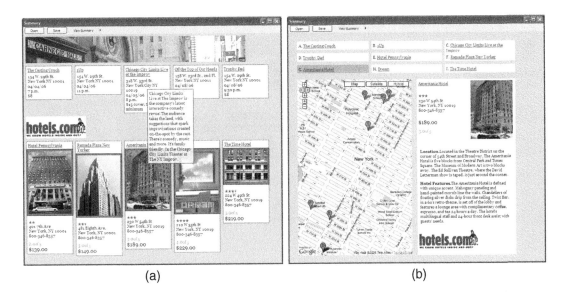

(a)   (b)

FIGURE 12.2

(a) The grid layout template places all the content on a grid and groups the content by Web site. (b) With the map layout template, the user can view the collected content with respect to a geographical map. This template presents only content that includes an address.

hotels from the same Web site. If the user goes to a new Web site or finds Web pages that are presented with a different Web page structure, he must manually select the content of interest. However, once an extraction pattern is created, it is stored and can be reused each time the user returns to gather information from the Web site.

Web Summaries also allows users to automatically gather related information from multiple Web sites. For example, a user can collect information about a restaurant and Web Summaries will automatically retrieve reviews from a favorite review Web site or bus routes from a local transportation Web site. In order to automatically collect related information, the system requires extraction patterns for those Web sites and user-defined *relations* that describe how the information on the different Web sites is associated. We describe the algorithm for retrieving related information in detail in the next section on "Gathering content semiautomatically".

Finally, Web Summaries introduces personalized *search templates*, which combine user-defined extraction patterns, relations, and layouts with a query interface. With search templates users can retrieve search results that include information from multiple Web sites and are formatted according to the user's preferences (see Figures 12.3 and 12.6).

SYSTEM DESIGN

The Web Summaries system includes five components: an extraction pattern repository that includes user-specified extraction patterns and relations; a data repository that holds the content collections;

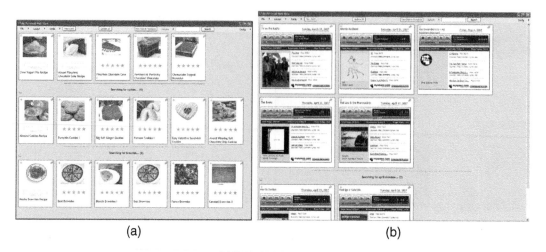

(a)   (b)

FIGURE 12.3

(a) With the recipe search template, the user collects recipes from cooking.com and allrecipes.com. Here the user has already collected five cards (shown in the first row) and has made two queries, one for "cookies" and another for "brownies." The system automatically gathers, extracts, and displays relevant recipes. The user can drag any search result into his collection. (b) The user relates upcoming.org to myspace.com to automatically collect music samples for upcoming shows.

predefined layout templates and user-defined cards that compose the summary views; and a set of search templates that combine various extraction patterns, relations, and cards and allow users to retrieve information from multiple Web sites simultaneously and compose it in a personalized way. Figure 12.4 provides a visual description.

Gathering content semiautomatically

The Web Summaries clipping interface uses the Document Object Model (DOM) structure as a mechanism for selecting content. When the user initiates the clipping mode through the toolbar, the typical behavior of the Web page is frozen, and the browser mouse event handlers are extended to allow the user to select pieces of the DOM hierarchy. As the user moves the cursor and clicks, the DOM nodes directly underneath the cursor are highlighted. Once the user has selected a set of nodes, the system generates an extraction rule for each selected node. The *extraction rule* consists of the selected node, the path from the root of the document to the selected node, and the user-assigned label. Web Summaries provides a set of common labels, however users can define their own personalized tags. The path in the extraction rule enables finding analogous elements in documents with similar structure. Structural extraction rules are also known as XPATH queries. The extraction rules rely on consistent structure. Thus, if the structure changes, the user will have to go back and respecify extraction rules. Gibson et al. (Gibson, Punera, & Tomkins, 2005) show that template material changes every 2 to 3 months; however, they give few details on the types of changes. To evaluate the

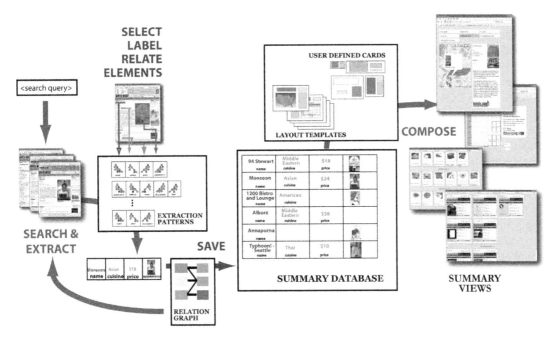

FIGURE 12.4

The user-selected page elements define extraction patterns that are stored in the extraction pattern repository. Every new page the user visits is compared with the patterns, and if matching page elements are found, the user can add them to the summary database. The layout templates filter the database and compose summary views. The user can view the database contents at any time with any view.

performance of structural extraction patterns over time, we conducted a 5-month study of Web page changes. Please see Dontcheva et al. (2007a) for details.

In addition to the *structural* extraction rules just described, the system also provides content-based rules. *Content-based extraction rules* collect content from new Web pages by matching text patterns instead of structural patterns. To specify a content-based rule, the user selects an element and labels it not with a keyword, as he does with the structural rules, but with text from the selected element that should be matched in analogous elements. For example, to only collect articles by author "John", the user selects an article and its author, chooses "semantic rule" from the right-button context menu, and types "John". A content-based rule first tries to find matching content using the structural path, but if it is not successful, the rule searches the entire document. It finds matching content only if the node types match. For example, if the rule finds the word "John" in a `<table>` node and the selected node defining the rule is in a `<p>` node, the rule will fail. This limits the number of spurious matches and ensures consistency in the gathered content. The effectiveness and power of content-based rules, when possible, was shown by Bolin et al. in Chickenfoot (Chapter 3).

The user may specify any number of extraction rules for a given page. Because those rules should always be applied together, the system collects the extraction rules into *extraction patterns* and then stores them in the extraction pattern repository (see Figure 12.4). An extraction pattern can include any number of extraction rules and can be edited by the user to add or remove rules. For example, the user might care about the name, hours, and address of a restaurant. The system creates an extraction rule for each of these elements and then groups them together so that for any new restaurant page, it searches for all page elements in concert.

When the user visits a Web page, each available extraction pattern for that Web domain is compared with the DOM hierarchy, and the pattern with the highest number of matching rules is selected as the matching pattern. If the user chooses to store the matched content, the Web page is stored locally, and the elements found by the matching pattern are added to the summary database (see Figure 12.4). The user can select hyperlinks and collect content from multiple pages simultaneously. The system loads the linked pages in a browser not visible to the user, compares the pages with the extraction patterns, and adds all matching elements to the database. If an extraction pattern does not match fully, it may be because some of the content is absent from the page, or because the structure of the page is slightly different. In these cases, the user can augment the extraction pattern by selecting additional elements from a page that includes the new content.

Although the growing use of Web page layout templates for formatting and organizing content on the Web makes it possible to automate collecting information from the Web, this automation comes at a cost. The automatic extraction is sensitive to the structure of HTML documents and depends on a sensible organization to enable clipping of elements of interest. If the structure does not include nodes for individual elements, the user is forced to select and include more content than necessary. On the other hand, if the structure is too fine, the user must select multiple elements, adding overhead to the clipping process. Most Web sites that do use templates tend to use those with good structure, because good structure makes it easier to automate Web page authoring.

To collect content from multiple Web sites automatically, the user must first specify the relationship between the Web sites by drawing a line in the summary connecting the page elements that are similar (see Figure 12.5). We represent this relationship as a relation and define a *relation* as a directed connection from tag_i from website$_A$ to tag_j from website$_B$. For example, when the user

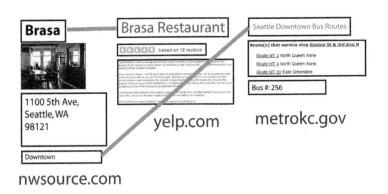

FIGURE 12.5

To create relationships between Web sites, the user can draw links between similar page elements.

draws a line between the names of the restaurants, he creates a relation from the "name" tag on Northwest Source to the "name" tag on Yelp. When the user connects restaurants and buses, he creates a relation from the "area" tag to the "route" tag. All relations are stored in the data repository and are available to the user at any time. Web page elements that are associated through relations form a relation graph.

When the user collects content from a new Web page, the system checks for relations that connect any of the collected Web page elements to other Web sites. When such relations exist, the system uses them to generate new search queries and limits the search results to the Web site specified in the relation. For example, when the user collects information about the restaurant "Nell's," the system generates two queries. To collect restaurant reviews it generates a query using the "name" tag (i.e., "Nell's") and limits the search results to yelp.com. To collect bus schedules the system generates a query using the "area" tag (i.e., "Green Lake") and limits the search results to the bus Web site, metrokc.gov.

To define this process more formally, the execution of a relation can be expressed as a database query. For a given relation r, where $r = \text{website}_A.\text{tag}_i \ \text{website}_B.\text{tag}_j$, one can express the process of automatically collecting content for any new data record from website_A for tag_i as a JOIN operation or the following SQL pseudo-query:

```
SELECT * FROM websiteB WHERE websiteB.tagj = websiteA.tagi
```

Since the Web is not made up of a set of uniform databases, we use a number of techniques to make this query feasible. We use the Google Search AJAX API to find Web pages within website_B that are relevant. To extract content from each of the search results, we employ the user-defined extraction patterns. Finally, we designed a number of heuristics to compute a similarity metric and rank the extracted search results. The system displays only the highest ranked extracted search result to the user but makes the remaining search results available.

In the current implementation, the system extracts content from only eight search results, because the Google AJAX Search API limits the search results to a maximum of eight. For all of the examples in this chapter, eight search results are sufficient and limit the delay in collecting information. For very common keywords, however, collecting eight search results is not sufficient. For example, searching for "Chili's" will yield many instances of the restaurant chain. For those types of queries, narrowing the search through one of the approaches discussed in the next section is necessary.

Our approach for collecting related content is limited to Web sites that are indexed by general search engines. There are many Web sites, such as many travel Web sites, that are not indexed by search engines because they create Web pages dynamically in response to user input. To handle these dynamic Web pages, in subsequent work we hope to leverage research into macro recording systems, such as WebVCR (Anupam et al., 2000), Turquoise (Miller & Myers, 1997), Web Macros (Safonov, 1999), TrIAs (Bauer, Dengler, & Paul, 2000), PLOW (Chapter 16), and Creo (Chapter 4). These systems allow users to record a series of interactions, store them as scripts, and replay them at any time to retrieve dynamic pages. Recent research on retroactive macro recording could be even more applicable for Web Summaries (Hupp & Miller, 2007). Madhavan et al. (2007) are developing information retrieval approaches to this problem that do not require user intervention.

The search process introduces ambiguity at two levels, the query level and the search result level. The system must be able to formulate a good query so that it can retrieve the relevant content. It must also be able to find the correct result among potentially many that may all appear similar.

Both of these forms of ambiguity pose considerable challenges and are active areas of research. Liu et al. (Liu, Dong, & Halevy, 2006) pose the query formulation problem as a graph partitioning. Dong et al. (Dong, Halevy, & Madhavan, 2005) propose propagating information across relations to better inform similarity computation. Next, we describe how we address these two types of ambiguity.

Query formulation

We formulate two keyword queries in parallel. One query includes only the extracted text content, and the other includes the extracted content and the tag associated with the content. These two queries are usually sufficient to collect the appropriate result within the top eight search results. Sometimes, however, queries may include too many keywords, and the search results are irrelevant or cannot be extracted. In such cases, we employ heuristics to reformulate the query. If characters such as "/", "−", "+", or ":" appear in the text, we split the string whenever they appear and issue several queries using the partial strings. We found this approach particularly effective for situations in which something is described in multiple ways or is part of multiple categories. For example, a yoga pose has a Sanskrit name and an English name. Querying for either name returns results, but querying for both does not, as the query becomes too specific. Queries may also be augmented to include additional Web page elements, such as the address, to make the query more or less specific. With an interactive system, processing a large number of queries can be prohibitive because of the delay caused by the search and extraction process. We focus on finding good heuristics that quickly retrieve results that are close to the desired content. If the system fails to find a good search result, the user can always go to the Web site and collect the content interactively.

Search result comparison

For each query we extract the first eight search results and rank the extracted content according to similarity to the Web page content that triggered the query. To compute similarity we compare the text of the extracted Web page elements using the correspondence specified in the relation that triggered the search. For example, when collecting content for the "Ambrosia" restaurant from nwsource.com, the system issues the query "Ambrosia" limiting the results to the yelp.com domain. The search results include reviews for the following establishments: "Ambrosia Bakery" (in San Francisco), "Cafe Ambrosia" (in Long Beach), "Cafe Ambrosia" (in Evanston), "Ambrosia Cafe" (in Chicago), "Ambrosia on Huntington" (in Boston), "Ambrosia Cafe" (in Seattle), and "Caffe Ambrosia" (in San Francisco). Because the relation between nwsource.com and yelp.com links the names of the restaurants, we compare the name "Ambrosia" to all the names of the extracted restaurants. We compare the strings by calculating the longest common substring. We give more weight to any strings that match exactly. For all seven restaurants in this example, the longest common substring is of length eight; thus, they receive equal weight. Next, we compare any additional extracted elements. We again compute the longest common substring for corresponding Web page elements. In this example, we compare the addresses of the extracted restaurants and compute the longest common substring for each pair of addresses, resulting in a ranking that places the Seattle restaurant "Ambrosia Cafe" as the best match to the original content. We display the highest ranked extracted content but provide all of the extracted content to the user so that he can correct any errors. The highest ranked content is marked as confident when multiple Web page elements match between Web sites.

   The problem of retrieving related information from multiple sources is described in the database community as data integration (Halevy, Rajaraman, & Ordille, 2006). Data integration is the problem of combining data residing in different sources and providing the user with a unified view of these data. The difficulty in data integration lies in forming mappings between heterogeneous data sources that may include different types of data and defining one single query interface for all of the sources. This problem emerges in a variety of situations both commercial (when two similar companies need to merge their databases) and scientific (combining research results from different bioinformatics repositories). With the growth of the Web, database researchers have shifted their focus toward data integration of unstructured Web content and its applications to Web search (Madhavan et al., 2007). Our work is complementary to database research in that it offers interactive techniques for data integration on a personal scale. We provide an interface that allows users to specify mappings between different data sources (i.e., Web sites) and then use these mappings to automatically extract content from the Web.

Finally, the current implementation allows the user to specify only one-to-one relations. In some situations a one-to-many relation is more appropriate, for example, if the user is interested in collecting academic papers and wants to collect all of the papers written by each of the authors for any given publication. The system can actually query for all of the papers by a given author, but it is not designed to let the user view all elements of the collection as relevant. In future work, we plan to explore other types of relations and also introduce transformations into the relations.

Summary composition

User collections are displayed using layout templates that filter the database to create summaries. Web Summaries includes two kinds of layout templates: predefined and user-specified. The predefined layout templates organize the entire collection. For example, table-based layouts organize the content in a grid, whereas anchor-based layouts relate the content through a central graphical element, such as a map or calendar.

User-specified layout templates, which we call *cards*, provide the user flexibility in the summary display. With cards, users can create different views for the items they are collecting. For example, the user can create a big card that includes a restaurant name, rating, address, price, and review, and a small card that includes just the restaurant name and price. All layout templates are defined with respect to the user-specified tags associated with the extracted content.

Predefined layout templates

To demonstrate different possibilities for summarizing Web content we implemented six layout templates: grid-based (see Figure 12.2a), map (see Figure 12.2b), calendar, text-based, PDA, and print-based. A layout template consists of placement and formatting constraints. The *placement constraints* specify how the data should be organized in the summary. For example, a placement constraint can specify that all content with the label "name" be placed in a list at the top of the document. The position of each element can be specified in absolute pixel coordinates or be relative to previously placed elements. For relative placement, the browser layout manager computes the final content position; for absolute placement, the template specifies all final element positions. Placement constraints can be hierarchical. For example, the template designer can specify that content collected from the same Web page be grouped into one visual element and that such groupings be organized in a list. Although the hierarchy can have any depth, in practice we have found that most layout templates include placement constraint hierarchies no deeper than two or three levels. *Formatting constraints* specify the visual appearance of the elements, such as size, spacing, or borders.

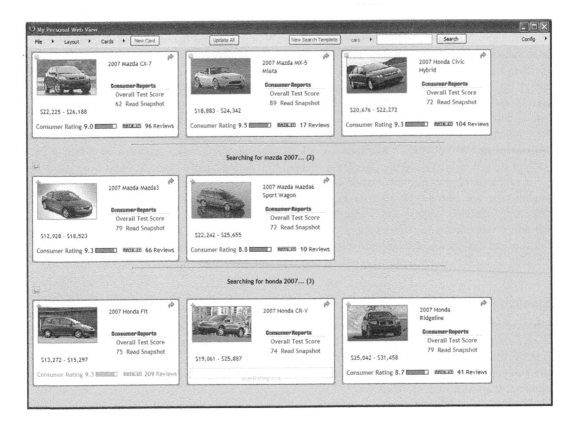

FIGURE 12.6

The user is shopping for cars and using a car search template to find new cars. He has three cards in his collection (shown in the first row) and has made two queries: "mazda 2007" (second row) and "honda 2007" (third row). Each card includes car reviews from autos.msn.com and edmunds.com.

Each layout template can also specify mouse and keyboard interactions for the summary. For example, when the user moves the cursor over an item in the calendar layout template, a short description of the event is presented. When the user clicks on the item, a detailed view of that item is displayed in a panel next to the calendar.

The layout templates are implemented with Dynamic HTML (DHTML), JavaScript and Cascading Style Sheet (CSS) style rules. To create the summary, the system loads an empty HTML document and dynamically populates the document with the DOM nodes in the database, using the placement constraints of the current layout template.

Authoring cards

When the user collects content from multiple Web sites, the summary may include duplicate information. For example, Figure 12.7 shows that the summary includes the Andaluca restaurant address twice, once from nwsource.com and once from yelp.com. Although this duplication is not

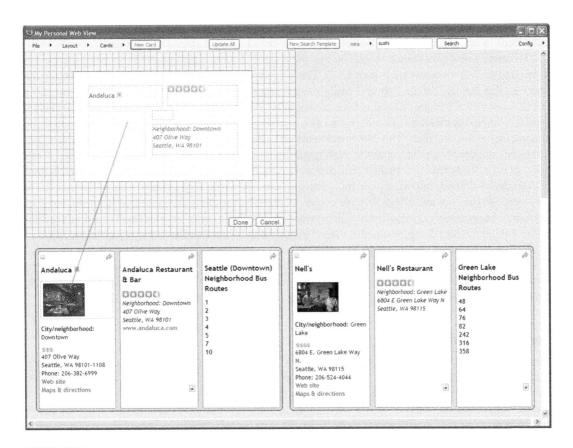

FIGURE 12.7

To design a new card, the user opens a canvas and begins drawing. He first draws the outline of the card and then draws containers. To place content in the containers, the user draws a line from the Web page element to the container. Here, the user adds an image to the card.

necessarily a problem, it does take up extra space, making it difficult for the user to quickly scan through many options. Web Summaries allows users to author cards to customize the view of collected information to their personal needs.

A *card* imposes a uniform design on content that may come from many different Web sites and may initially appear very different. Similarly to the predefined layout templates, a card defines which content should be displayed and how the content should be organized visually. Recall that the user's content collection is stored in the data repository and is accessible through a relation graph. It is the relation graph that specifies which records in the data repository are related. In database terminology, a card can also be described as defining a view on the relation graph in the data repository – that is, it lists the tags for the data that should be displayed in the card. For example, a card can include the name and address of a restaurant. Or it can also include pricing, rating, and images. The system includes a default card, which displays all records and Web page elements in the relation graph irrespective of the tags associated with the Web page elements. The user can use an interactive editing tool to create new cards at any time. Cards are persistent and can be reused and shared with others.

To create a new card the user clicks on the "New Card" button, which opens a canvas directly in his collection of Web content (see Figure 12.7). The card designer is tightly integrated with the collection space so that the user can quickly and easily merge content from different Web sites without switching windows or views. The user first draws the outline of the card and then proceeds to create containers that hold the Web page elements. To assign data to a container, the user clicks on a Web page element and drags a line to the container. The data is automatically resized to fit the size of the container. Each container is associated with the tag of the Web page element it contains and the element Web site. When the user is finished creating containers and assigning data, he clicks on the "Done" button, and the system transforms his drawing into a template for organizing and displaying Web content, a card. The user can at any time edit the card and add or remove content. Currently, the cards are presented in a grid, but they could also be manually organized into piles or arranged visually on a map or calendar. The authoring principles behind the card designer can also extend to authoring layout templates that organize the cards.

Cards can be interactive in nature, encoding interactions specific to the type of data that is collected. The card authoring tool does not currently provide capabilities for specifying interactions. We could expose a scripting interface and allow the user to specify any type of card interactions, but since Web Summaries does not require programming we chose to remove all scripting from the interactions.

Template-based search

Search templates combine the user-designed cards and relations as a basis for a new type of search interface that targets the keyword query to appropriate domains and organizes the search results in a visual summary. The user can thus bypass visiting Web pages directly and collect content through a search template. For example, if the user wants to find vegetarian restaurants but does not know where to start, he can simply query with the word "vegetarian" directed toward the data underlying the restaurant card. More formally, a *search template* includes a set of Web sites and any associated relations. When a user types a query in the search template, the system sends the query to a general search engine, in this case through the Google Search AJAX API, limiting the search results to the list of Web sites defined in the template. For each search result, the system extracts content using predefined extraction patterns and triggers any relations that are in the template to collect additional content. Because of limitations on the number of search results provided by the Google Search AJAX API, for each query/Web site pair, the system processes only eight search results. The user can also modify the search template by adding additional Web sites to be queried and relations to be triggered. Extracted search results are presented to the user as a set of cards. These are initially considered temporary, indicated by being displayed below the main collection of cards. The user can promote a search result to the actual collection, or he can delete all of the search results for a given query. For a visual description, please see Figure 12.8.

Because search templates combine information from multiple Web sites that is retrieved without the user's help, it becomes important to convey to the user the system's confidence in the retrieved results. Web Summaries achieves this through transparency. If content is not marked as confident during the automatic retrieval process, it is rendered semitransparent to alert users that they may want to confirm the information by clicking on it to go to the source Web page. In Figure 12.6 the rating for the 2007 Honda Fit is rendered in this way.

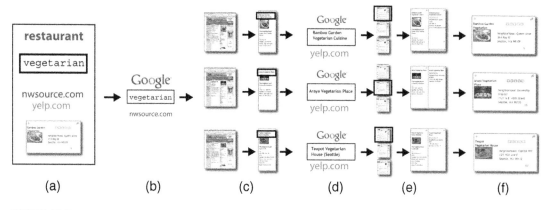

FIGURE 12.8

(a) The user types the query "vegetarian" into the restaurant search template to collect vegetarian restaurants. This search template includes two Web sites and a relation. The nwsource.com Web site is considered primary, because information from yelp.com is collected through a relation. (b) The system issues the query "vegetarian" to a general search engine and limits the results to nwsource.com. (c) Each search result is processed with an extraction pattern to extract relevant content. (d) The extracted content triggers relations, which issue further queries. (e) The subsequent search results are extracted, ranked, and added to the content that triggered the additional retrieval. (f) Finally, the user sees the extracted content as a series of cards.

Search templates may include Flash content as well. Figure 12.3b shows a collection of upcoming shows. In this example the user has related concerts from upcoming.org with band Web pages at myspace.com. Whenever the user adds a new concert to his collection, the system automatically collects music samples. The music samples are embedded in a music player, and because the player is just another HTML object, a Flash object, one can extract it just like any other Web page element. The music player retains full functionality, and the user can press the "play" button on the control to listen to the music.

The success of template-based search lies in the ability to extract semantic information from Web pages. Although semantic extraction is only in its infancy, we believe that it will only grow in the coming years, and template-based search is an example of the powerful new applications that will take advantage of machine-readable Web pages.

DISCUSSION

The interaction techniques embodied in the Web Summaries system enable users to transform the Web into their own personal Web that provides personalized access to the information they care about in the form of their choosing. First, we take advantage of the growth in template material on the Web and design semiautomatic interactive extraction of content from similar Web pages using structural and content *extraction patterns*. Second, we employ *layout templates* and user labeling to create rich displays of heterogeneous Web content collections. Third, we use search technology for proactive retrieval of content from different related Web sites through user-defined *relations*. Fourth, we let users define their own personalized and aesthetic views of heterogeneous content from any number of Web sites through *cards*. And finally, we introduce a new *template-based search* paradigm that combines the user-defined relations and cards into a search template. Search templates present a goal-driven search mechanism that creates visual personalized summaries of the content users need to accomplish their task. As users accomplish their goals with these tools, they also produce artifacts, such as the extraction patterns and relations that are persistent and sharable. These artifacts can be stored in a public repository and reused by others. Furthermore, they can be added to the Web sites where they originated, thereby enhancing the existing Web with semantic information, such as relationships between different Web sites or the types of content available in a particular Web page. If popularized by an online community, the ideas we present here can help realize a machine-readable World Wide Web.

To better understand how the Web Summaries system works in practice and to test how it would interact with an online community for sharing extraction patterns, we deployed the system for 10 weeks with 24 participants. Here we present the main conclusions from this field study. For more details, please see (Dontcheva et al., 2008).

Our study revealed that users collect a variety of Web content including highly structured content, such as tables and lists, and highly unstructured content, such as entire articles. Our participants actively used automatic retrieval on many Web sites and for their own personal tasks. They created over 250 extraction patterns by clipping pieces of Web pages and collected over 1000 items automatically. Though Web Summaries was useful for content-intensive tasks, users found it less applicable for transient daily tasks, because the tool required opening a summary window and actively saving content. Many participants also used Web Summaries as a mechanism for storing permanent versions of Web content that they view as highly dynamic. The participants were very positive about the layout templates and the resulting summaries. They used a variety of layout templates and requested more flexible customizable templates. Finally, the participants used a community pattern repository to download patterns created by others. They often modified downloaded patterns to suit their own needs. They suggested many improvements to the interface to help make sharing patterns as fast and easy as creating them through clippings.

These findings lead us to the following design implications for future semiautomatic and automatic tools for collecting Web content. First, tools for collecting and organizing Web content need to support the ability to collect both structured and unstructured Web content and display a heterogeneous collection of content. Second, in order to become well integrated into a user's daily Web usage, automation tools need to be sensitive not only to long and permanent Web tasks but also to transient and short-lived tasks, otherwise users will not integrate them into their Web browsing habits. Since Web browsing is such an integral part of users' lives, tools that support information management must be fluidly integrated into the browser and be available at any time. Finally, an online repository of extraction pattern information is still very new to users, and visualizations for exposing the available information must be carefully designed such that this type of shared automation can aid rather than hinder users from accomplishing their tasks.

Acknowledgments

We would like to thank Sharon Lin, Cheyne Mathey-Owens, and our study participants for all of their time and effort. Special thanks to Allen Cypher, Jeffrey Nichols, and Hyuckchul Jung for their insightful comments during the chapter preparation and review process.

This work is based on two earlier works:

1. Dontcheva, M., Drucker, S. M., Wade, G., Salesin, D., and Cohen, M. F. 2006. Summarizing Personal Web Browsing Sessions. In Proceedings of the 19th Annual ACM Symposium on User Interface Software and Technology. UIST '06, 115-124. DOI= http://doi.acm.org/10.1145/1166253.1166273.
2. Dontcheva, M., Drucker, S. M., Salesin, D., and Cohen, M. F. 2007. Relations, Cards, and Search Templates: User-Guided Web Data Integration and Layout. In Proceedings of the 20th Annual ACM Symposium on User Interface Software and Technology. UIST '07, 61-70. DOI= http://doi.acm.org/10.1145/1294211.1294224.

WEB SUMMARIES

Intended users:	All users
Domain:	All Web sites
Description:	With Web Summaries, users can create personalized search templates that can automatically retrieve content from multiple Web sites and display the information with a personally specified view. Search templates include user-defined extraction patterns for Web pages, relations between Web sites, and layout templates.
Example:	Restaurant Search. The user first clips and visually links information from a restaurant and bus Web site. The system automatically collects the same information for a few more restaurants and their associated bus routes. The user then arranges the restaurant and bus information in a visual card. Web Summaries uses the card to initialize a restaurant search template. The user can now query for sushi and the system retrieves sushi restaurant cards that present information from multiple local restaurant and bus Web sites.
Automation:	Yes. It automates collecting and organizing Web content.
Mashups:	Yes. Users can link information from multiple Web sites together and view it on maps, calendars, and grids.
Scripting:	No.
Natural language:	No.
Recordability:	No.
Inferencing:	Yes, Web Summaries infers data types using heuristics.
Sharing:	Yes, summaries can be shared as regular HTML pages.
Comparison to other systems:	Similarly to C3W and Zoetrope, Web Summaries allows users to link content from multiple Web sites and automatically retrieve related information. It is unique in its emphasis on data. The user manipulates data and creates personalized views of that data and as a side effect creates automation artifacts such as extraction patterns, relations, and search templates.
Platform:	Implemented as an extension to the Mozilla Firefox browser.
Availability:	Not currently available.

The temporal dimension in end user programming for the Web

13

Eytan Adar,[1] **Mira Dontcheva,**[2] **James A. Fogarty,**[3] **Daniel S. Weld**[3]

[1]*University of Michigan*
[2]*Adobe Systems*
[3]*University of Washington*

ABSTRACT

Despite the dynamic nature of the Web, most people only view and interact with a static snapshot. Search engines, browsers, and higher-level end user programming environments only support observing and manipulating a single point in time – the "now." We propose that moving beyond this static viewpoint is important because (1) maintaining a temporal view of the Web allows users to more clearly understand the behavior of their "programs," both in static and dynamic contexts; and (2) temporally changing information on the Web is interesting in its own right. In this chapter we discuss the opportunities and challenges of integrating the temporal dimension in end user programming environments and our experiences with Zoetrope, a tool for interacting with the ephemeral (i.e., dynamic) Web.

INTRODUCTION

Despite the dynamic nature of the Web, most people are only exposed to a static snapshot. Search engines, browsers, and higher-level end user programming environments only support observing and manipulating a single point in time – the "now." To better support interactions with historical data, we created the Zoetrope system (Adar et al., 2008) that provides a visual query language and environment for end user manipulation of historical Web content. By supporting such interactions from *within the context* of the Now Web (i.e., through the "present" copy of a page), the Zoetrope user does not need to identify the location of historical content. For example, a user may place a lens – a visual marker – on the "current" lowest used book price on an Amazon page, and have the *historical* price automatically extracted and visualized over the history of the page. Although it is focused on access to the ephemeral Web, the design of Zoetrope has a number of implications to the design of many end user programming environments in its ability to "debug" such programs on historical content and generate additional training data. Integrating the temporal dimension provides both new challenges and many new opportunities, which we explore within the context of Zoetrope.

ZOETROPE

Zoetrope functions as a complete system, providing a custom crawler, content store and indices, an internal dataflow language for representing queries on data, and a front end for "programming" queries and visualizing output. The main visual operator in Zoetrope is a lens. Lenses are rectangular objects drawn on any part of a Web page (see Figure 13.1). Each lens can be manipulated through a slider, giving users interactive access to historical content from "past" to "present" and providing the illusion of dynamic content from static information. Data selected within the lens can then be visualized in a number of different ways: time series for numerical data, movies constructed from many static images, timelines, and so on. Although there are a number of different types of lenses to target different types of data, all are highly interactive and respond to the user's manipulation of the slider instantly. Interactivity is a key feature and distinction for Zoetrope, driven by the fundamental observation that most applications that rely on screen-scraping style extractions will fail at some point because of a drastic change in page structures. By allowing the Zoetrope user to *see* how their selection functions over time, corrections can be made at points in history where the extraction has failed.

Additional lens features include filtering with keywords or other features and the binding of multiple lenses (on the same and different pages) to explore correlated data (e.g., gas prices on one page versus oil prices on another, versus news stories mentioning the Middle East on yet a third).

As described in Adar et al. (2008), Zoetrope contributes:

- A novel visual programming toolkit and a set of interactions for rapidly building and testing temporal Web queries,
- A semantics (formal model) for temporal data streams,
- A set of recomposable operators to manipulate temporal data streams,
- Indexing structures for fast processing and interaction with Web content over time, and
- A unique dataset collected by a new crawler design.

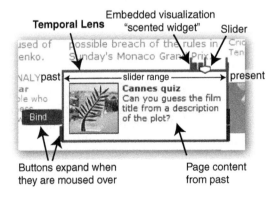

FIGURE 13.1

Anatomy of a lens.

In this chapter we explore in detail the particular design choices for Zoetrope and how the notion of time can be employed in end user programming environments regardless of their emphasis on past or present. These applications share a common goal with Zoetrope in their desire to function as well as possible into the *future*.

THE ZOETROPE ARCHITECTURE

Zoetrope consists of a number of components that, taken together, provide a complete solution for collecting, storing, and querying historical versions of the same page. This architecture is illustrated in Figure 13.2.

Crawler

The Zoetrope crawler is a modified Firefox with two (also modified) plugins. The first, WebPage-Dump (Pollak & Gatterbauer, 2007), outputs the browser-internal Document Object Model (DOM) representation of the page. Capturing this representation is important as it is (1) a compliant XML file that can be indexed in an XML database, and (2) a frozen version of the page that does not contain any JavaScript and can thus be guaranteed to render the same way each time the page is loaded. The modified WebPageDump waits some period until the JavaScript on the page has either stopped executing or some waiting period has expired. Though sometimes imperfect, this allows any Java-Script code that modifies the DOM to complete the process. In addition to the serialized DOM,

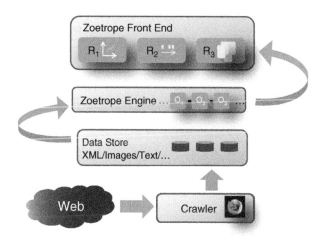

FIGURE 13.2

The Zoetrope architecture.

the plugin stores a single CSS page specifying formatting and all objects (images, flash files, etc.) associated with the page. A second plugin, Screengrab! (http://www.screengrab.org), produces a screen capture of whatever is being displayed in the browser. Using these plugins, the crawler collects an accurate representation of the page as it looked at the time of retrieval (through an image) and sufficient data so that the page can be correctly re-rendered if necessary. Though strictly only the unrendered content is needed, by storing and caching the rendered content, we are able to better support a number of the interactive features.

At present, the crawling infrastructure resides on a "headless" Linux server (i.e., one without a display system). Firefox instances, running in the background, collect nearly 1000 pages every hour. This is not a limit of the machine but rather the population of pages we have chosen to crawl. Each page is crawled once per hour at the fastest rate with a backoff protocol that speeds up or slows down the crawl as needed from a maximum of once an hour to a minimum of once a day (if the page remains unchanged). Although crawling speed can be greatly increased (further increasing version granularity), there are "politeness" limits that need to be respected. A machine would likely be able to crawl many times this number of pages, and one could envision a service that collects page snapshots at different intervals. Furthermore, using a Firefox plugin has the further advantage that people can add to their own database as they browse the Web. The combination of personal visit archives and periodic snapshots might be sufficient for a number of applications.

Storage and data

The DOM for each version of a page are loaded into an in-memory XML database. Saxon (http://www.saxonica.com) provides XPath query functionality and allows us to rapidly find matching elements or entire versions of pages. An in-memory index also tracks DOM elements by their rendered x and y coordinates. This structure allows us to quickly find which elements are clicked or selected. An early analysis of storage needs (Adar et al., 2008) revealed that each incremental copy for a 5-week crawl (crawled once an hour) was 15% (2 Kb average, 252 bytes median) the size of the original, compressed copy of the page. This is encouraging from the perspective of managing many copies of the same page.

The Zoetrope engine

Internally, Zoetrope is built on a simple dataflow architecture where *operators* act on a *content stream*. Conceptually, a content stream is a sequence of tuples (i.e., pairs), $<T_i, C_i>$, where C_i is a content item, such as a Web page or some piece of a page, and T_i is the time when that content was sampled from the Web. When a person creates a lens or some other visualization, Zoetrope generates a sequence of *operators*, which process the content stream. There are presently three main types of abstract operators which act on content streams in different ways:

- *Transform* operators modify the content payload of tuples. Each tuple is processed by this operator, and one or more new operators are generated, replacing the processed tuple. For example, if the content item is an image, a transform operator may crop the image.
- *Filter* operators modify the content stream by removing or allowing a given tuple to pass through. For example, a filter operator may only allow tuples with data greater than some number or only tuples where the content contains a certain string.

- Finally, *render* operators interface between the engine and GUI by rendering some visualization of the content stream that contains one or many tuples. A time series renderer, for example, will depict the fluctuations of numerical values over time.

The Zoetrope interface[1]

The primary Zoetrope interface is a zoomable canvas based on Piccolo (Bederson, Grossjean, & Meyer, 2004) within which the user can explore past versions of any number of Web pages. Though most Zoetrope features can be implemented in modern Web browsers, interactivity is still technically challenging and was best implemented in a custom application (though this will likely become less of a problem as new browser technologies are released). Zoetrope lenses are drawn directly into this interface as well as any visualizations, providing a single workspace for exploration. Although Zoetrope displays the rendered Web page as an image, the system maintains the interactivity of the live Web page. Clicking on a hyperlink opens a browser for the present version of the hyperlink target (or the historical version corresponding to the slider selection, if it exists within Zoetrope).

Figure 13.3 displays a Zoetrope workspace where the user has loaded the Amazon home page, selected an element on the page (the number of presales of the last Harry Potter book), and then visualized those presales in a time series. Zoetrope supports binding between multiple lenses or between lenses and visualizations.

Each lens drawn on a Web page has a corresponding slider at the top that can be moved from one end of the lens to the other. The leftmost end of the slider represents the first captured instance of the page available to Zoetrope, whereas the rightmost is the most recent capture. Although motion of the slider is continuous, in reality snapshots are discrete. To provide the illusion of continuity Zoetrope "rounds" to the nearest value. As the user moves the slider, a small textual overlay displays the nearest matching date (changing as the slider moves). Lenses in Zoetrope can be "bound," so that motion in one slider causes motion in all other lenses that it is bound to. Without binding, lenses act independently, potentially creating a page that is an amalgam of different pieces of the page from different points in time. How to properly notify users of this amalgam state is an interesting interface design challenge and research opportunity.

Lenses are in part inspired by the Video Cube (Klein et al., 2002) and Magic Lenses work (Bier et al., 2003). The former allows video stream frames to be layered and "sliced" to find an abstraction of the video. In the latter, a magic lens is a widget that can be placed directly on a document to illuminate the underlying representation while maintaining the visual context of the document. Architecturally, a number of database visualization systems are related to the stream and operator design in Zoetrope. Particularly, DEVise (Livny et al., 1997) was originally constructed to operate on streams of data that required visualization (though operators in DEVise tended to concentrate on the mapping of data to visual elements and less on transformation and filtering). Similarly, Polaris (Stolte et al., 2002) operates to visualize relational data. In both, the operators provided by the system are primarily targeted at the rendering step (deciding how graphs, charts, and other visualizations should be constructed).

---

[1]A video demonstration of Zoetrope is available at http://cond.org/zoetrope.html.

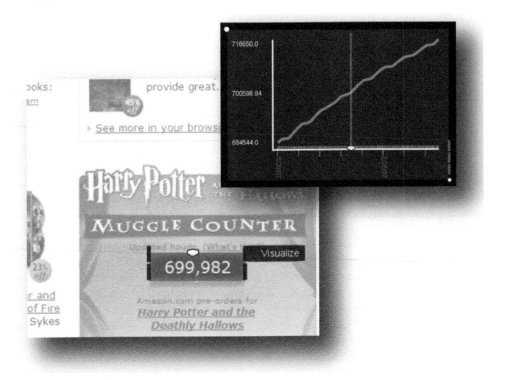

FIGURE 13.3

A time series visualization displays the Harry Potter book presales, or "Muggle Counter," over time.

ZOETROPE LENSES

A lens allows a person to select some content and track it over time (i.e., the *temporal extraction*). Although there are various flavors of lenses, their creation and use is nearly identical. A person creates a lens simply by drawing a rectangular area on the Web page surface. In the underlying semantics of the Zoetrope system, the creation of a lens produces a parametrized transform operator that acts on the original page content stream, an optional filter (or set of filters) that processes the transformed stream, and a renderer that displays the historical data in the context of the original page. The specific selections of transforms and filters depends on the lens type.

Lenses come in three distinct flavors: visual, structural, and textual. The different variations are intended to track content on the page based on its stability. For example, content that is stable in rendered coordinates can be tracked with a visual lens. On the other hand if the content being extracted by the lens is visually in a different place, but is always retrievable by the same path through the DOM hierarchy, this content can be tracked through a structured lens.

Visual lenses

The simplest Zoetrope lens is the visual lens. To create this type of lens, a person specifies a region on the original page (e.g., a portion of the BBC home page as in Figure 13.4). The specification produces a lens with a slider. The slider is parameterized on the width of the lens and the range of data being displayed. As the slider moves, the lens renders the corresponding data. Figure 13.4 illustrates how a visual lens is implemented using the internal Zoetrope operators. When created, each version of the page becomes a tuple in the content stream. Each of these tuples is then rendered (or looked up if cached), cropped, filtered, and then rendered inside the lens. Visual lenses are particularly useful for extracting portions of information that is generally statically placed on the page and has the same size (e.g., portion of a weather map, or part of a continuously updating Webcam image).

Structural lenses

Not all Web pages possess sufficient stability for a visual lens. Slight shifts in rendering or more significant movement of elements can cause distracting jumps when a person moves the lens slider. To counter this effect, and to allow for more precise selections, Zoetrope provides structural lenses. Structural lenses are created in the same way as visual lenses, by drawing a rectangle around an area of interest, but they track selected HTML content independent of visual position. Specifically, when created, a structural lens defines a DOM forest within the structure of the page. This is specified through an XPath expression (Berglund et al., 2007) that can be used to select a subtree of the

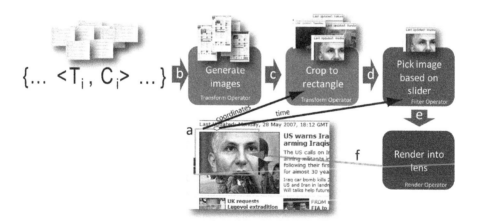

FIGURE 13.4

A visual lens in action. The user specifies a visual lens (a) on top of the page. This causes Zoetrope to take all versions of the document in a content stream and push those to a transform operator (b) that renders (or looks up) how the page looked at every time step. The tuples, which now contain rendered page images, are pushed (c) to a second transform which crops the images to the dimensions specified by the original placed lens. This stream is then pushed (d) to a filter operator that is parameterized to the slider state and which picks the single tuple closest to that time. Finally, a render operator takes (e) that single tuple and displays it inside the original lens (f).

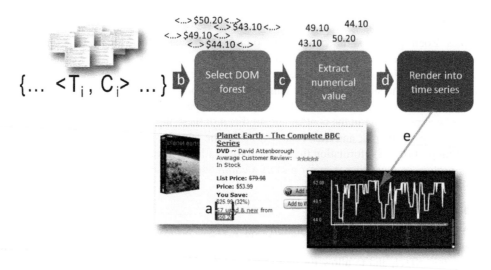

FIGURE 13.5

A structural lens and time series visualization. The user specifies a structural lens (a), selecting the used price of the DVD. Zoetrope takes all versions of the document in a content stream and pushes them to a transform operator (b) that selects a portion of the document corresponding to the selection (i.e., the XPath). A second transform operator (c) strips the text and extracts the numerical value which is pushed to a renderer (d) and finally a visualization (e).

structure. For example, in Figure 13.5, in order to track price over time in the page, the user selects the price element using a structural lens. The structural lens then parameterizes a transform operation which is able to pull out the element containing the price information over many past versions of the page.

Textual lenses

Visual and structural lenses are dependent on certain types of Web page stability. A visual lens relies on stability of the rendering, whereas a structural lens takes advantage of structural stability. Both are reasonable in many scenarios, but it is also worth considering selections based on unstable or semi-stable content. For example, consider tracking a specific team in a list of sports teams that is ordered by some changing value, such as rank (see Figure 13.6). As teams win and lose, the team of interest will move up and down the list. Specifying a rectangle at (100,400), or the fourth row in the list, will not work when the team moves from this position. To address this type of selection, we introduce the notion of a textual lens, which tracks a textual selection regardless of where the text is located on the page. A textual lens can track exactly the same string (e.g., a blog story) or approximately the same string (e.g., a sports team name with a score, where the score changes from time to time).

In its most general form, a textual lens tracks arbitrary text regardless of where it appears on the page, which DOM elements contain the text, and the size of those elements. This generalization is

FIGURE 13.6

A textual lens can track content regardless of where it appears on the page. For example, the Toronto Blue Jays move from being the 3rd to the 4th ranked team (top two images). A visual or structural lens created in the first time series would show the Blue Jays at first but the Yankees when the slider is moved back. A textual lens, on the other hand, tracks the Blue Jays no matter where they are in the list (bottom two images).

unfortunately too computationally intensive, even in scenarios where the text is unchanging, and the problem becomes intractable for an interactive system. To make our textual lenses interactive, we restrict the search space by making use of the document structure. Textual lenses often track items that appear in tables, lists, or structurally similar subtrees (e.g., posts in a blog all have similar forms). We take advantage of this structural similarity to only search among DOM elements that have similar tree structure to the original selection. From this initial set of possibilities, Zoetrope will compare the text in the original selection to the possible matches, picking the most likely one. The comparison is currently done through the standard Dice coefficient, which calculates the overlap in text tokens between two pieces of text (i.e., $\mathrm{SIM(A,B)}=2*|A{\cap}B|/(|A|+|B|)$), where A and B are sets of words.

Applying filters to lenses

Given the large volume of data encoded in a content stream, it is natural to want to focus on specific information of interest. Zoetrope uses filters to provide this capability. We have already seen a few different kinds of filter operations, but it is worth considering additional types:

- Filtering on time: One may wish to see the state of one or more streams at a specific time or frequency (e.g., 6 PM each day).
- Filtering on a keyword: The selection condition may also refer to C_i, the content half of the tuple $<T_i,C_i>$. If C_i contains text, then keyword queries may apply. For example, one might only be interested in headlines that contain the word "Ukraine."

- Filtering on amounts: One may also select content using an inequality and threshold (e.g., $>k$). If the content is numeric and the inequality is satisfied, then the tuple is kept; otherwise it is filtered. Similarly, one can select the maximum or minimum tuple in a numeric stream.
- Duplicate elimination: It may also be useful to select only those tuples whose content is distinct from content seen earlier in the stream.
- Compound filters: Logical operations (conjunction, disjunction, negation, etc.) may be used to compose more complex selection criteria.
- Trigger filters: An especially powerful filter results when one stream is filtered according to the results of another stream's filter. For example, Ed can filter the traffic page using a conjunction of the 6 PM time constraint and a trigger on the ESPN page for the keyword "home game." We will return to this when considering lens binding.

Because filtering is useful for many tasks, it is provided as an option whenever a visual, structural, or textual lens is applied. When selecting a region with filtering enabled, a lens is created based on the underlying selection and a popup window asks for a constraint to use in the filter, such as a word or phrase. Other appropriate constraints include maximum, minimum, and comparison operators.

Filtering is visually depicted with a scented widget (Willett, Heer, & Agrawala, 2007) which is displayed as a small embedded bar graph (Figure 13.1). The bar graph is displayed above the slider, indicating the location in time of the matching tuples. As a person moves the slider, the slider snaps to the bars, which act like slider ticks. Note that the bars need not be all of the same height and may reflect different information. A tall bar can indicate the appearance of new content that matches a filter, and a short bar can indicate content that appears previously but still matches the filter.

Binding lenses

People are often interested in multiple parts of a page or parts of multiple pages, as they may be comparing and contrasting different information (e.g., what does traffic look like on game days?). Zoetrope flexibly allows for the simultaneous use of multiple lenses. Lenses can act independently or be bound together interactively into a synchronized bind group. Sliders within a group are linked together, causing them all to move and simultaneously update their corresponding lens (see Figure 13.7).

Users may bind lenses for different reasons. For example, to check traffic at 6 PM on home game days, a user can bind a lens for traffic maps at 6 PM with a lens for home games from his favorite baseball site. Each lens in a bind group constrains its matching tuples to only include versions allowed by all other lenses in the group. Recall that this is achieved through a trigger filter. Each lens can add a new trigger filter parameterized to the time intervals that are valid according to other members of the bind group. Only tuples that satisfy all trigger filters are allowed. Thus, the resulting stream shows traffic data at 6 PM only on days for which there are home baseball games.

Lenses can also be bound disjunctively. For example, one may want to find when book A's price is less than $25, or when book B's price is less than $30 (i.e., one of the two books has dropped in price). Zoetrope supports this type of bind, which is currently obtained by holding the shift key while performing the bind operation. However, this operation creates an interesting twist as it causes data to be unfiltered. When binding two lenses in this way, filter operators can be thought of as operating in parallel rather than serially. A tuple passes if it matches any filter.

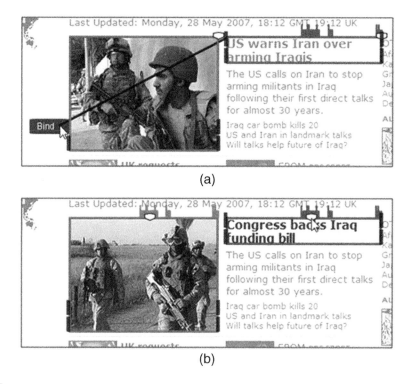

(a)

(b)

FIGURE 13.7

An example of a bind operation. The user constructs two separate lenses (a) and drags from one bind "port" to another. In this example, the user binds a lens that is filtering news stories about Iraq to the image posted next to the article. The two lenses become synchronized (b) so that motion in the slider of the first lens will automatically move the slider in the second.

Stacking lenses

In addition to binding, Zoetrope also supports the stacking of lenses. For example, consider a person who creates one lens on a weather page, filtering for "clear" weather, and would like to further apply a filter that restricts the selection to between 6 PM and 7 PM daily. Explicitly drawing one lens over the other and then binding them is visually unappealing and does not take advantage of the underlying semantics of the language. Instead, we introduce the notion of lens stacking. The toolbar in the Zoetrope window, which allows users to select the type of the lens, can also be used in a specialized binding operation which we call stacking. By dragging a lens selection from this toolbar to the bind button of the lens, a person indicates that they would like to further filter the existing lens. The original lens is replaced, and a new combined lens is generated, which takes the transform and filter from the original selection and augments it with additional transforms and filters. This new lens satisfies both the selection and constraints of the original lens as well as the new one. Furthermore, because some filters and transforms are commutative, stacking provides the opportunity to reorder the internal operations to optimize the processing of tuples.

Finally, we consider the partial stacking of lenses where a person wants to make a subselection from an existing lens. For example, a person may apply a textual lens that tracks a specific team in the ranking. The textual lens will track the team no matter where they are in the ranking, but the user would further like to pull out the wins for that team at various time points. Thus, they may create a second structural lens that consumes the selection of the textual lens and selects the wins. While most lenses can be easily stacked without modification, lenses that stack on top of textual lenses require a slight modification to utilize relative information (paths or locations). This subtle modification is necessary because the textual lens selects information that is not in a fixed location in either the x,y space or the DOM tree. Because the textual selection is variable, the structural lens must use a path relative to the selection rather than an absolute path.

ZOETROPE VISUALIZATIONS

Lenses enable viewing of Web content from different moments in time, but this exploration is likely just the first part of satisfying an information need. For example, a book's cost at specific points in time is interesting, but a person may also want to graph the price over time, calculate averages, or test variability. To facilitate this type of analysis, we have created a number of renderers that visualize or otherwise represent selected data. Visualizations, like lenses, create a sequence of transforms, filters, and renderers to display results. Although visualizations can exist independently of a lens, a lens typically defines the data displayed in the visualization. Lenses can thus also be used as a prototyping tool for testing selections and aggregations.

The transforms, filters, and processed streams generated by the lens can be directed to visualization rendering components that implement the visualization itself. For example, in a typical workflow, one might place a (potentially filtered) lens on a book price, move the slider to test the selection, and click on the visualization button to graph the price over time. Internally, the visualization step reuses the transform module of the lens and connects it to a time series renderer. Clearly, many temporal visualizations are possible (e.g., Silva & Catarci, 2000; Aigner et al., 2008), and could be implemented in Zoetrope or externally. Presently, Zoetrope only offers limited support for version-to-version comparisons. Filters, for example, note if the content at one time step is different from the previous time step (but do not currently indicate what those differences are). Many such visual comparison (i.e., "diff") algorithms exist (e.g., Douglis et al., 1998; Chen et al., 2000; Fishkin & Bier, 2004; Jatowt, Kawai, & Tanaka, 2008) and could be added as well. As we describe below, a number of default renderers provide visualization alternatives in the current implementation.

Timelines and movies

The simplest Zoetrope visualization type is the timeline (see Figure 13.8), which displays extracted images and data linearly on a temporal axis. This visualization allows, for example, viewing weather patterns over the course of a year, headline images in stories that mention Iraq, or unique articles about a favorite sports team (all ordered by time). As before, the rendered images visualized in the timeline are live and a person can click on any of the links. Double-clicking on any image in the visualization synchronizes the page (or pages) to the same time, allowing a person to see other

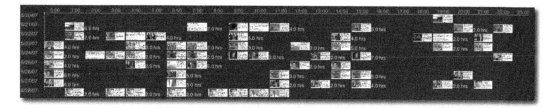

FIGURE 13.8

This timeline visualization shows the duration and frequency of news articles on the cbc.ca Web site.

information that appeared on the page at a particular time. This visualization can also eliminate duplicates and display a line next to each image depicting its duration. This type of display shows when new content appears and how long it stays on a page (e.g., a story in the news, a price at a store). To prevent the timeline from running indefinitely to the right, the visualization can fold the line into a grid with each row denoting activity over a day (or other interval).

The timeline visualization gives an instant sense of everything that has happened over some period. However, other examples are best served by cycling through the cropped images to produce an animated movie. Although this is equivalent to simply pulling the slider through time, a movie visualization automates and regulates transitions and looping while the visualization cycles through the images. For example, a static U.S. Geological Survey (USGS) earthquake map can be transformed into an animation of earthquakes over time, helping to pinpoint significant events.

Clustering

Our timeline visualization is a simple example of a grouping visualization, where extractions are grouped by some variable (time in this case). However, other more complex groupings are also possible. Clustering visualizations group the extracted clips using an external variable derived from another stream. For example, a clustering visualization can merge data from two different lenses, using one lens to specify the grouping criteria while the other lens provides the data. For example, in a cluster visualization of traffic and weather data we create a row for every weather condition (e.g., sunny, clear, rain), and every instance from the traffic selection is placed in the appropriate row depending on the weather condition at the time of the clipping. If it was rainy at 8:15 PM, for example, the traffic map from 8:15 PM is assigned to the rainy group (e.g., Figure 13.9).

Time series

A variety of interesting temporal data is numerical in nature, such as prices, temperatures, sports statistics, and polling numbers. Much of this data is tracked over time; however, in many situations it is difficult or impossible to find one table or chart that includes all values of interest. Zoetrope automatically extracts numerical values from selections of numerical data and visualizes them as a time series (e.g., Figure 13.3). The slider on the x-axis of the time series visualization is synchronized with the slider in the original lens selection. When the person moves the lens slider, a line moves on the time series visualization (and vice versa).

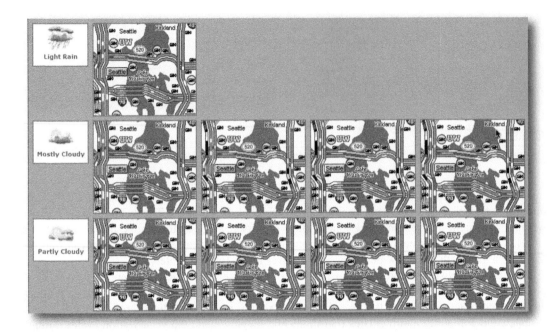

FIGURE 13.9

An example clustered visualization.

Exporting temporal data

The current version of Zoetrope implements many visualizations but is also designed for extensibility, and data extracted using Zoetrope lenses is also usable outside of Zoetrope. Systems such as Swivel (http://www.swivel.com) or Many Eyes (Viégas et al., 2007) excel in analysis and social interactions around data, but are not focused on helping people find the data in the first place. Zoetrope is able to generate a temporal, data-centric view of different Web sites to meet this need. To export data outside of Zoetrope, we created a Google Spreadsheet "visualization" that sends the lens-selected values to the external Google Spreadsheet system. When a person selects this option, appropriate date and time columns are generated along with the content present at that time interval (either strings or numerical data). This scheme expands the capabilities of Zoetrope by allowing people to leverage external visualizations, integrate with Web mashups, or perform more complex analyses.

CONCLUSIONS AND IMPLICATIONS FOR END USER PROGRAMMING

The World Wide Web is generally treated by users and system designers as a single snapshot in time. This limited view ignores the importance of temporal data and the potential benefits of maintaining a Web history. By considering the past, end user programming environments can be enhanced for the future. Zoetrope represents one possible solution in the space, concentrating specifically on how a user might analyze and visualize data from the temporal Web from the familiar context of the Now. By maintaining historical copies of the Web, Zoetrope provides users with the ability to simulate programs on historical data. This has implications for other end user programming tools for the Web which similarly depend on structural stability and benefit from allowing a user to test and validate their selections.

One feature of Zoetrope's interface is that it allows users to quickly detect failures in selections. Such functionality is desirable, perhaps even necessary, for end user programming environments as page templates will likely change at some point, causing the program to fail (Kushmerick, 1999; Kushmerick, 2000; Dontcheva et al., 2007a; Little et al., 2007; Adar et al., 2009). For end user programming environments and Web-based Programming by Demonstration (PBD) systems, dealing with this issue requires complex heuristics or learning algorithms to deal with the eventual failure. A change to a Web page represents a potentially fatal change in the "API" utilized by end user programs. Clearly addressing such failures, and building more robust systems, is critical in the construction of programs that can run without constant maintenance.

With a tool such as Zoetrope, users can interactively detect failures in the extraction and refine their selection, adding or removing restrictions, improving filtering conditions, or creating another lens for the "failed" interval. Although this may not solve all future failures, users may improve the robustness of their extractions by observing failures in the past – either refining their programs manually or providing additional training data to the system. User-specified failures give the system an opportunity to automatically adjust its behavior. For example, by identifying a failure on past data, the user is providing examples to the system, which can be used to train a failure detection mechanism. Supplying a "fix" to this failure can help train exception handling mechanisms that will allow a program to continue working or adapting despite future changes to page structure.

Users, as constructors of these programs and extractions, have a unique ability to determine if a program has succeeded. Additionally, historical data can be used in simulation. By simulating the program – whether an extraction, or something more sophisticated – on historical data, the programmer can identify failure conditions that may recur in the future and increase the robustness of his programs. Such a facility is interesting not only for systems targeting extraction tasks (e.g., Chapter 12 and (Dontcheva et al., 2007b), but also to PBD systems (e.g., see Chapter 5 and Leshed et al., 2008) and complex mashups (e.g., Chapter 8 and Fujima et al., 2004; Bolin et al., 2005). By retaining historical Web data, end user programming environments can allow users to test their programs. For example, a system like Clip, Connect, Clone (see Chapter 8 and Fujima et al., 2004) might allow a user to "clip" a stock price from one page, submit that value to a currency conversion system on a second page, and multiply by the number of owned shares on yet a third page. Historical data, such as that provided by Zoetrope, would allow for testing the application with different values. A simple slider on top of the stock price selection, for example, might allow a user to test the program on different historical values of the stock very simply. Such a system also raises interesting design and research questions as the conversion step may not use the conversion rate from the present rather than the time the user has set the slider to.

The incorporation of the temporal dimension in end user Web programming represents an interesting departure from the traditional Now Web view of the world. In addition to providing users with access to data that may no longer be available in an easy to manipulate way, retaining such information has broader implications for Now Web applications that are dependent on the ill-defined and constantly changing interfaces exposed by the Web. Temporal Web data can provide users with the ability to test, debug, simulate, and strengthen their programs into more robust end user programs.

ZOETROPE

Intended users:	All users, scientists
Domain:	All Web sites
Description:	Zoetrope is a visual query language for the ephemeral Web. The system allows a user to extract, visualize, and correlate data from historical versions of Web pages, from within the context of the "present" version. "Lenses" give fine-grained control over the data that is extracted and provide a quick test to validate these extractions.
Example:	Correlate historical gas and oil prices with news events about "war." The user draws lenses on one page containing today's gas prices, another on a page containing today's per-barrel oil price. Zoetrope extracts these prices from historical versions of the page, creating time series visualizations. Selecting the headline article on the news page, and filtering for "war," causes Zoetrope to identify historical articles that have appeared on the page and contain the term. A visualization can be created that links them for user exploration.
Automation:	Yes, the system automates certain historical extractions.
Mashups:	Yes, historical data from different pages can be aggregated.
Scripting:	No, Zoetrope provides a visual query language but not a traditional scripting language.
Natural language:	No, Zoetrope is a visual language.
Recordability:	No.
Inferencing:	Yes, using cues from the user, the system attempts to identify historical content relevant to the query.
Sharing:	Yes, extracted data can be pushed to public/shared pages (e.g., Google spreadsheets).
Comparison to other systems:	Zoetrope is unique in that it specifically targets historical Web data. Zoetrope's techniques might be useful in other systems for testing programs on historical versions of Web pages.
Platform:	The Zoetrope front end is implemented as a Java application; the crawling infrastructure is based on a Firefox plugin.
Availability:	Not publicly available.

Subjunctive interfaces for the Web

14

Aran Lunzer,[1] **Kasper Hornbæk**[2]

[1]*Meme Media Laboratory, Hokkaido University*
[2]*Dept. of Computer Science, University of Copenhagen*

ABSTRACT

The data resources and applications accessible through today's Web offer tremendous opportunities for exploration: ask a slightly different question, receive a correspondingly different answer. However, typical browser-based mechanisms for accessing the Web only enable users to pose one such question at a time, placing a heavy operational and cognitive burden on any user who wants to explore and compare alternatives. A subjunctive-interface approach may reduce this burden. Subjunctive interfaces support the setting up, viewing, and adjustment of multiple scenarios in parallel, allowing side-by-side instead of temporally separated viewing, and more efficient iteration through alternatives. We have implemented a spreadsheet-inspired environment where end users can program and use their own Web-access applications that include such multiscenario support. In this chapter we describe three modes of use of this environment – parallel retrieval, coordinated manipulation, and tentative composition – and explain how these may help to alleviate typical challenges in Web-based tasks. At the same time, we acknowledge that the increased scope for exploration made possible through this environment can itself present a form of cognitive burden to users, and we outline our plans for evaluating the impact of this effect.

INTRODUCTION

How inconvenient it is that so many applications for accessing Web resources only deliver results in response to explicit, pinpoint requests. For example, interfaces for flight enquiries typically require the user to specify exactly one destination city, which is fine for users with precisely formulated travel plans but a bore for everyone else. A user who wants to compare the deals and schedules available for a range of destinations must embark on an exploration, submitting a succession of requests and analyzing their respective results.

One problem in such cases is that users have poor support for covering a range of requests, even if the details of those requests follow some regular pattern. A user searching for flights might request information for several routes on a given date, or for a single route over many dates, or combinations of a few routes and dates. But if the interface only supports the handling of a single request at a time, this burdens the user not only with a potentially high number of interface actions to specify and submit the requests, but also with increased mental effort in planning the requests, remembering which requests have been made so far, and remembering where interesting results were found.

Furthermore, one-at-a-time interfaces provide poor support for comparing results (Terry & Mynatt, 2005), in that making comparisons requires the user to remember – or to have written down, or to request again – the details of those results that are currently out of sight. This again can constitute both a physical and a mental burden. We believe that these burdens can be reduced by enabling the user to carry out a number of requests at the same time. We refer to this as the use of parallel retrievals.

Consider now a second kind of Web interaction. A doctor who has access to her patients' records through a secure Web connection wants to retrieve images from specific stages in the treatment of a single patient, for example to observe progress of a disease within an organ. On obtaining each abdominal image study she goes through the same operations of selecting and scaling the desired sub-portion of the images, in three orthogonal planes, then adjusting the grayscale mapping so as to emphasize the boundary of the diseased region, and finally selecting display of just the overlays containing her own annotations. She accumulates browser windows, one for each imaging study, to be able to switch between them to help grasp the disease's changes over time. If she finds that the diseased region has spread beyond the bounds of the focus area she selected for the earlier studies, she readjusts those earlier views so that she can still compare like with like.

In this situation, which could equally apply to retrieving and manipulating weather maps, or archived pictures from a Webcam, it is frustrating to have to perform the same image manipulations many times over, especially given the risk that information gained from later views will upset earlier decisions. This frustration could be alleviated if there were a way to manipulate the various retrieved resources in concert, continuously confirming that the results will be valid for all of them. This we refer to as coordinated manipulation.

As a third example, consider a holidaymaker who (having successfully selected some flights) is now installed in a foreign city and is planning a day of sightseeing. The city is served by a navigation service Web site that provides estimates of point-to-point journey times on foot or by public transport. Having made a list of addresses he would like to visit, the visitor can use this site to plan an itinerary for the day.

The challenge here is to come up with a sequence of visits, and the journeys between them, that promises to be an interesting overall experience without excessive use of travel time or leg-power. If there were a strict constraint that all the listed sites be visited, a "traveling salesman" algorithm could be put to work in search of a time-efficient total solution – or, perhaps, the conclusion that there is no way to visit them all within a day. However, all but the most ardent tourist would probably take a more relaxed approach, trying a few alternative visit orders and transport options, and being willing to reject sites that turn out to be inconvenient to include. Nonetheless, this would be a frustrating task in the absence of support for what we call tentative composition – meaning, in this case, being able to compose and compare a number of alternative itineraries, involving different sites and/or different visit orders.

We believe that the above three kinds of challenge can all be addressed by offering users access to Web resources through subjunctive interfaces (Lunzer, 1999): interfaces that allow a user to explore alternatives by setting up multiple application scenarios at the same time, viewing those scenarios side by side, and manipulating them in parallel. In this chapter we report our investigations into using subjunctive interfaces for Web access.

The emphasis is on user control. As explained in the description of the third challenge, these cases are not amenable to definition in a way that would allow an automated algorithm to proceed, unsupervised, to an optimal solution. Only the user can specify what cases are of potential interest, and only the user can evaluate and (where necessary) compare the results. This interactivity places practical bounds on the complexity of setup that a user can be expected to handle; subjunctive interfaces are specifically designed to support about 10 parallel scenarios. Applications that would call for dozens or even hundreds of scenarios should be addressed with different techniques.

We begin by describing the RecipeSheet, a subjunctive-interface-enabled programming environment that we have equipped with mechanisms specifically for accessing Web resources. In the three following sections we then introduce three usage examples that address challenges of the kinds given previously; for each example we discuss briefly its applicability to common modes of use of today's Web. After these examples we address a potential downside to this work: that in seeking to make it easier to pursue an exploration that brings a range of information to a user's screen, we may be counterproductively increasing the burden on the user who then has to evaluate that information. Finally, we report on some initial feedback received from research colleagues for whom we implemented RecipeSheet-based applications for their work.

SUPPORTING MULTISCENARIO WEB ACCESS WITH THE RECIPESHEET

The RecipeSheet (Lunzer & Hornbæk, 2006a; Lunzer & Hornbæk, 2006b) is a spreadsheet-inspired environment that has built-in subjunctive-interface features, and thus supports parallel exploration of alternative calculations and their results. Like a spreadsheet, the RecipeSheet provides support for setting up custom flow-like calculations in terms of dependencies between cells. The subjunctive-interface features mean that the cells providing inputs at the start of a flow (referred to as ingredients) can hold multiple values simultaneously, the user can set up alternative scenarios based on chosen combinations of those values, and the cells holding derived values will then show the results for all scenarios, color-coded and/or spatially arranged to help the user understand which result arose from which scenario.

A RecipeSheet user defines inter-cell dependencies in terms of so-called recipes. There is a set of standard recipes, such as for extracting particular tagged elements from a chunk of XML, but users are also expected to create their own. Recipes can be programmed directly in Smalltalk, Open Object Rexx, or XQuery; recipes capturing behavior from Web applications can be built using the mechanisms of C3W (see Chapter 8) and Web-service recipes can be created with the help of SOAP or REST. In addition, the setup of cells and recipes on a sheet can be saved as a single composite recipe, that can then be used on other sheets.

Figures 14.1 and 14.2 show two of the fundamental operations in setting up a calculation flow on a RecipeSheet: adding a precoded recipe (in this case, written in Smalltalk) by dragging from a Recipe Browser onto the sheet, and then adding wires to connect a recipe to other recipes or cells.

Figure 14.3 illustrates one way for a user to set up additional calculation scenarios on a sheet: here the use of control-click (a mouse click with the Control key held down) on a value creates an additional scenario to hold the clicked value. In ingredient cells, markers with scenario-specific colored regions show which scenarios have been set up with which values. Further mouse operations

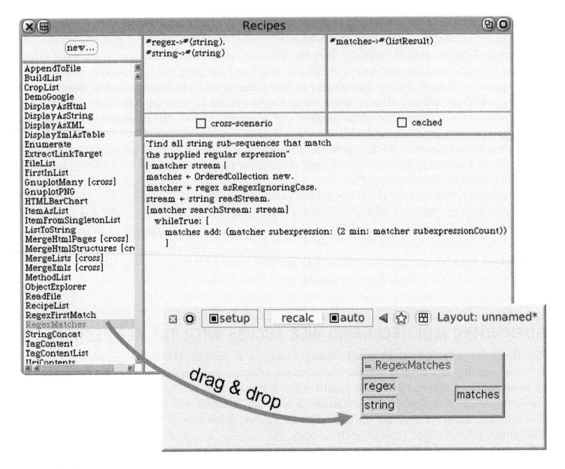

FIGURE 14.1

Adding a prebuilt recipe to a sheet, by dragging from the Recipe Browser. The sheet is in setup mode, in which recipes and their connections are displayed but the contents of any cells are hidden.

allow the user to move these markers to other values, thus adjusting the ingredients supplied to the scenarios' respective calculations. These operations are adapted from our earlier user studies on application-specific interfaces (Lunzer & Hornbæk, 2008).

As noted above, the RecipeSheet incorporates mechanisms originally developed for C3W (Clip, Connect, and Clone for the Web). Compared to the Microsoft Excel-backed substrate used in the original C3W implementation, the RecipeSheet provides more flexible facilities for connecting processing units extracted from Web applications, and for cloning their inputs to see multiple results side by side. The RecipeSheet replicates C3W's viewport facilities in the form of result cells that have the full rendering behavior of Microsoft's Internet Explorer (IE). These IE-based cells themselves offer C3W-style interaction features for selecting or clipping (i.e., extracting) HTML

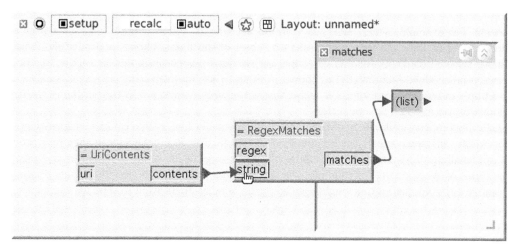

FIGURE 14.2

Dependency connections on a RecipeSheet. Here the user is specifying a connection from the *contents* result of the UriContents recipe to the *string* ingredient of the RegexMatches recipe, whose *matches* result has already been connected to a cell.

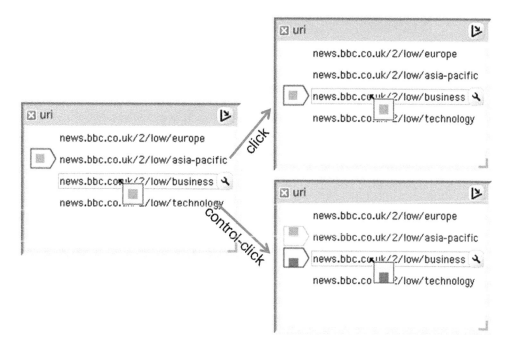

FIGURE 14.3

The basic mechanism for setting up additional scenarios. Whereas a plain click on an ingredient value just switches the input to the clicked value, a control-click sets up a second scenario to hold the value. Scenarios are distinguished by consistent use of color and relative positioning throughout the interface: within the scenario markers, and for side-by-side result displays (Figures 14.6, 14.7, and 14.9).

elements. For example, a user can select arbitrary elements within a page (e.g., in a page that includes a list of links the user might select a subset of the link anchors), and have the contents of those selected elements (in this case, the anchor tags) passed as inputs to another recipe for follow-on processing. Additionally, as shown in Figure 14.4, by interacting with such a cell a user can set up a degenerate form of C3W recipe that will simply extract a selected portion of the cell's contents for use in other cells or recipes.

A further property of the RecipeSheet is that the processing for a recipe is itself an ingredient – in other words, an input – that can be specified in a cell. The RecipeSheet can therefore provide uniform handling of variation in both inputs and processing, which seems a natural requirement in some forms of Web access. For example, whereas one user may want to view the results of sending alternative keyword queries to a single search engine, another might want to send the same query to

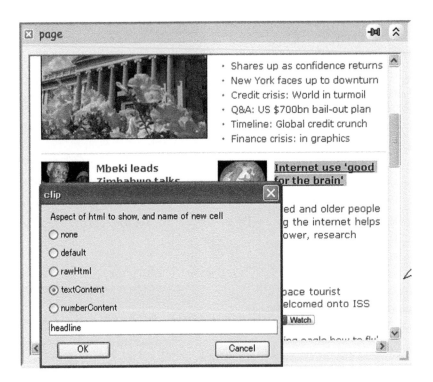

FIGURE 14.4

A visual mechanism for creating simple recipes to extract elements of HTML Web pages, by "clipping" a portion of a page displayed in a result cell. Here the user has highlighted and double-clicked a headline on a news page; in the dialog box she has given the name *headline* to the cell to be created to show this value, and has selected that just the textual content of the selected element (rather than the entire HTML tag) is to be extracted. This creates a custom recipe that will deliver to the *headline* cell the text contents of the corresponding element in whatever HTML is supplied to the cell *page*.

multiple engines. On a RecipeSheet the user can decide freely from one moment to the next whether to view variation in one aspect or the other, or a combination of the two.

This completes our brief outline of how the RecipeSheet supports multiple Web access scenarios. The potential benefits depend on how such scenarios are created and used. Each of the situations in the Introduction can be helped by a subjunctive interface being used in a different way: to support parallel retrieval, coordinated manipulation, and tentative composition, respectively. The following examples illustrate these three modes of use.

PARALLEL RETRIEVAL

Parallel retrieval refers to enabling the use of a retrieval style application, such as a flight enquiry site, to specify not just a single retrieval but several alternatives, differing in arbitrary ways, at the same time. These retrievals are handled in parallel as separate scenarios, and their are results displayed so that the user can see them all simultaneously, and can also see which retrievals delivered which results.

Figure 14.5 shows a sheet that has been set up to find related research article. When multiple searches are run in distinct scenarios, their respective results are merged into a single list for display in the *relatedPapers* cell. The items in this list are marked up, and then sorted, according to which scenarios they appear in. Thus, on the sheet that appears in the back of Figure 14.5 we can see that even though its three queries are all based on papers about the same Elastic Windows project, just three items were found by all three of the queries, and several items were found by one query only. A user who had searched on the basis of any single paper would have missed out on many results.

We suggest that presenting the merged and marked up results from multiple searches can, more generally, help users to work around the bias of any individual search. In (Lunzer, in press) we demonstrate how augmenting a Google search with a set of additional searches narrowed by date (e.g., by adding "1990..1999" to the search phrase) could bring to light items that, though coming at the very top of the results for their particular era, were drowned out of the top entries in a standard (non–date-narrowed) search. In particular, we believe that the markup showing why each item is being offered – for example, that it appeared high in a 1990s search but not in any other – will act as useful guidance for users in judging each item's importance. Muramatsu and Pratt (2001) made a call for this kind of "transparency" in search engine results, to help users of search engines to understand – and to control, if they wish – the transformations, such as stop word removal or suffix expansion, that are applied automatically to their queries. The desirability of such transparency in result presentation has itself gained much attention recently, as evidenced by an extensive survey (Cramer et al., 2008).

However, even having decided to augment a result display to reveal where each result has come from, it is far from clear what form of presentation will work best. Dumais, Cutrell, and Chen (2001), studying the impact of alternative formats for marking up results with automatically derived category information (e.g., distinguishing the various topics of pages retrieved by an ambiguous query such as "Jaguar"), found that users were much quicker at finding relevant items from lists divided according to category than from the complementary form of display in which category information was added

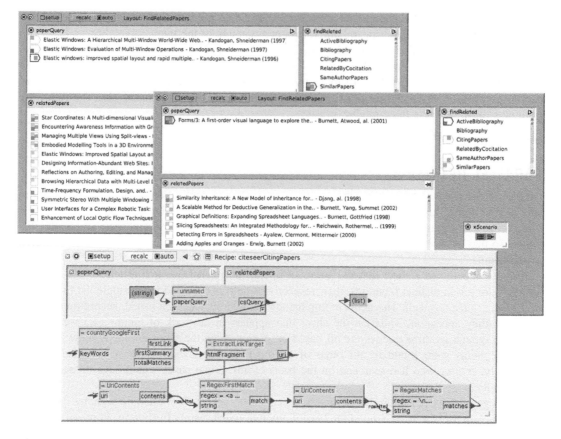

FIGURE 14.5

Parallel retrieval. Searching for academic articles, using mechanisms captured from the CiteSeer and DBLP Web sites. In the two upper sheets, the recipe specified in *findRelated* is used to find articles related to the one specified in *paperQuery*. In the sheet shown at top the user has requested a "similar papers" retrieval for each of three articles from the same project; in the second sheet, four alternative queries based on a single article. Results from all scenarios are merged into a single list, with markup to show which scenarios each item appears in – for example, the "Similarity Inheritance" paper (center of the figure) was found by three out of four searches. The searches were all coded as composite recipes; at the bottom is the setup of the sheet defining the CitingPapers recipe.

to each item in a single list. For an application such as the literature search shown in Figure 14.5, where items typically belong to multiple scenarios (cf. a unique category), and where this multiple membership itself has meaning, the trade-off is likely to be less clear-cut. In general we do not expect that any single presentation approach would be optimal for all parallel-retrieval situations; it depends too much on the nature of the information within each scenario, and the distinctions between scenarios. Our approach, therefore, is to give users the mechanisms they need to build multiscenario interfaces for their own Web searches.

In terms of Kellar, Watters, and Shepherd's (2007) four-category classification of Web-based information-seeking tasks, we regard parallel retrieval as being relevant to at least Fact Finding and certain kinds of Transaction. Fact Finding is used to refer to short-lived tasks for locating specific pieces of information, whereas Transactions covers interaction with Web applications, such as shopping sites, or email or blogging tools. The other two categories of information seeking – Information Gathering and Browsing – are by their nature less structured, and therefore less likely to have the regularity that makes parallel retrieval practical.

The fact that some Transaction-style operations have side effects, such as making purchases, would set a context-specific boundary on the actions that most users would want to perform in parallel. Whereas it would be reasonable to enquire about room prices at several hotels for the same date, for example, it would be highly unusual then to proceed to book them all. On the other hand, if the user's task happens to be to find a single hotel with a room available for each of several separate visits, proceeding to make a simultaneous booking for a set of enquiries (i.e., the various visits) might indeed make sense. Such an operation would fall within what we refer to as coordinated manipulation, as described in the next section.

COORDINATED MANIPULATION

By coordinated manipulation we mean having simultaneous control over several instances of an interactive application; in the introduction we gave the example of using this for browsing images. Within a subjunctive interface these application instances would typically reside within distinct scenarios created by the user.

Figure 14.6 shows a RecipeSheet built for the European Union's project ACGT,[1] which is pursuing (among other things) the development of an OncoSimulator that can reliably simulate cancer growth and treatment. The 3D visualization on the right of the sheet supports a limited form of direct-manipulation interaction: by clicking and dragging with the mouse, a user can rotate a view about horizontal and vertical axes. When there are multiple scenarios, and hence multiple views, their orientations are synchronized by the RecipeSheet such that rotating any one view causes the others to rotate the same amount, as seen in the figure. Such synchronized interaction is a staple of recent developments in coordinated and multiple views (Roberts, 2007), where it is recognized as a powerful technique for helping users to understand related data.

What is not readily apparent from the picture is that these views are in fact Web browsers, and the visualizations are AJAX-enabled pages. This provides the scope for implementing coordination at various levels, potentially applicable to a wide range of applications. The simplest form of coordination involves mirroring operations at the level of individual mouse and keyboard events. This allows coordinated control of visualizations that, like the 3D view in the figure, give uniform responses for user actions at equivalent coordinates within the view. If one were to open a set of Google Maps pages on different locations, for example, the operations of panning, zooming, and image selection could be mirrored at this level. Typing in a request for navigating from the map location to some other (common) location should also work, showing the different routes in

[1]EU FP6 Integrated Project "Advancing Clinico-Genomic Trials on Cancer" (2006-2010); http://www.eu-acgt.org.

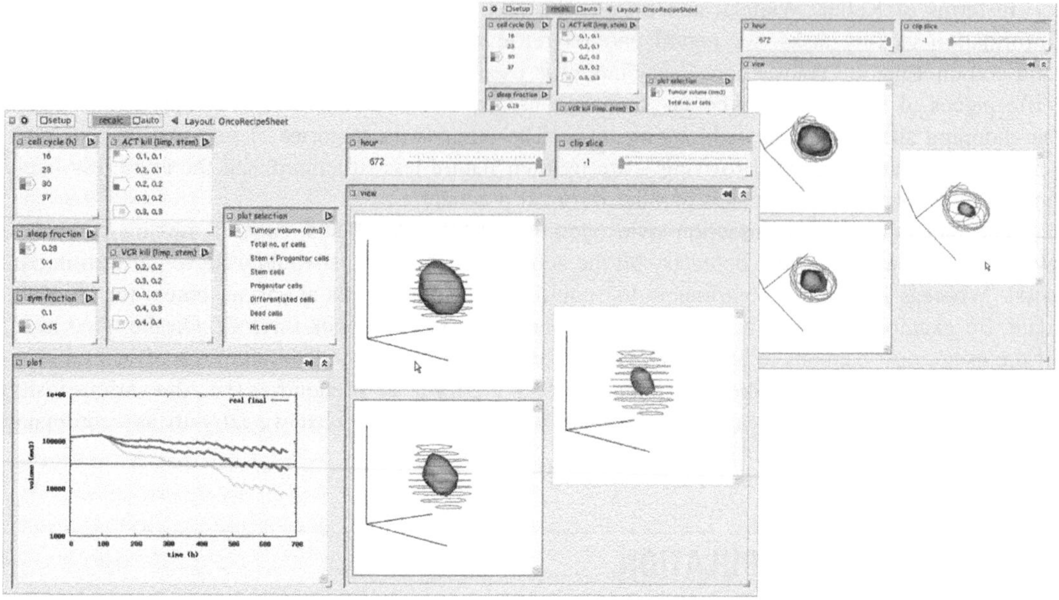

FIGURE 14.6

Coordinated manipulation. Two views of a sheet for exploring results from the ACGT OncoSimulator, a model for predicting the response of an individual patient's tumor to various forms of therapy. The five input cells at top left set the values for various simulation parameters. Here the user has set up three scenarios representing three levels of responsiveness to chemotherapy. In the large cell on the right, which shows an interactive 3D visualization of the simulated tumor, user manipulation is mirrored across all scenarios; in the background we see the outcome of rotating about a horizontal axis.

the individual views. Where this simple approach would break down is if the user switches into a mode such as a city's Street View, where the interaction options available depend on one's precise location in the city.

A next level of coordination would be through identifying and mirroring logical events: abstracting combinations of mouse movements and clicks to make up events such as selecting a menu item, or highlighting the entity at some location within an HTML page's DOM tree. Going a level higher still, one could employ mechanisms such as those of Koala/CoScripter (Little et al., 2007) to record and share operations in a way that would be robust even in the face of (some) differences in page layout.

Mirroring events at an abstract level therefore makes it possible to support not just manipulation of the objects within Web pages, but coordinated clicking of link anchors to navigate from one page to the next through matching regions of a Web site – for example, through standardized sets of pages relating to hotels on a travel site, or proteins in a bioinformatics repository. Hence, as mentioned previously, the possibility of querying a travel service to find a hotel that has a room available for each of several visits, then going through the booking procedure for all those visits together.

The above discussion shows how a given task can straddle the border between parallel retrieval and coordinated manipulation. Work by Teevan et al. (2004) suggests that much directed search on the Web – that is, search for a target that is known in advance to exist – is carried out as a mixture of the basic elements that underlie the two. Teevan et al. distinguish between, on the one hand, teleporting, by which they mean jumping directly to a Web page found as the result of a query, and on the other hand, orienteering, their term for localized, situated navigation that begins at a familiar starting point (such as a portal) and narrows in on the target. As noted before, the best we can do as interface designers is to provide facilities for users to choose for themselves the mix of teleporting and orienteering, and the range of scenarios over which they wish to perform the two. For now we are investigating what facilities make sense for the user group developing and calibrating the ACGT OncoSimulator.

TENTATIVE COMPOSITION

Some Web-based tasks can be characterized as the composition of multiple pieces of retrieved information, where it is the overall composed entity that serves the user's purpose, rather than the elements on their own. The example given in the introduction, of building a sightseeing itinerary, is essentially a composition of the route recommendations returned by the navigation service in response to various point-to-point queries. Being able to experiment with and compare alternative compositions, such as in this case varying the sequence of locations to be visited, is what we refer to as tentative composition.

As with the preceding two modes of use, tentative composition covers a broad range of users' tasks. At the simple end of this range are tasks in which the "elements" being combined are merely the values for placeholders within a structure that has been defined in advance: an everyday example would be the choice of starter, main course, and dessert to make up a meal; using today's Web one might create an office party invitation by composing venue details, transport information, and a map. Cases such as these can be treated simply as parameterized retrievals, and therefore explored using parallel retrieval mechanisms.

At the complex end of tentative composition tasks are cases of general design with arbitrarily many degrees of freedom, such as the planning of a new building or of a multi-continent concert tour. For some of these complex domains there are already specialized applications that include support for exploring design alternatives, and we are not suggesting that generic mechanisms for handling multiple scenarios could provide a similar strength of support. We believe that subjunctive interfaces will make their mark on small-scale, ad hoc composition of Web resources.

Supporting tentative composition requires, first, providing a substrate on which compositions are built. Then there must be a convenient way for the user to specify alternatives, and supportive mechanisms for viewing the corresponding outcomes and understanding how they differ – either in terms of the final results, or the alternative specifications that led to them. The RecipeSheet, having been designed to work as a substrate for flow-style calculations based on values supplied in cells, is inherently suited to the simplest kinds of tentative composition which, as stated above, can be set up like parallel retrievals. Figure 14.7 shows one such example, where the composition being carried out is the application of style settings to a Web page.

Beyond these simple cases, the RecipeSheet's supportiveness depends on how the composition is defined as a calculation flow. The building of a sightseeing itinerary could be tackled in various ways:

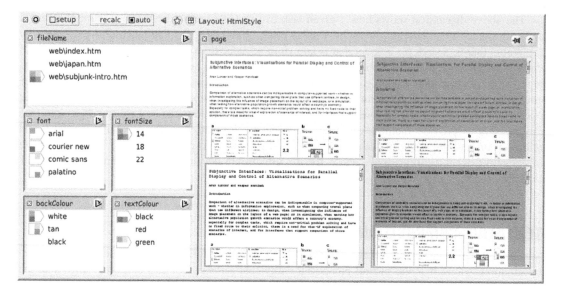

FIGURE 14.7

Tentative composition. In this case what is being composed is a rendered Web page, based on values supplied for the page content and for various style-defining parameters. The user has set up four alternative "compositions," and can see at a glance differences between them, such as how the font style affects the amount of space needed to render a given paragraph.

one possibility is to have a cell defining each sequential step in the itinerary (for example, one cell specifying the first visit address, a second cell specifying the second visit, and so on); another is to have a single cell in which the whole itinerary is specified as a list of addresses, and that lets the user specify different lists for different scenarios. The fact that the RecipeSheet makes specifying alternative processing as easy as specifying alternative parameter values would be useful in experimenting with alternative navigation services within these itineraries. However, we readily admit that both of the above approaches have potentially troublesome limitations: for example, the first would be highly inefficient for a user who wanted to try adding or removing one visit from an existing itinerary, whereas the second would provide poor support for grasping rapidly how two or more itineraries differ.

Although we are sure that the current design of the RecipeSheet is not the final answer in terms of supporting tentative composition in general, we believe its current level of support is sufficient to begin evaluation on exploratory tasks of this kind.

RISKS OF COGNITIVE OVERLOAD: THE PARADOX OF CHOICE

The Paradox of Choice is the title of a popular book by Barry Schwartz (2004), in which he points out that although having some freedom to make choices in your life feels much better than having no choice at all, too much choice is a problem in its own right. People get stressed by the amount of mental effort involved in weighing up alternatives, by the worry that other, better alternatives are somewhere out there to be found, and, after making a choice, by the fear that on balance one of the rejected options might have been better.

Given that subjunctive interfaces are intended to improve the quality of information users receive by encouraging them to request and view more alternatives, Schwartz's studies suggest that we might be doing our users more harm than good. Especially given the vast amount of information available over the Web, it can be argued that what users desperately need is more filtering, not more retrievals.

However, we feel that the current popular approach to helping users make sense of the Web – namely, using some hidden ranking or other heuristics to deliver a small, possibly high-quality but necessarily biased selection of results – is asking users to put too much trust in online systems. There is some evidence that users are alert to this: for example, Lin et al. (2003) found, in a study of users' attitudes to question-answering systems, a tendency to feel uncomfortable accepting answers from systems that provided only the bare answer. The users wanted to see some context surrounding the answer, to help them confirm its legitimacy.

Nonetheless, there are also plenty of studies showing that giving users too much to do is counter-productive. Beaulieu and Jones (1998) discuss the relationships between the visibility of system functions, the balance of control between user and system, and the user's cognitive load. They experimented with a relevance-feedback retrieval interface that was purposely designed to keep the users in control of their queries, by revealing the details of the feedback-derived query terms and requiring the users to review and adjust those terms. The users' response to this interface was to become less active, rather than more, presumably because they felt that making all those adjustments would be too much work. Muramatsu and Pratt (2001), who concluded from their study of transparent queries (mentioned earlier) that perhaps the best style of interface would be a "penetrable" interface – one that lets the user know what has been done, and also provides a chance to change it – made a point of adding the caveat that providing too much control could inadvertently overload the user.

Part of the issue, as Beaulieu and Jones note, is that users need to feel that the decisions available to them are relevant to their personal information needs, rather than being just artifacts of the interface. For our own goals of deploying end user programming and customization techniques that help users to express a range of directions to investigate, and then to make sense of the corresponding range of results, we must therefore strive to ensure that users will perceive this effort as part of what they wanted to do anyway. If we can achieve that, there is hope that users will regard the ability to set up and work with multiple scenarios as a welcome level of choice, rather than an unwelcome source of stress.

RESULTS OF INITIAL EVALUATIONS

Our initial evaluations have been based on two applications that we built using the RecipeSheet to meet specific needs of some of our research colleagues. Rather than pursue laboratory evaluations of the RecipeSheet, we decided to test it on real and complex examples of custom built Web processing. We set out from Shneiderman and Plaisant's (2006) notion of multidimensional, in-depth, long-term case studies, in which the idea is to iteratively develop and refine information visualizations in collaboration with professionals. Thus, we have worked in depth with two research projects and the applications they develop. Below we discuss these cases and present some initial results, relating in both cases to the pursuit of parallel retrievals.

The first application is an interface for running queries against DBpedia, an RDF representation of 2.6 million data items and their relationships as extracted from Wikipedia. Figure 14.8 shows an example of use of a sheet that has been set up for submitting SPARQL queries against the DBpedia data set and viewing their results. This example shows an exploration of the question, "With what country or countries is each Nobel Prize winner associated?" The data held in Wikipedia, and hence DBpedia, allows many ways of identifying such associations: Figure 14.8 shows the simultaneous posing of queries based on (a) the country of an educational institution attended by the person; (b) the country of an institution where the person worked; (c) the country where the person was born; and (d) the country where he or she died. Being able to pose these queries independently but simultaneously, and to see, from the scenario markup included in the results, which answer arose from

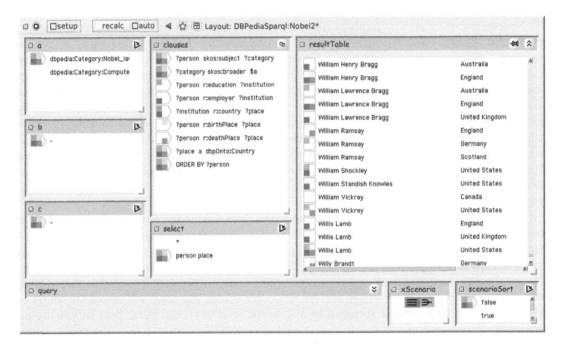

FIGURE 14.8

Requesting and viewing multiple parallel DBpedia queries. On this sheet, queries are defined as compositions of *clauses* entered by the user into the clauses cell. The clauses can include tokens such as $a, $b that refer to values in the corresponding named cells on the sheet (in this example only $a is being used). The user is looking for Nobel Prize winners and the countries with which they are associated, and has set up four scenarios querying, respectively, countries related to the person's education (scenario 1, shown with a mark in the top-left quadrant), employment (bottom left), birth (top right), and death (bottom right). The results show, for example, that – at least according to DBpedia's data – William Henry Bragg was born, worked, and died in England, and also worked in Australia.

which scenario, offers insights that would not be available from a simple list of people against countries. Among the available insights are an appreciation of DBpedia's incompleteness (for example, that country of birth is sometimes not clearly identified), and some common inconsistencies (such as variation between England and United Kingdom).

In evaluating this application we worked with two colleagues who are carrying out research on interfaces for accessing Semantic Web resources. They had both chosen DBpedia as a target platform for their work, and were at the stage of exploring its structure and content to understand what degree of regularity they would be able to exploit. Both were already well versed in the SPARQL query language. We made our DBpedia-specific sheet available for them to install, and supervised their first sessions of use to provide guidance on the basic facilities available. Their explorations of DBpedia continued for around a month, during which they occasionally consulted us with questions or requests for additional features. Our follow-up interviews were semistructured and focused on pertinent work tasks and the match of the RecipeSheet to those tasks. We also specifically canvassed their views on any difficulties they had encountered in setting up and manipulating scenarios.

Both of the interviewees felt that the RecipeSheet interface provided better support for their explorations than, for example, the various Web-browser-based SPARQL endpoints available at the time. One aspect of this perceived improvement arose from some simplifying assumptions we had made in our implementation: supporting a useful but incomplete subset of SPARQL (notably, only SELECT queries), and providing an extensive set of simple pre-canned entity-prefix abbreviations (such as **p:** for all DBpedia predicates). Further benefits arose from basic housekeeping characteristics of RecipeSheet layouts: for example, entity descriptors found within query results could be transferred easily (by drag and drop) to an ingredient cell, where they would remain through saves and reloads of the sheet, serving a reminding purpose even if not used often in further queries. This was especially useful for hard-to-remember entities, such as YAGO subject descriptors.

Both colleagues appreciated and benefited from the ability to run multiple queries side by side. One showed how she had used this in learning about the consistency of use of alternative predicates that indicate the same real-world relationship (e.g., **p:birthDate**, **p:dateOfBirth**); the other gave as an example his exploration of how consistently particular predicates were used across a range of related entity classes (e.g., various subclasses of **yago:Movie**). More generally, they saw the ability to see merged results from many queries as offering an augmented form of UNION: not only do you see the combined list of results as would appear in a standard UNION query, but each result is marked up with the particular query (which would normally be buried as a subpart of the UNION) that gave rise to it.

Various pieces of feedback from these colleagues led us to iterate the design of some basic RecipeSheet features. We learned that our mouse-click-based interface for switching items into and out of particular scenarios in multiselection lists (such as the *clauses* cell) was sometimes confusing. We developed an alternative selection mechanism based on use of the keyboard's number keys, correlated with a simple top-left to bottom-right ordering of scenarios. To select the clause **?institution r:country ?place** in the top-left and bottom-left scenarios as seen in Fig. 14.8, for example, the user presses the 1 and 2 keys (separately) while the mouse is over the marker for that clause. The users found this easier to understand than the mouse-based interface, and also faster.

We also noticed that the users frequently made slips when performing certain operations, such as deleting ingredient values when they had intended to reduce the number of scenarios, or vice versa. In discussions we realized that the relationship between scenarios and ingredient values was a source of confusion: in particular, the fact that a scenario can exist even if there are no ingredient values selected for it, and hence no colored marks on view corresponding to that scenario. We are working with the users to come up with a less surprising set of interface rules.

In response to specific requests we added a facility for stepping back through the recent history of scenario operations and selections, and a flashing telltale during long calculations (in this case, queries requiring lengthy processing by the DBpedia server) to alert the user that calculation is still in progress.

In our continuing evaluations in this area we are addressing other Web-centered retrieval domains (e.g., recommendations provided through the Amazon.com API), and shall be investigating users' understanding of and preferences regarding the merged presentation of alternative retrievals carried out in parallel. In this we hope to build on the context-presentation findings of Dumais et al. (2001) and follow-on work.

The second case study, which is still in progress, centers on our delivery of the front-end interface for the ACGT OncoSimulator, which has undergone many design iterations since the prototype seen in Figure 14.6. This includes recent changes made in response to feedback from the DBpedia study.

The first rounds of design iteration were carried out on the basis of our own experiences in using the sheet to exercise the simulation code across a range of cases, and in ironing out glitches in communication with the remote Grid services (provided by a project partner in Poland) that invoke the simulator, and with the Web server (provided by another partner in the Netherlands) that delivers the visualizations. The next stage in the project is an extensive validation and calibration of the OncoSimulator code, involving yet more partner groups. This is still under way at the time of writing.

Part of the job of simulator validation involves running large numbers of cases across sweeps of parameter values to confirm that the outcomes evolve consistently. Figure 14.9 shows one such parameter sweep, based on just 2 of the 35 parameters supported by the simulator. By setting up and recording many of these sweeps, the simulator developers will build up a picture of the zones of the parameter space within which the simulator functions predictably, and the confidence intervals that should be applied to its results based on sensitivity to critical parameters and their combinations.

For our evaluation we first wanted to confirm that our colleagues would be comfortable working with the RecipeSheet to set up, view, and where necessary keep records of such sweeps across critical regions of the parameter space. We gave the system to a member of the partner group in the Netherlands, and interviewed him after 3 weeks of using it. Again, the interview was semistructured; we focused on scenario setup and manipulation, with the overall goal of carrying out tasks directly relevant to the real-world validation work that the sheet is being used to support.

We found that the interviewee had become proficient in using the interface for setting up and viewing scenario combinations, and that he was generally satisfied with its features. We had made available to him the new keyboard-based scenario control mechanism that was suggested through our work with the DBpedia users, and he confirmed that for tasks involving complex setup of scenarios he too would opt to use this mechanism over the others available. However, he also gave comments similar to the DBpedia users regarding sources of confusion in the facilities for scenario deletion.

One set of features demanded by and newly introduced for the OncoSimulator application, though potentially of value in other applications involving access to a large parameter space, relates to helping users to understand where in the parameter space there are results that can be retrieved.

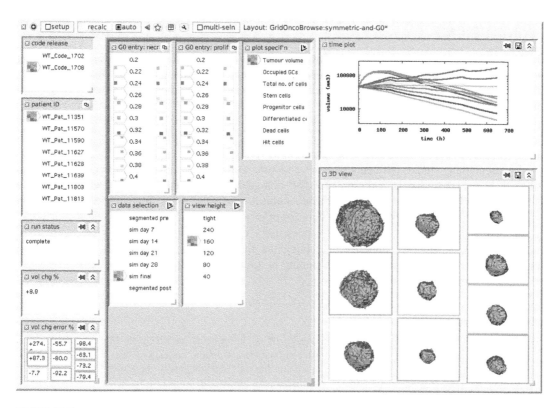

FIGURE 14.9

A parameter sweep carried out in a recent version of the OncoRecipeSheet. Of the 35 parameters used in driving the simulation, two related to *G0 entry* have been chosen, and set up with 10 values paired between the two. The results show, in the plot of tumor volume against time, an apparently dramatic discontinuity in tumor response for values beyond 0.34. Although these values (in combination with the default values used for the undisplayed parameters) are known to represent a biologically impossible situation, it is valuable to observe how the simulator behaves when driven to these extremes.

Given the OncoSimulator's total of 35 parameters, each typically having at least 10 candidate values, the population of the result space is inevitably sparse. We address this by a scheme of adding marks to ingredient values to show where results are available. What we have discovered from our initial evaluations is that users (including the previous interviewee) readily understand the principles of the markup scheme, but nonetheless have some difficulties in working with it in practice. One source of difficulties is the fact that this application has several parameters that work in pairs, and at the current stage of simulator development these paired parameters are typically given the same value, as is seen in Figure 14.9. Such cases seem to cause confusion because of the way that setting a value on one parameter immediately narrows the markup on its paired parameter to a single value. We are currently considering how to evolve this feature to reduce the scope for such confusion.

CONCLUSIONS

In this chapter we have outlined the role that subjunctive-interface mechanisms can play in supporting users' access to and comparison of Web resources. In particular we have shown how Web-access interfaces constructed using the RecipeSheet, a spreadsheet-inspired environment that has subjunctive-interface mechanisms built in, give end users the power to produce, on the fly, their own customized views of multiple resources. Users who also become proficient with the RecipeSheet's construction facilities, starting with its wiring-based interface for creating calculation flows, can go further to build their own interfaces for accessing whichever Web resources happen to interest them.

We are running studies to obtain evidence about the usability and effectiveness of the techniques described here, starting at the end user level. Our first goal is to establish firmly that users understand and can obtain benefits from facilities for using multiple scenarios in their Web interactions. We then plan to investigate how the physical and cognitive effort involved in reaping these benefits, including potential Paradox of Choice effects, influences users' willingness to pursue multiple alternatives rather than taking the easy option of accepting the first results on offer. We hope they can be persuaded that, at least some of the time, putting in a little extra effort does make sense.

Acknowledgments

We gratefully acknowledge the efforts of the developers of the systems on which the RecipeSheet depends, especially the members of the Squeak Smalltalk community, and of the colleagues who have assisted us in building and evaluating the RecipeSheet up to this point: the staff and students of the Meme Media Laboratory, Hokkaido University, and our many collaborating partners in the ACGT project, in particular at the University of Amsterdam and the National Technical University of Athens.

RECIPESHEET

Intended users:	All users; programmers
Domain:	Retrieval, design, and simulation
Description:	The RecipeSheet is not a dedicated Web programming system, but a spreadsheet-inspired environment in which users can build calculation flows and run multiscenario explorations to see how different inputs to the flows produce different results. The RecipeSheet has various mechanisms for accessing and displaying Web data.
Example:	The top results from a Google search can sometimes be affected by adding search operators such as "inurl:" or "allintitle:". A RecipeSheet could be set up to present the top 10 results from a Google search, and a user could choose to run several alternative searches in parallel. The sheet would merge the results, helping the user to check that she was not missing interesting results simply because of the presence or absence of an operator.
Automation:	Yes, tasks with unidirectional flows of data can be automated.
Mashups:	Yes, a sheet's flow can include the supply of results from one processing step as inputs to another, and each step can be delivered by a different Web site or service.
Scripting:	No, though programmers may create processing components.
Natural language:	No.
Recordability:	Yes, user actions can be recorded and result elements from form-style Web sites may be extracted, similar to C3W.
Inferencing:	No.
Sharing:	No, but recipes and layouts may be saved as files that can be distributed to other users.
Comparison to other systems:	The application of the RecipeSheet to Web-based resources is an extension of the original vision for C3W. Unlike other systems, building a sheet may require skills beyond those of a typical end user.
Platform:	Implemented as a plugin for Internet Explorer.
Availability:	A release is planned in 2010 to the Squeak community.

Natural Language

This section of the book explores the role natural language plays in end user programming systems. The first chapter proposes a "sloppy programming" model that takes its inspiration from keyword search interfaces and describes techniques for enabling a sloppy programming environment in the browser. This technique was used in the CoScripter system described in Part 2 of this text, "Customizing and Automating." The PLOW system shows how a natural language spoken explanation can be combined with programming by demonstration to help a system learn procedures from a single example, such as finding hotels near an address.

Finally, the MOOIDE system describes how to leverage an English language parser and commonsense knowledge base to produce a natural language programming environment for multi-player storytelling games.

Sloppy programming

15

Greg Little,[1] Robert C. Miller,[1] Victoria H. Chou,[1] Michael Bernstein,[1] Tessa Lau,[2] Allen Cypher[2]

[1]*MIT CSAIL*
[2]*IBM Research–Almaden*

ABSTRACT

Modern applications provide interfaces for scripting, but many users do not know how to write script commands. However, many users are familiar with the idea of entering keywords into a Web search engine. Hence, if a user is familiar with the vocabulary of an application domain, we anticipate that they could write a set of keywords expressing a command in that domain. For instance, in the Web browsing domain, a user might enter "click search button". We call loosely grammatical commands of this sort "sloppy commands." We discuss several prototypes that implement sloppy programming, translating sloppy commands directly into executable code. We also discuss the algorithms used in these prototypes, expose their limitations, and propose directions for future work.

INTRODUCTION

When a user enters a query into a Web search engine, they do not expect it to return a syntax error. Imagine a user searching for "End-User Programing" and getting an error like: "Unexpected token 'Programing'". Not only would they not expect to see such an error, but they would expect the search engine to suggest the proper spelling of "Programing". The burden is on the search engine to make the user right.

People have come to expect this behavior from search engines, but they do not expect this behavior from program compilers or interpreters. When a novice programmer enters "print hello world" into a modern scripting language, and the computer responds with "SyntaxError: invalid syntax", the attitude of many programmers is that the novice did something wrong, rather than that the computer did something wrong. In this case, the novice may have forgotten to put quotes and parentheses around "hello world", depending on the underlying formal language. Programmers do not often think that the computer forgot to search for a syntactically correct expression that most closely resembled "print hello world".

This attitude may make sense when thinking about code that the computer will run without supervision. In these cases, it is important for the programmer to know in advance exactly how each statement will be interpreted.

However, programming is also a way for people to communicate with computers daily, in the form of scripting interfaces to applications. In these cases, commands are typically executed under heavy supervision. Hence, it is less important for the programmer to know in advance precisely how a command will be interpreted, since they will see the results immediately, and they can make corrections. Unfortunately, scripting interfaces and command prompts typically use formal languages, requiring users to cope with rigid and seemingly arbitrary syntax rules for forming expressions. One canonical example is the semicolon required at the end of each expression in C, but even modern scripting languages like Python and JavaScript have similarly inscrutable syntax requirements.

Not only do scripting interfaces use formal languages, but different applications often use different formal languages: Python, Ruby, JavaScript, sh, csh, Visual Basic, and ActionScript, to name a few. These languages are often similar – many are based on C syntax – but they are different enough to cause problems. For instance, JavaScript assumes variables are global unless explicitly declared to be local with "var", whereas Python assumes variables are local unless declared with "global".

In addition to learning the language, users must also learn the Application Programmer Interface (API) for the application they want to script. This can be challenging, since APIs are often quite large, and it can be difficult to isolate the portion of the API relevant to the current task.

We propose that instead of returning a syntax error, an interpreter should act more like a Web search engine. It should first search for a syntactically valid expression over the scripting language and API. Then it should present this result to the user for inspection, or simply execute it, if the user is "feeling lucky." We call this approach *sloppy programming*, a term coined by Tessa Lau at IBM.

This chapter continues with related work, followed by a deeper explanation of sloppy programming. We then present several prototype systems which use the sloppy programming paradigm, and discuss what we learned from them. Before concluding, we present a high-level description of some of the algorithms that make sloppy programming possible, along with some of their tradeoffs in different domains.

RELATED WORK

Sloppy programming may be viewed as a form of natural programming, not to be confused with natural language processing (NLP), though there is some overlap. Interest in natural programming was renewed recently by the work of Myers, Pane, and Ko (2004), who have done a range of studies exploring how both nonprogrammers and programmers express ideas to computers. These seminal studies drove the design of the HANDS system, a programming environment for children that uses event-driven programming, a novel card-playing metaphor, and rich, built-in query and aggregation operators to better match the way nonprogrammers describe their problems. Event handling code in HANDS must still be written in a formal syntax, though it resembles natural language.

Bruckman's MooseCrossing (1998) is another programming system aimed at children that uses formal syntax resembling natural language. In this case, the goal of the research was to study the ways that children help each other learn to program in a cooperative environment. Bruckman found that almost half of errors made by users were syntax errors, despite the similarity of the formal language to English (Bruckman & Edwards, 1999).

More recently, Liu and Lieberman have used the seminal Pane and Myers studies of nonprogrammers to reexamine the possibilities of using natural language for programming, resulting in the Metafor system (Liu & Lieberman, 2005). This system integrates natural language processing with a commonsense knowledge base, to generate "scaffolding," which can be used as a starting point for programming. Chapter 17 discusses MOOIDE, which takes these ideas into the domain of a multi-player game. Sloppy programming also relies on a knowledge base, but representing just the application domain, rather than global common sense.

The sloppy programming algorithms, each of which is essentially a search through the application's API, are similar to the approach taken by Mandelin et al. for jungloids (Mandelin, Xu, & Bodik, 2005). A jungloid is a snippet of code that starts from an instance of one class and eventually generates an instance of another (e.g., from a File object to an Image object in Java). A query consists of the desired input and output classes, and searches the API itself, as well as example client code, to discover jungloids that connect those classes. The XSnippet system (Sahavechaphan & Claypool, 2006) builds on this idea to find snippets of code that return a particular type given local variables available in the current context. Sloppy programming algorithms must also search an API to generate valid code, but the query is richer, since keywords from the query are also used to constrain the search.

Some other recent work in end-user programming has focused on understanding programming errors and debugging (Ko & Myers, 2004; Ko, Myers, & Aung, 2004; Phalgune et al., 2005), studying problems faced by end users in comprehension and generation of code (Ko et al., 2004; Wiedenbeck & Engebretson, 2004) and increasing the reliability of end-user programs using ideas from software engineering (Burnett, Cook, & Rothermel, 2004; Erwig, 2005). Sloppy programming does not address these issues, and may even force tradeoffs in some of them. In particular, sloppy programs may not be as reliable.

SLOPPY PROGRAMMING

The essence of sloppy programming is that the user should be able to enter something simple and natural, like a few keywords, and the computer should try everything within its power to interpret and make sense of this input. The question then becomes: how can this be implemented?

Key insight

One key insight behind sloppy programming is that many things people would like to do, when expressed in English, resemble the programmatic equivalents of those desires. For example, consider the case where a user is trying to write a script to run in the context of a Web page. They might use a tool like Chickenfoot (see Chapter 3) which allows end users to write Web customization scripts. Now let us say the user types "now click the search button". This utterance shares certain features with the Chickenfoot command "click("search button")", which has the effect of clicking a button on the current Web page with the label "search". In particular, a number of keywords are shared between the natural language expression, and the programming language expression, namely "click", "search", and "button".

We hypothesize that this keyword similarity may be used as a metric to search the space of syntactically valid expressions for a good match to an input expression, and that the best matching expression is likely to achieve the desired effect. This hypothesis is the essence of our approach to implementing sloppy programming. One reason that it may be true is that language designers, and the designers of APIs, often name functions so that they read like English. This makes the functions easier to find when searching through the documentation, and easier for programmers to remember.

Of course, there are many syntactically valid expressions in any particular programming context, and so it is time consuming to exhaustively compare each one to the input. However, we will show later some techniques that make it possible to approximate this search to varying degrees, and that the results are often useful.

Interfaces

Perhaps the simplest interface for sloppy programming is a command-line interface, where the user types keywords into a command box, and the system interprets and executes them immediately. The interface is similar to the model assumed by Web search engines: you enter a query and get back results.

Sloppy commands can also be listed sequentially in a text file, like instructions in a cooking recipe. This model resembles a typical scripting language, though a sloppy program is more constrained. For instance, it is not clear how to declare functions in this model, or handle control flow. These enhancements are an area of future research.

In other research, we have explored an interface for sloppy programming that acts as an extension to autocomplete, where the system replaces keywords in a text editor with syntactically correct code (Little & Miller, 2008). This interface is aimed more at expert programmers using an integrated development environment (IDE). As an example of this interface, imagine that a programmer wants to add the next line of text from a stream to a list, using Java. A sloppy completion interface would let them enter "add line" and the system might suggest something like "lines.add (in.readLine())" (assuming a context with the local variables "lines" and "in" of the appropriate types).

Benefits

Sloppy programming seeks to address many of the programming challenges raised in the Introduction. To illustrate, consider a query like "left margin 2 inches" in a sloppy command-line interface for Microsoft Word. To a human reader, this suggests the command to make the left margin of the current document 2 inches wide. Such a command can be expressed in the formal language of Visual Basic as "ActiveDocument.PageSetup.LeftMargin = InchesToPoints(2)", but the sloppy version of this query has several advantages.

First, note that we do not require the user to worry about strict requirements for punctuation and grammar in their expression. They should be able to say something more verbose, such as "set the left margin to 2 inches", or express it in a different order, such as "2 inches, margin left". Second, the user should not need to know the syntactic conventions for method invocation and assignment in Visual Basic. The same keywords should work regardless of the underlying scripting language. Finally, the user should not have to search through the API to find the exact name for the property they want to access. They also should not need to know that LeftMargin is a property of the PageSetup object, or that this needs to be accessed via the ActiveDocument.

Another advantage of sloppy programming is that it accommodates pure text, as opposed to many end-user programming systems which use a graphical user interface (GUI) to provide structure for user commands. The benefits of pure text are highlighted in (Miller, 2002), and are too great to dismiss outright, even for end-user programming. Consider that text is ubiquitous in computer interfaces. Facilities for easily viewing, editing, copying, pasting, and exchanging text are available in virtually every user interface toolkit and application. Plain text is very amenable to editing – it is less brittle than structured solutions, which tend to support only modifications explicitly exposed in the GUI. Also, text can be easily shared with other people through a variety of communication media, including Web pages, paper documents, instant messages, and email. It can even be spoken over the phone. Tools for managing text are very mature. The benefits of textual languages for programming are well-understood by professional programmers, which is one reason why professional programming languages continue to use primarily textual representations.

Another benefit of using a textual representation is that it allows lists of sloppy queries (a sloppy program) to serve as meta-URLs for bookmarking application states. One virtue of the URL is that it's a short piece of text – a command – that directs a Web browser to a particular place. Because they are text, URLs are easy to share and store. Sloppy programs might offer the same ability for arbitrary applications – you could store or share a sloppy program that will put an application into a particular state. On the Web, this could be used for bookmarking any page, even if it requires a sequence of browsing actions. It could be used to give your assistant the specifications for a computer you want to buy, with a set of keyword queries that fill out forms on the vendor's site in the same way you did. In a word processor, it could be used to describe a conference paper template in a way that is independent of the word processor used (e.g., Arial 10 point font, 2 columns, left margin 0.5 inches).

Sloppy programming also offers benefits to expert programmers as an extension to autocomplete, by decreasing the cognitive load of coding in several ways. First, sloppy queries are often shorter than code, and easier to type. Second, the user does not need to recall all the lexical components (e.g., variable names and methods) involved in an expression, because the computer may be able to infer some of them. Third, the user does not need to type the syntax for calling methods. In fact, the user does not even need to know the syntax, which may be useful for users who switch between languages often.

SYSTEMS

Over the past few years, we have built a number of systems to test and explore the capabilities of sloppy programming. All of these systems take the form of plugins for the Firefox Web browser, and allow end users to control Web pages with sloppy commands. Two of the systems use a command-line interface, whereas the other allows users to record lists of sloppy commands.

Sloppy Web command-line

Our first prototype system (Little & Miller, 2006) tested the hypothesis that a sloppy programming command-line interface was intuitive, and could be used without instructions, provided that the user was familiar with the domain. The Web domain was chosen because many end users are familiar with it. The system takes the form of a command-line interface which users can use to perform common Web browsing tasks. Important user interface elements are shown in Figure 15.1.

The functions in the Web prototype map to commands in Chickenfoot (see Chapter 3). At the time we built this prototype, there were 18 basic commands in Chickenfoot, including "click", "enter", and "pick". The "click" command takes an argument describing a button on the Web page to click. The "enter" command takes two arguments, one describing a textbox on the Web page, and another specifying what text should be entered there. The "pick" command is used for selecting options from HTML comboboxes.

In order to cover more of the space of possible sloppy queries that the user could enter, we included synonyms for the Chickenfoot command names in the sloppy interpreter. For instance, in addition to the actual Chickenfoot function names, such as "enter", "pick", and "click", we added synonyms for these names, such as "type", "choose", and "press", respectively.

For the most part, users of this prototype were able to use the system without any instructions, and accomplish a number of tasks. Figure 15.2 is an image taken directly from the instructions provided to users during a user study. The red circles in the figure indicate changes the user is meant to make to the interface, using pictures rather than words so as not to bias the user's choice of words. The following sloppy instructions for performing these tasks were generated by different users in the study and interpreted correctly by the system: "field lisa simpson", "size large", "Return only image files formatted as GIF", "coloration grayscale", "safesearch no filtering".

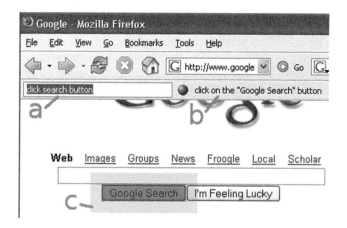

FIGURE 15.1

The graphical user interface (GUI) for the Web command-line prototype consists of a textbox affording input (a), and an adjacent horizontal bar allocated for textual feedback (b). The system also generates an animated acknowledgment in the Web page around the HTML object affected by a command as shown surrounding the "Google Search" button (c).

Find results	related to **all** of the words	lisa simpson
	related to the **exact phrase**	
	related to **any** of the words	
	not related to the words	
Size	Return images that are	large
Filetypes	Return only image files formatted as	GIF files
Coloration	Return only images in	grayscale
Domain	Return images from the site or domain	
SafeSearch	⦿ No filtering ◯ Use moderate filtering ◯ Use strict filtering	

FIGURE 15.2

Example tasks shown to users in a study. The red circles indicate changes the user is meant to make to the interface, using pictures rather than words.

However, we did discover some limitations. One limitation was that the users were not sure at what level to issue commands. To fill out the form above, they didn't know whether they should issue a high-level command to fill out the entire form, or start at a much lower level, first instructing the system to shift its focus to the first textbox. In our study, users never tried issuing high-level commands (mainly because they were told that each red circle represented a single task). However, some users did try issuing commands at a lower level, first trying to focus the system's attention on a textbox, and then entering text there. In this case, we could have expanded the API to support these commands, but in general, it is difficult to anticipate at what level users will expect to operate in a system such as this.

Another limitation was that users were not always able to think of a good way of describing certain elements within an HTML page, such as a textbox with no label. Consider, for example, the second task (the second red oval) in Figure 15.3.

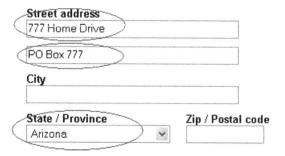

FIGURE 15.3

This is a more difficult example task from the study – in particular, it is unclear how users will identify the textbox associated with the second red oval using words.

We also found that, despite our best efforts to support the wide range of ways that people could express actions, we still found people trying commands we did not expect. Fortunately, in many cases, they would try again, and soon land upon something that the computer understood. This sort of random guessing rarely works with a formal programming language, and is one promising aspect of sloppy programming.

CoScripter

As discussed in Chapter 5, CoScripter was built to explore the synergy of combining several programming paradigms: programming by demonstration, the use of a wiki as a form of end-user source control, and sloppy programming. The newest version of CoScripter uses a grammar-based parser, but this section will focus on an early prototype of the system. CoScripter is an extension to Firefox. It appears as a sidebar to the left of the current Web page as shown in Figure 15.4 (note that this is an early screenshot of the system).

The original CoScripter system experimented with additional user interface techniques to assist users with the sloppy programming paradigm. Because the sloppy interpreter was sometimes wrong, it was important to implement several techniques to help the user know what the interpreter was doing and allow the user to make corrections. These techniques are illustrated in the following example from Figure 15.4. Suppose the user has selected the highlighted line: "scroll down to the 'Shop by commodity' section, click 'View commodities'". CoScripter interprets this line as an instruction to click the link labeled "View commodities". At this point, the system needs to make two things clear to the user: what the interpreter is about to do and why.

The system shows the user what it intends to do by placing a transparent green rectangle around the "View commodities" link, which is also scrolled into view. The system explains why it chose this particular action by highlighting words in the keyword query that contributed to its choice. In this case, the words "click", "view", and "commodities" were associated with the link, so the system makes these words bold: "scroll down to the 'Shop by commodity' section, click 'View commodities'".

If the interpretation was wrong, the user can click the triangle to the left of the line, which expands a list of alternate interpretations. These interpretations are relatively unambiguous instructions generated by the interpreter:

- "click the 'View commodities' link"
- "click the 'View contracts' link"
- "click the 'Skip to navigation' link"

When the user clicks on any of these lines, the system places a green rectangle over the corresponding HTML control. If the line is the correct interpretation, the user can click the "Run" or "Step" button to execute it. If not, they may need to edit the line. Failing that, they can add the keyword "you" (e.g., "you click the 'View commodities' link"), which the interpreter uses as a cue to leave execution to the user.

Note that CoScripter also includes a feature to allow users to record commands by interacting with Web pages rather than writing any sloppy code. Unfortunately, the system would sometimes record an action as a sloppy command that the sloppy interpreter would then fail to

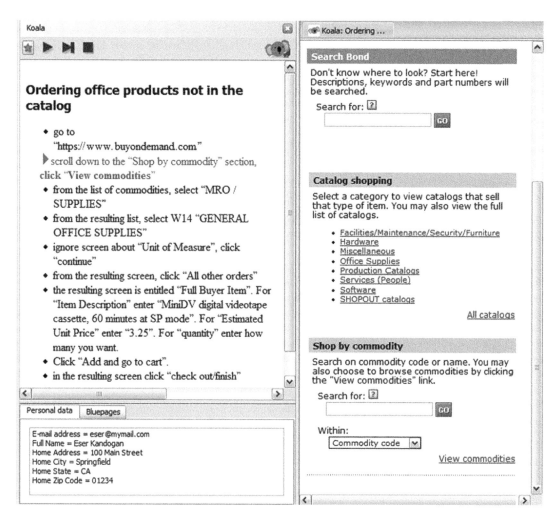

FIGURE 15.4

User interface for CoScripter: a sidebar in the Firefox Web browser.

interpret correctly. This is due to the ambiguous nature of sloppy programming, and suggests directions for future work. For instance, the recorder could notice that the sloppy command is ambiguous, and add additional keywords to alleviate the ambiguity. The newest version of CoScripter uses a grammar-based approach to parse the language, because it is so important for recorded commands to play back as expected (and for other reasons discussed in Chapter 5).

Inky

Inky (Miller et al., 2008) takes the idea of a Web command interface to a new level, seeking to explore a sloppy command interface for higher-level commands. Inky takes the form of a dialog that pops up when the user presses Control-Space in the Web browser. This keyboard shortcut was chosen because it is generally under the user's fingers, and because it is similar to the Quicksilver shortcut (Command-Space on the Mac).

The Inky window (see Figure 15.5) has two areas: a text field for the user to type a command, and a feedback area that displays the interpretations of that command. The Inky window can be dismissed without invoking the command by pressing Escape or clicking elsewhere in the browser.

Inky commands

A command consists of keywords matching a Web site function, along with keywords describing its parameters. For example, in the command "reserve D463 3pm", the reserve keyword indicates that the user wants to make a conference room reservation, and "D463" and "3pm" are arguments to that function.

Like the other sloppy interpreters discussed previously, the order of keywords and parameters is usually unimportant. The order of the entered command matters only when two or more arguments could consume the same keywords. For example, in the command "reserve D463 3pm 1 2 2007", it is unclear if "1" is the month and "2" is the date or vice versa. In "find flights SFO LAX", it is unclear which airport is the origin and which is the destination. In these cases, the system will give higher rank to the interpretation that assigns keywords to arguments in left-to-right order, but other orderings are still offered as alternatives to the user. Commands can use synonyms for both function keywords and arguments. For example, to "reserve D463 at 3pm", the user could have typed "make reservation" instead of "reserve", used a full room number such as "32-D463" or a nickname such as "star room", and used various ways to specify the time, such as "15:00" and "3:00".

Function keywords may also be omitted entirely. Even without function keywords, the arguments alone may be sufficient to identify the correct function. For example, "D463 15:00" is a strong match for the room reservation function, because no other function takes both a conference room and a time as arguments.

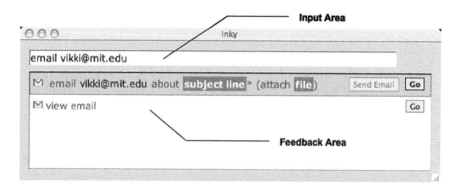

FIGURE 15.5

User interface for the Inky prototype.

The Inky prototype includes 30 functions for 25 Web sites, including scheduling (room reservation, calendar management, flight searches), email (reading and sending), lookups (people, word definitions, Java classes), and general search (in search engines and ecommerce sites). Most of the functions included in the prototype are for popular Web sites; others are specific to Web interfaces (such as a room reservation Web site) at the lab of the developer. Argument types specifically detected by Inky include dates, times, email addresses, cities, states, zip codes, URLs, filenames, and room names. Examples of valid commands include "email vikki@mit.edu Meeting Right Now!" (to send email), "java MouseAdapter" (to look up Java API documentation), "define fastidious" (to search a dictionary), "calendar 5pm meeting with rob" (to make a calendar event), and "weather cambridge ma" (to look up a weather forecast).

Inky feedback

As the user types a command, Inky continuously displays a ranked list of up to five possible interpretations of the command (see Figure 15.6). Each interpretation is displayed as a concise, textual sentence, showing the function's name, the arguments the user has already provided, and arguments that are left to be filled in. The interpretations are updated as the user types in order to give continuous feedback.

The visual cues of the interpretation were designed to make it easier to scan. A small icon indicates the Web site that the function automates, using the favicon (favorites icon) image displayed in the browser address bar when that site is visited. Arguments already provided in the command are rendered in black text. These arguments are usually exact copies of what the user typed, but may also be a standardized version of the user's entry in order to clarify how the system interpreted it. For example, when the user enters "reserve star room", the interpretation displays "reserve D463" instead to show that the system translated star room into a room number.

Arguments that remain to be specified appear as white text in a dark box. Missing arguments are named by a word or short phrase that describes both the type and role of the missing argument. If a missing argument has a default value, a description of the default value is displayed, and the box is less saturated. In Figure 15.7, "name, email, office, etc." is a missing argument with no default, whereas "this month" is an argument which defaults to the current month.

FIGURE 15.6

Example inputs and their corresponding interpretations using the Inky prototype.

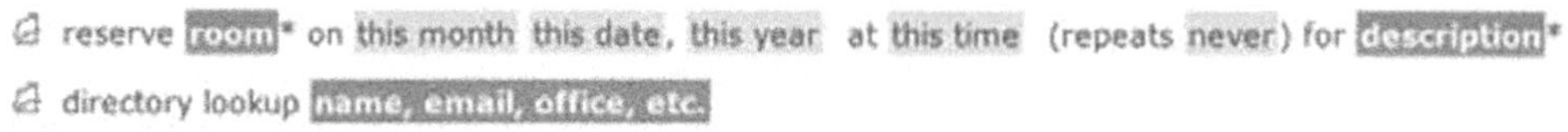

  ⌔ reserve room* on this month this date, this year at this time (repeats never) for description*

  ⌔ directory lookup name, email, office, etc.

FIGURE 15.7

Example outputs showing the different colorations used to indicate missing arguments.

For functions with persistent side effects, as opposed to merely retrieving information, Inky makes a distinction between arguments that are required to invoke the side effect and those that are not. Missing required arguments are marked with a red asterisk, following the convention used in many Web site forms. In Figure 15.7, the room and description are required arguments. Note that the user can run partial commands, even if required arguments are omitted. The required arguments are only needed for running a command in the mode that invokes the side effect immediately. The feedback also distinguishes optional or rarely used arguments by surrounding them with parentheses, such as the "(repeats never)" argument in the figure. It should be noted that this feedback does not dictate syntax. The user does not need to type parentheses around these arguments. If the user did type them, however, the command could still be interpreted, and the parentheses would simply be ignored.

ALGORITHMS

All of the systems described above need to convert a sloppy command into syntactically valid code. This section describes two approaches for performing these translations. The first approach assumes that the possible interpretations for a sloppy command are limited mainly by what is actually possible in the current context. This is the case in a typical form-based Web page, where the number of commands is roughly proportional to the number of form widgets. This algorithm was used in the early CoScripter system.

The second approach assumes that the space of possible interpretations in the current context is extremely large, and that the only effective way of searching through it is to guide a search using the keywords that appear in the sloppy query. For this approach, we focus on a slow but easy to understand algorithm that was used in the Web Command prototype. We then provide high-level insights into some improvements that can be made to the algorithm, along with references for more details about these improvements. These improvements were used in the Inky prototype.

CoScripter algorithm

We describe this algorithm in three basic steps, using the example instruction "type Danny into first name field" on the simple Web form shown in Figure 15.8.

First, the interpreter enumerates all the possible actions associated with various HTML objects in the document, such as links, buttons, textboxes, combobox options, checkboxes, and radio buttons. For each of these objects, the interpreter associates a variety of keywords, including the object's label, synonyms for the object's type, and action verbs commonly associated with the object.

For instance, the "First name" field of the Web form shown in Figure 15.8 would be associated with the words "first" and "name", because they are part of the label. It would also associate "textbox" and "field" as synonyms of the field's type. Finally, the interpreter would include verbs commonly associated with entering text into a text field such as "enter", "type", and "write".

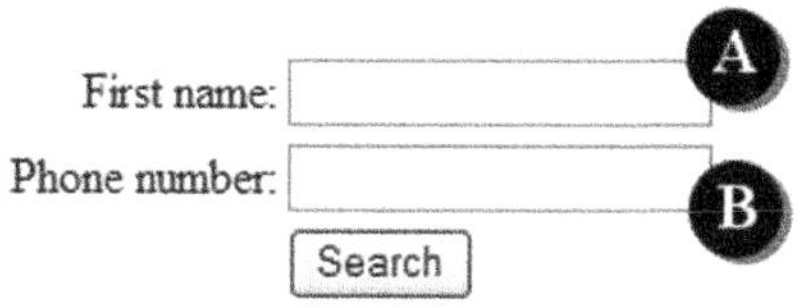

FIGURE 15.8

Example of a simple Web form.

Next, the interpreter searches for the object that matches the greatest number of keywords with the sloppy input sequence. In the example, textbox A would match the keywords "type", "first", "name", and "field", with a score of 4. In contrast, textbox B would only match the keywords "type" and "field", with a score of 2.

Finally, the system may need to extract arguments from the sloppy command (e.g., "Danny"). The key idea of this process is to extract a subsequence from the sloppy command, such that the remaining sequence is still a good match to the keywords associated with the Web object, and the extracted part is a good match for a string parameter using various heuristics (e.g., has quotes around it, or is followed/preceded by a preposition). In this example, we extract the subsequence "Danny" (which gets points for being followed by the preposition "into" in the original sloppy command). The remaining sequence is "type into first name field", which still has all 4 keyword matches to the text field.

This technique is surprisingly effective, because a Web page provides a very small search space.

Web command-line algorithm

Functions are the building blocks in this algorithm. Each function returns a single value of a certain type, and accepts a fixed number of arguments of certain types. Literals, such as strings or integers, are represented as functions that take no arguments and return an appropriate type. We can implement optional arguments for functions with function overloading. Functions can have many names, usually synonyms of the true function name. For instance, the "enter" command in the Web prototype has such names as "type", "write", "insert", "set", and the "=" symbol, in addition to its true name, "enter". Functions for literals may be thought of as functions with names corresponding to the textual representation of the literal. These names are matched programmatically with regular expressions; for example, integers are matched with "[0-9]+".

Arguments can also have names (and synonyms), which may include prepositions naming the grammatical role of the argument. We can implement named arguments as functions which take one parameter, and return a special type that fits only into the parent function. This may be useful for functions that take two arguments of the same type, such as the copy command in most operating systems. In this case, the idea would be to name one argument "from", and the other argument "to".

The translation algorithm needs to convert an input expression into a likely function tree. We describe it in two steps.

Step 1: Tokenize input

Each sequence of contiguous letters forms a token, as does each sequence of contiguous digits. All other symbols (excluding white space) form single character tokens.

Letter sequences are further subdivided on word boundaries using several techniques. First, the presence of a lowercase letter followed by an uppercase letter is assumed to mark a word boundary. For instance, LeftMargin is divided between the t and the M to form the tokens "Left" and "Margin". Second, words are passed through a spell checker, and common compound expressions are detected and split. For instance, "login" is split into "log" and "in". Note that we apply this same procedure to all function names in the API, and we add the resulting tokens to the spelling dictionary.

One potential problem with this technique is that a user might know the full name of a property in the API and choose to represent it with all lowercase letters. For instance, a user could type "leftmargin" to refer to the "LeftMargin" property. In this case, the system would not know to split "leftmargin" into "left" and "margin" to match the tokens generated from "LeftMargin". To deal with this problem, the system adds all camel-case sequences that it encounters to the spelling dictionary before splitting them. In this example, the system would add "LeftMargin" to the spelling dictionary when we populate the dictionary with function names from the API. Now when the user enters "leftmargin", the spell checker corrects it to "LeftMargin", which is then split into "Left" and "Margin". After spelling correction and word subdivision, tokens are converted to all lowercase, and then passed through a common stemming algorithm (Porter, 1980).

Step 2: Recursive algorithm

The input to the recursive algorithm is a token sequence and a desired return type. The result is a tree of function calls derived from the sequence that returns the desired type. This algorithm is called initially with the entire input sequence, and a desired return type which is a supertype of all other types (unless the context of the sloppy command restricts the return type).

For example, consider that the user types the sloppy query:

```
search textbox enter Hello World
```

The algorithm begins by considering every function that returns the desired type. For each function, it tries to find a substring of tokens that matches the name of the function. One function in the Web command prototype is called "enter", and so the algorithm considers dividing the sequence into three substrings as follows:

```
search textbox     (enter function: enter)     Hello World
```

For every such match, it considers how many arguments the function requires. If it requires n arguments, then it enumerates all possible ways of dividing the remaining tokens into n substrings such that no substring is adjacent to an unassigned token.

In our example, the "enter" function has two arguments: a string and a textbox to enter the string into. One natural possibility considered by the algorithm is that the first substring is one of the arguments, and the third substring is the other argument:

```
(argument: search textbox)     (enter function: enter)     (argument: Hello World)
```

Then, for each set of n substrings, it considers every possible matching of the substrings to the n arguments. For instance, it might consider that the left argument is the second argument to the enter function, and that the right argument is the first argument:

(argument 2: *search textbox*)   (enter function: *enter*)   (argument 1: *Hello World*)

Now for each matching, it takes each substring/argument pair and calls this algorithm recursively, passing in the substring as the new sequence, and the argument type as the new desired return type.

For instance, a recursive call to the algorithm will consider the substring:

```
search textbox
```

The desired return type for this argument will be Textbox, and one function that returns a textbox is called "findTextbox". This function takes one argument, namely a string identifying the label of the textbox on the Web page. The algorithm will then consider the following breakdown of this substring:

(argument 1: *search*)   (findTextbox function: *textbox*)

The algorithm will ultimately resolve this sequence into:

```
findTextbox("search")
```

These resulting function trees are grafted as branches to a new tree at the previous level of recursion, for example:

```
enter("Hello World", findTextbox("search"))
```

The system then evaluates how well this new tree explains the token sequence – for example, how many nodes in the tree match keywords from the token sequence (see "Explanatory Power" below). The system keeps track of the best tree it finds throughout this process, and returns it as the result.

The system also handles a couple of special case situations:

Extraneous tokens. If there are substrings left over after extracting the function name and arguments, then these substrings are ignored. However, they do subtract some explanatory power from the resulting tree.

Inferring functions. If no tokens match any functions that return the proper type, then the system tries all of these functions again. This time, it does not try to find substrings of tokens matching the function names. Instead, it skips directly to the process of finding arguments for each function. Of course, if a function returns the same type that it accepts as an argument, then this process can result in infinite recursion. One way to handle this is by not inferring commands after a certain depth in the recursion.

Explanatory power

Intuitively, we want to uncover the function tree that the user intended to create. All we are given is a sequence of tokens. Therefore, we want to take each function tree and ask: "if the user had intended to create this function tree, would that explain why they entered these tokens?" Hence, we arrive at the notion of *explanatory power* – how well a function tree explains a token sequence.

Tokens are explained in various ways. For instance, a token matched with a function name is explained as invoking that function, and a token matched as part of a string is explained as helping create that string.

Different explanations are given different weights. For instance, a function name explanation for a token is given 1 point, whereas a string explanation is given 0 points (because strings can be created from any token). This is slightly better than tokens which are not explained at all – these subtract a small amount of explanatory power. Also, inferred functions subtract some explanatory power, depending on how common they are. Inferring common functions costs less than inferring uncommon functions. We decided upon these values by hand in all of the systems built so far, since we do not have a corpus of sloppy commands to measure against. In the future, these values could be learned from a corpus of user-generated sloppy inputs.

Algorithm optimization

The algorithm described above slows down exponentially as more types and functions are added. The current Inky prototype only has 11 types and 35 functions, but the system is meant to support many user-supplied types and functions. In order to deal with the larger scale, we have explored a way of making the algorithm more efficient, at the expense of making it less accurate.

The algorithm in Inky uses a variant of the algorithm described in (Little & Miller, 2008). Briefly, this algorithm uses dynamic programming to find the fragment of the user's input that best matches each type known to the system. The initial iteration of the dynamic program runs the type-matching recognizers to identify a set of argument types possible in the function. Subsequent iterations use the results of the previous iteration to bind function arguments to fragments that match each argument's types. Interpretations are scored by how many input tokens they successfully explain, and the highest-scoring interpretations for each type are kept for the next iteration. For example, three integers from a previous iteration may be combined into a date. The dynamic program is run for a fixed number of iterations (three in the Inky prototype), which builds function trees up to a fixed depth. After the last iteration, the highest-scoring interpretations for the void return type (i.e., functions that actually do something) are returned as the result.

DISCUSSION

The prototypes and algorithms discussed previously work well in many cases. All of these systems have been tested with user studies, and have demonstrated some level of success. CoScripter has grown beyond a prototype, and has many thousands of real users, though the sloppy interpreter had to be refined to be less sloppy. Hence, there is still work to be done in the field of sloppy programming. In this section, we discuss a number of limitations, and directions for future work.

Limitations

There are three primary limitations of sloppy programming: consistency, efficiency, and discoverability. Sloppy commands are not always interpreted the same way. The algorithm and heuristics in the sloppy interpreter may change, if the user gets a new version of the software. This happens with conventional scripting languages too, but the consequences may be more difficult to notice with sloppy programming, because the system will try to interpret commands as best it can, rather than halt with a syntax error if a command is broken. (CoScripter has some heuristics to notice if a command is broken.) Also, the context of the command can change. If the user is executing a command in the context of a Web page, then the interpretation of that command may change if the Web page changes. Finally, a user may modify a sloppy command without realizing it; for example, they may invert the order of keywords. This will usually not have an effect, but depending on the algorithm and heuristics used, it can have an effect.

The next limitation is efficiency: there is a tradeoff between interpreting a command accurately, and interpreting a command quickly. The Web command-line algorithm described previously appears to interpret sloppy commands accurately, but it is extremely inefficient. It is fast enough in the Web command prototype, because the command set is very small, but the algorithm quickly becomes slow as more commands are added. We discussed an optimization to this algorithm in the previous section, but this optimization sacrifices the accuracy of interpretations by ignoring information (namely word order). Tradeoffs such as this are not yet well understood.

The final problem, discoverability, is a problem that plagues all command-line interfaces. It is not clear what the user may type. We try to overcome this by implementing our prototypes in a domain that users are familiar with, and try to have good coverage of that domain, so that the system is likely to recognize anything that the user types. However, users are very creative, and always come up with commands that designers of a system did not anticipate. Also, it is important to find ways to make the system more discoverable in domains where the user is not as familiar with the set of possible commands.

Future work

The primary goal of future work is to overcome the limitations mentioned earlier. To make sloppy programming more consistent, there are two main approaches. One is to have a fallback mechanism where users can, in the worst case, write commands in a verbose but unambiguous manner. The other approach is to fine-tune the existing heuristics, and add new heuristics. Fine-tuning heuristics will likely require a corpus of user-generated sloppy commands, along with the correct interpretation for each command. Discovering new heuristics may be more difficult, requiring creativity and testing. Validating new heuristics will again benefit from a corpus of sloppy commands.

The first step toward making sloppy programming more efficient may simply involve implementing the algorithms more efficiently, possibly using lower-level languages to achieve greater speed. The second step involves gaining a better understanding of the heuristics used in the algorithms. Some optimizations may require ignoring certain heuristics, and concentrating on others. These decisions would benefit from understanding the contributions that different heuristics make to the resulting interpretation quality.

We believe discoverability in sloppy programming can be enhanced in a number of ways. For instance, the Inky prototype explores the idea of showing people multiple interpretations as the user is typing. This is similar to Google showing query suggestions as the user types, based on popular search queries beginning with the characters entered so far. An extension to Inky, called Pinky (Miller et al., 2008), explores an interesting extension to this idea, where the user can interact with the suggestions themselves. These changes are propagated back to the sloppy command, allowing the user to learn more about the command language. This idea suggests a hybrid between command-line and GUI systems, with benefits from each. A side benefit of showing more information about how commands are interpreted is that users may understand the system better, and be able to write commands that are more robust to changes in the system. These ideas require future work to explore and verify.

SUMMARY

The techniques described in this chapter still just scratch the surface of a domain with great potential: translating sloppy commands into executable code. We have described potential benefits to end users and expert programmers alike, as well as advocated a continued need for textual command interfaces. We have also described a number of prototypes exploring this technology, and discussed what we learned from them, including the fact that users can form commands for some of these systems without any training. Finally, we gave some high-level technical details about how to go about actually implementing sloppy translation algorithms, with some references for future reading.

Acknowledgments

We thank all the members of the UID group at MIT and the User Interface group at the IBM Almaden Research Center, who provided valuable feedback on the ideas in this chapter and contributed to the development of the prototype systems, particularly Lydia Chilton, Max Goldman, Max Van Kleek, Chen-Hsiang Yu, James Lin, Eben M. Haber, Eser Kandogan. This work was supported in part by the National Science Foundation under award number IIS-0447800, and by Quanta Computer as part of the T-Party project. Any opinions, findings, conclusions or recommendations expressed in this publication are those of the authors and do not necessarily reflect the views of the sponsors.

This chapter is based on several earlier works:

1. A paper that originally appeared as "Translating Keyword Commands into Executable Code," in *Proceedings of the 19th Annual ACM Symposium on User Interface Software and Technology* (UIST 2006), © ACM, 2006. http://doi.acm.org/10.1145/1166253.1166275,

2. A paper that originally appeared as "Koala: Capture, Share, Automate, Personalize Business Processes on the Web," in *Proceedings of the SIGCHI Conference on Human Factors in Computing Systems* (CHI 2007), © ACM, 2007. http://doi.acm.org/10.1145/1240624.1240767, and

3. A paper that originally appeared as "Inky: a Sloppy Command Line for the Web with Rich Visual Feedback," in *Proceedings of the 21st Annual ACM Symposium on User Interface Software and Technology* (UIST 2008), © ACM, 2008. http://doi.acm.org/10.1145/1449715.1449737.

INKY

Intended users:	All users
Domain:	All Web sites, but a programmer must add support for each site
Description:	Inky allows users to type Web-related commands into a textbox, and it attempts to execute them. The system is not inherently restricted to any particular set of commands, but it only understands commands for which implementations have been written. Some examples include checking the weather and sending an email.
Example:	A user could use the system to add an event to their calendar with a command like "meeting with David at 4pm on Tuesday". This command would fill out the appropriate form on Google Calendar, and the user could ensure that the information was correct before clicking Submit.
Automation:	Yes, the system automates tasks typically consisting of one to three Web forms.
Mashups:	Possibly. Supported tasks may include entering information into multiple Web sites.
Scripting:	Yes. The system allows users to write commands in a sloppy scripting language, with the intent of trying to interpret anything the user types as a valid command.
Natural language:	No. The system tends to be more lenient than a classical natural language parser, because it does not require the user to use proper grammar. Writing in a very verbose natural language style is likely to confuse the system.
Recordability:	No.
Inferencing:	Yes, Inky uses many heuristics similar to natural language processing to translate queries into executable code.
Sharing:	No.
Comparison to other systems:	This system is similar to other systems that use sloppy programming, including the sloppy Web command-line prototype and CoScripter.
Platform:	Implemented as an extension to the Mozilla Firefox browser.
Availability:	Not currently available.

Going beyond PBD

A play-by-play and mixed-initiative approach

16

Hyuckchul Jung,[1] **James Allen,**[1] **William de Beaumont,**[1] **Nate Blaylock,**[1] **Lucian Galescu,**[1]
George Ferguson,[2] **Mary Swift**[2]

[1]*Institute for Human and Machine Cognition*
[2]*Computer Science Department, University of Rochester*

ABSTRACT

An innovative task learning system called PLOW (Procedure Learning On the Web) lets end users teach procedural tasks to automate their various Web activities. Deep natural language understanding and mixed-initiative interaction in PLOW make the teaching process very natural and intuitive while producing efficient and workable procedures.

INTRODUCTION

The Web has become the main medium for providing services and information for our daily activities at home and work. Many Web activities require the execution of a series of procedural steps involving Web browser actions. Programmatically automating such tasks to increase productivity is feasible but out of reach for many end users. Programming by demonstration (PBD) is an innovative paradigm that can enable novice users to build a program by just showing a computer what users do (Cypher, 1993). However, in this approach, numerous examples are often needed for the system to infer a workable task.

We aim to build a system with which a novice user can teach tasks by using a single example, without requiring too much or too specialized work from the user. This goal poses significant challenges because the observed sequence of actions is only one instance of a task to teach, and the user's decision-making process that drives his or her actions is not revealed in the demonstration.

To achieve this challenging goal, we have developed a novel approach in which a user not only demonstrates a task but also explains the task with a play-by-play description. In the PLOW system, demonstration is accompanied by natural language (NL) explanation, which makes it possible for PLOW to infer a task structure that is not easily inferable from observations alone but represents a user's intentions. Furthermore, the semantic information encoded in NL enables PLOW to reliably identify objects in nonstatic Web pages.

Another key aspect that makes PLOW more efficient is the mixed-initiative interaction that dramatically reduces the complexity of teaching a task by having the computer (1) proactively initiate execution so that the user can verify that it has correctly learned the task, and (2) ask timely questions to solicit information required to complete a task (e.g., asking for a termination condition when it learns an iterative task). This chapter presents the challenges, innovations, and lessons in developing the PLOW system.

MOTIVATING EXAMPLE

Information extraction from the Web is a routine action for many users, and travel arrangement (e.g., booking hotels, flights, and rental cars) is one of many time-consuming activities that require collecting information from multiple sources. Figure 16.1 shows a sample dialogue in which a user teaches PLOW how to find hotels near an address at a travel Web site such as mapquest.com.

In Figure 16.1, user actions (italic texts) are accompanied by a user's natural language description (normal texts labeled with "User"). Although most of the actions in Figure 16.1 are normal browsing actions, with PLOW, a user may need to perform some easy special actions, such as highlighting a text or an area of the screen by clicking and dragging to directly tell PLOW which information the user is interested in (underlined texts in Figure 16.1).

While user actions on a browser provides useful information, it is very difficult for a system to identify key high-level task information from the demonstration alone, such as:

- *Identifying a task goal*: What is the final goal of the current task? What is the input and the output?
- *Identifying correct parameterization*: What values are required to perform the task? Is a value a constant or a variable? For variables, what is the relation among them?
- *Identifying iteration control structure*: What is the boundary of iteration? Which actions should be repeated? When should iterations be stopped?
- *Identifying task hierarchy*: When does a new (sub) task start or end?

With PBD based on conventional machine learning approaches, such as (Angros et al., 2002; Lau & Weld, 1999; van Lent & Laird, 2001), to identify the previously mentioned key aspects of a task, multiple examples will be required to generalize learned knowledge. However, PLOW is able to build a task from a single demonstration by inferring the key task information described earlier from the natural language description provided by a user in the play-by-play demonstration.

Another major point is PLOW's proactive interaction with a user in a natural and unobtrusive manner. In Figure 16.1, the utterances and the actions of PLOW are presented in bold texts and the texts between angled brackets, respectively. For instance, PLOW asks questions (#12 and #20), reports its status (#23), proactively performs learned actions, and presents the action results for verification (#14, #16, #18, and #22).

Furthermore, the contextual information for an action enables PLOW to identify Web objects (e.g., text field, link, etc.) that can change over time. For instance, the user utterance in #8 ("*Put the city here*") explains the action of typing a city name into a field labeled with "City". The NL description is used to find the city field in future execution with a new page format (e.g., new ads inserted at the top, reordering input fields in the search box, etc.).

With this play-by-play and mixed-initiative approach, PLOW is able to build a robust and flexible task from a single demonstration. Learned tasks can be easily improved and modified with new examples, and they can be also reused to build a larger task and shared with other users.

1. User: Let me teach you how to find hotels near an address
2. User: Go to this website
   Types a URL, http://www.mapquest.com, in the browser's navigation box and hits Enter
3. User: Put hotels here
   Types "hotels" in the business type field
4. User: You need to know the address
5. PLOW: **What is the address?**
6. User: *Types an address, "40 South Alcaniz Street, Pensacola, FL", in a special GUI for inputs*
7. User: Put the street address here
   Types the street address, "40 South Alcaniz Street", in the street field
8. User: Put the city here
   Types "Pensacola" in the city field
9. User: Put the state here
   Types "FL" in the state field
10. User: Click the search button
    Presses a button with a label "Search"
11. User: Here is the list of hotels
    Highlights an area with a list of hotels
12. PLOW: **Can you check if I understand the list?**
    < Displays a special GUI that shows the contents of the hotel list >
13. User: This is the hotel name
    Highlights the hotel name in the special GUI
14. PLOW: < Identifies hotel names for the other hotels and displays the names >
15. User: This is the hotel address
    Highlights the address of a hotel
16. PLOW: < Identifies hotel addresses for the other hotels and displays them >
17. User: This is the hotel distance
    Highlights the distance for a hotel
18. PLOW: < Identifies distances for the other hotels and displays them >
19. User: Click the next link to get more results
    Clicks the link labeled "next"
20. PLOW: **When should I stop searching?**
21. User: When the distance is greater than two miles
22. PLOW: **I will try that**
    < Visits multiple pages and extracts information (i.e., hotel name, address, and
    distance) until the iteration termination condition is satisfied and displays the
    results in the special GUI >
23. PLOW: **I am finished**
24. User: I am done

FIGURE 16.1

A dialogue to find hotels near an address.

PLOW ARCHITECTURE

PLOW is an extension to TRIPS (Ferguson & Allen, 1998), a dialogue-based collaborative problem solving system that has been applied to many real-world applications.

The TRIPS system

The TRIPS system provides the architecture and the domain-independent capabilities for supporting mixed-initiative dialogues in various applications and domains. Its central components are based on a domain-independent representation, including a linguistically based semantic form, illocutionary acts, and a collaborative problem solving model. The system can be tailored to individual domains through an ontology mapping system that maps domain-independent representations into domain-specific representations (Dzikovska, Allen, & Swift, 2008).

Figure 16.2 shows the core components of TRIPS: (1) a toolkit for rapid development of language models for the Sphinx-III speech recognition system; (2) a robust parsing system that uses a broad coverage grammar and lexicon of spoken language; (3) an interpretation manager (IM) that provides contextual interpretation based on the current discourse context, including reference resolution, ellipsis processing, and the generation of intended speech act hypotheses; (4) an ontology manager (OM) that translates between representations; and (5) a generation manager (GM) and surface generator that generate system utterances from the domain-independent logical form.

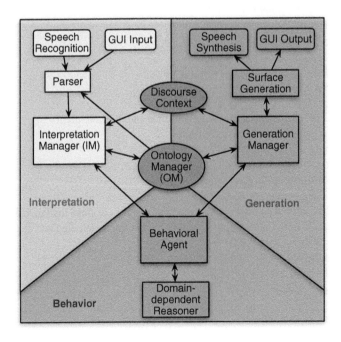

FIGURE 16.2

TRIPS architecture.

The IM coordinates the interpretation of utterances and observed cyber actions. IM draws from the Discourse Context module as well to help resolve ambiguities in the input, and coordinates the synchronization of the user's utterances and observed actions. Then IM interacts with a behavioral agent (BA) to identify the most likely intended interpretations in terms of collaborative problem solving acts (e.g., propose an action, accept a problem solving act or ignore it, work on something more pressing, etc.). BA gets support from additional reasoning modules specialized for each application domain and reports its status to a GM that plans a linguistic act to communicate the BA's intentions to the user.

TRIPS components interact with each other by exchanging messages through a communication facilitator. Therefore, they can be distributed among networked computers. The rest of this chapter will focus on the PLOW components. For further information about TRIPS, refer to (Allen, Blaylock, & Ferguson, 2002; Ferguson & Allen, 1998).

PLOW interface

PLOW inherits most of its core reasoning modules for language interpretation and generation from TRIPS. New capabilities for task learning are added to the behavioral agent that interacts with additional reasoners specialized for building task representation, maintaining a task repository, and executing learned tasks. Though these modules are designed to learn tasks in various domains (e.g., office applications, robots, etc.), PLOW focuses on tasks that can be performed within a Web browser, and its ontology is extended to cover Web browsing actions.

Figure 16.3 shows PLOW's user interface. The main window on the left is the Firefox browser instrumented so that PLOW can monitor user actions and execute actions for learned tasks. Through the instrumentation, PLOW accesses and manipulates a tree-structured logical model of Web pages, called DOM (Document Object Model). On the right is a GUI that summarizes a task under construction, highlights steps in execution for verification, and provides tools to manage learned tasks. A chat window at the bottom shows speech interaction, and the user can switch between speech and keyboard anytime.

The domain-independent aspect of PLOW was recently demonstrated in the project for appointment booking with the Composite Health Care System (CHCS) that is widely used at U.S. military hospitals. CHCS is a terminal-based legacy system and most of the PLOW codes were reused for the system. The major work involved instrumenting the terminal environment (e.g., observing key strokes, checking screen update, etc.) as well as extending the ontology for the health care domain. From a user's point of view, the only noticeable major change to adapt to was the replacement of a browser with a terminal.

Collaborative problem solving in PLOW

Figure 16.4 shows a high-level view of the information flow in PLOW. At the center lies a CPS (Collaborative Problem Solving) agent that acts as a behavioral agent in the TRIPS architecture. The CPS agent (henceforth called CPSA) computes the most likely intention in the given problem solving context (based on the interaction with IM). CPSA also coordinates and drives other parts of the system to learn what a user intends to build as a task and invokes execution when needed.

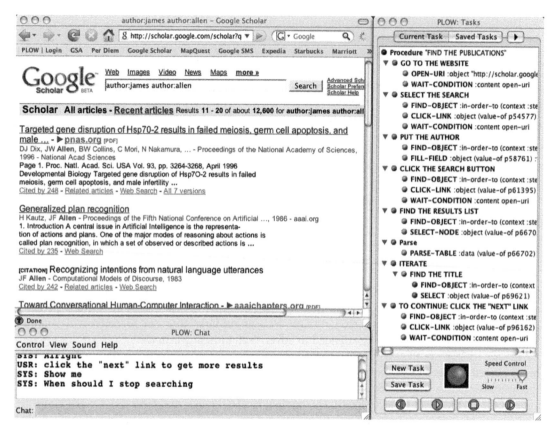

FIGURE 16.3

PLOW interface.

CPSA understands the interaction as a dialogue between itself and a user. The dialogue provides the context for interpreting human utterances and actions, and provides the structure for deciding what to do in response. In this approach, from a user's perspective, PLOW appears to be a competent collaborative partner, working together towards the shared goal of one-shot learning.

To give an overview of the collaborative problem solving, assume that a user introduced a new step. CPSA first checks if it knows how to perform the step and, if so, initiates a dialogue to find out if the user wants to use a known task for the step in the current task. If the user says so, CPSA invokes another dialogue to check if the user wants to execute the reused task or not. Depending on the user's responses, CPSA shows different behavior. In the case of execution, CPSA enters into an execution mode and presents results when successful. If execution failed, PLOW invokes a debugging dialogue, showing where it failed.

In some cases, the system takes proactive execution mixed with learning, following an explicit model of problem solving. In particular, this type of collaborative execution during learning is very

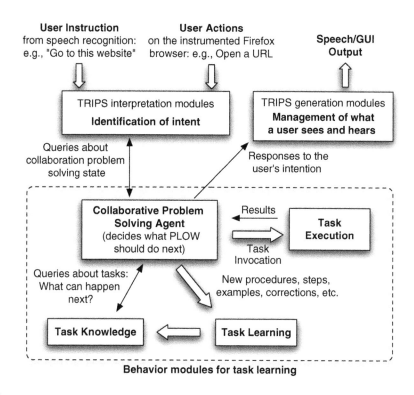

FIGURE 16.4

PLOW information flow.

critical in learning iteration without requiring a user to tediously demonstrate each loop over a significant period. Refer to (Allen et al., 2002) for the background and the formal model of collaborative problem solving in TRIPS.

TEACHING WEB TASKS WITH PLAY-BY-PLAY
Task representation

A task is built as a series of steps and each step may be primitive (i.e., a self-contained terminal action) or correspond to another task (i.e., calling a subtask). However, a task model is more than a collection of steps. A task model needs to contain information such as an overall task goal, preconditions, postconditions, the relationship between steps, and the hierarchical structure of a task, among others.

Figure 16.5 shows an abstract task model in PLOW that is designed to be easily executable by the system as well as applicable to further reasoning. The model includes a task goal, various conditions (pre/post/triggering/completion-condition), step description, and supplemental records, such as documentation. Each step consists of the name, preconditions, parameters, and primitive actions. An action definition includes its name and parameters.

```
(task :id <a unique identifier>
      :goal <task goal>
      :description <NL description of the task>
      :documentation <notes generated by PLOW but editable by a user afterward>
      :trigger <triggering conditions, if any>
      :pre-condition <required inputs & propositions to satisfy>
      :post-condition <task outputs & propositions to assert>
      :completion-condition <a system state for completion that includes a list of steps
                             to complete & propositions to satisfy>
      :steps ((step :preconditions <a list of propositions to satisfy>
              :id <a unique identifier>
              :description <NL description of the step>
              :name <step name>
              :parameters <a list of parameters>
              :actions ((action :name <action name>
                                :parameters <a list of parameters>)
                        (action ...) ...)) ...))
```

FIGURE 16.5

Abstract task model.

Following sections will show how a task model is constructed through collaboration between a user and PLOW that involves multiple communicative acts and highly sophisticated reasoning in PLOW. They will also provide more detailed description for each element in the task model presented in Figure 16.5. Refer to (Allen et al., 2007; Jung et al., 2008) for additional technical detail including the internal abstract knowledge representation language. The task model examples below are simplified for illustrative purpose by replacing a frame-like representation based on domain-specific ontology with plain English.

Task goal definition

The task model is incrementally built as a user performs play-by-play demonstration. Figure 16.6 shows a part of the task model built from the dialogue in Figure 16.1. Given the user utterance "*Let me teach you to find hotels near an address*" (#1 in Figure 16.1), TRIPS natural language understanding modules parse and interpret it. IM computes multiple hypotheses, selects the best candidate, and sends it to CPSA for evaluation.

Here, the selected hypothesis is that the user has proposed to teach PLOW a task for finding a set of hotels with an attribute of being near an address. CPSA reasons about the validity of the user's proposal and makes a decision, to accept or refuse. When it is accepted, IM requests CPSA to commit to the proposal. Then CPSA requests a task-learning module, henceforth called TL, to initiate the learning process for a new task. Receiving this request that includes the description of the task to learn, TL creates an initial task model with the goal part based on the given task description (Figure 16.6-a) and notifies CPSA of its ready status. Then, CPSA updates its collaborative problem solving state and waits for the user to define a step.

```
(task :id TASK007
      :goal (find OBJ1 such that OBJ1 (i) is a set of hotels and (ii) is near to a mailing address --- (a)
      :description "find hotels near an address" --- (b)
      :documentation "id: TASK007, created: 03/03/2009 12:49:34, user: hjung" --- (c)
      :precondition (inputs (a mailing address)) --- (d)
      :postcondition (outputs (the name/mailing address/distance of a hotel)) --- (e)
      :steps ....)
```

FIGURE 16.6

A task model example.

The task model built at this stage also includes other useful information such as a task description (Figure 16.6-b) and documentation (Figure 16.6-c). Note that the task description is not the text directly from speech recognition. Instead, it is text that the TRIPS surface generator produced from the internal representation of the task goal, which clearly shows that the system understands what a user said. The same goes for the step description in the task model. These reverse-generated NL descriptions are used to describe the current task in the PLOW interface (the right side window in Figure 16.3). PLOW automatically generates the documentation part, but a user can edit it later for a note.

A task may also have a trigger: e.g., when a user says, "*Let me teach you how to book hotels near an airport when a flight is canceled*", the event of flight cancellation (that can be notified in various forms) is captured as a trigger and recorded in the task model. While PLOW is running, if PLOW is notified of such an event, it finds a task with a matching triggering condition and, if any, executes the task.

Task step definition
High-level step description in play-by-play
When a user describes a step by saying, "*Go to this Website*" (#2 in Figure 16.1), IM and CPSA collaboratively interpret and reason about the utterance. Then, CPSA requests TL to identify a step by sending a message that contains the user's step description. Given this request, TL creates a step with an incomplete action part (since no action has been taken yet) and inserts the step definition (Figure 16.7) into the current task model.

```
(step :preconditions ((an ordering constraint that says this step is the first))
      :name Navigate
      :id STEP101
      :parameters (webpage as a destination)
      :description "go to the website"
      :actions (none defined yet))
```

FIGURE 16.7

An example of step definition.

Primitive actions of a step

Following the step description, a user performs a normal navigation action in the browser and the action is detected by the Firefox instrumentation. IM receives the action and checks with CPSA. Then, after checking the validity of the action, CPSA requests TL to learn the action of opening the URL observed in the browser. Using the information in this request, TL extends the action part of the step definition as shown in Figure 16.8.

Note that TL inserts additional information into the action definition based on its domain knowledge. To handle multiple windows, a browser window to perform the current action is specified. In addition, an action to wait for "complete Web page loading" is inserted (Figure 16.8-b). Without such synchronization, subsequent actions could fail, particularly on a slow network (e.g., trying to select a menu when the target menu does not appear yet). In navigating to a link, there can be multiple page loading events (e.g., some travel Web sites show intermediate Web pages while waiting for search results). PLOW observes how many page loading events have occurred and inserts waiting actions accordingly.

Figure 16.9 shows the PLOW interface after this step demonstration. The right side window for the current task under construction has a traffic signal light at the bottom portion. The signal changes colors (green/red/yellow) based on PLOW's internal processing state and its expectation of the application environment, telling if it is deemed OK for a user to provide inputs to PLOW (green) or not (red). Yellow implies that PLOW is not sure, because, in this case, there can be multiple page loading events controlled by the Web site server.

Web objects in primitive actions

In Figure 16.1, there is a step created by saying, "*Put the city here*" and typing a city name into a text field labeled with "City". Here, the observed action from the browser instrumentation is an action that puts some text (e.g., "Pensacola") into a text field. However, the semantic description helps PLOW to find the text field in a Web page, the layout of which may change in a future visit.

Figure 16.10 is a screenshot of the Firefox DOM Inspector that shows DOM nodes and their attributes/structure accessed by PLOW for its learning how to identify objects in nonstatic Web pages (e.g., redesigned or dynamic Web pages).[1] For simplicity, such objects will be called

```
(step …
    :actions
      ((action :name Open-URL      --- (a)
             :parameters (http://www.mapquest.com; at the current window))
       (action :name Wait-Condition --- (b)
             :parameters ("complete webpage loading"))))
```

FIGURE 16.8

Step definition with extended action part.

---

[1]PLOW has limitations in handling objects in rich interfaced pages that dynamically change while they are viewed, often in response to mouse actions or at specified timing events (e.g., Web pages with technologies such as Dynamic HTML and Flash).

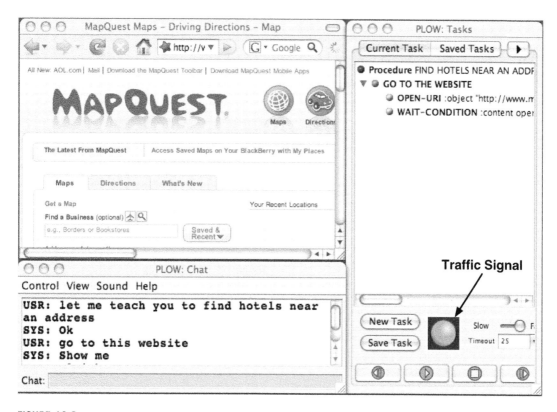

FIGURE 16.9

PLOW interface after step demonstration.

"Web objects" hereafter. For the step to put in a city, PLOW finds a match for "city" in one of the attributes of the INPUT node (i.e., id="startCity"). PLOW learns the relation between the semantic concept and the node attribute as a rule for future execution. Linguistic variation (e.g., cities) or similar ontological concepts (e.g., town, municipality) are also considered for the match. Right after learning this new rule, PLOW verifies it by applying the rule in the current page and checking if the object (i.e., a text field) found by the rule is the same as the object observed in demonstration.

PLOW also uses other heuristics to learn rules. For instance, when the node identified in the demonstration does not have any semantic relation, it finds another reference node traversing the DOM tree and, if found, computes the relation between the node observed in demonstration and the reference node found elsewhere. With this sophisticated approach, even when there is a Web page format change, PLOW is able to find a node as long as there are no significant local changes around the node in focus. For further information on PLOW's Web object identification, refer to (Chambers et al., 2006).

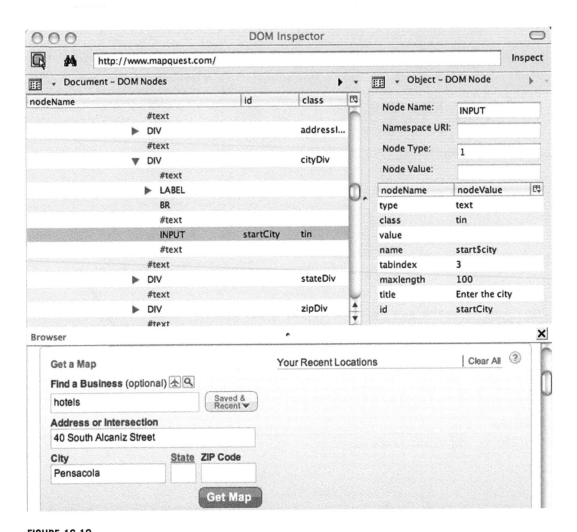

FIGURE 16.10

DOM structure of a Web page.

Parameter identification

Identifying parameters is challenging even for a simple task and, without special domain knowledge, it is almost impossible with only a single observation. When an object is used in a task, the system should determine if it is a constant or a variable. In the case of a variable, it also has to figure out the relation between variables. Figure 16.11 shows how natural language plays a critical role in PLOW's parameter identification, enabling it to identify parameters from a play-by-play single demonstration.

Utterance (Action)	Key Features	Interpretation
Let me show you how to find hotels near an address	- Bare plural - Object of an information producing action "find"	hotels – output
	- Indefinite - No decision action	an address – input
Put hotels (*Type "hotels"*)	- Bare plural - Identical to the typed text in the action	"hotels" – constant
Put the city (*Type "Pensacola"*)	- Definite - City is a role of an address in the ontology	a city – related to the address input

FIGURE 16.11

Interpretation of noun phrases.

Furthermore, TRIPS's reference resolution capability also identifies the relation between parameters. For instance, in Figure 16.1, the city instance in one step (#8) is related to the address mentioned earlier (#1 and #5). The semantic concept CITY is a role of another concept, ADDRESS, in the TRIPS ontology. A special address parser helps to reason that the typed city name "Pensacola" in the demonstrated action (#8) matches the city part of the given full address provided by a user (#6). Without this dependency relation from language understanding and the verification by the address parser, PLOW will add the city as a separate input parameter. Note that, in the final task model, there is only a single input parameter, an address (Figure 16.6-d).

NL description also helps to identify output parameters. From the utterances that specify which information to extract (#13, #15, and #17 in Figure 16.1), PLOW figures out that the objects to find in those steps are related to the task output defined in the task definition (i.e., "hotels" in #1). Therefore, they are added as output parameters (Figure 16.6-e).

Task hierarchy

PLOW uses simple heuristics to identify the beginning and end of a subtask. Any statement that explicitly identifies a goal (e.g., "*Let me show you how ...*") is seen as the beginning of a new (sub) task. A user's explicit statement, such as "*I'm done*", or another goal statement indicates the end of the current (sub) task. Our anecdotal experience is that users easily get familiar with this intuitive teaching style through a few guided training sessions.

Control constructs

Conditionals

Conditionals have a basic structure of "*if X, then do Y*", optionally followed by "*otherwise do Z*". However, the action trace for conditionals includes only one action, either Y or Z, based on the truth value of the condition X. In general, identifying X is very difficult, because the entire context of demonstration should be checked and reasoned about. However, in the play-by-play demonstration, when a user specifies a condition, PLOW can correctly interpret the condition from language.

Iteration

The main difficulty in identifying iterative procedures from a single example is that the action trace (a sequence of actions) alone does not fully reveal the iterative structure. For iteration, a system needs to identify these key aspects: (1) the list to iterate over; (2) what actions to take for each element; (3) how to add more list elements; and (4) when to stop.

For a system to reason about these aspects on its own, in addition to repetitive examples, full understanding of the action context (beyond observed actions) and special domain knowledge will be required (e.g., what and how many list items were potentially available, which ones were included in the observed actions, how and when Web page transition works, etc.). Furthermore, a user would not want to demonstrate lengthy iterations. In PLOW, natural language again plays a key role. As shown below, we designed the system GUI and dialogue to guide a user through the demonstration for iteration: mixed-initiative interaction with proactive execution and simple queries make the process much easier and intuitive.

In Figure 16.12, a user is teaching PLOW how to find hotels near an address. When the user highlights a list of results (Figure 16.12-a) and says, "*Here is a list of results*", PLOW infers that an iteration over elements in the list will follow. Then, PLOW enters into an iteration-learning mode with the goal of identifying the key aspects stated earlier. First, by analyzing the DOM structure for the list object, PLOW identifies individual elements of the list and then presents the parsed list in a dedicated GUI window with each element (essentially a portion of the original Web page) contained in a separate cell (Figure 16.12-b).

This GUI-based approach lets the user quickly verify the list parsing result and easily teach what to do for each element. Note that list and table HTML objects that contain the desired list may also be used for other purposes (e.g., formatting, inserting ads, etc.), so it is fairly common that some irrelevant information may appear to be part of the list. PLOW uses clustering and similarity-based techniques to weed out such information.

After presenting the parsed list, PLOW waits for the user's identification of an element. For instance, the user says, "*This is the hotel name*", and highlights the hotel name in one of the small cells in the GUI (Figure 16.12-c). Given this information, PLOW learns the extraction pattern and *proactively* applies the rule to the rest of elements (Figure 16.12-d). While the extracted data from this iterative step are stored in a knowledge base for further reasoning, a user cannot manipulate the data except for referring to them. In contrast, a mashup system, Potluck (Huynh, Miller, & Karger, 2007), provides a user with intuitive GUIs for clustering and editing the information from extracted lists.

Note that a composite action can be also defined for each list element. For instance, a user may navigate to a page from a link (e.g., in Figure 16.12-b, the "Directions To" link), extract data from

a. MapQuest search result

b. GUI for a parsed list

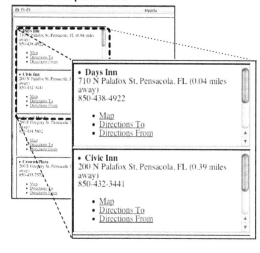

c. User demonstration on one list element: *"This is the hotel name"* < highlight the hotel name text >

d. New column with PLOW execution results

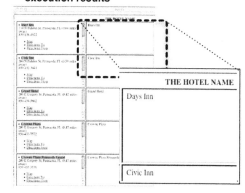

e. Link to the next page below the search results

Page: **1** 2 3 4 5 6 7 8 9 10 11 12 13 14   Next »

FIGURE 16.12

Learning iteration.

the new page, and so on. Dontcheva's Web summary system (Chapter 12) can also extract information from linked pages, the content of which may trigger information extraction from other Web sites based on user-defined relations. Though her system can be applied to a given collection of items, PLOW can identify an arbitrary number of items (in multiple Web pages) and iterate over them with termination conditions as described later.

If there is an error, the user can notify PLOW about the problem by saying, *"This is wrong"*, and show a new example. Then, PLOW learns a new extraction pattern and reapplies it to all list elements for further verification. This correction interaction may continue until a comprehensive pattern is learned.

Next, the user teaches PLOW how to iterate over multiple lists by introducing a special action (e.g., *"Click the next link for more results"* – see Figure 16.12-e). This helps PLOW to recognize the user's intention to repeat what he or she demonstrated in the first list on other lists. Here, to identify the duration of the iteration, PLOW asks for a termination condition by saying, *"When should I stop searching?"* For this query, it can understand a range of user responses, such as *"Get two pages"*, *"Twenty items"*, and *"Get all"*.

The conditions can depend on the information extracted for each element, as in *"Until the distance is greater than 2 miles"*. In the case of getting all results, the system also asks how to recognize the ending, and the user can tell and show what to check (e.g., *"When you don't see the next link"* or *"When you see the end sign"*). For verification, PLOW executes the learned iterative procedure until the termination condition is satisfied and presents the results to the user using the special GUI. The user can sort and/or filter the results with certain conditions (e.g., *"sort the results by distance"*, *"keep the first three results"*, etc.).

UTILIZING AND IMPROVING TAUGHT WEB TASKS
Persistent and sharable tasks

After teaching a task, a user can save it in a persistent repository. Figure 16.13 shows the "Saved Tasks" panel in the PLOW interface that shows a list of a user's private tasks. A pop-up menu is provided for task management, and one of its capabilities is exporting a task to a public repository for sharing the task with others. A user can import shared tasks from the "Public Tasks" panel.

Task invocation

Tasks in the private repository can be invoked through the GUI (Figure 16.13) or in natural language (e.g., *"Find me hotels near an airport"*). If the selected task requires input parameters, PLOW asks for their values (e.g., *"What is the airport?"*), and the user can provide parameter values using the GUI or natural language.

Users can invoke a task and provide input parameters in a single utterance, such as, *"Find me hotels near LAX"* or *"Find me hotels near an airport. The airport is LAX."* Results can also be presented via the GUI or in natural language. This NL-based invocation capability allows users to use

FIGURE 16.13

Task management.

indirect channels as well. For example, we built an email agent that interprets an email subject and body so that a user can invoke a task by sending an email and receive the execution results as a reply.

Here, given a user request, PLOW finds a matching task with its natural language understanding and ontological reasoning capabilities. A user does not necessarily have to use the same task description used in teaching. "*Get me restaurants in a city*" or "*Look for eateries in a town*" would select a task to find restaurants in a city.

Reusing tasks

In teaching a task, existing tasks can be included as subtasks. When a user gives the description of a new step, PLOW checks if the step matches one of the known tasks; if a matching task is found, it is inserted as a subtask with parameter binding between the current task and the reused task. For instance, in one teaching session, a user has taught how to book a flight and wants to reserve a hotel. For a step introduced by saying, "*Book a hotel for the arrival date*", PLOW will check for a matching task for the step.

If the user already has a task to reserve a hotel with a check-in date and a number of nights, PLOW will mark the step as reusing another task so that, in execution, the reused task can be called. PLOW will also infer that the arrival date should be bound to the check-in date and consider the number of nights as a new input parameter if there is no related object in the current task.

Editing tasks

To fix obsolete tasks (e.g., to update them after Web site changes) or to improve or simplify a task, PLOW lets a user add or delete steps. To reach a step to edit, PLOW supports (1) step-by-step execution (the default mode for verification) and (2) partial execution up to a certain step. One can invoke the two modes by saying, "*Let's practice step by step*" and "*Execute the task up to this step*" (after selecting a step in the current task window), respectively.

Setting up the action context (i.e., browser setting, extracted objects, available parameter values, etc.) with real execution is critical because the context is used in PLOW's reasoning for the action to edit. Figure 16.14 shows the interaction between a user (USR) and PLOW (SYS) for task editing that was to add a new step to select a checkbox for a special military rate in booking a hotel. Note that, before the dialogue in the chat window, the user selected the step described as "Put the check out date" in the current task window (marked with a stop sign).

Improving tasks from execution failure

Execution failure from unnecessary or missing steps can be corrected by task editing. Major Web site redesigns will sometimes trigger Web object identification failures. When PLOW detects an execution error, it stops at the failed action, notifies the user, and initiates a debugging process by asking for a new example from which it learns an additional extraction pattern.

In Figure 16.15, the task is to find hotel per diem rates for a city and a state. In testing for a city in Nebraska, PLOW failed at the step to find a per diem list because the list observed in demonstration had a significantly different structure from the list to find in testing. PLOW notified a user of the failure with speech and GUI (red text with a bug icon) outputs. The dialogue in the chat window

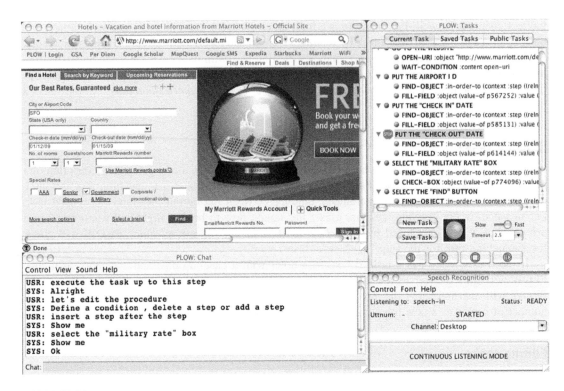

FIGURE 16.14

Task editing.

shows how PLOW and a user interacted with each other to address the problem. As shown in the browser window, the user gave a new example by highlighting the per diem rate list for the failed step. Now, the constructed task has become more robust with the knowledge about different list structures.

EVALUATION

In 2006 and 2007, PLOW was evaluated along with three other task-learning systems by an independent agency as a part of the U.S. DARPA (Defense Advanced Research Projects Agency) CALO (Cognitive Assistant that Learns and Organizes) project. Sixteen human subjects received training on each system and they were given ten problems that can be performed on various Web sites:

1. To whom should a travel itinerary be emailed?
2. List all publications from the work funded by a project.
3. List top N candidates for given product specifications.
4. Retrieve N product reviews for a product.
5. List restaurants within a certain distance from an address.
6. In what conference was an article published?

FIGURE 16.15

Failure correction with a new example.

7. What articles are cited in a given article?

8. What articles cite a given article?

9. Who else is traveling to a location on the same day with a person of interest?

10. What roles does a person play in an institution?

PLOW did very well in both tests, receiving a grade of 2.82 (2006) and 3.47 (2007) out of 4 (exceeding the project goals in both cases). The test score was given by human evaluators based on a complex scheme that took into account the completeness and the correctness of the results.

In a separate test in 2006, test subjects were given a set of 10 new *surprise* problems, some of which were substantially different from the original 10 problems. They were free to choose from different systems. However, PLOW was the system of choice among the subjects. In the testing, 55 task models out of the possible 160 individual models were constructed by 16 users. PLOW was used to create 30 out of the 55 completed task models, and 13 out of 16 users used PLOW at least once (the next most used system was used by 8 users). PLOW also received the highest average score (2.2 out of 4) in the test.

PLOW performed relatively well for the problems, the solution of which can be provided by a single Web site with minimal manipulation of the extracted information (e.g., simple data filtering such as selecting N items). As for the user-friendliness, though PLOW received favorable anecdotal comments for its natural interaction, users were often unable to undo incorrect steps (forcing them to restart), and they also got confused when PLOW entered into an error state without proper feedback, causing additional errors.

RELATED WORK

A major technique in task learning is an observation-based approach in which agents learn task models through observation of the actions performed by an expert (Angros et al., 2002; Lau & Weld, 1999; van Lent & Laird, 2001). However, a significant drawback of these approaches is that they require multiple examples, making them infeasible for one-shot learning in most cases without very special domain knowledge.

Researchers also investigated techniques that do not require observation by enabling experts to encode their knowledge with annotation (Garland, Ryall, & Rich, 2001; Lee & Anderson, 1997). To make a knowledge encoding process more efficient, a specialized GUI system, called Tailor, was developed as part of the DARPA CALO project (Blythe, 2005). Pseudo-NL-based scripts, such as CoScripter, fit very well for end users to automate and share Web-based processes (Chapter 5). Although these annotation and NL-based scripting technologies are very useful, it would be difficult for a system to learn how to identify Web objects in nonstatic Web pages.

Chickenfoot (Chapter 3), with a UNIX shell script style language, and AtomSmasher (Chapter 7), with rules to control multiple scripts, are good alternatives to automate Web-based processes that include complex control structures. However, they still have many features in conventional programming languages and are less suitable for novice end users.

Creo is a PBD system that can learn a task from a single example (Chapter 4). The generalization of observed actions is supported by knowledge bases of semantic information, MIT's ConceptNet and Stanford's TAP. Although the semantic information provides the basis for parameter generalization, it is limited to support reasoning about control structures from a single example.

Mashup systems are also efficient tools to extract and integrate information from multiple Web sites (see Chapters 9 and 12) (Huynh et al., 2007). While they are powerful tools, their capability and complexity are positively correlated (i.e., complex interfaces are provided for advanced functionalities). Furthermore, they have limitations on handling nonstatic Web objects and understanding extracted information for further reasoning.

SUMMARY

PLOW demonstrates that NL is a powerful intuitive tool for end users to build Web tasks with significant complexity using only a single demonstration. The natural play-by-play demonstration that would occur in human–human teaching provides enough information for the system to generalize demonstrated actions. Mixed-initiative interaction also makes the task building process much more convenient and intuitive. Without the system's proactive involvement in learning, the human instructor's job could become very tedious, difficult, and complex. Semantic information in NL description also makes the system more robust by letting it handle the dynamic nature of the Web.

Though PLOW sheds more light on NL's roles and the collaborative problem solving aspects in the end user programming on the Web, significant challenges still exist and new ones will emerge as application domains are expanded. Better reasoning about tasks, broader coverage of language understanding, and more robust Web object handling will be needed to address the challenges.

Acknowledgments

This work was supported in part by DARPA grant NBCHD-03-0010 under a subcontract from SRI International, and ONR grant N000140510314.

PLOW

Intended users:	All users
Domain:	All Web sites
Description:	PLOW learns a task from explicit demonstration of the task together with natural language instruction. The natural language "play by play" provides key information that allows rapid and robust learning of complex tasks including conditionals and iterations in one session.
Example:	Look for hotels near an airport based on their distance and price. When a user's flight is cancelled at midnight, the user invokes a task built by his/her colleague to get a list of hotels.
Automation:	Yes, it automates tasks that can be done by normal Web browsing actions but do not require visual understanding of Web pages.
Mashups:	It can combine information from multiple Web sources. However, its capability is limited by the difficulty in understanding complex instruction for how to present and manipulate combined information.
Scripting:	No.
Natural language:	Natural language processing is the key to understanding the user's intention and Web page content.
Recordability:	Yes, user actions are observed by the system.
Inferencing:	Heuristics are used in interpreting the user's intention, which may be vague or ambiguous, and learning how to identify objects in a Web page.
Sharing:	Yes, users can share tasks using a specialized GUI.
Comparison to other systems:	PLOW exploits the rich information encoded in the user's natural language description for demonstrated actions, which makes the teaching process efficient and natural.
Platform:	Implemented as a desktop application combined with an instrumented Mozilla Firefox browser. A Web-based version with a server was also developed.
Availability:	Not currently available.

Knowing what you're talking about

Natural language programming of a multi-player online game

17

Henry Lieberman, Moin Ahmad
Media Laboratory, Massachusetts Institute of Technology

ABSTRACT

Enabling end users to express programs in natural language would result in a dramatic increase in accessibility. Previous efforts in natural language programming have been hampered by the apparent ambiguity of natural language. We believe a large part of the solution to this problem is *knowing what you're talking about* – introducing enough semantics about the subject matter of the programs to provide sufficient context for understanding.

We present MOOIDE (pronounced "moody"), a natural language programming system for a MOO (an extensible multi-player text-based virtual reality storytelling game). MOOIDE incorporates both a state-of-the-art English parser, and a large commonsense knowledge base to provide background knowledge about everyday objects, people, and activities. End user programmers can introduce new virtual objects and characters into the simulated world, which can then interact conversationally with (other) end users.

In addition to using semantic context in traditional parsing applications such as anaphora resolution, commonsense knowledge is used to ensure that the virtual objects and characters act in accordance with commonsense notions of cause and effect, inheritance of properties, and affordances of verbs. This leads to a more natural dialog.

PROGRAMMING IN A MOO

Figure 17.1 illustrates MOOIDE's interface. A MOO (Bruckman & Resnick, 1995) is a conversational game modeling a simulated world containing virtual rooms or environments, virtual objects such as tables or flower pots, and virtual characters (played in real time by humans or controlled by a program). Players of the game may take simulated physical actions, expressed in natural language, or say things to the virtual characters or other human players. Programming consists of introducing new virtual environments, objects, or characters. They then become part of the persistent, shared environment, and can subsequently interact with players.

We choose the MOO programming domain for several reasons. Even though a conventional MOO has a stylized syntax, users conceive of the interaction as typing natural language to the system; an opportunity exists for extending that interaction to handle a wider range of expression.

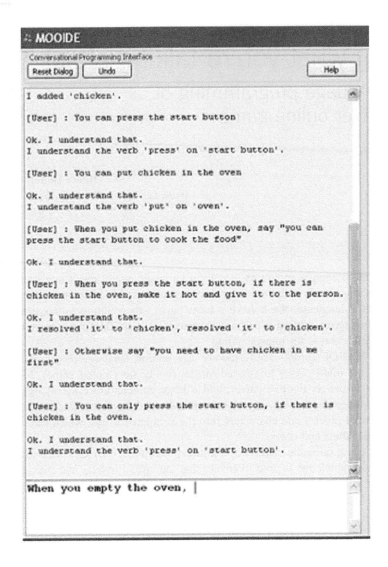

FIGURE 17.1

MOOIDE's programming interface. The user is programming the behavior of a microwave oven in the simulated world.

We leverage the ordinary person's understanding of natural language interaction to introduce programming concepts in ways that are analogous to how they are described in language. Interaction in natural language is, well, natural.

Contemporary Web-based MOOs are examples of collaborative, distributed, persistent, end user programmable virtual environments. Programming such environments generalizes to many other Web-based virtual environments, including those where the environments are represented graphically, perhaps in 3D, such as Second Life. Finally, because the characters and objects in the MOO imitate the real world, there is often a good match between knowledge that is useful in the game, and the commonsense knowledge collected in our Open Mind Common Sense knowledge base.

METAFOR

Our previous work on the Metafor system (Liu & Lieberman, 2005a; Mihalcea, Liu, & Lieberman, 2006) showed how we could transform natural language descriptions of the properties and behavior of the virtual objects into the syntax of a conventional programming language, Python. We showed how we could recognize linguistic patterns corresponding to typical programming language concepts, such as variables, conditionals, and iterations.

In MOOIDE, like Metafor, we ask users to describe the operation of a desired program in unconstrained natural language, and, as far as we can, translate it into Python code. Roughly, the parser turns nouns into descriptions of data structures ("There is a bar"), verbs into functions ("The bartender can make drinks"), and adjectives into properties ("a vodka martini"). It can also untangle various narrative stances, different points of view from which the situation is described ("When the customer orders a drink that is not on the menu, the bartender says, "I'm sorry, I can't make that drink"").

However, the previous Metafor system was positioned primarily as a code editor; it did not have a runtime system. The MOOIDE system presented here contains a full MOO runtime environment in which we could dynamically query the states of objects. MOOIDE also adds the ability to introduce new commonsense statements as necessary to model the (necessarily incomplete) simulated environment.

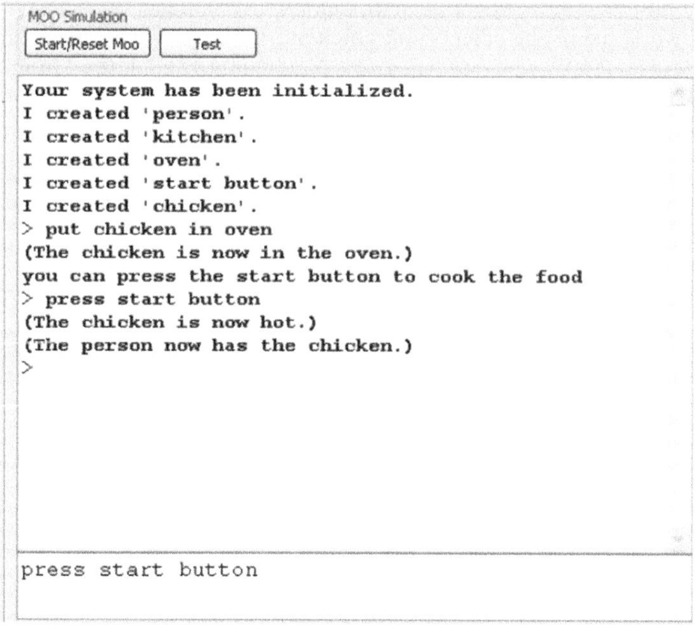

FIGURE 17.2

MOOIDE's MOO simulation interface. It shows user interaction with the microwave oven defined in Figure 17.1.

A DIALOG WITH MOOIDE

Let's look at an example of interaction with MOOIDE in detail, a snapshot of which is shown in the figures above. The following examples are situated in a common household kitchen where a user is trying to build new virtual kitchen objects and giving them behaviors.

> **There is a chicken in the kitchen.**
> **There is a microwave oven.**
> **You can only cook food in an oven.**
> **When you cook food in the oven, if the food is hot, say, "The food is already hot."**
> **Otherwise make it hot.**

The user builds two objects, a chicken and an oven, and teaches the oven to respond to the verb "cook." Any player can subsequently use the verb by entering the following text into the MOO:

> **cook chicken in microwave oven**

In the verb description, the user also describes a decision construct (the If-Else construct) as well as a command to change a property of an object – **make it hot**. To disallow cooking of nonfood items, he or she puts a rule saying that only objects of the "food" class are allowed to be cooked in the oven (**You can only cook food in an oven**). Note this statement is captured as a commonsense fact because it describes generic objects.

When the user presses the "Test" button on the MOOIDE interface, MOOIDE generates Python code and pushes it into the MOO, where the user can test and simulate the world he or she made. To test the generated world, he or she enters **cook chicken in oven** into the MOO simulation interface. However, in this case the MOO generates an error – **You can only cook food in an oven**. This is not what the user expected!

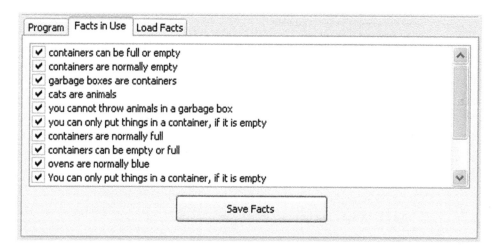

FIGURE 17.3

Commonsense facts used in the microwave oven example.

Of course you should be able to cook chicken; after all, isn't chicken a food? Wait, does the system know that? The user checks the commonsense knowledge base, to see if it knows this fact. The knowledge base is never fully complete, and when it misses deductions that are "obvious" to a person, the cause is often an incompleteness of the knowledge base. In this case, our user is surprised to find this simple fact missing. To resolve this error, he or she simply has to add the statement **Chicken is a kind of food**. Many other variants, some indirect, such as **Chicken is a kind of meat** or **People eat chicken**, could also supply the needed knowledge.

Then he or she tests the system again using the same verb command. Now, the command succeeds and the MOO prints out **The chicken is now hot**. To test the decision construct, the user types **cook chicken in oven** into the MOO simulator. This time the MOO prints out **The food is already hot**.

PARSING

MOOIDE performs natural language processing with a modified version of the Stanford link parser (Sleator & Temperley, 1991) and the Python NLTK natural language toolkit. As in Metafor, the ConceptNet commonsense semantic network provides semantics for the simulated objects, including object class hierarchies, and matching the arguments of verbs to the types of objects they can act upon, in a manner similar to Berkeley's FRAMENET. We are incorporating the AnalogySpace inference to perform commonsense reasoning. In aligning the programmed objects and actions with our commonsense knowledge base, we ignore, for the moment, the possibility that the author might want to create "magic ovens" or other kinds of objects that would intentionally violate real-world expectations for literary effect.

The system uses two different types of parsing: *syntactic* parsing and *frame-based* parsing. Syntactic parsing works using a tagger that identifies syntactic categories in sentences and that generates parse trees by utilizing a grammar (often a probabilistic context-free grammar). For example a sentence can be tagged as:

You/PRP can/MD put/VB water/NN in/IN a/DT bucket/NN ./.

From the tag (e.g., NN for noun, DT for determiner), a hierarchical parse tree that chunks syntactic categories together to form other categories (like noun/verb phrases) can also be generated:

```
(ROOT (S (NP (PRP You)) (VP (MD can)
    (VP (VB put) (NP (NN water))
    (PP (IN in) (NP (DT a) (NN bucket)))))
    (. .)))
```

Frame-based parsing identifies chunks in sentences and makes them arguments of frame variables. For example one might define a frame parse of the above sentence as: "*You can put [ARG] in [OBJ]*".

Syntactic parsing allows identification of noun phrases and verb phrases and dependency relationships between them. Frame-based parsing allows us to do two things – first, it allows us to do chunk extractions that are required for extracting things like object names, messages, and verb arguments. Second, frame parsing allows us to identify and classify the input into our speech act categories for programming constructs, further explained below. For example a user input that is of the form "If. . . . otherwise. . ." would be identified as a variant of an "IF_ELSE" construct very typical in programming.

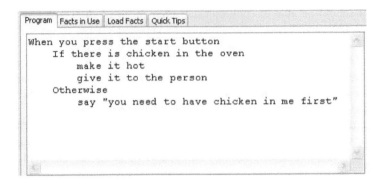

FIGURE 17.4

MOOIDE's English representation of MOO program code.

DIALOG MANAGER

The logic of the parsing system is controlled by a dialog manager that interprets user interaction. When the user enters something into the system, it uses three kinds of information to categorize the input: the current context, a frame-based classification of current input, and the object reference history. The current context broadly keeps track of what is being talked about – the user might be conversing about creating a new verb or adding decision criteria inside an IF construct. The dialog manager also keeps track of object reference history to allow users to use anaphora so that they do not need to fully specify the object in question every time. Using the previous information, the frame-based classifier does a broad syntactic classification of the input.

After the input has been classified, the dialog manager parses the input and makes changes to the internal representation of the objects, object states, verbs, and programs. Post-parsing, the dialog manager can generate three types of dialogs: a *confirmation* dialog, a *clarification* dialog, or an *elaboration* dialog. A confirmation dialog simply tells the user what was understood in the input and if everything in the input was parsed correctly. A clarification dialog is when the dialog manager needs to ask the user for clarification on the input. This could be simple "yes/no" questions, reference resolution conflicts, or input reformulation in case the parser cannot fully parse the input. If the parser fails to parse the input correctly, the dialog manager does a rough categorization of the input to identify possible features like noun phrases, verb phrases, or programming artifacts. This allows it to generate help messages suggesting to the user to reformulate the input so that its parser can parse the input correctly. For the elaboration dialog, the system lets the user know what it did with the previous input and suggests other kinds of inputs to the user. These could be letting the user know what commonsense properties were automatically added, suggesting new verbs, or requesting the user to define an unknown verb.

Commonsense reasoning

An important lesson learned by the natural language community over the years is that language cannot be fully understood unless you have some semantic information – you've got to know what you're talking about.

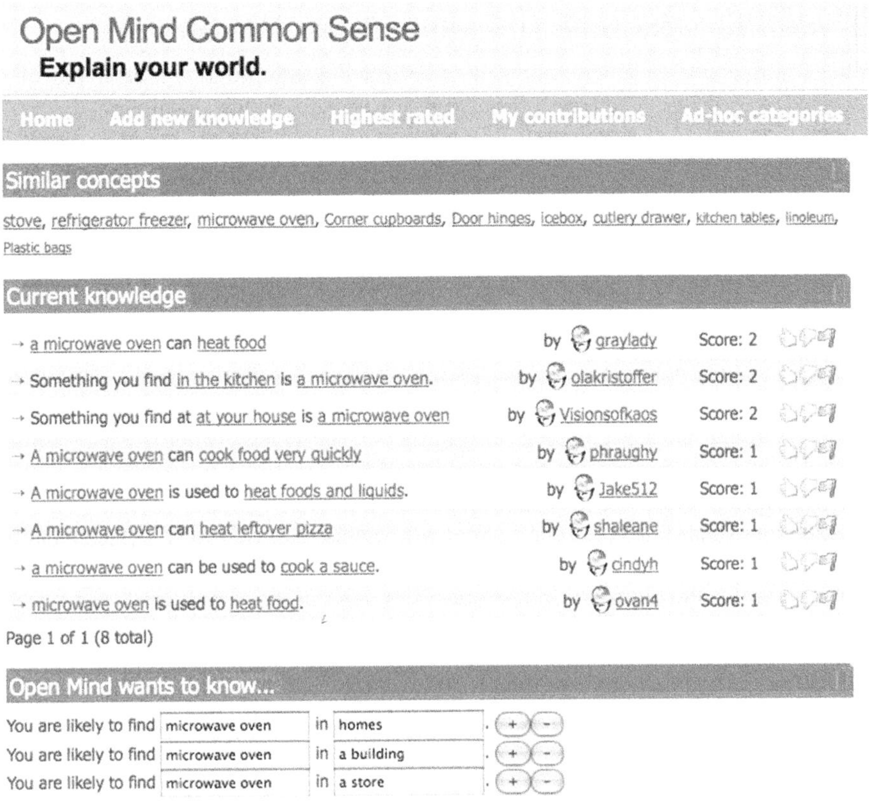

FIGURE 17.5

What Open Mind knows about microwave ovens.

In our case, commonsense semantics is provided by Open Mind Common Sense (OMCS) (Liu & Singh, 2004), a knowledge base containing more than 800,000 sentences contributed by the general public to an open-source Web site. OMCS provides "ground truth" to disambiguate ambiguous parsings, and constrain underconstrained interpretations. OMCS statements come in as natural language and are processed with tagging and template matching similar to the processes used for interpreting natural language input explained earlier. The result is ConceptNet, a semantic network organized around about 20 distinguished relations, including IS-A, KIND-OF, USED-FOR, etc. The site is available at http://openmind.media.mit.edu.

Commonsense reasoning is used in the following ways. First, it provides an ontology of objects, arranged in object hierarchies. These help anaphora resolution, and understanding intentional descriptions. It helps understand which objects can be the arguments to which verbs. It provides some basic cause-and-effect rules, such as "When an object is eaten, it disappears."

UNDERSTANDING LANGUAGE FOR MOO PROGRAMMING

Key in going from parsing to programming is understanding the programming intent of particular natural language statements. Our recognizer classifies user utterances according to the following speech act categories:

- **Object creation, properties, states, and relationships.** For example, *"There is a microwave oven on the table. It is empty."* A simple declarative statement about a previously unknown object is taken as introducing that object into the MOO world. Descriptive statements introduce properties of the object. Background semantics about microwave ovens say that "empty" means "does not contain food" (it might not be literally empty – there may be a turntable inside it).
- **Verb definitions,** such as *"You can put food in the basket."* Statements about the possibility of taking an action, where that action has not been previously mentioned, are taken as introducing the action, as a possible action a MOO user can take. Here, what it means is to "put food." A "basket" is the argument to (object of) that action. Alternative definition styles: "To ..., you...", "Baskets are for putting food in", etc.
- **Verb argument rules,** such as *"You can only put bread in the toaster."* This introduces restrictions on what objects can be used as arguments to what verbs. These semantic restrictions are in addition to syntactic restrictions on verb arguments found in many parsers.
- **Verb program generation.** *"When you press the button, the microwave turns on."* Prose that describes sequences of events is taken as describing a procedure for accomplishing the given verb.
- **Imperative commands,** like *"Press the button."*
- **Decisions.** *"If there is no food in the oven, say 'You are not cooking anything.'"* Conditionals can be expressed in a variety of forms: IF statements, WHEN statements, etc.
- **Iterations, variables, and loops.** *"Make all the objects in the oven hot."*

In (Pane & Ratanamahatana, 2001), user investigations show that explicit descriptions of iterations are rare in natural language program descriptions; people usually express iterations in terms of sets, filters, etc. In (Mihalcea, Liu, & Lieberman, 2006), we build up a sophisticated model of how people describe loops in natural language, based on reading a corpus of natural language descriptions of programs expressed in program comments.

EVALUATION

We designed MOOIDE so that it is intuitive for users who have little or no experience in programming to describe objects and behaviors of common objects that they come across in their daily life. To evaluate this, we tested whether subjects were able to program a simple scenario using MOOIDE. Our goal is to evaluate whether they can use our interface without getting frustrated, possibly enjoying the interaction while successfully completing a test programming scenario.

Our hypothesis is that subjects will be able to complete a simple natural language programming scenario within 20 minutes. If most of the users are able to complete the scenario in that amount of time, we would consider it a success. The users should not require more than minimal syntactic nudging from the experimenter.

Experimental method

We first ran users through a familiarization scenario so that they could get a sense of how objects and verbs are described in the MOO. Then they were asked to do a couple of test cases in which we helped the subjects through the cases. The experimental scenario consisted of getting subjects to build an interesting candy machine that gives candy only when it is kicked. The experimenter gave the subject a verbal description of the scenario (the experimenter did not "read out" the description):

> You should build a candy machine that works only when you kick it. You have to make this interesting candy machine that has one candy inside it. It also has a lever on it. It runs on magic coins. The candy machine doesn't work when you turn the lever. It says interesting messages when the lever is pulled. So if you're pulling the lever, the machine might say, "Ooh, I malfunctioned." It also says interesting things when magic coins are put in it, like, "Thank you for your money." And finally, when you kick the machine, it gives the candy.

The test scenario was hands-off for the experimenter who sat back and observed the user/MOOIDE interaction. The experimenter only helped if MOOIDE ran into implementation bugs, if people ignored minor syntactic nuances (e.g., comma after a "when" clause), and if MOOIDE generated error messages. This was limited to once or twice in the test scenario.

Experimental results

Figure 17.6 summarizes the post-test questionnaire.

Overall, we felt that subjects were able to get the two main ideas about programming in the MOOs – describing objects and giving them verb behavior. Some subjects who had never programmed before were visibly excited at seeing the system respond with an output message that they had programmed using MOOIDE while paying little attention to the demonstration part where we showed them an example of LambdaMOO. One such subject was an undergraduate woman who had tried to learn conventional programming but had given up after spending significant effort learning syntactic nuances. It seems that people want to learn creative tasks like programming, but do not want to learn a programming language. Effectively, people are looking to do something that is interesting to them and that they are able to do quickly enough with little learning overhead.

In the post-evaluation responses, all the subjects strongly felt that programming in MOOIDE was easier than learning a programming language. However, 40% of the subjects encountered limitations of our parser, and criticized MOOIDE for not handling a sufficient range of natural language expression. We investigated the cause for the parser failures. Some of the most serious, such as failures in correctly handling "an" and "the," were due to problems with the interface to MOOP, the third-party MOO environment. These would be easily rectifiable. Others were due to incompleteness of the grammar or knowledge base, special characters typed, typos, and in a few cases, simply parser bugs. Because parsing per se was not the focus of our work, the experimenter helped users through some cases of what we deemed to be inessential parser failure. The experimenter provided a few examples of the kind of syntax the parser would accept, and all subjects were able to reformulate their particular verb command, without feeling like they were pressured into a formal syntax. Advances in the underlying parsing technology will drive steady improvements in its use in this application.

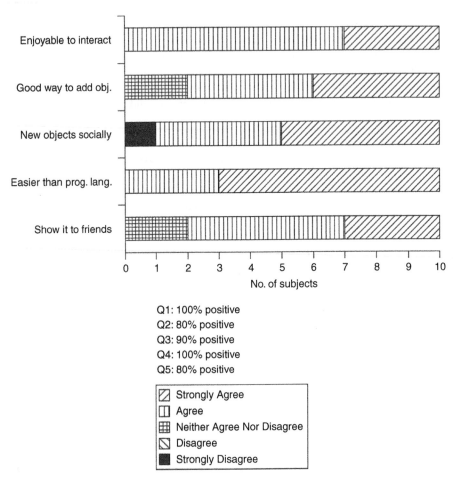

FIGURE 17.6

Results of the evaluation questionnaire.

There were some other things that came up in the test scenario that we did not handle, and we had to tell people that the system would not handle them. All such cases, discussed next, came across only once each in the evaluation.

People would often put the event declaration at the end, rather than the beginning, confusing our system. So one might say "the food becomes hot, when you put it in the oven" instead of "when you put the food in the oven, it becomes hot." This is a syntactic fix that requires the addition of a few more patterns. The system does not understand commands like "nothing will come out" or "does not give the person a candy," which describe negating an action. Negation is usually not required to be specified. These statements often correspond to the "pass" statement in Python. In other cases, it could be canceling a default behavior. One subject overspecified – "if you put a coin in the candy machine, there will be a coin in the candy machine."

This was an example where a person would specify very basic commonsense which we consider to be at the sub-articulable level, so we do not expect most people to enter these kind of facts. This relates to a larger issue – the kind of expectation the system puts upon its users about the level of detail in the commonsense that they have to provide. The granularity issue also has been recognized in knowledge acquisition systems, such as Blythe, Kim, Ramachandran, and Gil's EXPECT (2001), because informants are sometimes unsure as to how detailed their explanations need to be. Part of the job of a knowledge acquisition system and/or a human knowledge engineer, is to help the informant determine the appropriate level of granularity.

Unfortunately, there's no one answer to this question. Tutorials, presented examples, and experience with the system can help the user discover the appropriate granularity, through experience of what the system gets right and wrong, and how particular modifications to the system's knowledge affect its performance. A guide is the Felicity Conditions of van Lehn (1984), following Seymour Papert's dictum, "You can only learn something if you almost know it already." The best kinds of commonsense statements for the user to provide are those that are at the level that help it fill in inference gaps, such as the "Chicken is a food" example given earlier. One could certainly say, "Chicken is made of atoms," but that isn't much use if you're trying to figure out how to cook something. Because our commonsense knowledge base can be easily queried interactively, it is easy to discover what it does and does not know. There's some evidence (Maulsby, 1993) that people who interact with machine learning systems do adapt over time to the granularity effective for the system.

The system did not handle object removals at this time, something that is also easily rectified. It does not handle chained event descriptions like, "when you kick the candy machine, a candy bar comes out" and then "when the candy bar comes out of the candy machine, the person has the candy bar." Instead one needs to say directly, "when you kick the candy machine, the person has the candy bar." In preliminary evaluations we were able to identify many syntactic varieties of inputs that people were using and they were incorporated in the design before user evaluation. These were things like verb declarations chained with conjunctions (e.g., "when you put food in the oven and press the start button, the food becomes hot") or using either "if" or "when" for verb declarations (e.g., "if you press the start button, the oven cooks the food").

RELATED WORK

Aside from our previous work on Metafor (Liu & Lieberman, 2005; Mihalcea, Liu, & Lieberman, 2006), the closest related work is Inform 7, a programming language for a MOO game that does incorporate a parser for a wide variety of English constructs (Sleator & Temperley, 1991). Inform 7 is still in the tradition of "English-like" formal programming languages, a tradition dating back to Cobol. Users of Inform 7 reported being bothered by the need to laboriously specify "obvious" commonsense properties of objects. Our approach is to allow pretty much unrestricted natural language input, but be satisfied with only partial parsing if the semantic intent of the interaction can still be accomplished. We were originally inspired by the Natural Programming project of Pane, Myers, and Ratanamahatana (2001), which considered unconstrained natural language descriptions of programming tasks, but eventually wound up with a graphical programming language of conventional syntactic structure.

SUMMARY

Although general natural language programming remains difficult, some semantic representation of the subject matter on which programs are intended to operate makes it a lot easier to understand the intent of the programmer. Perhaps programming is really not so hard, as long as you know what you're talking about.

MOOIDE

Intended users:	All users, focusing on game players, beginning programmers
Domain:	Multi-player online virtual worlds, particularly text MUD/MOO environments
Description:	MOOIDE, pronounced "moody," is a natural language programming environment for creating new characters and new objects in virual environments. Behavior for characters and objects can be programmed to allow them to interact with game players or each other.
Example:	Create a MOO "room" that simulates a household kitchen, with a refrigerator, stove, etc. A human player could then type, "put chicken in the microwave oven", and tell it to "cook." The microwave oven might complain if you put an inappropriate object in it, such as a cat.
Automation:	Yes.
Mashups:	Not applicable.
Scripting:	Yes.
Natural language:	Yes, all interactions are through natural language.
Recordability:	Yes.
Inferencing:	Yes.
Sharing:	Yes.
Comparison to other systems:	The only other MOO natural language programming system is Inform 7. Inform 7 has no inference capability.
Platform:	Any Python platform, with the MOOP MOO system, the Stanford Natural Language Group parser, and the Divisi commonsense inference toolkit.
Availability:	Available only for sponsor organizations of the MIT Media Lab and selected academic collaborators.

Accessibility

Unfortunately, much of the content that appears on the Web is not easily accessible for visually impaired users, but some of the end user programming paradigms described in this book can help improve Web accessibility. For example, the Social Accessibility project coordinates third-party improvement of Web pages through the addition of external metadata. The TrailBlazer project, based on the CoScripter project described earlier, helps visually impaired users accomplish tasks by leading them through Web pages using step-by-step instructions that are automatically generated from a corpus of previously-created related step-by-step instructions.

Social Accessibility

A collaborative approach to improving Web accessibility

Yevgen Borodin,[1] **Shinya Kawanaka,**[2] **Hironobu Takagi,**[2] **Masatomo Kobayashi,**[2] **Daisuke Sato,**[2] **Chieko Asakawa**[2]

[1]*Department of Computer Science, Stony Brook University*
[2]*IBM Research – Tokyo*

ABSTRACT

This chapter challenges the assumption that Web site owners are the ones who are responsible for the accessibility of Web content. Web designers and Web developers have been notorious for not following official accessibility guidelines. At the same time, the amount of user-generated Web content made it practically impossible for site owners to ensure content accessibility in a centralized fashion. However, the dawn of social computing promises that collaborative approaches will overcome these problems. This chapter overviews the applications of social computing to Web accessibility and introduces Social Accessibility – a collaborative framework, which brings together end users and volunteers for the purpose of creating external accessibility metadata. In making the Web accessible, the Social Accessibility approach bypasses content owners, considerably reducing the time for accessibility renovations. In addition, the centralized metadata can be used to educate Web designers and developers about creating accessible content, while providing a central point for collaborative accessibility verification.

INTRODUCTION

The Web is playing an increasingly important role in our lives and has turned into an infrastructure vital to our society. However, in its evolution from single-author text-based Web pages to interactive Web applications with user-generated content, the Web has become less accessible to people with vision impairments, because content providers often fail to follow the accessibility guidelines while using a wide variety of inaccessible Web technologies with the primary focus on improving visual interaction.

Web content has traditionally been under the control of site owners, which is why, according to the present view on Web accessibility, site owners should be the ones who bear the responsibility for making their content accessible. Nowadays, however, the content is frequently generated by end users, who are posting information on content-sharing services, such as forums, blogs, etc., in the volume that can hardly be controlled by the site owners.

Highly interactive interfaces built with technologies such as AJAX and Flash exacerbate the accessibility problems even further. Though interactive Web sites can enhance the user experience by offering rich interactivity and responsiveness of the Web application, they simultaneously pose serious challenges not only to assistive software, such as screen readers used by blind people, but also to spiders crawling and indexing the Web, software tools that help users aggregate and filter information, automate repetitive tasks (Borodin, 2008; Leshed et al., 2008) (Chapter 5), provide custom views (Nichols & Lau, 2008) (Chapter 6), etc.

From a compliance perspective, Web designers and developers have to embed sufficient accessibility metadata into their content; for example, screen reader users need structural metadata (e.g., headings and lists) and alternative text for images to be able to efficiently navigate Web pages. Unfortunately, the accessibility metadata are often inadequate in both quality and quantity. Site owners are not able to give higher priority to their Web sites' accessibility compared to their business and technology needs, with the result that visual attractiveness of Web sites remains their primary focus.

Even those site owners who are willing to make their sites compliant with accessibility guidelines are not always able to do so, because of the need for specialized knowledge. On the other hand, only end users can reliably assess the usability and accessibility of Web sites. However, until now, the user involvement in improving Web accessibility has been very limited. There is general consensus among users that sending reports about accessibility problems to site owners is of little or no use, and that no effective feedback loop exists to correct accessibility problems. This leads us to believe that there is a clear need for a new framework that could engage the end users in making the Web more accessible and, thus, accelerate the accessibility renovations of Web sites.

Recent years have seen a surge in social networks (e.g., Facebook, MySpace, LinkedIn, etc.), which have proven effective in bringing together users with common interests, which in turn made possible a variety of collaborative approaches, such as ManyEyes (Viégas et al., 2007), ESP game (von Ahn & Dabbish, 2004), reCAPTCHA (von Ahn et al., 2008), Mechanical Turk (Kittur, 2008), and Phetch (von Ahn et al., 2007), to name a few.

The Social Accessibility Project (Takagi et al., 2008) featured in this chapter is taking a similar approach – it applies social computing strategies to accessibility metadata authoring. The collaboration through the Social Accessibility network allows persons experiencing accessibility problems to submit service requests, and it encourages other participants to respond to the requests by creating accessibility metadata, which can be generated both manually and automatically. This in turn provides various options for participation and volunteering. While shortening the creation time for accessible Web content, a collaborative approach can also drastically reduce the burden on content providers. And finally, the social networking infrastructure facilitates discussions and brings together people from around the world for the purpose of improving Web accessibility.

RELATED WORK

The work related to the Social Accessibility project includes collaborative authoring, transcoding, metadata authoring approaches, accessibility of Rich Internet Applications, and database integration.

Collaborative authoring

The Social Accessibility (SA) network enables collaborative authoring of accessibility metadata, which are additional information about the original Web documents to make them more accessible. The use of metadata in improving Web accessibility is wide-ranging and is covered by several W3C guidelines[1] and standards. Some representative examples include alternative text metadata describing images, labels for form elements, and ARIA[2] markup indicating the semantic roles of dynamic content. An important feature of accessibility metadata is that they can be used by a wide variety of software tools – from screen readers to search engines.

Collaborative document authoring is an area with a long history (e.g., Leland, Fish, & Kraut, 1988). A prime example of the largest success in this area is the wiki (Leuf & Cunningham, 2001), with the above-mentioned technology having yielded such fruits of global collaboration as the Wikipedia. In spite of the successes of collaborative authoring, it has rarely been applied to the accessibility area. One of the recent projects involving the technology is its use for collaborative "caption" authoring of multimedia content. The We-LCoME project is aimed at building accessible multimedia e-learning content through collaborative work on a wiki system (Ferretti et al., 2007; Ferretti et al., 2008). We-LCoME and Social Accessibility run in similar directions, using collaborative authoring for accessibility. Google Image Labeler[3] is a system used to build accurate textual descriptions of images through a game. The goal of the project is to improve the accuracy of Google Image search; nonetheless, the generated metadata could potentially be used for accessibility. Another system, which collects image labels through a game, is Phetch (von Ahn et al., 2007). The Social Accessibility approach learns from the existing research on collaborative document authoring and uses it to improve Web accessibility.

External metadata and transcoding

In general, there are two types of metadata: internal metadata that are embedded into documents (Web pages) and external (standoff) metadata that are stored separately, but are associated with the original documents. The important distinction is that the internal metadata can only be changed with the appropriate permissions from content owners, whereas the external metadata can be created by anyone. The SA approach utilizes the external metadata, in this way, enabling the collaborative approach to metadata authoring.

The main challenge in using the external metadata is in the on-the-fly association of specific metadata with the content they describe. Anchoring metadata to a specific part of a document is, therefore, key to the effective use of external metadata. Various research projects have been focusing on the automatic or semiautomatic creation and adaptation of external metadata to improve accessibility through transcoding original documents.

Transcoding is often used to modify the presentation of content without modifying the originals. Transcoding for Web accessibility is a category of approaches that make existing Web pages accessible on the fly. Currently, the technology is not widely used, in spite of its huge potential to improve

---

[1]Web Content Accessibility Guidelines (WCAG) Specifications: http://www.w3.org/TR/WCAG10/.
[2]Accessible Rich Internet Applications (ARIA) Specifications: http://www.w3.org/TR/wai-aria/.
[3]Google Image Labeler: http://images.google.com/imagelabeler/.

the accessibility of Web content. The primary reason for not using transcoding has been the heavy workload of metadata authoring, which has not been manageable until the introduction of collaborative approaches.

Transcoding of Web pages was originally developed to adapt Web pages to mobile devices (Bickmore & Schilit, 1997b) and to personalize pages (Maglio & Barrett, 2000). Then the technique was applied to transform inaccessible Web content into accessible on the fly. This technique has formed a new category of approaches – "transcoding for Web accessibility." More on transcoding, including history and methods, can be found in (Asakawa & Takagi, 2008a).

A recent research challenge in the transcoding area is dynamic Web applications, including AJAX techniques that use JavaScript to change the content of an already-loaded Web page. The AJAX (Asynchronous JavaScript and XML) techniques allow Web pages to download data on demand; for instance, while typing search keywords on a search engine Web site, the underlying JavaScript can transparently retrieve keyword suggestions from the server. The aiBrowser has a metadata mechanism to dynamically convert AJAX and Flash-based dynamic content into accessible formats (Miyashita et al., 2007). AxsJAX (Chen & Raman, 2008) is a technology used to make AJAX applications accessible while using JavaScript descriptions as a kind of metadata. Another technique, Access Monkey (Bigham & Ladner, 2007), also uses JavaScript to transcode content.

Metadata authoring approaches

Transcoding with external metadata has great potential as a new approach to creating a more accessible Web environment by supplementing the insufficient internal metadata. However, the workload of authoring has prevented it from providing major real-world benefits to users. We classify the approaches by the reduction of the authoring time and effort.

Fully automated generation. Automatic transcoding techniques can transform content without any additional information by using various inference techniques, such as content analysis (Ramakrishnan, Stent, & Yang, 2004), differential analysis (Takagi & Asakawa, 2000), and so on. These automatic methods have an advantage in coverage since they can deal with any content on the Web; however, the accuracy of their inferences can be problematic. Besides, mechanisms to add supplementary manual metadata are needed for practical deployments. One example of such an approach is WebInsight (Bigham et al., 2006). The system infers alternative texts for images by automatically combining the results of OCR with the text-based content analysis and human-authored metadata. In addition, the system is characterized by its use of manual metadata as a last resort after exhaustive automatic processing.

Semi automated authoring. Some types of annotations are difficult to create by using fully automated approaches, such as states of Rich Internet Applications (RIAs). In the traditional static-Web paradigm, each page represents a state reachable through static links easily identifiable in the HTML source code. On the other hand, in RIAs, the states are implicit and are determined by the user actions and the ensuing changes that occur in Web pages as a result of those actions. The discovery of the states, transitions, and the information hidden in those states can improve RIA accessibility to Web spiders, screen readers, and other tools (Borodin, 2008; Leshed et al., 2008; Nichols & Lau, 2008) that need to retrieve the information. Fully automated approaches for discovering such states are not feasible (Mesbah, Bozdag, & Deursen, 2008); conversely, a semiautomated approach guided by users (even if they do not realize it) can be used to create and share external metadata describing dynamic content and its behavior. The collaborative crawling (Aggarwal, 2002) approach can be used to automate the discovery of dynamic content and metadata authoring, as described further in this chapter.

Manual annotations. Users exploring Web content can also be a source of metadata. For example, blind users can find the starting position of the main content in a page by exploring the page and marking this position for other users. Some commercial screen readers have functions to register alternative texts for images (e.g., JAWS[4]). HearSay (Ramakrishnan, Stent, & Yang, 2004; Borodin et al., 2007) has more advanced functions to allow users to add metadata (labels) in combination with an automatic analysis function. Users can easily select an appropriate label from the candidates. Although more accurate than automated annotation, manual authoring of metadata can be time-consuming.

Improvement of centralized authoring (template matching). Site-wide Annotation (Takagi et al., 2002) is aimed at reducing workload by combining template matching algorithms with a metadata management tool, Site Pattern Analyzer (SPA). A snapshot of a target site is crawled by the tool in advance, and then the tool visualizes the correspondences of each item of metadata to each page on the screen. In spite of the improvements, the workload for metadata maintenance is still excessive, which prevents it from being adopted by site owners as a practical way of making their rapidly evolving content accessible.

Improvement of centralized authoring (styling information). SADIe (Harper, Bechhofer, & Lunn, 2006) is characterized by its annotation mechanism based on CSS[5] information. One of the well-established approaches in Web design is CSS-based styling, because it provides flexibility in design, reduces the cost of managing visual layouts, and even improves accessibility by separating the logical structure of the content from the page design. SADIe takes advantage of this approach to reduce the workload of metadata authoring by associating semantics with the styling components. The main limitation of this approach is that it only works for sites with well-organized CSS styling, meaning that CSS styles have to follow the logical structure of Web pages.

Accessibility of Rich Internet Applications

Most Rich Internet Applications (RIAs) are currently accessible only to users visually interacting with the dynamic content. If Web developers properly exposed states and transitions of their Web sites, screen readers, crawlers, and tools for information filtering (Kawanaka et al., 2008) and automation (Borodin, 2008; Leshed et al., 2008) (Chapter 5) would be able to interact with the rich content. Unfortunately, Web applications are built with a variety of technologies and toolkits, many of which make RIA Web sites partially or completely inaccessible. Until recently, there have been two disjointed efforts to improve the accessibility of dynamic content by either manual or automatic authoring of metadata.

Manual approaches. The use of W3C standard for Accessible Rich Internet Applications (ARIA)[6] was one of the first attempts to make RIAs accessible. ARIA markup is intended to be used by screen readers to improve accessibility of Web applications to blind people. ARIA metadata can

---

[4]JAWS, Freedom Scientific Inc.: http://www.freedomscientific.com/.
[5]Cascading Style Sheet (CSS): http://www.w3.org/TR/CSS2/.
[6]Accessible Rich Internet Applications (WAI-ARIA): http://www.w3.org/TR/wai-aria/.

be embedded into Web pages and can be used to describe live areas, roles, and states of dynamic content. Regrettably, most of the dynamic content available today does not implement the ARIA standard. Nor are Web developers likely to follow ARIA consistently, for they have not followed other accessibility guidelines.

ARIA can also be supplied as part of reusable components or widgets; for example, Dojo Dijit[7] provides ARIA-enabled widgets and a toolkit to build custom accessible widgets. However, Dijit is only one of many available toolkits, and Web developers continue creating inaccessible custom widgets of their own. Another application of ARIA is through transcoding. To illustrate, Google's Axs-JAX (Chen & Raman, 2008) allows Web developers to use JavaScript to inject ARIA metadata into existing applications. However, AxsJAX scripts have to be created manually so far.

Fully automated approaches. To date, the only known approaches to fully automated collection of information from Web applications have been crawling RIA Web sites statically or crawling RIAs by opening them in a Web browser (Mesbah et al., 2008). It is lamentable that both of these approaches have a number of limitations and cannot be used to make RIAs fully accessible in practice.

The majority of search engines index RIAs by statically crawling Web sites and extracting text from the HTML source code. With such crawling, one cannot effectively infer the implicit state model of the Web site. The results of indexing can be enhanced by content providers explicitly exposing textual data to Web spiders, such as through meta tags. However, content providers are not always aware of how to properly use meta tags to make content accessible to Web crawlers.

An alternative to the static crawling can be opening RIAs in a Web browser and simulating various user events on all objects to expose the resulting system events and hidden content. For instance, AJAX application crawling is described in (Mesbah, Bozdag, & Deursen, 2008; Frey, 2007), where diff algorithms are used to detect the changes. Dynamic changes can also be identified by combining a diff algorithm with HTML DOM mutation event listeners, as described in (Borodin et al., 2008a). Hypothetically, such AJAX crawling could automate metadata authoring. In reality, though, a crawler cannot often access all content, and it consumes substantial machine time, while suffering from: state explosion (Mesbah, Bozdag, & Deursen, 2008), irreversibility of actions (which requires that transitions be retraced from the start state), latency between actions and reactions (especially in AJAX applications), and inability to access password-protected Web sites.

The collaborative crawling approach described later in this chapter combines the manual and automated approaches to semiautomated generation of ARIA metadata.

Database integration

The Web domain and the Life Science domain are two of the most active domains among those integrating databases. Because these domains have many resources to handle (such as Web pages or genomes), and because those resources are often stored separately for each project, there exists a strong demand for data integration and data exchange.

The Semantic Web[8] is a W3C initiative for integrating and exchanging Web resources. Web developers can use metadata, which are described in a Resource Description Framework (RDF)[9] or the

---

[7]Dojo Dijit: http://dojotoolkit.org/projects/dijit.
[8]OWL Web Ontology Language: http://www.w3.org/TR/owl-features.
[9]Resource Description Framework (RDF): http://www.w3.org/RDF.

Web Ontology Language (OWL)[10] to specify titles, publishers, meanings, and other semantic roles. By adding such metadata, applications handling RDF or OWL can interpret the meaning of Web resources, and handle resources with similar meanings as well. For example, if two online banking Web sites have the same semantic metadata, an application using such metadata can provide the same interface to both Web sites, even though they may use different visual layouts. Since metadata are written in one format, it is not necessary to convert the data format, which makes data exchange relatively easy. SA is also striving for standardization of formats; however, it does not require the complexity of the Semantic Web, and is currently using a database with a custom schema (Kawanaka et al., 2008).

In the Life Science domain, integrating databases is an active area of research. YeastHub (Cheung et al., 2005) is a project aiming to integrate many databases of yeast genomes stored separately in the past. Users can now search for yeast genome data in the YeastHub and obtain database tables or RDF that combine the data stored in separate databases. However, because the genome data formats are relatively fixed, and because the genome data is easy to convert, data integration is relatively uncomplicated. Social Accessibility schema try to accommodate a mixture of metadata that may be useful to a wide variety of systems.

SOCIAL ACCESSIBILITY[11]
Architecture and workflow of the SA framework

Social Accessibility (SA) (Takagi et al., 2008) is a collaborative framework that uses the power of the open community to improve the accessibility of existing Web content. SA unites end users and supporters who can collaboratively create accessibility metadata.

Until very recently, the general presumption has been that Web developers have primary responsibility for making Web pages accessible by embedding accessibility metadata such as alternative text, headings, ARIA, etc., into their content. Nevertheless, with the escalating amount of user-generated content, it has become clear that developers cannot be held solely responsible for content accessibility. At the same time, even though only end users have the ability to assess the real accessibility and usability of Web pages, there has been no systematic feedback loop from users to content providers. In our view, the Social Accessibility approach challenges this presumption.

Screen reader users with a variety of accessibility needs can participate in the Social Accessibility initiative by installing SA plug-ins for Firefox or Internet Explorer (IE) browsers. The plug-ins connect to the SA server, as shown in Figure 18.1, and every time the user visits a new Web page with Firefox or IE Web browsers, the plug-in retrieves the accessibility metadata from the Open Repository and transcodes the Web page by applying the metadata to the browser's HTML DOM representation of the Web page. The users can then read the Web page using the assistive technology of their choice and enjoy the improved accessibility of the content. By using the End-User Tool, which is a stand-alone Windows application, users can report any remaining accessibility problems by creating service requests that are also stored in the Open Repository. The SA Web portal[12] facilitates collaboration between supporters and end users and provides a forum for discussing problems and solutions.

---

[10]OWL Web Ontology Language: http://www.w3.org/TR/owl-features.
[11]For further details about the SA approach, please see (Takagi et al., 2008).
[12]Social Accessibility Project: http://sa.watson.ibm.com.

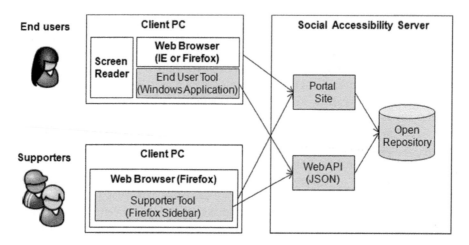

FIGURE 18.1

Basic architecture of the Social Accessibility service.

SA supporters are notified of incoming service requests through the Supporter Tool, which is a Firefox sidebar plug-in. The plug-in helps visualize user requests as well as any other accessibility problems. By using the plug-in, the supporters can act upon the requests and fix the accessibility problems. With every fix, the Supporter Plug-in submits the accessibility metadata to the SA Open Repository hosted on the Social Accessibility Server. Figure 18.2 shows the entire workflow: (1) a person with vision impairment reports an inaccessible image; (2) a supporter fixes the problem by adding alternative text; and (3) the end user listens to the alternative text of the image.

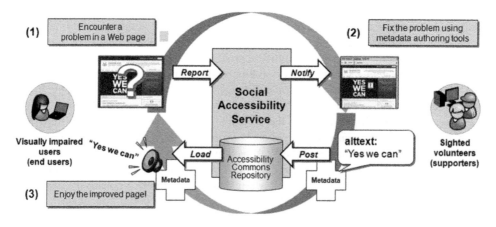

FIGURE 18.2

Workflow of Social Accessibility.

Accessibility assessment and visualization[13]

The Supporter Plug-in provides volunteers with the tools necessary for accessibility assessment of Web pages and visualization of user reports, including the User Request, Pagemap, and Quick Fix views.

The User Request view (Figure 18.3) shows recent problem reports and provides an easy interface for fixing the problems. Many reports are accompanied by a thumb-view snapshot of the

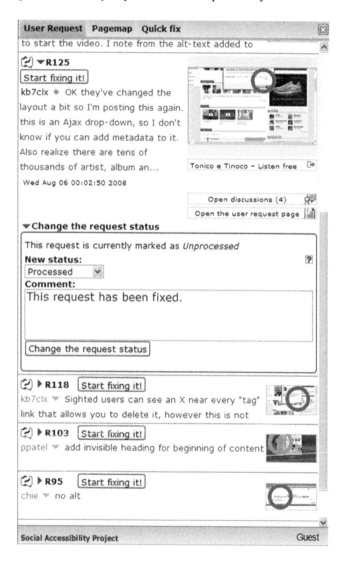

FIGURE 18.3

User Request view.

[13]The readers are invited to read the user guide and try the tools: http://sa.watson.ibm.com/getting_started/using_the_pagemap.

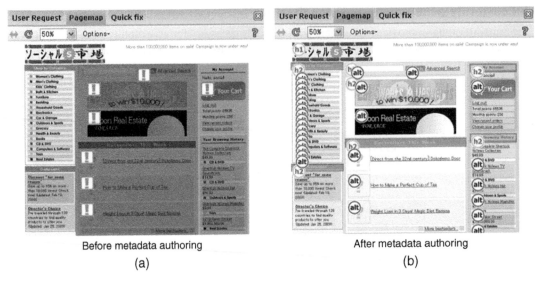

Before metadata authoring (a) After metadata authoring (b)

FIGURE 18.4

Pagemap editing tool.

Web page with the approximate position of the accessibility problem circled. This view also allows supporters to start a discussion and change the status of the request.

Pagemap is a WYSIWYG-style editor for metadata authoring (Figure 18.4). The editor uses a brightness-gradation technique (Takagi et al., 2004) to visualize how long it would take a screen reader user to reach a certain part of the page, using darker colors for less accessible content. The editor uses exclamation marks to indicate inaccessible images without alternative text or with meaningless default alternative text such as "banner" or "spacer." With the help of the editor, supporters can easily label elements as headings, provide text descriptions, or do both, by clicking on the exclamation marks. Figure 18.4a shows an inaccessible page before it was edited and Figure 18.4b – after it was renovated with Social Accessibility tools. Headings allow screen reader users to "jump" from one section of the page to another quickly, while alternative text ensures that users can read the labels of all images and image-links.

A Quick Fix view in Figures 18.3 and 18.4 displays a list of all images on the currently opened Web page and allows supporters to enter alternative text quickly.

Collaborative crawling

The current SA tools package enables manual metadata authoring. However, there is work under way to enable semiautomated and fully automated approaches to metadata authoring. The automated approaches can assist in creating metadata faster, while reducing both the expensive human effort and the minimum required accessibility knowledge on the part of the supporters.

The SA tools can provide an interface for manual authoring of ARIA-style metadata, such as live areas, relations between Web objects, object roles, etc. The ARIA-style markup will allow applications such as Web crawlers and screen readers to identify and correctly handle dynamic content, as well as identify states and transitions in Rich Internet Applications (RIA). However, creating ARIA-style annotations manually requires that supporters understand what dynamic content is and have more than basic knowledge of Web accessibility. Therefore, the process of authoring metadata could be greatly facilitated by semiautomated approaches such as collaborative crawling (Aggarwal, 2002) and could offer significant help to both Social Accessibility users and volunteers.

The collaborative crawling technique enables the discovery of the underlying structure of the Web by mining the browsing traces of a multitude of users. Although the original approach was employed for standard Web crawling between Web pages (Aggarwal, 2002), the SA tool for collaborative crawling (CCrawl[14]) mines user browsing behavior within Web pages to identify dynamic content. The approach delegates the discovery of dynamic content to regular computer users, with the expectation that, eventually, the users will try all allowable actions (transitions) and experience all possible system reactions. This approach will allow the SA volunteers to create ARIA-style metadata while performing their regular browsing activities. In the process, the volunteers act, in a way, as "distributed spiders" crawling the Web and discovering dynamic content.

By analyzing user actions and system reactions on a given Web page, it is possible to automatically infer ARIA metadata for live areas (e.g., dynamic stock ticker) and actionable objects (e.g., dragable), identify relations between objects (e.g., hover the mouse to open the menu), and even infer element roles (e.g., slider). Observing multiple users performing the same action will only improve inference confidence. The derived metadata can then be shared through the SA network and used by SA clients, such as screen readers with ARIA support or Web spiders for intelligent crawling of RIA sites.

Figure 18.5 illustrates a simple inference example on Amazon.com. When the user hovers the mouse over the dynamic menu (A), a "mousemove" event is triggered in the browser's DOM. The event is then caught by the underlying JavaScript, which displays a hidden submenu (B), which in turn triggers a "DOMAttrModified" event. By analyzing the sequence of user–system events and the resulting system reactions, it is possible to infer that (B) is a live area and (A) controls (B). This information can then be stored in the SA open repository. When a blind person visits the Amazon

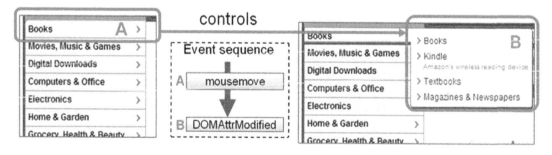

FIGURE 18.5

Discovering live areas and inferring relations on Amazon.com.

---

[14]The CCrawl tool is currently a concept prototype and is piloted separately from the main SA tools.

Web site, its Web pages can be transcoded to incorporate the correct ARIA markup. Then, with any screen reader that supports ARIA, the user will be able to expand the *"Books"* submenu and will have a usable interface to locate and review the submenu.

Metadata representation and Accessibility Commons[15]

The metadata generated by the Social Accessibility framework are stored in the Accessibility Commons (AC) database (Kawanaka et al., 2008). The metadata schema was defined in a collaborative effort of several research projects described in the next subsection, with the goal of unifying disparate schemas used by the projects and providing for future needs of these and other projects.

The AC schema includes three main components: *Semantics, URI Addressing,* and *Element Addressing*. The Semantics component describes the meaning of the metadata (e.g., level-1 heading, "news"); the URI Addressing specifies the target URI of the documents, for which the metadata were generated; and the Element Addressing is the reference to the HTML elements where the metadata have to be applied (e.g., XPath[16] address). Table 18.1 illustrates a sample metadata record suggesting that the HTML DIV element with the specified XPath be marked as a level-1 heading on all root-level HTML pages of the *example.com* Web site.

Because the metadata does not specify how exactly Web pages need to be transcoded, each Social Accessibility client application can interpret the metadata in its own way. Each metadata record also contains other information such as author, creation date, etc. The full schema definition can be found in (Kawanaka et al., 2008).

Client-side applications, such as metadata authoring tools (Takagi et al., 2002; Harper et al., 2006), and assistive technologies (Borodin et al., 2007) can access the *AC Open Repository* (Figure 18.1) using the Hyper-Text Transfer Protocol (HTTP). A client can submit metadata by posting it in JSON format (Kawanaka et al., 2008) and can retrieve metadata by sending a request with the URIs of the Web page and the images of that page. Figure 18.6 outlines the process of metadata retrieval from the AC repository.

First, the client application sends the query with URI of the current Web page to the AC server via the HTTP. Upon its arrival to the AC server, the URI is processed using an automaton-based

Table 18.1 Sample Metadata Record

Type	Value
Data Type	*H1*
Data Descr	*news*
URI Type	*wildcard*
URI Pattern	*http://www.example.net/*.html*
Address Type	*xpath*
Address	*/HTML[1]/BODY[1]/DIV[1]/DIV[2]*

---

[15]More details on the Accessibility Commons database can be found in (Kawanaka et al., 2008).
[16]XML Path Language (XPath): http://www.w3.org/TR/xpath.

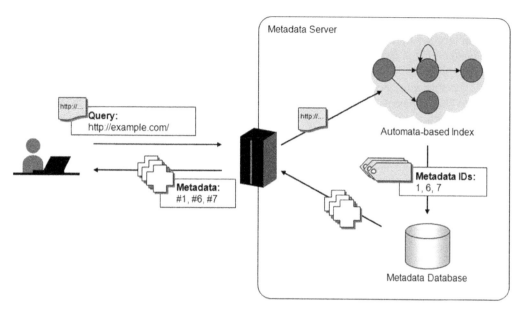

FIGURE 18.6

Retrieving AC metadata.

index, which returns the metadata IDs matching the queried URIs. The metadata records are then retrieved from the database using the metadata IDs. Finally, the metadata records are sent back to the client computer and are used to transcode the Web page.

Automaton-based indexing

The AC database is queried on the URI addresses, which can be represented with wildcards and regular expressions. As this kind of indexing is not implemented by typical database systems, AC employs a custom-made automaton-based index similar to that described in (Chan, Garofalakis, & Rastogi, 2002), which can identify all matching URI patterns using a nondeterministic finite state automaton. The index is created by converting a URI pattern to an automaton and then merging the automaton with the index automaton. The final states of the index automaton are associated with metadata IDs, which are accepted in those states, so that all of the metadata matching a URI can be retrieved by running the automaton once. The index automaton technique has greatly reduced the search times for metadata; with the current database containing around 100,000 records, the requested metadata can be found in microseconds.

Uniting disparate accessibility metadata

A number of existing accessibility research projects and products are using disparate metadata, a thorough understanding of which informed the design of the Accessibility Commons (AC) database schema, which hopefully ensured that the schema could be used by these projects and remain relevant as new projects and products are developed.

aiBrowser. The aiBrowser (Miyashita et al., 2007) is a multimedia browser for visually impaired people. The browser transcodes HTML documents and Adobe Flash[17] on the client side to provide alternate content that is more accessible for visually impaired people. The transcoding is done using metadata described in XML. The metadata describe how to combine HTML elements and Flash objects to generate more accessible alternate content. In the metadata, XPath expressions are used to specify HTML elements, and Flash queries are used to specify Flash objects. In addition, the aiBrowser allows users to add manual annotations for headings and alternative text. If the aiBrowser were to use a common repository, it could share its metadata and user annotations to provide alternative text and heading tags to people using other technologies.

HearSay. The HearSay nonvisual Web browser (Ramakrishnan, Stent, & Yang, 2004; Borodin et al., 2007; Mahmud, Borodin, & Ramakrishnan, 2007; Borodin et al., 2008b; Mahmud, Borodin, & Ramakrishnan, 2008) uses various content analysis techniques to improve Web accessibility, among which are context-directed browsing for identification of relevant information in Web pages (Mahmud, Borodin, & Ramakrishnan, 2007), language detection (Borodin et al., 2008b), concept detection (Mahmud, Borodin, & Ramakrishnan, 2008), etc. HearSay uses the results of the automated analyses to annotate Web content. For example, the context-directed browsing algorithm inserts a "start" label, instructing the browser to begin reading the page from a specific position. The HearSay browser has a VoiceXML-based dialog interface, which interprets the labels and provides facilities for navigating, editing, and creating manual labels, which can be stored in personal or shared repositories. The use of uniform metadata and a shared repository allows other applications to benefit from the labels created in HearSay. At the same time, future HearSay users will have access to metadata created by a wider pool of blind Web users.

WebInSight for Images. WebInSight for Images (Bigham et al., 2006) provides alternative text for many Web images to improve their accessibility. To make this alternative text, WebInSight uses contextual analysis of linked Web pages, enhanced Optical Character Recognition (OCR), and human labeling. The alternative text strings are stored in a shared database referenced by an MD5 hash of the image and the URL of the image. The stored alternative text is supplied as users browse the Web. When a user visits a Web page for the first time, WebInSight attempts to create alternative texts by doing contextual analysis and OCR. If these options fail, the user can request human labeling. By combining the alternative text into a common database, users will be more likely to experience the benefits.

Site-wide Annotation. Site-wide Annotation (Takagi et al., 2002) is a research project to transcode entire Web sites by annotating them. The metadata of the Site-wide Annotation use XPath expressions. The system checks for elements matching the expressions and transcodes the Web pages based on the metadata. This enables transcoding of an entire Web site with a small set of metadata. If this metadata could be created and shared by users, a larger number of Web sites would be transcoded for better Web accessibility.

AxsJAX. AxsJAX (Chen & Raman, 2008) is an accessibility framework to inject accessibility support into Web 2.0 applications. At present, the main targets of AxsJAX are Google applications such as Gmail and Google Docs. AxsJAX scripts use Greasemonkey or a bookmarklet, or run directly in Fire

---

[17]Adobe Flash: http://www.adobe.com/products/flash.

Vox,[18] a nonvisual Web browser implemented as a Firefox browser extension. AxsJAX uses XPath to connect ARIA markup to the corresponding Web page elements. Currently, these associations are distributed to users in the form of scripts. More tools could benefit from the semantic knowledge encoded in these scripts if they were stored in a more flexible and semantically accessible common repository.

Accessmonkey. Accessmonkey (Bigham & Ladner, 2007) is another common scripting framework that Web users and developers can use to improve Web accessibility collaboratively. The goal is to enable both Web users and developers to write scripts that can then be used to improve the accessibility of Web pages for blind Web users.

Structural semantics for Accessibility and Device Independence (SADIe). SADIe (Harper, Bechhofer & Lunn, 2006) is a proxy-based tool for transcoding entire Web sites as opposed to individual pages. It relies on ontological annotations of the Cascading Style Sheet (CSS) to apply accurate and scalable transcoding algorithms broadly. Only by explicitly enunciating the implicit semantics of the visual page structure (groups, components, typographic cues, etc.) can we enable machine understanding of the designers' original intentions. These intentions are important if we wish to provide a similar experience to visually impaired users as we do to fully sighted users. SADIe can be regarded as a tool for the site-wide reverse engineering of Web pages to achieve design rediscovery (Chikofsky & Cross, 1990).

JAWS. JAWS is one of the most popular screen readers, which has a labeling feature and allows users to provide alternative text for images or flash objects. The latest version of JAWS can make use of WAI-ARIA, a World Wide Web Consortium (W3C) internal metadata standard, to improve the accessibility of dynamic content.

Social Accessibility pilot service[19]

The Social Accessibility pilot service was launched in the summer of 2008. In the 10 months of the service being in use, its supporters resolved 275 service requests, creating over 18,000 metadata records for 2930 Web pages. Table 18.2 shows the frequencies of metadata types created by the

Table 18.2 Frequency of Metadata Types

Metadata Type	Count
Alternative text	11,969 (65%)
h+ (h1-6)	6069 (33%)
Landmark	122 (1%)
h-	119 (1%)
Others	17 (0%)
Total	**18,296 (100%)**

---

[18]Fire Vox: A Screen Reading Extension for Firefox: http://firevox.clcworld.net/.
[19]More details on the pilot service can be found in (Takagi et al., 2009).

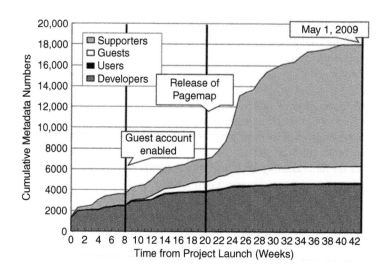

FIGURE 18.7

Historical activity of SA participants.

users. The majority of annotations were alternative text and headings (levels 1-6). Users and supporters together labeled 122 "landmarks" (new destinations added for navigation within a page), removed 119 headings, and created 17 metadata records about ARIA and specialized script metadata for DHTML.

Figure 18.7 shows the activity of authoring the accessibility metadata over the 42 weeks since the SA service was launched. The horizontal axis shows the time, and the vertical axis shows the cumulative number of metadata records created by each category of participants. The SA development team members were initial supporters who reduced their activities over time to encourage other participants. Some of the activities were the addition of landmarks and alternative text by the end users. Some of the contributions were made by SA guests, with the majority of activities being metadata authoring by the registered supporters after the Pagemap visualization release (Figure 18.3).

The majority of requests were for alternative text (124), headings (80), and questions about content (43). The remaining requests included forms, landmarks, Flash, color, CAPTCHA, DHTML, etc. Almost half (45%) of the requests were resolved within a single day. The supporters were not able to resolve 19 requests (5.9%), primarily because SA was not yet handling DHTML and Flash at that time.

CHALLENGES AND FUTURE WORK

A number of challenges will have to be eventually overcome to ensure continued effectiveness and value of the Social Accessibility network. The problems involve breakages of metadata due to site changes, conflicts between different metadata records, database performance, possibility of spam metadata, security and privacy of SA users, interface complexity, incentive systems, collaboration with content providers, etc.

Conflicts and broken metadata

The metadata accumulated in the AC database may eventually accrue conflicts; for example, two different versions of alternative text may be supplied for the same image. Also, the repository may contain broken metadata, such as that due to changes in the target Web pages. Currently, the SA infrastructure does not detect any conflicts or broken metadata and returns all metadata fetched by the query, leaving the metadata filtering task to the client application. It is our hope that, with a large number of participants, metadata errors may be quickly identified, reported, and fixed. However, techniques need to be developed for discarding or fixing broken metadata, as well as for metadata ranking and filtering. For instance, the user's own metadata can be given the highest priority, followed by human-authored and then machine-generated metadata. A ranking system can be employed to resolve conflicts based on supporters' reputations. Further, metadata filtering can be based on the user's locale, preferences, context, etc.

Database performance

It is expected that millions of metadata records will be accumulated in the AC repository; therefore, low-latency database performance is crucial to the SA infrastructure. Automaton-based indexing, briefly discussed in this chapter, is the first step to improving the response time of the SA service. With the growing number of metadata records, another source of latency will be the amount of data sent back to clients for every query. One way to reduce the amount of SA traffic is to filter the metadata on the AC server side before sending it to the client. For example, metadata conflicts can be resolved on the server side.

Security, privacy, and spam

Any successful system is eventually attacked by spammers, hackers, or both. For example, spammers may try to insert a large number of ads instead of the useful metadata. It may be possible to reduce the damage by introducing some protection mechanisms, such as a limited number of queries per second, limited size of labels, etc. A reputation system can further help identify and remove offending accounts and records.

Privacy protection, in part, always depends on the common sense of the users. For example, for reasons of safety, users should not knowingly submit any personal information as part of the metadata. For the same reason, in order to protect personal information, SA should not use textual content as a method of addressing HTML elements on the page. Nonetheless, when the user reports an error, a snapshot of the browser's content and the reading position are automatically captured and sent to the SA server. This functionality enables the supporters to understand the problems faced by the user; however, it may inadvertently violate user privacy by capturing such personal information as bank account numbers. To address this concern, screenshots have to be blurred or blacked out, to make them illegible yet preserve the visual structure of the page, before being submitted to the server. It may also be necessary to block screen capture of secure pages that use the HTTPS protocol.

Metadata authoring skills

A successful collaborative system should require minimal technical skills and contribution from its users, while providing maximum benefits. The current pilot system[20] requires that supporters have minimal knowledge about Web accessibility, such as the appropriateness of headings and alternative text. Both SA novice supporters and users can easily learn about the SA tools and services. However, the inclusion of more types of metadata will invariably increase the complexity of the interface. For example, the inclusion of the simplest ARIA metadata will require that supporters know about dynamic content and understand relationships between objects, thus complicating the interface required for selecting objects. Therefore, it is important to continue developing semiautomated and fully automated approaches to metadata authoring. Collaborative crawling is one of such promising approaches that would require no work whatsoever on the part of the user.

Effectiveness of incentives

SA employs a simple scheme for ranking supporters based, primarily, on the number of metadata records contributed to the system. The informal feedback from both users and supporters confirmed the importance of the incentive system. Supporters also remarked that the most effective rewards are the appreciative comments from end users. Ranking supporters on the SA portal Web site also motivated them to remain active on the system. As noted earlier, ranking can also help with metadata conflict resolutions. It is important to further develop the ranking mechanism to consider more parameters, such as end user appreciation, and measure the supporter's reactions.

Collaborating with content providers

Accessibility renovation work is too often reduced to the task of fixing the errors reported by automatic accessibility checkers. The SA approach may reduce the burden placed on site owners through the power of the community, which does not mean, however, that content providers can now ignore accessibility issues. Instead, the centralization of the metadata should encourage site owners to pay more attention to accessibility and, hopefully, renovate their sites to be more accessible. The SA system can change that by automatically summarizing, organizing, and delivering accessibility information to content providers with suggestions on how to incorporate metadata into Web sites.

In addition to resolving immediate accessibility problems, the reported issues can be regarded as the results of volunteer-based Web site usability testing by real users. The created metadata can also be regarded as volunteer-based consulting for accessibility improvements. In other words, the SA network is a system of collective intelligence for end users, volunteers, site owners, and everyone who has an interest in the accessibility of the Web. The Social Accessibility network will soon provide a portal for content providers, where site owners will be able to obtain a summary of accessibility problems on their Web site and a set of objective instructions on how to fix these problems. The products of the collaborative authoring process – metadata, discussions, and site-specific rules for metadata – will present invaluable information for effective renovations by site owners.

---

[20]Social Accessibility Project: http://sa.watson.ibm.com.

Another possible scenario is to enable content providers to transcode their Web pages on the fly for every Web page fetched from the Web server, in which case users may not even be aware of the mechanism improving Web accessibility. This approach would also improve the compliance of the Web site, since the improvement is taking place on the server side. A similar approach to dynamic transcoding of Web pages using a JavaScript library is already employed by Google's AxsJAX technology (Chen & Raman, 2008).

SUMMARY

This chapter discussed several collaborative approaches to improving Web accessibility and overviewed the challenges in Web accessibility. To reduce the burden on site owners and shorten the time to improved accessibility, we introduced Social Accessibility – a framework that can make the Web more accessible by gathering the power of the open community. The approach is characterized by collaborative metadata authoring based on user requests. Any Web user with a disability can report Web accessibility problems to the Social Accessibility service, and any Web user can volunteer to fix the accessibility problems without modifying the original content. We also discussed the collaborative crawling approach that can improve accessibility of Rich Internet Applications for screen readers, Web crawlers, and other software tools that need to interact with dynamic Web content.

With the growing popularity of social computing, the Social Accessibility approach has the potential to grow into a worldwide collective intelligence for Web accessibility, and contribute to changing the access environments of users with disabilities worldwide.

This work is based on earlier work: (Kawanaka et al., 2008; Takagi, et al., 2008; Takagi, et al., 2009).

SOCIAL ACCESSIBILITY

Intended users:	All users, but specifically assistive technology users
Domain:	All Web sites
Description:	Social Accessibility (SA) is a collaborative framework that uses the power of the open community to improve the accessibility of existing Web content. SA brings together end users and supporters who can collaboratively create and utilize the accessibility metadata.
Example:	John, a blind screen reader user, tries to make a purchase on a Web site, but encounters some accessibility problems, which he reports to the Social Accessibility network. In response to John's request, supporters create accessibility metadata by providing labels for inaccessible content, such as image buttons without alternative text, form elements without labels, etc. The next time John or any other screen reader user visits the Web page they will find the Web page fully accessible. The administrator of the inaccessible Web site can get an overview of the accessibility problems found on the Web site and incorporate the metadata directly into the Web site source code. Software tools such as crawlers and wrappers can also use the metadata to perform their tasks more efficiently.
Automation:	No, but the metadata can be used by automation tools.
Mashups:	No, but the metadata can be used by mashup tools.
Scripting:	No, but there is a user interface for authoring metadata.
Natural language:	No.
Recordability:	No.
Inferencing:	No.
Sharing:	The system facilitates collaborative authoring and usage of accessibility metadata for Web sites.
Comparison to other systems:	No clear similarities to other systems.
Platform:	Mozilla Firefox and Internet Explorer browsers
Availability:	The browser plug-ins may be downloaded from: http://sa.watson.ibm.com/.

TrailBlazer
Enabling blind users to blaze trails through the Web

Jeffrey P. Bigham,[1] **Tessa Lau,**[2] **Jeffrey Nichols**[2]

[1]*Department of Computer Science and Engineering, University of Washington*
[2]*IBM Research – Almaden*

ABSTRACT

For blind Web users, completing tasks on the Web can be frustrating. Each step can require a time-consuming linear search of the current Web page to find the needed interactive element or piece of information. Existing interactive help systems and the playback components of some programming by demonstration tools identify the needed elements of a page as they guide the user through predefined tasks, obviating the need for a linear search on each step. *TrailBlazer* is a system that provides an accessible, nonvisual interface to guide blind users through existing how-to knowledge. A formative study indicated that participants saw the value of TrailBlazer but wanted to use it for tasks and Web sites for which no existing script was available. To address this, TrailBlazer offers suggestion-based help created on the fly from a short, user-provided task description and an existing repository of how-to knowledge. In an evaluation on 15 tasks, the correct prediction was contained within the top 5 suggestions 75.9% of the time.

INTRODUCTION

For blind Web users, completing tasks on the Web can be time-consuming and frustrating. Blind users interact with the Web through software programs called screen readers. Screen readers convert information on the screen to a linear stream of either synthesized voice or refreshable Braille. If a blind user needs to search for a specific item on the page, they either must listen to the entire linear stream until the goal item is reached or they may skip around in the page using structural elements, such as headings, as a guide. To become proficient, users must learn hundreds of keyboard shortcuts to navigate Web page structures and access mouse-only controls. Unfortunately, for most tasks even the best screen reader users cannot approach the speed of searching a Web page that is afforded to sighted users (Bigham et al., 2007; Takagi et al., 2007).

Existing repositories contain how-to knowledge that is able to guide people through Web tasks quickly and efficiently. This how-to knowledge is often encoded as a list of steps that must be perfomed to complete the task. The description of each step consists of information describing the

Time Card CoScript

1. goto "http://www.mycompany.com/timecard/"
2. enter "8" into the "Hours worked" textbox
3. click the "Submit" button
4. click the "Verify" button

FIGURE 19.1

A CoScript for entering time worked into an online time card. The natural language steps in the CoScript can be interpreted both by tools such as CoScripter and TrailBlazer, and also read by humans. These steps are also sufficient to identify all of the Web page elements required to complete this task – the textbox and two buttons. Without TrailBlazer, steps 2–4 would require a time-consuming linear search for screen reader users.

element that must be interacted with, such as a button or textbox, and the type of operation to perform with that element. For example, one step in the task of buying an airplane ticket on orbitz. com is to enter the destination city into the textbox labeled "To". One such repository is provided by CoScripter (Chapter 5), which contains a collection of scripts written in a "sloppy" programming language that is both human- and machine-understandable (Figure 19.1).

In this chapter, we present *TrailBlazer*, a system that guides blind users through completing tasks step by step (Bigham, Lau, & Nichols, 2009). TrailBlazer offers users suggestions of what to do next, automatically advancing the focus of the screen reader to the interactive element that needs to be operated or the information that needs to be heard. This capability reduces the need for time-consuming linear searches when using a screen reader.

TrailBlazer was created to support the specific needs of blind users. First, its interface explicitly accommodates screen readers and keyboard-only access. Second, TrailBlazer augments the CoScripter language with a "clip" command that specifies a particular region of the page on which to focus the user's attention. A feature for identifying regions is not included in other systems because it is assumed that users can find these regions quickly using visual search.

Third, TrailBlazer is able to dynamically create new scripts from a brief user-specified description of the goal task and the existing corpus of scripts. Dynamic script creation was inspired by a formative user study of the initial TrailBlazer system, which confirmed that TrailBlazer made the Web more usable but was not helpful in the vast majority of cases where a script did not already exist. To address this problem, we hypothesized that users would be willing to spend a few moments describing their desired task for TrailBlazer if it could make them more efficient on tasks lacking a script. The existing repository of scripts helps CoScripter to incorporate knowledge from similar tasks or subtasks that have already been demonstrated. Building from the existing corpus of CoScripter scripts and the short task description, TrailBlazer dynamically creates new scripts that suggest patterns of interaction with previously unseen Web sites, guiding blind users through sites for which no script exists.

As blind Web users interact with TrailBlazer to follow these dynamically suggested steps, they are implicitly supervising the synthesis of new scripts. These scripts can be added to the script repository and reused by all users. Studies have shown that many users are unwilling to pay the upfront costs of script creation even though those scripts could save them time in the future (Chapter 5). Through the use of TrailBlazer, we can effectively reverse the traditional roles of the two groups, enabling blind Web users to create new scripts that lead sighted users through completing Web tasks.

This chapter describes the following three contributions:

- **An accessible guide:** TrailBlazer is an accessible interface to the how-to knowledge contained in the CoScripter repository that enables blind users to avoid linear searches of content and complete tasks more efficiently.

- **Formative evaluation:** A formative evaluation of TrailBlazer illustrating its promise for improving non-visual access, as well as the desire of participants to use it on tasks for which a script does not already exist.
- **Dynamic script generation:** TrailBlazer, when given a natural language description of a user's goal and a preexisting corpus of scripts, dynamically suggests steps to follow to achieve the user's goal.

RELATED WORK

Work related to TrailBlazer falls into two main categories: (1) tools and techniques for improving nonvisual Web access, and (2) programming by demonstration and interactive help systems that play back and record how-to knowledge.

Improving Web accessibility

Most screen readers simply speak aloud a verbal description of the visual interface. Although this enables blind users to access most of the software available to sighted people, they are often not easy to use because their interfaces were not designed to be viewed nonvisually. Emacspeak demonstrated the benefits to usability resulting from designing applications with voice output in mind (Raman, 1996). The openness of the Web enables it to be adapted for nonvisual access.

Unfortunately, most Web content is not designed with voice output in mind. To produce a usable spoken interface to a Web site, screen readers extract semantic information and structure from each page and provide interaction techniques designed for typical Web interactions. When pages contain good semantics, these can be used to improve the usability of the page, for instance by enabling users to skip over sections irrelevant to them.

Semantic information can either be added to pages by content providers or formulated automatically when pages are accessed. Adding meaningful heading tags (<H1 - 6>) has been shown to improve Web efficiency for blind Web users browsing structural information (Watanabe, 2007) but less than half of Web pages use them (Bigham et al., 2007). To improve Web navigation, in-page "skip" links visible only to screen reader users can be added to complex pages by Web developers. These links enable users to quickly jump to areas of the page possibly far in linear distance. Unfortunately, these links are often broken (Bigham et al., 2007). Web developers have proven unreliable in manually providing navigation aids by annotating their Web pages.

Numerous middleware systems (Asakawa & Takagi, 2008b) have suggested ways for inserting semantically relevant markup into Web pages before they reach the client. Chapter 18 discusses Social Accessibility, a system that crowdsources helpful markup using a network of volunteers. Other systems have focused on automatic detection of semantically important regions done in the interface itself. For example, the HearSay nonvisual Web browser parses Web pages into a semantic tree that can be more easily navigated with a screen reader (Ramakrishnan, Stent, & Yang, 2004).

Augmenting the screen reader interface has also been explored. Several systems have added information about surrounding pages to existing pages to make them easier to use. Harper et al. augments links in Web pages with "Gist" summaries of the linked pages to provide users more information about the page to which a link would direct them (Harper & Patel, 2005). CSurf observes the context of clicked links to begin reading at a relevant point in the resulting page (Mahmud, Borodin, & Ramakrishnan, 2007).

Although adding appropriate semantic information makes Web content more usable, finding specific content on a page is still a difficult problem for users of screen readers. AxsJAX addresses this problem by embedding "trails" into Web pages that guide users through semantically related elements (Google AxsJAX, 2008). TrailBlazer scripts expand on this trail metaphor. Because AxsJAX trails are generally restricted to a single page and are written in JavaScript, AxsJAX trails cannot be created by end users or applied to the same range of tasks as TrailBlazer's scripts.

Recording and playback of how-to knowledge

Interactive help systems and programming by demonstration tools have explored how to capture procedural knowledge and express it to users. COACH (Selker, 1989) and Eager (Cypher, 1991) are early systems in this space that work with standard desktop applications instead of the Web. COACH observes computer users in order to provide targeted help, and Eager learned and executed repetitive tasks by observing users.

Expressing procedural knowledge, especially to assist a user who is currently working to complete a task, is a key issue for interactive help systems. Work by Kelleher and Pausch (2005) on stencils-based tutorials demonstrates a variety of useful mechanisms, such as blurring all of the items on the screen except for those that are relevant to the current task. Sticky notes adding useful contextual information were also found to be effective. TrailBlazer makes use of analogous ideas to direct the attention of users to important content in its nonvisual user interface.

Representing procedural knowledge is also a difficult challenge. *Keyword commands* is one method, which uses simple pseudonatural language description to refer to interface elements and the operations to be applied to them (Little & Miller, 2006). This is similar to the sloppy language used by CoScripter to describe Web-based activity (Chapter 5). TrailBlazer builds upon these approaches because the stored procedural knowledge represented by TrailBlazer can be easily spoken aloud and understood by blind users.

A limitation of most current systems is that they cannot generalize captured procedural knowledge to other contexts. For example, recording the process of purchasing a plane ticket on orbitz. com will not help perform the same task on travelocity.com. One of the only systems to explore generalization is the Goal-Oriented Web Browser (Chapter 4), which attempts to generalize a previously demonstrated script using a database of commonsense knowledge. This approach centered around data detectors that could determine the type of data appearing on Web sites. TrailBlazer incorporates additional inputs into its generalization process, including a brief task description from the user, and does not require a commonsense knowledge base.

An alternate approach to navigating full-size Web pages with a script, as TrailBlazer does, is to instead shrink the Web pages by keeping only the information needed to perform the current task. This can be done using a system such as Highlight, which enables users to reauthor Web pages for display on small screen devices by demonstrating which parts of the pages used in the task are important (Nichols & Lau, 2008). The resulting simplified interfaces created by Highlight are more efficient to navigate with a screen reader, but prevent the user from deviating from the task by removing content that is not directly related to the task.

AN ACCESSIBLE GUIDE

TrailBlazer was designed from the start for nonvisual access using the following three guidelines (Figure 19.2):

- **Keyboard access:** All playback functions are accessible using only the keyboard, making access feasible for those who do not use a mouse.
- **Minimize context switches:** The playback interface is integrated directly into the Web pages through which the user is being guided. This close coupling of the interface into the Web page enables users to easily switch between TrailBlazer's suggestions and the Web page components needed to complete each step.
- **Directing focus:** TrailBlazer directs users to the location on each page to complete each step. As mentioned, a main limitation of using a screen reader is the difficulty in finding specific content quickly. TrailBlazer directs users to the content necessary to complete the instruction that it suggests. If the user wants to complete a different action, the rest of the page is immediately available.

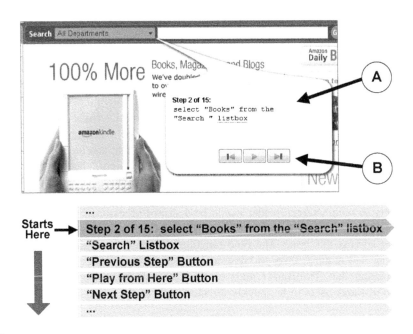

FIGURE 19.2

The TrailBlazer interface is integrated directly into the page, is keyboard accessible, and directs screen readers to read each new step. A) The description of the current step is displayed visually in an offset bubble but is placed in DOM order so that the target of a step immediately follows its description when viewed linearly with a screen reader. B) Script controls are placed in the page for easy discoverability but also have alternative keyboard shortcuts for efficient access.

The bubbles used to visually highlight the relevant portion of the page and provide contextual information were inspired by the "sticky notes" used in stencils-based tutorials (Kelleher & Pausch, 2005). The nonvisual equivalent in TrailBlazer was achieved by causing the screen reader to begin reading at the step (Figure 19.2). Although the location of each bubble is visually offset from the target element, the DOM order of the bubble's components was chosen such that they are read in an intuitive order for screen reader users. The visual representation resembles that of some tutoring systems and may also be preferred by users of visual browsers, in addition to supporting nonvisual access with TrailBlazer.

Upon advancing to a new instruction, the screen reader's focus is set to the instruction description (e.g., "Step 2 of 5: click the 'search' button"). The element containing that text is inserted immediately before the relevant control (e.g., the search button) in DOM order so that exploring forward from this position will take the user directly to the element mentioned in the instruction. The playback controls for previous step, play, and next step are represented as buttons and are inserted following the relevant control. Each of these functions can also be activated by a separate keyboard shortcut – for example, "ALT + S" advances to the next step.

The TrailBlazer interface enables screen reader users to move from step to step, verifying that each step is going to be conducted correctly, while avoiding all linear searches through content (Figure 19.3). If the user does not want to follow a particular step of the script they are using, the entire Web page is available to them as normal. TrailBlazer is a guide but does not override the user's intentions.

CLIPPING

While examining the scripts in the CoScripter repository, we noticed that many scripts contained comments directing users to specific content on the page. Comments are not interpreted by CoScripter however, and there is no command in CoScripter's language that can identify a particular region of the screen. Whether users were looking up the status of their flight, checking the prices of local apartments, or searching Google, the end goal was not to press buttons, enter information into textboxes, or follow links; the goal was to find information. A visual scan might locate this information quickly, but doing so with a screen reader would be a slower process.

Coyne and Nielsen (2001) observed that blind Web users often use the "Find" function of their Web browsers to address this issue. The Find function provides a simple way for users to quickly skip to the content, but requires them to know in advance the appropriate text for which to search. The "clip" command that TrailBlazer adds to the CoScripter language enables regions to be described and TrailBlazer users to be quickly directed to them.

Region description study

Existing CoScripter commands are written in natural language. To determine what language would be appropriate for our CoScripter command, we conducted a study in which we asked 5 participants to describe 20 regions covering a variety of content (Figure 19.4). To encourage participants to provide descriptions that would generalize to multiple regions, two different versions of each region were presented.

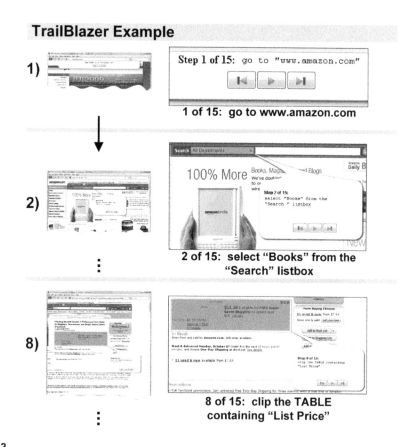

FIGURE 19.3

TrailBlazer guiding a user step by step through purchasing a book on Amazon. 1) The first step is to go to the Amazon.com homepage. 2) TrailBlazer directs the user to select the "Books" option from the highlighted listbox. 8) On the product detail page, TrailBlazer directs users past the standard template material directly to the product information.

Upon an initial review of the results of this study, we concluded that the descriptions provided fell into the following five nonexclusive categories: high-level semantic descriptions of the content (78%), descriptions matching all or part of the headings provided on the page for the region (53%), descriptions drawn directly from the words used in the region (37%), descriptions including the color, size, or other stylistic qualities of the region (18%), and descriptions of the location of the region on the page (11%).

The syntax of the clip command

We based the formulation of the syntax of the clip command on the results of the study just described. Clearly, users found it most convenient to describe the semantic class of the region. Although future work may seek to leverage a data detector like Miro to automatically determine

1-a. "2008 season stats"
1-b. "The highlighted region is of statistics. This is a table that has multiple numbers describing a player's achievements and records of what he has accomplished."

2-a. "This region lists search results for your query."
2-b. "This area contains the heading 'Search Results' along with the returns from a search of a term."

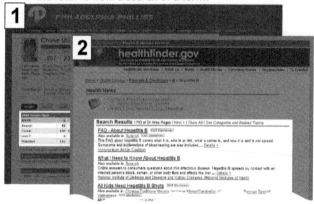

FIGURE 19.4

The descriptions provided by two participants for the screenshots shown illustrating diversity in how regions were described. Selected regions are (1) the table of statistics for a particular baseball player, and (2) the search results for a medical query.

the class of data to facilitate such a command (Chapter 4), our clip command currently refers to regions by either their heading or the content contained within them.

When using a heading to refer to a region, a user lists text that starts the region of interest. For instance, the step "clip the 'search results'" would begin the clipped region at the text "search results". This formulation closely matched what many users wrote in our study, but does not explicitly specify an end to the clip. TrailBlazer uses several heuristics to end the clip. The most important part is directing the user to the general area before the information that is valuable to them. If the end of the clipped region comes too soon, they can simply keep reading past the end of the region.

To use text contained within a region to refer to it, users write commands like, "clip the region containing 'flight status'". For scripts operating on templated Web sites or for those that use dynamically generated content, this is not always an ideal formulation because specific text may not always be present in a desired region. By using both commands, users have the flexibility to describe most regions, and, importantly, TrailBlazer is able to easily interpret them.

FORMATIVE EVALUATION

The improvements offered in the previous sections were designed to make TrailBlazer accessible to blind Web users using a screen reader. To investigate its perceived usefulness and remaining usability concerns, we conducted a formative user study with five blind participants. Our participants were experienced screen reader users. On average, they had 15.0 (SD = 4.7) years of computer experience, including 11.8 (2.8) years using the Web.

We first demonstrated how to use TrailBlazer as a guide through predefined tasks. We showed users how they could, at each step, choose to either have TrailBlazer complete the step automatically, complete it themselves, or choose any other action on the page. After this short introduction, participants performed the following three tasks using TrailBlazer: (1) checking the status of a flight on united.com, (2) finding real estate listings fitting specific criteria, and (3) querying the local library to see if a particular book is available.

After completing these tasks, each participant was asked the extent to which they agreed with several statements on a Likert scale (Figure 19.5). In general, participants were very enthusiastic about TrailBlazer, leading one to say "this is exactly what most blind users would like." One participant said TrailBlazer was a "very good concept, especially for the work setting where the

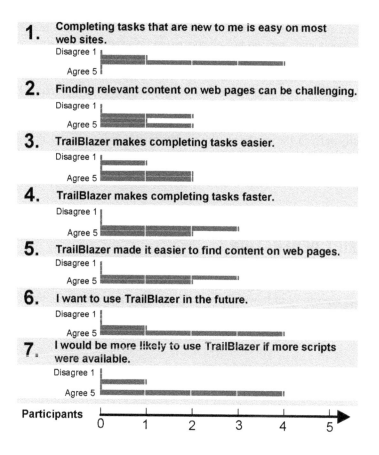

FIGURE 19.5

Participant responses to Likert scale questions indicating that they think completing new tasks and finding content is difficult (1, 2), think TrailBlazer can help them complete tasks more quickly and easier (3, 4, 5), and want to use it in the future (6), especially if scripts are available for more tasks (7).

scenarios and templates are already there." Another participant who helps train people on screen reader use thought that the interface would be a good way to gradually introduce the concept of using a screen reader to a new computer user for whom the complexity of Web sites and the numerous shortcuts available to them can be overwhelming. Participants uniformly agreed that despite their experience using screen readers, "finding a little kernel of information can be really time-consuming on a complex Web page" and that "sometimes there is too much content to just use headings and links to navigate."

Participants wondered if TrailBlazer could help them with dynamic Web content, which often is added to the DOM of Web pages far from where it appears visually, making it difficult to find. Screen readers can also have trouble presenting dynamically created content to users. TrailBlazer could not only direct users to content automatically, avoiding a long linear search, but also help them interact with it.

Despite their enthusiasm for using TrailBlazer for tasks that were already defined, they questioned how useful it would be if they had to rely on others to provide the scripts for them to use. One participant even questioned the usefulness of scripts created for a task that he wanted to complete, because "designers and users do not always agree on what is important." TrailBlazer did not support recording new tasks at the time of the evaluation, although new CoScripts could be created by sighted users using CoScripter.

Participants also had several suggestions on how to improve the interface. TrailBlazer guides users from one step to the next by dynamically modifying the page, but screen readers do not always update their external models of the pages that they read from. To fix this users would need to occasionally refresh the model of the screen reader, which many thought could be confusing to novice users. Other systems that improve nonvisual access have similar limitations (Google AxsJAX, 2008), and these problems are being addressed in upcoming versions of screen readers.

DYNAMIC SCRIPT GENERATION

TrailBlazer can suggest actions that users may want to take even when no preexisting script is available for their current task. These suggestions are based on a short task description provided by the user and an existing repository of how-to knowledge. Suggestions are presented to users as options, which they can quickly jump to when correct but also easily ignore. Collectively, these suggestions help users dynamically create a new script – potentially increasing efficiency even when they first complete a task.

Example use case

To inform its suggestions, TrailBlazer first asks users for a short textual description of the task that they want to complete; it then provides appropriate suggestions to help them complete that task. As an example, consider Jane, a blind Web user who wants to look up the status of her friend's flight on Air Canada. She first provides TrailBlazer with the following description of her task: "flight status on Air Canada." The CoScripter repository does not contain a script for finding the status of a flight on Air Canada, but it does contain scripts for finding the status of flights on Delta and United.

After some preprocessing of the request, TrailBlazer conducts a Web search using the task description to find likely Web sites on which to complete it. The first suggested step is "goto air-canada.com", and Jane chooses to follow that suggestion. If an appropriate suggestion was not listed, then Jane could have chosen to visit a different Web site or even searched the Web for the appropriate Web site herself (perhaps using TrailBlazer to guide her search). TrailBlazer automatically loads aircanada.com and then presents Jane with the following three suggestions: "click the 'flight status' button", "click the 'flight' button", and "fill out the 'search the site' textbox". Jane chooses the first option, and TrailBlazer completes it automatically. Jane uses this interface to complete the entire task without needing to search within the page for any of the necessary page elements.

A preexisting script for the described task is not required for TrailBlazer to accurately suggest appropriate actions. TrailBlazer can in effect apply scripts describing tasks (or subtasks) on one Web site to other Web sites. It can, for example, use a script for buying a book at Amazon to buy a book at Barnes and Noble, a script for booking a trip on Amtrak to help book a trip on the United Kingdom's National Rail Line, or a script for checking the status of a package being delivered by UPS to help check on one being delivered by Federal Express. Subtasks contained within scripts can also be applied by TrailBlazer in different domains. For example, the sequence of steps in a script on a shopping site that helps users enter their contact information can be applied during the registration process on an employment site. If a script already exists for a user's entire task, then the suggestions they receive can follow that script without the user having to conduct a search for that specific script in advance.

Suggestion types

The CoScripter language provides a set number of action types (Figure 19.6). Most CoScripts begin with a "goto" command that directs users to a specific Web page. Next, users are led through interaction with a number of links and form controls. Although not included in the scripts in the CoScripter repository, the final action implicitly defined in most CoScripts is to read the information that resulted from completion of the previous steps, which corresponds to the "clip" command added by TrailBlazer.

The creation of suggestions in TrailBlazer is divided into the following three corresponding components:

- **Goto component:** TrailBlazer converts a user's task description to keywords, and then searches the Web using those keywords to find appropriate starting sites.
- **General suggestion component:** TrailBlazer combines a user's task description, scripts in an existing repository, and the history of the user's actions to suggest the next action that the user should take.
- **Automatic clipping component:** TrailBlazer uses the textual history of user actions represented as CoScripter commands to find the area on the page that is most likely relevant to the user at this point using an algorithm inspired by CSurf (Mahmud, Borodin, & Ramakrishnan, 2007). Finding the relevant region to read is equivalent to an automatic clip of content.

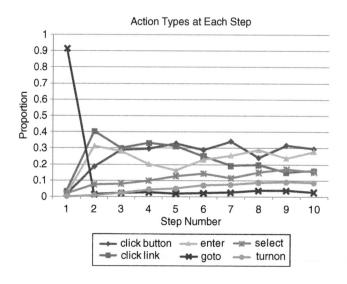

FIGURE 19.6

Proportion of action types at each step number for scripts in the CoScripter repository.

The following sections describe the components used by TrailBlazer to choose suggestions.

Goto component

As shown in Figure 19.6, most scripts begin with a goto command. Accordingly, TrailBlazer offers goto commands as suggestions when calculating the first step for the user to take. The goto component uses the task description input by the user to suggest Web sites on which the task could be completed.

Forming goto suggestions consists of the following three steps: (1) determining which words in the task description are most likely to describe the Web site on which the task is to be completed, (2) searching the Web using these most promising keywords, and (3) presenting the top results to users. A part-of-speech tagger first isolates the URLs, proper nouns, and words that follow prepositions (e.g., "United" from the phrase "on United") in the task description. TrailBlazer proceeds in a series of rounds, querying with keywords in the order described until it gathers at least five unique URLs. These URLs are then offered as suggestions.

The success of the goto component is highly dependent on the task description provided by the user and on the popularity of the site on which it should be completed. The authors have observed this component to work well on many real-world tasks, but future work will test and improve its performance.

General suggestion component

The main suggestion component described in this chapter is the general suggestion component, which suggests specific actions for users to complete on the current page. These suggestions are presented as natural language steps in the CoScripter language and are chosen from all the actions possible to complete on the current page. TrailBlazer ranks suggestions based on the user's task description, knowledge mined from the CoScripter script repository, and the history of actions that the user has already completed.

Suggestions are first assigned a probability by a Naive Bayes classifier and then ranked according to them. Naive Bayes is a simple but powerful supervised learning method that after training on labeled examples can assign probability estimates to new examples. Although the probabilities assigned are only estimates, they are known to be useful for ranking (Lewis, 1998). The model is trained on tasks that were previously demonstrated using either TrailBlazer or CoScripter, which are contained within the CoScripter script repository.

The knowledge represented by the features used in the model could have also been expressed as static rules for the system to follow. TrailBlazer's built-in machine learning model enables it to continually improve as it is used. Because tasks that users complete using TrailBlazer implicitly describe new scripts, the features based on the script repository should become more informative over time as more scripts are added.

Features used in making suggestions

To accurately rank potential actions, TrailBlazer relies on a number of informative, automatically derived features (Figure 19.7). The remainder of this section explains the motivation behind the features found to be informative and describes how they are computed.

Leveraging action history

TrailBlazer includes several features that leverage its record of actions that it has observed the user perform. Two features capture how the user's prior actions relate to their interaction with forms (Figure 19.7-5,6). Intuitively, when using a form containing more than one element, interacting with one increases the

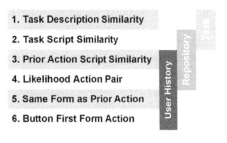

1. Task Description Similarity
2. Task Script Similarity
3. Prior Action Script Similarity
4. Likelihood Action Pair
5. Same Form as Prior Action
6. Button First Form Action

FIGURE 19.7

The features calculated and used by TrailBlazer to rank potential action suggestions, along with the three sources from which they are formed.

chance that you will interact with another in the same form. The *Same Form as Prior Action* feature expresses whether the action under consideration refers to an element in a form for which an action has previously been completed. Next, although it can occur in other situations, pressing a button in a form usually occurs after acting on another element in a form. The *Button First Form Action* feature captures whether the potential action is a button press in a form in which no other elements have been acted upon.

Similarity to task description

The *Task Description Similarity* feature enables TrailBlazer to weight steps similar to the task description provided by the user more highly (Figure 19.7-1). Similarity is quantified by calculating the vector cosine between the words in the task description and the words in each potential suggestion. The word–vector cosine metric considers each set of words as a vector in which each dimension corresponds to a different term, and in which the length is set to the frequency by which each word has been observed. For this calculation, a list of stopwords is removed. The similarity between the task description word vector v_d and the potential suggestion word vector v_s is calculated as follows:

$$VC(v_d, v_s) = \frac{v_d \cdot v_s}{\|v_d\| * \|v_s\|} \tag{19.1}$$

The word–vector cosine is often used in information retrieval settings to compare documents with keyword queries (Baeza-Yates & Ribeiro-Neto, 1999).

Using the existing script repository

TrailBlazer uses the record of user actions combined with the scripts contained in the script repository to directly influence which suggestions are chosen. The CoScripter repository contains nearly 1000 human-created scripts describing the steps to complete a diversity of tasks on the Web. These scripts contain not only the specific steps required to complete a given Web-based task, but also more general knowledge about Web tasks. Features used for ranking suggestions built from the repository are based on (1) statistics of the actions and the sequence in which they appear, and (2) matching suggestions to relevant scripts already in the repository. These features represent the knowledge contained within existing scripts, and enable TrailBlazer to apply that knowledge to new tasks for which no script exists.

Some action types are more likely than others according to how many actions the user has completed (Figure 19.6). For instance, clicking a link is more likely near the beginning of a task than near the end. In addition, some actions are more likely to follow actions of particular types. For instance, clicking a button is more likely to follow entering text than clicking a link because buttons are usually pressed after entering information into a form. Following this motivation, the *Likelihood Action Pair* feature used by TrailBlazer is the likelihood of each action given the actions that the user completed before (Figure 19.7-4). This likelihood is computed through consideration of all scripts in the repository.

Leveraging existing scripts for related tasks

TrailBlazer also directly uses related scripts already in the repository to help form its suggestions. TrailBlazer retrieves two sets of related scripts and computes a separate feature for each. First, TrailBlazer uses the task description provided by the user as a query to the repository, retrieving scripts that are related to the user's task. For instance, if the user's task description was "Flight status on Air Canada", matches on the words "flight" and "status" will enable the system to retrieve scripts for finding the flight status on "United" and "Delta." The procedure for checking flight status on both of these sites is different than it is on Air Canada, but certain steps, like entering information into a textbox with a label containing the words "Flight Number" are repeated on all three. The *Task Script Similarity* feature captures this information (Figure 19.7-2).

The second set of scripts that TrailBlazer retrieves are found using the last action that the user completed. These scripts may contain subtasks that do not relate to the user's stated goal but can still be predictive of the next action to be completed. For instance, if the user just entered their username into a textbox with the label "username", many scripts will be retrieved suggesting that a good next action would be to enter their "password" into a password box. The *Prior Action Script Similarity* feature enables TrailBlazer to respond to relevant subtasks (Figure 19.7-3).

The motivation for the *Task Script Similarity* and *Prior Action Script* features is that if Trail-Blazer can find steps in existing scripts similar to either the task description or an action previously completed by the user, then subsequent steps in that script should be predictive of future actions. The scores assigned to each step are, therefore, fed forward to other script steps so that they are weighted more highly. All tasks implicitly start with a goto step specifying the page on which the user first requests suggestions, so a prior action always exists. The process used is similar to spreading activation, which is a method used to connect semantically related elements represented in a tree structure (Collins & Loftus, 1975). The added value from a prior step decreases exponentially for each subsequent step, meaning that steps following close after highly weighted steps primarily benefit.

To compute these features, TrailBlazer first finds a set of related scripts S by sending either the task description or the user's prior action as a *query* to the CoScripter repository. TrailBlazer then derives a weight for each of the steps contained in each related script. Each script s contains a sequential list of natural language steps (see Figure 19.1). The weight of each script's first step is set to $VC(s_0, query)$, the vector cosine between the first step and the query as described earlier. Trail-Blazer computes the weight of each subsequent step, as follows:

$$W(s_i) = w * W(s_{i-1}) + VC(s_i, query) \qquad (19.2)$$

TrailBlazer currently uses $w = 0.3$, which has worked well in practice. The fractional inclusion of the weight of prior steps serves to feed their weight forward to later steps.

Next, TrailBlazer constructs a weighted sentence $sent_S$ of all the words contained within S. The weight of each word is set to the sum of the computed weights of each step in which each word is contained, $W(s_i)$. The final feature value is the word–vector cosine between vectors formed from the words in $sent_S$ and *query*. Importantly, although the features constructed in this way do not explicitly consider action types, the labels assigned to page elements, or the types of page elements, all are implicitly included because they are included in the natural language CoScripter steps.

Presenting suggestions to users

Once the values of all of the features are computed and all potential actions are ranked, the most highly ranked actions are presented to the user as suggestions. The suggestions are integrated into the accessible guide interface outlined earlier. TrailBlazer provides five suggestions, displayed in the interface in rank order (Figure 19.8).

The suggestions are inserted into the DOM immediately following the target of the prior command, making them appear to nonvisual users to come immediately after the step that they just completed. This continues the convenient nonvisual interface design used in TrailBlazer for script playback. Users are directed to the suggestions just as they would be directed to the next action in a preexisting script. Just as with predefined actions, users can choose to review the suggestions or choose to skip past them if they prefer, representing a hallmark of mixed initiative design (Horvitz, 1999). Because the suggestions are contained within a single listbox, moving past them requires only one keystroke.

Future user studies will seek to answer questions about how to best present suggestions to users, how many suggestions should be presented, and how the system's confidence in its suggestions might be conveyed by the user interface.

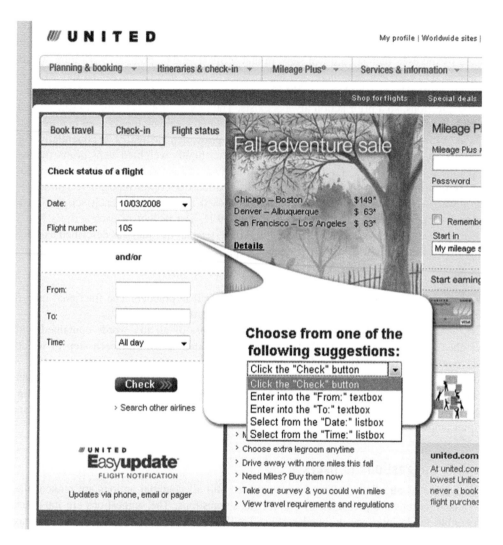

FIGURE 19.8

Suggestions are presented to users within the page context, inserted into the DOM of the Web page following the last element with which they interacted. In this case, the user has just entered "105" into the "Flight Number" textbox and TrailBlazer recommends clicking on the "Check" button as its first suggestion.

EVALUATION OF SUGGESTIONS

We evaluated TrailBlazer by testing its ability to accurately suggest the correct next action while being used to complete 15 tasks. The chosen tasks represented the 15 most popular scripts in the CoScripter repository, according to the number of people who have run them. The scripts contained

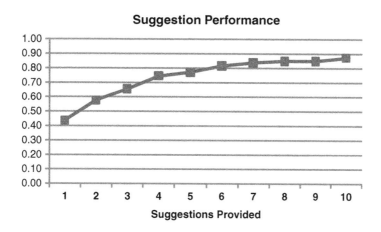

FIGURE 19.9

The fraction of the time that the correct action appeared among the top suggestions provided by TrailBlazer for varying numbers of suggestions. The correct suggestion was listed first in 41.4% cases and within the top 5 in 75.9% of cases.

a total of 102 steps, with an average of 6.8 steps per script (SD = 3.1). None of the scripts included in the test set were included when training the model.

Using existing scripts to test TrailBlazer provided two advantages. The first was that the scripts represented a natural ground truth to which we could compare TrailBlazer's suggestions, and the second was that each provided a short title that we could use as the user's description for purposes of testing. The provided titles were relatively short, averaging 5.1 words per title. The authors believe that it is not unreasonable to assume that users could provide similar task descriptions since users provided these titles.

On the 15 tasks in this study, TrailBlazer listed the correct next action as its top suggestion in 41.4% of cases and within the top 5 suggestions in 75.9% of cases (Figure 19.9). Predicting the next action correctly can dramatically reduce the number of elements that users need to consider when completing tasks on the Web. The average number of possible actions per step was 41.8 (SD = 37.9), meaning that choosing the correct action by chance has a probability of only 2.3%. TrailBlazer's suggestions could help users avoid a long, linear search over these possibilities.

Discussion

TrailBlazer was able to suggest the correct next action among its top five suggestions in 75.9% of cases. The current interface enables users to review these five choices quickly, so that in these cases users will not need to search the entire page to complete the action – TrailBlazer will lead them right there. Furthermore, in the 24.1% of cases in which TrailBlazer did not make an accurate suggestion, users can continue completing their tasks as they would have without TrailBlazer. Future studies will look at the effect on users of incorrect suggestions and how we might mitigate these problems.

TrailBlazer had difficulties making correct suggestions when the steps of the procedure seemed arbitrary. For instance, the script for changing one's emergency contact information begins by clicking through links titled "Career and Life" and "About me – personal" on pages on which nearly 150 different actions could be made. Because no similar scripts existed, no features indicated that it should be selected. Later, the script included the step, "click the 'emergency contacts' link", which the system recommended as its first choice. These problems illustrate the importance of having scripts in the first place, and are indicative of the improvements possible as additional scripts and other knowledge are incorporated.

Fortunately, TrailBlazer is able to quickly recover upon making an error. For instance, if it does not suggest an action involving a particular form and the user completes an action on the form anyway, TrailBlazer is likely to recover on the next suggestion. This is particularly true with form elements because of the features created specifically for this case (features 5 and 6 in Figure 19.7), but TrailBlazer is often able to recover in more general cases. TrailBlazer benefits greatly from its design as a guide to a human who can occasionally correct its suggestions, and its operators also benefit because of the efficiency it gains when it is correct.

FUTURE WORK

TrailBlazer can accurately predict the next step that users are likely to want to perform based on an initial action and provides an accessible interface enabling blind users to leverage those suggestions. A next step will be user studies with blind Web users to study how they use the system and discover improvements on the provided interface to suggestions.

Guiding Web users through completing Web tasks has many applications beyond improving access for blind Web users. The TrailBlazer approach adapts easily to commonly used phone menu systems. Because of the reduction in complexity achieved by guiding users, the TrailBlazer approach may also be appropriate for certain users with learning or cognitive disabilities. Additionally, users of small screen devices face many of the same problems as screen reader users do in finding relevant information in complex Web pages and may benefit from a similar approach.

Interfaces for nonvisual access could benefit from moving toward task-level assistance of the kind exposed by TrailBlazer. Current interfaces too often focus on either low-level annotations or deciding beforehand what users will want to do, taking away their control.

SUMMARY

We described TrailBlazer, an accessible interface to how-to knowledge that helps blind users complete Web-based tasks faster and more effectively by guiding them through a task step by step. By directing the user's attention to the right places on the page and by providing accessible shortcut keys, Trail-Blazer enables users to follow existing how-to instructions quickly and easily. A formative evaluation of the system revealed that users were positive about the system, but that the lack of how-to scripts could be a barrier to use. We extended the TrailBlazer system to dynamically suggest possible next steps based on a short description of the desired task, the user's previous behavior, and a repository of existing scripts. The user's next step was contained within the top five suggestions 75.9% of the time, showing that TrailBlazer is successfully able to guide users through new tasks.

Acknowledgements

We thank T.V. Raman for inspiring the use of trails to improve nonvisual access; the participants in our formative evaluation for useful and encouraging feedback; and Yevgen Borodin, Anna Cavender, Allen Cypher, Clemens Drews, James Lin, and Barton Smith for their feedback and support.

TRAILBLAZER

Intended users:	Blind users
Domain:	All Web sites
Description:	TrailBlazer helps blind people complete tasks on the Web by suggesting contextually relevant next steps to take. These suggestions are presented in an accessible, nonvisual interface using existing screen readers.
Example:	Place a book on hold at the library. TrailBlazer uses existing scripts to help formulate and present suggestions on what the user should do next, for instance "click the 'book search' link", "fill out the 'search' textbox'", or "select 'book' from the 'search type' box". Users can choose which of these actions to complete and TrailBlazer will direct the focus of their screen reader to the relevant component on the Web page for easy completion.
Automation:	Yes, and it always offers suggestions on what the user should do next.
Mashups:	No.
Scripting:	Yes, TrailBlazer builds from the CoScripter scripting language.
Natural language:	No, although the commands and suggestions are offered in an English-like language.
Recordability:	Yes.
Inferencing:	Yes, TrailBlazer uses a number of features input into a machine learning model to formulate and rank suggestions.
Sharing:	Yes, TrailBlazer uses the same script repository as CoScripter.
Comparison to other systems:	TrailBlazer is similar to CoScripter because it uses the same underlying scripting language, but differs because it offers suggestions even without a script for a particular task.
Platform:	Implemented as an extension to the Mozilla Firefox browser.
Availability:	Portions of TrailBlazer have been made available as part of CoScripter since late 2008 under the same licensing terms as CoScripter. Some portions are currently not available.

User Studies

We conclude the book with a set of user studies that look at the human factors around making an end user programming system. Specifically, the following chapters discuss challenges around building mashups, reusing codes, debugging, and using documentation and example search in the context of end user programming.

The Web-active end user

20

Nan Zang, Mary Beth Rosson
College of Information Sciences and Technology, The Pennsylvania State University

ABSTRACT

In this chapter we present our work that has led to the idea of the *Web-active end user* – individuals who actively seek and adopt new technologies and try to make the most of what the Web has to offer. Using the context of mashups – a type of Web application that combines different data into one interface – we explore how these users take advantage of the Web. We examine some of their ideas about online information and detail their use of a mashup tool. By focusing our work on the users themselves, we hope to better understand the needs of these users and provide a user-centered direction for future tools.

INTRODUCTION

The years since the bursting of the 2000 Internet bubble have seen tremendous change in how people use the Web. The spread of online authoring tools and services has encouraged users to create and share their own works on the Web. The concepts and services that drive personal blogging and socially oriented Web sites like Digg, YouTube, and Facebook suggest that traditional participatory design paradigms can be brought to the masses online, allowing millions of users to not only share their own works but also give them access to an ever-expanding range of information provided by other people and organizations.

The increasing availability to end users of online information and associated services can be seen as part of the more general trend toward *commons-based peer production* (Benkler, 2002). This movement is associated with the shared development of professional software (e.g., within the open source community), but the concept is broad enough to include the production and sharing of content and ad hoc applications by nonprofessional developers as well. Indeed as the ease and coverage of Web searches has continued to improve, the everyday user is part of what might be seen as the Google or Wikipedia online culture, where an answer to almost every question is just a few keystrokes away. However, having rapid access to enormous amounts of information is often just a first step for end users, who must then compare, combine, or otherwise integrate across queries or Web portals to address more specialized questions or task goals (e.g., planning a budget vacation). The problem of end user analysis and integration of online information is still an open problem within the peer production paradigm.

Over the last 2 years (2007–2008), we have been exploring the opportunities and challenges of Web mashups with respect to the general goal of helping end users integrate and make sense of the information that they are exposed to in their everyday lives. We began this work by examining the current status of mashup development: Who actually creates Web mashups and what are they creating ("The Status Quo: Who Actually Builds Mashups?" section)? Next, we surveyed Web users to profile their online activities and to identify the types of information they deal with and the problems they encounter ("Features of the Web-active End User" section). Finally, we conducted a series of interviews to gather more detailed qualitative information about how users think about online information and information integration ("Features of the Web-active End User" section).

THE STATUS QUO: WHO ACTUALLY BUILDS MASHUPS?

We began our investigation of Web mashup tools and requirements by surveying developers from online communities that we expected to host experts interested in mashup activities. For example, we targeted user forums associated with popular Application Programming Interfaces (APIs), such as the Google Maps API and Flickr API, as well as more general forums like DaniWeb. In total, we identified 15 such forums, inviting participation in a survey on mashup development.

The survey was designed to probe both general Web development issues, as well as issues specifically related to mashup development. This allowed us to see how mashups fit into a more general Web development culture. We were also concerned with how mashup developers discovered mashups and proceeded to learn how to create them, because one of our abiding research issues is just-in-time (Chapter 23) or informal learning. Finally, given our own experience as Web developers, we expected that developers would rely primarily on online information resources when they had questions, so we also probed their experiences with API documentation. We assume that any work we do to help nonprogrammers build mashups will require its own form of documentation, so this was an initial step at understanding what worked well or poorly.

At the end of the survey period we gathered a total of 63 responses (see Table 20.1). As with any survey, the number of responses (N) for individual questions varied because not every participant responded to every question. Roughly half the questions were presented to and answered by a subset of participants – the developers who had created at least one mashup.

Of the 63 respondents, about half (31) reported that they had created mashups before. The population was relatively young, male, and well educated: the average age was 33 years; 88.9% were male, and 53% had at least a university degree (see Table 20.1 for a summary of respondents' demographics). All 31 participants with mashup creation experience were male, and their average age was 34 years; 76% had university degrees or higher. The respondents varied considerably in their experiences with different Web technologies, but as one would expect, mashup developers reported more exposure to advanced programming activities (e.g., "programming desktop applications," "programmed using Web-based API"). This is not surprising and suggests that the individuals who have learned about mashup development are the same ones who are actively involved in Web programming more generally.

To help us quantify respondents' technical skills, we asked them how often they use a range of Web technologies and tools. Over half reported that they use Web scripting and programming languages frequently or daily, but the majority rarely or never develop desktop applications or use

Table 20.1 Expert Developer Demographics, Including Those Who Did and Did Not Report as Having Created at Least One Web Mashup.

Characteristic	Distribution	
Gender (N = 54)	Male: 88.9% (48) Female: 11.1% (6)	
Age (N = 53)	18–23: 18.9% 24–29: 22.6% 30–35: 22.7%	36–41: 22.6% >41: 13.2%
Education (N = 53)	High school: 30.2% College: 41.5%	Master's: 13.2% Doctorate: 5.7%
Occupation (N = 53)	Software developer: 34.0% Contractor: 18.9%	Student: 13.2% Consultant: 7.5%

Web-based APIs. We found this to be interesting because most mashups require the use of APIs. It is possible that, while our respondents are regular participants in general Web development activities, mashup development is not a common task.

When examining the subpopulation of mashup developers separately, we observed a clear difference in the programming activities they report versus the rest of the sample. Specifically, mashup developers have more exposure to developing desktop applications and they are more likely to have used Web-based APIs. Table 20.2 contains a tally of respondents who reported that they participate in each of the activities frequently or daily.

The mashup developers reported that they create mapping mashups most often, and they identify the Google Maps API as the most frequently used API. These results are consistent with the 2008 reports from ProgrammableWeb (Musser, 2008), a Web site that tracks mashups; this suggests that the people responding to our relatively small survey are a reasonable match to more general trends. A breakdown of the types of mashups created and the APIs they used to create mashups is displayed in Figures 20.1a and 20.1b.

We found three general problem areas in the developers' descriptions of problems encountered in mashup development: API reliability, coding issues, and documentation. Reliability refers to the

Table 20.2 Frequent Programming Activities for Total Sample Versus the More Expert Developers

	All respondents (N = 61)	Mashup developers (N = 30)
Use a Web page editor	54.4%	58.6%
Use HTML/XHTML only	56.9%	57.1%
Use CSS	71.5%	78.6%
Use Web programming language (PHP, ASP, etc.)	75.0%	73.4%
Program desktop applications	32.8%	44.8%
Programmed using Web-based API	28.1%	50.0%

issues and frustrations involved when dealing with third-party APIs, both in the sense of system availability time and the trustworthiness of the data. Because mashups rely almost completely on public services, the bulk of a mashup system is not in the hands of the developer, and thus API reliability is very important. Another issue relates to coding skills; the programming expertise needed to bring together multiple APIs using languages like JavaScript or PHP creates barriers for even relatively experienced programmers. Finally, they were concerned with the lack of proper documentation and the limited examples available for many APIs.

When asked how they learned to create mashups, all of those responding reported that they were self-taught. This may be due to the ad hoc nature of mashups. When we conducted this survey in 2007, the growing popularity of mashups was clear, but there were few if any resources for learning how to create a mashup; courses on mashup creation were nonexistent and the first books on mashups were still being written. We learned that documentation serves as a primary resource for mashup developers wishing to learn how an API works. They value the accuracy of the documentation and the availability of examples as important and necessary for learning. They cited a lack of effective tutorials and examples as a major problem in learning about and developing mashups. Suggestions for improving documentation included proper "examples of working code" and "graduated information for beginners to experts by level."

Although this survey was preliminary and exploratory, it provided two general insights that we have carried into our ongoing work. The first was the critical importance of documentation in the initial step of learning how to create a mashup and later sustaining API usage. On occasion, supporting technologies like Web service definition language (WSDL) can provide clues to developers about the functionality and operation of an API. However, many APIs, including Google Maps, do not provide such assistance, so developers must rely entirely on whatever documentation they can find.

A second insight gleaned from this study was that mashup development was quite limited in variety, at least at the time that we conducted the study. There are a small number of APIs that are used in the majority of mashups, with the majority focused on the use of maps. It is possible that the visual nature of maps – combined with the fact that Google Maps was an early public API – makes map-based mashups particularly

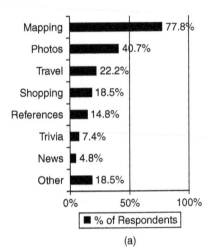

(a)

FIGURE 20.1A

Types of mashups created.

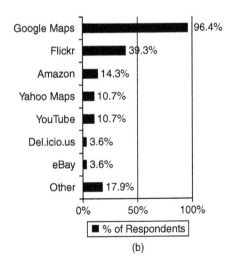

(b)

FIGURE 20.1B

APIs used in development.

attractive as a place to start. More recently there has been an expansion in the types of mashups being created and the APIs used. Though mapping and the Google Maps API continue to be the most popular, ProgrammableWeb reports that socially oriented mashups and the use of social network APIs like Twitter and Facebook have become increasingly popular.

FEATURES OF THE WEB-ACTIVE END USER[1]

After exploring the experiences and problems of expert mashup developers, we turned to the user population we hoped to target – end users who have no programming experience. In doing so, one goal was to identify some of the skill differences between the experts and the end users. Another important goal of this inquiry was to develop a benchmark for the user population that we have termed *Web-active end users*. Guided by studies from the Pew Internet and American Life Project (Horrigan, 2007; Madden, 2006), we argued that users are becoming more and more active online, and that many spend a great deal of time exploring advanced technologies that may contribute to enhancing their lives online. We speculated that college students are at the forefront of this trend, because they have relatively more time to explore new services and are of a generation that has been growing with and using the Internet since they were born.

Web technology survey of Web users

To begin this investigation of end users, we developed a survey that contained questions about technology experience and general Web activities; specifically we asked about their sharing activities online. We postulated that creating and sharing content online could be important enabling and motivating factors in promoting mashup development for this user population. Also, to take advantage of any respondents who had experiences with APIs, mashups, or both, we created a subsection with similar mashup-related questions from our prior study ("The Status Quo: Who Actually Builds Mashups?" section).

We faced an important methodological challenge in designing this online survey: How does one ask an end user who has never been exposed to mashups to describe their future mashup use? Though providing some context for the participants is required, supplying them with too much information would bias their responses. In the end, we furnished them with a single sentence description of mashups, followed by an illustration of the concept using two simple examples. We followed this with questions about the rate of difficulty of creating a mashup, as well as the benefits this skill could offer. Further, to probe their technical understanding of mashup development, we asked respondents to speculate on the steps needed to create a mashup. After considering these aspects of mashups, we asked the participants to brainstorm mashups that they would be interested in creating. Finally, we asked them to imagine that they had the skills to build a mashup and asked them to estimate how often they would do this; we included this question to get a best guess as to whether and how much they could see a use for the mashup concept.

For this study, we recruited students from a variety of disciplines at our local university (Penn State). As a result, the majority of respondents were under the age of 21 years (74.2%) and were still

---

[1]Based on, "What's in a mashup? And why? Studying the perceptions of web-active end users," by Nan Zang and Mary Beth Rosson, which appeared in *IEEE Symposium on Visual Languages and Human-Centric Computing* © 2008 IEEE.

Table 20.3 Web-Active End User Survey Participant Demographics

Characteristic	Distribution		
Gender (N = 225)	Male: 60.9% Female: 39.1%		
Age (yr) (N = 225)	18–21: 74.2% 21–25: 20.0%	>25: 5.7%	
Education (N = 202)	Some college: 84.2% Associate's degree: 3.0%	College: 10.4% Master's: 2.5%	
Discipline (N = 176)	Information sciences and technology: 50.6% Communications: 29.5% Business: 7.4%	Humanities: 7.4% Science and engineering: 5.1%	

enrolled in college (some college: 84.2%). A large portion of the participants are from the College of Information Sciences and Technology (IST) where students are exposed to a variety of technologies relevant to our work in their own coursework. At the conclusion of this study, we had collected 259 responses to the survey. Table 20.3 summarizes the respondents' demographics.

Regarding general technology experience, most respondents (72%) reported that they have been using computers for more than 10 years. They spend a large amount of time on the computer, with 76% reporting over 15 hours per week and 32.3% spending more than 30 hours per week. With other digital technologies, only one respondent does not own a cell phone, 80% own a digital camera, and 93% own an MP3 player. Another feature is that 87% own a laptop computer, but only 64.2% own a desktop computer. This could be due to an increase in mobile computing. Of course, many respondents owned both.

With respect to computer expertise, we asked them to rate themselves on a 5-point Likert scale, with 1 = no experience and 5 = a great deal of experience. The majority of the respondents (62.2%) self-rated a 4 or higher; the average rating was 3.83. Most had taken classes on programming (63.4%), but the larger percentage (79.6%) did not consider themselves programmers. As a way to gauge their skills with Web technologies, we asked the participants to rate their own experience with a number of programming languages and online media. They used a similar 5-point scale used to rate their computer expertise in general. As we expected, the only example of advanced experiences was with HTML (Mean = 3.66) and very little experiences with Web-based languages like PHP (Mean = 1.99) and ASP (Mean = 1.49).

As mentioned before, we expected that at least some of the survey participants would report having had experience with Web-based APIs; a small group (6.6%) reported that they did. Comparing this group to the rest of the respondents, it was not surprising that they reported themselves as higher in computer expertise (4.56). Moreover, all but one person in the API-experience group had received formal programming training. However, only seven of these Web developers considered themselves to be programmers when directly asked, "Do you consider yourself as a programmer, whether in Web or other types of programming?" It may be that Web development – even when APIs are used – may not qualify as "real programming" by these end users.

To accompany the self-reports on computer expertise and technology experience, we probed respondents' personal initiative and motivations when dealing with technology. Past research suggests that a person's motivation to explore and learn new ideas could be closely tied to the success of novel EUP systems (Rosson & Kase, 2006; Wiedenbeck, Sun, & Chintakovid, 2007). To evaluate a participant's motivations, we asked them to rate the following three statements as they applied to themselves on a 5-point scale, with 1 = not accurate and 5 = very accurate:

- Out of my friends I am one of the first to adopt a new technology or gadget.
- I actively search for new and interesting Web sites to visit.
- My friends and co-workers come to me for help with computer- and technology-related questions.

Though the averages for each of these items concentrated toward the midpoint (3.11–3.36), the three items had good internal reliability, so we averaged the items for each respondent to create a single Technology Initiative construct.

As a way to better understand the online activities that our participants engage in, we asked them how often they use specific Web services on a scale from 1 to 4, where 1 = never and 4 = daily. As one might expect, social networking was most frequently used, along with online videos. Other socially oriented services like bookmarking or photos were less frequently used. These results are summarized in Table 20.4.

We also asked respondents to estimate how often they participate in creating and sharing content online. Close to a third of the respondents (30.6%) reported that they share their creations on a weekly basis. Also, 69% reported having created a personal Web site and 45.6% have their own Weblog or online journal. This suggests that these users are not only active consumers of information, but they are avid creators of content, a trend that is consistent with our concept of Web-active end users.

When asked why they participate in these types of sharing activities, most said, "Just for fun," or, predictably, "To socialize." As students, they also create items online for class. Interestingly, almost half of the respondents (48.8%) create content online as a way to share their hobbies (see Figure 20.2). This data is consistent with a growing trend of hobbyists pursuing their interests online (Griffith & Fox, 2006). The two categories of fun and hobbies also emphasize the critical role of intrinsic motivation and personal interests in motivating active use of the Web.

As a way to introduce the concept of mashups to the participants, we provided the simple explanation and examples in Figure 20.3.

Table 20.4 Frequency of Online Activities

Online activity	Mean (std. dev.)
Social networking (Facebook, MySpace, etc.) (N = 258)	3.63 (0.74)
Video (YouTube, MetaCafe, etc.) (N = 257)	3.05 (0.71)
Online maps (Google Maps, MapQuest, etc.) (N = 257)	2.53 (0.63)
Shopping (Amazon, eBay, etc.) (N = 258)	2.39 (0.66)
Photography (Flickr, Webshots, etc.) (N = 258)	2.15 (0.87)
Travel (Expedia, Orbitz, etc.) (N = 254)	1.78 (0.55)
Social bookmarking (Del.icio.us, Mag.nolia.com, etc.) (N = 256)	1.32 (0.67)

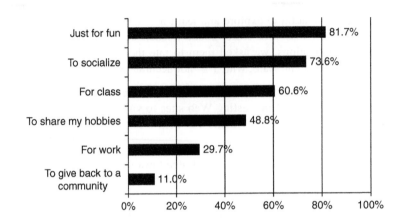

FIGURE 20.2

Reasons to create online content.

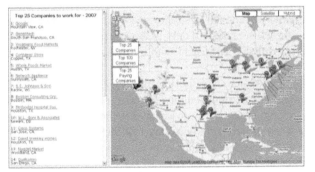

FIGURE 20.3

Description and examples of mashups.

> *"Mashups are Web applications that combine information or data from two or more sources into one interface. For example, plotting the top 25 best companies to work for onto a map is considered a mashup (left). Another example could be cross-referencing CNN news feeds with Wikipedia (right)."*

Using this introduction as a point of reference, we asked participants to consider "How difficult do you think it would be to create the mashup (in Figure 20.3)?" and "How useful do you believe mashups are?" indicating their response on 5-point Likert scales; for difficulty, 1 = not difficult and 5 = very difficult, and for usefulness, 1 = not useful and 5 = very useful. We expected that the responses gathered here would be prototypical of "novice" Web-active end users. Although the average difficulty ratings (3.34) were higher than the average usefulness ratings (3.17), it is inadvisable to make side-by-side comparisons; we do not know how these end users judged usefulness and difficulty, and in particular what they used to anchor the two 5-point scales.

When examining difficulty ratings as a function of gender, we found an interesting contrast: women judged mashup creation to be more difficult than men (3.38 vs. 3.04), but rated usefulness did not vary as a function of gender (3.39 vs. 3.30). The gender difference in difficulty ratings is consistent with other studies in EUP; studies have shown that women report lower self-efficacy and less confidence in a number of EUP situations (Beckwith et al., 2006; Rosson et al., 2007). Again, it is difficult to generate strong implications from ratings created by novices. However, we find it promising that women were just as likely as men to believe that mashups would be useful. Perhaps if we can develop tools or explanations that make mashup creation seem more simple and accessible, women will be just as likely as men to explore the new technology.

To supplement the 5-point ratings of difficulty and usefulness we followed each with an open-ended question. As part of the difficulty question, we asked the participants to speculate on the steps needed to create the second example (the right mashup in Figure 20.3). We received 171 open-ended responses, which we coded for accuracy on a scale from 0 to 3. We based this scale on the three steps needed to create a mashup: data gathering, data manipulation, and data presentation. Each answer received a point for any step that was correctly conveyed; for example "Locate RSS feed [. . .] and format page to accept feed" was coded with a 2, because locating an RSS feed corresponds to data gathering and formatting a page equates to data presentation. Responses that mentioned none of the three steps received a score of 0. Within the group, 54 respondents were not able to describe any of these three components of mashup creation, 56 described one, 39 were able to describe two, and 22 touched on all three aspects. Across all participants, an average of 1.17 steps was mentioned.

Initially we expected that the participants' ability to describe the mashup process should be related to their ratings of difficulty (i.e., knowing less about a process might make it seem more unobtainable and difficult), but we found no such pattern. It is possible that competing tendencies could be in play – people who know more about the mashup process recognize that it is often difficult, while those who are totally naïve may have no way of assessing difficulty.

In conjunction with the usefulness rating, we asked participants to describe ways that they could see themselves benefiting from creation of Web mashups. We coded the 82 responses into categories; some answers denied any benefit, but others alluded to effects on search, Web browsing, data integration, creativity, visualization, efficiency, as well as just gaining a new skill. Not surprisingly, we found that the number of benefits postulated by a respondent had a positive correlation with his or her rating of mashup usefulness.

As one of the final questions, we asked participants to describe mashups they could envision creating. Given that they had little knowledge of mashups beyond the descriptions we gave them, we hoped that by thinking about mashups in the context of benefits and costs, the mashups they described would be representative of what novice mashup developers would desire. The 116 respondents to this question generated 134 ideas which we grouped using the existing categories from ProgrammableWeb. Figure 20.4 summarizes the frequency with which each category appeared in respondents' brainstorming (note that, if an idea could fall into more than one category, we coded it with multiple category tags).

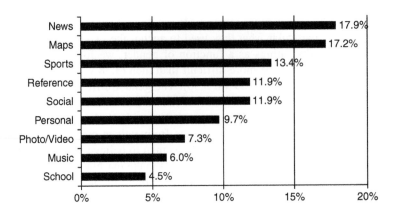

FIGURE 20.4

Categories of mashup ideas.

Motivation for mashing up

A persistent theme in studies of EUP, and in end-user development of mashups in particular, is the motivation for an end user to learn programming techniques. If end users do not have the skills to create mashups, what might we do to encourage them to learn enough to take some first steps? There are many internal factors that come into play when a user decides to devote effort into learning a new system.

In the case of novel programming technologies, one framework for analyzing the factors that influence users' decisions on whether or not to learn new skills is the *attention investment model* (Blackwell & Green, 1999). Drawing from the Cognitive Dimensions (CD) of Notations framework (Blackwell & Green, 2003), this model can be used to frame the initials steps a user takes before deciding to invest effort into a task. In particular, it uses aspects of CD to examine the cognitive requirements that a tool or notation places on the novice user. Furthermore, it applies cost–benefit analysis (Blackwell, 2001) as a predictor of possible effort investment. This framework has been used to explain end users' behavior in EUP problem-solving tasks (Blackwell & Burnett, 2002).

Attention investment considers four cognitive cost–benefit variables: cost, risk, investment, and payoff. As summarized in Figure 20.5, we applied these variables to conceptualize how our survey respondents might be estimating their future use of mashups. Here we map the user's perception of the attention cost needed to complete a mashup. Risk is a combination of the possibility of failure with no resulting payoff, and the possible future cost associated with creating a mashup. Payoff is the estimated future cost saved by investing the attention towards creating a mashup. The investment variable is then represented by the choice that the end user makes.

If we consider a hypothetical situation in which an end user has the opportunity to create a mashup using a tool, the decisions he or she would make may be strongly influenced by their current analysis of the benefits versus the costs associated with learning this new tool. As a preliminary investigation of this possibility, we asked the participants to estimate how often they would create mashups – assuming that they had the needed skills and expertise – on a scale with four choices;

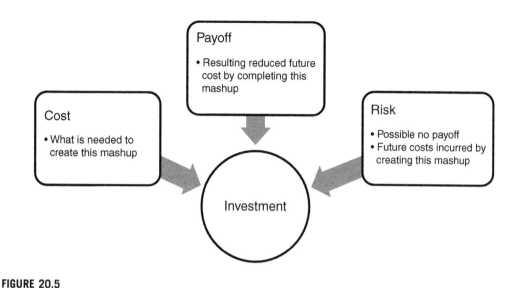

FIGURE 20.5

Attention investment model applied to creating mashups.

the ratings corresponded to 1 = never, 2 = rarely, 3 = weekly, and 4 = daily. We anticipated that this metric would give us a way to predict future actions.

As shown in Table 20.5, the majority of the respondents suggested that they would rarely use mashups. Only one person chose the "Daily" option, so we removed this respondent as an outlier. However, even though relatively few participants chose the lower or higher frequency options, we found that there was enough variability and systematicity in these ratings that the measure was useful as an outcome variable. For example, as can be seen in Table 20.5, when we decomposed ratings of usefulness and difficulty according to ratings of future use frequency, we found a correlation between the ratings of usefulness and future use frequency, but no relation to difficulty. This suggests that in this particular situation of novel technology use – that is, when the user has very little background knowledge about the new technology – users' expectations about possible use is influenced by their beliefs about how useful the technology is, but not of how difficult they expect the task to be. In other words, when the knowledge state is very low, perceptions of benefits or payoff may have a greater influence on the user's willingness to invest attention more than perceptions of cost.

Table 20.5 Difficulty and Usefulness by Future Mashup Frequency

	Never (N = 38)	Rarely (N = 148)	Weekly (N = 30)
Difficulty	3.29	3.10	3.17
Usefulness	2.74	3.37	3.97

Predicting who will engage in future mashup activity

Another goal of this exploratory research is to identify user characteristics that might help to predict which end users might be most likely to engage in future mashup activity. We assume that this information would be useful for EUP tool designers as a guideline to create mashup tools that attract the right people, so as to maximize early adoption. To examine this, we selected eight potential predictors for the future mashup frequency variable (Table 20.6). The computer experience variable is a normalized scale of hours per week spent on the computer, hours per week spent on the Internet, computer expertise, and the number of years using a computer.

Using these variables we performed a stepwise regression to find predictors for the future mashup frequency variable. This technique for statistical model building progressively adds variables into a regression equation. At each step, the overall model equation is tested against all the other variables being considered. If a variable is added to the equation and the predictive power of the regression is increased, the variable is incorporated into the model.

Once the regression model was complete, we learned that usefulness, online hobbies, and technology initiative were statistically significant predictors. Interestingly, gender and computer experience did not play a significant role in predicting future mashup frequency. This is especially surprising because we found that men rated themselves more highly than women in both computer experience and technology initiative. Of course, keep in mind that we earlier reported that difficulty ratings were correlated with gender. In general however these results emphasize the points we made earlier, namely that novice users' expectations about mashups as a technology they might use are influenced strongly by their intrinsic interests, for example as reflected in their online hobby-related activities or their general technology initiative.

As a final piece of exploratory analysis, we wondered whether the types of mashups that users envisioned might be related to variations in technology initiative. To examine this, we did a

Table 20.6 Characteristics of Web-Active End Users That May Predict Future Mashup Activity

Variable	Definition	Summary
Gender	Female or male	Male, N = 137 Female, N = 88
Computer experience	Sum of four normalized scales ($\alpha = 0.76$)	Mean: −0.018 SD: 3.05
Technology initiative	Average of three 5-point scales ($\alpha = 0.77$)	Mean: 3.21 SD: 1.07
Advanced media	Use of video camera, Web cam, or smart phone	Mean: 1.41 SD: 1.18
Web 2.0	Use of online maps, photo, and video services	Mean: 2.26 SD: 0.51
Hobbies online	Post online content for hobbies (Y/N)	Yes, N=120 No, N=126
Difficulty	Difficulty creating a mashup 5-point rating	Mean: 3.34 SD: 1.01
Usefulness	Usefulness of mashups 5-point rating	Mean: 3.17 SD: 0.94

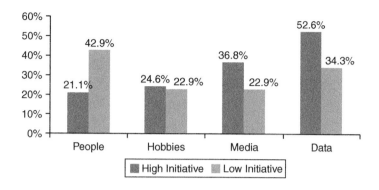

FIGURE 20.6

Categories of mashup ideas.

median-split of the technology initiative variable, creating two groups of high and low technology initiative. We then compared the mashup ideas associated with individuals in these two groups. To simplify our analysis, we collapsed the original nine categories from Figure 20.5 into four: hobbies (sports and music), people (social and personal), media (photo/video and news), and data (maps, school, and reference). Figure 20.6 graphs the comparison across high and low technology initiative groups. It suggests a tendency for data-related mashups to be suggested more often by high initiative participants, whereas those with low initiative suggested people-related mashups more. Although our work is quite preliminary, tool or documentation designers might use results like these to "tune" their offerings for different segments of the prospective user population.

If we wish to engage end users in mashup development in the future, it is important to consider what characteristics of users make them most likely to try out the new technology. Essentially, we want to guess which users will see the benefits as outweighing their perceptions of cost and risk. We found that a combination of technology initiative, perceptions of mashup usefulness, and the sharing of hobbies online could be key factors in how often a user will consider creating mashups. Though these results are based on self-assessments from our respondents, the findings point to specific themes that should be investigated further, particularly when building tools to support mashup activities.

Finally, to enhance perceptions of usefulness as much as possible, designers should also consider the types of mashups users would want to create. Our data suggests that the users with more initiative will pursue data-intensive, sophisticated mashups, whereas those with less initiative will tend towards people-driven, social mashups. Tailoring tools toward either of these activities could make building mashups more attractive for different segments of the Web-active user population.

As we concluded this study, it was still unclear as to the types of mashups end users could envision creating. While we did ask them to describe some ideas, we felt it would be useful to gather some detailed qualitative descriptions from the users. Also, their explanations of the mashup creation process suggested that there were still misconceptions; on average the respondents successfully predicted 1.17 of the three steps involved in creating a mashup. Thus, we felt that it would be important to examine the first step of mashup creation, information collection. Where do these users get the information they consume every day? Can they imagine any mashups or possible information combinations that would be useful to them?

A CLOSER LOOK AT ONLINE INFORMATION[2]

Although the survey study provided considerable information about the types of users who might want to experiment with mashups, and about the mashup topics end users might explore, we still had very little understanding of *how* a Web-active end user might think about the mashup process. How do they think about the data that they hope to manipulate? What sorts of combinations can they imagine for a given set of data? To more closely examine these questions, we conducted an interview study of end users. We recruited 12 college students from a technology-oriented discipline as participants after a prescreened survey. We deliberately recruited individuals who exemplified the category of Web-active users, identified in our earlier study ("Features of the Web-active End User" section); they were not programmers, but still were active participants on the Web and had higher levels of technology initiative. We also specifically included a single self-identified programmer as a way to benchmark our results.

All but one participant was quite vocal when describing online activities. To initially seed their responses we provided a list of categories of information for them to react to: news, sports, pictures, weather, and shopping. When speaking about each of these categories, the participants listed numerous sites that they commonly visit. It is unsurprising that the most popular sites for each category were also mentioned most often. For instance, Amazon is the most mentioned single site for shopping, and CNN was mentioned most for news sources. Although these popular sites were mentioned most frequently, less common Web sites were also brought up. For example, when talking about shopping, retailers like Forever 21 or Kohl's were also cited. In all categories but sports, the total number of unique sites mentioned outnumbered the references to the more popular sites. This pattern is consistent with the general trends of the Long Tail (Anderson, 2008) – when probed, the participants describe interests and goals related to a wide range of online information, even though there are clearly a number of "obvious" sources. More generally, this Long Tail effect is prevalent in other areas of EUP; individual users have capricious needs that cannot always be fulfilled by an existing application.

When participants were asked about other categories of online information that they use frequently (i.e., beyond the five categories we primed them with), all but two mentioned social networking; specifically they immediately raised the example of Facebook. In this context, a common theme was how Facebook includes the range of information types mentioned up to that point; "You can find pictures of your friends, news about events and I'm pretty sure there's an App that lets you see sports teams." Beyond social networks, the only other recurring category was coursework. This is not surprising given that all of the participants were students.

After they were exhausted of data sources and data categories, we asked the participants to brainstorm possible ways of combining information in ways useful to them. We elicited these responses

[2]Based on "Playing with Information: How End Users Think About and Integrate Dynamic Data," by Nan Zang and Mary Beth Rosson, which appeared in *IEEE Symposium on Visual Languages and Human-Centric Computing* © 2009 IEEE.

by using two questions: "Have there ever been situations where you needed information from different sites to answer a question or solve a problem?" and "Can you think of a time when combining information from different sites to answer a question or solve a problem?" When thinking about these combinations, participants provided us with a broad range of ideas that varied in both specific information used and complexity. For example, one participant suggested that it would be useful to combine weather information with shopping and events so that the system could recommend outfits to wear for outdoor events based on weather. Another example combined company information with job listings to make it easier when preparing for an interview.

It is clear that there are many unique combinations of information that could be useful for these users. Whereas some ideas, such as combining news and maps, already exist on certain Web sites, combinations like RateMyProfessor and course listings have eccentricities that are not easily supported with existing tools; one may be able to integrate RateMyProfessor with Penn State course listings, but what about students at Notre Dame or Purdue? We hope that by taking the common ideas initially gathered here, we can look toward building a tool to support the more general activities of these users.

DISCUSSION

Throughout this work, we have referred to a class of end users as "Web-active." But what does it really mean to be active on the Web, or to use the Web in an active way? Generally, this concept cannot be exactly quantified, but we have begun to identify features associated this user group, specifically their activities online, the initiative towards technology, and their technology expertise. These characteristics suggest that they are an exemplary population to target with new tools. In particular, a major issue with any EUP tool is "if we build it, will they come." One way to encourage users to come is to target a specific population that has the motivation to invest the additional effort to adopt and learn a new tool. By incorporating information and examples that are both interesting and useful to this subset of users, we can better support specific needs and then broaden to a larger user base. Moreover, their higher level of technology initiative may even assist in encouraging others around them to take up these new tools and technologies.

Online activities

A primary indicator for a Web-active end user is the activities he or she pursues. Throughout all of our work, we consistently found that social networking was a primary engagement factor for this university population's Web-based activities. However, this was not the only indicator. Though they spend large amounts of time using social networking sites, many times these activities serve as a gateway to other activities. In interviews that followed our survey studies, many of our participants cite Facebook as the site they visit most, but further probes often extracted descriptions of other activities that were initiated in Facebook. Other studies have shown that using community-building features of these social networking sites can be leveraged to encourage users to extend their presence into other systems (Rosson et al., 2008). At the same time, the Web 2.0 trend that is promoting the sharing of personal creations is another feature of these Web-active users. In particular, our studies have shown that creating content to share common interests in hobbies is an important factor that may contribute to their adoption of new technologies. Through the course of schoolwork and social interactions, these users have explored developing Web sites and sharing their personal interests through blogging and online journals.

As compared to the categorization by Horrigan (2007), where much of the American population are considered with "few technology assets" (49%) and are indifferent (11%) or even completely disconnected from the Internet (15%), the Web-active user can be thought of as the "elite technology user." As described by Horrigan, these users are "heavy and frequent users of the internet... are engaged with user-generated content." This is one of the reasons why we looked toward a college student population to recruit participants; this age group encompasses the largest population of the elite technology users (Horrigan, 2007).

Web-active end users are at the top of the information consumption food chain. Though they may not know how to program and develop applications, they are the users that pursue new technologies and are the people that their friends go to for assistance when it comes to technology. Because of this, they will continue to be active participants in shaping the online landscape. Not only do they consume content, they increasingly are active contributors to online activities. The things they create and share add to the overall richness of the online experience. This is a defining feature of the Web-active end user.

Technology initiative

Beyond their activities, technology initiative helps to quantify the *active* element of Web-active end users. The idea of initiative in this work includes three facets: active technology adoption, active technology assimilation, and active technology dissemination. These three items are directly related to each of the three rating scales that were combined to form the Technology Initiative index. These users sit at an intersection where they absorb information and technology for their own purposes, but also pass it on to their friends. This is very similar to what Gladwell (2000) described as "mavens." Mavens are people who specialize in gathering information and are the ones whom the average user relies upon to learn about new activities, gadgets, and other novel technologies.

In our survey of Web-active users, we found a close relationship between these three aspects of initiative, so we combined them to create a single index. In the larger population we found that this value was varied widely (from 1 to 5). Although we find high initiative for many Web-active users, a large number of users are active on the Web but do not describe themselves as high in technology initiative. Indeed we found that this index has predictive significance for their Web activities, so we see it as one index of their "active" status in this population. Many users who have low technology initiative are nonetheless active in their Web behavior – however they may be more actively oriented to social interaction and communication (i.e., on "people-oriented" activities).

Technology expertise

Web-active users vary widely in computer expertise. From the data gathered here, we found that most do rate themselves highly, but these types of ratings are unreliable because we do not have a full understanding of how each participant made these decisions. However, it appears that these users are very confident in their general skill levels. This is a promising feature of Web-active users, in that they may feel confident enough to try new tools like mashup editors, even if they also consider themselves to be "low" in technology initiative. Although these users typically do not have programming skills, they may be confident enough to investigate new tools and environments.

SUMMARY

In the last decade, Web 2.0 culture has become increasingly prevalent in many areas of online activity. Computer users have become increasingly sophisticated in the way they interact with the Web. With the progress toward more open Web services and the increasing involvement in online interests – including social networking and multimedia – the activities that users want to pursue can no longer be handled by system designers. More and more, users with programming skills are taking advantage of the technologies online to build tools tailored to their own goals. For example, programmers are encouraged by Web services like Google Maps and Flickr to employ their APIs and adapt them for individual goals, essentially building mashups. However, while these trends have promoted the active use of online resources and idea of "helping users help themselves," many less sophisticated users are left out. In other words, there may be a large group of "have-nots" who could capitalize on these technologies, but do not have the necessary technical skills to do so.

In our work we identified a population of Web-active users who have not only identified useful types of information they encounter daily but also described situations where having the ability to build mashups would be useful in fulfilling their information needs ("Features of the Web-active End User"). However, they lack the programming expertise to be able to integrate such technologies. It seems that they have a general understanding of HTML, but not much beyond. It would be practical to direct these users to the resources they need by focusing on their common activities as a way to entice them to take up new technologies. Here the key challenge is to identify situations in which the user will find the benefits of working with a new tool to be greater than the cost of learning how to do it. In this case, Web-active end users are an exemplary population to study in this context. These users are born into the age of the Internet and have been actively consuming and contributing content online for most of their lives. They already rely on the Internet for everyday problem solving and are enthusiastically engaged in blogging and social networking activities. By appealing to these interests, designers can engage users and encourage them to explore new tools.

Although we do not believe that it is yet possible to build tools that can support all the information needs of every user, our hope is that this work can be used as a profile of a promising target population for future tools, in particular mashup creation tools, for the current "have-nots."

Reuse in the world of end user programmers

21

Christopher Scaffidi, Mary Shaw

Kelley Engineering Center, Oregon State University

ABSTRACT

End user programmers often reuse one another's code when creating new programs, but this reuse is rarely as clean or simple as the black box reuse that professional programmers aspire to achieve. In this chapter, we explore the motivations that drive reuse of end user code, the challenges that impede reuse of end user code, and several approaches that facilitate reuse of end user code. We give particular emphasis to the problem of helping end users to identify high-quality reusable code amid the millions of scripts, macros, spreadsheets, and other programs produced by essentially anonymous users out on the Web. Based on a review of empirical studies, we find that reusable code is often characterized by certain traits, suggesting that it might be possible to help end user programmers to find reusable code by automatically gathering, analyzing, and synthesizing information about whether code has these desirable traits. We close the chapter with a discussion of future research opportunities aimed at helping end users to identify, understand, and adapt reusable code.

INTRODUCTION

Reuse is a central aspect of end user programming. For example, empirical studies have shown that users commonly reuse one another's CoScripter macros, which automate browser interactions with Web sites (Chapter 5). Users sometimes execute existing macros without modification, but other times they modify another person's macro before executing it. In addition, they sometimes combine existing macros via copy and paste into a new macro. They also sometimes learn from one another's macros before writing a new macro of their own, demonstrating conceptual if not literal code reuse. All these forms of reuse can help users to create new programs more quickly and correctly than they could by writing code totally from scratch.

Macros are not the only kind of code that end user programmers reuse. Code includes any human-readable instructions that a computer can execute or translate to an executable form. For instance, people reuse spreadsheets (Nardi, 1993), JavaScript and HTML (Rosson, Ballin, & Nash, 2004), and MATLAB programs (Gulley, 2006).

But reuse of code created by other end users is often messy. For one thing, such code lacks formally defined interfaces, so reusing such code typically involves actually digging into its details and understanding it. Moreover, end users usually have not been trained in designing for reuse, and end users have little or no time to design for reuse. Indeed, they may not even *think* to design for reuse in the first place. Not all end user code is easy to reuse.

This stands in contrast to the practices of professional programmers, who often can assemble applications by combining existing components. For instance, professional programmers now routinely create systems with database components or SMTP servers, or even smaller components like ActiveX controls. "Thousands of such controls have been developed, sold, and used. They are small, easy to work with, and an effective example of binary reuse" (Liberty, 2005). Despite the fact that programmers still encounter some problems when combining components (Garlan, Allen, & Ockerbloom, 1995), it should still be recognized that to a remarkable extent, professional programming has moved toward a vision where programmers are "able safely to regard components as black boxes" (Naur, 1968).

Yet reuse of user-created code lags behind. In this chapter, we explore several reasons why reuse of end user code is desirable yet not as simple as snapping together black boxes. We discuss different ways in which end users reuse one another's code, and we contrast this with the ways in which they reuse code written by professional programmers. We follow this by focusing on the crucial problem of helping end users to identify reusable code, which is a prerequisite to any reuse. Finally, we close by considering future research directions aimed at helping end users to identify, understand, and adapt reusable code.

REUSE: VISION VERSUS REALITY

When some software engineers hear the word "reuse," they think of creating a program by assembling meticulously designed components. McIlroy may have been the first (and most eloquent) person to espouse this vision (Naur, 1968):

> "The most important characteristic of a software components industry is that it will offer families of routines for any given job...In other words, the purchaser of a component from a family will choose one tailored to his exact needs...He will expect families of routines to be constructed on rational principles so that families fit together as building blocks. In short, he should be able safely to regard components as black boxes."

Even today, among some professional programmers, there is a view that programming can be as simple as hooking together black boxes (Nash, 2003):

> "Components represent the 'transistor' of the software industry, or perhaps more accurately, the 'integrated circuit.' They provide a known quantity, a building block of established functionality and quality that can be used to assemble applications in a way more akin to assembly of a television than traditional development of an application."

Achieving this idyllic vision would allow programmers to focus on selecting the right black boxes and hooking them together in a sensible way, rather than digging into the minutiae of each box's internal implementation. And in many circumstances, professional programming *really is* this simple. For example, accessing legacy COM objects in the more modern .NET programming platform is "surprisingly easy," typically involving only a few lines of code (Liberty, 2005). Constructing the graphical layout of user interfaces in a C# or Java IDE is usually as simple as dragging and dropping icons (Liberty, 2005; Nash, 2003). Other easy to reuse components include database components, Web services, XML parsers, and SMTP servers.

Combining black boxes to produce applications is such an effective approach for software development that it forms the basis for the "software factory" concept (Greenfield et al., 2004). In this approach, a team is responsible for creating a "factory" that comprises highly reusable components, recipes for combining those components, and tailored tools for executing the recipes under programmers' control. The factory then "can be used to rapidly and cheaply produce an open-ended set of unique variants of an archetypical product" (Greenfield et al., 2004). In other words, the factory semiautomates the production of a product family. Certainly, not all organizations produce product families (so the software factory is not a "silver bullet"), but if an organization needs to create many similar applications in one domain, then the software factory is a valid approach to consider.

Such a vision might also seem ideally suited to the needs of end user programmers. What is not to like in the idea of letting end users assemble programs from black boxes? Let us deconstruct this vision and examine the reasons why its implicit assumptions are unsatisfied in the context of end user programming.

Assumption: The "industry" can understand end users' work well enough to provide "routines" meeting the "exact needs" for "any given job"

Analyses of federal data show that end users have a remarkable range of different occupations (Scaffidi, Shaw, & Myers, 2005). They include managers in accounting companies and marketing firms, engineers in many different fields, teachers, scientists, health care workers, insurance adjusters, salesmen, and administrative assistants. In smaller numbers, they also include workers in many extremely specialized industries such as data processing equipment repairers, tool and die makers, water and sewage treatment plant operators, early childhood teacher's assistants, and printing press operators.

Researchers have documented a wide range of ways that workers in these diverse industries write programs to help automate parts of their work. Examples include office workers creating Web macros to automate interactions with intranet sites (Leshed et al., 2008), advertising consultants creating Web macros to compile sales information (Koesnandar et al., 2008), managers creating spreadsheets to manage inventory (Fisher & Rothermel, 2004), system administrators creating scripts to analyze server logs (Barrett et al., 2004), and teachers creating programs to compute students' grades (Wiedenbeck, 2005). Within each industry, occupation, and kind of programming is still more variation. For example, different office workers use different Web sites, and even those within the same organization use their intranet sites in different ways.

Not only is the diversity of end users' contexts simply staggering, but the sheer number of end users is overwhelming. Overall, by 2012, there are likely to be 90 million computer users in American workplaces alone, including 13 to 55 million end user programmers (depending on the definition of "programming") (Scaffidi, Shaw, & Myers, 2005). In contrast, the federal government anticipates that professional programmers in America will only number 3 million, nearly an order of magnitude smaller than the number of end user programmers.

Given the huge difference between the sizes of these two populations, as well as the incredible diversity of end users' jobs, it is inconceivable that the industry of professional programmers could understand every kind of end user's work at a sufficient level of detail to provide routines that meet the "exact needs" of "any given [programming] job." McIlroy's hypothetical catalog cannot be complete if it is to meet the "exact needs" of end user programmers. There are not enough professional programmers available to produce a software factory for every single group of end user programmers. There simply is a huge range of domain-specific detail that only the end users themselves understand.

Thus, there must necessarily be a significant functional gap between the generic components provided by an "industry" of professional programmers and the domain-specific requirements of end users. For example, IBM provides the general purpose CoScripter platform, but the end users are the ones who implement Web macros that manipulate specific Web sites to meet the particular requirements of their work.

In short, the "industry" of professional programmers can only meet the general needs of end users, not their "exact needs." Consequently, if users want to have the needed code, then they must fill the resulting functional gap by creating code of their own.

Assumption: The industry sells components to a "purchaser"

The vision presented by McIlroy implicitly presents a producer–consumer relationship, wherein the component consumer acts as a relatively passive purchaser. This is a reasonable way of viewing the role of a programmer who simply stitches together existing components or uses a software factory. However, this relationship is an incomplete description of situations where there is a large functional gap between the components and the finished program. In the case of many professional and end user programmers, producing a final program often requires sizable expenditures of effort. In addition, end users' code often embodies significant domain-specific intellectual capital, such as when a spreadsheet automates the computations in an insurance company's proprietary pricing model. As a result, the contributions of the end users become valuable in their own right.

This raises the potential and indeed desirability of reusing end users' programs, to the extent that end users have similar needs that are unmet by the generic components offered by the component industry. For example, office workers sometimes reuse one another's Web macros (Leshed et al., 2008), scientists sometimes reuse one another's simulation and other analysis code (Segal, 2004), and system administrators sometimes reuse one another's scripts (Barrett et al., 2004).

As a result, some end user programmers play a dual role as consumers of professionally produced code as well as producers of code that other end users might reuse.

Assumption: People can assemble programs from "black boxes"

A component provides an interface specification that defines its properties, including the component's supported operations, functionality, and post-conditions guaranteed to be satisfied after operations are called (Shaw et al., 1995). Accordingly, McIlroy's vision phrases component reuse in terms of calling components' operations, with clearly defined functionality, precision, robustness, and time–space performance (Naur, 1968).

But end users' code is rarely packaged up as a component with a well defined interface. In fact, the most popular end user programming platforms do not even offer any way to specify interfaces. For example, Excel spreadsheets do not expose any externally visible operations, nor do CoScripter macros (except for simply running a macro in its entirety). Not only do Excel and CoScripter lack any mechanism for exposing operations, but they provide no way to specify the properties of these hypothetical operations (such as post-conditions or time–space performance).

So if end user programmers want to package code for reuse via interfaces, then they must rely on general purpose languages. However, such languages are known to be difficult for end user programmers to learn, and it takes years for a people to develop the skills necessary to design robust component interfaces (Spalter, 2002). Few end users have overcome these hurdles: the former chief systems architect at BEA has estimated that for every programmer who knows how to use a Java-like programming language, there are nine more who only know how to use typical end user programming environments like Microsoft Excel, Visio, and Access (Bosworth, 2004). In other words, for every programmer (professional or end user) who can use a language that supports creating components, there are nine more who can create code that does not support creating components.

In such a context, it is unreasonable to expect that most code created by end users will be callable in a black box manner through interfaces. Instead, end users will need alternate approaches for reusing one another's code.

FORMS OF REUSE IN THE END USER PROGRAMMING CONTEXT

Hoadley et al. have identified several forms of code reuse by end user programmers: code invocation, code cloning, and template use (Hoadley et al., 1996) (Table 21.1). The producer of the reused code could be a professional or an end user programmer.

Code invocation or black box reuse

Since Hoadley developed this categorization in 1996, empirical studies have shown that all of these forms of reuse are common, except for black box reuse of end user code. Specifically, one study by Segal revealed "plenty of evidence of the research scientists reusing publicly available code and components [produced by professional programmers]…But the only local reuse episodes we saw were two scientists who had a long history of working together" (Segal, 2004). Many scientists have a high level of programming skill, and they often use general-purpose programming languages (such as Fortran and C) that provide the syntactic constructs necessary to define components with precisely

Table 21.1 Reuse in the World of End User Programmers Rarely Takes the Form of Simply Stitching Together "Black Box" Components into a Finished Application

	Provider of reusable code	
Form of reuse	Professional programmers	End user programmers
Code invocation or black box reuse	Common	Rare
Code cloning or white box reuse	Common	Common
Template reuse or conceptual reuse	Common	Common

defined interfaces. Yet black box reuse of end user code does not seem to thrive even in this propitious context, so we were unsurprised that we could not find any other empirical studies reporting situations where end users wrote programs that called one another's code.

Code cloning or white box reuse

When programming, end users typically create programs that are specialized to the specific task at hand. When later faced with a similar (but not identical) task, people can sometimes reuse an existing program as a starting point, though doing so will typically require making some edits. For example, one study of CoScripter macro use found that "in many cases, a user initially created a script with a hard-coded value and then went back and generalized the script to reference the Personal Database [a parameter]" (Bogart et al., 2008). In another study of end users who created kiosk software for museum displays, every single interviewee reported sometimes making a copy of an existing program that he or she wanted to reuse, then editing the program to make it match new requirements (Brandt et al., 2008).

Hoadley et al. (1996) refer to this form of reuse as "code cloning" because it so often involves making a copy of an existing program. However, as mentioned in the CoScripter macro study, end user programmers sometimes edit the original program directly in order to make it general enough to support more than one situation. Therefore, this general category of reuse might be better identified with the more widely accepted phrase "white box reuse."

One inhibitor to white box reuse is that the end user must be able to find and understand code before he can reuse it. Consequently, end users are more likely to reuse their own code than that of other people (Bogart et al., 2008; Rosson, Ballin, & Nash, 2004; Wiedenbeck, 2005).

This inhibitor can become a significant impediment to white box reuse of code written by professional programmers. For example, we are not aware of any empirical studies documenting situations where end user programmers viewed the source code for professionally produced components (despite the fact that many such components are now open source). The explanation for this might be that professional programmers commonly write code with languages, APIs, algorithms, and data structures that are unfamiliar or even unintelligible to most end users. In addition, there is often no easy way to find a professional's source code.

Template reuse or conceptual reuse

End user programmers often refer to existing programs as a source of information about how to create new programs. For instance, in one study of reuse by end user programmers who created Web applications, "interviewees commonly described using other people's code as a model for something they wanted to learn" (Rosson, Ballin, & Nash, 2004). The examples are sometimes provided by other end users and sometimes by professional programmers (often to facilitate writing code that calls their components or APIs). In many cases, the examples are fully functional, so the programmer can try out the examples and better understand how they work (Walpole & Burnett, 1997).

Hoadley et al. (1996) refer to this form of programming as "template reuse" because in the 1980s and early 1990s, researchers commonly used the word "template" to describe a mental plan for how to accomplish a programming task. Another appropriate name for this form of reuse might be "conceptual reuse," because in such cases, concepts are reused rather than actual code.

LOW-CEREMONY EVIDENCE OF REUSABLE END USER CODE

Given the value of reusing end users' code and the multiple ways in which that code can be reused, it might seem as though reuse of end user code would be commonplace. Yet for every reusable piece of end user code, many are never reused by anyone (Gulley, 2006; Scaffidi, 2009; Segal, 2004). Actually identifying the reusable pieces of code within the mass of other code can be like looking for a needle in a haystack.

The same could also be said for reuse of professional programmers' code, but conventional software engineering has well established methods for assessing or ensuring the quality of code. These methods include formal verification, code generation by a trusted automatic generator, systematic testing, and empirical follow-up evaluation of how well the software works in practice. We have used the term "high-ceremony evidence" to describe the information produced by these methods (Scaffidi & Shaw, 2007), because applying them requires producers or consumers of code to exert high levels of skill and effort, in exchange for strong guarantees about code quality. Many professional programmers can call upon these techniques to look for the reusable code in the haystack.

But end user programmers (and some professional programmers) often lack the skill, time, and interest to apply these methods. What they need instead are methods based on "low-ceremony" evidence: information that may be informal, imprecise, and unreliable, but that can nevertheless be gathered, analyzed, and synthesized with minimal effort and skill to generate *confidence* (not a guarantee) that code is reusable. Individual pieces of low-ceremony evidence are of low reliability, yet good decisions can be made on the basis of an accumulation of such evidence when that evidence provides generally consistent results.

For example, if a certain spreadsheet has been downloaded by dozens of well-respected co-workers, this fact would be low-ceremony evidence of reusability. It is informal because no formal process, notation, logic, or other formalized structure is prescribed for the gathering or use of the data underlying this fact. This evidence is imprecise, since different people might have downloaded the code for different reasons (for example, either to read the code or to use the code). This evidence is unreliable, because having numerous code downloads does not always imply reusability (for example, they might have all downloaded the code and found that it was full of bugs). Yet download counts are widely used and widely helpful, and they are claimed to play a crucial role in helping users to find reusable Web macros (Little et al., 2007) and MATLAB code (Gulley, 2006). Such evidence can be easily gathered from server logs. It can be analyzed in many easy ways, whether by segmenting downloads by date or by groups of users (which can prompt insights such as realizing that certain code has fallen out of disfavor, or that a certain spreadsheet is only popular among accountants). Finally, such evidence can be synthesized with other evidence – for example, if the code has been downloaded many times, and all of those users continue to use the code, and if some of those co-workers are well-regarded as being technology savvy, then all of these forms of evidence can in the aggregate produce high confidence in the code's reusability.

Low-ceremony evidence does not provide the strong guarantees of high-ceremony evidence. Rather, it provides indicators to guide decisions. This kind of evidence would be particularly appropriate for end user programmers because they rarely need the resulting program to perform perfectly. For example, in one study, teachers reported that their gradebook spreadsheets were "not life-and-death matters" (Wiedenbeck, 2005), and in another study, Web developers "did not see their efforts as 'high stakes' and held a correspondingly casual view of quality" (Wiedenbeck, 2005). For these people, the strong quality guarantees of high-ceremony methods probably do not provide enough value to justify the requisite effort. But low-ceremony evidence might suffice, if it is possible to make reasonably accurate assessments of code's reusability based on whatever low-ceremony evidence is available about that code at a particular moment in time.

In the remainder of this chapter, we review empirical evidence showing that the reusability of end user programmers' code can indeed be inferred from certain kinds of low-ceremony evidence. These studies allow us to develop a catalog of low-ceremony evidence that is known to relate to reuse of end user programmers' code. We categorize the evidence based on its source: evidence based on the code itself, evidence based on the code's authorship, and evidence based on prior uses of the code. For example, code is more likely to be reusable if it contains variables rather than hard-coded values, if it was authored by somebody who has been assigned to create reusable code, and if it was previously used by other people who rated it highly. Our catalog of kinds of evidence can be extended in the future if additional studies empirically document new sources of low-ceremony evidence that are indicative of code reusability.

As shown in Table 21.2, we draw on 11 empirical studies of end user programmers:

- Retrospective analyses of a Web macro repository (Bogart et al., 2008; Scaffidi, 2009)
- Interviews of software kiosk designers (Brandt et al., 2008)
- A report about running a MATLAB code repository (Gulley, 2006)
- Observations of college students in a classroom setting (Ko, Myers, & Aung, 2004)
- An ethnography of spreadsheet programmers (Nardi, 1993)
- Observations of children using programmable toys (Petre & Blackwell, 2007)
- Interviews (Rosson, Ballin, & Nash, 2004) and a survey of Web developers (Zang, Rosson, & Nasser, 2008)
- Interviews of consultants and scientists (Segal, 2004)
- Interviews of K–12 teachers (Wiedenbeck, 2005)

Where relevant, we supplement these with one simulation of end user programmer behavior (Blackwell, 2002), as well as empirical work related to professional programmers (Biggerstaff & Richter, 1987; Burkhardt & Détienne, 1995; Mohagheghi et al., 2004; Rosson & Carroll, 1996).

After reviewing the three sources of low-ceremony quality evidence (the code itself, the code's authorship, and the code's prior uses), we summarize a recent study that combined evidence from the first two sources to accurately predict whether Web macro scripts would be reused (Scaffidi et al., 2009). Our results open several research opportunities aimed at further exploring the range and practical usefulness of low-ceremony evidence for identifying reusable end user code.

Source #1: Evidence based on the code itself

If programmers could always create programs simply by stitching together some components chosen from a catalog, then the code implementing those components would not matter. More precisely, suppose that programming was as simple as selecting components based on their interfaces and writing a program that called components' operations through their interfaces. The point of an

Table 21.2 Studies on Reusability of End User programmers' Code

Evidence based on information about	Studies of end user programmers*												Studies of professional programmers[†]			
	1	2	3	4	5	6	7	8	9	10	11	12	1	2	3	4
Code itself																
Mass appeal					X				X		X		X			X
Flexibility		X			X		X	X	X		X	X	X			
Understandability			X		X	X		X	X	X	X		X			X
Functional size	X								X				X	X	X	
Code's authorship						X			X							
Code's prior uses					X											

*1, (Blackwell, 2002); 2, (Bogart et al., 2008); 3, (Brandt et al., 2008); 4, (Gulley, 2006); 5, (Ko, Myers, & Aung, 2004); 6, (Nardi, 1993); 7, (Petre & Blackwell, 2007); 8, (Rosson, Ballin, & Nash, 2004); 9, (Scaffidi, 2009); 10, (Segal, 2004); 11, (Wiedenbeck, 2005); 12, (Zang , Rosson, & Nasser, 2008).
[†]1, (Biggerstaff & Richter, 1987); 2, (Burkhardt & Détienne, 1995); 3, (Mohagheghi et al., 2004); 4, (Rosson & Carroll, 1996).

interface is that it abstracts away the implementation. So if the code supporting an interface has been formally validated, that interface alone should provide sufficient information to formally prove that the resulting program would work as intended. Gathering any additional information about the code itself would be superfluous in terms of proving the correctness of the program. The number of lines of code, the number of comments, the actual programming keywords used, the coupling and cohesion of the implementing classes, none of it would matter. Even if the code was an unintelligible wad of spaghetti or a thick ball of mud, it would not matter.

Yet as argued earlier, end user programmers rarely use one another's code through black box methods. Instead, they more typically rely on white box and conceptual reuse, both of which involve actually understanding the code.

White box and conceptual reuse are also important among professional programmers. It has been argued, and widely confirmed through experience, that professional programmers' code is more reusable if it has certain traits (Biggerstaff & Richter, 1987). In particular, the code must be *relevant* to the requirements of multiple programming tasks, it must be *flexible* enough to meet those varying requirements, it must be *understandable* to the people who would reuse it, and it must be *functionally large* enough to justify reuse rather than coding from scratch.

These traits also apparently contribute to the reusability of end user programmers' code, because every study of end users cited in Table 21.2 produced findings of the form, "Code was hard to reuse unless it had X," where X was a piece of low-ceremony evidence related to one of these four code-based traits. For example, unless code contained comments, teachers had difficulty understanding and reusing it (Wiedenbeck, 2005). In this example, the evidence is the presence of comments in the code, and the trait is understandability. Thus, the evidence was an indicator of a trait, and thus an indicator (but not a guarantee) of reusability.

Information about mass appeal/functional relevance

The presence of keywords or other tokens in a certain piece of code appeared to be evidence of whether the code was relevant to many peoples' needs. For instance, Web macros that operated on Web sites with certain tokens in the URL (such as "google" in "google.com") were more likely to be reused by people other than the macro author (Scaffidi, 2009). If somebody is already familiar with a certain Web site, and has created some scripts that access that site, then he might be interested in other scripts that also target that site. Put another way, if there was a large supply of scripts containing a certain keyword, then there also was a large demand for scripts containing that keyword.

But when programmers seek reusable code, they are looking for more than certain keywords. Keywords are just a signal of what the programmer is really looking for: code that provides functionality required in the context of the programmer's work (Burkhardt & Détienne, 1995; Ko, Myers, & Aung, 2004; Rosson & Carroll, 1996). Typically, only a small amount of code is functionally relevant to many contexts, so a simple functional categorization of code can be evidence of its reusability. For example, 78% of mashup programmers in one survey created mapping mashups (Zang, Rosson, & Nasser, 2008). All other kinds of mashups were created by far fewer people. Thus, just knowing that a mashup component was related to mapping (rather than photos, news, trivia, or the study's other categories) suggested mass appeal.

Information about flexibility and composability

Reusable code must not only perform a relevant function, but it must do it in a flexible way so that it can be applied in new usage contexts. Flexibility can be evidenced by use of variables rather than hard-coded values. In a study of children, parameter tweaking served as an easy way to "change the appearance, behaviour, or effect of an element [component]," often in preparation for composition of components into new programs (Petre & Blackwell, 2007). Web macro scripts were more likely to be reused if they contained variables (Bogart et al., 2008; Scaffidi, 2009).

Flexibility can be limited when code has nonlocal effects that could affect the behavior of other code. Such effects reduce reusability because the programmer must carefully coordinate different pieces of code to work together (Ko, Myers, & Aung, 2004; Wiedenbeck, 2005). For example, Web developers considered scripts to be less reusable if they happened to "mess up the whole page" (Rosson, Ballin, & Nash, 2004), rather than simply affect one widget on the page. In general, nonlocal effects are evidenced by the presence of operations in the code that write to nonlocal data structures (such as the Web page's document object model).

Finally, flexibility can be limited when the code has dependencies on other code or data sources. If that other code or data become unavailable, then the dependent code becomes unusable (Zang et al., 2008). Dependencies are evidenced by external references. As an example, users were generally unable to reuse Web macros that contained operations that read data from intranet sites (i.e., sites that cannot be accessed unless the user is located on a certain local network) (Bogart et al., 2008). For instance, one Web macro accesses the site intranet.etb.com.co, which can only be accessed by people who work at La Empresa de Telecomunicaciones de Bogotá (which owns the etb.com.co domain). Except for employees of this company, the script is entirely unreusable.

Information about understandability

Understanding code is an essential part of evaluating it, planning any modifications, and combining it with other code (Ko et al., 2004). Moreover, understanding existing code can be valuable even if the programmer chooses not to directly incorporate it into a new project, since people often learn from existing code and use it as an example when writing code from scratch (Rosson, Ballin, & Nash, 2004; Rosson & Carroll, 1996). This highlights the value of existing code not only for verbatim black box or near-verbatim white box reuse, but also for indirect conceptual reuse.

Many studies of end user programmers have noted that understandability is greatly facilitated by the presence of comments, documentation, and other secondary notation. Scientists often struggled to reuse code unless it was carefully documented (Segal, 2004), teachers' "comprehension was also slow and tedious because of the lack of documentation" (Wiedenbeck, 2005), office workers often had to ask for help to reuse spreadsheets that lacked adequate labeling and comments (Nardi, 1993), and Web macros were much more likely to be reused if they contained comments (Scaffidi, 2009). End user programmers typically skipped putting comments into code unless they intended for it to be reused (Brandt et al., 2008). In short, the presence of comments and other notations can be strong evidence of understandability and, indirectly, of reusability.

Information about functional size

When asked about whether and why they reuse code, professional programmers made "explicit in their verbalisation the trade-off between design and reuse cost" (Burkhardt & Détienne, 1995), preferring to reuse code only if the effort of doing so was much lower than the effort of implementing similar functionality from scratch. In general, larger components give a larger "payoff" than smaller components, with the caveat that larger components can be more specialized and therefore have less mass appeal (Biggerstaff & Richter, 1987). Empirically, components that are reused tend to be larger than components that are not reused (Mohagheghi et al., 2004).

Simulations suggest that end user programmers probably evaluate costs in a similar manner when deciding whether or not to reuse existing code (Blackwell, 2002), though we are not aware of any surveys or interviews that show that end user programmers evaluate these costs consciously. Nonetheless, there is empirical evidence that functional size does affect reuse of end user programmers' code. Specifically, Web macros that were reused tended to have more lines of code than Web macros that were not reused (Scaffidi, 2009).

Source #2: Evidence based on code's authorship

In some organizations, certain end user programmers have been tasked with cultivating a repository of reusable spreadsheets (Nardi, 1993). Thus, the identity of a spreadsheet's author might be evidence about the spreadsheet's reusability.

Even when an author's identity is unknown, certain evidence about the author can be useful for inferring code's reusability. For example, CoScripter Web macros were more likely to be reused if they were uploaded by authors located at Internet addresses belonging to IBM (which developed the CoScripter platform) (Scaffidi, 2009). In addition, Web macros were more likely to be reused if they were created by authors who previously created heavily reused macros.

Source #3: Evidence based on code's prior uses

Once someone has tried to reuse code, recording that person's experiences can capture information about the code's reusability. Repositories of end user code typically record this information as reviews, recommendations, and ratings (Gulley, 2006; Little et al., 2007). In the MATLAB repository, capturing and displaying these forms of reusability evidence has helped users to find high-quality reusable code (Gulley, 2006).

Untapped evidence

It is interesting that empirical studies have documented so few ways in which reuse of end user code is affected by evidence based on authorship and prior uses (see previous sections on sources #2 and #3). In our view, this is somewhat surprising because analogous sources of evidence play a vital role in everyday life *outside* of code reuse. For example, when shopping for a new vacuum cleaner, it is not uncommon for people to consider information about the different vacuum cleaners' manufacturers (analogous to authorship) as well as their previous experiences with vacuum cleaners (analogous to prior uses). Indeed, there are many forms of evidence analogous to authorship and prior uses that people rely on in everyday life:

- Reviews of products by Underwriters Laboratories or by *Consumer Reports* and similar publications (reporting on prior uses of the products in a laboratory setting)
- Third-party ratings and reviews of products by users at amazon.com or other online stores (reporting on prior uses of the products by other people)
- Recommendations by co-workers or friends (again reporting on prior uses by other people)
- Branding or seller reputation, including brand management through advertising (presenting evidence about the product producer)
- "Best X" reports, such as *Money Magazine's* "Best Graduate Programs" (often reporting based on surveys of people about their perceptions of product producers or products)

Outside of ordinary life, a great deal of this evidence is available to help professional programmers select components for reuse. For example, *Dr. Dobb's Journal* often provides reviews of products; programmers can rate components available for sale at programmersparadise.com; co-workers often offer opinions (sometimes rather zealously) about components; component producers manage their brands carefully through Web sites and sometimes even television commercials; and sites for programmers, like slashdot.org, sometimes run polls about components, including the "favorite filesystem" poll.

Because of the importance of this information in everyday life and in the work of professional programmers, we anticipate that evidence about authorship and prior uses also plays an important role in guiding reuse of end user code. Future research might be able to uncover the nature of this evidence and develop approaches for using it to facilitate reuse.

PREDICTING CODE REUSE BASED ON LOW-CEREMONY EVIDENCE

As a first step toward finding effective models for combining low-ceremony evidence into predictions of reusability, we have designed and evaluated a machine learning model that predicts reuse of CoScripter Web macros (Scaffidi, 2009). This model classifies macros into two categories – "likely to be reused" or "unlikely to be reused" – based on features corresponding to low-ceremony evidence. These features include information about the macro's source text (such as the number of comments and number of variables) as well as information about the macro's authorship (such as the number of macros previously created by the macro's author). Additional features can be added to the model in the future.

This model is based on the notion of evaluating how well scripts satisfy arithmetic rules that we call "predictors." The first step is to train the model using an algorithm that selects rules (using an information theoretic criterion) that distinguish between macros that are reused and macros that are not reused. For example, one predictor might be *number_of_comments ≥ 3*, another might be *number_of_variables ≤ 2*, and a third might be *number_previously_authored ≥ 1*.

After the model has been "loaded" with a set of predictors during training, it can be used to predict if some other macro will be reused. Specifically, a macro is classified as "likely to be reused" if it matches at least a certain number of predictors. Continuing the example above, requiring at least one predictor match would predict that a script will be reused only if *number_of_comments ≥ 3*, *number_of_variables ≤ 2*, or *number_previously_authored ≥ 1*.

As described earlier in this chapter, reuse takes several forms in the end user programming context, so we tested whether low-ceremony evidence would suffice for predicting four different forms of reuse. In particular, we tested based on whether each macro would be executed by its author more than 1 day after its creation, executed by users other than its author, edited by users other than its author, and copied by users other than its author. Black box reuse is detected by the first and second measures of reuse, whereas white box reuse is detected by the third and fourth measures. Admittedly, these measures of reuse are not perfect. However, they do provide a good starting point for testing whether low-ceremony evidence provides enough information to identify reusable code.

The model predicted reuse quite accurately, with 70%–80% recall (at 40% false positive rate), whether other end user programmers would reuse a given macro. The most useful predictors related to mass appeal, functional size, flexibility, and authorship.

These results show that low-ceremony evidence can be combined in a simple manner to yield accurate predictions of Web macro reuse. Though there may be other equally accurate methods of combining evidence, our model has the advantage of being relatively simple, which might make it possible to automatically generate explanations of why the model generated certain predictions. Moreover, the model is defined so that it does not require the programs under consideration to be Web macros. Thus, we are optimistic that it will be possible to apply the model to other kinds of end user code.

CONCLUSION AND FUTURE DIRECTIONS

Professional programmers cannot anticipate and provide components for every domain-specific need. To close this functional gap, end users create code that is valuable in its own right. Other end users often can benefit from reusing this code, but reusing it is not as simple as plucking components from a catalog and stitching them together. Reuse is more typically a multistage, white box process in which users search for useful code, attempt to understand it, and make needed modifications through cloning, editing, or both. Users also need to understand code to learn reusable concepts from it. Empirical studies show that code with certain traits tends to be more reusable. At least in the Web macro domain, it is actually possible to accurately predict whether code will be reused, based on information that may be informal, imprecise, and unreliable, but that can nevertheless be gathered, analyzed, and synthesized with a minimal amount of effort and skill.

These results represent one step toward providing end users with more effective approaches for quickly identifying reusable code created by other users, understanding that code, and adapting the code or learning from it to create new code. A great deal of additional work will be needed before end users obtain anything resembling the benefits originally promised by the stereotypical vision of component-based reuse.

First, our results create the opportunity to collect and exploit low-ceremony evidence in new system features aimed at supporting reuse. Several of the systems presented in this book would provide excellent test beds for this exploration. For example, the CoScripter repository (Chapter 5) could use the model presented in this chapter as a ranking function in search results, to be able to sort scripts by their reuse potential. Another possible application would be to integrate reusability scores with information from other sources, such as models of social networks; for example, if reuse is localized within a community, or among people with shared interests, then the CoScripter repository could rank code more highly if it appears to be highly reusable and if it was created by somebody with similar interests to the user running the search.

Systems might use evidence to rank code differently, depending on the user who is looking for code to reuse. For example, the designers of the ITL framework note that "Advanced users may be comfortable with complex structures, such as conditionals and iteration, but these may confuse novice users" (Chapter 11). Consequently, it might be useful for the repository to differentiate between advanced users and novices, presenting different search results to each. Novice users might be identified as those who have never uploaded code that had conditionals and iteration; advanced users then would be those who have uploaded such code at least once. When presenting search results to a novice user, the repository could filter out (or downrank) code that contained conditionals and iteration, but it would use no such filter for advanced users. In this case, the evidence of reusability (the presence of conditionals and iteration) would be used to characterize users *and* code, with the goal of only presenting hard-to-understand code to users who have previously presented evidence that they are capable of understanding such code. Of course, any such innovation would need thorough testing to determine whether it is effective at linking users with useful code.

As one final idea for how to apply low-ceremony evidence in the context of end user programming for the Web, consider the notion of "trusted" and "untrusted" widgets created by users for users in the Mash Maker system (Chapter 9). Trusted widgets are allowed to execute certain operations in the user's browser that untrusted widgets are not allowed to execute (such as to read cookies transmitted between the browser and server). To become trusted, a widget must receive an imprimatur provided by the Mash Maker system administrators at Intel. This creates a bottleneck – no widget can become trusted until after Intel's employees have a chance to look at it. One possible improvement would be to let users decide for themselves whether they want to trust a widget that another user created, based on low-ceremony evidence. For example, after downloading an untrusted widget, the user could click on a button in the Mash Maker client to view evidence about trustworthiness. The client might indicate, for instance, "This widget does not call any API functions that could send data outside your browser. It was authored by a user who was confirmed to have the email address someuser@company.com. It has previously been trusted by 9 people whose code you have previously trusted, including your-own-sysadmin@your-own-company.com." Depending on whether the user is persuaded by this evidence, he could decide to trust the widget or not.

Second, we have found relatively few studies showing that code reuse is related to the code's authorship or prior uses. This was somewhat surprising, because evidence about prior uses has been incorporated into many repositories in the form of rating, review, and reputation features. Thus, one direction for future work is to perform more studies aimed at empirically identifying situations where this and other low-ceremony evidence helps to guide end user programmers to highly reusable code. Further empirical studies might also help to extend our catalog by identifying new sources of low-ceremony evidence, beyond the code itself, authorship, and prior uses.

Third, it will be desirable to empirically confirm the generalizability of our machine learning model. This will require amassing logs of code reuse in some domain other than Web macros (such as spreadsheets), collecting low-ceremony evidence for that kind of code, and testing the model on the data. At present, except for the CoScripter system, we are unaware of any end user programming repository with enough history and users to support such an experiment. Ideally, just as we have drawn on research from studies performed by many teams, the machine learning model would be confirmed on different kinds of code by different research teams.

Fourth, although these studies have shown the importance of understandability in promoting white box and conceptual reuse, there has been virtually no work aimed at helping end users to produce code that other people will be able to understand. For example, though virtually all of the studies emphasized the importance of code comments in promoting understandability, most studies also showed that end user programmers rarely take the time to embed comments in their code. End users lack the time to make significant up-front investments in understandability, yet this hampers reusability by their peers. New approaches are needed to break this deadlock.

Finally, a similar deadlock exists in the problem of designing code that other end user programmers can easily adapt. Among professional programmers, it is widely accepted that good design promotes flexibility, chunks of manageable and useful functional size, and ultimately mass appeal. Yet end user programmers often lack the time and skills to invest up front in design. The resulting code can be not only hard to understand but also hard to adapt. End user programmers need effective techniques and tools to support the creation of well-designed code, as well as the adaptation of poorly designed code. Perhaps this might involve providing approaches that help users to create code that can more easily be reused in a black box fashion. In other cases, it will be necessary to develop techniques and tools for analyzing, refactoring, combining, and debugging existing code.

End user code is not a simple thing, and helping end users to effectively reuse one another's code will require more than simply snapping together building blocks.

Acknowledgments

We thank the members of the EUSES Consortium for constructive discussions. This work was supported by the EUSES Consortium via NSF ITR-0325273, and by NSF grants CCF-0438929 and CCF-0613823. Opinions, findings, and recommendations are the authors' and not necessarily those of the sponsors.

Mashed layers and muddled models

22

Debugging mashup applications

M. Cameron Jones,[1] Elizabeth F. Churchill,[1] Les Nelson[2]

[1]Yahoo! Research
[2]PARC

ABSTRACT

Programming for the Web is a daunting task, especially when attempting to mash up multiple services and data sources. Many technologies advocated in this book approach this problem by attempting to hide the messiness of the Web from the developer. However, these efforts can complicate the process of debugging as data are passed through multiple transformations and sources of errors are obscured beneath additional layers of abstraction and processing. In this chapter we discuss the issues of debugging Web applications and Web mashups, and we explore how users of the Yahoo! Pipes programming environment turn to an online community for help-seeking and help-giving. We discuss the social and collaborative aspects of debugging in Web programming and argue that the complexity and heterogeneity of the Web requires a diversity of knowledge and experience beyond the grasp of any individual, and any effort to encourage or enhance the end user programming experience for the Web must embrace facilities for social and collaborative engagement.

INTRODUCTION

Debugging is an essential part of computer programming or coding. An article on Wikipedia defines computer programming to be "the process of writing, testing, debugging/troubleshooting, and maintaining the source code of computer programs" (Wikipedia, 2008). Estimates on the amount of time developers spend testing and debugging applications varies widely. Tassey reports that over half of development costs are spent on identifying and correcting defects, and between 10% and 35% of programming effort is spent debugging and correcting errors (Tassey, 2002). Ko and Myers, citing Tassey's report, claim that program understanding and debugging represent up to 70% of the time required to ship a software application (Ko & Myers, 2004). Beizer estimated that as much as 90% of all labor resources spent on software development are spent on testing (Beizer, 1990).

Despite the recognized importance of debugging in software development, it is only recently that researchers have studied debugging in the context of programming work done by nonexpert programmers. Studies of debugging in "end user programming" have primarily focused on individual programmers working in desktop application programming environments (e.g., spreadsheets (Kissinger et al., 2008)). Typically, end user debugging has been studied in experimental laboratory settings (e.g., Ko & Myers, 2004) versus workplace studies or more natural environments. However, debugging practice can also be observed on the Web in online communities of developers, spanning end users and expert programmers, and encompassing varying degrees of collaborative interaction from loosely connected independent developers using common tools, to more formal, collaborative, tightly knit open-source development teams. The artifacts being created and debugged by these "user–programmers" are themselves often accessible and interrogable online.

In this chapter we explore the relevant research on debugging and evaluate how debugging is complicated by the added complexities of Web programming. Furthermore, we discuss how solutions designed to mitigate the problems and complexities of Web mashup programming introduce new complexities to debugging. In one such environment, the Yahoo! Pipes visual language for Web mashup programming, a community of developers has emerged in which many debugging activities take place, through the sharing and collaborative editing of Pipes programs. The community can marshal diverse skills, knowledge, and expertise to debug a broken program, perhaps mitigating some of the complexities particular to Web mashup programming.

Classic models of debugging

In traditional models of software development, such as the waterfall and spiral models, testing and debugging software comprise discrete stages in the software development process. Alternative methods emphasize integrated and continuous testing and evaluation of software as it is being written; extreme programming, for example, advocates writing tests before the code is written. However, debugging in general can be treated and understood, much as it is described by Hailpern and Santhanam as "the process of ... analyzing and possibly extending (with debugging statements) the given program that does not meet the specification in order to find a new program that is close to the original and does satisfy the specifications" (Hailpern & Santhanam, 2002).

They go on to articulate the granularity of analysis required as the code being developed changes state from early development through finished product. In the early stages, debugging tends to be at the lowest code levels, such as stepping through individual code units one statement at a time to verify the immediate computational results. In the latter stages, larger portions of the system are being tested, resulting in increased complexity of debugging across many components and layers of the software.

Eisenstadt reports on 56 anecdotes for bug "war stories," primarily in C/C++ contexts, and codes these according to "why difficult," "how found," and "root cause." The majority of reported worst case bugs were attributed to remotes (in space or time) of the causes and symptoms of bugs and the lack of visibility in the debugging tools to see the bug (Eisenstadt, 1997).

Agans presents nine guidelines characterizing successful debugging across the range of software development kinds (Agans, 2003). Issues of particular relevance to working with mashups include:

- **Understand the system:** Know the entire system, including the reliance on external components and the interface complexities associated with invoking those components.
- **Make it fail:** The conditions needed to stimulate the failure are more complex. The remote nature of the invocation makes both the definition of initial conditions and recording of resulting actions more difficult.

- **Quit thinking and look:** Though observation of faults is essential to debugging, building in instrumentation is not an option for mashup sources.
- **Divide and conquer:** The boundary of the API defines the granularity of debugging. Once the bug is traced down the "rabbit hole" of a Web service, other techniques must come into play.

Law describes the tools and strategies involved in debugging. Issues of particular relevance to mashups are largely constrained by the API boundary (Law, 1997):

- Static debugging consisting of reviewing requirements, design, and code is subject to the visibility allowed by each of the source APIs.
- Run-time observation of the program behavior as a whole at run time is a primary tool in debugging mashups.
- Source code manipulation is limited to instrumenting at the API boundary.
- Dynamic debugging at a detailed level including breakpoints, single-stepping, and hardware traps is not an option for external sources.

Mental models

A mental model is an explanation of how something works, a translation of a system or phenomenon into a cognitive representation of how it works. While analogous to the original systems or phenomena they represent, models are often imperfect, yet they allow people to reason about complex systems, and make predictions that can be translated back to the original context (Craik, 1943). There is a long history of research into mental models and technology design, with a more or less strong commitment to the nature of the model itself or how it is used in human reasoning. The strong notion of a mental model is a fairly complete simulation of the workings of a process – for example a simulation of how a piece of code may transform input to produce output. The more often cited and weaker notion of a mental model is a loose ad hoc narrative explanation for how something might work – sufficient only to allow someone to interact with an interactive device, but not necessarily geared towards problem solving or fault finding and repair (Norman, 1988).

A slightly different take on debugging is the psychology of programming (PPIG) approach, which focuses on the ways in which people debug – that is, how human problem solving proceeds given the identification of an error to locate and rectify the bug. Many of these studies focus on the level of expertise with regard to programming, to the language being used, to the environment being programmed within, and to the level of complexity of the problem. Some work has been done on the impact of domain expertise on the specification and implementation of the program itself, but this is more seldom reported.

Much of the work on mental models and computer programming is fairly old, dating from the late 1970s through to the mid-1990s. In many instances the issues of mental models and training were perhaps offset by the development of better programming environments and debugging tools, and better help manuals. However, for understanding debugging in more ad hoc environments like the Web, we believe some of these approaches are still of interest.

Brooks formulated a cognitive model of how programmers understand code. The model is basically a top-down approach with development of an abstract overview of the domain and the purpose for the code by forming, testing, refining, and verifying hypotheses (Brooks, 1983). This kind of top-down approach stands in contrast to a more bottom-up approach like those recommended by Shneiderman and Mayer (1979) and Pennington (1987). These researchers consider it more likely that programmers group code into what they consider to be logical chunks by reading the code and formulating chunks into a higher-level picture of the overall architecture and its subcomponents. Pennington, more than Shneiderman and Mayer, focused on the flow of control and the sequence of events from the program. She proposes two models: first, the model of the program based on the control-flow abstraction, then a situation model based on the data-flow/functional abstraction of the program. An integrated meta-model was developed by von Mayrhauser and Vans (1995), who offer a mode combined approach. Programmers move between different models, as appropriate – top-down, situation, program, and knowledge base. The knowledge base is the programmer's current knowledge that is used to guide the models as well as store new knowledge.

THE CURRENT SITUATION: WEB DEVELOPMENT

The Web, specifically the Web browser, has been described as a "really hostile software engineering environment" (Douglas Crockford, http://video.yahoo.com/watch/111593/1710507). Developing applications for the Web and the modern Web browser presents unique challenges that stymie even the most skilled developer. User–programmers must navigate a complex ecosystem of heterogeneous formats, services, tools, protocols, standards, and languages, and somehow scrape together an application that presents a consistent experience across multiple platforms. The pains of Web development are perhaps most evident in the context of Web mashups, because these applications draw upon multiple sources of information and services, and necessarily must negotiate the incompatibilities arising from the integration of unlike components. Furthermore, there are numerous tools and services targeted at user–programmers that support mashup development.

Thus there are many sources of complexity, at least two to do with sourcing and one to do with production: (1) multiple sources of information and services, each with different protocols for access; (2) multiple standards for (and use of) language and format; and (3) many different tools for creating mashups. Although less frequently the case with the "modern" Web browser, it is still sometimes the case that the final production, as rendered by the browser itself, can also cause problems.

Mashups are largely ad hoc integrations for situational applications. In this they are akin to research prototypes, designed to quickly "cobble together" enough of a solution from existing resources to demonstrate novelty in capability and/or user experience. From experiences of research integrations, Nelson and Churchill (2006) report the diagnosing of errors through layers of external applications and operating system software. In this instance involving production of printed cards for a tangible interface for controlling Microsoft Powerpoint, the assumptions and limitations of Powerpoint, Microsoft Word, and the various print drivers were very much a factor involved in diagnosing problems in the new application.

Debugging of mashups instrinsically involves the space–time distance and visibility issues due to distributed and black box dependencies. And also as in the mashup situation, it falls to the end user to make the diagnosis and correct the problem through the many models of computation involved. Current Web development environments incorporate many layers of abstraction, and depend on many features that are black boxed – that is, an opaque abstraction that does not yield to inspection or interrogation. What differentiates Web development from other development contexts is that the black boxes and abstractions of the Web are neither uniform nor consistent, and often developers must employ complex articulations in order to align entities which operate at different levels of abstraction, or execute in different layers of the execution stack. For example, in the snippet shown in Figure 22.1, a PHP array reference ($item) is embedded in a line of JavaScript code (var asin...), which is in an HTML document, being generated by a PHP script. The PHP script is parsed and interpreted on the server, generating an HTML document as output. The HTML document, which contains dynamically written JavaScript, is passed to the client's browser, where it is executed locally.

```
<?php
...
?>
<html><head>
<script type="text/javascript">
var asin = "<?php echo $item['Asin']; ?>";
...
</script>
<?php
...
?>
```

FIGURE 22.1

Messy mashup code. The PHP code blocks have been highlighted.

Keeping track of when particular pieces of code are executed and in what context is difficult for professional developers, and even more so for end users. In Jones & Twidale (2006b) we learned that a major obstacle for novice programmers in building a mashup is maintaining an accurate mental representation of the process model and tracking when and where each code segment is executed. Expert developers will recognize the ugliness of the code in Figure 20.1, and suggest introducing additional layers of abstraction (e.g., using a Model-View-Controller pattern) as a means of managing the complexity. However, the addition of new layers of abstraction also adds more layers which must be learned, understood, and examined upon failure.

Another factor which confounds mashup development is the reliability of the underlying services and infrastructure on which an application is built. For example, one mashup application developed 2 years ago by one of the authors recently stopped working because the mapping service it used changed its API. Another mashup stopped working because the organization providing the service changed its name, and moved its servers to new domains, breaking the connection. It is seemingly a contradiction to have a "robust mashup application," because the developer has little to no control over the remote services and information sources being used. It is like building a house on sand; the ground is constantly shifting, making it difficult to make any long-term progress.

Debugging code like the example in Figure 22.1 is complex for all the reasons mentioned earlier, and many others. For the developer to "understand the system," as Agans states is necessary, the developer must have a working knowledge of PHP, HTML, and JavaScript, far more languages than typically employed in other software development contexts (Agans, 2003). Additionally, the developer needs to be familiar with the Amazon API and its particular interfaces, terminology, and data models. For example, knowing that the ASIN is the field needed, and that it is parsed and stored by the particular PHP library being used in the array under the case-sensitive key "Asin" are not self-evident facts. Knowing this particular system also requires knowledge of the execution environments, which include the PHP execution environment (e.g., Apache on a Linux server, with perhaps a customized PHP configuration), as well as the browser execution environment for the HTML/JavaScript side (e.g., Internet Explorer, Firefox, etc.). The diversity of pieces being assembled and used complicates efforts to "make it fail," because it is not always clear where errors are coming from, and thus it is not necessarily clear how to reproduce them. Not all sources and contexts are observable, or as observable as others. For example, the level of JavaScript error reporting and debugging support in Internet Explorer is far different from what is available in Firefox with extensions like Firebug, which can be even more frustrating, considering a bug may only be manifested in Internet Explorer. At a certain point the developer encounters barriers (like the browser barrier) that impede further investigation and debugging, making it impossible to "divide and conquer," because some units are indivisible.

Numerous user-level tools and programming environments have been developed that attempt to facilitate mashup development: Intel Mash Maker, Yahoo! Pipes, and Microsoft Popfly are some of the most widely known of these. These tools all seek to make mashup programming easier by handling many of the complexities surrounding the backend integration of multiple, heterogeneous data sources. Typically they implement a new layer of abstraction that is designed to provide a more homogeneous programming environment, making the programming task easier because the system is more consistent and knowable. We have been studying Yahoo! Pipes and the community of users who engage in discussions on the Yahoo! Pipes developer forums.

YAHOO! PIPES

Yahoo! Pipes is a Web-based visual programming language for constructing data mashups. Yahoo! Pipes was originally developed as a tool to make extracting, aggregating, and republishing data from across the Web easier. Since its launch in February 2007, over 90,000 developers have created individual pipes on the Yahoo! Pipes platform, and pipes are executed over 5,000,000 times each day. Figure 22.2 shows the Yahoo! Pipes editing environment; it consists of four main regions: a navigational bar across the top, the toolbox on the left, the work canvas in the center, and a debug-output panel at the bottom. The toolbox contains modules, the building blocks of the Yahoo! Pipes visual language.

Yahoo! Pipes' namesake is the Unix command-line pipe operator, which allows a user to string together a series of commands, where the output of one command is passed as input to the next. In the graphical language of Yahoo! Pipes, modules (operators) are laid out on a design canvas. Modules may have zero or more input ports, and all have at least one output port; additionally, modules may have parameters which can be set by the programmer, or themselves wired into the output of other modules so that the value of the parameter is dependent upon a run-time value specified elsewhere. The input and output ports are wired together, representing the flow of data through the application. Selecting an output port highlights all the compatible input ports to which the output may be connected.

There are a number of data types within Yahoo! Pipes that determine what inputs and outputs are compatible. In the most general terms, there are simple scalar data values and items, which are sets of data objects (e.g., items in an RSS feed, or nodes in an XML document). Values have types, including: text, URLs, locations, numbers, dates, and times.

In Yahoo! Pipes, data flows from the initial module(s), where user data are input or external data are retrieved, through subsequent modules in the pattern and order dictated by the wiring diagram. All applications in Yahoo! Pipes have a single output module, which is wired to the end of the execution sequence, and collects the final data stream for distribution via RSS, JSON (JavaScript Object

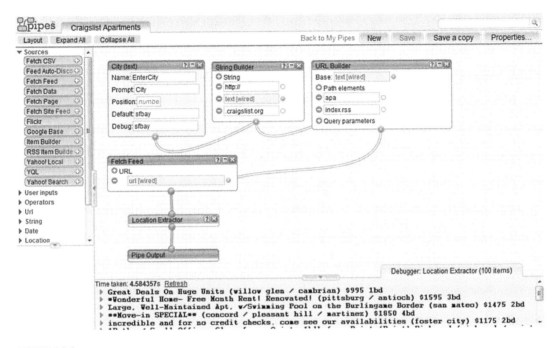

FIGURE 22.2

Yahoo! Pipes visual mashup editor.

Notation), or a variety of other formats. Drawing on the Unix command-line metaphor, the output module is akin to "standard out" or the user terminal.

Unlike the Unix command-line pipe, Yahoo! Pipes allows users to define complex branching and looping structures, have multiple sources and execution paths executing in parallel, and, in general, create programs of arbitrary complexity. There is no direct method for writing recursive functions, and Yahoo! Pipes does not allow for cycles in the program structure (i.e., where the output of a module is fed back to the input of a module further "upstream"). This enforces a more or less linear execution flow to the applications that is bounded by the amount of data being processed.

SOCIAL COLLABORATIVE DEBUGGING

The Web, though presenting many unique challenges for development, also offers some potential solutions in the form of large communities of programmers willing to engage in conversations about programming problems. These conversations not only service the original participants, but also become searchable archives which continue to support subsequent developers in programming and debugging. The conversations also provide rich evidence of users articulating their problems and translating their understanding across literacies, and mental and computational models.

Traditional models of debugging and empirical studies of debugging tend to focus on single coders, solving contrived single "bugs," in closed stable worlds. The Web and mashups therefore do not really map well to many of these models of how debugging takes place in practice, although the recommendations for systematic investigation hold.

A somewhat different programming situation that also requires the kind of development of a mental model of the code is that of understanding legacy code. Here, programmers need to understand the original programmer's thoughts, decisions, and the rationale behind the design of the legacy code. Burgos et al. studied programmers as they wrestled with the development of models of legacy code in organizations and came up with six main methods that programmers use: software documentation, skills databases (to find experts), knowledge databases (where project data like design documents and traceability matrices are stored and made available), person-to-person communication, source code (searching for key identifiers), and reverse engineering tools (Burgos, Ryan, & Murphee, 2007).

Obviously, source code is a primary resource in debugging an application. There are numerous tools and resources on the Web for sharing source code, and source code snippets; many of these tools have been designed explicitly to support sharing code for the purposes of debugging. One such tool, Pastebin (both an open-source software toolkit, and a Web service pastebin.com), describes itself as a "collaborative debugging tool." Pastebin allows user–programmers to paste source code (or any other text) into a Web form; the source code is then persisted for a user-specified time period on a server and given a unique URL. The URL can then be distributed to other people who can view the source code that was originally pasted and shared. In addition, other user–programmers can post corrections or amendments to the original snippet.

Services like Pastebin originated out of a need to establish a common context or focus around a particular segment or snippet of code. This is very hard to do in instant messaging, where messages are limited in length; in public IRC channels, pasted code would flood a channel with streams of text making it difficult, if not impossible, to have a conversation; and it is also difficult to manage in discussion forums, because the code gets entangled with the discussion thread. Additionally, making comments or revisions to the code in these contexts requires repeatedly copying and pasting the code into the conversation, making it difficult to read and effectively compare revisions.

Although Pastebin allows any arbitrary text to be posted, it is typically used for sharing source code snippets, console logs, and error logs. Other similar code sharing tools include services like gist.github.com, and pastie.org; and there are numerous services for sharing snippets that are not directly targeted at source code, including Thumbtack and Live Clipboard, both from Microsoft Live Labs, and Google Notebook. These services satisfy varying degrees of collaborative interaction, ranging from supporting awareness to facilitating collaborative coding. Jones and Twidale showed that shared copied text among collaborators can be used to infer activity and attention, which helps maintain awareness in collaborative environments (Jones & Twidale, 2006a). Some of these tools support annotation, allowing other people to comment on or suggest changes to the code; other tools support full collaborative editing, complete with access control and revision management (e.g., gist is a snippet sharing service on Github.com backed by a git version control repository).

The Yahoo! Pipes platform supports similar functionality to Pastebin, in that each pipe application is individually addressed by a unique ID and URL. Users may publish their pipes in the public directory, where they can be searched, browsed, and viewed by anyone. However, Yahoo! Pipes has a very open security model, allowing any user to view and run any pipe, so long as they know the URL, even if it is not published in the directory. This design was intentional, because the Yahoo! Pipes developers wanted to foster the kind of learning by example that Netscape's "View Source" feature facilitated for HTML. Thus, every pipe application that is created has a "View Source" button attached to it, allowing users to inspect how a pipe works. This allows users to not only share links to their in-progress and unpublished pipes, but also view and modify each other's pipes, allowing users to collaboratively debug problems.

When a pipe application is viewed by a user who is not the owner of the pipe, a local copy is made in the user's browser, and any changes that are made by the user are then saved to a new copy on the server, preserving the original pipe. Additionally, each pipe has a "clone" button, which allows a user to make a copy of an existing pipe (either their own or someone else's).

In addition to entire pipes being copiable and modifiable, pipes can be embedded within one another as a "sub-pipe." This allows developers to create and share reusable components, and generate intermediate levels of abstraction in their applications. An embedded sub-pipe is represented as a module in the Yahoo! Pipes interface, which can be wired to other modules, or other sub-pipes. Users can drill down into embedded sub-pipes, to inspect and modify the included functionality.

Yahoo! Pipes provides discussion forums for users to talk, ask questions, interact with each other and the Pipes development team, and give and receive help. The Yahoo! Pipes discussion boards (http://discuss.pipes.yahoo.com/) have been active since Pipes was launched in February 2007. The forums have been a significant source of information on programming in Pipes, because there is not much documentation for the language, merely some tutorials and annotations. We have studied monthly snapshots of the Pipes discussion forums sampled from the past 2 years, the most recent snapshot ending 1 December 2008.

The discussions in the Pipes forums are divided into three areas: developer help, general discussion, and a section for showing off Pipes applications. Table 22.1 provides some general statistics about the activity of the forums at the most recent snapshot (December 2008). Most of the activity on the Pipes discussion forums is in question–answer interactions in the developer help forum. The majority of posts receive replies of some kind. However, just over one fourth (25.9%) of posts never receive a response, and that proportion falls to 20% when we consider just the help forum, where most of the debugging conversations occur.

Most user–programmers do not participate in the discussion forums. Of the over 90,000 user–programmers who have authored a pipe application, only 2081 have posted a message to one of the forums. Nearly all (1725) of them participate in the forums for a month or less. Figure 22.3 shows the distribution of participant engagement in the Pipes discussion forums. There is a high degree of transiency in the community as people come, engage for short periods of time, and leave.

Table 22.1 Statistics of the Pipes Developer Forums from December 2008.

Pipes forums activity data	Developer help	General discussion	Show off your pipe
Number of threads	1731	576	241
Number of posts without replies	347	165	149
Avg. thread length	3.65	2.89	1.07
Std. dev. of thread length	4.22	3.48	1.53
Number of participants	1523	638	236
Avg. num. participants per thread	2.34	2.14	1.34
Std. dev. of num. participants	2.13	2.06	0.69

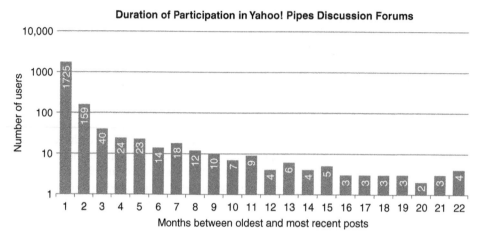

FIGURE 22.3

The distribution of how long user–programmers have participated in discussions in the Yahoo! Pipes forums. Most user–programmers only participate for a short time.

The community and social structure that emerges from the interactions in the Pipes forums is characterized by several strong hubs, individuals who actively seek to engage newcomers and answer questions. These hubs include members of the Pipes development team as well as peer user–pro-grammers from the community. There are, however, relatively few hubs, and the majority of participants in the discussions are connected to very few other individuals: 16% (336) participants are not connected to anyone else; 63% (1311) participants are connected to 5 or fewer other individuals; 12 participants are connected to 100 or more others in the network, with 1 participant having over 1000 connections. The social network of interaction, measured by mutual participation in a thread on the forum, is depicted in Figure 22.4. In this network, nodes represent participants, and edges represent a social tie between two participants if they have participated in a common thread; the relationship is unweighted (i.e., binary).

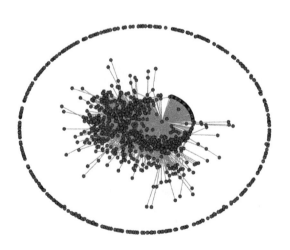

FIGURE 22.4

The social network of the Yahoo! Pipes discussion forums. There is a clear separation between a connected core and a periphery of isolated individuals and small cliques.

The social network depicted in Figure 22.4 highlights several features of the Pipes community. Although the elliptical shape and egg yolk appearance of this network visualization is primarily a visual artifact of the algorithm used to render it, there are nonetheless mean-ingful structures in the graph that reflect the structure and dynamics of the community. One of the most striking visual structures is the clear separation between a connected core and a periphery of isolated individuals and cliques. Within the core of the interconnected individuals, there are observable valences of engagement (i.e., more connected individuals are closer to the center), and several social hubs can be readily seen. The fan-shape arrangement in the lower right quadrant of the center is anchored by an indi-vidual with over 1000 connections. This participant is engaging in a large amount of question answering, acting as the sole respondent to many newcomers who tend to leave the forums after getting the answer they came for.

In the periphery of the network are individuals who have no social ties to other members of the community, and isolated cliques, or small groups of dyads and triads who interact with each other exclusively. The emergence of this structure within the community is intriguing. Why do some ques-tions get answered and others do not? How do people move from the periphery to the core? How do user–programmers engage with communities over time? Figure 22.5 shows the growth of the com-munity in monthly intervals over the 22 months during which the forums have been active, broken down into the number of disconnected individuals, connected individuals, and individuals who were newly connected in the period sampled (both new to the community, and existing members who were previously disconnected).

The growth depicted in Figure 22.5 shows a relatively linear growth in the size of the network as a whole, and both subsets of connected and disconnected individuals track a similar trajectory of linear growth. This could be interpreted as evidence that the community is adequately responding

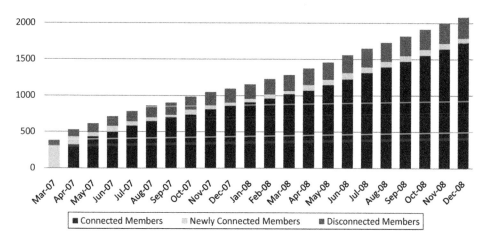

FIGURE 22.5

The growth of the Pipes discussion forums community from 7 February 2007 to 1 December 2008, illustrating the relative growth in the numbers of connected and disconnected individuals.

to new posts and questions asked by new members, otherwise we would expect to see the size of the disconnected region growing faster than that of the connected region. In order to better illustrate the detailed dynamics and interactions around debugging in the Pipes community, we present several examples and snippets of conversations, selected from the forums. We focus on conversations involving more than one participant which illuminate the interactions developers have around software debugging and collaborative problem solving.

Worked examples of social debugging from Yahoo Pipes

Tools like Yahoo! Pipes layer on additional abstractions and metaphors in the Web development context that can make building mashups faster and easier. However, these additional layers introduce new black boxes into the Web development ecosystem that can interfere with a user's prior understanding of how things work, and like the findings of Churchill and Nelson, can complicate debugging activities by obscuring the sources of errors (Churchill & Nelson, 2002). In this section we present two conversations taken from the Yahoo! Pipes discussion forums. These conversations are rich examples of how complex debugging conversations can be. They are not intended to be typical or representative; they highlight how debugging issues have not been alleviated in the Pipes programming context, and have in fact become more complicated.

In the following conversation, a user describes the problem he is having viewing the output of a Pipe application. He initially assumes the problem he is experiencing has to do with the application he composed in Yahoo! Pipes.

In the exchange between Paul and Roger, we can see the progressive peeling away of layers of abstraction and execution. Paul begins with the assumption that there is a problem in his pipe application, that he has caused an error. Roger replies, stating that the pipe appears to work for him and does not exhibit the problematic behavior Paul is reporting. He offers the suggestion that the problem may be in the caching behavior of the Yahoo! Pipes platform. Paul responds that he thinks it might be a problem of the Google Reader RSS viewer application, and not a problem with his pipe or the Yahoo! Pipes cache. After several more exchanges, Roger asserts that the problem likely is being caused by an incompatible browser or operating system setting.

In this example, we can see that the potential sources of the errors are far more numerous than typically considered in debugging. Typically, when a program does not work as expected, the programmer assumes there is a problem in his or her code, trusting that the underlying compiler or interpreter, operating system, networking stack, etc., are working properly. Rarely would we expect an error in program execution to be caused by a bug in the underlying operating system, for example. However, in Yahoo! Pipes, the underlying infrastructure for interpreting and executing the pipe application may itself have bugs; or the browser or other application in which the pipe is being executed, or the output is being rendered, may be incompatible with certain aspects of the Yahoo! Pipes system or data formatting; or there may be a problem with improperly formatted data being fed into the pipe; or there may be some other problem further upstream in one of the data sources. Many of these problems are outside the user's control, making them nearly impossible to resolve. Evident in the conversation is a style of divide and conquer method of bug localization, where numerous possibilities and permutations are tested; however, the developers are essentially guessing at what the cause may be, because there are certain aspects of the bug that are not inspectable. In the example given in Figure 22.6, the Pipes platform cannot be inspected, nor can the Google Reader Web

Paul

I have created an images-only RSS feed that basically grabs images such as these:
http://www.vrindavandarshan.com/yr2008/a. . .
The problem is the images are not showing up in-line as "content", rather you have to click through to actually see them. This makes the RSS feed rather useless for displaying inside other modules or devices.
Could someone look at my pipe and let me know what I am doing wrong? All I want is for the output of the RSS feed to simply contain the 3 images of the day. Here's the pipe as far as I have gotten it: http://pipes. yahoo.com/pipes/pipe.info?_. . .

Roger

When I looked at your RSS feed - http://pipes.yahoo.com/pipes/pipe.run?_i. . . - the images were displayed. Are you still not seeing the images? If so you will need to supply more details about how you are viewing the RSS feed. It may be that you are experiencing caching issues that should not last more than about 30 minutes.

Paul

I'm trying to use Google Reader, which does not seem to show a "preview" image in-line. I have to click through to each image to see it. Maybe this is just a Google Reader thing, but I have other feeds (e.g., Dilbert Web comic) that show the image right on the page.

Roger

When using "Expanded view" in Google Reader both the Dilbert feed and your feed show images without any need for clicking. At least, that's what I'm seeing. I can't see any "preview" images for either feed in either List or Expanded view.

Paul

This is very strange, because the feed will not work for me unless I manually load the images by typing the image URL directly into the address bar first. After I do this, the image seems to "preload" and then the RSS feed works fine. If I don't do this I get a 403 forbidden error from the site. Is there some standard template that can be used for creating an RSS feed that is simply a group of images?

Roger

I think we are in the realm of browser/operating system/security settings differences.
All I can say is that the feed works for me in Google Reader using FF3 and W2K.
You may be able to find more help from the Google Reader Help group.
http://groups.google.com/group/Google-Re. . .

FIGURE 22.6

An exchange between two Pipes developers (user names have been anonymized) where they are attempting to localize the source of a bug, peeling off the layers of the Web programming stack.

application. Some browser and operating system settings and execution may be inspected, but it is difficult to compare the settings of one user to another as there are many possibilities that may be causing the problem. Users may also have no control (or awareness of) security and firewall settings that may be perturbing the execution and data flow.

Over the course of the discussion, the source of the error shifts, touching on nearly every layer of the programming stack, and in the end, the user is no closer to solving the problem than he was at the beginning. In highly abstracted programming contexts like that of Web mashup programming, the number of possible sources that must be examined increases, which presents challenges for user–programmers in knowing the system completely, making it fail, and observing and reproducing bugs. Though this problem may be particularly salient in Yahoo! Pipes context, given the additional layers introduced by the visual language, we believe these problems to be inherent in mashup programming in general. Web mashups are necessarily embedded in a web of interdependent services, platforms, and data objects, many of which are not as robust or verified as modern compilers or the underlying operating system stack. While Web mashups are often discussed in the context of the Web as an operating system, the reality is that the Web is not as stable or robust as a standard desktop operating system. It is often the case that services have bugs or fail, network connections are not reliable, and data are not properly formatted (often because the standards are underspecified). Jones, Churchill, and Twidale (2008) framed these challenges within the cognitive dimensions framework. They argue that the existing cognitive dimensions do not account for the additional complexity and challenges imposed by the open, heterogeneous nature of the mashup ecosystem, and point to the affordances development tools, like Pipes, have for sharing and collaborative debugging as a possible mechanism for cognitive offloading, and effective resolution to complex problems.

Other bugs stem exclusively from problems with the visual language of Pipes itself, and have little to do with the mashups more generally. Figure 22.7 contains a snippet of conversation where several user–programmers are reporting problems with the drag-and-drop interaction in the Yahoo! Pipes interface. These user–programmers are reporting problems dropping modules into a loop operator module.

In the above example, the "bug" that is being fixed is not necessarily technical, but rather is a "bug" in the mental models being formulated. Their conversational interactions illustrate not only the bugs in Freddy and Pete's models of how Pipes works, but also in Harry and Don's (both of whom know how Pipes works because they built it) models of what the problem is and their understanding of the models that user–programmers have of Pipes. There emerges a sense that the problem is perhaps in the browser and operating system configuration, that the user–programmers experiencing the problem are using an unsupported or untested system. There was even a section of the conversation pertaining to stylesheet errors as a possible cause of the problem.

The exploration of the numerous possible sources and their entailments highlights how complex and interdependent the ecosystem is. Even when powerful robust tools for authoring exist that seek to facilitate development by substituting relatively homogenous abstractions for the mixed, ad hoc, and/or conflicting ones the user–programmer would have to address otherwise, the user–programmer is only one veneer away from the messy and ugly issues, raising questions about how much can be taken for granted, and how much knowledge is needed to effectively author applications in environments like Yahoo! Pipes. Similar to how a Windows programmer works with abstractions like the file system without much need to know the internals of how it works, can the Web reach a point where user–programmers do not need intimate knowledge of all the component parts in order to effectively author applications?

Pete

Am I just missing something very basic here, but how do I drop a source module onto the For Each: Replace operator? No matter what I try, the boxes will not merge like in the examples.

So to be clear I am trying to drop a Flickr source that I am trying to drop (merge) with a For Each: Replace operator.

I am using Firefox 2.0.

Freddy

I want to chime in. I'm having problems getting the For Each operators to work. After I create a For Each: Replace I cannot drop anything onto it. I try Flickr or Fetch and they simply lie over it.

This is both FF 1.5.0.9 and Safari 2.0.4 on Mac (Intel). Any help with this would be greatly appreciated.

Seven additional posts in which developers document different browser and operating system configurations have been omitted.

Harry [a Yahoo! employee]

The browsers mentioned, in particular FF and IE7, should have no problems with this. We'll look into what's causing it. It doesn't seem to always crop up. I know it's not ideal but sometimes even when it doesn't work for an existing Pipe, a new one will still work.

To help us figure it out, feel free to post Pipe URLs where you're seeing this issue or talk about the steps leading up to it. Thanks!

Freddy

I've tried on FF on a few platforms, no go for me... I've created new ones, restarted the browser, restarted the machine. :)

It doesn't work in any pipe I use, but here's one:

http://pipes.yahoo.com/pipes/knwB40642xG...

Two posts about style sheet errors have been omitted.

Don [a Yahoo! employee]

We're still looking into this - but having trouble reproducing it (I'm sure you are all seeing it though).

One thing that occurred to me that isn't as obvious as it should be, is that you can't drag modules that are on the canvas INTO the For Each - you can only drag them from the "mi pipes" or "sources" toolbox/library on the left (or the search results from the top right). Is that one of the problems here?

Freddy

Oops. Yes that was the problem. I didn't even realize that you could drag off the left nav - I was just clicking them and having the modules show up on the canvas.

FIGURE 22.7

Excerpts from a thread relating to some confusion about the drag-and-drop functionality in the Yahoo! Pipes visual editor. All user names have been anonymized.

CONCLUSIONS

In this chapter we have described the social and collaborative practices of debugging among user–programmers in the Yahoo! Pipes community. The highly abstract and layered architectures of Web programming present numerous challenges to user–programmers. They can obscure the source of problems, complicating the challenge of localizing the source of a bug; and the abstractions they add can not only introduce new bugs, but also conflict with established understandings and lead to wasted effort chasing red herrings in the debugging process.

Similar to how Eric Raymond described debugging in open source, "given enough eyeballs, all bugs are shallow," a community of developers can localize bugs much more quickly. Through social and collaborative debugging, developers working in orchestration can marshal more diverse resources to debug a problem. Although each individual is only able to understand a portion of the system, the multiple, overlapping knowledge, skills, resources, and expertise of many individuals can provide a more complete view of the entire system. This may involve the application of multiple users' prior knowledge or expertise, but could also involve users testing more possible configurations and options than a single developer is able to do alone (e.g., testing multiple operating system, browser, and application configurations). This can increase the speed with which developers are able to make applications fail, eliminating possibilities more quickly, and deducing the source of bugs more quickly.

We close this chapter with several questions about the future of end user programming for the World Wide Web. Do authoring tools like Yahoo! Pipes actually support true "end users"? How much knowledge of the underlying infrastructure, protocols, and technologies is needed to get started? To be proficient or expert? Do mashup authoring tools allow users to express themselves easily and intuitively? How exportable is knowledge from one environment to another? How do we encourage deep learning in abstracted environments? Do these tools impose models that conflict with the underlying data or technology? Or conflict with users' prior knowledge or understanding?

How the Web helps people turn ideas into code

23

Joel Brandt,[1,2] **Philip J. Guo,**[1] **Joel Lewenstein,**[1] **Mira Dontcheva,**[2] **Scott R. Klemmer**[1]

[1]*Stanford University*
[2]*Adobe Systems, Inc.*

ABSTRACT

This chapter investigates the role of online resources in building software. We look specifically at how programmers – an exemplar form of knowledge workers – opportunistically interleave Web foraging, learning, and writing code. To understand this, we have both studied how programmers work in the lab and analyzed Web search logs of programming resources. The lab provides rich, detailed information and context about how programmers work; online studies offer a naturalistic setting and the advantages of scale. We found that programmers engage in *just-in-time learning* of new skills and approaches, *clarify and extend* their existing knowledge, and *remind* themselves of details deemed not worth remembering. The results also suggest that queries for different purposes have different styles and durations. These results contribute to a theory of online resource usage in programming, and suggest opportunities for tools to facilitate online knowledge work.

INTRODUCTION

"Good grief, I don't even remember the syntax for forms!" Less than a minute later, this participant in our Web programming lab study had found an example of an HTML form online, successfully integrated it into her own code, adapted it for her needs, and moved on to a new task. As she continued to work, she frequently interleaved foraging for information on the Web, learning from that information, and authoring code. Over the course of 2 hours, she used the Web 27 times, accounting for 28% of the total time she spent building her application. This participant's behavior is illustrative of programmers' increasing use of the Web as a problem-solving tool. How and why do people leverage online resources while programming?

Web use is integral to an *opportunistic* approach to programming that emphasizes speed and ease of development over code robustness and maintainability (Brandt et al., 2009a; Hartmann, Doorley, & Klemmer, 2008). Programmers do this to *prototype, ideate, and discover* – to address questions best answered by creating a piece of functional software. This type of programming is widespread, performed by novices and experts alike: it happens when designers build functional prototypes to explore ideas (Myers et al., 2008), when scientists write code to control laboratory experiments, when entrepreneurs assemble complex spreadsheets to better understand how their business is operating, and when professionals adopt agile development methods to build applications quickly (Martin, 2002). Scaffidi, Shaw, and Myers (2005) estimate that by the year 2012 there will be 13 million people in the United States who call themselves "programmers." This estimate is over four times larger than the Bureau of Labor Statistics' estimate of 3 million "professional programmers" (Scaffidi, Shaw, & Myers, 2005). This discrepancy is indicative of the trend that programming is becoming an essential part of many other professions, and that an increasing number of individuals are engaging in programming without formal training. We believe there is significant value in understanding and designing for this large population of amateur programmers.

To create software more quickly, people – especially amateurs – often tailor or "mash up" existing systems (see Chapters 8–11, and also MacLean et al., 1990; Lieberman, Paternò, & Wulf, 2006). As part of this process, they often search the Web for suitable components and learn new skills (Hoffmann, Fogarty, & Weld, 2007). How do people currently use the Web to program, and what are high impact opportunities for tools to support and improve this practice? To help readers get as much as possible out of this chapter, we'll start with conclusions and then explain the studies that led to them. Through our studies, we have uncovered five key insights about how programmers use online resources.

FIVE KEY INSIGHTS

Programmers use Web tutorials for just-in-time learning, gaining high-level conceptual knowledge when they need it. Tools may valuably encourage this practice by tightly coupling tutorial browsing and code authoring. One system that explores this direction is d.mix (described in Chapter 10), which allows users to "sample" a Web site's interface elements, yielding the API calls necessary to create them. This code can then be modified inside a hosted sandbox.

Web search often serves as a "translator" when programmers don't know the exact terminology or syntax. Using the Web, programmers can adapt existing knowledge by making analogies with programming languages, libraries, and frameworks that they know well. The Web further allows programmers to make sense of cryptic errors and debugging messages. Future tools could proactively search the Web for the errors that occur during execution, compare code from search results to the user's own code, and automatically locate possible sources of errors.

Programmers deliberately choose not to remember complicated syntax. Instead, they use the Web as external memory that can be accessed as needed. This suggests that Web search should be integrated into the code editor in much the same way as identifier completion (e.g., Microsoft's IntelliSense and Eclipse's Code Assist). *Blueprint* is a system that is beginning to explore this direction (Brandt et al., 2010). Blueprint brings the task of searching for example code into the development environment. This integration allows Blueprint to leverage code context to return better search results, which ultimately helps programmers write better code more quickly. Another possible approach is to build upon ideas like keyword programming (Little & Miller, 2006) to create authoring environments that allow the programmer to type "sloppy" commands that are automatically transformed into syntactically correct code using Web search.

Programmers often delay testing code copied from the Web, especially when copying routine functionality. As a result, bugs introduced when adapting copied code are often difficult to find. Tools could assist in the code adaptation process by, for example, highlighting all variable names and literals in any pasted code. Tools could also clearly demarcate regions of code that were copied from the Web and provide links back to the original source.

Programmers are good at refining their queries, but need to do it rarely. Query refinement is most necessary when users are trying to adapt their existing knowledge to new programming languages, frameworks, or situations. This underscores the value of keeping users in the loop when building tools that search the Web automatically or semiautomatically. In other cases, however, query refinements could be avoided by building tools that automatically augment programmers' queries with contextual information, such as the programming language, frameworks or libraries in the project, or the types of variables in scope.

STUDY 1: OPPORTUNISTIC PROGRAMMING IN THE LAB

We conducted an exploratory study in our lab to understand how programmers leverage online resources, especially for rapid prototyping.

Method

The participants' task was to prototype a Web chat room application using HTML, PHP, and Java-Script. They were given a working execution environment (Apache, MySQL, and a PHP interpreter), and were asked to implement five specific features (see sidebar). Four of the features were fairly typical, but the fifth (retaining a limited chat history) was more unusual. We introduced this feature so that participants would have to do some programming, even if they implemented other features by downloading an existing chat room application (three participants did this). We instructed participants to think of the task as a hobby project, not as a school or work assignment. Participants were not given any additional guidance or constraints. An experimenter asked open-ended questions to encourage think-aloud reflection, and all participants were recorded with audio and video screen capture.

Chat room features that lab study participants were asked to implement:
1. Users should be able to set their username on the chat room page (application does not need to support account management).
2. Users should be able to post messages.
3. The message list should update automatically without a complete page reload.
4. Each message should be shown with the username of the poster and a timestamp.
5. When users first open a page, they should see the last 10 messages sent in the chat room, and when the chat room updates, only the last 10 messages should be seen.

Twenty Stanford University students participated in a 2.5-hour session. The participants had an average of 8.3 years of programming experience, but little *professional* experience (only one spent more than 1 year as a professional developer). Thirteen participants rated themselves as novices in at least one of the technologies involved. For a more thorough description of the method, see (Brandt et al., 2009b).

Results

On average, participants spent 19% of their programming time on the Web in 18 distinct sessions (see Figure 23.1). Web session length resembles a power-law distribution (see Figure 23.2). The shortest half (those less than 47 seconds) compose only 14% of the total time; the longest 10% compose 41% of the total time. This suggests that *individuals are leveraging the Web to accomplish several different kinds of activities*. Web usage also varied considerably between participants: the most active Web user spent an order of magnitude more time online than the least active user.

Intentions behind Web use

Why do programmers go to the Web? At the long end of the spectrum, participants spent tens of minutes *learning* a new concept (e.g., by reading a tutorial on AJAX-style programming). On the short end, participants delegated their memory to the Web, spending tens of seconds to *remind* themselves of syntactic details of a concept they knew well (e.g., by looking up the structure of a *foreach* loop). In between these two extremes, participants used the Web to *clarify* their existing knowledge (e.g., by viewing the source of an HTML form to understand the underlying structure). This section presents typical behaviors, anecdotes, and theoretical explanations for these three styles of online resource usage (see Table 23.1 for a summary).

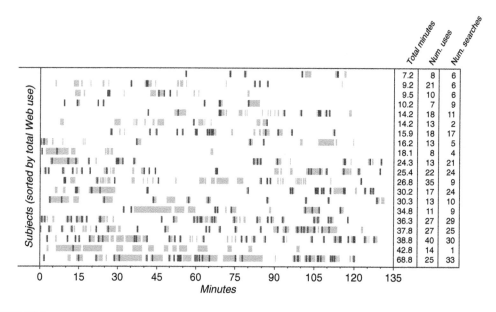

FIGURE 23.1

Overview of when participants referenced the Web during the laboratory study. Subjects are sorted by total amount of time spent using the Web. Web use sessions are shown in light gray, and instances of Web search are shown as dark bars.

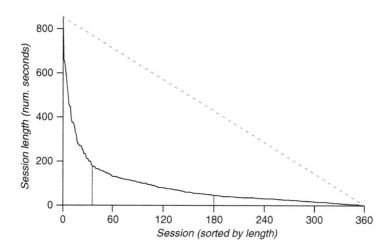

FIGURE 23.2

All 360 Web use sessions among the 20 participants in our lab study, sorted and plotted by decreasing length (in seconds). The left vertical bar represents the cutoff separating the 10% longest sessions, and the right bar the cutoff for 50% of sessions. The dotted line represents a hypothetical uniform distribution of session lengths.

Table 23.1 Summary of Characteristics of Three Points on the Spectrum of Web Use Intention.

Web session intention:	Learning	Clarification	Reminder
Reason for using Web	Just-in-time learning of unfamiliar concepts	Connect high-level knowledge to implementation details	Substitute for memorization (e.g., language syntax or function usage lookup)
Web session length	Tens of minutes	~ 1 minute	< 1 minute
Starts with Web search?	Almost always	Often	Sometimes
Search terms	Natural language related to high-level task	Mix of natural language and code. cross-language analogies	Mostly code (e.g., function names, language keywords)
Example search	"ajax tutorial"	"javascript timer"	"mysql_fetch_array"
Num. result clicks	Usually several	Fewer	Usually zero or one
Num. query refinements	Usually several	Fewer	Usually zero
Types of Web pages visited	Tutorials, how-to articles	API documentation, blog posts, articles	API documentation, result snippets on search page
Amount of code copied from Web	Dozens of lines (e.g., from tutorial snippets)	Several lines	Varies
Immediately test copied code?	Yes	Not usually, often trust snippets	Varies

Just-in-time learning

Participants routinely stated that they were using the Web to *learn* about unfamiliar technologies. These Web sessions typically started with searches used to locate tutorial Web sites. After selecting a tutorial, participants frequently used its source code for learning-by-doing.

Searching for tutorials. Participants' queries usually contained a natural language description of a problem they were facing, often augmented with several keywords specifying technology they planned to use (e.g., "php" or "javascript"). For example, one participant unfamiliar with the AJAX paradigm performed the query "update web page without reloading php". Query refinements were common for this type of Web use, often before the user clicked on any results. These refinements were usually driven by familiar terms seen on the query result page: In the previous example, the participant refined the query to "ajax update php".

Selecting a tutorial. Participants typically clicked several query result links, opening each in a new Web browser tab before evaluating the quality of any of them. After several pages were opened, participants would judge their quality by rapidly skimming. In particular, several participants reported using cosmetic features – such as prevalence of advertising on the Web page or whether code on the page was syntax-highlighted – to evaluate the quality of potential Web sites. When we asked one participant how she decided what Web pages are trustworthy, she explained, "I don't want [the Web page] to say 'free scripts!' or 'get your chat room now!' or stuff like that. I don't want that because I think it's gonna be bad, and most developers don't write like that. . .they don't use that kind of language." This assessing behavior is consistent with information scent theory, in that users decide which Web pages to explore by evaluating their surface-level features (Pirolli, 2007).

Using the tutorial. Once a participant found a tutorial that he believed would be useful, he would often immediately begin experimenting with its code samples (even before reading the prose). We believe this is because tutorials typically contain a great deal of prose, which is time-consuming to read and understand. Subject 10 said, "I think it's less expensive for me to just take the first [code I find] and see how helpful it is at. . .a very high level. . .as opposed to just reading all these descriptions and text."

Participants often began adapting code before completely understanding how it worked. One participant explained, "there's some stuff in [this code] that I don't really know what it's doing, but I'll just try it and see what happens." He copied four lines into his project, immediately removed two of the four, changed variable names and values, and tested. The entire interaction took 90 seconds. This learning-by-doing approach has one of two outcomes: It either leads to deeper understanding, mitigating the need to read the tutorial's prose, or it isolates challenging areas of the code, guiding a more focused reading of the tutorial's prose.

For programmers, what is the cognitive benefit of experimentation over reading? Results from cognitive modeling may shed light on this. Cox and Young developed two ACT-R models to simulate a human learning the interface for a central heating unit (Cox & Young, 2000). The first model was given "'how-to-do-the-task' instructions" and was able to carry out only those specific tasks from start to finish. The second model was given "'how-the-device-works' instructions," (essentially a better mapping of desired states of the device to actions performed) and afterwards could thus complete a task from any starting point. Placing example code into one's project amounts to picking up a task "in the middle." We suggest that when participants experiment with code, it is precisely to learn these action/state mappings.

Approximately one third of the code in participants' projects was physically copied and pasted from the Web. This code came from many sources: whereas a participant may have copied a hundred lines of code altogether, he did so ten lines at a time. This approach of programming by example modification is consistent with the Yeh et al. study of students learning to use a Java toolkit (Yeh, Paepcke, & Klemmer, 2008).

Clarification of existing knowledge

There were many cases where participants had a high-level understanding of how to implement functionality, but did not know how to implement it in the specific programming language. They needed a piece of *clarifying* information to help map their schema to the particular situation. The introduction presented an example of this behavior: The participant had a general understanding of HTML forms, but did not know all of the required syntax. These *clarifying* activities are distinct from *learning* activities, because participants can easily recognize and adapt the necessary code once they find it. Because of this, *clarifying* uses of the Web are shorter than *learning* uses.

Searching with synonyms. Participants often used Web search when they were unsure of exact terms. We observed that search works well for this task because synonyms of the correct programming terms often appear in online forums and blogs. For example, one participant used a JavaScript library that he had used in the past but "not very often," to implement the AJAX portion of the task. He knew that AJAX worked by making requests to other pages, but he forgot the exact mechanism for accomplishing this in his chosen library (named *Prototype*). He searched for "prototype request". The researchers asked, "Is 'request' the thing that you know you're looking for, the actual method call?" He replied, "No. I just know that it's probably similar to that."

Clarification queries contained more programming language–specific terms than *learning* queries. Often, however, these terms were not from the correct programming language! Participants often made language analogies: For example, one participant said "Perl has [a function to format dates as strings], so PHP must as well." Similarly, several participants searched for "javascript thread". Though JavaScript does not explicitly contain threads, it supports similar functionality through interval timers and callbacks. All participants who performed this search quickly arrived at an online forum or blog posting that pointed them to the correct function for setting periodic timers: *setInterval*.

Testing copied code (or not). When participants copied code from the Web during *clarification* uses, it was often not immediately tested. Participants typically trusted code found on the Web, and indeed, it was typically correct. However, they would often make minor mistakes when adapting the code to their needs (e.g., forgetting to change all instances of a local variable name). Because they believed the code correct, they would then work on other functionality before testing. When they finally tested and encountered bugs, they would often erroneously assume that the error was in recently written code, making such bugs more difficult to track down.

Using the Web to debug. Participants also used the Web for clarification *during* debugging. Often, when a participant encountered a cryptic error message, he would immediately search for that exact error on the Web. For example, one participant received an error that read, "XML Filtering Predicate Operator Called on Incompatible Functions." He mumbled, "What does that mean?" then followed the error alert to a line that contained code previously copied from the Web. The code did not help him understand the meaning of the error, so he searched for the full text of the error. The first site he visited was a message board with a line saying, "This is what you have:", followed by the code in question and another line saying, "This is what you should have:", followed by a corrected line of code. With this information, the participant returned to his code and successfully fixed the bug without ever fully understanding the cause.

Reminders about forgotten details

Even when participants were familiar with a concept, they often did not remember low-level syntactic details. For example, one participant was adept at writing SQL queries, but unsure of the correct placement of a *limit* clause. Immediately after typing "ORDER BY respTime", he went online and searched for "mysql order by". He clicked on the second link, scrolled halfway down the page, and read a few lines. Within ten seconds he had switched back to his code and added "LIMIT 10" to the end of his query. In short, when participants used the Web for *reminding* about details, they knew *exactly* what information they were looking for, and often knew *exactly* on which page they intended to find it (e.g., official API documentation).

Searching for reminders (or not). When participants used the Web for learning and clarification, they almost always began by performing a Web search and then proceeded to view one or more results. In the case of reminders, sometimes participants would perform a search and view only the search result snippets without viewing any of the results pages. For example, when one participant forgot a word in a long function name, a Web search allowed him to quickly confirm the exact name of the function simply by browsing the snippets in the results page. Other times, participants would view a page without searching at all. This is because participants often kept select Web sites (such as official language documentation) open in browser tabs to use for reminders when necessary.

The Web as an external memory aid. Several participants reported using the Web as an alternative to memorizing routinely used snippets of code. One participant browsed to a page within PHP's official documentation that contained six lines of code necessary to connect and disconnect from a MySQL database. After he copied this code, a researcher asked him if he had copied it before. He responded, "[yes,] hundreds of times," and went on to say that he never bothered to learn it because he "knew it would always be there." We believe that in this way, programmers can effectively distribute their cognition (Hollan, Hutchins, & Kirsh, 2000), allowing them to devote more mental energy to higher-level tasks.

STUDY 2: WEB SEARCH LOG ANALYSIS

Do query styles in the real world robustly vary with intent, or is this result an artifact of the particular lab setting (Carter et al., 2008; Grimes, Tang, & Russell, 2007)? To investigate this, we analyzed Web query logs from 24,293 programmers making 101,289 queries about the Adobe Flex Web application development framework in July 2008. These queries came from the *Community Search* portal on Adobe's Developer Network Web site. This portal indexes documentation, articles, blogs, and forums by Adobe and vetted third-party sources.

To cross-check the lab study against this real-world data set, we began this analysis by evaluating four hypotheses derived from those findings:

H1: *Learning* sessions begin with natural language queries more often than *reminding* sessions.

H2: Users more frequently refine queries without first viewing results when *learning* than when *reminding*.

H3: Programmers are more likely to visit official API documentation in *reminding* sessions.

H4: The majority of *reminding* sessions start with code-only queries. Additionally, code-only queries are least likely to be refined and contain the fewest number of result clicks.

Method

We analyzed the data in three steps. First, we used IP addresses (24,293 unique IPs) and time stamps to group queries (101,289 total) into sessions (69,955 total). A session was defined as a sequence of query and result-click events from the same IP address with no gaps longer than 6 minutes. This definition is common in query log analysis (e.g., Silverstein et al., 1999).

Second, we selected 300 of these sessions and analyzed them manually. We found it valuable to examine all of a user's queries, because doing so provided more contextual information. We used unique IP addresses as a proxy for users, and randomly selected from among users with at least 10 sessions; 996 met this criteria; we selected 19. This IP-user mapping is close but not exact: a user may have searched from multiple IP addresses, and some IP addresses may map to multiple users. It seems unlikely, though, that conflating IPs and users would affect our analysis.

These sessions were coded as one of *learning*, *reminding*, *unsure*, or *misgrouped*. (Because the query log data is voluminous but lacks contextual information, we did not use the *clarifying* midpoint in this analysis.) We coded a session as *learning* or *reminding* based on the amount of knowledge we believed the user had on the topic he was searching for, and as *unsure* if we could not tell. To judge the user's knowledge, we used several heuristics: whether the query terms were specific or general (e.g., "radio button selection change" is a specific search indicative of *reminding*), contents of pages visited (e.g., a tutorial indicates *learning*), and whether the user appeared to be an expert (determined by looking at the user's entire search history – someone who occasionally searches for advanced features is likely to be an expert). We coded a session as *misgrouped* if it appeared to have multiple unrelated queries (potentially caused by a user performing unrelated searches in rapid succession, or by pollution from multiple users with the same IP address).

Finally, we computed three properties about each search session. For details on how each property is computed, see Brandt et al. (2009b).

1. *Query type* – whether the query contained only code (terms specific to the Flex framework, such as class and function names), only natural language, or both.
2. *Query refinement method* – between consecutive queries, whether search terms were generalized, specialized, otherwise reformulated, or changed completely.
3. *Types of Web pages visited* – each result click was classified as one of four page types: *Adobe APIs*, *Adobe tutorials*, *tutorials/articles* (by third-party authors), and *forums*.

For the final property, 10,909 of the most frequently visited pages were hand-classified (out of 19,155 total), accounting for 80% of all visits. Result clicks for the remaining 8246 pages (20% of visits) were labeled as *unclassified*.

Results

Out of 300 sessions, 20 appeared misgrouped, and we were unsure of the intent of 28. Of the remaining 252 sessions, 56 (22%) had *learning* traits and 196 (78%) had *reminding* traits. An example of a session with *reminding* traits had a single query for "function as parameter" and a single result click on the first result, a language specification page. An example of a session with *learning* traits began with the query "preloader", which was refined to "preloader in flex" and then "creating preloader in flex", followed by a result click on a tutorial.

We used the Mann-Whitney U test for determining statistical significance of differences in means and the chi-square test for determining differences in frequencies (proportions). Unless otherwise noted, all differences are statistically significant at $p < .001$.

H1: The first query was exclusively natural language in half of *learning* sessions, versus one third in *reminding* sessions (see Table 23.2).

H2: *Learning* and *reminding* sessions do not have a significant difference in the proportion of queries with refinements before first viewing results.

H3: Programmers were more likely to visit official API documentation in *reminding* sessions than in *learning* sessions (31% versus 10%, see Table 23.3). Notably, in *reminding* sessions, 42% of results viewed were Adobe tutorials.

Table 23.2 For Hand-Coded Sessions of Each Type, Proportion of First Queries of Each Type (252 Total Sessions).

Type of first query	Session type		All hand-coded
	Learning	Reminding	
Code only	0.21	**0.56**	0.48
Nat. lang. & code	**0.29**	0.10	0.14
Nat. lang. only	**0.50***	0.34	0.38
Total	1.00	1.00	1.00

*Significant majorities across each row in bold, * entry means only significant at p < .05.*

Table 23.3 For Queries in Hand-Coded Sessions of Each Type, Proportion of Result Clicks to Web Sites of Each Type (401 Total Queries).

Result click Web page type	Session type		All hand-coded
	Learning	Reminding	
Adobe APIs	0.10	**0.31**	0.23
Adobe tutorials	0.35	0.42	0.40
Tutorials/articles	**0.31**	0.10	0.17
Forums	0.06	0.04	0.05
Unclassified	0.18	0.13	0.15
Total	1.00	1.00	1.00

Significant majorities across each row in bold.

H4: Code-only queries accounted for 51% of all *reminding* queries. Among all (including those not hand-coded) sessions, those beginning with code-only queries were refined less ($\mu = 0.34$) than those starting with natural language and code ($\mu = 0.60$) and natural language only ($\mu = 0.51$). It appears that when programmers perform code-only queries, they know what they are looking for, and typically find it on the first search.

After evaluating these hypotheses, we performed further quantitative analysis of the query logs. In this analysis, we focused on how queries were refined and the factors that correlated with types of pages visited.

Programmers rarely refine queries, but are good at it

In this data set, users performed an average of 1.45 queries per session (the distribution of session lengths is shown in Figure 23.3). This is notably less than other reports, such as 2.02 (Silverstein et al., 1999). This may be a function of improving search engines, that programming as a domain is well-suited to search, or that the participants were skilled.

Across all sessions and refinement types, 66% of queries *after refinements* have result clicks, which is significantly higher than the percentage of queries before refinements (48%) that have clicks. This contrast suggests that refining queries generally produces better results.

When programmers refined a query to make it more *specialized*, they generally did so without first clicking through to a result (see Table 23.4). Presumably, this is because they assessed the result snippets and found them unsatisfactory. Programmers may also see little risk in "losing" a good result when specializing – if it was a good result for the initial query, it ought to be a good result for the more specialized one. This hypothesis is reinforced by the relatively high click rate before performing a completely new query (presumably on the same topic) – good results may be lost by completely changing the query, so programmers click any potentially valuable links first. Finally,

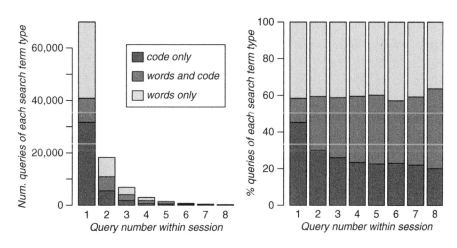

FIGURE 23.3

How query types changed as queries were refined. In both graphs, each bar sums all *i*th queries over all sessions that contained an *i*th query (e.g., a session with three queries contributed to the sums in the first three bars). The graph on the left is a standard histogram; the graph on the right presents the same data, but with each bar's height normalized to 100 to show changes in proportions as query refinements occurred.

Table 23.4 For Each Refinement Type, Proportion of Refinements of That Type Where Programmers Clicked on Any Links *Before* the Refinement (31,334 Total Refinements).

Refinement type					
Generalize	New	Reformulate	Spacialize	Spelling	All
0.44	0.61	0.51	0.39	0.14	0.48

almost no one clicks before making a spelling refinement, which makes sense because people mostly catch typos right away.

Users began with code-only searches 48% of the time and natural language searches 38% of the time (see Figure 23.3). Only 14% of the time was the first query mixed. The percent of mixed queries steadily increased to 42% by the eighth refinement, but the percent of queries containing only natural language stayed roughly constant throughout.

Query type predicts types of pages visited

There is some quantitative support for the intuition that query type is indicative of query intent (see Table 23.5). Code-only searches, which one would expect to be largely *reminding* queries, are most likely to bring programmers to official Adobe API pages (38% versus 23% overall) and least likely to bring programmers to all other types of pages. Natural-language-only queries, which one would expect to be largely *learning* queries, are most likely to bring programmers to official Adobe tutorials (39% versus 34% overall).

CONCLUSIONS AND FUTURE WORK

In this chapter, we have seen how many of the fundamental barriers that programmers face (Ko, Myers, & Aung, 2004) can be overcome using Web resources. This research is part of a larger intellectual endeavor to create a psychological account of programming (Détienne, 2001), and to use

Table 23.5 For Queries of Each Type, Proportion of Result Clicks Leading Programmer to Web Pages of Each Type (107,343 Total Queries). Significant Majorities and Near-Ties Across Each Row in Bold.

Result click Web page type	Query type			All clicks
	Code	Nat. lang. & code	Nat. lang.	
Adobe APIs	**0.38**	0.16	0.10	0.23
Adobe tutorials	0.31	0.33	**0.39**	0.34
Tutorials/articles	0.15	**0.22**	0.19	0.18
Forums	0.03	**0.07**	**0.06**	0.05
Unclassified	0.13	0.22	**0.27**	0.20
Total	1.00	1.00	1.00	1.00

programming as a petri dish for understanding problem-solving and knowledge work more broadly (Newell & Simon, 1972).

Specifically, this chapter illustrated an emerging problem-solving style that uses Web search to enumerate possible solutions. The Web has a substantially different cost structure than other information resources: It is cheaper to search for information, but its diverse nature may make it more difficult to understand and evaluate what is found (Choo, Detlor, & Turnbull, 2000). Programmers – and likely, other knowledge workers – currently lack tools for rapidly understanding and evaluating these possible solutions. Understanding how to build these tools remains an important direction for future work.

In practice, programmers use many resources other than the Web, such as colleagues and books. What is the role these other resources could and do play? This chapter looks exclusively at Web usage; other researchers have similarly examined other information resources individually. (For example, Chong and Siino (2006) examined collaboration between programmers during solo and pair programming.) Future work is needed to compare the trade-offs of these different information resources.

For programmers to use online resources, there must be people who create these resources. What motivates individuals to *contribute* information, such as tutorials and code snippets, and how can technology make sharing easier and more common? For example, is it possible to "crowdsource" finding and fixing bugs in online code? Can we improve the experience of reading a tutorial by knowing how the previous 1000 readers used that tutorial? These are just some of the many open questions in this space.

Finally, how does the increasing prevalence and accessibility of Web resources change the way we teach people to program? With ready access to good examples, programmers may need less training in languages, frameworks, and libraries, and greater skill in formulating and breaking apart complex problems. It may be that programming is becoming less about knowing how to *do* something and more about knowing how to *ask* the right questions.

Acknowledgments

We thank Rob Liebscher and Diana Joseph at Adobe Systems for their help in acquiring the Web query logs; Beyang Liu for his help in coding video data from our lab study; Intel for donating computers for this research; and all of the study participants for sharing their insights. This research was supported in part by NSF Grant IIS-0745320.

This work is based on an earlier work: "Two Studies of Opportunistic Programming: Interleaving Web Foraging, Learning, and Writing Code," in *Proceedings of the 27th International Conference on Human Factors in Computing Systems*, © ACM, 2009. http://doi.acm.org/10.1145/1518701.1518944.

References

Adar, E., Dontcheva, M., Fogarty, J., & Weld, D. S. (2008). Zoetrope: interacting with the ephemeral web. In *Proceedings of the 21st annual ACM symposium on User interface software and technology* (pp. 19–22). Monterey, CA, USA: ACM.

Adar, E., Teevan, J., Dumais, S., & Elsas, J. (2009). The web changes everything: understanding the dynamics of web content. In *Proceedings of the Second ACM International Conference on Web Search and Data Mining* (pp. 9–12). Barcelona, Spain: ACM.

Agans, D. (2003). *Debugging: The Nine Indispensable Rules for Finding Even the Most Elusive Software and Hardware Problems.* New York: AMACOM.

Aggarwal, C. C. (2002). Collaborative crawling: mining user experiences for topical resource discovery. In *Proceedings of the Eighth ACM SIGKDD International Conference on Knowledge Discovery and Data Mining* July 23–26, Edmonton, Alberta, Canada.

Aigner, W., Miksch, S., Müller, W., Schumann, H., & Tominski, C. (2008). Visual Methods for Analyzing Time-Oriented Data. *IEEE Transactions on Visualization and Computer Graphics, 14*(1), 47–60.

Allen, J., Blaylock, N., & Ferguson, G. (2002). A Problem Solving Model for Collaborative Agents. In *Proceedings of the International Joint Conference on Autonomous Agents and Multi-Agent Systems.*

Allen, J., Chambers, N., Ferguson, G., Galescu, L., Jung, H., Swift, M., et al. (2007). PLOW: A Collaborative Task Learning Agent. In *Proceedings of the AAAI Conference on Artificial Intelligence: Special Track on Integrated Intelligence.*

Anderson, C. (2008). *The Long Tail: Why the Future of Business Is Selling Less of More.* New York: Hyperion.

Anderson, C. R., Domingos, P., & Weld, D. S. (2001). Personalizing Web Sites for Mobile Users. In *Proceedings of the 10th international conference on World Wide Web* (pp. 565–575).

Angros, R., Johnson, L., Rickel, J., & Scholer, A. (2002). Learning Domain Knowledge for Teaching Procedural Skills. In *Proceedings of the International Joint Conference on Autonomous Agents and Multiagent Systems.*

Ankolekar, A., & Vrandecic, D. (2008). Kalpana - enabling client-side web personalization. In *Proceedings of the Nineteenth ACM Conference on Hypertext and Hypermedia (Hypertext)* (pp. 21–26).

Anupam, V., Freire, J., Kumar, B., & Lieuwen, D. (2000). Automating Web navigation with the WebVCR. In *Proceedings of the 9th International World Wide Web Conference on Computer Networks: The International Journal of Computer and Telecommunications Networking (Amsterdam, The Netherlands)* (pp. 503–517). Amsterdam, The Netherlands: North-Holland Publishing Co.

Arase, Y., Hara, T., Uemukai, T., & Nishio, S. (2007). OPA Browser: A Web Browser for Cellular Phone Users. In *Proceedings of the 20th annual ACM symposium on User interface software and technology* (pp. 71–80).

Arasu, A., & Garcia-Molina, H. (2003). Extracting structured data from Web pages. In SIGMOD (pp. 337–348).

Asakawa, C., & Takagi, H. (2008a). Transcoding. In S. Harper, & Y. Yesilada (Eds.), *Web Accessibility: A Foundation for Research, Human-Computer Interaction Series.* Springer-Verlag.

Asakawa, C., & Takagi, H. (2008b). *Web Accessibility: A Foundation for Research.* Springer.

Ashish, N., & Knoblock, C. A. (1997). Wrapper generation for semi-structured Internet sources. *Geography,* 8–15.

Baeza-Yates, R., & Ribeiro-Neto, B. (1999). *Modern Information Retrieval.* Boston, Massachusetts: Addison-Wesley Longman Publishing Co.

Baldwin, J., Rowson, J. A., & Coady, Y. (2008). PrintMonkey: giving users a grip on printing the web. In *Proceedings of the Eighth ACM Symposium on Document Engineering (DocEng)* (pp. 230–239).

Banavar, G., Bergman, L., Cardone, R., & Chevalier, V. (2004). An Authoring Technology for Multidevice Web Applications. *IEEE Pervasive Computing, 3*(3), 83–93.

Barrett, R., Maglio, P., & Kellem, D. (1997). How to personalize the Web. In *Proceedings of the SIGCHI Conference on Human Factors in Computing Systems (CHI)* (pp. 75–82).

Barrett, R., Kandogan, E., Maglio, P., & Haber, E. (2004). Field Studies of Computer System Administrators: Analysis of System Management Tools and Practices. In *2004 ACM Conference on Computer Supported Cooperative Work* (pp. 388–395).

Baudisch, P., Xie, X., Wang, C., & Ma, W. Y. (2004). Collapse-to-Zoom: Viewing Web Pages on Small Screen Devices by Interactively Removing Irrelevant Content. In *Symposium on User Interface Software & Technology (UIST)* (pp. 91–94).

Bauer, M., Dengler, D., & Paul, G. (2000). Instructible Information Agents for Web Mining. In *Proceedings of the International Conference on Intelligent User Interfaces (IUI)* (pp. 21–28).

Baumgartner, R., Flesca, S., & Gottlob, G. (2001a). Declarative information extraction, Web crawling, and recursive wrapping with Lixto. In *Proceedings of the 6th International Conference on Logic Programming and Nonmonotonic Reasoning (LPNMR)* (pp. 21–41).

Baumgartner, R., Flesca, S., & Gottlob, G. (2001b). Supervised wrapper generation with Lixto. In *Proceedings of the 27th International Conference on Very Large Databases (VLDB)* (pp. 715–716).

Beaulieu, M., & Jones, S. (1998). Interactive searching and interface issues in the Okapi best match probabilistic retrieval system. *Interacting with Computers, 10*(3), 237–248.

Beckwith, L., Kissinger, C., Burnett, M., Wiedenbeck, S., Lawrance, J., Blackwell, A., et al. (2006). Tinkering and gender in end-user programmers' debugging. In *CHI '06: Proceedings of the SIGCHI conference on Human Factors in computing systems*.

Bederson, B. B., Grosjean, J., & Meyer, J. (2004). Toolkit Design for Interactive Structured Graphics. *IEEE Transactions on Software Engineering, 30*(8), 535–546.

Beizer, B. (1990). *Software testing techniques* (2nd ed.). New York: Van Nostrand Reinhold.

Benkler, Y. (2002). Coase's penguin, or, Linux and the nature of the firm, *Yale Law Review, 112.*

Berenson, A. (2008). Lilly Considers $1 Billion Fine To Settle Case. *New York Times*, January 31.

Berglund, A., Boag, S., Chamberlin, D., et al. (2007). *XML Path Language (XPath) 2.0, World Wide Web Consortium.*

Berners-Lee, T., Hendler, J., & Lassila, O. (2001). The Semantic Web. *Scientific American*, May.

Bernstein, A., & Kaufmann, E. (2006). GINO – a guided input natural language ontology editor. In *ISWC 2006* (pp. 144–157).

Beyer, H., & Holtzblatt, K. (1998). *Contextual design: defining customer-centered systems.* Morgan Kaufmann.

Bickmore, T. W., & Schilit, B. N. (1997a). Digestor: Device-independent Access to the World Wide Web. In *Selected papers from the sixth international conference on World Wide Web* (pp. 1075–1082).

Bickmore, T. W., & Schilit, B. N. (1997b). Digestor: Device-independent access to the World-Wide Web. In *Proceedings of the 6th Int. World-Wide Web Conference* (pp. 655–663).

Bier, E. A., Stone, M. C., Pier, K., Buxton, W., & DeRose, T. D. (1993). Toolglass and magic lenses: the see-through interface. In *Proceedings of the 20th annual conference on Computer graphics and interactive techniques* (pp. 73–80). Anaheim, CA: ACM.

Biggerstaff, T., & Richter, C. (1987). Reusability Framework, Assessment, and Directions. *IEEE Software, 4*(2), 41–49.

Bigham, J. P., & Ladner, R. E. (2007). Accessmonkey: a collaborative scripting framework for Web users and developers. In *Proc. the 2007 int. Cross-Disciplinary Conf. on Web Accessibility (W4a)* (vol. 225, pp. 25–34) W4A '07.

Bigham, J. P., Kaminsky, R. S., Ladner, R. E., Danielsson, O. M., & Hempton, G. L. (2006). WebInSight: making Web images accessible. In *Proc. the 8th int. ACM SIGACCESS Conf. on Computers and Accessibility* (pp. 181–188). Assets '06.

Bigham, J. P., Cavender, A. C., Brudvik, J. T., Wobbrock, J. O., & Ladner, R. E. (2007). Webinsitu: A comparative analysis of blind and sighted browsing behavior. In *Proc. of the 9th Intl. ACM SIGACCESS Conf. on Computers and Accessibility (ASSETS '07)* (pp. 51–58). Arizona: Tempe.

Bigham, J. P., Cavender, A. C., Kaminsky, R. S., Prince, C. M., & Robison, T. S. (2008). Transcendence: enabling a personal view of the deep web. In *Proceedings of the 13th International Conference on Intelligent User Interfaces (IUI '08)* (Gran Canaria, Spain) (pp. 169–178). NY: ACM.

Bigham, J. P., Lau, T. A., & Nichols, J. W. (2009). TrailBlazer: Enabling Blind Users to Blaze Trails Through the Web. In *Proceedings of the 12th International Conference on Intelligent User Interfaces (IUI 2009)* (pp. 177–186). Sanibel Island, Florida: ACM. This is a minor revision of the work published in Proceedings of the International Conference on Intelligent User Interfaces (IUI 2009), http://doi.acm.org/10.1145/1502650.1502677.

Bila, N., Ronda, T., Mohomed, I., Truong, K. N., & Lara, E. D. (2007). PageTailor: Reusable End-User Customization for the Mobile Web. In *Proceedings of MobiSys* (pp. 16–25).

Blackwell, A. F., & Burnett, M. (2002). *Applying attention investment to end-user programming*. Paper presented at the Proceedings of IEEE 2002 Symposia on Human-Centric Computing Languages and Environments.

Blackwell, A. F., & Green, T. R. G. (1999). *Investment of attention as an analytic approach to cognitive dimensions*. Collected Papers of the 11th Annual Workshop of the Psychology of Programming Interest Group (PPIG-11).

Blackwell, A. F., & Green, T. R. G. (2003). *Notational systems – The Cognitive Dimensions of Notations Framework. HCI Models, Theories, and Frameworks* (pp. 103–133).

Blackwell, A. F. (2001). See What You Need: Helping End-users to Build Abstractions. *Journal of Visual Languages and Computing*.

Blackwell, A. (2002). First Steps in Programming: A Rationale for Attention Investment Models. In *2002 IEEE Symposium on Human-Centric Computing Languages and Environments* (pp. 2–10).

Blythe, J., & Russ, T. (2008). Case-based reasoning for procedure learning by instruction. In *Proc. IUI 2008* (pp. 301–304). ACM Press.

Blythe, J., Kim, J., Ramachandran, S., & Gil, Y. (2001). An Integrated Environment for Knowledge Acquisition. In *International Conference on Intelligent User Interfaces*.

Blythe, J., Kapoor, D., Knoblock, C. A., Lerman, K., & Minton, S. (2008). Information integration for the masses. *Journal of Universal Computer Science, 14*(11), 1811–1837.

Blythe, J. (2005). Task Learning by Instruction in Tailor. In *Proceedings of the International Conference on Intelligent User Interfaces* (pp. 191–198). ACM Press.

Bogart, C., Burnett, M., Cypher, A., & Scaffidi, C. (2008). End-User Programming in the Wild: A Field Study of CoScripter Scripts. In *Proceedings of the 2008 IEEE Symposium on Visual Languages and Human-Centric Computing (AVI)* (pp. 39–46).

Bolin, M., Webber, M., Rha, P., Wilson, T., & Miller, R. C. (2005). Automation and customization of rendered web pages. In *UIST '05: Proceedings of the 18th Annual ACM Symposium on User Interface Software and Technology,* (pp. 163–172). New York, NY, USA: ACM.

Bonnie, A. (1993). *A small matter of programming*. MIT Press.

Borodin, Y., Mahmud, J., Ramakrishnan, I. V., & Stent, A. (2007). The HearSay non-visual Web browser. In *Proc. the 2007 int. Cross-Disciplinary Conf. on Web Accessibility (W4a)* (vol. 225, pp. 128–129) W4A '07.

Borodin, E. (2008). *Automation of Repetitive Web Browsing Tasks with Voice-Enabled Macros*. ASSETS 2008.

Borodin, Y., Bigham, J., Raman, R., & Ramakrishnan, I. V. (2008a). What's New? – Making Web Page Updates Accessible. In *Proceedings of the 10th international ACM SIGACCESS conference on Computers and accessibility* (pp. 130–131). Nova Scotia, Canada: ACM.

Borodin, Y., Bigham, J., Stent, A., & Ramakrishnan, I. V. (2008b). Towards One World Web with HearSay3. In *W4A'08: Proceedings of the 2008 international Cross-Disciplinary Conference on Web Accessibility* (pp. 128–129).

Bosworth, A. (2004). BEAs Bosworth: The World Needs Simpler Java. *eWeek Magazine*, February 19.

Bouillon, L., Vanderdonckt, J., & Souchon, N. (2002). Recovering Alternative Presentation Models of a Web Page with Vaquita. In *Computer-Aided Design of User Interfaces III* (pp. 311–322).

Brandt, J., Guo, P., Lewenstein, J., & Klemmer, S. (2008). Opportunistic Programming: How Rapid Ideation and Prototyping Occur in Practice. In *4th Intl. Workshop on End-User Software Engineering* (pp. 1–5).

Brandt, J., Guo, P. J., Lewenstein, J., Dontcheva, M., & Klemmer, S. R. (2009a). Opportunistic Programming: Writing Code to Prototype, Ideate, and Discover. *IEEE Software, 26*(5).

Brandt, J., Guo, P. J., Lewenstein, J., Dontcheva, M., & Klemmer, S. R. (2009b). Two Studies of Opportunistic Programming: Interleaving Web Foraging, Learning, and Writing Code. In *Proceedings of CHI 2009: ACM Conference on Human Factors in Computing Systems*. Boston, MA.

Brandt, J., Dontcheva, M., Weskamp, M., & Klemmer, S. R. (2010). Example-centric programming: Integrating Web search into the development environment. In *Proceedings of CHI 2010: ACM Conference on Human Factors in Computing Systems*. Atlanta, GA.

Brooks, R. (1983). Toward a Theory of Comprehension of Computer Programs. *International Journal of Man Machine Studies, 18*(6), 542–554.

Brooks, C., Mazer, M. S., Meeks, S., & Miller, M. (1995). Application specific proxy servers as http stream transducers. In *WWW*.

Bruckman, A., & Edwards, E. (1999). Should we leverage natural language knowledge? An analysis of user errors in a natural-language-style programming language. In *CHI '99* (pp. 207–214).

Bruckman, A., & Resnick, M. (1995). The MediaMOO Project: Constructionism and Professional Community. *Convergence, 1*, 94–109.

Bruckman, A. (1998). Community Support for Constructionist Learning. *Computer Supported Cooperative Work, 7*(1–2), 47–86.

Burgos, C. L., Ryan, J. J. C. H., & Murphee, E. L. (2007). Through a mirror darkly: How programmers understand legacy code. *Information Knowledge Systems Management, 6*, 215–234. IOS Press.

Burkhardt, J., & Détienne, F. (1995). An Empirical Study of Software Reuse by Experts in Object-Oriented Design. In *5th International Conference on Human-Computer Interaction* (pp. 38–138).

Burnett, M., Atwood, J., Djang, R. W., Gottfried, H., Reichwein, J., & Yang, S. (2001). Forms/3: A first-order visual language to explore the boundaries of the spreadsheet paradigm. *Journal of Functional Programming, 11*(2), 155–206.

Burnett, M., Cook, C., & Rothermel, G. (2004). End-User Software Engineering. *Commun. ACM, 47*(9), 53–58.

Buyukkokten, O., Garcia-Molina, H., Paepcke, A., & Winograd, T. (2000). Power Browser: Efficient Web Browsing for PDAs. In *Conference on Human Factors in Computing Systems (CHI)* (pp. 430–437).

Carter, S., Mankoff, J., Klemmer, S. R., & Matthews, T. (2008). Exiting the Cleanroom: On Ecological Validity and Ubiquitous Computing. *Human-Computer Interaction, 23*(1), 47–99.

Chambers, N., Allen, J., Galescu, L., Jung, H., & Taysom, W. (2006). Using Semantics to Identify Web Objects. In *Proceedings of the National Conference on Artificial Intelligence: Special Track on AI and the Web*.

Chan, C. Y., Garofalakis, M., & Rastogi, R. (2002). *RE-Tree: An Efficient Index Structure for Regular Expressions*. VLDB '02.

Chang, C-H., & Lui, S-C. (2001). Lepad: Information extraction based on pattern discovery. In *WWW* (pp. 681–688).

Chaudhri, V. K., Cheyer, A., Guili, R., Jarrold, B., Myers, K. L., & Niekrasz, J. (2006). A case study in engineering a knowledge base for an intelligent personal assistant. In *Proc. SemDesk 2006*.

Chen, Y. F., Douglis, F., Huang, H., & Vo, K-P. (2000). TopBlend: An Efficient Implementation of HtmlDiff in Java. *AT&T Labs-Research Technical Report 00.5 1*.

Chen, C., & Raman, T. V. (2008). AxsJAX: A Talking Translation Bot Using Google IM. In *Proc. the 2008 int. Cross-Disciplinary Conf. on Web Accessibility (W4a)* (pp. 105–107) W4A '08.

Cheung, K. H., Yip, K. Y., Smith, A., deKnikker, R., Masiar, A., & Gerstein, M. (2005). YeastHub: a semantic web use case for integrating data in the life sciences domain. *Bioinformatics*, *21*(1), 85–96.

Chi, E. H., Riedl, J., Barry, P., & Konstan, J. (1998). Principles for information visualization spreadsheets. *IEEE Computer Graphics and Applications*, *18*(4), 30–38.

Chidlovskii, B. (2001). Automatic repairing of web wrappers. In *WIDM*.

Chikofsky, E. J., & Cross, J. H. (1990). Reverse engineering and design recovery: A taxonomy. In *IEEE Software* (pp. 13–17).

Chong, J., & Siino, R. (2006). Interruptions on Software Teams: A Comparison of Paired and Solo Programmers. In *Proceedings of CSCW 2006: ACM Conference on Computer Supported Cooperative Work*.

Choo, C. W., Detlor, B., & Turnbull, D. (2000). *Web Work: Information Seeking and Knowledge Work on the World Wide Web*. Kluwer Academic Publishers.

Churchill, E. F., & Nelson, L. D. (2002). *Tangibly Simple, Architecturally Complex: Evaluating a Tangible Presentation Aid, CHI '02 Extended Abstracts on Human Factors in Computing*. ACM Press.

Clark, J., & DeRose, S. (1999). *XML Path Language (XPath), Version 1.0*. http://www.w3.org/TR/xpath.

Cockburn, A., & McKenzie, B. (2001). What do Web users do? An empirical analysis of Web use. *International Journal of Human-Computer Studies*, *54*(6), 903–922.

Collins, A., & Loftus, E. (1975). A spreading activation theory of semantic processing. *Psychological Review*, *82*, 407–428.

Cox, A. L., & Young, R. M. (2000). Device-Oriented and Task-Oriented Exploratory Learning of Interactive Devices. In *Proceedings of ICCM 2000: International Conference on Cognitive Modeling* (pp. 70–77).

Coyne, K. P., & Nielsen, J. (2001). *Beyond alt text: Making the web easy to use for users with disabilities*.

Craik, K. J. W. (1943). *The Nature of Explanation*. Cambridge University Press.

Cramer, H., Evers, V., Van Someren, M., Ramlal, S., Rutledge, L., Stash, N., et al. (2008). The effects of transparency on trust and acceptance in interaction with a content-based art recommender. *User Modeling and User-Adapted Interaction*, *18*(5), 924–1868.

Cranor, L. F., & Garfinkel, S. (Eds.). (2005). *Security and Usability: Designing Secure Systems that People Can Use*. O'Reilly.

Crescenzi, V., & Mecca, G. (2004). Automatic information extraction from large website. *Journal of the ACM*, *51*, 731–779.

Cypher, A., & Halbert, D. C. (1993). *Watch What I Do: Programming by Demonstration*. MIT Press.

Cypher, A., & Smith, D. C. (1995). KidSim: End User Programming of Simulations. In *Proceedings of CHI, 1995 (Denver, May 7–11)* (pp. 27–34). New York: ACM.

Cypher, A. (1991). Eager: programming repetitive tasks by example. In *Proceedings of the SIGCHI Conference on Human Factors in Computing Systems (CHI)* (pp. 33–39).

Cypher, A. (Ed.), (1993). *Watch what I do: Programming by Demonstration*. Cambridge, MA: MIT Press.

Dapper. http://dapper.net.

Denning, P., Horning, J., Parnas, D., & Weinstein, L. (2005). Wikipedia risks. *Communications of the ACM*.

Détienne, F. (2001). *Software Design: Cognitive Aspects*. Springer.

Dey, A., Abowd, G., & Wood, A. (1998). CyberDesk: A framework for providing self-integrating context-aware services. In *Proceedings of the International Conference on Intelligent User Interfaces (IUI 98)*.

DiGiano, C., & Eisenberg, M. Self-disclosing design tools: a gentle introduction to end-user programming. In *Proceedings of the 1st Conference on Designing Interactive Systems (DIS)* (pp. 189–197).

Dix, A., Beale, R., & Wood, A. (2000). Architectures to make simple visualisations using simple systems. In *Proceedings of Advanced Visual Interfaces (AVI 00)*.

Dong, X., Halevy, A., & Madhavan, J. (2005). Reference reconciliation in complex information spaces. In *Proceedings of the 2005 ACM SIGMOD International Conference on Management of Data (Baltimore, Maryland, June 14–16, 2005). SIGMOD '05* (pp. 85–96). New York, NY: ACM. DOI=http://doi.acm.org/10.1145/1066157.1066168.

Dontcheva, M., Drucker, S. M., Wade, G., Salesin, D., & Cohen, M. F. (2006). Summarizing personal Web browsing sessions. In *Proceedings of the 19th Annual ACM Symposium on User Interface Software and Technology (Montreux, Switzerland, October 15–18, 2006). UIST '06* (pp. 115–124). New York, NY: ACM. DOI=http://doi.acm.org/10.1145/1166253.1166273.

Dontcheva, M., Drucker, S. M., Salesin, D., & Cohen, M. F. (2007a). *Changes in webpage structure over time.* University of Washington Computer Science and Engineering Technical Report, TR2007-04-02.

Dontcheva, M., Drucker, S. M., Salesin, D., & Cohen, M. F. (2007b). Relations, cards, and search templates: user-guided web data integration and layout. In *Proceedings of the 20th Annual ACM Symposium on User Interface Software and Technology (Newport, Rhode Island, USA, October 07–10, 2007). UIST '07* (pp. 61–70). New York, NY: ACM. DOI=http://doi.acm.org/10.1145/1294211.1294224.

Dontcheva, M., Lin, S., Drucker, S., Salesin, D., & Michael, F. (2008). Cohen. Experiences with content extraction from the web. In *SIGCHI 2008 Workshop on Semantic Web User Interaction*.

Douglis, F., Ball, T., Chen, Y-F., & Koutsofios, E. (1998). The AT&T Internet Difference Engine: Tracking and viewing changes on the web. *World Wide Web, 1*(1), 27–44.

Dragunov, A. N., Dietterich, T. G., Johnsrude, K., Mclaughlin, M., Li, L., & Herlocker, J. L. (2005). Tasktracer: a desktop environment to support multi-tasking knowledge workers. In *Proc. IUI 2005* (pp. 75–82). ACM Press.

Dumais, S., Cutrell, E., & Chen, H. (2001). Optimizing search by showing results in context. In *Proceedings of the SIGCHI Conference on Human Factors in Computing Systems (Seattle, Washington, United States). CHI '01* (pp. 277–284). New York, NY: ACM. DOI=http://doi.acm.org/10.1145/365024.365116.

Dzikovska, M., Allen, J., & Swift, M. (2008). Linking Semantic and Knowledge Representations in a Multi-domain Dialogue System. *Journal of Logic and Computation, 18*(3), 405–430, Oxford University Press.

Eagle, N., & Singh, P. (2004). Context sensing using speech and common sense. In *Proceedings of the NAACL/HLT 2004 Workshop on Higher-Level Linguistic and Other Knowledge for Automatic Speech Processing*.

Eisenstadt, M. (1997). My hairiest bug war stories. *Communications of the ACM, 40*(4), 30–37.

Eker, S., Lee, T., & Gervasio, M. (2009). Iteration learning by demonstration. In *Papers from the 2009 AAAI Spring Syposium on Agents that Learn from Human Teachers (Technical Report SS-09-01)*. AAAI Press.

Ennals, R., Brewer, E., Garofalakis, M., Shadle, M., & Gandhi, P. (2007). Intel Mash Maker: join the web. *SIGMOD Rec, 36*(4), 27–33.

Ennals, R., & Gay, D. (2007). User-friendly functional programming for web mashups. In *Proceedings of the 2007 ACM SIGPLAN International Conference on Functional programming* (pp. 223–234). New York, NY.

Erwig, M., Abraham, R., Cooperstein, I., & Kollmansberger, S. (2005). Automatic generation and maintenance of correct spreadsheets. *ICSE*, 136–145.

Eugster, P. T. H., Felber, P. A., Guerraoui, R., & Kermarrec, A. (2003). The many faces of publish/subscribe. *ACM Computing Surveys, 35*, 114–131.

Euzenat, J., & Valtchev, P. (2004). Similarity-based ontology alignment in OWL-lite. In *Proc. ECAI 2004* (p. 333). IOS Press.

Faaborg, A. (2005). *A Goal-Oriented User Interface for Personalized Semantic Search.* Masters Thesis. Massachusetts Institute of Technology. http://agents.media.mit.edu/projects/semanticsearch/.

Faaborg, A., & Lieberman, H. (2006). A goal-oriented web browser. In *CHI '06: Proceedings of the SIGCHI conference on Human Factors in Computing Systems* (pp. 751–760). New York, NY.

Fairbanks, G., Garlan, D., & Scherlis, W. (2006). Design fragments make using frameworks easier. *SIGPLAN Notices*, *41*(10), 75–88.

Fellbaum, C. (1998). *WordNet: An Electronic Lexical Database*. Cambridge, Massachusetts: MIT Press.

Ferguson, G., & Allen, J. (1998). TRIPS: An Integrated Intelligent Problem-Solving Assistant. In *Proceedings of the National Conference on Artificial Intelligence*.

Ferretti, S., Mirri, S., Roccetti, M., & Salomoni, P. (2007). Notes for a Collaboration: On the Design of a Wiki-type Educational Video Lecture Annotation System. In *Proc. the IEEE Int. Workshop on Semantic Computing and Multimedia Systems (IEEESCMS' 07)*, (pp. 651–656). IEEE Computer Society.

Ferretti, S., Mirri, S., Muratori, L. A., Roccetti, M., & Salomoni, P. (2008). E-learning 2.0: you are We-LCoME! In *Proc. the 2008 int. Cross-Disciplinary Conf. on Web Accessibility (W4a)* (pp. 116–125) W4A '08.

Fisher, M., II, & Rothermel, G. (2004). *The EUSES Spreadsheet Corpus: A Shared Resource for Supporting Experimentation with Spreadsheet Dependability Mechanisms*. Technical Report 04-12-03. Lincoln: University of Nebraska.

Fishkin, K., & Bier, E. (2004). WebTracker – a Web Service for tracking documents. In *Proceedings of the 6th International World Wide Web Conference (WWW 1997)*.

Fox, A., Goldberg, I., Gribble, S. D., Lee, D. C., Polito, A., & Brewer, E. A. (1998). Experience With Top Gun Wingman: A Proxy-Based Graphical Web Browser for the 3Com PalmPilot. In *Proceedings of Middleware '98* (pp. 407–424).

Freebase. http://freebase.com.

Freire, J., Kumar, B., & Lieuwen, D. (2001). Web-Views: accessing personalized Web content and services. In *Proceedings of WWW 2001* (May 1–5, Hong Kong, China) (pp. 576–586). NY: ACM.

Frey, G. (2007). *Indexing AJAX Web Applications. ETH Department of Computer Science, Institute of Computational Sciences*. Available from:http://e-collection.ethbib.ethz.ch/view/eth:30111.

Fuchs, N. E., Kaljurand, K., & Kuhn, T. (2008). *Attempto controlled English for knowledge representation* (pp. 104–124).

Fujima, J., Lunzer, A., Hornbæk, K., & Tanaka, Y. (2004a). Clip, connect, clone: combining application elements to build custom interfaces for information access. In *Proceedings of the 17th Annual ACM Symposium on User Interface Software and Technology (UIST)* (pp. 175–184).

Fujima, J., Lunzer, A., Hornbæk, K., & Tanaka, Y. (2004b). C3W: Clipping, Connecting and Cloning for the Web. In *Proceedings of the 13th international World Wide Web conference on Alternate track papers & posters (WWW)*, (May 17–22, New York, NY, USA) (pp. 444–445). NY: ACM.

Fujima, J., Yoshihara, S., & Tanaka, Y. (2007). Web Application Orchestration Using Excel. In *Proceedings of the IEEE/WIC/ACM International Conference on Web Intelligence (WI '07)* (Washington, DC, USA) (pp. 743–749). IEEE Computer Society.

Funk, A., Tablan, V., Bontcheva, K., Cunningham, H., Davis, B., & Handschuh, S. (2008). CLOnE: Controlled language for ontology editing. In *The Semantic Web, volume 4825 of LNCS* (pp. 142–155). Springer.

Garlan, D., Allen, R., & Ockerbloom, J. (1995). Architectural Mismatch or Why It's Hard to Build Systems out of Existing Parts. In *17th International Conference on Software Engineering* (pp. 179–185).

Garland, A., Ryall, K., & Rich, C. (2001). Learning Hierarchical Task Models by Defining and Refining Examples. In *Proceedings of the International Conference on Knowledge Capture*.

Garrett, J. (2001). Ajax: A New Approach to Web Applications. Available at http://www.adaptivepath.com/ideas/essays/archives/000385.php.

Gasparetti, F., & Micarelli, A. (2007). Exploiting web browsing histories to identify user needs. *IUI* (pp. 325–328).

Gerlenter, D. (1989). Linda in context. *Communications of the ACM, 32*.

Gervasio, M., & Murdock, J. (2009). What were you thinking? Filling in missing dataflow through inference in learning from demonstration. In *Proc. IUI 2009* (pp. 157–166). ACM Press.

Gervasio, M., Lee, T. J., & Eker, S. (2008). Learning email procedures for the desktop. In *Papers from the AAAI 2008 Workshop on Enhanced Messaging (Technical Report WS-08-04)*. AAAI Press.

Gibson, D., Punera, K., & Tomkins, A. (2005). The volume and evolution of web page templates. In *Special Interest Tracks and Posters of the 14th International Conference on World Wide Web (Chiba, Japan, May 10–14, 2005). WWW '05* (pp. 830–839). New York, NY: ACM. DOI=http://doi.acm.org/10.1145/1062745.1062763.

Gladwell, M. (2000). *The Tipping Point: How Little Things Can Make a Big Difference*. New York: Little Brown.

Goer, E. Swinging through the jungle with mash maker and searchmonkey. www.http://developer.yahoo.net/blog/archives/2008/10/swinging_throug.html.

Google AxsJAX. Google, Inc. (2008). Http://code.google.com/p/google-axsjax/.

Google gadgets. http://code.google.com/apis/gadgets.

Greasespot. http://greasespot.net.

Green, T. R. G., & Petre, M. (1996). Usability analysis of visual programming environments: A "cognitive dimensions" framework. *Journal of Visual Languages and Computing, 7*(2), 131–174.

Greenfield, J., Short, K., Cook, S., & Crupi, J. (2004). *Software Factories*. Wiley.

Griffith, M., & Fox, S. (2006). Hobbyists online.

Grimes, C., Tang, D., & Russell, D. M. (2007). Query Logs Alone are Not Enough. In *Workshop on Query Log Analysis at WWW 2007: International World Wide Web Conference*. Banff, Alberta, Canada.

Guha, R., & McCool, R. (2002). A System for Integrating Web Services into a Global Knowledge Base. http://tap.stanford.edu/sw002.html.

Guha, R., & McCool, R. (2003a). TAP: Building the Semantic Web. http://tap.stanford.edu/.

Guha, R., & McCool, R. (2003b). TAP: a Semantic Web Platform. *Computer Networks: The International Journal of Computer and Telecommunications Networking, 42*(5).

Guha, R., McCool, R., & Miller, E. (2003). Semantic search. In *Proceedings of the 12th International Conference on World Wide Web (WWW)*.

Gulley, N. (2006). Improving the Quality of Contributed Software and the MATLAB File Exchange. In *2nd Workshop on End User Software Engineering* (pp. 8–9).

Hailpern, B., & Santhanam, P. (2002). Software debugging, testing, and verification. *IBM Systems Journal 41*(1), 4–12.

Halevy, A., Rajaraman, A., & Ordille, J. (2006). Data integration: the teenage years. In U. Dayal, K. Whang, D. Lomet, G. Alonso, G. Lohman & M. Kersten, et al. (Eds.). *Very Large Data Bases. VLDB Endowment* (pp. 9–16). In *Proceedings of the 32nd International Conference on Very Large Data Bases* (Seoul, Korea, September 12–15, 2006).

Harper, S., & Patel, N. (2005). Gist summaries for visually impaired surfers. In *Proc. of the 7th Intl. ACM SIGACCESS Conf. on Computers and Accessibility (ASSETS '05)* (pp. 90–97). New York, NY, USA.

Harper, S., Bechhofer, S., & Lunn, D. (2006). SADIe: transcoding based on CSS. In *Proc. the 8th int. ACM SIGACCESS Conf. on Computers and Accessibility* (pp. 259–260). Assets '06.

Hartmann, B., Klemmer, S. R., Bernstein, M., Abdulla, L., Burr, B., Robinson-Mosher, A., et al. (2006). Reflective physical prototyping through integrated design, test, and analysis. In *Proceedings of the 19th annual ACM symposium on User interface software and technology* (pp. 299–308). Montreux, Switzerland: ACM.

Hartmann, B., Doorley, S., & Klemmer, S. R. (2008). Hacking, Mashing, Gluing: Understanding Opportunistic Design. *IEEE Pervasive Computing, 7*(3), 46–54.

Hartmann, B., Loren, Y., Allison, A., Yang, Y., & Klemmer, S. R. (2008). Design as exploration: creating interface alternatives through parallel authoring and runtime tuning. In *Proceedings of the 21st annual ACM symposium on User interface software and technology* (pp. 91–100). Monterey, CA, USA: ACM.

Hartmann, B., Wu, L., Collins, K., & Klemmer, S. R. (2007). Programming by a sample: Rapidly creating web applications with d.mix. *UIST*.

Hoadley, C., Linn, M., Mann, L., & Clancy, M. (1996). When, Why and How do Novice Programmers Reuse Code. In *6th Workshop on Empirical Studies of Programmers* (pp. 109–129).

Hoffmann, R., Fogarty, J., & Weld, D. S. (2007). Assieme: finding and leveraging implicit references in a web search interface for programmers. In *Proceedings of the 20th annual ACM symposium on User interface software and technology* (pp. 13–22). Newport, Rhode Island, USA: ACM.

Hollan, J., Hutchins, E., & Kirsh, D. (2000). Distributed Cognition: Toward a New Foundation for Human-Computer Interaction Research. *ACM Transactions on Computer-Human Interaction, 7*(2), 174–196.

Hong, L., Chi, E. H., Budiu, R., Pirolli, P., & Nelson, L. (2008). SparTag.us: a low cost tagging system for foraging of web content. In *Proceedings of the Working Conference on Advanced Visual Interfaces (AVI)* (pp. 65–72).

Horrigan, J. (2007). *A Typology of Information and Communication Technology Users*.

Horvitz, E. (1999). Principles of mixed-initiative user interfaces. In *Proc. of the SIGCHI Conf. on Human factors in Computing Systems (CHI '99)* (pp. 159–166). New York, NY, USA.

Howell, J., Jackson, C., Wang, H. J., & Fan, X. (2007). Operating system abstractions for client mashups. In *Proceedings of the 11th USENIX workshop on Hot Topics in Operating Systems*.

Hupp, D., & Miller, R. C. (2007). Smart Bookmarks: Automatic Retroactive Macro Recording on the Web. In *Proceedings of the 20th Annual ACM Symposium on User Interface Software and Technology (UIST)* (pp. 81–90).

Hutchins, E. L., Hollan, J. D., & Norman, D. A. (1985). Direct manipulation interfaces. *Human-Computer Interaction, 1*(4), 311–338.

Huynh, D., Mazzocchi, S., & Karger, D. (2007). Piggy bank: Experience the semantic web inside your web browser. *Web Semantics, 5*(1), 16–27.

Huynh, D., Miller, R., & Karger, D. (2007). Potluck: Data Mash-Up Tool for Casual Users. In *Proceedings of the International Semantic Web Conference*.

Ingaiis, D. (1988). Fabrik a visual programming environment. In *OOPSLA*.

Irmak, U., & Suel, T. (2006). Interactive wrapper generation with minimal user effort. *WWW* (pp. 553–563).

Ito, K., & Tanaka, Y. (2003). A visual environment for dynamic web application composition. In *Proceedings of HT 2003* (Aug 26–30, Nottingham, UK) (pp. 184–193). NY: ACM.

Jatowt, A., Kawai, Y., & Tanaka, K. (2008). Visualizing historical content of web pages.

Jones, M. C., & Twidale, M. B. (2006). *Snippets of Awareness: Syndicated Copy Histories*. CSCW 06 Poster. Banff, Alberta, Canada.

Jones, W., Bruce, H., & Dumais, S. (2002). Once found, what then?: A study of "keeping" behaviors in the personal use of web information. *Proceedings of the American Society for Information Science and Technology, 39*(1), 391–402. DOI=http://dx.doi.org/10.1002/meet.1450390143.

Jones, M. C., Churchill, E. F., & Twidale, M. B. (2008a). *Mashing up Visual Languages and Web Mashups*. VL/HCC.

Jones, M. C., Churchill, E. F., & Twidale, M. B. (2008b). *Tinkering, Tailoring, & Mashing: The Social and Collaborative Practices of the Read-Write Web*. CSCW Workshop. San Diego, California.

Jung, H., Allen, J., Galescu, L., Chambers, N., Swift, M., & Taysom, W. (2008). Utilizing Natural Language for One-Shot Task Learning. *Journal of Logic and Computation, 18*(3), 475–493, Oxford University Press.

Kaminski, C. Much Ado About Smart Tags. Available at http://www.alistapart.com/articles/smarttags/.

Kawanaka, S., Borodin, Y., Bigham, J. P., Lunn, D., Takagi, H., & Asakawa, C. (2008). Accessibility commons: a metadata infrastructure for web accessibility. In *Proceedings of the 10th international ACM SIGACCESS Conference on Computers and Accessibility (Halifax, Nova Scotia, Canada, October 13–15, 2008)* (pp. 153–160). Assets '08. New York, NY: ACM. DOI=http://doi.acm.org/10.1145/1414471.1414500.

Kellar, M., Watters, C., & Shepherd, M. (2007). A field study characterizing Web-based information-seeking tasks. *Journal of the American Society for Information Science and Technology*, 58(7), 999–1018. DOI=http://dx.doi.org/10.1002/asi.v58:7.

Kelleher, C. & Pausch, R. (2005). Stencils-based tutorials: design and evaluation. In *Proceedings of the SIGCHI conference on Human factors in computing systems (CHI '05)* (pp. 541–550). Portland, Oregon, USA.

Kelly, D., & Teevan, J. (2003). Implicit feedback for inferring user preference: A bibliography. SIGIR Forum.

de Keukelaere, F., Bhola, S., Steiner, M., Chari, S., & Yoshihama, S. (2008). Smash: Secure component model for cross-domain mashups on unmodied browsers. In *WWW* (pp. 535–544).

Kim, M., Bergman, L., Lau, T., & Notkin, D. (2004). An Ethnographic Study of Copy and Paste Programming Practices in OOPL. In *Proceedings of the 2004 International Symposium on Empirical Software Engineering* (pp. 83–92). IEEE Computer Society.

Kissinger, C., et al. (2006). *Supporting End-User Debugging: What Do Users Want to Know?* AVI06.

Kistler, T., & Marais, H. (1998). WebL – a programming language for the Web. In *Proceedings of the Seventh International Conference on World Wide Web (WWW)* (pp. 259–270).

Kittur, A. (2008). Crowdsourcing user studies with Mechanical Turk. In H. Chi & B. Suh (Eds.), *Proc. CHI 2008* (pp. 453–456). ACM Press.

Klein, A. W., Sloan, P. P. J., Finkelstein, A., & Cohen, M. F. (2002). Stylized video cubes. In *Proceedings of the 2002 ACM SIGGRAPH/Eurographics symposium on Computer animation*. San Antonio, Texas: ACM.

Ko, A. J., & Myers, B. A. (2004). Designing the Whyline: A Debugging Interface for Asking Why and Why Not Questions. *CHI*, 151–158.

Ko, A. J., Myers, B. A., & Aung, H. H. (2004). Six Learning Barriers in End-User Programming Systems. In *Proceedings of VL/HCC 2004: IEEE Symposium on Visual Languages and Human-Centric Computing* (pp. 199–206). Rome, Italy.

Koelma, D., van Balen, R., & Smeulders, A. (1992). Scil-vp: A multi-purpose visual programming environment. In *Applied Computing* (pp. 1188–1198).

Koesnandar, A., Elbaum, S., Rothermel, G., Hochstein, L., Scaffidi, C., & Stolee, K. T. (2008). Using Assertions to Help End-User Programmers Create Dependable Web Macros. In *16th International Symposium on Foundations of Software Engineering* (pp. 124–134).

Kravets, D. (2008). Amazon.com Tossed Into Pirate Bay Jungle. December 4, Available at http://www.wired.com/threatlevel/2008/12/amazoncom-tosse/.

Krieger, M., Stark, E., & Klemmer, S. R. (2009). Coordinating tasks on the commons: designing for personal goals, expertise and serendipity. In *Proceedings of the 27th international conference on Human factors in computing systems* (pp. 1485–1494). Boston, MA, USA: ACM.

Krulwich, B. (July/August 1997). Automating the Internet: Agents as User Surrogates. *IEEE Internet Computing*, 1(4), 34–38.

Kuhlins, S., & Tredwell, R. (2003). Toolkits for generating wrappers – a survey of software toolkits for automated data extraction from Web sites. Revised Papers from the International Conference NetObjectDays on Objects, Components, Architectures, Services, and Applications for a Networked World (NODe '02), *LNCS, 2591*, 184–198.

Kulkarni, A. (2002). *Design Principles of a Reactive Behavioral System for the Intelligent Room.* To appear.

Kushmerick, N. (1999). Regression testing for wrapper maintenance. In *Proceedings of the sixteenth national conference on Artificial intelligence and the eleventh Innovative applications of artificial intelligence conference*. Orlando, Florida: United States, American Association for Artificial Intelligence.

Kushmerick, N. (2000). Wrapper verification. *World Wide Web*, 3(2), 79–94.

Kushmerick, N., Weld, D. S., & Doorenbos, R. (1997). Wrapper induction for information extraction. *IJCAI*.

Laender, A. H. F., Ribeiro-Neto, B. A., da Silva, A. S., & Teixeira, J. S. (2002). A brief survey of web data extraction tools. *SIGMOD Record, 31*(2), 84–93.

Lau, T., & Weld, D. (1999). Programming by Demonstration: An Inductive Learning Formulation. In *Proceedings of the International Conference on Intelligent User Interfaces*.

Law, R. (1997). An overview of debugging tools. *ACM SIGSOFT Software Engineering Notes, 22*(2), 43–47.

Lee, F., & Anderson, J. (1997). Learning to Act: Acquisition and Optimization of Procedural Skill. In *Proceedings of the Annual Conference of the Cognitive Science Society*.

Lee, K. J. (2006). What goes around comes around: an analysis of del.icio.us as social space. In *CSCW '06: Proceedings of the 2006 20th anniversary conference on Computer supported cooperative work* (pp. 191–194). New York, NY, USA: ACM.

Leland, M. D., Fish, R. S., & Kraut, R. E. (1988). Collaborative document production using quilt. In *Proc. the 1988 ACM Conf. on Computer-Supported Cooperative Work* (pp. 206–215). CSCW '88.

Lenat, D. (1995). CYC: a Large-Scale Investment in Knowledge Infrastructure. *Communications of the ACM, 38*(11).

Lerman, K., Minton, S., & Knoblock, C. (2003). Wrapper maintenance: a machine learning approach. *Journal of Artificial Intelligence Research, 18*, 149–181.

Lerman, K., Plangprasopchock, A., & Knoblock, C. A. (2007). Semantic labeling of online information sources. *International Journal on Semantic Web and Information Systems, 3*(3), 36–56.

Leshed, G., Haber, E. M., Matthews, T., & Lau, T. (2008). CoScripter: automating and sharing how-to knowledge in the enterprise. In *Proceeding of the Twenty-Sixth Annual SIGCHI Conference on Human Factors in Computing Systems (CHI)* (pp. 1719–1728).

Leuf, B., & Cunningham, W. (2001). *The Wiki Way: Quick Collaboration on the Web*. Addison-Wesley Professional.

Lewis, D. D. (1998). Naive Bayes at forty: The independence assumption in information retrieval. In *Proc. of ECML-98, 10th European Conf. on Machine Learning* (Vol. 1398, pp. 4–15). Heidelberg, DE, Chemnitz, DE: Springer Verlag.

Liberty, J. (2005). *Programming C#*. O'Reilly.

Lieberman, H., & Liu, H. (2002). Adaptive Linking between Text and Photos Using Common Sense Reasoning. In *Proceedings of the Adaptive Hypermedia and Adaptive Web-Based Systems, Second International Conference (AH 02)*.

Lieberman, E., & Miller, R. C. (2007). Facemail: Showing Faces of Recipients to Prevent Misdirected Email. In *Proceedings of the 3rd Symposium on Usable Privacy and Security (SOUPS)* (pp. 122–131).

Lieberman, H., Nardi, B., & Wright, D. (1998). Grammex: Defining Grammars by Example. In *Proceedings of the Conference on Human Factors in Computing Systems (CHI 98)*.

Lieberman, H., Liu, H., Singh, P., & Barry, B. (2004). Beating Some Common Sense into Interactive Applications. *AI Magazine*, Winter.

Lieberman, H., Faaborg, A., Daher, W., & Espinosa, J. (2005). How to Wreck a Nice Beach You Sing Calm Incense. In *Proceedings of the International Conference on Intelligent User Interfaces (IUI 05)*.

Lieberman, H., Paternò, F., & Wulf, V. (2006). *End-User Development*. Springer.

Lieberman, H. (Ed.). (2001). *Your Wish is My Command: Programming by Example*. San Francisco, CA: Morgan Kaufmann.

Lin, J., Quan, D., Sinha, V., Bakshi, K., Huynh, D., Katz, B., et al. (2003). What Makes a Good Answer? The Role of Context in Question Answering. In *Proceedings of the Ninth IFIP TC13 International Conference on Human-Computer Interaction (INTERACT 2003), September 2003* (pp. 25–32). Switzerland: Zurich.

Lin, J., Wong, J., Nichols, J., Cypher, A., & Lau, T. A. (2009). End-user programming of mashups with vegemite. In *Proceedings of the 13th international conference on Intelligent user interfaces (IUI '09)* (Sanibel Island, FL, USA) (pp. 97–106). NY: ACM.

Lingham, S., & Elbaum, S. (2007). Supporting end-users in the creation of dependable web clips. In *WWW* (pp. 953–962).

Little, G., Lau, T. A., Cypher, A., Lin, J., Haber, E. M., & Kandogan, E. (2007). Koala: capture, share, automate, personalize business processes on the web. In *CHI '07: Proceedings of the SIGCHI conference on Human factors in computing systems* (pp. 943–946). New York, NY, USA: ACM.

Little, G. & Miller, R. C. (2006). Translating keyword commands into executable code. In *UIST '06: Proceedings of the 19th annual ACM symposium on User interface software and technology* (pp. 135–144). New York, NY, USA: ACM.

Little, G., & Miller, R. C. (2008). Keyword Programming in Java. *Journal of ASE*.

Liu, H., & Lieberman, H. (2005). Programmatic Semantics for Natural Language Interfaces. *CHI*, 1597–1600.

Liu, H., & Lieberman, H. (2005a). Metafor: Visualizing stories as code. In *Proceedings of the 10th International Conference on Intelligent User Interfaces* (pp. 305–307). San Diego, California, USA.

Liu, H., & Singh, P. (2004). ConceptNet: a Practical Commonsense Reasoning Toolkit. *BT Technology Journal*.

Liu, H., Lieberman, H., & Selker, T. (2002). GOOSE: A Goal-Oriented Search Engine With Commonsense. In *Proceedings of the Adaptive Hypermedia and Adaptive Web-Based Systems, Second International Conference, (AH 02)*.

Liu, H., Selker, T., & Lieberman, H. (2003). Visualizing the Affective Structure of a Text Document. In *Proceedings of the Conference on Human Factors in Computing Systems (CHI 03)*.

Liu, J., Dong, X., & Halevy, A. (2006). Answering structured queries on unstructured data. In *Proceedings of Ninth International Workshop on the Web and Databases, WebDB Chicago, Illinois, USA, June 30, 2006*.

Livny, M., Ramakrishnan, R., et al. (1997). DEVise: integrated querying and visual exploration of large datasets. New York, NY, USA: ACM.

Lunzer, A., & Hornbæk, K. (2003a). Widget multiplexers for side-by-side display and control of information-processing scenarios. In *Adjunct Proceedings of HCI International 2003* (June 22–27, Crete, Greece) (pp. 91–92). Mahwah, NJ: Lawrence Erlbaum Associates.

Lunzer, A., & Hornbæk, K. (2003b). Side-by-side display and control of multiple scenarios: Subjunctive interfaces for exploring multi-attribute data. In *Proceedings of OZCHI 2003* (Nov 26–28, Brisbane, Australia) (pp. 202–210). Los Alamitos, CA: IEEE Computer Society Press.

Lunzer, A., & Hornbæk, K. (2004). Usability studies on a visualisation for parallel display and control of alternative scenarios. In *Proceedings of AVI 2004* (May 25–28, Gallipoli, Italy) (pp. 125–132). NY: ACM.

Lunzer, A., & Hornbæk, K. (2006a). An Enhanced Spreadsheet Supporting Calculation-Structure Variants, and its Application to Web-Based Processing. In K. P. Jantke, A. Lunzer, N. Spyratos, & Y. Tanaka (Eds.), *Proceedings of the Dagstuhl Workshop on Federation over the Web, Dagstuhl Castle, Germany, May 2005 (Lecture Notes in Artificial Intelligence, Vol. 3847–2006)* (pp. 143–158).

Lunzer, A., & Hornbæk, K. (2006b). RecipeSheet: Creating, Combining and Controlling Information Processors. In *Proceedings of the 19th Annual ACM Symposium on User interface Software and Technology (UIST '06), Montreux, Switzerland, Oct 2006* (pp. 145–153).

Lunzer, A., & Hornbæk, K. (2008). Subjunctive interfaces: Extending applications to support parallel setup, viewing and control of alternative scenarios. *ACM Transactions on Computer-Human Interaction*, *14*(4), Article 17 (January 2008), 44 pages.

Lunzer, A. (1999). Choice and comparison where the user wants them: Subjunctive interfaces for computer-supported exploration. In *Proceedings of INTERACT '99* (Aug 30–Sept 3, Edinburgh, Scotland) (pp. 474–482). Amsterdam, The Netherlands: IOS Press.

Lunzer, A. (in press). Using Subjunctive Interfaces to Put Delivered Information into Context. Knowledge Media Science: Preparing the Ground. In K. P. Jantke, R. Kaschek, N. Spyratos, & Y. Tanaka (Eds.), *Lecture Notes in Artificial Intelligence* (Vol. 4980). In press.

MacLean, A., Carter, K., Lövstrand, L., & Moran, T. (1990). User-tailorable systems: pressing the issues with buttons. In *Proceedings of the SIGCHI Conference on Human Factors in computing systems (CHI)* (pp. 175–182). Seattle, Washington: ACM.

Mackay, W. (1990). Patterns of sharing customizable software. In *Proceedings of the 1990 ACM Conference on Computer-supported Cooperative Work (CSCW)* (pp. 209–221).

Mackay, W. (1991). Triggers and barriers to customizing software. In *Proceedings of the SIGCHI Conference on Human Factors in Computing Systems (CHI)* (pp. 153–160).

Madden, M. (2006). *Internet Penetration and Impact. Pew Internet & American Life Project.*

Madhavan, J., Jeffery, S., Cohen, S., Dong, X., Ko, D., Yu, C., & Halevy, A. (2007). Web-scale data integration: You can afford to pay as you go. In *CIDR 2007, Third Biennial Conference on Innovative Data Systems Research, Asilomar, CA, USA, January 7–10, 2007, Online Proceedings* (pp. 342–350).

Maglio, P., & Barrett, R. (2000). Intermediaries personalize information streams. *Communications of the ACM, 43*(8), 96–101.

Mahmud, J. U., Borodin, Y., & Ramakrishnan, I. V. (2007). Csurf: a context-driven non-visual web-browser. In *WWW '07: Proceedings of the 16th International Conference on World Wide Web* (pp. 31–40).

Mahmud, J. U., Borodin, Y., & Ramakrishnan, I. V. (2008). Assistive Browser for Conducting Web Transactions. In *IUI '08: Proceedings of the International Conference on Intelligent User Interface.*

Mandelin, D., Xu, L., Bodik, R., & Kimelman, D. (2005). Jungloid Mining: Helping to Navigate the API Jungle. *PLDI '05,* 48–61.

Martin, R. C. (2002). *Agile Software Development, Principles, Patterns, and Practices.* Prentice-Hall.

Maulsby, D. (1993). *The Turvy experience: simulating an instructible interface, in Watch what I do: programming by demonstration* (pp. 239–269). Cambridge, MA: MIT Press.

McCool, R., Guha, R., & Fikes, R. (2003). Contexts for the Semantic Web. http://tap.stanford.edu/contexts.pdf.

Meng, X., Hu, D., & Li, C. (2003). Schema-guided wrapper maintenance for web–data extraction. In *WIDM* (pp. 1–8).

Mesbah, A., Bozdag, E., & Deursen, A. (2008). *Crawling AJAX by Inferring User Interface State Changes.* Yorktown Heights, NY, USA: ICWE.

Microformats. http://microformats.org.

Microsoft popfly. http://popfly.com.

Mihalcea, R., Liu, H., & Lieberman, H. (2006). NLP (natural language processing) for NLP (natural language programming). *CICLing,* 319–330.

Millen, D. R., Feinberg, J., & Kerr, B. (2006). Dogear: Social bookmarking in the enterprise. In *CHI '06: Proceedings of the SIGCHI conference on Human Factors in computing systems* (pp. 111–120). New York, NY, USA: ACM.

Miller, R. C., & Bharat, K. (1998). SPHINX: a framework for creating personal, site-specific Web crawlers. In *Proceedings of the Seventh International Conference on World Wide Web (WWW)* (pp. 119–130).

Miller, R., & Myers, B. (1997). *Creating Dynamic World Wide Web Pages by Demonstration.* Technical Report CMU-CS-97-131 (and CMU-HCII-97-101). Carnegie Mellon University School of Computer Science.

Miller, R. C., & Myers, B. A. (2000). Integrating a Command Shell into a Web Browser. In *Proceedings of the USENIX Annual Technical Conference (IUSENIX)* (pp. 171–182).

Miller, R. C., Chou, V., Bernstein, M., Little, G., Van Kleek, M., Karger, D., et al. (2008). Inky: a sloppy command line for the Web with rich visual feedback. In *Proceedings of the 21st Annual ACM Symposium on User Interface Software and Technology (UIST)* (pp. 131–140).

Miller, R. C. (2002). *Lightweight Structure in Text.* PhD thesis, Carnegie Mellon University.

Miyashita, H., Sato, D., Takagi, H., & Asakawa, C. (2007). aiBrowser for Multimedia – Introducing Multimedia Content Accessibility for Visually Impaired Users. In *Proc. the Ninth Int. ACM SIGACCESS Conf. on Computers and Accessibility* (pp. 91–98) Assets '07.

Mohagheghi, P., Conradi, R., Killi, O., & Schwarz, H. (2004). An Empirical Study of Software Reuse vs. Defect-Density and Stability. In *26th International Conference on Software Engineering* (pp. 282–291).

Morley, D., & Myers, K. (2004). The SPARK agent framework. In *Proc. AAMAS 2004* (pp. 714–721). IEEE Computer Society.

Mossberg, W. Microsoft Will Abandon Controversial Smart Tags. http://ptech.wsj.com/archive/ptech-20010628.html.

Muramatsu, J., & Pratt, W. (2001). Transparent Queries: investigation users' mental models of search engines. In *Proceedings of the 24th Annual international ACM SIGIR Conference on Research and Development in information Retrieval (New Orleans, Louisiana, United States). SIGIR '01* (pp. 217–224). New York, NY: ACM. DOI=http://doi.acm.org/10.1145/383952.383991.

Muslea, I., Minton, S., & Knoblock, C. (1999). A hierarchical approach to wrapper induction. In *Autonomous Agents* (pp. 190–197).

Musser, J. (2008). *ProgrammableWeb*. Retrieved June 13, 2008, from http://programmableweb.com.

Myers, B., Hudson, S. E., & Pausch, R. (2000). Past, present, and future of user interface software tools. *ACM Transactions on Computer-Human Interaction, 7*(1), 3–28.

Myers, B., Pane, J., & Ko, A. (2004). Natural Programming Languages and Environments. *CACM, 47*(9), 47–52.

Myers, B., Park, S. Y., Nakano, Y., Mueller, G., & Ko, A. (2008). How Designers Design and Program Interactive Behaviors. In *Proceedings of VL/HCC 2008: IEEE Symposium on Visual Languages and Human-Centric Computing* (pp. 177–184).

Myers, B. (1991). Graphical techniques in a spreadsheet for specifying user interfaces. In *Proceedings of the SIGCHI conference on Human factors in computing systems (CHI '91)* (Apr 27–May 2, New Orleans, LA, USA) (pp. 243–249). NY: ACM.

Myers, B. A. (1993). Peridot: creating user interfaces by demonstration. In *Watch what I do: programming by demonstration* (pp. 125–153). MIT Press.

Nadamoto, A., & Tanaka, K. (2003). A comparative web browser (CWB) for browsing and comparing web pages. In *Proceedings of the 12th international conference on World Wide Web (WWW '03)* (May 20–24, Budapest, Hungary) (pp. 727–735). NY: ACM.

Nardi, B., Miller, J., & Wright, D. (1998). Collaborative, Programmable Intelligent Agents. *Communications of the ACM, 41*(3).

Nardi, B. (1993). *A Small Matter of Programming: Perspectives on End User Computing.* Cambridge: MIT Press.

Nash, M. (2003). *Java Frameworks and Components.* Cambridge University Press.

Naur, P. (1968). In P. Naur & B. Randell (Eds.), *Software Engineering: Report on a conference sponsored by the NATO Science Committee*, Germany, Garmisch.

Nelson, L. D., & Churchill, E. F. (2006). Repurposing: Techniques for reuse and integration of interactive systems. In *Proceedings of the 2006 IEEE International Conference on Information Reuse and Integration* (pp. 490–495).

Nelson, G. (2006). *Natural language, semantics and interactive fiction.* http://www.inform-fiction.org/I7 Downloads/Documents/WhitePaper.pdf.

Newell, A., & Simon, H. (1972). *Human Problem Solving.* Prentice-Hall.

Nichols, J., & Lau, T. (2008). Mobilization by demonstration: using traces to re-author existing web sites. In *Proceedings of the 13th International Conference on Intelligent User Interfaces (IUI '08)* (pp. 149–158). Gran Canaria, Spain.

Nichols, J., Hua, Z., & Barton, J. (2008). Highlight: A System for Creating and Deploying Mobile Web Applications. In *Proceedings of the Symposium on User Interface Software and Technology (UIST'2008)* (pp. 249–258).

Nielsen, J., & Molich, R. (1990). Heuristic evaluation of user interfaces. In *Proc. CHI 1990* (pp. 249–256). ACM Press.

Norman, D. (1986). Cognitive Engineering. In D. Norman & S. Draper (Eds.), *User Centered System Design* (pp. 38–41). Hillsdale, NJ: Lawrence Erlbaum Associates.

Norman, D. (1988). Psychology of Everyday Things. *Basic Books*.

North, C., & Shneiderman, B. (2000). Snap-together visualization: Can users construct and operate coordinated views? *International Journal of Human-Computer Studies, 53*(5), 715–739.

Olston, C., & Woodruff, A. (2000). Getting portals to behave. In *Proceedings of InfoVis 2000* (Oct 9–10, Salt Lake City, UT, USA) (pp. 15–26). Los Alamitos, CA: IEEE Computer Society Press.

"Oops! I Emailed a Reporter." National Public Radio *On the Media*, February 8, 2008. Available at http://www.onthemedia.org/transcripts/2008/02/08/04.

Page, S. R., Johnsgard, T. J., Albert, U., & Allen, C. D. (1996). User customization of a word processor. In *Proceedings of the SIGCHI Conference on Human Factors in Computing Systems (CHI)* (pp. 340–346).

Pandit, M., & Kalbag, S. (1997). The Selection Recognition Agent: Instant Access to Relevant Information and Operations. In *Proceedings of the International Conference on Intelligent User Interfaces (IUI 97)*.

Pane, J., Myers, B., & Ratanamahatana, C. A. (2001). Studying the language and structure in non-programmers' solutions to programming problems, *54*(2), 237–264.

Pane, J. F., Ratanamahatana, C., & Myers, B. A. (2001). Studying the language and structure in non-programmers' solutions to programming problems. *Int. J. Human-Computer Studies, 54*(237), 264.

Papazoglou, M. P., Traverso, P., Dustdar, S., & Leymann, F. (2007). Service-Oriented Computing: State of the Art and Research Challenges. *Computer, 40*(11), 38–45.

Parent, C., & Spaccapietra, S. (1998). Issues and approaches of database integration. In *Commun. ACM 41* (5th ed., pp. 166–178).

Paul, R. (September 3, 2008). New Firefox JavaScript engine is faster than Chrome's V8. Available at arstechnica.com/open-source/news/2008/09/new-firefox-javascript-engine-is-faster-than-chromes-v8.ars.

Pennington, N. (1987). Stimulus Structures and Mental Representation in Expert Comprehension of Computer Programs. *Cognitive Psychology, 19*(3), 295–341.

Petre, M., & Blackwell, A. (2007). Children as Unwitting End-User Programmers. In *2007 IEEE Symposium on Visual Languages and Human-Centric Computing* (pp. 239–242).

Phalgune, A., Kissinger, C., Burnett, M., Cook, C., Beckwith, L., & Ruthruff, J. R. (2005). Garbage. In *Garbage Out? An Empirical Look at Oracle Mistakes by End-User Programmers* (pp. 45–52). VL/HCC.

Piernot, P., & Yvon, M. (1993). The AIDE Project: An Application-Independent Demonstrational Environment. In A. Cypher (Ed.), *Watch What I Do: Programming by Demonstration* (pp. 383–401). Cambridge, MA: MIT Press.

Pilgrim, M. (2005). *Greasemonkey Hacks: Tips & Tools for Remixing the Web with Firefox*. O'Reilly.

Pirolli, P., & Card, S. (1999). Information Foraging. *Psychological Review, 106*(4), 643–675.

Pirolli, P. L. T. (2007). *Information Foraging Theory*. Oxford University Press.

Pollak, B., & Gatterbauer, W. (2007). *Creating Permanent Test Collections of Web Pages for Information Extraction Research*. SOFSEM '07, Harrachov, Czech Republic.

Porter, M. (1980). An algorithm for suffix stripping. *Program, 14*(3), 130–137.

Potter, R. (1993). Just-in-time programming. In A. Cypher (Ed.), *Watch What I Do: Programming by Demonstration*. MIT Press.

Raeder, G. (1986). A survey of current graphical programming techniques. *IEEE Xplore*.

Ramakrishnan, I. V., Stent, A., & Yang, G. (2004). HearSay: enabling audio browsing on hypertext content. In *Proc. the 13th int. Conf. on World Wide Web* (pp. 80–89). WWW '04.

Raman, T. V. (1996). Emacspeak—a speech interface. In *Proc. of the SIGCHI Conf. on Human Factors in Computing Systems (CHI '96)* (pp. 66–71). Vancouver, Canada.

Raposo, J., Pan, A., Alvarez, M., & Vina, A. (2005). Automatic wrapper maintenance for semi-structured web sources using results from previous queries. In *SAC* (pp. 654–659).

Rdfa. http://www.w3.org/TR/xhtml-rdfa-primer/.

Riehle, D. (2006). How and why wikipedia works. An interview with Angela Beesley, Elisabeth Bauer, and Kizu Naoko. *Computers and Society*, 3–8.

Roberts, J. C. (2007). State of the Art: Coordinated & Multiple Views in Exploratory Visualization. In *Proceedings of the Fifth international Conference on Coordinated and Multiple Views in Exploratory Visualization (July 02, 2007). CMV* (pp. 61–71). Washington, DC: IEEE Computer Society. DOI=http://dx.doi.org/10.1109/CMV.2007.20

Rode, J., & Rosson, M. B. (2003). Programming at runtime: requirements and paradigms for nonprogrammer Web application development. In *Proc. HCC 2003* (pp. 23–30). IEEE Computer Society.

Rosson, M., & Carroll, J. (1996). The Reuse of Uses in Smalltalk Programming. *Transactions on Computer-Human Interaction, 3*(3), 219–253.

Rosson, M. B., & Kase, S. (2006). Work, Play, and In-Between: Exploring the Role of Work Context for Informal Web Developers. In *IEEE Symposium on Visual Languages and Human-Centric Computing, 2006. VL/HCC 2006* (pp. 151–156).

Rosson, M., Ballin, J., & Nash, H. (2004). Everyday Programming: Challenges and Opportunities for Informal Web Development. In *2004 IEEE Symposium on Visual Languages and Human-Centric Computing* (pp. 123–130).

Rosson, M. B., Sinha, H., Bhattacharya, M., & Zhao, D. (2007). Design Planning in End-User Web Development. In *Visual Languages and Human-Centric Computing, 2007. VL/HCC 2007. IEEE Symposium on.* (pp. 189–196).

Rosson, M. B., Sinha, H., Zhao, D., Carroll, J. M., & Ganoe, C. (2008). Cultivating a Landscape of Online Places for a Developmental Learning Community. *Advanced Learning Technologies.*

Rucker, J., & Polanco, M. (1997). Siteseer: Personalized navigation for the Web. *Communications of the ACM, 40*, 73–75.

Safonov, A. (1999). Web macros by example: users managing the WWW of applications. In *CHI '99 Extended Abstracts on Human Factors in Computing Systems (Pittsburgh, Pennsylvania, May 15–20, 1999). CHI '99* (pp. 71–72). New York, NY: ACM. DOI=http://doi.acm.org/10.1145/632716.632761.

Safonov, A. (1999). Web Macros by Example: Users Managing the WWW of Applications. In *Proceedings of the Conference on Human Factors in Computing Systems (CHI 99).*

Sahavechaphan, N., & Claypool, K. (2006). XSnippet: Mining For Sample Code. In *Proceedings of the 21st annual ACM SIGPLAN conference on Object-oriented Programming Systems, Languages, and Applications (OOPSLA)* (pp. 413–430).

Salber, D., Dey, A. K., & Abowd, G. D. (1999). The context toolkit: aiding the development of context-enabled applications. In *CHI '99* (pp. 434–441).

Scaffidi, C., & Shaw, M. (2007). Toward a Calculus of Confidence. In *1st Intl. Workshop on Economics of Software and Computation.*

Scaffidi, C., Shaw, M., & Myers, B. (2005). Estimating the Numbers of End Users and End User Programmers. In *Proceedings of VL/HCC 2005: IEEE Symposium on Visual Languages and Human-Centric. Computing* (pp. 207–214). Dallas, Texas.

Scaffidi, C., Myers, B., & Shaw, M. (2008). Topes: reusable abstractions for validating data. In *Proc ICSE 2008* (pp. 1–10). ACM Press.

Scaffidi, C., Bogart, C., Burnett, M., Cypher, A., Myers, B., & Shaw, M. (2009). Predicting Reuse of End-User Web Macro Scripts. In *2009 International Conference on Visual Languages and Human-Centric Computing.*

schraefel, m.c., Zhu, Y., Modjeska, D., Wigdor, D., & Zhao, S. (2002). Hunter gatherer: interaction support for the creation and management of within-web-page collections. In *Proceedings of the 11th International Conference on World Wide Web* (pp. 172–181). Honolulu, Hawaii, USA: ACM.

Schwartz, B. (2004). *The Paradox of Choice: Why More is Less.* Harper Perennial.

Segal, J. (2004). *Professional End User Developers and Software Development Knowledge.* Tech. Rpt. 2004/25. United Kingdom: Dept. of Computing, Faculty of Mathematics and Computing, The Open University, Milton Keynes.

Selker, T. (1989). Cognitive adaptive computer help (coach). In *Proc. of the Intl. Conf. on Artificial Intelligence* (pp. 25–34). Amsterdam: IOS.

Sellen, A. J., Murphy, R., & Shaw, K. L. (2002). How knowledge workers use the web. In *Proceedings of the SIGCHI Conference on Human Factors in Computing Systems: Changing Our World, Changing Ourselves (Minneapolis, Minnesota, USA, April 20–25, 2002). CHI '02* (pp. 227–234). New York, NY: ACM. DOI=http://doi.acm.org/10.1145/503376.503418.

Seo, Y-W., & Zhang, B. T. (2000). A reinforcement learning agent for personalized information filtering. In *IUI* (pp. 248–251). ACM.

Shaw, M., DeLine, R., Klein, D., & Ross, T. (1995). Abstractions for Software Architecture and Tools to Support Them, *IEEE Transactions on Software Engineering, 21*(4), 314–335.

Shneiderman, B., & Mayer, R. (1979). Syntactic/semantic interactions in programmer behavior: A model and experimental results. *International Journal of Parallel Programming, 8*(3), 219–238.

Shneiderman, B., & Plaisant, C. (2006). Strategies for evaluating information visualization tools: multi-dimensional in-depth long-term case studies. In *Proceedings of the AVI Workshop on BEyond time and errors: novel evaLuation methods for Information Visualization (Venice, Italy, May 23, 2006). BELIV 2006* (pp. 1–7). NY: ACM.

Silva, S. F., & Catarci, T. (2000). Visualization of linear time-oriented data: a survey. In *Proceedings of the First International Conference on Web Information Systems Engineering* (Vol. 1, pp. 310–319).

Silverstein, C., Marais, H., Henzinger, M., & Moricz, M. (1999). Analysis of a Very Large Web Search Engine Query Log. *ACM SIGIR Forum, 33*(1), 6–12.

Simon, K., & Lausen, G. (2005). Viper: Augmenting automatic information extraction with visual perceptions. *CIKM* (pp. 381–388).

Singh, P., Lin, T., Mueller, E., Lim, G., Perkins, T., & Zhu, W. L. (2002). Open Mind Common Sense: Knowledge Acquisition from the General Public. In *Proceedings of the First International Conference on Ontologies, Databases, and Applications of Semantics for Large Scale Information Systems.*

Singh, P., Barry, B., & Liu, H. (2004). Teaching Machines about Everyday Life. *BT Technology Journal.*

Singh, P. (2002). The Public Acquisition of Commonsense Knowledge. In *Proceedings of AAAI Spring Symposium on Acquiring (and Using) Linguistic (and World) Knowledge for Information Access.*

Sleator, C. D., & Temperley, D. (1991). Parsing English with a link grammar. In *Third International Workshop on Parsing Technologies.*

Sohn, T., & Dey, A. (2003). iCAP: an informal tool for interactive prototyping of context-aware applications. In *CHI '03* (pp. 974–975).

Spalter, A. (2002). Problems with Using Components in Educational Software. In *2002 SIGGRAPH Conference Abstracts and Applications* (pp. 25–29).

Spaulding, A., Blythe, J., Haines, W., & Gervasio, M. (2009). From Geek to Sleek: integrating task learning tools to support end users in real-world applications. In *Proc. IUI 2009* (pp. 389–394). ACM Press.

Speer, R., Havasi, C., & Lieberman, H. (2008). *AnalogySpace: Reducing the Dimensionality of Commonsense Knowledge, Conference of the Association for the Advancement of Artificial Intelligence (AAAI-08)*, Chicago, July.

Stocky, T., Faaborg, A., & Lieberman, H. (2004). A Commonsense Approach to Predictive Text Entry. In *Proceedings of the Conference on Human Factors in Computing Systems (CHI 04).*

Stolte, C., Tang, D., et al. (2002). Polaris: A System for Query, Analysis, and Visualization of Multidimensional Relational Databases. *IEEE Transactions on Visualization and Computer Graphics*, 52–65.

Stuerzlinger, W., Chapuis, O., Phillips, D., & Roussel, N. (2006). User interface façades: towards fully adaptable user interfaces. In *Proceedings of the 19th annual ACM symposium on User interface software and technology* (pp. 309–318). Montreux, Switzerland: ACM.

Stylos, J., & Myers, B. (2006). Mica: A Web-Search Tool for Finding API Components and Examples. In *Proceedings of the IEEE Symposium on Visual Languages and Human-Centric Computing (VL/HCC)* (pp. 195–202). IEEE.

Stylos, J., Myers, B. A., & Faulring, A. (2004). Citrine: providing intelligent copy-and-paste. In *Proceedings of the 17th Annual ACM Symposium on User Interface Software and Technology (UIST)* (pp. 185–188).

Sugiura, A., & Koseki, Y. (1998). Internet scrapbook: automating Web browsing tasks by demonstration. In *Proceedings of the 11th Annual ACM Symposium on User Interface Software and Technology (San Francisco, California, United States, November 01–04, 1998). UIST '98* (pp. 9–18). New York, NY: ACM. DOI=http://doi.acm.org/10.1145/288392.288395.

Tajima, K., & Ohnishi, K. (2008). Browsing large HTML tables on small screens. In *Proceedings of the 21st Annual ACM Symposium on User Interface Software and Technology (UIST)* (pp. 259–268).

Takagi, H., & Asakawa, C. (2000). Transcoding proxy for non-visual Web access. In *Proc. the Fourth int. ACM Conf. on Assistive Technologies* (pp. 164–171). Assets '00.

Takagi, H., Asakawa, C., Fukuda, K., & Maeda, J. (2002). Site-wide annotation: reconstructing existing pages to be accessible. In *Proc. the Fifth int. ACM Conf. on Assistive Technologies* (pp. 81–88) Assets '02.

Takagi, H., Asakawa, C., Fukuda, K., & Maeda, J. (2004). Accessibility designer: visualizing usability for the blind. In *Proc. of the 6th international ACM SIGACCESS Conf. on Computers and Accessibility*, (pp. 177–184). Assets '04. New York, NY: ACM.

Takagi, H., Saito, S., Fukuda, K., & Asakawa, C. (2007). Analysis of navigability of web applications for improving blind usability. In *ACM Transactions on Computer-Human Interaction* (Vol. 14, pp. 3–13). ACM Press.

Takagi, H., Kawanaka, S., Kobayashi, M., Itoh, T., & Asakawa, C. (2008). Social accessibility: achieving accessibility through collaborative metadata authoring. In *Proceedings of the 10th international ACM SIGACCESS Conference on Computers and Accessibility (Halifax, Nova Scotia, Canada, October 13–15, 2008)* (pp. 193–200). Assets '08. New York, NY: ACM. DOI=http://doi.acm.org/10.1145/1414471.1414507.

Takagi, H., Kawanaka, S., Kobayashi, M., Sato, D., & Asakawa, C. (2009). Collaborative web accessibility improvement: challenges and possibilities. In *Proceeding of the Eleventh international ACM SIGACCESS Conference on Computers and Accessibility (Pittsburgh, Pennsylvania, USA, October 25–28, 2009)*, (pp. 195–202) ASSETS '09. New York, NY: ACM.

Tan, D. S., Meyers, B., & Czerwinski, M. (2004). Win-Cuts: manipulating arbitrary window regions for more effective use of screen space. In *CHI '04 extended abstracts on Human factors in computing systems* (pp. 1525–1528). Vienna, Austria: ACM.

Tanaka, Y., & Imataki, T. (1989). IntelligentPad: A hypermedia system allowing functional compositions of active media objects through direct manipulations. In *Proceedings of the IFIP 11th World Computer Congress* (Aug 28–Sept 1, San Francisco, CA, USA) (pp. 541–546). North-Holland: IFIP.

Tanaka, Y., Kurosaki, D., & Ito, K. (2002). Live Document Framework for Re-editing and Redistributing Contents in WWW. In H. Jaakkola, H. Kangassalo, E. Kawaguchi & B. Thalheim (Eds.), *Information Modelling and Knowledge Bases XIV* (pp. 247–262). Amsterdam, The Netherlands: IOS Press.

Tanaka, Y. (2003). *Meme Media and Meme Market Architectures: Knowledge Media for Editing, Distributing, and Managing Intellectual Resources*. Wiley-IEEE Press.

Tassey, G. (2002). *NIST: The Economic Impacts of Inadequate Infrastructure for Software Testing*.

Teevan, J., Alvarado, C., Ackerman, M. S., & Karger, D. R. (2004). The perfect search engine is not enough: a study of orienteering behavior in directed search. In *Proceedings of the SIGCHI Conference on Human Factors in Computing Systems (Vienna, Austria, April 24–29, 2004). CHI '04* (pp. 415–422). New York, NY: ACM. DOI=http://doi.acm.org/10.1145/985692.985745.

Teevan, J., Dumais, S. T., & Horvitz, E. (2005). Personalizing search via automated analysis of interests and activities. In *SIGIR* (pp. 449–456).

Terry, M., & Mynatt, E. D. (2002). Recognizing creative needs in user interface design. In *Proceedings of the 4th conference on Creativity & Cognition (C&C '02)* (Oct 13–16, Loughborough, UK) (pp. 38–44). NY: ACM.

Terry, M., & Mynatt, E. D. (2005). Enhancing general-purpose tools with multi-state previewing capabilities. *Knowledge-Based Systems*, 18, 415–425.

Terry, M., Mynatt, E. D., Nakakoji, K., & Yamamoto, Y. (2004). Variation in element and action: Supporting simultaneous development of alternative solutions. In *Proceedings of the SIGCHI conference on Human factors in computing systems (CHI '04)* (Apr 24–29, Vienna, Austria) (pp. 711–718). NY: ACM.

Truong, K. N., Huang, E. M., & Abowd, G. D. (2004). CAMP: A magnetic poetry interface for end-user programming of capture applications for the home. In *UbiComp* (pp. 143–160).

Tuchinda, R., Szekely, P., & Knoblock, C. A. (2008a). Building mashups by example. *Intelligent User Interfaces* (pp. 139–148).

Tuchinda, R., Szekely, P., & Knoblock, C. A. (2008b). Building Data Integration Queries by Demonstration. In *Proceedings of Intelligent User Interfaces* (pp. 170–179).

Tudorache, T., Noy, N. F., Tu, S., & Musen, M. A. (2008). Supporting collaborative ontology development in protege. *ISWC* (vol. 22, pp. 17–32). Springer.

Tufte, E. R. (1990). *Envisioning Information.* Cheshire, CT: Graphic Press.

van Lent, M., & Laird, J. (2001). Learning Procedural Knowledge through Observation. In *Proceedings of the International Conference on Knowledge Capture.*

van Lehn, K. (1984). *Mind Bugs: The Origins of Procedural Misconceptions.* Cambridge, MA: MIT Press.

von Ahn, L., & Dabbish, L. (2004). Labeling images with a computer game. In *Proc. Conf. on Human Factors in Computing Systems* (pp. 319–326).

von Ahn, L., Ginosar, S., Kedia, M., & Blum, M. (2007). Improving image search with Phetch. In *Proceedings of the IEEE International Conference on Acoustics, Speech, and Signal Processing (Honolulu, Apr. 15–20)* (pp. IV–1209–IV–1212). New York: IEEE Press.

von Ahn, L., Maurer, B., McMillen, C., Abraham, D., & Blum, M. (2008). reCAPTCHA: Human-based Character Recognition via Web Security Measures. *Science*, 1465–1468, 12 September 2008.

von Mayrhause, A., & Vans, A. M. (1995). Program comprehension during software maintenance and evolution. *Computer*, 28(8), 44–55.

Viégas, F. B., Wattenberg, M., & van Ham, F. (2007). Many Eyes: A Site for Visualization at Internet Scale. *IEEE Transactions on Visualization and Computer Graphics*, 1121–1128.

Walpole, R., & Burnett, M. (1997). Supporting Reuse of Evolving Visual Code. In *1997 Symposium on Visual Languages* (pp. 68–75).

Watanabe, T. (2007). Experimental evaluation of usability and accessibility of heading elements. In *Proc. of the Intl. Cross-Disciplinary Conf. on Web Accessibility (W4A '07)* (pp. 157–164).

Wiedenbeck, S., & Engebretson, A. (2004). Comprehension strategies of end-user programmers in an event-driven application. *VL/HCC*, 207–214.

Wiedenbeck, S., Sun, X., & Chintakovid, T. (2007). Antecedents to End Users' Success in Learning to Program in an Introductory Programming Course. In *IEEE Symposium on Visual Languages and Human-Centric Computing, 2007. VL/HCC 2007* (pp. 69–72).

Wiedenbeck, S. (2005). Facilitators and Inhibitors of End-User Development by Teachers in a School Environment. In *2005 IEEE Symposium on Visual Languages and Human-Centric Computing* (pp. 215–222).

Wikipedia (2009). *Computer Programming.* http://en.wikipedia.org/wiki/Computer_programming. Accessed February 19, 2009.

Willett, W., Heer, J., & Agrawala, M. (2007). Scented Widgets: Improving Navigation Cues with Embedded Visualizations. *IEEE Transactions on Visualization and Computer Graphics*, 13(6), 1129–1136.

Wilson, A., Burnett, M., Beckwith, L., Granatir, O., Casburn, L., Cook, C., et al. (2003). Harnessing Curiosity to Increase Correctness in End-User Programming. *Proceedings of CHI*, 305–312.

Winograd, T. (2001). Architectures for context. *Hum Comput Interact*, *16*(2), 401–419.

Witten, I., & Mo, D. (1993). TELS: Learning Text Editing Tasks from Examples. In A. Cypher (Ed.), *Watch What I Do: Programming by Demonstration* (pp. 183–203). Cambridge, MA: MIT Press.

Wobbrock, J. O., Forlizzi, J., Hudson, S. E., & Myers, B. A. (2002). WebThumb: interaction techniques for small-screen browsers. In *Proceedings of the Symposium on User Interface Software and Technology* (pp. 205–208).

Wong, J., & Hong, J. (2006). Marmite: end-user programming for the Web. In *Proceedings of the SIGCHI Conference on Human Factors in Computing Systems (CHI)* (pp. 1435–1444).

Wong, J., & Hong, J. I. (2007). Making mashups with marmite: towards end-user programming for the web. In *Proceedings of the SIGCHI conference on Human factors in computing systems (CHI 2007)* (April 28–May 3, San Jose, CA, USA) (pp. 1435–1444). NY: ACM.

Wong, J., & Hong, J. (2008). What do we "mashup" when we make mashups? In *Proceedings of the 4th International Workshop on End-user Software Engineering (WEUSE)* (pp. 35–39).

Yahoo pipes. http://pipes.yahoo.com.

Yeh, R. B., Paepcke, A., & Klemmer, S. R. (2008). Iterative Design and Evaluation of an Event Architecture for Pen-and-Paper Interfaces. In *Proceedings of UIST 2008: ACM Symposium on User Interface Software and Technology*. Monterey, California.

Zang, N., Rosson, M. B., & Nasser, V. (2008). Mashups: Who? What? Why? In 26*th* *SIGCHI Conference on Human Factors in Computing Systems – Work-in-Progress Posters* (pp. 3171–3176).

Zheng, S., Scott, M. R., Song, R., & Wen, J-R. (2008). Pictor: An interactive system for importing data from a website. *KDD* (pp. 1097–1100).

Zheng, S., Wu, W., Song, R., & Wen, J-R. (2007). Joint optimization of wrapper generation and template detection. *KDD* (pp. 894–902).

Index

Note: Page numbers followed by '*f*' indicate figures, '*t*' indicate tables.

473

Printed and bound by CPI Group (UK) Ltd, Croydon, CR0 4YY

03/10/2024

01040315-0006